The Oxford Book of
New Zealand Writing
Since 1945

The Oxford Book of New Zealand Writing Since 1945

chosen by

MacDonald P. Jackson
and
Vincent O'Sullivan

Auckland
Oxford University Press
Oxford   Melbourne   New York

Oxford University Press

Oxford   London   Glasgow
New York   Toronto   Melbourne   Auckland
Kuala Lumpur   Singapore   Hong Kong   Tokyo
Delhi   Bombay   Calcutta   Madras   Karachi
Nairobi   Dar Es Salaam   Cape Town
and associates in
Beirut   Berlin   Ibadan   Mexico City   Nicosia

First published 1983
Introductions and selection © MacDonald P. Jackson
and Vincent O'Sullivan 1983

ISBN 0 19 558097 4

Cover design by John McNulty
Photoset in Baskerville by Whitcoulls Ltd, Christchurch
Printed by Hing Yip Printing Co, Hong Kong
Published by Oxford University Press
Trentham House, 28 Wakefield Street, Auckland, New Zealand

Contents

POETRY

J. R. HERVEY

Born in 1889 in Southland, he was ordained an Anglican priest, and from 1915 to 1938, served in various parishes in Canterbury. He suffered from ill-health over many years, and died in 1958.

EILEEN DUGGAN

Born in 1894 in Tua Marina, Marlborough, and educated at Victoria University. Apart from one year as a schoolteacher, and another as a university lecturer in history, her life (in Wellington) was devoted to her writing, which included journalism. She died in 1972.

A. R. D. FAIRBURN

Born in 1904 in Auckland, and apart from three years in England in the early nineteen thirties, lived there all his life. A versatile writer and a gifted artist, he worked as journalist, radio script-writer, and union secretary, and, for the last six years of his life, lecturer at the art school at Auckland University. He was a lively and busy commentator on social and political life. He died in 1957.

CHARLES BRASCH

Born in 1909 in Dunedin, and educated at Oxford. He worked as an archaeologist in Egypt, then as a teacher and civil servant in England. He returned to New Zealand in 1947, when he was the main force behind the establishment of the quarterly *Landfall*, which he edited for twenty years. Although he often travelled abroad, he lived mostly in Dunedin, and his autobiography, *Indirections*, was published in 1980. He died in 1973.

BASIL DOWLING

Born in 1910 at Southbridge, Canterbury, and educated at Canterbury University, Knox Theological College, Dunedin, and Westminster College, Cambridge. Ordained a Presbyterian minister, he later worked in labouring jobs and as a librarian, and since 1951 as a schoolmaster in England. He lives in Rye, East Essex.

CHARLES SPEAR

Born in 1910 in Owaka, South Otago, and educated at Canterbury and Otago Universities. A man of wide-ranging scholarship, he taught in the English Department at Canterbury University for twenty-seven years. Since his retirement in 1976 he has lived in London.

ALLEN CURNOW

Born in 1911 in Timaru, and educated at Canterbury and Auckland Universities, and St John's Theological College, Auckland. From 1935 to 1948 he worked for the *Press*, in Christchurch, then in journalism in London before joining the English Department at Auckland University in 1951. He retired as Associate Professor in 1977. He has also written plays, and edited *The Penguin Book of New Zealand Verse*, 1960.

DENIS GLOVER

Born in 1912 in Dunedin, and educated at Canterbury University. Founder of the Caxton Press in the 1930s, he served with the Royal Navy in World War II, and was awarded the D.S.C. A distinguished typographer and book designer, he died in 1980.

PAUL HENDERSON

Born in 1913 in Leithfield, Canterbury, she lived in or near Christchurch for most of her life. She also published fiction under her own name of Ruth France. She died in 1957.

M. K. JOSEPH

Born in 1914 in England, and educated at Auckland University and Oxford. After service in the British Army in World War II, he returned to New Zealand, and taught English at Auckland University until shortly before his death in 1981.

GLORIA RAWLINSON

Born in Haapai, Tonga, in 1918, and came to New Zealand in 1924. Most of her life she has lived in Auckland.

MARY STANLEY

Born in Christchurch in 1919, and educated at Auckland University. She taught in several schools, and lived in Auckland until her death in 1980.

RUTH DALLAS

Born in Invercargill in 1919, and for many years has lived in Dunedin. As well as her poetry, she has published seven children's novels.

HUBERT WITHEFORD

Born in 1921 in Wellington, and educated at Victoria University. Apart from a brief return, he spent the years from 1953 to 1981 in London, working at the Central Office of Information. He now lives in Wellington.

KEITH SINCLAIR

Born in 1922 in Auckland, and educated at Auckland University. He served with both the army and the navy during World War II. An eminent and prolific historian, he is Professor of History at Auckland University. His Pelican *A History of New Zealand*, 1959, remains a literary as well as scholarly achievement.

KENDRICK SMITHYMAN

Born in 1922, he has lived mostly in or around Auckland, where since World War II he has worked as a teacher, first in primary schools, later at the University of Auckland.

HONE TUWHARE

Born in 1922 in Kaikohe, he belongs to the Ngapuhi hapus Ngati Korokoro, Ngati Tautahi, Te Popoto, and Uri-O-Hau. He worked as a boilermaker, and was active in trade-union affairs. He has spent time in Germany as the guest of the German government, and in recent years has lived in Dunedin.

JANET FRAME

Born in 1924 in Dunedin. She grew up in Oamaru, was briefly a student and a teacher, and has devoted her life to writing. She spent five years in London, and on several occasions has lived and worked at the Yaddo Foundation, the writer's colony in Saratoga Springs, New York. She now lives in Wanganui.

LAURIS EDMOND

Born in 1924 in Hawkes Bay, and educated at Victoria University. She spent much of her life in country towns, taught English and French in secondary schools, and edited the Post Primary Teachers' *Journal*. She lives in Wellington, and in recent years has written several plays.

ALISTAIR CAMPBELL

Born in 1925 in Rarotonga, his father a New Zealand Scot and his mother from Tongareva in the Northern Cook Islands. Educated at Victoria University, he has worked for many years in educational publishing in Wellington. He has also published plays and children's stories.

W. H. OLIVER

Born in 1925 in Feilding, and educated at Victoria University and Oxford. The founding editor of *Comment*, a quarterly of current affairs and the arts, he has published several historical works, including *The Story of New Zealand*, 1960, and edited *The Oxford History of New Zealand*, 1980. He is Professor of History at Massey University, Palmerston North.

RAYMOND WARD

Born in 1925 in London, and educated at King's College, London University. He had three years war service with the Royal Navy, then taught for several years before coming to New Zealand in 1959. He has lived since then in Dunedin.

JAMES K. BAXTER

Born in 1926 in Dunedin, and attended Otago and Victoria Universities. He spent some years in England as a schoolboy, and in 1958 visited India. Otherwise he lived mostly in Dunedin and Wellington, until towards the end of his life he established his community at Jerusalem on the Wanganui River. He worked at several jobs, but his energies were mainly directed to an enormous production of poetry, drama, criticism and social commentary. He died in 1972.

CHARLES (MIKE) DOYLE

Born in 1928 in England, and educated at Auckland University, he has lived for many years in Canada, where he is Professor of English at the University of Victoria, British Columbia. He has published widely in several countries, and has written books of criticism.

ALISTAIR PATERSON

Born in 1929 in Nelson, and educated at Canterbury and Victoria Universities. After a career as a teacher in the Royal New Zealand Navy, he now works with the Education Department in Auckland.

OWEN LEEMING

Born in 1930 in Christchurch, and educated at Canterbury University. He studied composition in Paris, and worked as a producer for the B.B.C. before settling in France, where he has lived for several years.

C. K. STEAD

Born in Auckland in 1932, and educated at Auckland University and the University of Bristol. Also a critic and editor, he is Professor of English at Auckland University.

GORDON CHALLIS

Born in 1932 in Wales, he settled in New Zealand in 1953, and took a degree from Victoria University. He has worked in England as a journalist, and lived in Spain. He is now a social worker.

KEVIN IRELAND

Born in Auckland in 1933, he lived for many years in London, and more recently in Ireland. He has written, as well as poetry, the libretti for two operas: 'The Snow Queen' (BBC Third Programme, 1982), and 'The Man Who Made Good' (British Arts Council Commission, 1982).

PETER BLAND

Born in 1934 in Yorkshire, and emigrated to New Zealand when he was twenty. In Wellington he worked for broadcasting and as a freelance journalist, and was a co-founder of Downstage Theatre. He returned to live in London in 1969.

FLEUR ADCOCK

Born in New Zealand in 1934, spent the war years in England with her family, and returned to live in Wellington in 1947. Educated at Victoria University, where she read Classics. In 1963 she settled in London and worked as a librarian in the Foreign and Commonwealth Office until 1979, when she resigned to become a freelance writer. She edited *The Oxford Book of Contemporary New Zealand Poetry* in 1982.

VINCENT O'SULLIVAN

Born in 1937 in Auckland, and educated at Auckland University and Oxford. For several years an academic, he now lives in Wellington as a freelance writer and editor. He edited the Oxford *Anthology of Twentieth Century New Zealand Poetry*, 1971.

K. O. ARVIDSON

Born in 1938 in Hamilton, and educated at Auckland University. He has taught English in Australian Universities, and at the University of the South Pacific, Fiji. He now teaches at Waikato University.

MICHAEL JACKSON

Born in 1940 in Taranaki, and educated at Auckland University and Cambridge. An anthropologist, he teaches at Massey University, Palmerston North.

RACHEL McALPINE

Born in 1940 in Fairlie, and educated at Massey, Canterbury and Victoria Universities. She has written five plays, and works at the Correspondence School in Wellington. She was the first writer to take part in the Australia-New Zealand Writers' Exchange, in 1982.

DAVID MITCHELL

Born in 1940, he lives in Auckland and works as an art-teacher with the Education Department.

ELIZABETH SMITHER

Born in 1941 in New Plymouth, where she lives with her husband, the painter Michael Smither. She writes journalism, children's stories, and a weekly verse column for the local paper.

PETER OLDS

Born in 1944 in Christchurch, he spent much of his life in Auckland, but in recent years has lived in Dunedin.

BRIAN TURNER

Born in 1944 in Dunedin. A committed South Islander, he works as a publisher's editor and freelance writer, especially on sport and environmental issues. He has written the text for *Images of Coastal Otago*.

SAM HUNT

Born in Castor Bay, Auckland in 1946. He lives as a full-time writer and performer.

BILL MANHIRE

Born in 1946 in Invercargill, and educated at Otago University and University College, London. He teaches English at Victoria University.

IAN WEDDE

Born in 1946 in Blenheim, and educated at Auckland University. As a child he lived in East Pakistan and England, as well as New Zealand, and travelled widely after graduating, spending two years in Amman, Jordan. He has worked at various labouring jobs, and also written for cabaret and radio. He lives in Wellington.

MURRAY EDMOND

Born in 1949 in Hamilton, and educated at Auckland University. He has worked extensively in experimental and educational theatre, and for the last three years has been actor, director and writer for Town and Country Players in Wellington.

PROSE

FRANK SARGESON

Born in 1903 in Hamilton. He quickly gave up his intention to become a solicitor, travelled in Europe in the late 1920s, was briefly a public servant, and worked as both sheep-farmer and market-gardener before committing himself to freelance journalism, and fiction. During the Depression he built himself a hut at Takapuna, Auckland, and later a house on the same site that was his home until his death in 1982.

RODERICK FINLAYSON

Born in Auckland in 1904, he spent his childhood summers in the Bay of Plenty, among the people he later wrote of. He began writing in the 1930s, when he was out of work much of the time. He now lives at Weymouth, on the Manukau Harbour.

JAMES COURAGE

Born in 1903 in Christchurch, and educated at Oxford. He was for ten years the manager of a bookshop in Hampstead, then gave his time more to writing. He wrote several plays, and died in 1963.

A. P. GASKELL

Born in Kurow, North Otago, in 1913, and educated at Otago University. In both primary and secondary teaching, he spent his professional life in several country and city schools in the North and South Islands.

DAN DAVIN

Born in 1913 in Invercargill, he was educated at Otago University, and Oxford. During the Second World War he had a distinguished military career with the New Zealand Army, and was awarded the M.B.E. From the end of the war until his retirement in 1979, he was with the Clarendon Press, Oxford.

JOHN REECE COLE

Born in 1916 in Palmerston North. Served as a pilot during World War II, and trained as a librarian. He worked in library development in New Zealand and South East Asia, and was one time Librarian of the Alexander Turnbull Library. He lives at Karaka Bay, Wellington.

MAURICE DUGGAN

Born in 1922 in Auckland, where he lived for most of his life. He travelled in Europe, and worked for many years in advertising. He died in 1974.

DAVID BALLANTYNE

Born in 1924 in Auckland. A widely experienced journalist, he worked for a number of years in London before returning to Auckland where he now lives. He has written also for stage and television.

JANET FRAME

(See biographical note above)

O. E. MIDDLETON

Born in 1925 in Christchurch. He worked at a variety of jobs, travelled widely, and studied at the Sorbonne in 1955-56. Since 1970 he has lived in Dunedin.

RENATO AMATO

Born in 1928 in Potenza, Southern Italy, he studied law at the University of Turin, and became a freelance writer in Rome. He came to New Zealand in 1954, and worked at labouring jobs before resuming legal studies at Victoria University. He lived in Wellington for several years before his death in 1964.

NOEL HILLIARD

Born in 1929 in Napier, he began work as a journalist on the *Southern Cross*. At various times he has worked as a labourer, teacher, sub-editor, proofreader, and full-time writer. He lives at Titahi Bay near Wellington.

YVONNE DU FRESNE

Born in 1929, she grew up in a Danish-French Huguenot community in the Manawatu. She has had a full-time teaching career, and lives in Wellington.

BARRY MITCALFE

Born in 1930, he is the author of twenty books, including translations and children's fiction. He is the founder of the Coromandel Press.

PHILIP MINCHER

Born in 1930 in Auckland, where he continues to live. He has written widely for radio.

MAURICE GEE

Born in 1931 in Whakatane, Bay of Plenty, he grew up in Henderson, and was educated at Auckland University. He worked as a teacher, casual labourer, and librarian, before becoming a full-time writer. His novel *Plumb* won the British James Tait Black Memorial Prize in 1978. He lives in Nelson.

MAURICE SHADBOLT

Born in Auckland in 1932. He is the author of sixteen books and his first stage play, *Once on Chunuk Bair*, was professionally performed in 1982.

C. K. STEAD

(see biographical note above)

KATHLEEN CRAYFORD

Born in 1930 in London, and educated at South East Essex Technical College. She emigrated to New Zealand in 1962, graduated from Victoria University, Wellington, and works in an office in Christchurch.

RUSSELL HALEY

Born in 1934 in Dewsbury, England, and educated at Auckland University. A prolific radio playwright, he lives in Auckland, and teaches at the Auckland Technical Institute.

WARREN DIBBLE

Born in 1935. He now lives in Australia.

JOY COWLEY

Born in 1936 in Levin. She has lived on a farm in the Manawatu, and, for the last twelve years, in Wellington. She has also published children's books,.and worked for radio and film.

VINCENT O'SULLIVAN

(see biographical note above)

PATRICIA GRACE

Born in 1937 in Wellington, she is Maori of Ngati Raukawa descent. A teacher by training, she published her first children's book in 1982.

MARGARET SUTHERLAND

Born in 1941 in Auckland. She trained as a nurse before marrying, and now lives in Auckland.

OWEN MARSHALL

Born in 1941 in Te Kuiti, but brought up Blenheim and Timaru. Educated at Canterbury University, he teaches at Waitaki Boys' High School, Oamaru.

MICHAEL HENDERSON

Born in Nelson in 1942, and educated at Canterbury University. After graduating in law, he held a diplomatic appointment with the Department of Foreign Affairs, before taking up a Teaching-Writer Fellowship at the University of Iowa. He now lives at Motueka.

CHRIS ELSE

Born in 1942 in Hull, England, and emigrated to New Zealand in 1956. After Auckland University and Auckland Teachers' College, he taught in Auckland, Albania, and London, before working as a bookseller. He is now a computer programmer and lives in Wellington. He has written for both radio and stage.

MICHAEL MORRISSEY

Born in 1942 in Auckland, where he lives as a full-time writer. As well as fiction and poetry, he has written for both stage and radio.

WITI IHIMAERA

Born in 1944 in Gisborne, he belongs to Te Whanau a Kai, subtribe of Te Aitanga a Mahaki and Rongowhakaata, and has close links with other tribes including Ngati Porou, his mother's people. Educated at Victoria University, he is a diplomat with the Department of Foreign Affairs. He has co-edited an anthology of Maori writing in the 1970s, *Into the World of Light*.

MICHAEL GIFKINS

Born in Wellington in 1945, and educated at Auckland University, he is a freelance publishing consultant in Auckland.

IAN WEDDE

(see biographical note above)

KERI HULME

Born in 1947 of Ngai Tahu, Orkney Scots and English descent. She grew up in the South Island, and has worked at journalism and various labouring jobs. She lives at Okarito on the West Coast.

STEVAN ELDRED-GRIGG

Born in Greymouth in 1952, and educated at Canterbury University and Australian National University. Most of his life has been spent in Canterbury, and he has published important historical works on that province.

Acknowledgements

For permission to reproduce copyright passages grateful acknowledgement is made to the publishers and copyright holders of the following:

Poetry:

Fleur Adcock, *The Eye of the Hurricane* (A. H. & A. W. Reed, 1964); *Tigers* (OUP, 1967); *High Tide in the Garden* (OUP, 1971); *The Scenic Route* (OUP, 1974); *The Inner Harbour* (OUP, 1979). K. O. Arvidson, *Riding the Pendulum: Poems 1961-69* (OUP, 1973). James K. Baxter, *Collected Poems* (OUP, 1979). Peter Bland, *My Side of the Story, Poems 1960-64* (Mate Books, 1964); *The Man with the Carpet Bag* (Caxton Press, 1972); *Mr Maui* (London Magazine Editions, 1976). Charles Brasch, *The Estate and Other Poems* (Caxton Press, 1957); *Ambulando* (Caxton Press, 1964); *Not Far Off* (Caxton Press, 1969); *Home Ground* (Caxton Press, 1974). Alistair Campbell, *Kapiti: Selected Poems, 1947-1971* (Pegasus Press, 1972); *Dreams, Yellow Lions* (Alister Taylor, 1975). Gordon Challis, *Building* (Caxton Press, 1963). Allen Curnow, *Collected Poems* (A. H. & A. W. Reed, 1974); *An Incorrigible Music* (AUP/OUP, 1979); *You Will Know When You Get There* (AUP/OUP, 1982). Ruth Dallas, *Country Road and Other Poems, 1947-52* (Caxton Press, 1953); *The Turning Wheel* (Caxton Press, 1961); *Day Book* (Caxton Press, 1966); *Shadow Show* (Caxton Press, 1968); *Walking on the Snow* (Caxton Press, 1976); *Steps of the Sun* (Caxton Press, 1979). Basil Dowling, *Canterbury and Other Poems* (Caxton Press, 1949); *The Unreturning Native and Other Poems* (Nag's Head Press, 1973). Charles Doyle, *Distances* (Paul's Book Arcade, 1963); *Messages for Herod* (Collins, 1965); *Malahat Review* 26 (April 1973). Eileen Duggan, *More Poems* (Allen & Unwin, London, 1951). Lauris Edmond, *In Middle Air* (Pegasus Press, 1975); *Salt from the North* (OUP, 1980). Murray Edmond, *End Wall* (AUP/OUP, 1981). A. R. D. Fairburn, *Collected Poems* (Pegasus Press, 1966). Janet Frame, *The Pocket Mirror* (Pegasus Press, 1967). Denis Glover, *Selected Poems* (Penguin Books, 1981). Paul Henderson, *The Halting Place* (Caxton Press, 1961). J. R. Hervey, *Man on a Raft, More Poems* (Caxton Press, 1949); *She Was My Spring* (Caxton Press, 1974); *Landfall* (vol. 35, 1955). Sam Hunt, *Collected Poems, 1963-80* (Penguin Books, 1980). Kevin Ireland, *Face to Face* (Pegasus Press, 1963); *Educating the Body* (Caxton Press, 1967); *A Grammar of Dreams* (Wai-te-ata Press, 1975); *Orchids, Hummingbirds, and other poems* (AUP, 1974); *Literary Cartoons* (Islands/Hurricane, 1977). Michael Jackson, *Latitudes of Exile* (John McIndoe, 1975); *Wall* (John McIndoe, 1980). M. K. Joseph, *The Living Countries* (Paul's Book Arcade, 1959); *Inscription on a Paper Dart* (AUP, 1974). Owen Leeming, *Venus is Setting* (Caxton Press, 1972). Rachel McAlpine, *Zig-zag up a Thistle, Surprise surprise* (unpublished poems). Bill Manhire, *The Elaboration* (Square and Circle, 1972); *The Young New Zealand Poets* (Heinemann, 1973); *How to Take Your Clothes Off at the Picnic* (Wai-te-ata Press, 1973); *Good Looks* (AUP/OUP, 1982). David Mitchell, *Pipe Dreams in Ponsonby* (Stephen Chan, 1971). Peter Olds, *Freeway* (Caveman Press, 1974); *Doctor's Rock* (Caveman Press, 1976); *Beethoven's Guitar* (Caveman Press, 1980). W. H. Oliver, *Fire Without Phoenix: Poems 1946-54* (Caxton Press, 1957); *Out of Season* (OUP, 1980). Vincent O'Sullivan, *Revenants* (Prometheus Books, 1969); *From the Indian Funeral* (John McIndoe Press, 1976); *Butcher & Co.* (OUP, 1977); *Brother Jonathan, Brother Kafka* (OUP, 1980); *Landfall* 138 (June 1981). Alistair Paterson, *Birds Flying* (Pegasus Press, 1973). Gloria Rawlinson, *Of Clouds and Pebbles* (Paul's Book Arcade, 1963); *NZ Poets Read Their Work* (Waiata Recordings, 1974). Keith Sinclair, *Songs for a Summer* (Pegasus Press, 1952); *A Time to Embrace* (Paul's Book Arcade, 1963); *The Firewheel Tree* (AUP/OUP, 1973). Elizabeth Smither *Here Come the Clouds* (Alister Taylor, 1975); *You're Very Seductive William Carlos Williams* (John McIndoe, 1978); *The Legend of Marcello Mastroianni's Wife* (AUP/OUP, 1981); *Casanova's Ankle* (OUP, 1981). Kendrick Smithyman, *The Blind Mountain* (Caxton Press, 1950); *Inheritance* (Paul's Book Arcade, 1962); *Flying to Palmerston* (AUP/OUP, 1968); *Earthquake Weather* (AUP, 1972); *The Seal in the Dolphin Pool* (AUP, 1974); *Dwarf with a Billiard Cue* (AUP/OUP, 1978). Charles Spear, *Twopence Coloured* (Caxton Press, 1951). Mary Stanley, *Starveling Year* (Pegasus Press, 1953). C. K. Stead, *Crossing the Bar* (AUP/OUP, 1972); *Quesada* (The Shed, 1975); *Walking Westward* (The Shed, 1979). Brian Turner, *Ladders of Rain* (John McIndoe, 1978); *Ancestors* (John McIndoe, 1981). Hone Tuwhare, *No Ordinary Sun* (Blackwood & Janet Paul, 1965); *Come Rain Hail* (Bibliography Room of

University of Otago, 1970); *Sap-wood & Milk* (Caveman Press, 1972); *Something Nothing* (Caveman Press, 1974). Raymond Ward, *Settler and Stranger* (Caxton Press, 1965). Ian Wedde, *Made Over* (Stephen Chan, 1974); *Earthly: Sonnets for Carlos* (Amphedesma Press, 1975, and the Author); *Castaly* (AUP/OUP, 1980); *Islands* 31 (June 1981). Hubert Witheford, *The Lightning Makes a Difference* (Brookside Press, 1962, and the Author); *A Native, Perhaps Beautiful* (Caxton Press, 1967); *A Possible Order* (Ravine Press, Middlesex, 1980).

Prose:

Renato Amato, *The Full Circle of the Travelling Cuckoo* (Whitcombe and Tombs, 1967). David Ballantyne, *And the Glory* (Hale, London, and Whitcombe and Tombs, 1963). John Reece Cole, *It Was So Late and Other Stories* (AUP/OUP, 1978). James Courage, *Such Separate Creatures* (Caxton Press, 1973). Joy Cowley, *NZ Listener* (5 March 1965); *Islands* 29 (June 1980). Kathleen Crayford, *Landfall* 127 (September 1978). Dan Davin, *Selected Stories* (Hale, London and VUP/Price Milburn, 1981). Warren Dibble, *Landfall* 81 (March 1967). Yvonne Du Fresne, *Farvel and Other Stories* (VUP/Price Milburn, 1980). Maurice Duggan, *Collected Stories* (AUP/OUP, 1981). Stevan Eldred-Grigg, *NZ Listener* (2 December 1978). Chris Else, *Dreams of Pythagoras* (Voice Press, 1981). Roderick Finlayson, *Brown Man's Burden* (AUP/OUP, 1973). Janet Frame, *The Lagoon and Other Stories* (Caxton Press, 1961); *The Reservoir: Stories and Sketches* (George Braziller, New York, 1963); *Landfall* 75 (September 1965); *Cornhill Magazine* (Spring 1970); *NZ Listener* (17 March 1979 and 9 June 1979). A. P. Gaskell, *All Part of the Game* (AUP/OUP, 1978). Maurice Gee, *A Glorious Morning, Comrade* (AUP/OUP, 1975). Michael Gifkins, *Islands* 30 (October 1980). Patricia Grace, *Waiariki* (Longman Paul, 1975); *The Dream Sleepers and Other Stories* (Longman Paul, 1980). Russell Haley, *Landfall* 136 (December 1980). Michael Henderson, *Islands* 1 (Spring 1972); Noel Hilliard, *Islands* 28 (March 1980); *Landfall* 140 (December 1981). Keri Hulme, *NZ Listener* (17 January 1976). Witi Ihimaera, *Pounamu Pounamu* (Heinemann, 1972); *The New Net Goes Fishing* (Heinemann, 1977). Owen Marshall, *The Master of Big Jingles* (John McIndoe, 1982). O. E. Middleton, *Selected Stories* (John McIndoe, 1976). Philip Mincher, *Landfall* 85 (March 1968). Barry Mitcalfe, *I Say, Wait for Me* (Outrigger, 1976). Michael Morrissey, *Landfall* 125 (March 1978). Vincent O'Sullivan, *The Boy, The Bridge, The River* (John McIndoe and A. H. & A. W. Reed, 1978); *Dandy Edison for Lunch and Other Stories* (John McIndoe, 1981). Frank Sargeson, *The Stories of Frank Sargeson* (Penguin, 1982). Maurice Shadbolt, *The Presence of Music: Three Novellas* (Cassell, London, 1967). C. K. Stead, *Five for the Symbol* (Longman Paul, 1981). Margaret Sutherland *Getting Through and Other Stories* (Heinemann, 1977). Ian Wedde, *The Shirt Factory and Other Stories* (VUP/Price Milburn, 1981).

Introduction

Poetry

The year in which the Second World War ended saw the publication of Allen Curnow's first Caxton *Book of New Zealand Verse*. Among those poets whose work formed the staple of that anthology, R. A. K. Mason and Ursula Bethell are lamented casualties of our time limit, which also bars those admirable poems by which in the war years Curnow and Charles Brasch helped shape our national consciousness. Curnow saw in pakeha discovery and settlement of New Zealand a dubious history of miscalculation and failure, a re-enactment of the Fall, while Brasch's elegiac cadences evoked a 'silent land' where 'Lives like a vanishing night-dew drop away'. Rootlessness, isolation, spiritual impoverishment were the themes. 'To introduce the landscape to the language' – the longing was for what the Welsh call *cydymdreiddiad*, which has been glossed as 'that subtle knot of interpenetration, which . . . grows in time . . . between a territory and its people and their language, creating a sense of belonging to a particular stretch of the earth's surface'. Fortunately, Curnow is still writing, and Brasch continued to develop and surprise, evolving in the last decade of his life a new style – naked, gaunt, sinewy – in which to chart his quest for some undisputed ground for faith to stand on. 'Cry Mercy' struggles to earn the muted affirmation of its close. Something of a late-Yeatsian temper animates 'Ergo Sum', and 'Shoriken' inclines to an eastern metaphysic. A life-time's fastidiousness in the choice and arrangement of words is behind the concentrated perfection of the valedictory 'Winter Anemones'.

Denis Glover also remained productive until his death in 1980. Much of his work is versified buffoonery, and even the serious poems are apt to fluctuate uneasily between the highflown and the comic-bathetic. His mature love poetry is clear-sighted and direct, but the heart of his *œuvre* remains the 'Sings Harry' sequence, in which under cover of a persona he gave unembarrassed expression to a pastoral vision that embraces tussock and cabbage-tree. A pure homespun lyricism sets fading human aspirations against a backdrop of sea, mountains, lakes, hills. (Hervey's 'The Return' draws on similar emotion.) Nowhere in our verse is the tug of land on spirit more fully realized.

A. R. D. Fairburn's finest love lyrics predate 1945, but even a handful of his later poems confirms Curnow's impression of 'one who reconciled in a singular way, in his lyric style, the English and the traditional with the modern, the regional, and the personal'. 'Tom's a-Cold', with its echo of the disguised Edgar in *King Lear*, grounds itself in the tradition of those anonymous Elizabethan ballads in which the crazed Tom o' Bedlam bewails his lost mistress Maudline. 'The Estuary', vividly localized, characteristically holds the intense moment against the flow of time. Fairburn's metrical skill is well illustrated in 'Song at Summer's End', with its subtle quickenings and retardations of the four-beat line. And it was not till 1952 that Fairburn published the most satisfying of his long poems, 'To a Friend in the Wilderness' (written in 1949), in which he dramatizes a recurrent conflict, between engagement and withdrawal, present even in the opening poem of *He Shall Not Rise* (1930). Here the ancient debate between town and country, the active and the contemplative life, assumes a personal urgency, as the poet wavers between a private Arcady on the Mahurangi peninsula, north of Auckland, and a metropolis where social concern sours into disgust and despair. Retreat is envisaged not as mere evasion, but as joyous submission to nature's imperatives. The poem has the bare minimum of intellectual structuring: it lives in its rhythms, in the rich particularity of its loving evocation of a northern littoral, in the ebb and flow of feeling as it moves through its resolution to the coda's dying fall. Few later New Zealand poets – Campbell, Arvidson, and Wedde on occasions, Stead in those sections of 'Quesada' not sabotaged by grenades of self-conscious punning – have risked such Romantic fullness of sentiment.

II

New Zealand poetry has followed the twentieth century British and (especially) American trend towards the abandonment, or merely sporadic use, of rhyme and traditional metres. It has also reflected the social and poetic *Zeitgeist* in its growing distrust of afflatus, of anything that Pound might have mocked as 'sonorous – like the farting of a goose'.

Some poets have avoided grandiloquence through an imagist or gnomic brevity. Hubert Witheford, introduced to readers of Curnow's Caxton book through 'Elegy in the Orongorongo Valley', with its plangent rhythms and lush diction, has pared utterance to the pithy exactitude of 'The Staying of the Magi', which says all that need be said about youth, age, and the sources of joy in a memorable thirteen words. Ruth Dallas, receptive to oriental influences, has sought to emulate a Japanese potter, whose jar 'was uneven, casual, easy, nonchalant; . . . seemed almost accidental, but was not', often achieving this difficult ease when neatly sketched visual images combine to yield their modest commentary on man, time, and nature. Kevin Ireland, proclaiming that 'thin men/write gaunt poems', in which 'each word/sticks out/like a rib', has cultivated an epigrammatic wit, and in *Literary Cartoons* (1977) 'set down a sequence of troubled jests'.

Among newer poets, Bill Manhire and Elizabeth Smither have been similarly terse. Manhire explained: 'The chief joy of the short lyric I take to be its ability to carry the reader out of the sequential, linear world into its own moment: as it were, Snap'. Manhire's sidesteps of idiom, image, or narrative are always gracefully executed. His poems administer a series of mild shocks to the reader's imagination. Smither has the same power to startle, though sometimes gratuitously. She can skewer male sexual vanity or encapsulate the *outré* in a dozen mannered lines.

Of course all these poets have at times needed more room to manœuvre. Dallas, for example, has used dramatic monologue to reveal states of mind, as in 'An Old Woman Thinks of Death' or the extract from 'Jackinabox' where the grumbling caretaker of a camping ground carries more than a hint of a personified super-ego, vainly attempting to control a larrikin libido. And although Sam Hunt, Chrysler Valiant troubadour, describes himself as 'a tapper out of poems on table-top, sand-dune or bar; a hummer of roadsongs', a traditional craftsmanship serves more ambitious ends in such poems as 'My Father Today' and 'Birth of a Son'.

Other poets have opted not for the intensity of contraction but for that fashionable expansive mode in which everything within a wide-ranging field of awareness is hustled onto the page. In reviewing James K. Baxter's transitional collection, *Pig Island Letters* (1966), Charles Brasch diagnosed a tendency to write poetry rather than poems, so that instead of growing individually from unique occasions, the items seemed 'chopped off arbitrarily from a continuous poetic conveyor-belt'. Several of our poets would, with Baxter, repudiate Brasch's 'Apollonian' criteria, commending a Dionysiac openness to experience and an art less of packaging than of 'process'.

The catchcry points to the increasing influence of American theory and practice, particularly a broad stream that flows from Whitman, through Pound, Williams, Olson and the Black Mountain, New York, and Beat poets to diverge into many channels, for which Donald Allen's *The New American Poetry* (1960), revised as *The Postmoderns* (1982), forms some kind of catchment area. This is a poetry of 'open form', 'projective techniques', 'composition by field', the 'variable foot', and the 'breath group'. Its spoor is the uppercase ampersand. Yet the more talented New Zealand poets who thus disclose their allegiances draw on the tradition in markedly different ways. They are aware too that many of the finest living American poets were not rounded up into Allen's postmodernist flock.

Ian Wedde is the virtuoso of his generation. 'I tend to quest about like a dog backtracking & crisscrossing a terrain in search of an odour's source', he has said of his methods. Wedde's is a finely tuned contemporary sensibility. He projects its responses with *esprit*, and the poetic gifts on display are all but dazzling. His poems have wit, momentum, grace, and relish the haecceity of things. In idiom, tone, and movement 'Pathway to the Sea' has an insistent modernity that makes 'To a Friend in the Wilderness' seem a product of another era. Yet, for all its 'disorderly development &/the large number of/non-sequiturs', Wedde's poem has a firm narrative structure, and even a moral – spelt out explicitly enough for any Victorian. But it is a moral rooted in experience that we share with the poet as he so engagingly re-creates it for us in all its mental and physical detail. The poem actualizes the exuberant play of mind and personality over a train of back-yard events.

David Mitchell's verse, closely associated with the poetry-reading circuit, is scored on the page for oral delivery. It sings a distinctive music, created partly by the radical redeployment and fragmentation of a traditional prosody, partly by the blending into one register of pop vernacular and nineteenth-century poeticisms. It is verse that can accommodate pipis and unicorn, mandrake root and barber's chair, and it is toughened by intimacy with pain. And if Peter Olds can recall Kerouac or Corso, the zany vitality of this kiwi chloropromazine freak is entirely his own.

Reading New Zealand verse chronologically one discerns a gradual change in the relationship between 'image' and 'meaning'. Traditionally, poetry has linked an inner world of thoughts and feelings to an outer world of objects and events, encouraging description and narration of particulars to serve as correlatives for emotion or to expand into more general statement; 'encouragement' being a matter of selecting and arranging the sensory details, presenting them through language that carries a certain connotative loading, and adding direct comment. Poems have, to borrow Howard Nemerov's analogy, comprised both photograph and caption. But the drift of modern poetry is towards a less assertive relation between concrete image and abstract meaning, so that the caption is, as it were, insinuated into the photograph itself, phenomena being allowed to generate their own significance with a minimum of explicit interpretation. When this tendency is carried to extremes – so that not only is comment eschewed, but the other ways of eliciting meaning are also neglected – the reader experiences the poem as a hodgepodge of fragmentary perceptions or as a snapshot by a randomly pointed camera lens. 'A poem should not mean but be', but would 'An empty doorway and a maple leaf' affect us quite so deeply had we been given no clue that this image stands 'For all the history of grief'? We might have supposed it had something to do with Canadian immigration policy. The couplet gains its resonance from the juxtaposition of concrete and abstract.

Although New Zealand poets have in the last few decades become more suspicious of overt statement, the bulk of our best verse continues to generalize the particular through metaphor, to provide what Robert Frost called 'the pleasure of ulteriority', as in the subtle close of Fleur Adcock's 'The Soho Hospital for Women'. With the simple dual-purpose phrase 'how little I needed in fact' her chronicle of events and personages broadens out into an acquired wisdom. As the American poet Richard Wilbur declares, 'I like it when the ideas of a poem seem to be necessary aspects of the things or actions which it presents – stretching away and yet always adhering, like shadows'.

III

Of central importance to post-war New Zealand poetry has been the development of Allen Curnow and James K. Baxter into poets of extraordinary scope and power. The older man's *Collected Poems 1933-1973* (1974) proved to be a milestone and not a tombstone. The volume is a coherent record of those encounters with experience through which an acute poetic intelligence of a sceptical modern cast has struggled, with ever-increasing technical resource, to locate self in space and time. In the fifties the stylistic clarity of Curnow's performances on national themes gave way to more densely textured verse, crowded with images linked in a complex network of puns and assonances. But a poem such as 'Spectacular Blossom', no less than earlier pieces in which a personal malaise found its reflection in our island colony's past and present, transmutes a New Zealand reality into a broader truth, as it apprehends and fuses into a unity of the imagination life and death, youth and age, male and female, sacrifice and generation; for it fashions a pohutukawa tree in the image of both a young girl and an old man, and in its accompanying detail assimilates the local and familiar to the ritualistic, the archetypal, and the timeless.

The sequence *Trees, Effigies, Moving Objects* (1972) broke a long silence. In a lively contemporary style, marked by sudden shifts of register, Curnow, responding to new pressures, grapples with old concerns, to which the title points: *trees* for the living world around us, *effigies* for those constructs of the human mind which mediate between the raw physical facts and our experience of them, *moving objects* for a nervous sense of flux and fragmentation; through the sequence blows a chill wind of change. Public and private considerations merge, and the tension between *here* and *there* (now particularized as Washington D.C.) is explored yet again.

Curnow's next volume (1979) renders the 'incorrigible music' of an earth that, in Shakespeare's phrase, 'devours her own sweet brood'. In an irredeemably fallen world, to live is to kill. The cruel paradoxes of sacrifice have often fired Curnow's imagination. 'The stain of blood that writes an island story' has written the whole history of the human race. In *You Will Know When You Get There* (1982) the dominant theme is mortality. If the long modernist poem can be said to essay a new heterogeneity of matter and tone, promoting a strenuous imaginative activity in the reader seeking to grasp its suppressed interconnections and gain a sense of the whole, 'Organo ad Libitum' is the most powerful New Zealand addition to the genre.

In introducing his anthologies Curnow traced the emergence of an indigenous poetry, partly as a history of response to the physical situation and contours of these islands. A new generation of poets, mainly based in Wellington and several of them immigrants, argued that his selections for the *Penguin Book of New Zealand Verse* (1960) slighted new talents not readily drafted under a nationalist banner. Louis Johnson, in editing eleven issues of *New Zealand Poetry Yearbook* between 1951 and 1964, provided them with a forum; Baxter (1962) accused Curnow of a fixation on 'Kiwi stuff, bush broodings, seacoast broodings, mountain broodings, by poets who still think of London as the centre of the cultural universe'. Johnson himself turned to the domestic and the suburban for his subject matter, exploring social and inter-personal anxieties more commonly the novelist's province. In his best pieces a Freudian symbolism conveys a Freudian understanding. Peter Bland confronted the Welfare State with wry humour; Gordon Challis built elegant verbal icons from his insights as a working psychotherapist; and Owen Leeming, in 'The Priests of Serrabonne' (a sort of extended 'Church Going') anatomized a lost faith. But the most eloquent new voice was that of James K. Baxter.

Baxter burst upon Wellington in the forties, a teenage prodigy, a local Dylan Thomas or Rimbaud. He died in 1972, aged forty-six, barefooted and bearded pastor to drop-outs and drug-addicts, guru and social critic, 'scapegoat taking upon himself the burden of tribal guilt' (his own words twenty years earlier), founder of a new Jerusalem in the Maori settlement of that name on the banks of the Wanganui river. Alcoholic, Public Servant, Catholic Convert, Family Man, Burns Fellow intervened.

His is the most ample talent yet to appear among our poets. In their various metamorphoses his life and work, always growing out of each other, are nonetheless a continuum, following lines already laid down in those provocative 'notes on modern poetry' published as *The Fire and the Anvil* (1955). There a coherent view of art is outlined; it is touched on or elaborated in *Aspects of Poetry in New Zealand* (1967) and the talks and essays in *The Man on the Horse* (1967). It sees poetic activity as therapeutic – for the poet and for his society. Artistic creation is for Baxter a process of integration, whereby the anarchic, sexual, aggressive energies of the unconscious (the Freudian id, if you like) are brought into the total personality. 'Agonies, desires, and dilemmas which the housewifely mind has cast out on the rubbish-heap must be unearthed and exposed to the sun'. Outcast, hobo, criminal, junky, bohemian, vandal, pirate, hell's angel, tomcat – each is seen by the poet as *alter ego*, figure for the free creative-destructive core of the psyche. Baxter's career was the most vital reaction yet against 'the Calvinist ethos which underlies our determinedly secular culture like the bones of a dinosaur buried in the suburban garden plot – *work is good; sex is evil; do what you're told and you'll be alright; don't dig too deep into yourself*', an ethos breeding rigidity and neurosis.

'What happens is either meaningless to me, or else it is mythology', Baxter once said, and much of his work (as of his life) coheres around enactment of the ancient seasonal myth of separation, death, and rebirth, as paradigm of psychic and spiritual pilgrimage. Descent into the self's underworld has various guises: exploration of a cave, return to the womb of the pub, obliteration of the ego through the sexual act or the steady contemplation of death. In coastal 'hollow place', on park bench, at the centre of the labyrinth, or between the thighs of Hine-nui-te-po an apprehension of inner chaos releases the creative springs.

Baxter's output was abundant. The *Collected Poems* (1979) amount to more than six hundred pages. Their symbols strike deep, and Baxter's work exhibits in full measure the creator's 'love of the world, and a wish that it should respond to his love'. Of the enduring worth of such well shaped structures as 'The Fallen House', 'Wild Bees', 'The Homecoming', 'Lament for Barney Flanagan', and 'Perseus' there can be no doubt.

His last poems may yet prove even more valuable. Back in 1965 he described his constructions as of two kinds, 'a strait-jacket of formal rhetoric, with full rhymes and references to Greek mythology, fathered by Robert Lowell', and 'a loose hen-coop, erected by rule-of-thumb bush carpentry, . . . with half-rhymes and speech rhythms'. His *Jerusalem Sonnets* (1970) affected a new compromise. Each unit of what is in effect a single poem consists of fourteen unrhymed, irregular, paired lines – a form borrowed from Lawrence Durrell's 'The Soliloquy of Hamlet'. This keeps the 'poetic conveyor-belt' moving, but permits the poet to parcel experience in manageable segments. The last phase of Baxter's career is, poetically, a triumphant vindication of the course that Brasch saw him taking in *Pig Island Letters*. The Jerusalem verse has immediacy (sustained even in his sestinas) and an unmistakable authenticity. More important, the man himself has become so assured, the personality so authoritative, that simply by projecting it entire, by way of spontaneous, casual-seeming talk, he creates the 'memorable speech' of poetry. It is as if the essential creative impulse had already gone into fashioning the life. The poetry of Baxter's Jerusalem period has the cohesion and richness of a singular self in a singular situation – a situation affording easy access to Christian thought and symbol, Maori myth and folk-lore, a rural New Zealand setting that declares life's simplicities, and a cast of characters. And Baxter's foreknowledge of his own imminent death is a constant source of strength.

Historically, the positives of our poetry have been tied to landscape or sexual love. The significance of Baxter's social experiment, and of the poetry associated with it, lies in its synthesis of humanist, Christian, and Maori tribal values in a potent ideal of community, founded on *aroha* or *caritas*, 'the love present in each man's heart which will bring him to heaven and to God and join him to his fellow men'. This is poetry not of dogma but of vision.

IV

Where Baxter assumed the role of prophet, his near-contemporary Kendrick Smithyman epitomizes the poet-craftsman, the contriver of 'verbal contraptions' (in Auden's phrase). If, as Robert Frost quipped, poetry is 'what gets lost in translation', Smithyman, our least translatable poet, might be accounted our most poetic. Certainly his·is a mind that meets Auden's notorious criterion of the poetic: it revels in 'riddles and all other ways of not calling a spade a spade'.

His verse is oblique, intricate, allusive, 'conceited' in the Jacobean sense, peppered with puns, and sometimes unrewardingly obscure. But the way of saying represents a way of seeing, obsessive in descrying correspondences. Smithyman nods towards an older view of poetry as cultivated entertainment, where a game-playing delight in the resources of language and the formation of pattern dominates the creative drive, the play becoming serious when the deeper levels of personality are engaged. His study of New Zealand poetry, *A Way of Saying* (1965), is in part a rationalization of his own poetic strategy. There he distinguishes between the 'romantic' and 'academic' strains in our verse; his own verse is obviously 'academic' as in the course of the discussion he defines the term – a poetry with its own inbuilt defence-works of irony and wit.

The personality emerging· from Smithyman's eight volumes is sane, good-humoured, quirky, and in the least histrionic way compassionate. A strong sense of human limitation is accompanied by a strong sense of human worth and dignity. Smithyman can celebrate love in its most everyday manifestations, accept frailty and eccentricity with a wry affection, take pleasure in virtue however unspectacular its form. No other New Zealand poet can more deftly capture the lineaments of a particular locale. He responds to historical process. And he can convey psychological states of the city-dweller, as in 'Flying to Palmerston', which, through a specific occasion and setting, images dislocation, unease, distraction, suspense.

In reviewing Charles Doyle's anthology, *Recent Poetry in New Zealand* (1965), designed to supplement Curnow's Penguin, David Moody named Charles Spear and M. K. Joseph among a small group of poets who had made 'authoritatively distinct contributions to New Zealand poetry since the war' (*Landfall*, 78). This still seems perceptive. *Twopence Coloured* (1951) looks like verbal cameo-work, but Spear's 'studiously minor' muse is (as he claims) 'attuned to doom'. A post-war temper infiltrates the trim stanzas of a Rhymers Club aesthete, and disturbing, sharply focused details loom from a phantasmagoria in miniature of historical, literary, and personal anecdote.

Joseph is unmistakably one of Smithyman's 'academics', for whom a poem remains 'an artefact made with words', in which a cultivated mind disports, or meditates on the seen and the unseen. He is moved, and can move the reader, by abstractions, which he elucidates by way of exempla from the visible world. 'On the Exercise of Freewill in the Lifting of an Arm' has obvious enough antecedents, but what other New Zealand poet could conduct a philosophical argument in relaxed blank verse to the point where the bland voice of the logician rises to something akin to passion?

Over the last few decades several gifted poets have shown staying-power, notably C. K. Stead and Alistair Campbell. 'Hard. Bright. Clean. Particular.' The opening line of the first poem in Stead's *Crossing the Bar* (1972) inevitably proffers itself as true of a small yet fascinating body of verse, difficult to characterize. In attempting the Baxterian sonnet Stead suspected 'an unconscious wish to exorcise that dour Kiwi ghost'. The wraiths of many poets, living and dead, haunt Stead's pages. Alert to technical innovations, he has the expertise to write well in any mode, and has lately found a new direction. But to cull snippets from his experiments in open form (as in 'Walking Westward') is to distort the essential nature of such poetry. Campbell has always followed his own path. *Mine Eyes Dazzle* (1950), a best-seller, had 'glamour or incandescence' (as Baxter called it) and a vibrant energy. Campbell's poems are shapely and lucid. In *Sanctuary of Spirits* (1963) an endemic violence, elsewhere projected into landscape, is strikingly personalized in the warrior figure of Te Rauparaha.

Hone Tuwhare turned poet in middle age. The lyrics of *No Ordinary Sun* (1964), with their vivid animistic imagery, haunting free-verse cadences, and muscular vigour, make a direct appeal to the senses and emotions. In the title poem a tree, addressed in subtly chosen human terms, is imagined as victim of nuclear holocaust; animism, the 'pathetic fallacy', generates the feeling here, as in Campbell's early verse. Tuwhare, R. A. K. Mason suggested in a foreword, drew 'his main strength from his own people'. His poetry owes something to the oratory of the marae, and is suffused with a Maori love of the land and nostalgia for lost ways of life and thought. In his later volumes the tone is less certain; the poet tends to become self-conscious and to strike uncomfortable neo-sophisticate poses or indulge in strained whimsy, but there is an extension of range into colloquialism and anecdote. A poem such as 'Drunk' achieves a satisfying double perspective, presenting both the ludicrous behaviour of a drunk as seen by the detached spectator and the mental life of the drunk, the pain and need, as experienced from the inside; and the comic lament of the Maori statue in downtown Auckland hits a characteristic note of bemused badinage.

Among the generation who began publishing in the early sixties it is to Vincent O'Sullivan that one turns for the most persuasive matching of productivity to talent. His poems are always elegantly wrought, rhythmically alive, rich in imagery and specific reference, much of it quarried abroad by a visitor conscious enough of a contrasting homeland. Some of his strongest early poems rework Greek mythology to expose relationships and states of mind. His 'Butcher' poems take the tradition of Glover's 'Harry' songs a step closer to drama, especially now that Butcher's cousin Baldy, the intellectual, has joined the cast. Butcher, amiable dealer in flesh and blood and guts, is created with a novelist's empathy and given a line of racy shop-talk which in an entirely original way weds the indigenous to time-honoured poetic concerns. O'Sullivan moves easily between the colloquial and the eloquent. In *Brother Jonathan, Brother Kafka* (1980), a sequence of sixteen-line units divided into unrhymed quatrains, circumstances surrounding a visit to New England converge to force an intense emotional and intellectual stock-taking, and to discipline the poet's copious skills. The voice is perfectly modulated. O'Sullivan attends to nuances of word and idiom and packs his observations into the verse, so as to achieve what Kevin Ireland has aptly called 'the verbal equivalent of focal depth'.

A satisfying feature of the last decade has been a rise in the number of women writing good verse. *Private Gardens: An Anthology of New Zealand Women Poets* (1977), edited by Riemke Ensing, has thirty-five contributors. In 1975 three women published their first collections: Rachel McAlpine, Elizabeth Smither, and Lauris Edmond. Although they differ considerably in style and poetic character all, like Mary Stanley and 'Paul Henderson' (Ruth France) before them, have written interestingly about people and relationships.

Fleur Adcock has been publishing over a much longer period, and she, too, records incidents involving mother and child, woman and husband, lover, friend. Her verse, supple and assured, has continued to delight since she first staked her claim to our attention with that urbane testimony to a classical education, 'Note on Propertius I.3'. In 1965 she said: 'I tend to admire poetry which can wear a formal dress lightly and naturally'. In an apt verse tribute to her second volume, *Tigers* (1967), Charles Brasch wrote (in 'Saying a World') of the 'grace and crispness' of her 'detached, distinct' voice, in 'saying-songs that talk/People, animals', poems 'Disclosing a tiger-cool/Simulacre of mind and being'. Her manner is always equable and decorous, but may be astringent, and many poems are tense with intuited menace, their composure holding nightmare at bay. In her latest collections her 'saying-songs' fall mainly into syllabics or freer forms. A poem such as the beautiful 'Kilpeck', so exact in its delineation of complex feeling through a faultless selection of external details, she considered in 1977 'typical of the way I now work'. Yet in the last section of 'The Soho Hospital for Women' she reverts to a most effective use of rhyme.

V

Twenty years ago critical debate about New Zealand verse centred on 'content'. Yet Curnow's insistence that 'Reality must be local and special at the point where we pick up the traces', often interpreted as a prescription for poetry that sported a national badge, was the statement of a simple truth, a recognition that we exist in space and time and that poems emerge from the attempt to embody in words a poet's experience in a given here and now. The demand was for particularity of reference, for the verbal rendering of the visible and palpable stuff of the world we inhabit. Recent arguments have been about 'poetics', theories of procedure and form. But the underlying issue is still poetry's relationship to phenomena. Ironically, Curnow has now felt obliged to stress the importance of those intellectual processes whereby poetry has always ordered the 'phenomenal welter'. Again his seems the voice of common sense, but poets follow their instincts, and we must look for good poems wherever we can find them. Poetry, said Howard Nemerov, offering a minimal definition, 'is a way of getting something right in language'. New Zealand poetry is increasingly heterogeneous. A greater range of experience has been getting into our poems, which assume various configurations on the page and voice-patterns in the mind. But the best, whatever their modes, have the indispensable appeal of 'language doing itself right'.

Allen Curnow's comments on Fairburn are from *The Penguin Book of New Zealand Verse* (1960), p.319. Poets' prose statements are from *Recent Poetry in New Zealand* (1965), ed. Charles Doyle (Baxter, Adcock); *The Young New Zealand Poets* (1973), ed. Arthur Baysting (Manhire, Wedde); and *Private Gardens: An Anthology of New Zealand Women Poets* (1977), ed. Riemke Ensing (Adcock). Baxter's other remarks are from his prose works mentioned in the text, and (on *caritas*) from an interview with J. E. Weir in *Landfall*, 111 (September 1974). Hunt's comment is from *Landfall*, 122 (June 1977), Dallas's from her collection *Walking on the Snow* (1976). Brasch's review of *Pig Island Letters* is reprinted in Charles Brasch, *The Universal Dance* (1981). My references to American poet Howard Nemerov are to his book *Figures of Thought* (1978), and Richard Wilbur's statement is in *Poet's Choice* (1962), ed, Paul Engle and Joseph Langland. 'A poem should not mean but be' and the couplet rhyming a maple leaf and grief are from Archibald MacLeish's famous poem, 'Ars Poetica'. Curnow's recent critical theorizing, mentioned in Section V, is 'Olson as Oracle: "Projective Verse" Thirty Years On', *New Zealand Through the Arts: Past and Present* (Turnbull Library, 1982).

MacDonald P. Jackson

Prose

The short story, like matagouri, has a capacity for survival at times and in places where larger forms are not much in evidence. During the Second World War there were few New Zealand novels, and no drama to speak of. But in 1945 there were a dozen odd publications that accepted short stories. *New Zealand New Writing* had worked to what one would call a consistent standard over three years, but the publication terminated with the ending of the war. The hand-set little magazine *Arena* was for a time the one serious literary journal, until Charles Brasch in 1947 established *Landfall*. Brasch possessed an editorial flair that encouraged and guided most of the writers in this collection. Under his own hand for twenty years, and with other editors since, *Landfall* has been the tested survivor in a field where titles continue to rise and fall. Their number and life span fluctuates, but such journals as *Fernfire, Numbers, Here & Now, Mate, Climate,* and *Islands* particularly, were prominent among those that first gave standing room to new talents, or helped set new directions. University publications too turn up impressive lists of writers who began to find their feet in, for instance, Otago's *Critic*, Auckland's *Kiwi*, Victoria's *Spike*. *Te Ao Hou* for several years was the important focus for Maori writing. And over several decades the New Zealand Broadcasting Corporation, both through radio and the weekly journal the *Listener*, has taken hundreds of short stories to an audience far wider than any within the reach of other publications.

There are few writers in this anthology whose work has not consistently appeared in one or more of these places.

II

At the end of the War, New Zealand fiction of a kind that would have an appeal beyond local readers did not make up more than a short row of books. Even less did it comprise anything that might be called a strong tradition. But it was also true that the country's two best known writers had each established an *œuvre* that clearly led in different directions. Almost thirty years before, Katherine Mansfield had brought the tradition of European Impressionism to the English short story. With *Prelude* especially she had given her fiction the glancing, associative method of the film, anticipating techniques in prose that already distinguished the poetry of some of her contemporaries. She invented for herself a narrative form that now seems the obvious inheritance of any short story writer. At home, in deliberate opposition, and almost alone, Frank Sargeson had set up a simpler alternative. He quickly struck his own distinctive line, and his readers in the nineteen thirties and forties caught eagerly at the sound of their own voices. New Zealanders had never heard themselves quite so clearly as they did in those tight, low-key stories of men for whom speech often seemed an imposition.

Mansfield's writing was subtle, delicate at times to the point of preciosity (so its opponents thought), drawing new boundaries with its form and presentation. Here was the individual voice, as in most Modernist prose, staking its claim to change what had been thought of as fixed. Sargeson's way, once the choice was made for the local and indigenous, meant a preference for the laconic, and for the broader strokes defining a society rich enough in passions, but short on subtlety. (His later strained ornateness was to offer decoration when immediacy tapered off.)

Almost all the stories collected in this anthology turn to one or other of those traditions. There are those writers whose talents led them to attempt something quite new, and the greater number whose emphasis lay rather on depicting New Zealand life more accurately, but in ways already more or less laid down. Both approaches have attracted fine writers. But this simple yet real division has meant that insistent social realism, with often enough a deliberately uneventful prose as the most appropriate instrument for expressing a no-frills society, became the dominant tradition of New Zealand fiction. Those who have been least touched by that predilection, writers like Janet Frame and Maurice Duggan, the Maurice Gee of *Plumb* and the novelist M. K. Joseph, are those who have found styles that draw more from complex individual minds than they do from what society offers, or from what New Zealand writing had to hand. Language developed as private configuration, rather than the attempt to make it serve as a kind of verbal camera, is what the best of our fiction achieves.

Ideas have seldom burgeoned quickly or moved with much speed in a society whose ambitions, as Samuel Butler observed in 1863, seemed 'far better adapted to develop and maintain in health the physical than the intellectual nature.' To expect anything else, at least in the context of our colonial beginnings, would be to misunderstand history. Yet the limitations remain. From the start we have been a community so jealously derivative from Britain that in recent decades we have come desperately to fear the thought of invigorating our genetic pool from any other source. As a Pacific people we are almost rabidly European, yet we suspect all but a small corner of Europe. We are a country that from the 1980s can look back at intelligently alert political government for fewer than twenty years in the entire century. Our national assertiveness is partly that of a community less sure of its own character as the decades proceed; or if more sure at particular points, less happy with what it sees. And it is here that one comes closest to the note sounded most often in our fiction: the idea that for most of us self-definition is likely to emerge from a litany of negatives, or dreams that failed, or sourness in unexpected places.

In the forty odd stories brought together here, the fact that over three quarters are shaped about distress or disillusion of some kind may not in itself be such a significant thing to note. One could say the short story *anywhere* has tended to move in such dimensions. It is the novel that gives us the feel of a society in its broader workings, and the short story with its comparatively simpler set of events that lights a flare behind the single character, catching him or her off-guard, exposing the pathos of ordinary lives. But that explanation stops too short. It does not explain why acts of violence are at the centre of well over half the stories here; why fantasy or fun or the absurd crops up in no more than half a dozen stories; why it is that there are so few in which men and women are seen in any kind of relationship that might be taken as admirable. One concedes there is always a risk in assuming that art reflects society in its domestic particulars. But when a one-to-one realism is the predominant mode in most of these stories, certain conclusions begin to bear down rather insistently. To think those reflections are not the business of the literary critic would be to miss the point of what fiction does for most of those who read it.

There can be few comparisons so disconcerting or ironical as that between what the novelist John Mulgan wrote when, as a member of the British Army he met up with fellow New Zealanders in the African desert in 1942, and sentences from another fine novelist, written a quarter of a century further on. Mulgan had been struck by those 'quiet and shrewd and sceptical' men, without the 'tired patience' or the 'automatic discipline' of the English. In the flush of optimism, he wrote 'If the old world ends now with this war, as well it may, I have had visions and dreamed dreams of another New Zealand that might grow into the future on the foundations of the old. This country would have more people to share it. They would be hard-working peasants from Europe that know good land, craftsmen that love making things with their own hands, and all men who want the freedom that comes from an ordered, just society. There would be more children in the sands and sunshine, more small farms, gardens, and cottages. . . . Few would be rich, none would be poor. They would fill the land and make it a nation.' (*Report on Experience*, 1947.)

In her novel *A State of Siege* (1966) Janet Frame looks coldly at what that vivid hope of Mulgan's had become. 'Perhaps, after all, in a land where bulldozers were people, motor-mowers were people, where all things were people except, it seemed, the people themselves, she might be taking risks in trying to paint the islanders, for their teeth might be the fangs of bulldozers filled with clay, and their hair might be still, marigold petals, their faces grey mudflats pimpled with weeds, their eyes mangrove pools.'

Admittedly hers is the vision of an intensely symbolic writer, a kind of antipodean Kafka for whom human personality is crushed not by the intractability of laws and systems, but by its own humanity – by what novelists in one way or another have been celebrating for two hundred years. Not all of us believe that to be normal, to be suburban, to live surrounded by that clutter of machines, gadgets, tidiness, control, all that becomes the paraphernalia of violence and guilt in her novels, is necessarily to be on the side of the obtuse or the damned. Yet Frame's gift is to tilt the mirror in a way that effectively condemns. Her belief is that an individual's language is as close as we shall come to what once was called truth – the right and appropriate relation between things. The claims of language itself are the last human flurry. A knack with images, the achievements of private speech, is all that an autistic child has to pit against her killers in that splendid apocalyptic novel, *Intensive Care* (1970). But Frame's unique voice does not prevent her setting out very clearly what is true of a number of New Zealand writers. Many are forced to a kind of existential stance, the need to build from the ground up the set of values to which allegiance might be given.

For generations the changes have been rung on the old but potent fact of this country's isolation – of writer from community, community from its parent and from indigenous culture, of present-day New Zealanders from whatever moral forces first settled here. And the alienation, of course, which is the stock-in-trade of twentieth century literature. Yet surprisingly few critics have written on why writers are so seemingly cut off from their public; why a strong Protestant ethos has ended up for many as hypocrisy, suspicion, dullness. Patrick Evans has noted the *political* belief amongst us that 'individual dissent . . . may have a malign and external origin.'

As they read the writers of almost any other country, New Zealand pakehas may feel dismayed at how much there is to draw on *there*, which most of us here must do without. Little folklore, for example. Nothing in the way of songs or traditional music that is really our own. No festivals in any true sense. No traditions of marvellous exaggeration or rhetoric or satire or regionalism. (How much of our admiration for Albert Wendt's recent novels has to do with his drawing so richly on his Samoan background?) The little enough we start with leads at times to defensively extravagant claims – that 'Godzone' syndrome of political leaders, airline publicity, vice-regal speeches, brewery calendars. It ends with almost all good prose writers in the country feeling that they are locked into a system that claims meagre loyalty.

I would hazard putting forward this other reason as well. Many of the story writers in this anthology came from a working-class or non-conformist childhood, with its attendant virtues and limitations. They then became part of a society where those values for the most part have been betrayed over and over, and mostly by those from a similar background. So many of us grow into a world where we are uncomfortable; it does not continue in any satisfactory way what childhood and adolescence, what we learned at home or were told about our country at school, actually prepared us for. We are cut off from that, even as we are prevented by a hoary intellectual fashion from accepting that there can be much rewarding human feeling in what we loosely call that middle class where most of us have come to live. Our caginess with both definitions and allegiances may have much to do with why that staple of the English novel, a sense of social fabric, is a rare thing in our fiction.

One may suppose that is why so much of our story telling reverts to childhood for its values, and sees so much adult life in terms of betrayal. This is a common theme in Maurice Gee. It is at the centre of our one fine political fable, Michael Henderson's *The Log of a Superfluous Son* (1975). That inventive and witty book finds in our meat trade a convincing emblem for military involvement in the East. Its young protagonist, caught up in inevitable corruptions, looks back to childhood on the land: 'there in the hills on the farm where you grew and dreamed before you heard the language of leaders and legitimation, before you considered limits first and before everything was located, and lost. . . . Ah yes and you were Baldur battling Fenris and nothing was little.'

How often something like that is declared in our fiction. It is as though there is no other time but childhood when many feel at home. I am sure too that it leads to so many New Zealanders never wearying of returning to talk of the Depression, to the city riots, to the 1951 wharf strike, to those few times in officially peaceful years when at least some men and women knew a sense of community through upheaval. (The massive resistance to the 1981 Springbok tour inevitably joins that list.) It is why we cannot afford to be sceptical when we read in writers like Dan Davin that war gave something to New Zealanders that they seldom felt in peacetime. For violence, whatever else, is the possibility of something new. In Maurice Shadbolt's most important novel, *Strangers and Journeys* (1972), the main events arise out of violence and protest, from brief group efforts to achieve that elusive dream, the just society. Those efforts collapse into disparate and solitary men acting out very personal dramas. It is nicely appropriate that the artist in the novel paints canvases like Colin McCahon's, sombre love-pictures for a land of bitter men. Paintings with such titles as *A Land with No Heroes*, and *Can Anyone Save Us Here?* The make-shift resolutions that the novel comes to are the business of men acting privately. Society has no share in them.

Yet any tradition that is worth its salt is going to have at some point one set of values clearly drawing against another. In New Zealand fiction, that contrary pull is most apparent in stories written by Maoris, or stories by pakehas who find their touchstones in Maori life. Polynesians, unlike most of us, lay claim to a solid world of people who share their values, who would ask much the same things from the future, who reverence a common past. I doubt that there are many New Zealanders who read Patricia Grace and Witi Ihimaera, Roderick Finlayson and Noel Hilliard, and not envy their certainty, that part of their experience which draws on a communal source. Against *aroha*, what he called 'the powerful bond of love that springs from a tribal matrix', James K. Baxter could see in his own world only pakeha suburbia, 'never once happy, never at peace'. For many writers besides Baxter, the enemy of tribal values is first and always the city. Noel Hilliard has looked with the hardest eye at Maori urban life, working most accurately with the language of his characters. But in any Maori fiction, the measure of degradation is the distance travelled from the tribal centre. Ihimaera's 'The Gathering of the Whakapapa' (1972) is an impressive account of precisely what that centre means. An old man who puts off dying until he has completed the ancestral tree is asked whether the *whakapapa* really matters. 'Oh yes! Because it gives me unison with the universe. It tells me that I am not alone or ever will be. It weaves me into a pattern of life that began at world's creation and will be there at world's end. . . . Although I will die, the pattern will not be broken.'

There are few pakeha writers who would claim anything like this, and probably none who did not agree that for western writers anywhere, nostalgia is hardly a fruitful road. Yet regret for what our own society does not possess explains what even thirty years ago one critic called the 'disproportionately numerous' number of Maoris in our fiction. It is another way of putting to ourselves that our post-European patterns are fragmentary, at times privately symbolic, almost always a matter of construction rather than what has been handed down. It also implies how fiction cannot help but become a moral act.

III

A single story is read for itself, but an anthology often is taken as a kind of national dress. Any collection from the same cultural background will throw certain tendencies into relief, and encourage us to remark that what may merely be a feature in one work becomes a theme – perhaps an obsession – as it occurs in a dozen others. You simply cannot hear forty people from one country, and not pick up the sounds that they share. Yet a common social stance is not in the first place what brings us to a book. What draws us is the way any writer sets off with the inheritance of one time, at one place, and turns it so that while what emerges is clearly from no other source, even more clearly it is the shaping of one mind. When one reads in Joy Cowley's 'The Silk' of the tiny figure gesturing from the bridge, or of Maurice Duggan's Miss Laverty receiving the broken record, one is not too much concerned with whether old age is a predominant theme in so many other stories, or that Miss Laverty's return to her room places her with similar characters who live alone. One may of course observe it, and statistics make their point. It is not even the event of the snipping scissors or the plangent tune at last coming to an end that holds our attention, although each is brilliantly placed for its effect. In every good story, however much what is depicted matters for itself, there is something else that matters more. The exuberance or refinement of style, the fact of delight in language working to its given end, is what brings us back to any piece of fiction. Style is what breaks a tradition into the components that interest us. Maurice Gee and Owen Marshall may write more centrally from their society than do most of our short story writers, but that is not at the last why we admire them. Our admiration, as with writers as different as Yvonne du Fresne or Margaret Sutherland or the fabulist Chris Else, is for the flexing of language under the direction of one voice. That is to say only what any decent writer assumes. The verbal patterns of fiction are not the gifts of the reporter, but those of the illusionist.

There is a difference, then, in how we read an anthology, and the stories that make it up. But there is no problem about a story working as 'art', and also leaving us with what may as well be called a 'moral point' – an arranged view of how we live, which is not simply a snapshot. Each of these stories has been chosen because at some point reality is picked up and rubbed in a way that had not quite been done before. Something is seen that any of us might have observed; the way it comes to us could be provided only by one mind. However modestly, every story works towards that 'figure in the carpet' that Henry James spoke of. Whatever exists is *in* the fiction, however we choose to take up references to what lies beyond it, or use the story as a flashlight across our lives. And there is a fine phrase of Janet Frame's to suggest what only the best will direct at us: 'the imaginative force . . . trained to see the invisible, the intangible, the real.'

Vincent O'Sullivan

Note

The selections of prose and verse were made jointly late 1981 and early 1982. We were able to add some works published in 1982, but not, unfortunately, Allen Curnow's longish 'Organo ad Libitum'. We had planned to include a story by Ronald Hugh Morrieson, but permission was refused by John Barnett of Longman Paul. We had originally included poems by Louis Johnson, but unfortunately he later withdrew his permission. Portions of the poetry introduction have been revised from an article on New Zealand writing in *Thirteen Facets*, ed. Ian Wards, 1978.

Sincere thanks are due to the following: Nicole Jackson and Caroline Macdonald for many hours' work on proof-reading, and the former for ordering and typing the bibliography; Moira O'Byrne and Mark Houlahan for help with xeroxing and with gathering information.

Since the editors were in separate countries while much of this anthology was being selected and typeset, we thank Anne French for gracefully and efficiently meeting the extra demands that this situation made on her as publisher's editor.

MacD. P. J.
V. O'S.

J. R. HERVEY

I Have Made Friends with Time

I have made friends with time although I have seen
His fingers close on many a meek treasure:
Friends, although in the time of the dark visit
There was no silver word of recompense.

Time makes no contract, softens with no pledge
The onset of events, but like the seasons
His moods return so that today lies
A petted lover but tomorrow dies.

Yet I have made friends with time,
Having taken his cloud-burst of pain
As earth takes the rain,
And in the threatening twilight
Have been as an evening lark in whose throat
Day lingers though lost over the mountains.

Friends with time although
He brings death like a blow,
For then I shall no more walk with mystery
Speaking but telling nothing like the sea,
No more be wistful with winds,
No more with the necessity of the lark
Publish the day to the dark. . . .

And all this
At the turn of the road,
Or beyond the secretive hills.

The Return

Her childhood could not believe in those mountains
But growing up under them
Her youth learned to kneel to their greatness.

Finding, however, a love higher than mountains,
She departed into an equable domesticity,
Rude, nevertheless, with a dark rush of duties,
And caught in cascading trivialities.

But love kept a silence in her heart,
And snow-bright memories rose
Out of a scene distant as juvenility,
A tranquillizing retrospect.

And these stood guard until time
In his more tender guise as deliverer
Nudged her into the narrowness of age.

Where hungering for a waft of the freedom in which she began
And with past loyalties stirring like lilies,
She returned to the former wilderncss
Where she had lost her childhood like a silver trinket,
And to the mountains and their old redeeming friendship,
Feeling so safe under mountains.

Children among the Tombstones

The O so gay
Among the text-strewn graves at play –
Says nothing the heaven-telling story
To inmates of the earlier glory.

Mourning the wrangle
Between life and death a carven angel –
Too near the beginning to see the end
They danced with time the trumped up friend.

And sprinkled over
With loves and flowers and songs to cover
From ghosts and stones so down to death,
And mounded hints that hold their breath.

To party laughs
They could invite the epitaphs,
Wiseacre text and monument –
No death, no death, the word was sent.

From the wide eyed
Of world without end was nothing to hide,
Necropolis nurse of endless play,
No death, no death whistled the day.

EILEEN DUGGAN

Shades of Maro of Toulouse

Where are the words that broke the heart with beauty?
This is the age of the merely clever.
As pâté de foie gras
Demands the grossened geese,
You must pass satiety
Because without morbidity
There is no caste,
No cachet.
You have not lived.
Also, whether with or without,
Use erudition,
Shrug in tags in strange tongues,
And leer by ellipses.
To play it your way –
Ex pede Herculem,
But from your foot, oh seldom Apollo!
Or have it then,
Sus Minervam!

In one breath decry reason and avow it;
Demand it of others but claim to transcend it;
Refuse to return to a hope you have failed.
There is human respect in even apostasy,
And the metaphysical is above creeds!

Write of the poor but not for them.
The aim is altruism.
It enables savants to evade
Where charity would demand
Contacts.

There is somewhat which flatters,
Which sends the thumbs to the armpits
In this role of dialectical defender.

I speak not of those humble
Who grieve for a world awry
And own themselves frustrate
Save in random will:
Who hold reason is the mate of truth,
Not a bleak, rabid spider
That eats its espouser;
Who husk hate
And in beauty
Cry for the moon,
Not the paraselene
Of those afraid to talk in their sleep
Lest they be intelligible.

Oh, God, in these our days,
Our dreadful days,
Give us simplicity,
Give us passion,
To write not of
But to and for man!

Contrast

It was so cold the skyline seemed to splinter
As the ice in the puddles cracked beneath the camels.
The great statute that we know as winter,
Unsoftened yet by any Spring amendment,
Was full enforced – a sumptuary law,
Forbidding earth undue indulgence
In leaf and flower, in hip and haw.

The caravan swayed like a ship under canvas when its
        topsails belly in the wind,
And the Magi looked over the rolling dunes
As a sailor to shore in his mind.
Their light in the dusk was like a lantern at a mast-head,
Seen dipping, the bluer for the salt air, afar off;
And their thought was deep and slow and undulating
Like the rising and falling of a galley in the sea's trough –
All very leisurely as demand great distances –
And the star, as slow as reason, undulated too.

Ah but the shepherds on the hill above the grotto,
Like a bolt from the blue,
Hurtled headlong, helter-skelter, wild-foot, down the cragside,
As fast as instinct – no conjecture, no dismay!
They had not watched for years; they had not calculated;
But they knew the way.

Augury

The heart can bear great omens
Of terror to fall,
But a soft dread or a slow threat
Fear most of all!

A sign as light as thistle-seed
Bodes the wildest pain.
When down flies on a still day,
Say wind, see rain!

A. R. D. FAIRBURN

For an Amulet

What truly is will have no end,
although denied by friend or foe,
and this I tell to foe and friend
as onward to the grave we go.

The candle in my little room
gives light but will not bake the host.
I share my certainty with Hume,
my candle with the Holy Ghost.

The Estuary

The wind has died, no motion now
in the summer's sleepy breath. Silver the sea-grass,
the shells and the driftwood, fixed in the moon's vast crystal.
Think: long after, when the walls of the small house
have collapsed upon us, each alone,
far gone the earth's invasion
the slow earth bedding and filling the bone,
this water will still be crawling up the estuary,
fingering its way among the channels, licking the stones;
and the floating shells, minute argosies
under the giant moon, still shoreward glide
among the mangroves on the creeping tide.

The noise of gulls comes through the shining darkness
over the dunes and the sea. Now the clouded moon
is warm in her nest of light. The world's a shell
where distant waves are murmuring of a time
beyond this time. *Give me the ghost of your hand:
unreal, unreal the dunes,
the sea, the mangroves, and the moon's white light,
unreal, beneath our naked feet, the sand.*

Tom's a-Cold

Where is my love that has no peer,
   where wanders she, among what brakes,
along what hillside cold and drear
   above the tarns and hollow lakes?
I hear the whirlwind shake the sky,
   I feel the worm within me gnaw,
for she is lost, and lost am I,
   alone upon my bed of straw.

Beyond the door blasts of black air,
   the rain descending on the wind;
I know my love is wandering there

with ragged clothes and hair unpinned.
I shall not lead her through the door
  and lay my hand upon her wrist,
O she must roam for evermore
  through rain and dark, or moonlit mist.

My love was fairer than the sun,
  her breast beneath my hand was warm,
but she has left me all alone
  in midmost darkness of the storm.
I hear the sleet upon the thatch,
  the thunder by the lightning hurled;
I know she will not lift my latch
  before the ending of the world.

Song at Summer's End

Down in the park the children play
rag-happy through the summer day
with dirty feet and freckled faces,
laughing, fighting, running races.
Dull against the smoky skies
the summer's heavy burden lies,
leaden leaves on tired trees
lacking supple limbs like these.

The skyline shows the shape of life,
tomorrow's world of sweat and strife,
fifty stacks and one grey steeple.
Down the street come factory people,
folk who used to play on swings,
dodging chores and apron-strings
to wrestle on the grass and run
barefoot with the fleeting sun.

Some of the kids are sailing boats;
the first leaf drops unheeded, floats
and dances on the muddy pond.
Shadows from the world beyond
lengthen, sprawl across the park;
day rolls onward towards the dark.
From the clock-tower, wreathed in smoke,
Time speaks gravely, stroke on stroke.

Down on my Luck

Wandering above a sea of glass
  in the soft April weather,
wandering through the yellow grass
  where the sheep stand and blether;
roaming the cliffs in the morning light,

hearing the gulls that cry there,
not knowing where I'll sleep tonight,
  not much caring either.

  I haven't got a stiver
    the tractor's pinched my job,
  I owe the bar a fiver
    and the barman fifteen bob;
  the good times are over,
    the monkey-man has foreclosed,
  the woman has gone with the drover,
    not being what I supposed.

  I used to get things spinning,
    I used to dress like a lord,
  mostly I came out winning,
    but all that's gone by the board;
  my pants have lost their creases,
    I've fallen down on my luck,
  the world has dropped to pieces
    everything's come unstuck.

Roaming the cliffs in the morning light,
  hearing the gulls that cry there,
not knowing where I'll sleep tonight,
  not much caring either,
wandering above a sea of glass
  in the soft April weather,
wandering through the yellow grass
  close to the end of my tether.

To a Friend
in the Wilderness

For Douglas Robb

FOR GOD'S SAKE let it rip, let go the rope,
the weight is dead against you. Toss in your hand,
the cards are stacked. You're jostled off the course,
get off your horse. Our land
is conquered, lost: homunculus supreme
sits on the world's back: the weevil is in the sack.
Come, leave the fool to his triumph. Like sand
it will slip through the bones of his hand.
I'm tired of writing, and I'm tired of waiting:
no answer – and it's six months since you wrote.
I'm pleading with you now, not just inviting.
Listen: when Kelly went he left me his boat,
the sun is on the sea and the fish are biting,
the garden is full, the fruit begins to fall.
For God's sake chuck it, join me and share my crust,
the world well lost. Make life a long week-end.

Old friend, dear friend,
your voice comes to me through the scrawled words

like a bell ringing in the riotous midnight,
like news of peace through static.
                    I hear the leaves
rustle above your door. On the sun-baked path
the cat lies dreaming. Noon-tranced, the pig
sleeps in the shade. Your house stands,
a cavernous rock in a sea of light. In the passage
a wisp of breeze or a poltergeist stirs the cobweb.
The sun is exalted, climbs
to his throne of noon. In the crystal heat the cicadas
crackle on sunlit walls, on pea-sticks dried and splintered,
and among the macrocarpas:
from thistle to cloudless blue the world is vibrant.
Even the inner rooms are pervaded with noon,
the whole world a hot room hung with green leaves.

Beyond the pampas bushes
the sea snores on the shingle, boils lazily among the rocks.
There lie the umber weeds, combings
from the sea's hair, there sparkle
salt crystals on the pearl and amber shells.
No need to tell me of these things, no need
for letters. I am with you, and we sit again
on the old log half-buried in the sand,
sucking our pipes, happy to talk of things
we shall never understand, our smoke wreathing
on the still air in the pattern of our thoughts,
eyes narrowed in the glare
of sun and sea to watch the falling wave
that holds the summer in its green concave.

Come with me now, past the Maori grave,
past the straggling fig-tree like a map of London
along the track and over the wooden bridge.
Once more we climb the cliff-path sweating and silent
and stand at the high point, by the crumbling edge,
the sea beneath us, the winds' dancing-floor
deserted now and shining: my nostalgia
Laocöon to the giant pohutukawa.
High noon, intensity of light and sadness.
Landward the far-off hills are walls of blue
fringing the valley floor, broad map of summer. The deepening green
foretells the fall of leaves, and friendship's end,
all that we are, all that we love,
dissolved and lost in the darkness of the molecule.
Time takes us on his back and lumps us along,
hope hardens, and the wind blows from the grave;
our wound is mortal, no hand can heal us,
no fingers can unweave
the solid strands of doom. The seasons turn
and take us with them, our cycloid curve
bounds faster towards eternity. We age,
and like a beleaguered army fall to grief and rage
and curse the king we serve, the name of war.

But on that shore
despair withers in the sun, in the salt air,
love goes gloveless, faith is naked, the eye
stares at the skeleton fact, the doomed lips
smile at truth revealed, cry welcome
to the flux, the fire, the fury,
the dance of substance on the needle-point of mind,
the kiss of clay, the flame of the sea, the reek
of the flesh, the animal beauty of the stars.
Your leisure grows like a tree, wrapping its roots
round the earth to which it belongs;
and thoughts pass huge and slow across your mind
like cloud-shadows over the purple sea.
You can take time like Mithridates,
unscathed will drink eternity.

March will die into April, autumn
will age and be grey as a pensioner, May
will fade in a mist, the day come
when the tui no longer spangles the scarlet
flax-flowers with his song,
when the dawn brings sleet and the bees are quiet
and the morning thrush is dumb.
Winter will come with a blast of wind and a flourish of chilling showers,
and the sea will moan, and the driftwood, whiter grown,
be swept in heaps like bones,
and the bodies of dead sea-birds
will lie beyond the lash of the wave,
the sea will rave and the surf cast rags of kelp on the shore;
the creeks will rise and the streams with yellow water run,
and the mud be cold and deep about your door.
The wind in the dark will roar
and the midnight fill with dread,
but the driftwood fire will still
be warm at the midmost core,
at the beating heart of the storm.
Then like a smile from the dead
or a song from the granite rock
spring will come with its four
blue eggs that mirror the sky
in the nest in the privet hedge,
with a blush of green on the willow
and buds on the sycamore,
and the thrush in the macrocarpa
telling the time of life.
The starling in the gutter
will splash in the shining air,
and spiders make of their spittle
great cities in the grass,
the fantail flit in the tea-tree,
turn cartwheels over the mare,
young violets charm the wind,
even the dun unsmiling
bush at the head of the stream
hold up its darling flowers

to kiss the robe of the sun.
The time of doubt will pass,
faith and fact will be one.

I have no wish to circle the globe,
have no desire to travel
beyond my chosen acre: would choose
to live in peace in one place
and make my life one stay:
there is much to unravel, and much to piece together.
I would pick up a shell and scan it for half a day,
wander the paths of childhood, traverse the way
that is lost for ever;
I would think of the living, so restless in their sleep,
I would dream of the dead with their quiet faces,
see in my little room
the world stretched on the great rack of doom.

I could be happy, in blue and fortunate weather,
roaming the country that lies between you and the sun,
over the hills, fold after fold,
following the gradual sheeptracks, winding slowly
past gullies flecked with the ragwort's curse
or golden with the uneconomic gorse
to the tops of the skyhills where in time of drought
the danthonia shines like a flame that consumes the summer.
I could be happy roaming chancefoot
over those hills in the soft autumn rain,
or wandering in winter wildness. I would come again
like a shot from a gun, like a train,
like a stallion with streaming mane,
like a woman wild with the pain
and the joy of love. I would come
and live on the land, live off it,
go fishing with terns and shags,
set snares for pheasant and rabbit,
if need be walk in rags –
I would come if it were not so
that something says to me, No.
Is it hope, or fear, or habit
that has this power to restrain,
or the dim voice of a prophet?
Or a ghost within my brain?

But me no buts! You're leading me a dance.
Now what have you been reading, to queer your guts?
Ralph Waldo Trine? A sentimental tract
aiming to prove that miracle is fact,
or saying that modern men, given a chance,
are better lovers than haters? Or some sermon
drooling of Christian witness, moral fitness?
Philosophers and priests and men of letters
are the Devil's politicians on the stump,
gulling their betters,
history a running sore on Nature's rump,

the world a den of madmen. Let's be spectators
on this other planet, governed by us alone,
broad as desire, yet small enough to be
reflected in the eye of gull or gannet.
Let them steal watches or wives, cut throats or capers,
kill time or cousins german,
light beacon-fires of progress, or stinking tapers,
while we transmute the metal of their folly,
turn all their leaden doubts and self-communings,
their servile posturings, attitudes of conscience
to golden shuttlecocks, and have some sport.
Raffle your birthright, sell your chattels, come,
be quit of it all: the maggot heap of money,
the haunted room, the desperate street,
the revolving wheels and the withered hand,
the tedious week, the circular task; the cheapjack
building Utopia, the salesman bleating of Christ,
the unhappy poor envying the unhappy rich,
evil barring the door, the sorner in the sun-room,
despair in every heart, the world at the mercy
of a maniac with a comic moustache, or a peasant
riding the Apocalypse; or of the smooth
cut-throats in black with their balance-sheets and Bibles;
law married to madness, knowledge to error,
our children numbered for the shambles.
Will you escape these things? Or will you endure them?
Who will cure them? Tell me, when terror
lightens the sky, what will you answer then?

Again? Old friend, you're clever,
you know my thoughts. You tempt me with your talk
when the mood is blackest and I think of waves
breaking for ever.
How can I make this difficult decision
who have children to rear to the same
most difficult decision? Shall I teach them
to inhabit this world, to inherit
the slough of my doubt, the fury of my despair,
patiently to repeat each crime and blunder,
get knowledge piecemeal and too late, lose wonder
staring at the mocking image each generation
holds up to the next; breeding, begetting their kind,
or bleeding and dying
in a lunatic war in a distant land for a lost cause?
Shall I endure these things? Or shall I
break the circle,
bring them to live in the innocence of your world,
train them in stone-age crafts, using
such simple gear as might be stored in a cave,
or stowed in an ark? Facing absolute power,
shall I become the absolute economist,
the dark philosopher, to circumvent the Devil?
The way would be hard: but a harder may emerge
from speeches, campaigns, and talks-at-the-highest-level.

Safe in your wilderness of sea and mountain,
far from this wilderness that men have built,
you need not fear the universal plague,
terror and mortal madness, need not hear
that sound the heart makes when the mother grieves
for the murdered child, the voice of helpless guilt.
Your days are not mixed with violence, the years
suffer a gentle death, die slowly, fall like leaves.
Sometimes at night the cries of wild birds seem
the inward voice of doom, sometimes you dream
the hills fall down, the sea comes rushing in,
but morning brings the sunlight on the sill,
the blackbird shouting. Yours
is the weather shore, where many windless dawns
of mist and cloud take root upon those hills
and flower in sudden storm: but hail and thunder
are Nature's rhetoric, lifting the spirit up
heaven-high, re-kindling wonder.

Why am I not beside you, flesh and spirit?
I could be happy serving my time to the earth,
living in luminous poverty, apprenticed
to a blind, unthinkable future. I could be happy
even when the house had fallen, its rotten eaves
tangled in blackberry; well content to sleep
under the raupo hearing the rain on the leaves
rustling in darkness; glad to sweat in the sun,
and wash my body in the sea.

But I am held like the constant moon;
though chaos is my earth I hold my orbit.
Let me speak bluntly: no man, essaying sanity,
putting off vanity,
looking calmly at the world, looking it in the eyes,
could find in soul or sense an innocent love.
The fool prospers, the coward lies in silk,
the pimp is full of honour; the brave and wise
stand silent at the crowd's edge
while liars fumble with their lies.
Fate is witless: the irrational bolt will fall
where least deserved, or most, or not at all:
and at the last
we are lost in abstract death. Leave the matter there
and the hand would freeze on the instant, the heart stop,
the breath melt into air. Why
do we struggle to hold the heat of this fire of being
against the chill of Nothing, wrestle in pain
to sustain this tension between the ideal
and the real, between desire and defeat; to square
beauty with bounden duty, the innocent act
with the metaphysical fact? The heavens are silent.
Doctrines are many and doctors two a penny.
Truth in her time-flight scatters a million fragments,
and the paper-chase is endless. Knowledge is bought
and sold on margins. Mirrors,

of fear concave, of power convex, distort.
What we are taught is often
tautology, or lies. We are fools if we think
that an absolute absolves, or that it will soften
the impact of brute fact. Neither priest nor sage
scanning the skies, neither sacred nor secular page,
gives a standard spelling for Ought; and many who save
their breath for their porridge are virtuous and wise,
while others who are most voluble
practise in error. All this I admit
out of my mother-wit. We are come of age
this side of death when we know that in terms of thought
these problems are insoluble.

What is our lodestar, then? All that is human,
kin to us, born of woman (O sea ever-living,
mother of all, falling in sunlight, breaking
over the rocks for ever, taking and giving!);
whatever knows it is mortal,
and shapes a god out of nothing, an image of beauty
from paint or stone or air; whatever is bound
by the phallic will, by the logic of generation,
and having at heart an irreducible faith
is impelled to gamble against statistical truth;
whatever hurts and is hurt, and knows about pain
as a devil sitting at the end of the bed or the brain;
whatever is gay and has courage to travel by night –
this is our map and compass and destination.
We must make our chart from the record of measurements, soundings,
the remembrance of wrecks, and follow our changing course
by the stars, and the set of the tides, and the slant of the wind;
we must yield to the terms of our being, allow
neither Church nor State to establish patent rights
over our natural joys, the heart's affections.
We know in the instant of joy that our warrant is sure,
our faith not vain, our being not belied by death.

Old rebel, what is there left for me to say?
This only: till at length
I reach the end of action, the last of my strength,
I cannot sever the bond,
destroy the documents, cut the cord
of my origin and being. This is my world.
These people are my clansmen, my accomplices.
I share the crime. This guilt is my reprieve:
I am alive, and I do not mean to leave
till the game is up, and my hand has lost its power.
These are my people. Till seventy times seven
I am committed to them,
which is neither a matter for pride nor a cause for grief:
does the shaken leaf
lay claim to the earth, or condemn
the wind that blows out of heaven?
These are my flesh and blood since time began,
their folly is my folly, their joy my joy,

caught in this mortal predicament, girl and boy,
busy matron, sad-faced successful man,
prim saint and puzzled sinner,
grim loser and bad winner, pimp and peeping Tom,
snotty-nosed cherub, anonymous letter writer,
sleek parasite and host, master and slave,
owl-eye, chew-cud, wolf-jaw, ferret-face,
all of them one in the image of man
which I bear in my heart a burden to the grave.

Old friend, dear friend, some day
when I have had my say, and the world its way,
when all that is left is the gathering in of ends,
and forgathering of friends,
on some autumn evening when the mullet leap

in a sea of silver-grey,
then, O then I will come again
and stay for as long as I may,
stay till the time for sleep;
gaze at the rock that died before me,
the sea that lives for ever;
of air and sunlight, frost and wave and cloud,
and all the remembered agony and joy
fashion my shroud.

CHARLES BRASCH

The Ruins

I have seen them still and clear in the bareness of dawn,
Strong hulls of shadow by no sunlight feigned.
I have watched them troubling the wind, rooted, opaque.
Air was about them; a dead leaf from their ivies
Rustling freed itself and fell coldly;
Trees kept their settled distance, grasses,
These grasses I touch now,
Knelt softly against the bruised face of the stone,
And birds in early wide-eyed flight
Skirted them as though making their constant passage.
Yet there is nothing here, nothing but the grasses
Of a level space open to the sea's quiet.

Can it be that what is to come is already here –
That the preparations are made, and what they point to
By some happy conjunction
May grow visible and seem even now to be?
That the air makes advances, drawing on the future
For these ripe clairvoyant moments, to load
Some artless plot of earth with burdens
That time lays up for it, and that the mind
Inexplicably sharpened may perceive
Through the loud deliverances of sense
Other shapes and workings, the undreamed of issue
Of currents unmarked or misconstrued?

But it is seldom that time opens unguarded
Or that I am able to see,
For if I look and wait there is only the careless now.
So this mild afternoon
The level space lies innocent, no walls
Lift up serpent wreaths of ivies
That bind their stones in a knot of death,
The wind flows unparted
Where I shall always see them cleaving it,
And sinks into the distance, or turns away
Into another era,
And is lost, lost in the sea's quiet.

Autumn, Thurlby Domain

What news for man in a broken house, old trees
And ruined garden dying among the hills?
Nothing is here to distract or to surprise,
Nothing except the plainness of stone walls
And trunks unleafing, what has been planted and grows,
What has been built to stand; that now fails,
Having served its time,
And goes back ripe to the earth from which it came.

What news? Are old age and decay so new
They put us out of countenance, offend
Lives that have long forgotten how to grow
And die, and do not care to understand
The elemental language of sickle and plough,
Of nursery and orchard, sun and wind,
That speak to us everywhere
With the same untroubled intimacy as here?

What we have found before we shall find again,
No new thing; age and youth seem strange to us
Who can no longer relight the morning sun,
Bring each day to birth in that bitter stress
And eddying joy that mark the life of a man
As years ring a tree; only in loss,
All knowledge stripped away,
We stumble towards our naked identity.

All civilizations, all societies,
Die with a dying house. These walls beheld
Rites of birth, marriage and death, customary days
Of equable happiness, dear hope unfulfilled,
Heart practised in patience and hand grown wise;
All human glory men have dreamed or hailed
Lived here in embryo or
Epitome, and dies in character.

What ceremony does autumn hold this afternoon
With green-gold bough and golden spire – what rite
Of pirouetting poplar-dancers, to crown
The dying year, the death of man's estate,
With brilliance so raptly and so lightly worn?
In celebration of death we consummate
Our vows to place and time,
In sickness and in health to live and die with them.

Self to Self

'Out of this thoughtless, formless, swarming life
What can I find of form and thought to live by,
What can I take that will make my song news?'

'Where nothing is, a seed may yet be sown.
Does not chaos cry for the forming hand?
Thought and form be the new song you choose.'

'But if this outward chaos only mirrors
Chaos within, confusion at the heart,
How can I start, where settle to begin?'

'The formless and the thoughtless then your theme;
Knowing disorder like the palm of your hand,
Set up house there, amid the stench and din,

And be at home in your own darkness, naming
Hand and mouth first, wall and ceiling, then all
That hurts you or offends, without as within,

All that you hate, that maddens, that merely is –
The ants, the dumb oxen, the golden calves
(For there is nothing you have the right to refuse);

And when you have bent before them, made them one
With the waste heart, they will obey your word,
Out of disorder bring you song for news.'

'To work in what I fear, subject my weakness
To power, surrender speech for an idiot dumbness? –
O worse than death, the very self to abuse.'

'What have you left to lose, disorder's own?
Only from incarnation of disorder
Can order spring, and you must end to begin,
If you would sing you must become news.'

Ambulando

i

In middle life when the skin slackens
Its loving clasp of our loose volumes,
When the bone tree stiffens and its well-jointed branches
Begin to creak, to droop a little,
May the spirit hold out no longer for
Old impossible terms, demanding
Rent-free futures where all, all is ripeness,
But cry pax to its equivocal nature and stretch
At ease with wry destiny,
Supple as wind bowing in every reed.

ii

Now that the young with interest no longer
Look on me as one of themselves
Whom they might wish to know or to touch,
Seeing merely another sapless greyhead,
The passport of that disguise conducts me
Through any company unquestioned,
In cool freedom to come and go
With mode and movement, wave and wind.

iii

Communicate with stones, trees, water
If you must vent a heart too full.
Who will hear you now, your words falling

As foreign as bird-tongue
On ears attuned to different vibrations?
Trees, water, stones:
Let these answer a gaze contemplative
Of all things that flow out from them
And back to enter them again.

iv

I do not know the shape of the world.
I cannot set boundaries to experience.
I know it may open out, enlarged suddenly,
In any direction, to unpredictable distance,
Subverting climate and cosmography,
And carrying me far from tried moorings
So that I see myself no more
Under some familiar guise
Resting static as in a photograph,
Nor move as I supposed I was moving
From fixed point to point;
But rock outwards like the last stars that signal
At the frontiers of light,
Fleeing the centre without destination.

Mountain Lily

Higher than birds climb from their marble forest
The mountain lily nests
In shade among scrawled rocks and snow-grass plumes,
Where veins of water tremble down from snow
By antlered heads tossing and snuffing at the wind's mouth.
It rears in shade broad leaves cupped for tear-drops
Of rainbow water, and snow-moulded flowers
– Standards of white dawn –
That gaze with golden eye
Through veiling and unveiling of cloudy sky
Into star-eyes hidden from staring noon.
All day shadowed alone, it rises at last
Borne on its lunar wave into worlds of air,
Spreading dark leaf-wings to the late sun.

from *In Your Presence*

I read your signature
In the rose and in the rock and in the fabling sea,
And follow through every when and where
The lines of your face and the print of your hand.
Yet write for me sharper on eye and ear
Your form and name, my living bread,

That I may never go hungry more,
But even in the farthest galleries of air
Wake and sleep as though in your hand.

*

Morepork, shrewd sentry owl,
Watching night pass,
Sleepless, censorial,
Never heed us;

We have love's work to do,
We shall not stir
While your grave star-show
Turns in the air;

Driving the world round
We, by our rites,
Burnish your darkness and
Fuel those lights.

Cry Mercy

Getting older, I grow more personal,
Like more, dislike more
And more intensely than ever –
People, customs, the state,
The ghastly status quo,
And myself, black-hearted crow
In the canting off-white feathers.

Long ago I lost sight of
That famous objectivity,
That classic, godlike calm
For which the wise subdue
Their poisonous-hot hearts,
Strength of arm and righteous
Tongue, right indignation.

To know all, to bear all
Quietly, without protest,
To bend never breaking,
To live on, live for another
Day, an equable morning –
Is that what men are born for?
Is that best of all?

To each his own way,
For each his particular end.
Judging one another
By inner, private lights
Fortuitous as ourselves,
We leave some other to judge
By impersonal sunlight

Objective, as we hope,
In the after-world, if any,
What we have made of ourselves,
How we have laid out
That miserly talent, gift
Bestowed on us at the start
For the problematical journey.

How shall I make excuse
That I am not with those
Who lost the loving word
In sumps of fear and hate,
Convicts, displaced persons,
Castaways even of hope?
On them too a sun rises:

Any of us may be hunted
Among them any day.
What certainties assure
Another dawn will wake me
Or the galaxy swim on?
To live is to remember
Remembering to forget.

I lay down no law
For myself or my neighbour.
I search for can and must
Along the broken flare-path,
Pitching left and right
Shaken by voices and thunders,
By other lights, by looms
Of chaos, and my self-shadow.

Liking and disliking,
Unloving and wanting love,
Nearer to, farther from
My cross-grained fellow mortals,
On my level days I cry mercy
And on my lofty days give thanks
For the bewildering rough party.

Man Missing

Someone else, I see,
Will be having the last word about me,
Friend, enemy, or lover
Or gimlet-eyed professor.
Each will think he is true
To the man he thinks he knew
Or knows, he thinks, from the book.
Each will say, Look!
Here he is, to the life,
On my hook or knife;
And each, no doubt, having caught me

Will deal with me plainly, shortly
And as justly as he can
With such a slippery no-man.

Well, I'll be quite curious,
Watching among the dubious
Dead, to see what they make
Of this antique: Genuine, or Fake?
Myself, I've hardly a clue;
I know how I feel, what I do,
But how true my feelings are
And why I perform a particular
Act is quite beyond me,
Analyse and prod me
As I will, as they will,
Nothing quite fills the bill;
And the man writing this now
Is gone as he makes his bow.

Gone, for I never can bind
My seesaw will or mind
That keeps changing with the weather,
Not only from bad to better
And back, but changing aim
And course, myself still the same,
And looking everywhere
I find no centre anywhere,
No real self, only a sort
Of unthought self-conscious thought;
A house with no one at home,
Where any visitor is welcome
To name, try, spare or pan
A genuinely missing no-man.

Ergo Sum

Pretences, discontents –
Leaves of my raging tree,
Self-hate and self-deceit,
All shameful rancours that
Loathing cannot disown,
It is you keep me warm
In the chill fever of
Mood-modes I must try on,
Daily, hourly practising.

To make, unmake, remake,
Unmask and discover,
To cloak, bluff and confess,
These are the ritual
Twistings and contortions
That bedevil relations

Of one, two and many
In self's game of self-will
In pursuit of its living.

Self scatters itself in
A swarm of witnesses
Against itself, and is
Stronger being scattered
In many that attest
By question, evasion,
Self-confirming doubt, all
Continuities that
Are covert forms of growing.

I die therefore I am:
Dying out of myself,
Dying into myself,
Sieved and sea-changed through
The calendar of roles,
Disguises, feints, black-outs,
Worn down by treadmill thoughts,
Torn by the harrow
And heartburn of becoming.

Who am I to command
A self and its leaf-selves
Living dispersed through all
With the salt grains of the sea?
I follow, obeying a word
That leads in whirling dance
Through the cloud of days
And the cries of living and dead
To the last leaf-burning.

Shoriken

1

Feel the edge of the knife
Cautiously –
Ice-keen
It lies against your cheek
Your heart
Will pierce at once if you should stir
Yet offers
A pillow loving to your head
A sword to cross the malevolent sea.

Note. Shoriken is the Japanese name of one of the eight Taoist Immortals. A kakemono by Motonobu in the British Museum shows him crossing the sea, balanced on the edge of his sword.

2

The wood of the world harbours
Lamb and lion, hawk and dove.
A world of lions alone
Or a world of doves – would it
Capture our headstrong devotion
Harness the wolf-pack of energies
That unsparing we spendthrift
Earning our lives till death?
Where in its white or black would be work for love?

3

The merciless strike with swords
With words
With silences
They have as many faces as the clouds
As many ruses as the heart
The fountains of their mercy never run dry.

4

In a world of prisoners
Who dare call himself free?

5

Every mark on your body
Is a sign of my love.
Inscribed by the years, you tell
Unwittingly
How we travelled together
Parted and met again
Fell out sometimes, then made peace.
Crowsfoot, scar, tremulous eyelid
Are not matters for shame
But passages of the book
We have been writing together.

6

Giver, you strip me of your gifts
That I may love them better.

7

To remember yesterday and the day before
To look for tomorrow

To walk the invisible bridge of the world
As a tightrope, a sword edge.

8

What wages are due to you
Unprofitable servant?
You come asking for wages?
Fifty years long you have breathed
My air, drunk my sweet waters
And have not been cut down.
Is it not a boon, living?
Do not your easy days mark
The huge forbearance of earth?

9

The bluntest stones on the road will be singing
If you listen closely
Like lilies or larks
Those that may stone you to death after.

10

Rising and setting stars
Burn with the same intensity
But one glows for the world's dark
One whitens into tedious day.

11

All yours that you made mine
Is made yours again.

12

To speak in your own words in your own voice –
How easy it sounds and how hard it is
When nothing that is yours is yours alone

To walk singly yourself who are thousands
Through all that made and makes you day by day
To be and to be nothing, not to own

Not owned, but lightly on the sword edge keep
A dancer's figure – that is the wind's art
With you who are blood and water, wind and stone.

13

One place is not better than another
Only more familiar
Dearer or more hateful
No better, only nearer.

14

He is earth, dying to earth.
The charge of life spends itself
Wears, wears out.
His sole enemy is the self
That cannot do otherwise
Than live itself to death
            death
The desert sand
That dries all tears
            death
Our rest and end.

15

Selfless, you sign
Your words mine.

16

To cross the sea is to submit to the sea
Once venture out and you belong to it
All you know is the sea
All you are the sea
And that sword edge itself a wave-crest of the sea.

Winter Anemones

The ruby and amethyst eyes of anemones
Glow through me, fiercer than stars.
Flambeaux of earth, their dyes
From age-lost generations burn
Black soil, branches and mosses into light
That does not fail, though winter grip the rocks
To adamant. See, they come now
To lamp me through inscrutable dusk
And down the catacombs of death.

BASIL DOWLING

Mushrooms

We went to look for stragglers on a ridge
Beyond the upland pasture, where the rough
Scrub country rolled away. But what we saw,
Or what I now remember was near home
Beside the neat green oatfield, a score or so
Mushrooms among the daisies and dandelions
And dewy wine-red sorrel, like a flock
Of sheep and lambs looked down on from a height;
Domes of old vellum, and buttons coy and small
White as new gloves; and scattered here and there
Some kicked by cows, showing their fleshy gills.
That morning we walked far and soaked our boots
Along the wet sheep-tracks, but now my thoughts
Stay in that mushroom paddock to recover
Childhood and all sweet mornings, dew, and grass.

The Unreturning Native

Above the sounds that echo eerily
    Still in my mind
I hear those Valkyries of wild sea wind,
    Though now they blow more kind.

Of all lost faces one remains with me:
    The downcast face
Of that dark, woebegone, uprooted race,
    But now it haunts me less.

That raw, harsh landscape in my memory
    Once seemed hostile,
But tones more truthfully with human ill
    Than gentle vale and hill.

Old friends beloved and loving faithfully
    There yet abide
To press their soft assault upon that pride
    Which even from love would hide.

No, may that love, that land, and that blown sea,
    Though never again
Present to prick my heart and eyes, remain
    As constant as my pain.

Rebel and Recluse

Once hot and arrogant
To set the world to rights
I gave my days and nights

To protest, and would rant
On soapbox or on stage
Against the folly of war,
That monstrous popular
Folly of every age,
But most condemned in ours.
In passionate argument
With all who came I spent
My spiritual powers
Like water, and not least,
When I could no more speak
As rebel or heretic,
On minister and priest
My narrow searchlight fell
And on the evaded word
Once uttered by their Lord,
'Resist not; do not kill.'

Now everything, alas,
Which then I so decried,
Pointed and prophesied
Again has come to pass,
And though I honour all
And pour on them my praise
Who shared those ardent days
Or knew a prison cell,
I no more fling my life
At moral barricades,
Or rush upon the blades
Of intellectual strife,
But know the sturdiest breeds
Of evil have their term
And die of the deep worm
Their own corruption feeds.

I am like Egypt's king
That Joseph did forewarn,
And filled his barns with corn
Against long hungering;
Or like that poet of old
Who in an evil time
Conned the secrets of rhyme
As a miser cons his gold,
Or on a terrace sat
Making his verses scan,
While Vandal, Goth and Hun
Hammered upon the gate.

A Memory of Goose Bay

Silence is absolute but for the sea
Swishing among the rocks there endlessly,
And here in bush a bellbird at high noon
Tapping a row of tumblers with a spoon.

Glenmark

Here are the proud gates, guarded by old trees;
There the long winding drive, and over there
The soaring slopes of tussock hills, with sheep
Like maggots on a rabbit's tawny pelt.
This is high country. Lives were always, here,
Lived in the shadow of magnificence
And silence (when the great winds were at rest),
Which must have given them some dignity
Beyond their own, and saved their acts
From pettiness and triviality,
Or so I fancy in a meaner time
When space has shrunk, and people flock to cities
Where human nature's dwarfed, and the deadly beat
Of too much contact sickens gentle souls.
There, like a ground-plan, stretches what remains
Of the great mansion that the millionaire,
Old Moore, had hardly built when fire destroyed it.
That must have been a sight from the dazzled windows
Of those five workers' homes, from one of which
My father might have watched, or rather run
To organise a desperate bucket-chain
To save what could be saved. Do those tall trees
Remember how their lower leaves were scorched?
Only they could remember, as only they,
The tallest of them, could remember now
The pioneers who manned this famous station
(More like a wild protectorate than farm)
And now are in their graves. Those grassy mounds,
Once flower beds, might be untended graves,
And all is quiet as a country church.
This page or half page of our history
Is precious to me, human history;
The sort one finds, outside the history books,
In gossip, and in yarns around campfires,
And precious even more because my father
Served here his hard apprenticeship with sheep.

CHARLES SPEAR

O Matre Pulchra . . .

When you whom Jules de Goncourt's prose
Had placed on shallow, leaf-strewn steps,
Against a tower, slate-roofed and rose,
When you gaze in your mirror's depths,

Dear worldling, do you understand
My seeing in those raffish eyes,
Instead of ladies of the land,
My landlord's fancy lady rise?

The Disinherited

They cared for nothing but the days and hours
Of freedom, and in silent scorn
Ignored the worldly watchers and the powers,
Left staples shattered and uptorn,
Filed window-bars and dynamited towers.

What was their wisdom whom no vice could hold?
Remote as any gipsy rover,
They stared along the cliffs, mauve fold on fold,
And watched the bees fly over.

From velvet hills, trees in the river-bed,
From glassy reefs in skeins of foam,
They reared the shell of vision and of words unsaid
To be their haunting and their earthly home.

Christoph

The wind blew strongly like the voice of fate
Through cheerless sunlight, and the black yawl strained
And creaked across the sullen slate
Of Zuider Zee. That night it rained;

The Hook of Holland drenched in diamonds lay
Far southward; but the exile coming home
Turns back to hours like golden tissues stacked away,
And sees no more the sulky, weltering foam,
But only roses, or white honey in the comb.

Environs of Vanholt I

White and blue, an outspread fan,
The sea slopes to the Holmcliff, and the dawn
Spins vaporous spokes across the Broken Span
To light up Razor Drop and Winesael Yawn.

Beanpod sleeps out beside his malt-filled pot;
Behind him lies the still and silver land;
No atom bomb drops from a shapely hand,
But birds of boding in a greasy knot
Pick at the rusted corpse half-hid in sand.

The Prisoner

I walked along the winding road;
It was high summer; on one side
Behind pale foliage sinuously flowed
The hand-sown wheat in rustling pride.

Grey sprawling stone, before me towered the school;
I touched the chapel-corner through the hedge,
Traced dimly in the window's painted pool
Three mitres and the shield with rope and wedge.

Deep peace! Yet there was panic terror shut inside;
The bronze bells rolled and reeled in flowing tide.
Against that shock time buckled to resist,
And no sound pierced the loneliness, no voices cried;
Only the great towers trembled in the pouring mist.

Vineta

Fire in the olive groves throughout the night,
And charred twigs crackling like the living coal;
The flame-splash spread across the wounded height;
Came flash on cannon flash and thunder-roll;
Then through the black smoke roared the bomber flight:
He crouched part-stricken in his shallow hole.

Strangely, at last he put his arms aside
And seemed to drift away. It was the rising tide
That heaped its star-shot depths upon a sunken town
Of brittle amber. There he thought to drown
Against a church haled over on its side,
So with the torpid ghosts he laid him down;
But pain and breath were not so easily denied.

Animae Superstiti

Some leagues into that land I too have fared;
The diligence along the causeway sped,
While from the left a giant planet glared
Across the restless marsh with face of lead.

In number we were four: you, child, and I;
The swordsman next, who wore his mocking air
Of Papal Zouave, fencing master, spy,
And last the golliwog with vacant, saxe-blue stare.

Onward we whirled; you slept disturbed in mind,
And from your hand the English roses fell;
Europe by lamplight far behind,
We clove the white fog's shifting swell.

So for an hour, and then I must return,
And you with your creatures ply insensate flight.
Broken I stood beneath the frontier light,
Till through the endless marsh I could discern
No wheels, no sound, only the airs of night.

Scott-Moncrieff's Beowulf

In the curdled afterglow of night
The long ship leaves the cliff, the ness, the cave;
Unending arcs of icy light
Flicker about her on the climbing wave;

And coming close fierce warriors crowd
To shout across the Swan's Way. See! They pass.
She drives through trailing veils of cloud,
And time pours down like rain on weeping glass.

From a Book of Hours

Bearing white myrrh and incense, autumn melts
Through flower and fruit and combed blonde straw;
Thunder looms on the mountain forest-belt;
The winter firewood purrs beneath the saw.

Our garden scents upbillow like the veils
Of Solomon's Temple, shimmer in the rain,
And all is peace. Slowly the daylight fails,
And voice and lute bring back the stars again.

1894 in London

Like torn-up newsprint the nonchalant snow
Creaked down incessantly on Red Lion Square.
Clock chimes were deadbeats. Clang! Nowhere to go!
The cabbies drove with marble stare,
The snowed-up statues had a pensive air.

Inside the pub the spirits flowed,
And Sal and Kate the guardees' tanners shared;
Out in the dusk the newsboys crowed,
And to infinity the lamp-posts flared,
The gas-blue lilies of the Old Kent Road.

Old England's blue hour of unmeasured nips,
The Quiet Time for Dorian Gray,

The day off for the barmaid's hips,
Prayer-Book revision time down Lambeth way.

At Dawn

Balancing, sliding, like a sheet of lace,
The tide sailed up the murmuring strand,
Drowned rock and shell in rill and race,
Wheeling on planes of marbled sand.

The shipwrecked man against a violet sky
Splashed like a drunken god, fell prone, embraced
The earth and slept. He heard not now the cry
Rent from the feathered, heartless breast on high
And moving through the blackness of the waste.

It was so innocent, the sleeping man,
The bowing waves to chime the empty hours,
Pink-cameo cliffs ablaze with trail and fan
Of mauve and purple fuchsia flowers.

God Save the Stock

Dusk falters over shelf and chair,
Carnation webs of shadows hold
A symbol in that tranquil air,
A candle's hoop of uncoined gold.

He writes reports in sweet repose –
The Jews require new management;
Korea soothed with flowing prose,
He writes in charmed astonishment.

The horn-rimmed prefect on the primrose path
Commands success with lip upcurled.
Fare well, Commander of the Bath,
And good luck, playboy of the western world!

Promised Land

Dispart the frost-white boughs, and lo!
The world of winter, mile on mile;
Wind-wavy seas of unplumbed snow,
Then endless peaks and one defile.

The high elect would fear to cross
Those wastes unconquerable, ideal:
There lies your path; count all as loss,
Cast armour by, lay down your steel;

For you shall walk the sheer gulf's brink,
Through glass-blue caves all brittle spars

And flaws. Thereafter you shall sink,
Snowblind in slush, beneath the stars.

Escape

Against deep seas blue-black like mussel-shells
The island arched its bluffs and stony scarps,
Which, wave-rocked, tolled in winter time like bells,
Or chimed to spring as sweet as Irish harps.

Above, a fool's crown of canary cloud,
Moulded by mighty winds to dizzy height,
Leaned to the isle like press of sail o'erbowed,
And sunshine pierced the eyes with swords of light.

This have we chosen, far from friends and home,
This space of barren rock and crimson heath,
With cliffs of quaking honey-comb
And the tides of death in the galleries beneath.

Remark

High-coiffed the muse in green brocade
Hears waltzes that are not for her,
And haunts, by time yet unbetrayed,
A breath-dimmed pane's curved lavender.

Studiously minor, yet attuned to doom,
Like an old gramophone this modish muse –
She may grow spiteful in a little room,
Attack the glass with crystal shoes,
Get airborne on a witches' broom.

ALLEN CURNOW

At Dead Low Water

i

At dead low water, smell of harbour bottom,
Sump of opulent tides; in foul chinks twirl
Weed and whorl of silt recoiling, clouding
The wan harbour sighing on all its beaches.

The boat was not deliberately abandoned
But tied here and forgotten, left afloat
Freakishly, bobbing where the summers foundered,
Jarring each wave the jetty's tettered limbs;

Worm carves wave polishes original shapes,
Bolt and knot give way, gaps in the decking
Turn up again, driftwood on other sands.
All drifts till fire or burial.

Life, trapped, remembers in the rancid shallows
What crept before the enormous strides of love
When the word alone was, and the waters:
Goes back to the beginning, the whole terror

Of time and patience. Keel and bolt are frilled
With the shrimp's forest, all green-bearded timbers.
Salt rocky chink, nude silted cleft give off
Birth smell, death smell. Mute ages tread the womb.

ii

Nervous quiet not calm possesses
Sea water here, the wave turns wary
Finding itself so far inland.

The father with the child came down
First thing one morning, before any
Dreamt of visiting the beach; it was

Daylight but grey, midsummer; they
Crossed high-water mark, dry-shod,
Derelict shells, weed crisped or rotting,

Down to the spongy rim, slowly
Without fear, stepping hand in hand
Within an inch of the harmless sea

Pure, unfractured, many miles,
Still steel water sheathed between
Once violent hills, volcanic shapes.

O memory, child, what entered at the
Eye, ecstasy, air or water?
What at the mouth? But carefully

Morning by morning incorruption
Puts on corruption; nervously
Wave creeps in and lingers over

Tideswept heaps where the fly breeds:
Memory flows where all is tainted,
Death with life and life with death.

Twenty years. A child returned
Discerns in quicksand his own footprint
Brimming and fading, vanishing.

iii

Failed at the one flood we do not count
On miracles again, and you may say
We die from now; while each amazed migrant
Waves back, and cannot tear his eyes away

From his own image, the weeping threatening
Accusing thing, and knows death does not rid
Him even of the deformed sunk sifted thing,
Memory's residue; because the dead,

Father and child, still walk the water's edge:
A kindness, an inconsequent pastime, froze
In time's tormented rock, became an age
When tropics shifted, buried rivers rose,

Meaningless but for individual pain
No death, no birth relieves or lunar pulses drown.

From *Tomb of an Ancestor*

I

In Memoriam, R.L.M.G.

The oldest of us burst into tears and cried
Let me go home, but she stayed, watching
At her staircase window ship after ship ride
Like birds her grieving sunsets; there sat stitching

Grandchildren's things. She died by the same sea.
High over it she led us in the steepening heat
To the yellow grave; her clay
Chose that way home: dismissed, our feet

Were seen to have stopped and turned again down hill;
The street fell like an ink-blue river
In the heat to the bay, the basking ships, this Isle
Of her oblivion, our broad day. Heaped over

So lightly, she stretched like time behind us, or
Graven in cloud, our farthest ancestor.

Old Hand of the Sea

Old hand of the sea feeling
Blind in sunlight for the salt-veined beaches
O setting on a tide my bearded boat a-sailing
Easy as the bird's breast that barely touches

Immemorial deeps of death:
Here, now, my harbour, child's play pool,
Sifter of sunk bright treasure, breaker of earth,
Is monster and lover of the gazing soul.

Horizons bloomed here on the globes of eyes,
Here grieving fog fastened those lids with tears
Disfiguring, transfiguring; holidays
Nested like bird or girl. All disappears

But the salt searching hand. Oh sightless tides
What blossom blows to you from spring hillsides?

Eden Gate

The paper boat sank to the bottom of the garden
The train steamed in at the white wicked gate,
The old wind wished in the hedge, the sodden
Sack loved the yellow shoot;

And scampering children woke the world
Singing Happy Doomsday over all the green willows
That sprang like panic from the crotch of the cold
Sappy earth, and away in the withered hollows

A hand no warmer than a cloud rummaged
At the river's roots: up there in the sky
God's one blue eye looked down on the damaged
Boy tied by the string of a toy

And saw him off at the gate and the train
All over again.

To Forget Self and All

To forget self and all, forget foremost
This whimpering second unlicked self my country,

To go like nobody's fool an ungulled ghost
By adorned midnight and the pitch of noon
Commanding at large everywhere his entry,
Unimaginable waterchinks, granular dark of a stone?
Why that'd be freedom heydey, hey
For freedom that'd be the day
And as good a dream as any to be damned for.

Then to patch it up with self and all and all
This tousled sunny-mouthed sandy-legged coast,
These painted and these rusted streets,
This heart so supple and small,
Blinding mountain, deafening river
And smooth anxious sheets,
And go like a sober lover like nobody's ghost?
Why that'd be freedom heyday, hey
Freedom! That'd be the day
And as good a dream as any to be damned to.

To sink both self and all why sink the whole
Phenomenal enterprise, colours shapes and sizes
Low like Lucifer's bolt from the cockshied roost
Of groundless paradise: peeled gold gull
Whom the cracked verb of his thoughts
Blew down blew up mid-air, where the sea's gorge rises,
The burning brain's nine feathering fathom doused
And prints with bubbles one grand row of noughts?
Why that'd be freedom heyday, hey
For freedom, that'd be the day
And as good a dream as any to be damned by.

Elegy on My Father

Tremayne Curnow, of Canterbury, New Zealand, 1880–1949

Spring in his death abounds among the lily islands,
There to bathe him for the grave antipodean snows
Fall floodlong, rivermouths all in bloom, and those
Fragile church timbers quiver
By the bourne of his burial where robed he goes
No journey at all. One sheet's enough to cover
My end of the world and his, and the same silence.

While in Paddington autumn is air-borne, earth-given,
Day's nimbus nearer staring, colder smoulders;
Breath of a death not my own bewilders
Dead calm with breathless choirs
O bird-creation singing where the world moulders!
God's poor, the crutched and stunted spires
Thumb heavenward humorously under the unriven

Marble November has nailed across their sky:
Up there, dank ceiling is the dazzling floor
All souls inhabit, the lilied seas, no shore

My tear-smudged map mislimned.
When did a wind of the extreme South before
Mix autumn, spring and death? False maps are dimmed,
Lovingly they mock each other, image and eye.

The ends of the earth are folded in his grave
In sound of the Pacific and the hills he tramped singing,
God knows romantically or by what love bringing
Wine from a clay creek-bed,
Good bread; or by what glance the inane skies ringing
Lucidly round; or by what shuffle or tread
Warning the dirt of miracles. Still that nave

He knelt in puts off its poor planks, looms loftier
Lonelier than Losinga's that spells in stone
The Undivided Name. *Oh quickening bone*
Of the Mass-priest under grass
Green in my absent spring, sweet relic atone
To our earth's Lord for the pride of all our voyages,
That the salt winds which scattered us blow softer.

The Eye Is More or Less Satisfied
with Seeing

Wholehearted he can't move
  From where he is, nor love

Wholehearted that place,
  Indigene janus-face,

Half mocking half,
  Neither caring to laugh.

Does true or false sun rise?
  Do both half eyes tell lies?

Cradle or grave, which view's
  The actual of the two?

Half eyes foretell, forget
  Sunrise, sunset,

Or closed a fraction's while
  Half eyes half smile

Upon light the spider lid
  Snares, holds hid

And holds him whole (between
  The split scarves of that scene)

Brimming astride a pulse
  Of moon-described eyeball's

Immobile plenitude –
  Flower of the slight stemmed flood.

Snap open! He's all eyes, wary,
  Darting both ways one query,

Whether the moonbeam glanced
  Upon half to whole enhanced,

Or wholly the soul's error
  And confederate mirror.

Keep in a Cool Place

A bee in a bloom on the long hand of a floral
Clock can't possibly tell the right time
And if it could whatever would the poor bee do with it
In insufferably hot weather like this?

Everything white looks washed, at the correct distance
And may be the correct distance. You could eat
Our biggest ship sweet as sugar and space can make her.
Every body's just unwrapped, one scrap of a shaving

Left for luck or the look, the maker's seal intact,
Glad to be genuine! The glassy seaside's
Exact to the last detail, tick of a tide,
Fluke of the wind, slant of a sail. The swimmers

On lawns and the athletes in cosy white beds have visitors
And more flowers. Poor bee! He can make up time
At frantic no speed, whether tick or tock,
Hour or minute hand's immaterial. That's

Exactly how it is now. It is. It is
Summer all over the striped humming-top of the morning
And what lovely balloons, prayer-filled (going up!) to fluke
For once and for all the right time, the correct distance.

Spectacular Blossom

Pohutukawa Trees, Auckland

Mock up again, summer, the sooty altars
Between the sweltering tides and the tin gardens,
All the colours of the stained bow windows.
Quick, she'll be dead on time, the single
Actress shuffling red petals to this music,
Percussive light! So many suns she harbours
And keeps them jigging, her puppet suns,

All over the dead hot calm impure
Blood noon tide of the breathless bay.

Are the victims always so beautiful?

Pearls pluck at her, she has tossed her girls
Breast-flowers for keepsakes now she is going
For ever and astray. I see her feet
Slip into the perfect fit the shallows make her
Purposefully, sure as she is the sea
Levels its lucent ruins underfoot
That were sharp dead white shells, that will be sands.
The shallows kiss like knives.

Always for this
They are chosen for their beauty.

Wristiest slaughterman December smooths
The temple bones and parts the grey-blown brows
With humid fingers. It is an ageless wind
That loves with knives, it knows our need, it flows
Justly, simply as water greets the blood,
And woody tumours burst in scarlet spray.
An old man's blood spills bright as a girl's
On beaches where the knees of light crash down.
These dying ejaculate their bloom.

Can anyone choose
And call it beauty? – The victims
Are always beautiful.

He Cracked a Word

He cracked a word to get at the inside
Of the inside, then the whole paper bag full
The man said were ripe and good.
The shrunken kernels
Like black tongues in dead mouths derided
The sillinesses of song and wagging wisdom.
These made a small dumb pile, the hopping shells
Froze to the floor, and those made patterns
Half-witted cameras glared at, finding as usual
Huge meteorites in mouseland.
What barefaced robbery!
He sat, sat, sat mechanically adding
To the small dumb pile, to the patterns on the floor,
Conscious of nothing but memories, wishes
And a faint but unmistakable pricking of the thumbs,
The beginnings of his joy.

A Small Room with Large Windows

i

What it would look like if really there were only
One point of the compass not known illusory,
All other quarters proving nothing but quaint
Obsolete expressions of true north (would it be?),
And seeds, birds, children, loves and thoughts bore down
The unwinding abiding beam from birth
To death! What a plan!
      Or parabola.
You describe yours, I mine, simple as that,
With a pop and a puff of nonchalant stars up top,
Then down, dutiful dead stick, down
(True north all the way nevertheless).

One way to save space and a world of trouble.

A word on arrival, a word on departure.
A passage of proud verse, rightly construed.
An unerring pen to edit the ensuing silences
(That's more like it).

ii

    Seven ageing pine trees hide
Their heads in air but, planted on bare knees,
Supplicate wind and tide. See if you can
See it (if this is it), half earth, half heaven,
Half land, half water, what you call a view
Strung out between the windows and the tree trunks;
Below sills a world moist with new making where
The mangrove race number their cheated floods.
Now in a field azure rapidly folding
Swells a cloud sable, a bad bitching squall
Thrashes the old pines, has them twitching
Root and branch, rumouring a Götterdämmerung.
Foreknowledge infects them to the heart.
         Comfortable
To creak in tune, comfortable to damn
Slime-suckled mangrove for its muddy truckling
With time and tide, knotted to the vein it leeches.

iii

In the interim, how the children should be educated,
Pending a decision, a question much debated
In our island realms. It being, as it is,
Out of the question merely to recognize
The whole three hundred and sixty degrees,
Which prudence if not propriety forbids,
It is necessary to avail oneself of aids

Like the Bible, or no Bible, free swimming tuition,
Art, sex, no sex and so on. Not to direct
So much as to normalize personality, protect
From all hazards of climate, parentage, diet,
Whatever it is exists. While, on the quiet,
It is understood there is a judgment preparing
Which finds the compass totally without bearing
And the present course correct beyond a doubt,
There being two points precisely, one in, one out.

iv

A kingfisher's naked arc alight
Upon a dead stick in the mud
A scarlet geranium wild on a wet bank
A man stepping it out in the near distance
With a dog and a bag
                        on a spit of shell
On a wire in a mist
                        a gannet impacting
Explode a dozen diverse dullnesses
Like a burst of accurate fire.

From *Trees, Effigies, Moving Objects*

I

Lone Kauri Road

The first time I looked seaward, westward,
it was looking back yellowly,
a dulling incandescence of the eye of day.
It was looking back over its raised hand.
Everything was backing away.

Read for a bit. It squinted between the lines.
Pages were backing away.
Print was busy with what print does,
trees with what trees do that time of day,
sun with what sun does, the sea
with one voice only, its own,
spoke no other language than that one.

There wasn't any track from which to hang
the black transparency that was travelling
south-away to the cold pole. It was cloud
browed over the yellow cornea which I called
an eyeball for want of another notion,
cloud above an ocean. It leaked.

Baldachin, black umbrella, bucket with a hole,
drizzled horizon, sleazy drape,
it hardly mattered which, or as much

what cometing bitchcraft, rocketed shitbags,
charred cherubim pocked and pitted the iceface
of space in time, the black traveller.
Everything was backing away.

XI

Two Pedestrians with One Thought

Things are things carried
away by the wind like this
big empty carton which
bumps as it skids as it
arse-over-kites over
anything else that's loose
dust, for instance, while
    all the little angels
    ascend up ascend up
things are things emptied
on the tip of the wind
arsey-versey vortically
big print for instance
APPLE JUICE nothing in the
world ever catches its
carton again where the
wind went ƎƆIUႱ Ǝ⅃ԀԀⱯ
loose as the dust or the
water or the road or the
blood in your heels while
    all the little angels
    ascend up on high
    all the little
God!
That was close, that bus
bloody nearly bowled the
both of them the dog with his
hindleg hiked and
APPLE JUICE bumped off the
wind's big boot
        angels
    ascend up
hang on there
as long as you can
you and your dog before the
wind skins the water off the
road and the road off the
face of the earth
        on high
     which end up?
     Arse end up
full beam by daylight
this funeral goes grinning, a
lively clip, a tail wind, the
grave waiting

hang on to your hands
anything can happen
once where the wind went
fingers you feel to be
nailed so securely
can come loose too
hold on to your ears and
run dog run while
simply, silverly
they walk in the wind that is
rippling their trousers
Hiroshima Harry and the
dandy Dean
dust free dusted while
 all the little angels
 ascend up ascend up
with
Plato in the middle
holding out his diddle in the
way souls piddle from a
very great height and
dead against the wind,
dead against the wind.

XII

Magnificat

Who hasn't sighted Mary
 as he hung hot-paced
by the skin of the humped highway
 south from Waikanae
three hundred feet above the
 only life-size ocean?
Tell me, mother of mysteries,
 how far is time?

Twelve electric bulbs
 halo Mary's head,
a glory made visible
 six feet in diameter,
two hundred and forty-five feet
 of solid hill beneath.
Tell me, mother of the empty grave,
 how high is heaven?

Mary's blessed face
 is six-and-a-half feet long,
her nose eighteen inches,
 her hands the same.
Conceived on such a scale,
 tell me, Dolorosa,
how sharp should a thorn be?
 how quick is death?

Mary's frame is timbered
   of two-by-four,
lapped with scrim and plastered
   three inches thick.
Westward of Kapiti
   the sun is overturned.
Tell me, Star of the Sea,
   what is darkness made of?

Mary has a manhole
   in the back of her head.
How else could a man get down there
   for maintenance, etc?
Mary is forty-seven feet,
   and that's not tall.
Tell me, by the Bread in your belly,
   how big is God?

I AM THE IMMACULATE
   CONCEPTION says
Mary's proud pedestal.
   Her lips concur.
Masterful giantess,
   don't misconceive me,
tell me, mother of the Way,
   where is the world?

From *An Incorrigible Music*

Canst Thou Draw Out Leviathan with an Hook?

I

An old Green River knife had to be scraped
of blood rust, scales, the dulled edge scrubbed
with a stone to the decisive whisper of steel
on the lips of the wooden grip.

You now have a cloud in your hand
hung blue dark over the waves and edgewise
luminous, made fast by the two brass rivets
keeping body and blade together, leaving
the other thumb free for feeling
how the belly will be slit and the spine severed.

The big kahawai had to swim close
to the rocks which kicked at the waves
which kept on coming steeply steaming,
wave overhanging wave
in a strong to gale offshore wind.

The rocks kicked angrily, the rocks
hurt only themselves, the seas without a scratch
made out to be storming and shattering,

but it was all an act that they ever broke
into breakers or even secretively
raged like the rocks, the wreckage of the land,
the vertigo, the self-lacerating
hurt of the land.
                         Swimming closer
the kahawai drew down the steely cloud
and the lure, the line you cast
from cathedral rock, the thoughtful death
whispering to the thoughtless,

Will you be caught?

II

Never, let them die of the air,
pick up your knife and drive it
through the gills with a twist,
let the blood run fast,
quick bleeding makes best eating.

III

An insult in the form of an apology
is the human answer to the inhuman
which rears up green roars down white,
and to the fish which is fearless:

if anyone knows a better it is a man
willing to abstain from his next breath,
who will not be found fishing from these rocks
but likeliest fished from the rip,

white belly to wetsuit black, swung copular
under the winching chopper's bubble,
too late for vomiting salt but fluent at last
in the languages of the sea.

IV

A rockpool catches the blood,
so that in a red cloud of itself
the kahawai lies white belly uppermost.

Scales will glue themselves to the rusting blade
of a cloud hand-uppermost in the rockpool.

V

Fingers and gobstick fail,
the hook's fast in the gullet,

the barb's behind the root
of the tongue and the tight
fibre is tearing the mouth
and you're caught, mate, you're caught,
the harder you pull it
the worse it hurts, and it makes
no sense whatever in the air
or the seas or the rocks
how you kick or cry, or sleeplessly
dream as you drown.

A big one! a big one!

A Balanced Bait in Handy Pellet Form

Fluent in all the languages dead or living,
the sun comes up with a word of worlds all spinning
in a world of words, the way the mountain answers
to its name and that's the east and the sea *das meer,*
la mer, il mare Pacifico, and I am on my way to school

barefoot in frost beside the metalled road
which is beside the railway beside the water-race,
all spinning into the sun and all exorbitantly
expecting the one and identical, the concentric,
as the road, the rail, the water, and the bare feet run

eccentric to each other. Torlesse, no less,
first mountain capable of ice, joined the pursuit,
at its own pace revolved in a wintry blue
foot over summit, snow on each sunlit syllable,
taught speechless world-word word-world's ABC.

Because light is manifest by what it lights,
ladder-fern, fingernail, the dracophyllums
have these differing opacities, translucencies;
mown grass diversely parched is a skinned 'soul'
which the sun sloughed; similarly the spectral purples

perplexing the drab of the dugover topsoil
explain themselves too well to be understood.
There's no warmth here. The heart pulsates
to a tune of its own, and if unisons happen
how does anybody know? Dead snails

have left shells, trails, baffled epigraphy
and excreta of such slow short lives,
cut shorter by the pellets I 'scatter freely',
quick acting, eccentric to exorbitant flourishes
of shells, pencillings, drab or sunlit things

dead as you please, or as the other poet says,
Our life is a false nature 'tis not in
the harmony of things. There we go again, worrying

the concentric, the one and identical, to the bone
that's none of ours, eccentric to each other.

Millions die miserably never before their time.
The news comes late. Compassion sings to itself.
I read the excreta of all species, I write
a world as good as its word, active ingredient
30 g/kg (3%) Metaldehyde, in the form of a pellet.

From *You Will Know When You Get There*

A Reliable Service

.The world can end any time
it likes, say, 10.50 am
of a bright winter Saturday,

that's when the *Bay Belle*
casts off, the diesels are picking
up step, the boatmaster leans

to the wheel, the white water
shoves Paihia jetty back.
Nobody aboard but the two of us.

Fifteen minutes to Russell
was once upon a time
before, say, 10.50 am.

The ketch slogging seaward
off Kororàreka Point,
the ensign arrested in

mid-flap, are printed and
pinned on a wall at the end
of the world. No lunch

over there either, the place
at the beach is closed. The *Bay
Belle* is painted bright

blue from stem to stern.
She lifts attentively. That
will be all, I suppose.

A Touch of the Hand

Look down the slope of the pavement
a couple of kilometres, to where it empties
its eyeful of the phantoms of passers-by

into mid-morning light which tops it up again
with downtown shadows. There has to be a city
down there and there is, and an 'arm of the sea',

a cloud to sprinkle the pavement, a wind
to toss your hair, otherwise your free hand
wouldn't brush it from your eyes, a welcome

touch of sincerity. As they pass down hill
away from you, their backs, and uphill towards you
their faces, the ages, the sexes, the ways

they are dressed, even one 'smile of recognition',
beg an assurance the malice of your mind
withholds. Look down, confess it's you or they:

so empty your eye and fill it again, with
the light, the shadow, the cloud, the other city,
the innocence of this being that it's the malice

of your mind must be the ingredient making
you possible, and the touch which brushes
the hair from your eyes on the slope of the pavement.

You Will Know When You Get There

Nobody comes up from the sea as late as this
in the day and the season, and nobody else goes down

the last steep kilometre, wet-metalled where
a shower passed shredding the light which keeps

pouring out of its tank in the sky, through summits,
trees, vapours thickening and thinning. Too

credibly by half celestial, the dammed
reservoir up there keeps emptying while the light lasts

over the sea, where it 'gathers the gold against
it'. The light is bits of crushed rock randomly

glinting underfoot, wetted by the short
shower, and down you go and so in its way does

the sun which gets there first. Boys, two of them,
turn campfirelit faces, a hesitancy to speak

is a hesitancy of the earth rolling back and away
behind this man going down to the sea with a bag

to pick mussels, having an arrangement with the tide,
the ocean to be shallowed three point seven metres,

one hour's light to be left and there's the excrescent
moon sponging off the last of it. A door

slams, a heavy wave, a door, the sea-floor shudders.
Down you go alone, so late, into the surge-black fissure.

DENIS GLOVER

Sings Harry

Songs

I

These songs will not stand –
The wind and the sand will smother.

Not I but another
Will make songs worth the bother:
   The rimu or kauri he,
   I'm but the cabbage tree,
     Sings Harry to an old guitar.

II

If everywhere in the street
Is the indifferent, the accustomed eye
Nothing can elate,
It's nothing to do with me,
     Sings Harry in the wind-break.

To the north are islands like stars
In the blue water
And south, in that crystal air,
The ice-floes grind and mutter,
     Sings Harry in the wind-break.

At one flank old Tasman, the boar,
Slashes and tears,
And the other Pacific's sheer
Mountainous anger devours,
     Sings Harry in the wind-break.

From the cliff-top a boy
Felt that great motion,
And pupil to the horizon's eye
Grew wide with vision,
     Sings Harry in the wind-break.

But grew to own fences barbed
Like the words of a quarrel;
And the sea never disturbed
Him fat as a barrel,
     Sings Harry in the wind-break.

Who once would gather all Pacific
In a net wide as his heart
Soon is content to watch the traffic
Or lake waves breaking short,
     Sings Harry in the wind-break.

III

When I am old
    Sings Harry
Will my thoughts grow cold?
Will I find
    Sings Harry
For my sunset mind
Girls on bicycles
Turning into the wind?

Or will my old eyes feast
Upon some private movie of the past?
    Sings Harry.

Fool's Song

All of a beautiful world has gone
– Then heigh ho for a biscuit,
And a buttered scone.
For a dog likes his biscuit
And a man his buttered scone,
    Sings Harry.

I Remember

I remember paddocks opening green
On mountains tussock-brown,
And the rim of fire on the hills,
And the river running down;

And the smoke of the burning scrub,
And my two uncles tall,
And the smell of earth new-ploughed,
And the antlers in the hall,
    Sings Harry.

Then Uncle Jim was off to the wars
With a carbine at his saddle
And was killed in the Transvaal
– I forget in just what battle.

And Uncle Simon left the farm
After some wild quarrel,
Rolled his blanket and rode off
Whistling on his sorrel.

My father held to the land
Running good cattle there,
And I grew up like a shaggy steer
And as swift as a hare
While the river ran down.

But that was long ago
When the hawk hovered over the hill
And the deer lifted their heads
And a boy lay still
By the river running down,
      Sings Harry.

Once the Days

Once the days were clear
Like mountains in water,
The mountains were always there
And the mountain water;

And I was a fool leaving
Good land to moulder,
Leaving the fences sagging
And the old man older
To follow my wild thoughts
Away over the hill,
Where there is only the world
And the world's ill,
      Sings Harry.

Lake, Mountain, Tree

Water brimmed against the shore
Oozing among the reeds,
And looking into the lake I saw
Myself and mountains and weeds.

From the crystal uttermost ridge
Dwarfed was the river's course;
Cloud-shouting, to the world's edge
I rode a whole island for my horse.

Forlorn at the last tree,
Grey shingle bruised our bones;
But there holding tenaciously
Were roots among stones.

Knowing less now, and alone,
These things make for me
A gauge to measure the unknown
– Lake, mountain, tree,
      Sings Harry.

The Casual Man

Come, mint me up the golden gorse,
Mine me the yellow clay
– There's no money in my purse

For a rainy day,
   Sings Harry.

My father left me his old coat,
Nothing more than that;
And will my head take hurt
In an old hat?
   Sings Harry.

They all concern themselves too much
With what a clock shows.
But does the casual man care
How the world goes?
   Sings Harry.

A little here, a little there –
Why should a man worry?
Let the world hurry by,
I'll not hurry,
   Sings Harry.

Thistledown

Once I followed horses
And once I followed whores
And marched once with a banner
For some great cause,
   Sings Harry.
But that was thistledown planted on the wind.

And once I met a woman
All in her heart's spring,
But I was a headstrong fool
Heedless of everything,
   Sings Harry.
– I was thistledown planted on the wind.

Mustering is the life:
Freed of fears and hopes
I watch the sheep like a pestilence
Pouring over the slopes,
   Sings Harry.
And the past is thistledown planted on the wind.

Dream and doubt and the deed
Dissolve like a cloud
On the hills of time.
Be a man never so proud,
   Sings Harry.
He is only thistledown planted on the wind.

The Park

The river slower moved
And the birds were still.

Leaf and tree in silence hung
Breathless on the plunging sun.

Now came still evening on,
And suddenly the park was full of pedals,
   Sings Harry.

Mountain Clearing

It was a friendly and a private place
   Sings Harry.
Where a moss-grown track beside the stream
Led to the clearing in the birches. The face
Of the dark hill above was darkling green.

And in the morning came the sound of the axe
   Sings Harry.
Or the bush-buried shot at mountain deer;
The river talked to the stones and swamp-smothered flax,
And the hut smoke rose clear.

That was a good place to be camping in
   Sings Harry.
Where we unsaddled and hobbled the horses,
Heading over Honeycomb Pass and Mount Thin
For sheep and heat and dust and a hundred water-courses.

The Flowers of the Sea

Once my strength was an avalanche
   Now it follows the fold of the hill
And my love was a flowering branch
   Now withered and still.

Once it was all fighting and folly
   And a girl who followed me;
Who plucked at me plucked holly,
   But I pluck the flowers of the sea,
   Sings Harry,

   *For the tide comes
   And the tide goes
   And the wind blows.*

Themes

What shall we sing? sings Harry.

Sing truthful men? Where shall we find
The man who cares to speak his mind:
Truth's out of uniform, sings Harry,
That's her offence
Where lunacy parades as commonsense.

Of lovers then? A sorry myth
To tickle tradesmen's palates with.
Production falls, wise men can prove,
When factory girls dream dreams of love.

Sing of our leaders? Like a pall
Proficiency descends on all
Pontific nobodies who make
Some high pronouncement every week.

Of poets then? How rarely they
Are more than summer shadow-play.
Like canvassers from door to door
The poets go, and gain no ear.

Sing of the fighters? Brave-of-Heart
Soon learns to play the coward's part
And calls it, breaking solemn pacts,
Fair Compromise or Facing Facts.

Where all around us ancient ills
Devour like blackberry the hills
On every product of the time
Let fall a poisoned rain of rhyme,
    Sings Harry,
But praise St Francis feeding crumbs
Into the empty mouths of guns.

What shall we sing? sings Harry.

Sing all things sweet or harsh upon
These islands in the Pacific sun,
The mountains whitened endlessly
And the white horses of the winter sea,
    Sings Harry,

On the Headland

Wrapped in the sea's wet shroud
The land is a dream, is a cloud.
The mist and the sun
Have made it their own,
    Sang Harry,
And hand on hips
Watched the departing ships.

From *Arawata Bill*

The Crystallised Waves

Snow is frozen cloud
Tumbled to the ravine,
The mist and the mountain-top
Lying between.

The cloud turns to snow or mist,
The mist to the stream,
The stream seeks out the ocean
All in a geographer's dream.

What are the mountains on high
But the crystallised waves of the sea,
And what is the white-topped wave
But a mountain that liquidly weaves?

The water belongs to the mountain.
Belongs to the deep;
The mountain beneath the water
Suckles oceans in sleep.

How are the tops in the dawn?

For Myself and a Particular Woman

Why didn't I know before
That to be disarmed
Is greater than to be victor,
That to disarm yourself
Makes yourself conqueror.

Embrace victory or defeat
Without pride or rancour,
Taking what turns up
Wary of elation, seeking no solution
That can be predicted or designed,
Yet facing what must befall knowing,
Flatly, love is all.

Forgive to be forgiven,
Leavening the bread of living.

The past is past; future
Who can knowingly foretell?
The present measures all.

Theocritus viii, 53

Not for me fat far-off lands
Nor guarantee of meat money

Nor even a medal gained
Trimming seconds off the wind.

No. Beneath this rock I sit
You in my arms, fond
Watching my sheep graze,
The rolling blue beyond.

PAUL HENDERSON

Elegy

1

Morning after death on the bar was calm;
There was no difficulty in looking for the boy's body.
The boat had been found in the dark, overturned,
And at dawn the men went out again
To search the beaches and sweep, in the boats, offshore.
The mountains to the north stood up like sepulchres
Rising white-boned out of a black sea.
The flat hymnal of light lay asleep in the sky
And sang morning in a minor key
To wake the wheeling flights of birds
That, curious, mark down all drifting wrack
And disabled drowned bodies.

2

He should not have attempted the bar, of course;
The tide was ebbing but he was making for home.
On the wide sea with night falling,
Only the open, small yacht to uplift him,
He must have felt, well, try it.

Moments make miniature green globes in the mind;
Light flaring on dark from house windows
As the lifeboat slid out on the ways;
Searchlight like an awed moon at sea
Probing the black night and white breakers,
A drawn will of the anxious, twining a tight knot
In the shadows of Shag Rock; car lights
A stereoscopic, too brutal revelation of tears.

The shocked boy saying that his friend was gone;
That they'd found the boat, turned turtle,
But that Jack was lost, they couldn't find him.

O weep all night for this drowned youth,
Waiting in the rock's black arms for the foreseen time
Of lifeboat returning, lonely, in the small hours;
Of certainty frozen in the immutable shape of hands;
Of a boy's boat is no bond, nor even a safe coffin.

Get some sleep, if you can; by now he's dead,
The water is too cold, it is almost winter.

3

Yet at dawn they were searching the beaches.
In the immense dawn distances the groups of men

Walked like little pins over the sandspits
And the morning light broke bitterly like snowflakes
On the sun-dazed self-conscious sea
That tight-lipped along the beaches hides
Its dreadful truths, its doused, its double-drowned boys
Lying like Jonahs in a beast's belly.

The sun rose on a silver-lidded sea that lapped
Over the sandbanks like turning shillings,
Making enormous shadows which, when reached,
Were nothing at all. In such confusion
Of light and lazing sand-pipers and lumps of seaweed
How find in this vast soul of silver and of sand
All that is left of one boy?

Yet at noon the beast opened its lips,
Or perhaps it was just that, with the sun higher,
The light was no longer tricky, but anyway
The boy was spewed up, and the body was seen
Floating face down, in a life-jacket, beyond the surf.

So is the sea-god fed, and one more sacrifice
Strewn on the waves. No fairer limbs
Are demanded, their separate toll will delay
Disaster in the mind's millennial time and kiss
The countless bare noons where there are no shadows.

It was easy enough then to go out on surf-skis,
Into the light that by afternoon would be blue,
And bring in the boy's body, for a calmer burial.

I Think of Those

Sometimes I think of those whose lives touch mine
Too briefly; who, by a look or word, show me
A little of what lies beneath, but, leaving then,
Because we are trained to silence, they are shut away.

How shall I tell one friend from casual passer
Who am walled also in self; and cannot say
Do not hesitate; here is a love without fear;
The mind in its lonely prison forfeits today

As well as its yesterdays; and black tomorrows
Are chained with the hooded falcon on time's wrist
Unknowing and therefore unenvious of ecstatic arrow
Flight when the dark bird is released.

Yet I come to you in these words as surely
As though you were here surprised again at my eyes,
Though if this be all, if there is never any
If there is never between us more, no such awakening dies.

M. K. JOSEPH

Mercury Bay Eclogue

(For Rachel and David)

I

The child's castle crumbles; hot air shimmers
Like water working over empty sand.
Summer noon is long and the brown swimmers
For fear of outward currents, lie on land.
With tumbleweed and seashells in its hand
The wind walks, a vigorous noonday ghost
Bearing gifts for an expected guest.

Hull down on horizon, island and yacht
Vanish into blue leaving no trace;
Above my head the nebulae retreat
Dizzily sliding round the bend of space
Winking a last red signal of distress.
Each galaxy or archipelago
Plunges away into the sky or sea.

In the dry noon are all things whirling away?
They are whirling away, but look – the gull's flight,
Stonefall towards the rainbows of the spray
Skim swim and glide on wing up to the light
And in this airy gesture of delight
See wind and sky transformed to bless and warn,
The dance, the transfiguration, the return.

The turning wheels swing the star to harbour
And rock the homing yacht in a deep lull,
Bring children to their tea beneath the arbour,
Domesticate the wind's ghost and pull
Islands to anchor, softly drop the gull
Into his nest of burnished stones and lead
The yachtsmen and the swimmers to their bed.

II

A shepherd on a bicycle
Breaks the pose of pastoral
  But will suffice to keep
  The innocence of sheep.

Ringing his bell he drives the flock
From sleepy field and wind-scarred rock
  To where the creaming seas
  Wash shoreward like a fleece.

The farmer and his wife emerge
All golden from the ocean-surge
    Their limbs and children speak
    The legend of the Greek.

The shadowy tents beneath the pines
The surfboards and the fishing-lines
    Tell that our life might be
    One of simplicity.

The wind strums aeolian lyres
Inshore among the telephone wires
    Linking each to each.
    The city and the beach.

For sunburnt sleepers would not come
If inland factories did not hum
    And this Arcadian state
    Is built on butterfat.

So children burn the seastained wood
And tell the present as a good
    Knowing that bonfires are
    Important as a star.

And on his gibbet the swordfish raised
With bloody beak and eye glazed
    Glares down into the tide
    Astonishment and pride.

Machine once muscled with delight
He merges now in primitive night;
    The mild and wondering crowd
    Admire the dying god
    Where Kupe and where Cook have trod.

III

Over the sea lie Europe and Asia
    The dead moulded in snow
The persecution of nuns and intellectuals
    The clever and the gentle
The political trials and punishment camps
    The perversion of children
Men withering away with fear of the end.

Fifteen years of a bad conscience
    Over Spain and Poland
Vienna Berlin Israel Korea
    Orphans and prostitutes
Unburied the dead and homeless living
    We looked on ruined cities
Saying, These are our people.

We sat in the sun enduring good luck
  Like the stain of original sin
Trying to be as God, to shoulder
  The world's great sorrow
Too shaken to see that we hadn't the talent
  That the clenching heart is a fist
And a man's grasp the reach of his arm.

Be still and know: the passionate intellect
  Prepares great labours
Building of bridges, practice of medicine.
  Still there are cows to be milked
Students to teach, traffic direction
  Ships unloading at wharves
And the composition of symphonies.

IV

The poets standing on the shelf
Excavate the buried self
Freud's injunction they obey
Where id was, let ego be.

Yeats who from his tower sees
The interlocking vortices
Of the present and the past,
Shall find the centre hold at last.

Eliot whose early taste
Was for the cenobitic waste
Now finds the promise of a pardon
Through children's laughter in the locked garden.

Pound in his barbed-wire cage
Prodded into stuttering rage
Still earns reverence from each
Because he purified our speech.

Cavalier or toreador
Is Campbell expert to explore
The truthful moment when we face
The black bull in the arid place.

And Auden who has seen too much
Of the wound weeping for the healer's touch
A surgeon in his rubber gloves
Now cauterizes where he loves.

The summer landscape understood
The morning news, the poet's mood,
By their imperatives are defined
Converging patterns in the mind.

V

Come fleet Mercury, messenger of gods and men
Skim with your winged sandal the resounding surf
Quickly come bearing to all things human
Celestial medicine for their tongueless grief.
Heaven's thief and merchant, here is your port
Lave with your gifts of healing and of speech
All mortals who shall ever print with foot
These silent hills and this forsaken beach.

Come sweet Venus, mother of men and beasts
While meteors fall across the yellow moon
Above the hills herded like sleeping beasts,
Gently come, lady, and with hand serene
Plant fruits of peace where by this mariner's mark
The torrents of your sea-begetting roar
And trouble in their dreams of glowing dark
These sleeping hills and this forbidden shore.

Come swift ship and welcome navigators
Link and line with your instruments this earth
To heaven under the propitious stars,
Show forth the joined and fortune-bearing birth
And set this fallen stone a meteorite
Where Mercury and Venus hand in hand
Walk on the waters this auspicious night
And touch to swift love this forgotten strand.

Distilled Water

From Blenheim's clocktower a cheerful bell bangs out
The hour, and time hangs humming in the wind.
Time and the honoured dead. What else? The odd
Remote and shabby peace of a provincial town.
Blenkinsopp's gun? the Wairau massacre?
Squabbles in a remote part of empire.
Some history. Some history, but not much.

Consider now the nature of distilled
Water which has boiled and left behind
In the retort rewarding sediment
Of salts and toxins. Chemically pure of course
(No foreign bodies here) but to the taste
Tasteless and flat. Let it spill on the ground,
Leach out its salts, accumulate its algae,
Be living: the savour's in impurity.
Is that what we are? something that boiled away
In the steaming flask of nineteenth century Europe?
Innocuous until now, or just beginning
To make its own impression on the tongue.

And through the Tory Channel naked hills
Gully and slip pass by, monotonously dramatic

Like bad blank verse, till one cries out for
Enjambement, equivalence, modulation,
The studied accent of the human voice,
Or the passage opening through the windy headlands
Where the snowed Kaikouras hang in the air like mirage
And the nation of gulls assembles on the waters
Of the salt sea that walks about the world.

Scientist's Song

If an equation could solve itself
The mathematician would be on the shelf.

The verb to be is always present tense
The fern is signed in the cut fern
Frost turns to flowers beneath the lens
Cold will burst stone and bruised flints burn
Roses and carnations burst
From a handful of seed as dry as dust.

The sunflower keeps perpetual noon
Dust falling in a glass marks time
Flood and folly attend the moon
Hollow rocks in the valleys chime
The tree on which a little bird sings
Registers centuries in its rings.

Lenslike a pebble of ice ignites
Dried fronds, and the barked kauri
Lets fall its amber stalactites
To be a beetle's cemetery
The standing stone above the tomb
Is sealed with sap of odorous gum.

Cavities and crystals take
Their shape in the cooling stone
Wax and the flower's juices make
The bees' familiar hexagon
Smoked glass and spectroscope conceal
Six-pointed stars turning in a wheel.

Mammoths fresh in caves of ice
Visit the hunter in his dream
And the iceberg's contours take the precise
Logic of a theorem
The mathematician and the mammoth
Lie down in a perpetual sabbath.

From *Pastiches*

Mr Eliot Goes to Canterbury

A poet was there of our compaignye,
A proper man, so God his soule gye,

Albe that melancolique was his hewe.
His countenaunce was as a hawke in mewe,
Or as an egle soch as men descrie
Upon the hills of Trace or Caucasie.
And as he prycketh forth he syngeth stille
With doleful chere: 'O cruelle is Aprille.'
Ful manie a short sentence did he yiv
Upon the objectiv correlativ,
Of Dant and Virgil and of manie oun,
And of the classique traditioun.
He hadde y-wryten of the waste londe
And of the hollwe men, I understonde,
And of Suine y-nekked like the ape,
And for the nones in Frensshe wold he jape.
Quartettes he endyted, and the lay
That clerks yclepeden AEsc Wednesday:
And eek had made, as ye shal here in plas,
Of that ful blisful martir Saint Thomas.
Of all the English makers was he flour
And eke a veray parfit publishour.

Mars Ascending

(For Jet Morgan and Sandro Botticelli)

I

A continental cloud of yellow dust
Storms over Lacus Solis; dull and hoar
Are the lichenous prairies; polar frost
Dissolves into unseasonable thaw.

Out there, down here, something is amiss:
Flood takes a town, grenades kill a child,
What has been will be, what might be is,
The nations rage and the desert runs wild.

Somehow our future, age or violence,
Measured by clocks or strata, mirrors there
For stargazers to see with instruments
The white-patched poles, the dust, the thinning air.

II

Mars ascends in golden armour
Venus in shell of dark lies sleeping
Children gaze at night-sky window

Children in their beds lie sleeping
Mars unbars the shining window
Venus unpins the golden armour

Venus clouds the curtained window
Mars now in her lap lies sleeping
Children steal the golden armour.

On the Exercise of Freewill in the
Lifting of an Arm

'Necessity is the recognition of freedom.'

Time (so they say) is irreversible:
The white clock-faces with their idiot grin
Face one way only and with whirligig hands
Like a policeman at a busy intersection
Signal all traffic up a one-way street
And since time (we agree) is irreversible
Each separate act conforming to time's law
Commits itself into an unknown future.
I lift my arm and cannot not have lifted
The bone and sinew: I let it fall, its falling
Lies heavy and immovable on the past
As the statue of Ozymandias
Since time (you know) is irreversible.

The act (we incline to say) is free
But freedom is a means, not end.
There's no such thing as a perpetual freedom
For freedom is a condition precedent
And the act (so the act's self implies) is free
Free to the act. Yet in the action
Freedom is subsumed: once acted
You are committed to the act. The arm lies,
Children are born, a meal digests,
Birds fall from the air, the sun grows hotter.
Freedom to act, but once the act committed
You are committed to the act
And even not to act is a decision
Not to act. Free before the act, and after
Bound, and the act is free yet, acted,
Is committed, since time is irreversible.

Necessity and freedom are experienced facts.
Since truth (being one) is indivisible
Freedom is an aspect of necessity,
Necessity the passive conjugation
Of freedom, and since truth is indivisible
The statue wills its fall, the child its day,
Old men their grave, all things their proper station.
When the idiot clock-mask drops, beneath
Is seen a countenance angelical,
Freedom to act, necessity to act,
Need to accept the freely-taken course.
The arm lifts, lifts the bone and sinew
Linked in an act of necessary freedom
Since truth is indivisible is truth.

Girl, Boy, Flower, Bicycle

This girl
Waits at the corner for
This boy
Freewheeling on his bicycle.
She holds
A flower in her hand
A gold flower
In her hands she holds
The sun.
With power between his thighs
The boy
Comes smiling to her
He rides
A bicycle that glitters like
The wind.
This boy this girl
They walk
In step with the wind
Arm in arm
They climb the level street
To where
Laid on the glittering handlebars
The flower
Is round and shining as
The sun.

Cinema

Sunken in each his individual night
They sit, the shoppers and the men in raincoats;
The children squirm; a finger like an insect
Rustles a paper bag; the lovers sigh
Beneath the blinding barrage of the white
Dream shot into their dark, and their hearts
Are the rectangle upon which intersect
The crystal vision and the vitreous eye.

Though daylight solve their equation and redeem
This dance of phantoms in the shadowed hall,
I live the lens, the dazzle and the dream
As sunk in my separate darkness I recall
Plato once said that all we are and have
Is shadows dancing on the wall of a cave.

The Drunkard and the Crane

Drifting in fogs of booze
The drunkard on the bench
Watches the passing dollies
And belches for his lunch.

The liquor-loosened jowl
Quivers with vile regret,
The carious teeth maul
A sodden cigarette.

Miles above his head
The solemn crane uprears
Easily its swinging load
Of girders to the stars.

Across the granite sky
Delicate masons climb
Building incessantly
Their glittering honeycomb.

On our primordial swamp
They daringly erect
An airy metallic camp
And tower of intellect.

Elegy in a City Railyard

Slategrey stonegrey smokegrey
The fag-end of evening smoulders away.
The girl from the store and the produce-broker
The teacher the wharfie the city clerk
The sportsgoods man and the barroom joker
Have all gone into the companionable dark.
The ledger is closed: the hand comes down
Carefully blotting the graph of skylines
Scribbled across the dove-coloured town.
Like a woolworth diamond, Jupiter shines
On a sky as soft as an eiderdown.

Creme-de-menthe, ember-red, amber
The lights glow out and the day fails.
Tyres burr on the road's camber
As they take the bridge above the fan of rails
Shining like lead and the sheeted steam
Tinged from below with boiler fires.

The roundhouse is silent – there seem
No live things here except the tyres
Of the buses, and the piston's push and haul
And the signal's unintelligible call
And the searchlights in their tall martian machine
Knifing the grey September weather
Where the voices of night come home between
The engines talking quietly together.

GLORIA RAWLINSON

The Hare in the Snow

Afraid and trackless between storm and storm
Runs the mountain hare blinded with snow,
Digs in its dazzle her last desperate form
But seeks a refuge not a death below.

What shall our utmost clarity unlock?

Where she had rooted for her darkened hope
Time, immense, unhumbled, turns with the sun
Stripping snows down to adamantine rock:
All that's left of grief on the bright slope
Discover now – a small crouched skeleton.

From Ur to Erewhon

Long since my father sailing the Euphrates
anchored his heart to a village and there
watched the brick suburbs like a rose unfold
the city of the moon god – of Nannar.
My mother singing devils from the door
found life above the millstone's daily meed
sweet as the cake she mixed on festive days
of oil and honey wheat and poppyseed.

But Lord Storm lashed the river Lord Storm lit a fire
an evil fire in the hearts of enemies
our city died in flames even as foretold
on night's enormous tablet writ with stars.
And I was taken by the river's fury
Stop, cried a pebble to the flood
Wait, sang a reed but the waters rushed me
down to the scarlet weir of sinew and blood.

I know not to what ocean flows the river
but it rolls five thousand years to Erewhon
where you my brother fencing the wilderness
pause to see your mattock strike a bone.
Remember as you lay the fragment bare
the cake eaten the perished city the river moved away
the bush felled the vanished bird the bomb exploded –
and me the sister you buried but yesterday.

Then – And Again

Then was the brown Waikato gripped by cicadas
on post, willow and paddock strumming and zizzing

harsh as sandpaper, but making the world listen
for whatever we said of love they said it louder
          all in the beat and tune
          of their maori chanting
          ta ra ra, te kita kita
          ta ra ra, te kita kita

By the river blazing with sky, among osiers
they went mad, hooked on their own joy;
to be human was to be overridden
I felt their fever crackling into my brain.
          Live, O day of our sun
          for ever, for ever,
          ta ra ra, te kita kita
          ta ra ra, te kita kita

A long hot road in the fading summer,
and fruit-stalls: cloudy-purple grapes,
watermelon slices crisp as frost,
a carton of peaches, a carton of pears,
          and you, love, and you, love,
          in cicada country
          ta ra ra, te kita kita
          ta ra ra, te kita kita

Providence bottled in syrup, stored for winter.
It's not enough. So much succumbs to the cold.
Behind the drizzling walls when indifferent fangs
rip our days apart I want to take that disc
from its sleeve in my head, and in defiance
          play it over and again
          to the edge of sleep
          ta ra ra, te kita kita
          ta ra ra

MARY STANLEY

The Wife Speaks

Being a woman, I am
not more than man nor less
but answer imperatives
of shape and growth. The bone
attests the girl with dolls,
grown up to know the moon
unwind her tides to chafe
the heart. A house designs
my day an artifact
of care to set the hands
of clocks, and hours are round
with asking eyes. Night puts
an ear on silence where
a child may cry. I close
my books and know events
are people, and all roads
everywhere walk home
women and men, to take
history under their roofs.
I see Icarus fall
out of the sky, beside
my door, not beautiful,
envy of angels, but feathered
for a bloody death.

Sestina

The body of my love is a familiar country
read at the fingertip, as all children learn
their first landscape. This is the accepted face
secure of harm, in whose eye I am at home
and put on beauty as the thorn in autumn wears
its bright berry, the sky its haycock summer of cloud.

And here in a miracle season no storms cloud
our halcyon day nor prophet stains a green country
with wry mouth twisted to what vision wears
his own griefs. Music is struck off rocks, we learn
the sun ripening behind walls of flesh, the bird called home
pilgrim tracing with sure wing a world's face.

He whom I love is more near than this one face
shaped for me at my beginning, dispersed like cloud
in death's careless weather. At the end we come home
to the same bed, fallen like stones or stars in a country
no one travels. Only the mindless winds learn
our history, yet for us each man his mourning wears.

We are what we have been. The living creature wears
like trees his grain of good and evil years. The face

is schooled by daily argument of pain to learn
disguises for the private wound. None knows what country
lies under the shut skull, or dazzling beacon of cloud
beckons the always outcast through stubborn exile home.

This dear shell, this curve my hand follows, is home
also to the stranger I may not meet, who wears
deeper than tears his secret need. He walks a country
I cannot touch or reach, where the remembered face
burns under brittle glass of winter, and every cloud
holds in its core of ice the dream I may not learn.

Or is he Orpheus, leaving my daylight kingdom to learn
Eurydice for whom he enters the dark god's home?
Hermes, show him this woman, in her cerecloth cloud
of sleep! She is not prey to the subtle worm which wears
already at my cheek. No word unlocks her face
or voice answers him out of that silent country.

Yet always we ride out winter and the face
of famine. We return, and O then morning wears
mountains, our signal joy climbing a cloud.

Put Off Constricting Day

Husband, put down Spinoza, Pericles,
the seventeenth century, even the new
nemesis striding after doll or moll.
Private eye or dick, they'll crack the case
as wide as any yawn I'll give, waiting
for bed and casual goodnight.
                              And now
put off constricting day, let sleep release
the obedient body from necessities
of action and response imposed by wills
other, alien, indifferent or hating.

Am I another such, not wife, nearer
than these, more culpable of harm and pain?
Or less, not noticed but by my default?
Look now, before you sleep, am I not still
the one you sought on winter-walking streets,
adding your breath, lonely, to fog and rain?
Then the incendiary blood burned up to spill
its brilliant meteors, crystals of fire
ardent to strike, in doubly shared assault,
from the expectant flesh an answering heat.

RUTH DALLAS

Milking before Dawn

In the drifting rain the cows in the yard are as black
And wet and shiny as rocks in an ebbing tide;
But they smell of the soil, as leaves lying under trees
Smell of the soil, damp and steaming, warm.
The shed is an island of light and warmth, the night
Was water-cold and starless out in the paddock.

Crouched on the stool, hearing only the beat
The monotonous beat and hiss of the smooth machines,
The choking gasp of the cups and rattle of hooves,
How easy to fall asleep again, to think
Of the man in the city asleep; he does not feel
The night encircle him, the grasp of mud.

But now the hills in the east return, are soft
And grey with mist, the night recedes, and the rain.
The earth as it turns towards the sun is young
Again, renewed, its history wiped away
Like the tears of a child. Can the earth be young again
And not the heart? Let the man in the city sleep.

The Boy

Miraculously in the autumn twilight, out of
The wet-grass smell of the apple, out of the cold
Smooth feel of it against his shrunken fingers,
He made the boy; he was not there before,
A boy in the trailing apple branches hiding,
Surprising us like the cobwebs hung with rain
That suddenly shone from the darkness under the leaves.

Out of the apple he made the boy, the apple
So pensively turned and turned in the rainy twilight,
Cold yellow apple out of his childhood heavy
Again in his hand. So quietly he stood,
Under dark leaves, shoulders and grey head bent,
Cupped fingers gnarled and knotty as old twigs,
He seemed at first another apple tree.

Then he made the boy, the boy who still
In autumn twilight shakes, when no wind stirs,
The yellow apples from the trees, or swings
On the oldest boughs; but he was not the boy;
We could in a moment see the tight-skinned apple
Fall and open into roots and leaves,
But never the hands grow into the boy's young hands.

From *Letter to a Chinese Poet*

17

Beating the Drum

Warming a set of new bones
In the old fire of the sun, in the fashion
Of all men, and lions, and blackbirds,
Finding myself upon the planet earth,
Abroad on a short journey
Equipped with heart and lungs to last
Not as long as a house, or a peony rose,
Travelling in the midst of a multitude
Of soft and breathing creatures
In skins of various colours, feathers, fur,
A tender population
For a hard ball spinning
Indifferently through light and dark,
I turn to an old poem,
Fresh as this morning's rose,
Though a thousand summers have shed their blooms
Since the bones that guided brush or pen
Were dust upon the wind.
So men turned to a carved stick
That held the lonely history of the tribe.

Round the sun and round the sun and round.

We have left the tree and waterhole
For a wilderness of stars.

Round the sun and round the sun and round.

I sing the carvers of sticks and the makers of poems,
This man who worked on ivory,
That one who shaped a fine jar,
And the man who painted a cave wall
By the light of fire.
                    Reminded in the noon hour
              With the sun warm upon the bone
        Under the canopy of the climbing rose,
That man is cut down like a flower,
I sing the makers
Of all things true and fair that stand
When the wind has parted
The warm and obedient bones of the hand;
All those I sing,
And among them name your name,
Who left the earth richer than when they came.

The rose is shaken in the wind,
      Round the sun
            The petals fall
                  And round the sun and round.

Evening

Snow still patches the mountain;
The city grows numb with frost.
I pile logs on an open fire,
Listen for a while to music,
Then open my books and read.
When I look up I half-expect to see
My father still seated at the table,
Re-assembling the stopped clock,
My mother's head bent over her sewing,
My grandmother resting in her favourite chair.
Once I gave little thought to the snow outside,
Was unmoved by a city silenced.

Viewing the Cherry Blossom

The cherry blossom falters,
                    is spent.
Petals rain down
                in pink showers.
Pink snow
           gathers underfoot.
Doll-like
          the people stroll
Under
         the spring trees,
Leisurely
        as figures
In a Hiroshige print.

           The blossom they sigh for,
The scene,
          is the same,
Now,
      and in time to come.
Only the spectators
               change.

Envoy

The blackbird sings as clearly
  On the cemetery wall,
The meadow blooms more fairly
  Where no feet fall;
    When the winds of heaven sigh
      Last year's threadbare leaves
      Rise up and dance their ancient reel
      For men and women passing by,
Or nobody at all.

Shadow Show

Watch, now.
From this black paper,
If I cut a silhouette,
Hands blown sideways by unceasing winds,
Shoulders bowed under a burden,
Knees bent,
A birdsclaw foothold on the earth,
You could say that I made a tree,
Storm twisted.

Or a woman, or a man.

In Central Otago

Seek foliage and find
Among cracked boulders
Scab of lichen, thyme.

Seek a burgeoning tree
Discover
Upended witches' brooms.

Seek grass and tread
Stiff sheet of ice drawn
Over the land dead.

Moon country.
No one could live here,
In the houses squat on shingle.

Fields scorched,
Snow gripping the mountains;
Nothing could recover

From such desolation,
Jack Frost's sheep-run,
Mirror of the bleak mind.

But come back in a month –
See blanketing the slits
And sockets of the land's skeleton

Square eiderdowns of peach-bloom,
Old crone, Plum, unpick
A feather mattress from a bald stone.

A Warm Evening

I clip back the periwinkle.
Its blue eye looks at me.

My shoulder-joints burn
From wielding the hedge-shears.

I rest on the veranda
And look out at the harbour and hills.

Wind has ruffled the water,
Leaving pathways of calm.

Sun whitens the breast of a sea-bird
And lights windows on the opposite shore.

Sweat I saw on my father's brow
Like rain, cools now on mine.

The periwinkle smiles. I see
Who is going to win at this game.

An Old Woman Thinks of Death

O gather me, gather,
Gather, Lord,
For I am grown weary
That once stood steady
As a lamp-flame.
My tongue turns dry.
It is hard to give a little light.
Toppling, I am toppling,
Put out your hand
Put out

Pussyfoot Death
Taking the mother and leaving the father
Mad, selling the beds from under the boys,
Mad with drink and grief

  (*sings*) 'And what will poor Robin do then
        Poor thing?
        He'll hide his head under his wing.'

That was in my schoolbook.

I had taken his breakfast in as usual,
I would have heard him if he had cried out.

O gather me, O gather me
I have outlived my companions,
I am a lamp burning on
Into day

Reverie

Memories, dancers queueing in the wings,
Honey-bleed, erupt from shattered combs;
Now in foot-and-spot-light pivot
To a breathing from the stalls.

Was it so? And so?

The boards were swept, aseptic, bare,
For NOW to caper,
THIS MORNING and THIS EVENING to wrestle.
Tight-packed as capsuled thistle-seeds,
The dancers,

Till musing fanned them forth.

Am I the author? Their conductor?
Or an abstraction by the dancers dreamed?
They bow, form chains and shuffle, swing.
Like birds they are flung free.

Dead men lightly leave their tombs.

From *Jackinabox*

7

Behold, the windmill of the camping ground!

I nail up the signs: DON'T WASTE WATER.
PLACE YOUR RUBBISH IN THE BINS PROVIDED.
CAMP HERE. THIS WAY TO CARETAKER'S RESIDENCE.
PERSONS ARE NOT PERMITTED IN THE PLANTATION.

To my care the keys are entrusted.
I, alone, can lock or unlock
The men's toilets and the women's toilets.
This is a remote spot, you understand,
Between the road and the sand-dunes.

In the winter, wild ducks quack in the lagoons.
And the neighbouring surf may shake the earth,
But you could stand all day in the camping ground
And see nothing but padlocked cabins.

It is then that I make the ground tidy.
I paint the rubbish bins and chop wood.
Biking on a fine afternoon from my bach,
Which is round the first bend in the road.

If you offered me a mansion in the city
I wouldn't take it, on a winter's afternoon,

When the bins are upside down and the wood stacked
Neatly, ready to burn under the outside coppers.

But summer! That is different.
Tents. Trailers. No one reading the notices.
I prefer not to speak about it.

This much I will say. Every year, however vigilant,
I find the signposts turned the wrong way round.
Yes. And sometimes sunk in the lagoons.

HUBERT WITHEFORD

The Gap

The wall is broken there. But briars hide it
And green luxuriant boughs are stubborn there.
After the mouldering path has disappeared you find it,
Go all the way. Be lost. Stand still and look around.
And hear perhaps a bird, perhaps some feral sound
Scuffling among the foliage and your fear.
Your fear? Not what you knew before,
That ever-clutching, narrowing constraint,
A broader thing. Almost, the touch of awe,
Meeting what is not you. Not hostile, not concerned,
The wood around you waits.
And you must wait – and watch. Stand in the gentle rain.
Put down your heavy load.

King of Kings

The Emperor (you've heard?) went by this road.
Ahead, police, postillions, cuirassiers;
Behind, ambassadors, air-marshals, equerries,
And, all around, this mild, unjubilant crowd.
I saw the Emperor?
Well, no. It seemed important to be there.
I'd travelled far. Spent my life's savings, too.
But, while I looked at the half-witted horsemens' plumes
And thought of some of what was wrong with me,
I saw his back, receding down new streets.

Cloud Burst

The fuchsia and I seem happy now.
Up from the sun-hard soil the rain is bouncing
And lightning bursts out of the afternoon.
The radio
Crackles with anger much more lively than the dim
Threats of peace-loving statesmen that it drowns.
Closer
Reverberations. Flower-pots overflow.
Even the heart
Has burst its calyx of anxieties;
The spouting
Cascades superbly into two brown shoes
Put carefully – by someone else – out in the yard.
The lightning makes a difference to the room.

The Displacement

How can I look at my unhappiness
As it puts its hand over the side
Of the crumbling old well
And hooks itself up?
I know without opening my eyes
It is ugly,
It is mine.

It is really not unhappiness at all,
Who is to tell what it is?
It is something pressing up toward the light;
I call it ugly but feel only it is obscene,
A native, perhaps beautiful, of the vasty deep.

Barbarossa

Addiction to the exceptional event –
That flaw
In something like *My Childhood Days in X*,
And fault-line – as from the Aleutians
Down the Pacific to where I was when
It opened wide one day when I was ten.

The town-hall whistle blows. It's five
To twelve. Now homewards, slow,
Turning a legend like a stone, sea-worn,
Red-streaked. The bearded Emperor in the German cave
Sits in his armour; when will he wake and go
Clanking into the light to lead his hordes?

The gutters heave.
            Upon the rumbling ground
I balance. I sit down.
A stop to stories of the death of kings.
I watch the telegraph
Poles. A great hand plucks the strings.

Upon the other coast Napier, too, sways
Most irrecoverably: flames. Looters are shot
By landing-parties near the gutted shops.
Half a hill
Spilt on the coast-road; squashed in their ancient Fords
The burghers sit there still.

Mokau Estuary, 5 a.m., November, 1943

There has been time enough since the cold dawn wind
Dampened my forehead on the sea-sliced hill.

And now a dank nostalgia laps the beach
Below; around the faint light crude penumbra spill.

My country is submerged and falsified,
For what I do not want the tears unfold.

Now, to the midnight underground slides in,
Smooth as escaping life, the *Circle Line*.

Dazed yet awakening I know the doors
Seal me within such final carriages

And feel as then I did not, under the sun rise,
How keen the edge of morning in that cold.

Upon Westminster Bridge

I look in the direction I think a poem may come
Around the corner, up river, past Chelsea.
Beneath, laden with garbage, glide the barges against the stream,
To my right the agreeable towers of a failing democracy,

Quite some way to my left that place
Where I work – in Hercules Road, North Lambeth.
It faces policemen's flats. These fill the space
Where Blake amid his naked garden sat.

Crowd not upon me witnesses. Back, infernal Wordsworth!

Bondage

Watching the lightning
On the Bassin d'Arcachon
Link the sea to the sky,
Atlantic with Gironde,

I sit, and there might be
Just the cold glass in my hand,
Far storm, the tropic breeze,
The *plage* – neon-lit, abandoned.

But flashing in my skull
I feel that other chain
From cell to clattering cell
Saying

'You have been here too long' and 'Go
Back. Tell her to come'.
Blaze, forked conjunctions,
Who dares to stand alone?

The Arena

The life drains out. In drops and spurts it flows
And, as it runs, I move. In stops and goes.

Lurching, spasmodic, I draw nearer to
The obscure centre I have turned around,
My forty years – say 'God', say 'sex',
But know the sensual bound
While strength leaks
Out, of life within, the race against the wheel
Spun faster every month, each month more fell.

A wound takes time and resurrection more.
Slowly I cross this room,
What will have died before I reach a door?

White Goddess

When will she come again –

The milk-white muse,
Whose wings, spread sheer, close in
Over the nightmare and the activeness?
'Like any living orgasm'
As the man stranded there,
At the bright-bottled bar,
Anxiously says of his roses.

They, too, are in question.

Words of Love

Cold is my fear
But near is your cold hand
I take in mine.

Cold are the dead
And near
But differently,

Who wait
Without forgiveness
And lie

Outside
Or too far in.
You wait with me.

The Staying of the Magi

Asking again and again
'Where has the magic gone?'
And the answer
'Here'.

An 18th Century Painting of Wildfowl

Surprised
The visible
Proves to be playing about.

Pure
In the peacock tail
Is the place we are.

Mind
Is the delectable,
The mill, the ground.

KEITH SINCLAIR

Memorial to a Missionary

Thomas Kendall, 1778–1832, first resident missionary in New Zealand, author of The New Zealanders' First Book *(1815), grandfather of the Australian poet, H. C. Kendall.*

Instructed to speak of God with emphasis
On sin and its consequence, to cannibals
Of the evil of sin, he came from father's farm,
The virtuous home, the comfortable chapel,
The village school, so inadequately armed,
His mail of morals tested in drawing-rooms,
Not war, to teach his obscure and pitied pupils.

There were cheers in Clapham, prayers in Lincolnshire,
Psalms on the beaches, praise, O hope above.
Angels sang as he built the south's first school,
For Augustine had landed with the love
Of God at the Bay; he would speak for his aims were full
Of Cranmer, Calvin; would teach for he brought the world
Of wisdom, dreamed of the countless souls to save.

But though he cried with a voice of bells none heard,
For who was to find salvation in the sounds
Of English words? The scurrilous sailors spoke
More clearly with rum and lusting, so he turned
To the native vowels for symbols, sought to make
The Word of God anew, in the tribes' first book
Laying in Christ's advance a path of nouns.

Seeking the Maori name for sin, for hell,
Teacher turned scholar he sat at Hongi's feet
And guns were the coin he paid for revelation.
To the south men died when Hongi spent his fees.
Wrestling with meanings that defied translation,
Christian in seeking truth found sorcery,
Pilgrim encountered sex in philosophy.

A dreaming hour he spent at that mast of a tree,
And apple of his eye his mother withheld was that love,
The night of feeling, was pure and mooned for man,
Woman was made of earth and earth for wife.
In following their minds he found the men
And reached for a vision past his mother-land,
Converted by heathen he had come to save.

He drank the waters of the underworld
Lying all day in the unconverted flesh,
Entangled in old time, before Christ's birth,
Beyond redemption, found what a nest of bliss,

A hot and mushroom love lay fair in the fern
To suck from his soul the lineaments of desire,
And leave despair, O damned undreamed of pleasures.

To cure the sick at soul the little doctor
Sought out an ardent tonic far too hot,
Though not forbidden, for his infirmity.
With the south on his tongue and sweet he had forgotten
His mission, thirsted for infinities
Of the secret cider and its thick voice in the throat,
Bringing the sun all a-blossom to his blood.

But as sudden and in between such dawns his conscience
Sharpened his sins to prick his heart like nails.
The hell the Christian fears to name was heaven
To his fierce remorse and heaven and hell
Were the day and night in his life and wasted him
With their swift circling passions, until he cursed
In prayers but hated the flush of his concupiscence.

Did he fall through pride of spirit, through arrogance
Or through humility, not scorning the prayers
Of savages and their intricate pantheon?
He lacked the confident pity of his brethren.
To understand he had to sympathize,
Then felt, and feeling, fell, one man a breath
In the human gale of a culture's thousand years.

The unfaithful shepherd was sent from the farm of souls
To live, a disgraceful name in the Christian's ear,
A breathing sin among the more tolerant chiefs.
An outcaste there, or preaching where he fled
To Valparaiso from devils and reproof,
Or coasting logs round Sydney, still he strove
To find the life in the words his past had said.

Drowning off Jervis Bay, O the pain,
For death is a virgin rich in maidenheads
And memories, trees two hundred feet and tall.
The sea is a savage maiden, in her legs
Sharp pangs no missionary drank before,
And the immortality that Maui sought.
O move to Hawaiki, to the shadow of Io's breath.

No man had died such a death of dreams and storms,
For drowning with memories came that expected devil.
He was racked on the waves and spirit wrecked he wept
For his living sins, each tear-drop swimming with evil.
O soul be chang'd into little water drops
And fall into the ocean ne'er be found!
Dying he shrank from that chief who would seize him for ever.

But there no tohunga met him, angels flew
To draw his frightened soul quivering to heaven,
Bright there, bright in the open life of light.

Trying to speak known words that the unbelievers
Might know what was said and bring their ears to Christ,
He had sung with the spirit, prayed with the understanding,
Thus saved the soul he had paid to save the heathen.

His was the plough, he turned the sacred soil
Where others reaped, a pioneer in Christ's
New clearing, strove with unswerving will
Amidst the roots, the rotting stumps and compost
Of the mind to make a bed where the gospel
Might lie down in the breeding sun and grow
A crucifix of leaves, O flowers of crosses.

Immortal in our mouths, and known in heaven,
Yet as we praise we wish him greater – left
On our fractured limb of time, not yet possessed,
Where north will not meet south, of the south's lost gift.
Taught of the sinful flesh he never sensed
That to reach for truth was to reach for God, nor found
God immanent in the cannibals' beliefs.

Father he left us a legacy of guilt,
Half that time owed us, who came from the north, was given:
We know St Paul, but what in that dreaming hour,
In that night when the ends of time were tied – and severed
Again and so ever – did he learn from the south?
He could not turn to teach his countrymen,
And lost, (our sorrow), lost our birthright for ever.

The Parakeet

Shadows of bars suggest perhaps,
If memory slumbers behind
Those jewelled eyes, eucalypts
Festooned with bark strips, ribboned
With light. But his scream echoes
From farther than Bimberi Peak
Before a word or thought arose
To sing or check the slash of beak.
Clapper in a wire bell, voice
Of a demon in a nun's dream,
Chiming, enticing, then raucous
With a mad, a mindless glee;
His glaze was baked in a volcanic kiln.
Was his the first loudness to rage
Glittering over a slow, reptilian
Earth? Anachronism caged
He sits, a focus of unease –
As though, a sailor's pet, he might
Spout blasphemies to greet the visitors.
Perhaps (his own augur) it is not the light
Of past that keeps him spry: he wakes
Us to an instant's fear that this
May be the sunrise he awaits,

His inheritance of flame, a citrus
Strip in smoking morning, wing-slashed,
And Sydney a screeching desert.

The Grin

When I see a girl
quite absurdly happy
I think of you
coming to meet me.
Only those truly in love
smile that strange smile.
As a gannet,
wings fanned in the wind,
brakes on its nested rock
joyfully open-billed,
so I home in
to you with this wild grin.

KENDRICK SMITHYMAN

Anzac Ceremony

The bird that bears our branchy future flies
suddenly from the thicket and the saddest clown
turning to tell his message of too much grief
puts up his hand for the charity of one leaf,
cries for affection. No one hears or replies.
Will there be never or ever where he may lie down?

I drove my brother bleeding away from my porch.
I, full-fed, sent my sister afraid and hungry away.
She took her strength from the blood he gave,
she bound his wound, she brought water to lave;
their hurt is healed that now is my reproach.
What difficult word is there which I must say?

Who can forgive me, now being still and alone
with the touch of power, the saintly healing touch?
At the scarred and brothel kiss I cannot baulk,
I shall walk with the beggar and with the idiot talk,
abandon my goods, give my warm bed to the clown,
my sister's loss redeem, speak my brother's speech.

From *Considerations*

'High in the Afternoon the Dove'

High in the afternoon the dove
winds melancholy to his mate
a thread of music, monotone
upon the languid afternoon.
The language of his simple love
spills phrases, breaking through the heat.

Heraldic and primeval birds
reflect from their neglected tree
the clemency we did not know,
the charity we could not say,
who kept behind our uncouth words
a terrifying privacy.

Returned to memory they wind
ingenuously, note under note,
our pain commingled with their song,
the pain of music which must hang
like heat stiff on a lazy wind,
stabbing our history to the heart.

After

Put your man down somewhere
in a good lasting soil.
Do not think, bitterly, there
goes the sum of love and toil.

He was so part of you:
you bred him from your fall
into his own; today you endow
your life with his burial.

What was he, this manchild
childman? A doll of stone,
a sop for whatever ailed
you once, a weakness outgrown.

Waikato Railstop

Two suicides, not in the one season
   exactly, as we count what is materially
a season: principally I remember for
this railstop a so ordinary quality,
   so neutral, it may be
     distinguished for,

by, what was unusual there, as though
   intensely they cut peepholes through February's
smoke and haze revealing, instantaneous and all-
summing, purest motives, marrying perdition
   with action. Do not, please,
     misrepresent

the hamlet as an enthusiasm
   for the mortuary-minded in a death-centred
democracy. That certain young women should find
themselves unseasonably with child is to be
   understood and even
     an interest

to those on outlying farms. There was also
   an engineer who built an aircraft in his backyard,
which he could not fly; ambition was not licensed
to go soaring. Such an ascent measures most days'
   custom of being flat.
     You may set off

one day from another if you wish or
   if you can, skirting their outlook in the sandy
pinebelts while the Highway on the slight ridge above
consigns traffic elsewhere and a rake of coal-cars
   retreating south does not
     hurry, clacking

into the crossing and out, nor disturbs
   mynahs and bulbuls from their squabbling. Let orchard
and vineyard tally freights of purpose; you do well
or wither and rot where, to entertain your summer
   listening, the child's play
      musketry of

gorsepods fusillades at no target big
   enough to miss. Admiring does not get you far.
Wattleseeds crushed underfoot stink as from a knoll
you track further across the swamp ravelling out
   and winding mazily
      acres of peat

smoke their signals but no one, slouching hot,
   cares to separate smoke hulk from thundery cumulus.
Noon massed above blackens cloudland and a cuckold
below, seething skein by skein impartially.
   Outside the billiard room
      a truck backfires.

Alarm Without Excursion

'To know my deed, 'twere best not know myself. (*Knocking
   within*)'
                         Macbeth, II, i

After lovemaking, starkly unbound
   again, being returned each to each
we were dozing (you remember) and almost slept
   when there was a sound
of knocking at the front door but no footsteps crept
unlawfully or ribaldly cracked brash
down the path, no word said but the ground
bass of the nightwind – then my flesh

still warm from you cowardly took chill
   as furtively I lay to hear
if someone spoke, but would not get and look.
   What is it broods ill
for your bravo-lover to unman him so? that shook
his complacency, his woman hunched near
urging that he rush baresark on the hill
and challenge whatever prowled there.

What knocked the door? Only air's hollow
rough hand, or a pouncing cat; perhaps a lost fellow
benighted some ages since . . .
I do not know. I do not want to know.

Parable of Two Talents

Somewhere I read how, long since oh very
Long ago a certain Knight (most certain

In his faith) fought with the Beast
Who was his unbelief, his lack-faith contrary
In all contrarieties; but again,
    Again the Beast would hoist
Himself up from injudiciously being dead
    And not done with
    However he bled,
Stank or staggered, a corrupt patch-pelt
Scurfy verminous draggletail, caricature
    Of piety's detestably impure
Other. And the Knight – how was it he felt?

Variously he felt, variously. There was his pride
Going triumphantly before his fall
With his humility, taxed
Excessive – the Beast was, and could not be, denied.
He felt this way and that while temporal
    Lords, lords spiritual passed
Before him deferential. So he retired
    To a wilderness
    Where his absurd
Pitying servile victim followed him,
His handy monster who sustained him in that place.
    There in his hour Beast washed his tired face,
Digged deep, and chose to die, a lasting whim.

Man and a Brute lie proper in one pit,
Whom warring could not sunder: how deep should
We read the tale? I give it
No commentary, but wonder (an autumn night
Dropping dropping leaves from a dying wood)
    What medieval wit
Intended how far, how much is left unsaid;
    And sit, your virtue's
Beast, my day not played
Wholly away or so far undone
That I cannot see marriage and this parable
    Could have some truck: you, admirable
And chaste vowed to your Brute. And how alone

Should either face the wilderness who have
So much together fought, so much one mind,
So little understanding,
So much need? Flaunt handsome on your high horse and brave
My scruffy riots; they will again down, bend
    Their craggy knee, commending
Their deathly due the tax of a humbled blood
    night of autumn,
    moonshine pricking the wood
that is a wilderness as I trick
No one (you less than any) with this metaphor
    In which I hide what I should declare
Plainly, a debt that needs no rhetoric.

Hint for the Incomplete Angler

Not too far north from where I write set dawn
Before your bow precisely. Out there, cast
The kingfish from his feeding while you prey.

Smug blue worms will peck at your neat craft's side.
Show due respect then while you steal the tide.

There was a fisherman once who did things right.

For more than forty years he pulled fish out.
By line, net or pot God's plenty hauled to pout
And puff on the bottomboards, to smack
Themselves silly and die, else were tossed back
Until they swelled a right size for the pan
He kept on the wall by his sink. That man
Had long outgrown the truth of simple tales
Which said if he stroked his arm he showered scales,
That said for years he nourished an old mermaid
All to himself in his bach. Friend, he was staid,
Ordinary, and (it may be) none too bright,
But who could come godlike home with that high light
Morning on morning, to be sane as we
Would claim we are? Yet he did fittingly
More than we'd dream, and with more dignity.

For when he couldn't heave any more at the net,
When the old man snapper clung too hard, he set
His nose to the sea away out east of the Head
To give what was due from good years to the tide.

Watch for the worms as you go, at your dinghy's side.

Flying to Palmerston

'his air/of lost connections . . .'

1

Queen Street, horror
of what is altogether
bearable, where have I seen
that girl's face, that face, before?

Flight 523 departs twelve fortyfive.
Potplants in the Airways lounge
do not breathe; immobile, they flower
in an air of being suspended.
A quarter after one you will take
one pill to keep away a certain situation.

Do not be nervous, I write to myself.
The flowers have not fallen however
pallid are stalks of the lily.

2

The lily is marked. The Indian woman
wears a caste mark on her forehead;
she sits dead centre of the lounge, poised
for flight. She is equidistant from
all points here of calculated reason.

The entrance doors (one knows how
the trick is worked) open as you approach.
Look, Mum, no hands will
do you quite nicely. Thank you, m'am.

Courtesy anticipates your burden.

3

Beyond the door that no hands open
a moonface Chinese wanders.
His reason is calculated. On his forehead
a blue tattoo like a star. Bullet wound?
Stigmata? At the centre. Not dead.
Not likely.

4

Queen Street, horror
of what is altogether
bearable, where have I seen
that girl's face before?

5

The girl, I mean, is on display
in a store window, tranquillised
perhaps, which is why she can
sit so long so still. But why

was her throat cut? And why
does she not bleed – this is
how horror accrues to us who want
to pass by on another side
calculating our reasons, we see

that her head probably never sat
very comfortably on her shoulders
but it was bearable, tolerated.

Below her jawline the mortal
thread is revealed, a gap continuous
around the further side. Out of sight.

6

Issues from the darkness within
no blood. The not even dead
pallid in an air of absence
suspended, displayed, comment
on Queen Street. But where

have I seen before me that face?

7

Twelve fortytwo. A bus is at the door.
No longer a person. You are now
in flight. A Flight.

Reminiscence

Nacreous, inciting you to touch
and to stroke (it would be) in wonder
that what held wit could so be flesh
remarkably, biding suave under
a schoolgirl's fusty navy gym –
am I quite fool if it amaze
me yet, pondering *What dimension*
properly was hers or what guise,
who then moved in, not of, our world?
until our little learning crouched appalled
that one should have been born again,
perfect anachronist, a Helen.

Or thus she seemed, at seventeen,
when scholarship and critical sense
both were lightly worn; not so pain,
I guess now. Was it merely prurience
which piled a fire the next years slaked?
Or is it that there must be one
whom the Mystery endows, compact
of impossibilities undone
only in waking dreams? You schemed –
so did we, all of us, who skulked condemned
as painful cowards of no act,
insensible none could be correct.

Colville

That sort of place where you stop
long enough to fill the tank, buy plums,
   perhaps, and an icecream thing on a stick
while somebody local comes
   in, leans on the counter, takes a good look
     but does not like what he sees of you,

intangible as menace,
a monotone with a name, as place
   it is an aspect of human spirit
(by which shaped), mean, wind-worn. Face
   outwards, over the saltings: with what merit
     the bay, wise as contrition, shallow

as their hold on small repute,
good for dragging nets which men are doing
   through channels, disproportioned in the blaze
of hot afternoon's down-going
   to a far fire-hard tide's rise
     upon the vague where time is distance?

It could be plainly simple
pleasure, but these have another tone
   or quality, something aboriginal,
reductive as soil itself – bone
   must get close here, final
     yet unrefined at all. They endure.

A school, a War Memorial
Hall, the store, neighbourhood of salt
   and hills. The road goes through to somewhere else.
Not a geologic fault
   line only scars textures of experience.
     Defined, plotted; which maps do not speak.

Idyll

Adam and Eve, without serpent
or guile, all night the river *duetto*,
voices that were steps and stairs.
Those smallest rapids in the gorge
spelled out sleep for jittery timbers,
lulling coves and sandbars.
Sang, right through the night, just loud
enough to tell they kept their distance
from your doorstep which was
a pair of honeysuckle trees,
Adam and Eve left and right by the path
which you took, to rinse a bucket of washing,
where we lifted any bucket of water.
We drank the last light.

And sank the last of the whisky,
letting the fire go blank.
Indefinite as smoke upstream,
a stag roared. Nightfall,
a truckload of kids cruised the road
spotting for possums with a .22,
but went off before long,
maybe to tickle trout.

We also, we were illicit, apart from
our eiron's habitual domain,
vulnerable. Whatever anyone means by
life is not in our hands. You are lived
by. Most of twenty-four hours
of each/any/every day,
when the little white faithful pills work
as quietly as the sisters
at the hospital of Mater Misericordiae
where they shot you full of gold
salts, copper salts, salts of tears
not without failing.
How, elementary, is your will free?

The malformed path ended at
those honeysuckle trees, rewarewa.
The river's name rightly is Waiata.
Vulnerable, we could not
distinguish good from evil. Our
sin was original. It was content.

The Seal in the Dolphin Pool

One side of the tank, a glass wall.
People swim the aquarium corridor's air.
Uninteresting avaricious fish,
they butt nose to glass. Eyes enlarge.
The mouths work. When they move away,
no trail of bubbles sweeps behind them.

Dolphins must be familiar with such quirks,
whose milieu is water full of noises
(as islands may be) and signal systems.
Towards silence the corridor darkens.
They try to communicate, a cognitive
well-disposed folk caring to cooperate,
believing that another species
implies limitation. Success will
only slowly arrive, altering the nature
of codes exchanged and of rewards.

They cooperate, yes, also they compete:
for applause, to impress, as custom
agreeable to some characters.

Tough on others, that trait.
One, the outsider inside their community,
a seal whose eyes hint at innocence,
less shrewd if yet undeceived. He learns
a small man's problem in the big
man's world, how to compete, how to defend.
He has the small man's answer, comedy.

On fine edge of satire. He cannot totally
discredit what they do well,
gesture, movement, but he may clown.
For viewers he discovers once
more the staples. Play upon pathos, fools'
holiness, incongruity, defect of
mechanical surety . . . he runs his routines
through. All come pat, out of the book.

That's what you think. He's neither
college freshman nor intellectual.
We mistake him. He does not plan
to mime. He is surrounded by water
and noise, which is what he adapts.
Sound as movement, motion as sound,
who cannot suppose the enormity,
silence, on the glass's further side.

They dance. He sings, buffo,
shamelessly scooping his notes, sliding
into falsetto, plunging
the bass, hamming like hell, mugging,
doing his thing. Nobody understands
that every small man cramps a tenor who struggles
to get out. He does not

grasp the why of it, why the fish
people out there do not hear him
(hard enough, he tries) although they move
their mouths distinctly exhaling
as in response, or reaction. Puzzling
hits deeper, than any sound plummeted.

Science Fiction

That original gift is first taken
from them. Their valley at the end of
a working day can no longer taste
like a glass of cool water, like a beer
from a pool in the creek beyond hay paddocks
where they lowered bottles thoughtfully
before the baler got moving,
                              cannot taste
silence easing again from the Forest
following afternoon generously downriver,
spreading across the flats, threading

poplars, stepping subtly over fences, tending
to the valley's mouth almost
where is Ocean. There, gave up.

This was the given. Kill the baler's engine.
Flip over switches in the milking shed.
For a while, sultry, overborne, they could expect
silence. Not more.

The butcher less often hands out meat but drinks
with a faceless operative before his shop's
closing time. The school's consolidated.
Postal services are erratic. The garage will
still sell petrol although uncertain
about current prices. You cannot talk
to the man you were advised to see
at the cheese factory – the factory is abandoned.
It has a use, housing heavy duty vehicles,
hauler units, structural steel frames.
Nobody was there; nobody worries
afraid of loss, or interference.
Their caravan camp is along the main road,
between deserted houses. Oldfashioned
roses, *their* neighbours.
Nearby, elaborate concrete work is said to be
a new bridge. It's wide enough for
a landing pad.

Until you leave the valley you do not quit
sound of presence, the rig whining
upslope from the highway, a drilling outfit
reported to have tapped natural
gas at ten thousand feet. That is
the story put around. They are aliens.
They have strange accents. They do not understand
that silence is a value. We have seen their kind
on television. In this rejected place
only invaders have a future to project.
They do not expect to find oil.

HONE TUWHARE

Time and the Child

Tree earth and sky
reel to the noontide beat
of sun and the old man
hobbling down the road.
Cadence –

of sun-drowned cicada
in a child's voice shrilling:
. . . are you going man?

Where are going man where
The old man is deaf
to the child.
His stick makes deep
holes in the ground.
His eyes burn to a distant point

where all roads converge. . . .
The child has left his toys
and hobbles after the old
man calling: funny man funny man

funny old man funny
Overhead the sun paces
and buds pop and flare.

Burial

In a splendid sheath
of polished wood and glass
with shiny appurtenances
lay he fitly blue-knuckled
and serene:

*hurry rain and trail him
to the bottom of the grave*

Flowers beyond budding
will not soften the gavel's
beat of solemn words
and hard sod thudding:

*hurry rain and seek him
at the bottom of the grave*

Through a broken window
inanely looks he up;
his face glass-gouged and bloodless

his mouth engorging clay
for all the world uncaring. . . .

Cover him quickly, earth!
Let the inexorable seep of rain
finger his greening bones, deftly.

Tangi

I did not meet her
on the bordered path
nor detect her fragrance
in the frolic of violets
and carnations.

She did not stroll riverward
to sun-splash and shadows
to willows trailing garlands
of green pathos.

Death was not hiding in the cold rags
of a broken dirge:
nor could I find her
in the cruel laughter of children,
the curdled whimper of a dog.

But I heard her with the wind
crooning in the hung wires
and caught her beauty by the coffin
muted to a softer pain –
in the calm vigil of hands
in the green-leaved anguish
of the bowed heads
of old women.

The Old Place

No one comes
by way of the doughy track
through straggly tea tree bush
and gorse, past the hidden spring
and bitter cress.

Under the chill moon's light
no one cares to look upon
the drunken fence-posts
and the gate white with moss.

No one except the wind
saw the old place
make her final curtsy
to the sky and earth:

and in no protesting sense
did iron and barbed wire
ease to the rust's invasion
nor twang more tautly
to the wind's slap and scream.

On the cream-lorry
or morning paper van
no one comes,
for no one will ever leave
the golden city on the fussy train;
and there will be no more waiting
on the hill beside the quiet tree
where the old place falters
because no one comes any more

no one.

Not by Wind Ravaged

Deep scarred
    not by wind ravaged nor rain
    nor the brawling stream:
    stripped of all save the brief finery
    of gorse and broom; and standing
    sentinel to your bleak loneliness
    the tussock grass –

O voiceless land, let me echo your desolation.
    The mana of my house has fled,
    the marae is but a paddock of thistle.
    I come to you with a bitterness
    that only your dull folds can soothe
    for I know, I know
    my melancholy chants shall be lost
    to the wind's shriek about the rotting eaves.

Distribute my nakedness –
    Unadorned I come with no priceless
    offering of jade and bone curio: yet
    to the wild berry shall I give
    a tart piquancy; enhance for a deathless
    space the fragile blush of manuka. . . .

You shall bear all and not heed.
    In your huge compassion embrace
    those who know no feeling other
    than greed:
    of this I lament my satisfaction
    for it is as full as a beggar's cup:
    no less shall the dust of avaricious men
    succour exquisite blooms with
    moist lips parting
    to the morning sun.

No Ordinary Sun

Tree let your arms fall:
raise them not sharply in supplication
to the bright enhaloed cloud.
Let your arms lack toughness and
resilience for this is no mere axe
to blunt, nor fire to smother.

Your sap shall not rise again
to the moon's pull.
No more incline a deferential head
to the wind's talk, or stir
to the tickle of coursing rain.

Your former shagginess shall not be
wreathed with the delightful flight
of birds nor shield
nor cool the ardour of unheeding
lovers from the monstrous sun.

Tree let your naked arms fall
nor extend vain entreaties to the radiant ball.
This is no gallant monsoon's flash,
no dashing trade wind's blast.
The fading green of your magic
emanations shall not make pure again
these polluted skies . . . for this
is no ordinary sun.

O tree
in the shadowless mountains
the white plains and
the drab sea floor
your end at last is written.

The Girl in the Park

The girl in the park
      saw a nonchalant sky
      shrug into a blue-dark
      denim coat.

      The girl in the park
      did not reach up to touch
      the cold steel buttons.

The girl in the park
      saw the moon glide
      into a dead tree's arms
      and felt the vast night
      pressing.
      How huge it seems,
      and the trees are big she said.

The stars heard her
and swooped down perching
on tree-top and branch
owl-like and unblinking.

The grave trees,
as muscular as her lover
leaned darkly down to catch
the moonrise and madness
in her eyes:
the moon is big, it is very big
she said with velvet in her throat.

An owl hooted.
The trees scraped and nudged
each other and the stars
carried the helpless
one-ribbed moon away. . . .

The girl in the park
does not care: her body swaying
to the dark-edged chant
of storms.

Old Man Chanting in the Dark

Where are the men of mettle?
are there old scores
left to settle?
when will the canoes leap
to the stab and kick
the sea-wet flourish
of pointed paddles?
will the sun play again
to the skip of muscles
on curved backs bared
to the rain's lash
the sea's punch?
to War! to War!

where are the proud lands
to subdue – and women?
where are the slaves
to gather wood for the fires
stones for the oven?
who shall reap
the succulent children whimpering
on the terraced hill-top?

no more alas no more
no raw memory left
of these
nor bloody trophies:
only the fantail's flip

to cheeky war-like postures
and on the sand-hill
wry wind fluting
the bleached bones marrowless

Drunk

When they hustled him out
at closing time he had
forty cents clutched in
his hands for another drink

Rain stabbed the streets
with long slivers of light
He picked his way
gingerly treading the golden
non-existent stairs
to the fried-fish shop

Whirling pin-points
of coloured lights confused
him: and when people appeared
to converge on him he swerved
to avoid them and collided
with a post

He sensed a sea of receding
faces picked himself up
and promptly emptied his guts
on the footpath fervently calling
for his bleeding mate Christ
who was nowhere to be seen

Later wearing a stiff mask
of indifference
he pissed himself in the bus

At work the next morning
he moved with effort in the hollow
silence of a self-built tomb:
unaware of the trapped mortal
crouching there

To a Maori Figure Cast in Bronze outside
the Chief Post Office, Auckland

I hate being stuck up here, glaciated, hard all over
and with my guts removed: my old lady is not going
to like it

I've seen more efficient scare-crows in seed-bed
nurseries. Hell, I can't even shoo the pigeons off

Me: all hollow inside with longing for the *marae* on
the cliff at Kohimarama, where you can watch the ships
come in curling their white moustaches

Why didn't they stick me next to Mickey Savage?
'Now then,' he was a good bloke
Maybe it was a Tory City Council that put me here

They never consulted me about naming the square
It's a wonder they never called it: Hori-in-the-gorge-at-
bottom-of-Hill. Because it is like that: a gorge,
with the sun blocked out, the wind whistling around
your balls (your balls mate) And at night, how I
feel for the beatle-girls with their long-haired
boy-friends licking their frozen finger-chippy lips
hopefully. And me again beetling

my tent eye-brows forever, like a brass monkey with
real worries: I mean, how the hell can you welcome
the Overseas Dollar, if you can't open your mouth
to poke your tongue out, eh?

If I could only move from this bloody pedestal I'd
show the long-hairs how to knock out a tune on the
souped-up guitar, my *mere* quivering, my *taiaha* held
at the high port. And I'd fix the ripe *kotiros* too
with their mini-*piupiu*-ed bums twinkling: yeah!

Somebody give me a drink: I can't stand it

A Fall of Rain at Miti-Miti

Drifting on the wind, and through
the broken window of the long house
where you lie, incantatory chant
of surf breaking, and the Mass
and the mountain talking.

At your feet two candles puff the
stained faces of the *whanau*, the vigil
of the bright madonna. See, sand-whipped
the toy church does not flinch.

E moe, e te whaea: wahine rangimarie

Mountain, why do you loom over us like
that, hands on massive hips? Simply
by hooking your finger to the sea,
rain-squalls swoop like a hawk, suddenly.
Illumined speeches darken, fade to metallic
drum-taps on the roof.

Aanei nga roimata o Rangipapa.

Flat, incomprehensible faces: lips moving
only to oratorical rhythms of the rain:

quiet please, I can't hear the words.

And the rain steadying: black sky leaning
against the long house. Sand, wind-sifted
eddying lazily across the beach.

And to a dark song lulling: *e te whaea, sleep.*

JANET FRAME

O Lung Flowering Like a Tree

O lung flowering like a tree
a shadowy bird bothers thee
a strange bird that will not fly away
or sing at break of day and evening.

I will take my knife
I will cut the branch of the tree
he clings to and will not let go
then the wide sky can look in
and light lay gloss
on the leaves of blood beating with life.

Oh yes, tomorrow I will take my knife
and the light and I will look in,
O plagued lung flowering like a tree,
said the surgeon.

Yet Another Poem About a Dying Child

Poets and parents say he cannot die
so young, so tied to trees and stars.
Their word across his mouth obscures
and cures his murmuring good-bye.
He babbles, *they say*, of spring flowers,

who for six months has lain
his flesh at a touch bruised violet,
his face pale, his hate clearer
than milky love that would smooth over
the pebbles of diseased bone.

Pain spangles him like the sun,
He cries and cannot say why.
His blood blossoms like a pear tree.
He does not want to eat or keep
its ugly windfall fruit.

He does not want to spend or share
the engraved penny of light
that birth put in his hand
telling him to hold it tight.
Will parents and poets not understand?

He must sleep, rocking the web of pain
till the kind furred spider will come
with the night-lamp eyes and soft tread
to wrap him warm and carry him home
to a dark place, and eat him.

Rain on the Roof

My nephew sleeping in a basement room
has put a sheet of iron outside his window
to recapture the sound of rain falling on the roof.

I do not say to him, The heart has its own comfort for grief.
A sheet of iron repairs roofs only. As yet unhurt by the demand
that change and difference never show, he is still able
to mend damages by creating the loved rain-sound
he thinks he knew in early childhood.

Nor do I say, In the travelling life of loss
iron is a burden, that one day he must find
within himself in total darkness and silence
the iron that will hold not only the lost sound of the rain
but the sun, the voices of the dead, and all else that has gone.

When the Sun Shines More Years Than Fear

When the sun shines more years than fear
when birds fly more miles than anger
when sky holds more bird
sails more cloud
shines more sun
than the palm of love carries hate,
even then shall I in this weary
seventy-year banquet say, Sunwaiter,
Birdwaiter, Skywaiter,
I have no hunger,
remove my plate.

Some Will Be for Burning

Some will be for burning, not all.
In the deep sky trees may lean, and men,
to take their hot gold coin, and some,
not all, will be for burning.

In autumn many trees have ashes for leaves;
the willow and the silver poplar
have paid the penalty of fire
no creek or soft rain will smother;

and there are men whose footfall on earth
is like the smoke and whisper of leaves.

But some will be for staying cold and whole
like stone in growth of moss, the green ember
kindled by creek water and soft rain.

Dialogue

'People are strange?'

'Yes. They gave the rat of fear a brilliantine hairdress,
smoothed its bristle, preened its whiskers.
Clean and harmless as an ultra-bomb or refined plague
it followed like a poodle at the heels of their God.

'For exercise it walked upon the faith-lit Common
Ground of superstition; for breeding purposes it used
the free steepled stud opposite the Town Hall, the reserved
shelves of libraries, and cinemas showing expurgated films.

'How it earned the approval of their domestic hearts!
But – secret in the night, as the Rat of Fear, it gnawed
the stale furred slices of love, the half-tasted meal,
the torn letter of demand, refusal, transition
– all the overflowing garbage of their guilt.'

'People are strange?'

'Yes, after the indifference of bees and lions
to small print, fossils, promises and disaster funds.'

Mother and Daughter

Gay strawberry tassels hang from the arbutus.
Irresistibly persuaded, raindrops separate
from clinging leaves. Water easily will let go
its trembling hold when earth force reaches up to tug it free.

Half-green, half-yellow, the sycamores are shabby with waiting.
Their windmill seeds, knowing
the routine, travel blindfold past withered
stalks that languidly admit, It can happen here.

Custom lies heavier than death upon the scene.
The watching eye must look away to discover
Proserpine ugly, unpredictably human,
abhorring white lilies, roses, saffron flowers,

while her mother, blond Ceres, does not care so late
to tramp cornfield and street to discover where,
in what underground hovel, with whom
her wayward daughter sleeps six months of the year.

Yet concern and love are told still in the moss-burning strawberries
and the young raindrops, without will, sliding into the earth,
and the wind, awake all night, helping in the search for what is lost,
and the glistening white face of the frost against the morning window.

The Flowering Cherry

These cherries are not wine-filled bowls for thirsty birds
nor ornaments of the house where sky's the ceiling.
These are the pawnbroker tree's discreet sign,
the wine, tear and blood drops of bondage,
the tree's relentless advantage
taken of the poverty that came when, warmed
with familiar memory of what had been
and had been and would be but is never known
entirely or believed until it is born,
we saw the cherry tree in flower, and at once spent
a life's rich astonishment.

'Why should I be bound to thee?'
Blake asked of the myrtle tree. Why?
He killed to escape. Blood flowed beneath the tree:
a father's blood, an old man's, who must have known
how to bargain with all possession
that makes a tree, a house, a sky into a prison
and each man see the marks of chains upon his skin.

The cherry tree flowers earlier than most,
falls as snow while snow is still falling
sweeps into us and through us and we taste
the flower as fruit, we eat the first
full-blown light unfolded out of winter darkness.
Then, as if the bloom were gone, the tree will hide
in wine-coloured shade and pawn signs to pursue its trade.

And we are prisoners then, borrowing wonder
to redeem the pledge; or too poor, too ill,
too far away to make the necessary journey,
we plead in writing for the tree's mercy. Why
should a lifetime of marvelling be spent
on this first view of spring light, this burst of cherry snow?
Why should the tree house our treasure in blood?

When next you pass the flowering cherry now, in September,
look closely at the cool dark wine house
where the blackbirds sing for their supper
where the human senses sing for their survival.

LAURIS EDMOND

August, Ohakune

All night in winter the dogs howled
up the hill in the mad woman's house –
she had forty living inside,
half starved, truculent, snarling
at all who came; but only kids
would creep along the derelict track:
half choked with fear they stalked phantoms,
found their nightmare, an ancient stag,
eyeless, ghastly holes gouged
by rats, above the blackened door.
They smothered screams – and went back,
in daylight only . . .
                          Further off
we could hear the river
intermittently tapping its menacing morse
and the morepork call through the dark;
at last the frost hunted us in
to take shelter in a cold uneasy sleep.

Over all was the mountain, Snow Queen
of an old tale, brilliant and deadly, brooding
on the fate of frozen villages.

Before a Funeral

The great bright leaves have fallen
outside your window
they lie about
torn by the season from
the beggared cherry trees.
In your room, alone,
I fold and hide away
absurd, unnecessary things –
your books, still ready and alert,
it seems, for understanding,
clothes, dry and cold,
surprised in holding still
to hairs upon the collars,
handkerchiefs in pockets,
socks, awry, not ready for
the queer neglect of death.

Mechanically useful, I make
preparations for some possible
impossible journey no one
will ever take; work will help
they tell me, and indeed

your room is now nothing
but things, and tidy.
I have put away your life.

Out in the autumn garden
a sharp rapacious wind
snatches the brilliant booty
of the leaves. The blackened branches
groan. They knot, and hold.
And yet the cold will come.

Scar Tissue

Wellington is an old crone
all gaps, teeth knocked out;
daily, watchers stare
at waving arms that claw
walls into rubble.
A case of indecent exposure
occurred last week:
bed, wardrobe, blue wallpaper
swinging high – drunken, ridiculous,
skin peeled off and bricks falling
into the crawling pit where puddles show
the sea still seeps under the Quay.

I used to walk this way on windy nights
past Barretts roaring doorway
stinking of beer and early closing
up the old steps, not then assaulted
by the big drills, nor lit
by simpering shops,
but dark, clay-smelling, convolvulus
and periwinkle sprawling on the stones
and fennel, ripe and strong,
grasping the bank. There,
a few yards from the rattling trams,
I would come to you, breathless from running;
I remember the wind wrapping us,
your hands cold inside my coat
and the shreds of our voices whirled up up high
into a torn corner of sky.

Long afterwards I still was shaken
when I passed, the bitter wind could still
sting me to tears. But no more –
a pulse has dulled in the flesh;
I feel it less.
Today they've got a new instrument,
a great iron ball that smashes at
the city's trembling past.
I gape with the rest, say
with the same dull voice I know
it has to go.

Round Oriental Bay

This is my city, the hills and harbour water
I call home, the grey sky racing over headlands,
awkward narrow streets that stirred me long ago
– it's half a lifetime since I first came in
wonderment and savoured here prodigious
conversations, gravid with abstractions, in Mount
Street cemetery; read Eliot; acted plays that
occupied us night long – planning, having visions,
making love with all the light sweet leisure
of the young till startled by the dawn we walked
still softly laughing to our dingy old addresses,
returning later for the talking, always talking,
in the drowsy gorse on Varsity Hill.

What else? The shared penury, our monumentally
naïve political convictions; our cleverness
(the 'vicious little circle' marvelling at its
brilliance for a fragile funny summer term);
our simplicity – 'If you won't marry me
I'll wait for you for ever' – ah, it was all
for ever . . . and now what's left of it, that
passion so intense there was a kind of moral
splendour in it, those helpless loyalties?

The bell of Saint Gerard's booms gently in the dusk;
the city's strict oblongs of light are new,
but in these hills the past is soaked like blood
that soaks a battlefield; the restless water grinds
the pebbled beach, before the island's dark hump
opens the winking red eye of the buoy; above me
lights wake too in gabled houses – the battered,
windswept, hill-top houses that still stand
and face the constant beating of the weather.

The Beech Tree

It's over, the rending shudder,
the crack; the tree's despatched –
and with it the long-settled
communities of green gossiping,
rapt occupations of birds,
the shared calamities of weather.
We crowd beside the stump, watch
sap like a kind of bleeding ooze
out of the packed encircling
substance of the wood; this
morning's act exposed
a century's patterned industry,
the years' circumferences
gathered cell by inching cell
out of the inner and the outer
lives of growth and weather.

And I think how in us too such
cycles move, how silently our accidents
and errors, the slowly multiplying
comprehension of our loss, our joy,
accumulate till every season of
the heart's engrained within us.

I tell you, friend or lover, all
who touch my life, I cannot lose you
even by forgetting until death destroys
the ordered secret kingdom of my body.

After Chagall

'Intensity and detachment: court both.'

The streets of my city grow old and small,
they are turning into a Russian village;
great waves of indigo light carry me up
and up into a populous sky; I attenuate,
turn upside down and float, the air streams
past billowing like iris blue chiffon, I
come to you on a house top where you are
playing on a red guitar the old songs
of the people; stars dance in the angle
of your elbow; we touch and our bodies
merge in a moving cloud of light turning
to paradisal green. There is no sound
but the hum of our hearts. The painter
is right, the real world could never
contain us. This is intensity.

Now the air thickens, the radiant company
darkens – bodies, birds, cows, violins and
harvest moons come drifting down, they
coalesce; we blink and look again at men
in suits smoking and talking of the news
in the morning paper; women's heads
repose on shoulders, mouths talk and eat,
bodies merely breathe. I struggle, choking
on the denseness of the air, look everywhere
but cannot find you. When it no longer hurts
to stand still and fit into the strict shape
of my skin – that will be detachment.

The Names

Six o'clock, the morning still and
the moon up, cool profile of the night;
time small and flat as an envelope –
see, you slip out easily: do I know you?
Your names have still their old power,
they sing softly like voices across water.

Virginia Frances Martin Rachel Stephanie
Katherine – the sounds blend and chant
in some closed chamber of the ear, poised
in the early air before echoes formed.
Suddenly a door flies open, the music
breaks into a roar, it is everywhere;

now it's laughter and screaming, the crack
of a branch in the plum tree, the gasping
and blood on the ground; it is sea-surge
and summer, 'Watch me!' sucked under
the breakers; the hum of the lupins, through
sleepy popping of pods the saying of names.

And all the time the wind that creaked in
the black macrocarpas and whined in the wires
was waiting to sweep us away; my children who
were my blood and breathing I do not know you:
we are friends, we write often, there are
occasions, news from abroad. One of you is dead.

ALISTAIR CAMPBELL

Hut Near Desolated Pines

Cobwebs and dust have long
Deadened an old man's agony.
The choked fireplace, the chair
On its side on the mud floor,
May have warmed an old man's
Bones or propped them upright
While his great head nodded;
Fantastical images may have stirred
His mind when the wind moaned
And sparks leapt up the chimney
With a roar. But what great gust
Of the imagination threw wide
The door and smashed the lamp
And overturned both table and chair . . .?
A rabbiter found him sprawled
By the door – no violence, nothing
To explain, but the hungry rats
That scurried over the fouled straw.
A foolish lonely old man
With his whiskers matted with dung.
Since when birds have stuffed the chimney
With straw, and a breeze flapped
Continually through the sack window;
And all the while the deft spiders
Doodled away at their obituaries,
And the thin dust fell from the rafters . . .
Nothing but cobwebs and dust
Sheeting an old man's agony.

At a Fishing Settlement

October, and a rain-blurred face,
And all the anguish of that bitter place.
It was a bare sea-battered town,
With its one street leading down
On to a shingly beach. Sea winds
Had long picked the dark hills clean
Of everything but tussock and stones
And pines that dropped small brittle cones
On to a soured soil. And old houses flanking
The street hung poised like driftwood planking
Blown together and could not outlast
The next window-shuddering blast
From the storm-whitened sea.
It was bitterly cold; I could see
Where muffled against gusty spray
She walked the clinking shingle; a stray
Dog whimpered and pushed a small
Wet nose into my hand – that is all.

Yet I am haunted by that face,
That dog, and that bare bitter place.

The Return

And again I see the long pouring headland,
And smoking coast with the sea high on the rocks,
The gulls flung from the sea, the dark wooded hills
Swarming with mist, and mist low on the sea.

And on the surf-loud beach the long spent hulks,
The mats and splintered masts, the fires kindled
On the wet sand, and men moving between the fires,
Standing or crouching with backs to the sea.

Their heads finely shrunken to a skull, small
And delicate, with small black rounded beaks;
Their antique bird-like chatter bringing to mind
Wild locusts, bees, and trees filled with wild honey –

And, sweet as incense-clouds, the smoke rising, the fire
Spitting with rain, and mist low with rain –
Their great eyes glowing, their rain-jewelled, leaf-green
Bodies leaning and talking with the sea behind them:

Plant gods, tree gods, gods of the middle world . . . Face downward
And in a small creek mouth all unperceived,
The drowned Dionysus, sand in his eyes and mouth,
In the dim tide lolling – beautiful, and with the last harsh

Glare of divinity from lip and broad brow ebbing . . .
The long-awaited! And the gulls passing over with shrill cries;
And the fires going out on the thundering sand;
And the mist, and the mist moving over the land.

From *Elegy*

II

Now He is Dead

Now he is dead, who talked
Of wild places and skies
Inhabited by the hawk;

Of the hunted hare that flies
Down bare parapets of stone,
And there closes its eyes;

Of trees fast-rooted in stone
Winds bend but cannot break;
Of the low terrible moan

That dead thorn trees make
On a windy desolate knoll;
Of the storm-blackened lake

Where heavy breakers roll
Out of the snow-bred mist,
When the glittering air is cold;

Of the Lion Rock that lifts
Out of the whale-backed waves
Its black sky-battering cliffs;

Of the waterfall that raves
Down the black mountain side,
And into a white cauldron dives.

VII

The Laid-out Body

Now grace, strength and pride
Have flown like the hawk;
The mind like the spring tide,

Beautiful and calm; the talk;
The brilliance of eye and hand;
The feet that no longer walk.

All is new, and all strange –
Terrible as a dusty gorge
Where a great river sang.

Bitter Harvest

The big farm girl with the dumb prophetic body
And shoulders plump and white as a skinned peach
Goes singing through the propped-up apple boughs.

Behind her steps an ancient Jersey cow
With bones like tent-poles and udder swinging.

And last a hairy boy who with a fishing-pole
Drives youth and age before him, flanked by boulders
More yielding than his love. O bitter harvest

When drought affirms and plenitude denies!
Well, let them pass. Assuredly the boy
Will drop his worm into a dusty hole

And fish up . . . death, and the ancient cow
On which so much depends will clear the moon.

From *Sanctuary of Spirits*

IX

Against Te Rauparaha

'*Kei hea koutou kia toa* – Be brave
that you may live.'
                    Hongi Hika

The records all agree
you were a violent, a pitiless man,
        treacherous as an avalanche
poised above a sleeping village.
        Small, hook-nosed as a Roman,
haughty, with an eagle's glance,
        Caligula and Commodus
                were of your kin.

        Kapiti floats before me,
and the shadows round the island
                prickle
like the hairs of my scalp.
        Shadows of war canoes
                splinter the bright sea.
And I hear on the cliff below
        the low cry of a chief:
        '*Ka awe te mamae!*
                Alas, the pain!'

Ironical to think your island pa,
        once drenched with the blood
                of men and whales,
has since become a sanctuary for birds.
Would this make sense to you, I wonder.
        That life is holy would seem
a dubious proposition to you,
        old murderer –
                most laughable.

        Pathetic ghost!
Sometimes you hoot despairingly
                across the valley,
and my small daughter sobs in her sleep,
        convinced an engine is pursuing her.
Black as anthracite,
        issuing in steam
                out of the bowels of the hill,
yours is a passable imitation, I'll allow.
But where is the rage that terrorised the coast?
the towering pride not to be withstood?
        Imperial violence . . .!
                Imperial poppycock!
I saw you slink away in the moonlight –
a most solitary, attenuated ghost

      reduced to scaring little girls.
The worst that you can do is raise a storm
      and try to tear my roof off . . .

      But why deceive myself?
I know you as the subtlest tormentor,
      able to assume at will
the features of the most intimate terrors.

Remember Tama who betrayed his friends,
   guests on his *marae*,
to the murderous vengeance of Hakitara –
Pehi and forty others,
         all great chiefs,
      impiously butchered in their sleep!
How, spider-clever, you again escaped
      to spin a web and snare him.
         And how Te Hiko, Pehi's son,
glared at him for fully half an hour,
      lifted Tama's upper lip
         with a forefinger
and tapped the wolfish teeth,
         crying wildly:
'These teeth ate my father!'

         Tamaiharanui
who strangled in the night
      his beautiful daughter
         that she might not be a slave.
But afterwards
      plump goose for a widow's oven,
         plucked of his honour,
what remained of Tama
      but a victim for a ritual vengeance?

Tama and Hiko too were of your kin,
   and vengeful Hakitara – violent men,
      crazed with the lust for blood!
Who would have guessed that they were also
      dutiful sons, affectionate fathers?
or that, decorous on the *marae*,
      they entertained their guests
         with courtly ease?

Scarer of children, drinker of small girls,
      your malicious eye stares down
         out of the midday sun,
blasting the seed in the pod,
      choking the well with dust.

These teeth ate my father –
      ate the heart of the bright day!

Insidious enmity!
   I know you by these signs:

the walls crack without cause,
      heads show pointed teeth,
leer and fall away,
      the dog barks at nothing,
whimpers and hides his head,
      and something wild
darts into the night
      from under my window . . .
YOU – Te Rauparaha!

The wind rises,
      lifts the lid off my brain –

Madman, leave me alone!

Gathering Mushrooms

Dried thistles hide his face.
Look closely –
that's your enemy.
Ants carry away his flesh,
but still he grins.
You know him by his thumbs
round and white,
breaking the earth like mushrooms,
coated with fine sand.

A bony finger flicks a bird
into your face,
daisies snap at your heels,
nostrils
flare in the ground
that you believed was solid –
and a dark wind rides
the whinnying tussock up the hillside.

Gather your mushrooms then,
and if you dare
ignore the thin cries of the damned,
issuing through the gills.

Sick of running away
you drop in the soaking grass.
Through tears
you watch a snail climbing a straw
that creaks and bends
under its weight,
and note how tenderly it lifts
upon its shoulder
the fallen weight of the sky.

Why Don't You Talk to Me?

Why do I post my love letters
in a hollow log?
Why put my lips to a knothole in a tree
and whisper your name?

The spiders spread their nets
and catch the sun,
and by my foot in the dry grass
ants rebuild a broken city.
Butterflies pair in the wind,
and the yellow bee,
his holsters packed with bread,
rides the blue air like a drunken cowboy.

More and more I find myself
talking to the sea.
I am alone with my footsteps.
I watch the tide recede
and I am left with miles of shining sand.

Why don't you talk to me?

The Gunfighter

You will see him any day in Te Kuiti
or Cannons Creek,
immaculate in black
and triggered like a panther on the prowl.

Conscious of all eyes,
but indifferent to all except the heroine
watching from behind lace curtains,
doom walks the main street of a small town.

Is it fear or admiration that widens
those lovely eyes?
He knows her eyes are on him,
but gives no sign he knows –
he has a job to do.

The sun has reached high noon,
the shadows stand with flattened palms
against the walls of buildings
or shrink back into doorways.
The heroine lets fall the curtain,
she has fallen –
drilled clean through the heart with love.

Now he stands alone
in the pool of his own shadow,
his wrists flexible as a dancing girl's,

his palms hovering like butterflies
over the blazing butts of his sixguns.

The streets are cleared,
the township holds its breath –
for the gunfighter, the terrible gunfighter
is in town.

Love Song for Meg

It was the way
   the sun came sidling
through the branches –
   points of light
exploding into stars
   as the wind,
eddying overhead,
   delicately sprung
the leaves apart.
   I remember most
your eyes and then
   your silence.
Light's undertow,
   backwash of green
from the dull silver
   of decaying trees.
It was the way
   your green eyes
widened and turned black.
   Black and gold
sang the leaves,
   the water rose
in the secret pool
   where all afternoon
I tickled trout –
   rose gently
and carried us away
   in summer sleep.

Dreams, Yellow Lions

When I was young
I used to dream of girls
and mountains.

Now it is water I dream of,
placid among trees, or lifting
casually on a shore

where yellow lions come out
in the early morning
and stare out to sea.

Memo to Mr Auden, 29/8/66

Re your 'Musée des Beaux Arts', Mr Auden,
The Old Masters may have never been wrong,
But we regret that you were often wrong,
Sometimes appallingly, as in 'Miss Gee'.
As Mother's little boy with close-set eyes,
You might have thrown fewer stones at birds
And more at Mother who may have been to blame.
Suffering is a personal thing, but we believe
You see it rather as a spectacle – a public thing.
Suffering is a small girl screaming to her mother
That the torturer's horse has run her sister down.
As to the children skating on the pond,
One cry of anguish from the girl in labour
Will stop them all – excepting Mother's boy
Who will skate on . . . Mr Auden, not all the aged
Reverently, passionately await the miraculous birth.
Some may have been stone-throwers in their youth,
And that same cry will pierce them with cruel delight.
The Old Masters knew that. You must have known that.
But you chose to write of doggy dogs and a horse
With an innocent behind – mere stage props, Mr Auden.
And as to that dreadful martyrdom, admit you willed it
Into happening so you could write about it.
Mr Auden, you are the ploughman in Bruegel's 'Icarus'
Following a stage prop. You are the delicate
Expensive ship that sees something amazing, perhaps
Even tragic – a boy falling out of the sky,
But you have a poem to finish and sail calmly on.

W. H. OLIVER

In Radcliffe Square, Oxford

On a wet and wintry dusk in Radcliffe Square
While a gusty wind torn between pinnacles
Volleyed the sound of bells from wall to wall,
A man and a woman were busy quarrelling
Under a corner gas-lamp, splayed on the sheer
Cliff of the library wall.

He in a uniform, she young and resentful,
Were standing at two arms' distance, eloquent
So caught in disgust and despair, more than in words
The ignorant wind whipped from their twisting lips.
That was the surface, a trivial hate: their money,
Merchandise, or souls, the issue.

Walls, spire and pinnacles, commemorating
Our Blessed Lady and all hallowed souls
Observed the decline of their love. St Mary's
Tower of bell notes boomed around the square
Echoing welcome welcome welcome into heaven;
Had not one clear note for these dead.
Cobble stones gleamed; a dark dome shoved the clouds;
Heaven was everywhere present everywhere full
Of foreboding.

They, separating, left the square empty
As the bells became still. Then the shouldering dome and the spire
Springing to heaven on a crutch of stone
Were lost in a scurry of rain. Heaven was everywhere
Present, everywhere mourned their loss.

In the Fields of My Father's Youth

1

In the fields of my father's youth, now bountiful and green,
I walked and stared, half-recollecting each
New but anticipated emblem of a past
once legendary, now more remote than legend,
remembering all he had told for the delight of children:
folk-habits, succession of seasons and lives,
the dim procession of my ancestors
walking through centuries this treadmill lane.

Its trench between stone bramble-plaited hedges
wound where the contour made a passage easy,
past fertile hills where he had worked all seasons,
last of the peasant line who broke this earth.
Mill and manor, farm house, cottages,
kept up an easy, sociable conversation:

a discourse of rank and degree, proud and humble
linked by its cautious line in a common life.

I celebrated every moderate hope
that lay embedded in the lane's hard clay
feeling myself made radical once more;
and celebrated, too, the manor house,
crown of the country, elegant, discreet
as well-worn riches, sweet as piety.

2

How many hopes were trenched in the secretive lane?
I populated every crossroad with
a host of suicides impaled on hate:
passionate, modest, impossible hopes, denied
in life and death the four unwinding roads
which lead, whichever way, to difference.
When it was moonlight, how many bones
jangled together at Black Cross and White Cross
as an army of lost liberators gaped for flesh?
How great a multitude of dreams? Not his,
at the end. They leapt across an era and a world and pitched
full-flighted, ready to flower, on an empty island,
travelled the dust and gravel of a new highroad
linking, not age to age, but moderate hope to hope.

Solitude, dream, their pinched and starving hopes,
his and my ancestors', he brought to breed
in the raw clay and timber of a settlement
new and elsewhere; not anywhere
the manor's grace could mock their stuntedness.

3

His dream is fulfilled in an acre of fertile ground;
took body in a house, a family;
in leisure, fruit and flowers, company;
work winning ease, children bringing home
children for grandparents, warmth for autumn.
The dream is fulfilled in an empty island town,
a street of stucco shops and iron verandahs
perched on the site of a violated forest;
a temporary borough pitiable
beneath the winter snow range meditating
flood and disaster in the final spring –
not yet. Clay gapes in cuttings and the soil runs down
each winter river; land is dying; yet
there will be life in it enough for him,
enough for the dream to flourish and express
a permanent hope lodged in impermanence,

given, in one brief life, a chance to live
apart from that perpetual English rite:
one taken chance, then newness, all things strange.

Till that time fall from the mountain and the sky
I think the innumerable peasantry within
his hand and eye, the ground bass of that theme
particular skill and courage elaborate,
are strong and sappy in his acre garden
and, I expect, are happy as never on earth
moving in his disguises among strawberry frames,
directing the growth of flowers round a house.
They are prodigal there who died in paucity
and, having raised a county's fodder and crops,
delight themselves in more luxurious harvests.

And I think they talk through the words of poetry
he writes to me here in England, telling me
of the growth and profit and joy of his fruitful acre
as once in passion and in oratory
they stood on platform, soapbox, with the jobless,
full of the argument of state, rebelliously
talking down privilege, arguing equal rights.
That dream flower faded, cynically abused;
the song of equality became a bribe
offered abroad by immoral political apes,
while good men reeled in the wake of procureurs.

There is only the garden full of surprising fruit.

4

The lane led away to the by-pass, to the rail,
to the university town, this desk, these words.
Can I who live by his flight relinquish either
the peasant's dream or the eloquent manor house?
Both were his first and every birthday gift.

All those who sleep in tears within my seed
will reach, if I do not, the breaking point
where loyalties depart and go their ways
separate, hostile, taking up their arms
to meet in battle on the disputed field
of England's and our own heart's heritage.

That will be time for treasons and for faith.

Solstice

The day marks the end of the year,
five years, fifty, more, any number.
It began cool and grey, a light wind turning the leaves,
high mackerel clouds roofing the green space.

Then the blade of the sun struck through. I hacked
the spring's wild growth, shoulders stinging,
harder and leaner under a clear light.
Now the late sun slants into the enclosure.
The fire settles into ash, wood I had hewed
at the meridian from a dead orange tree,
hard, good burning. Light catches in my glass
and gleams, bright in the darkening day.
I look into the dying sun with open eyes.

RAYMOND WARD

Watching Snow

You were standing at the window, silently
when the first flakes began to fall
between the houses, to settle in the boughs
of the leafless elm and in the yard below;
and so intently were you watching them
spin through the early winter gloom
to catch in fences, heap the window sill,
you did not notice when I spoke to you.

So I fell silent, too. But no,
not just because the snow enchanted me:
the way you stood there like a memory
re-awakened so much tenderness
I had thought buried long ago,
nostalgic, maternal as the falling snow,
that I was glad when you made no reply.
Nearness enough to watch you standing there,

and as intently as you watched the snow:
it gathered slowly, darkening your hair
and shoulders, till your outline only, drained
like a negative, at last remained,
sharp against the window veiled with steam.
You must have known that I was watching you,
pierced by the memory a snowflake clears,
or why were you also, when you turned, in tears?

Solo for Clarinet

I am always meeting him. In his rags
or in his extra special clothes, he
lands on both feet from out of nowhere.
Like new.
        A springy disconcerting number
with a slouch hat skimming one ear
like a spun lariat, or a tray load
tilting on a waiter's palm;
alternatively, rubbed right forward
astonishing his nose.
             Definitely
not the man-in-the-street. Not
Everyman. Nothing like that.
Himself: as water is inclined
to be liquid and fire flame;
and with as little interest
in the habit of name.
             Snakily
on his toes he confronts me, his hat
like a rubber ball bobbing on

a seal's nose; while he cranes
his neck to see me in the round
with a stare like Picasso's.
Ants I can't shake off, his eyes
stalk round my chin, file through
my shirt, my trousers, bite my skin
till I am itching all over.

Immediately I begin to wriggle
pivoting, he slithers off –
as a gorilla might in clothes –
and I slump like a ransacked house
with broken windows.

JAMES K. BAXTER

High Country Weather

Alone we are born
    And die alone;
Yet see the red-gold cirrus
    Over snow-mountain shine.

Upon the upland road
    Ride easy, stranger:
Surrender to the sky
    Your heart of anger.

The Bay

On the road to the bay was a lake of rushes
Where we bathed at times and changed in the bamboos.
Now it is rather to stand and say:
How many roads we take that lead to Nowhere,
The alley overgrown, no meaning now but loss:
Not that veritable garden where everything comes easy.

And by the bay itself were cliffs with carved names
And a hut on the shore beside the Maori ovens.
We raced boats from the banks of the pumice creek
Or swam in those autumnal shallows
Growing cold in amber water, riding the logs
Upstream, and waiting for the taniwha.

So now I remember the bay and the little spiders
On driftwood, so poisonous and quick.
The carved cliffs and the great outcrying surf
With currents round the rocks and the birds rising.
A thousand times an hour is torn across
And burned for the sake of going on living.
But I remember the bay that never was
And stand like stone and cannot turn away.

To my Father

Today, looking at the flowering peach,
The island off the shore and waves that break
Quiet upon the rocks and level beach –
We must join forces, you and I, remake
The harbour silted and the city bombed
And all our hopes that lie now fire-entombed.

Your country childhood helped to make you strong,
Ploughing at twelve. I only know the man.
While I grew up more sheltered and too long
In love with my disease; though illness can

Impart by dint of pain a different kind
Of toughness to the predatory mind.

There is a feud between us. I have loved
You more than my own good, because you stand
For country pride and gentleness, engraved
In forehead lines, veins swollen on the hand;
Also, behind slow speech and quiet eye
The rock of passionate integrity.

You were a poet whom the time betrayed
To action. So, as Jewish Solomon
Prayed for wisdom, you had prayed
That you might have a poet for a son.
The prayer was answered; but an answer may
Confound by its exactness those who pray.

Finding no fault in you, I have been tempted
To stay your child. But that which broke
(Nature) the navel-cord, has not exempted
Even your light and sympathetic yoke.
It is in me your own true mettle shows;
Nor can we thus be friends till we are foes.

This you know well, but it will bear repeating –
Almost you are at times a second self;
Almost at times I feel your heart beating
In my own breast as if there were no gulf
To sever us. And you have seemed then rather
An out-of-time twin brother than a father.

So much is true; yet I have seen the time
When I would cut the past out, like a cancer,
Which now I must digest in awkward rhyme
Until I move 'in measure like a dancer'.
To know an age where all our loves have scope:
It is too much for any man to hope.

You, tickling trout once in a water-race;
You, playing cards, not caring if you lost;
You, shooting hares high on the mountain face;
You, showing me the ferns that grow from frost;
You, quoting Burns and Byron while I listened;
You, breaking quartz until the mica glistened.

These I remember, with the wind that blows
Forever pure down from the tussock ranges;
And these remain, like the everlasting snows,
Changeless in me while my life changes;
These, and a thousand things that prove
You rooted like a tree in the land's love.

I shall compare you to the bended bow,
Myself the arrow launched upon the hollow
Resounding air. And I must go

In time, my friend, to where you cannot follow.
It is not love would hope to keep me young,
The arrow rusted and the bow unstrung.

We have one aim: to set men free
From fear and custom and the incessant war
Of self with self and city against city –
So they may know the peace that they were born for
And find the earth sufficient, who instead
For fruit give scorpions and stones for bread.

And I sit now beside the wishing-well
And drop my silver down. I will have sons
And you grandchildren yet to tell
Old tales despite the anger of the guns:
Leisure to stroll and see Him unafraid
Who walked with Adam once in the green shade.

Elegy for an Unknown Soldier

There was a time when I would magnify
His ending; scatter words as if I wept
Tears not my own but man's. There was a time.
But not now so. He died of a common sickness.

Nor did any new star shine
Upon that day when he came crying out
Of fleshy darkness to a world of pain
And waxen eyelids let the daylight enter.

So felt and tasted, found earth good enough.
Later he played with stones and wondered
If there was land beyond the dark sea rim
And where the road led out of the farthest paddock.

Awkward at school, he could not master sums.
Could you expect him then to understand
The miracle and menace of his body
That grew as mushrooms grow from dusk to dawn?

He had the weight though for a football scrum
And thought it fine to listen to the cheering
And drink beer with the boys, telling them tall
Stories of girls that he had never known.

So when the War came he was glad and sorry,
But soon enlisted. Then his mother cried
A little, and his father boasted how
He'd let him go, though needed for the farm.

Likely in Egypt he would find out something
About himself, if flies and drunkenness
And deadly heat could tell him much – until
In his first battle a shell splinter caught him.

So crown him with memorial bronze among
The older dead, child of a mountainous island.
Wings of a tarnished victory shadow him
Who born of silence has burned back to silence.

Wild Bees

Often in summer, on a tarred bridge plank standing,
Or downstream between willows, a safe Ophelia drifting
In a rented boat – I had seen them come and go,
Those wild bees swift as tigers, their gauze wings a-glitter
In passionless industry, clustering black at the crevice
Of a rotten cabbage tree, where their hive was hidden low.

But never strolled too near. Till one half-cloudy evening
Of ripe January, my friends and I
Came, gloved and masked to the eyes like plundering desperadoes,
To smoke them out. Quiet beside the stagnant river
We trod wet grasses down, hearing the crickets chitter
And waiting for light to drain from the wounded sky.

Before we reached the hive their sentries saw us
And sprang invisible through the darkening air,
Stabbed, and died in stinging. The hive woke. Poisonous fuming
Of sulphur filled the hollow trunk, and crawling
Blue flame sputtered – yet still their suicidal
Live raiders dived and clung to our hands and hair.

O it was Carthage under the Roman torches,
Or loud with flames and falling timber, Troy!
A job well botched. Half of the honey melted
And half the rest young grubs. Through earth-black smouldering ashes
And maimed bees groaning, we drew out our plunder.
Little enough their gold, and slight our joy.

Fallen then the city of instinctive wisdom.
Tragedy is written distinct and small:
A hive burned on a cool night in summer.
But loss is a precious stone to me, a nectar
Distilled in time, preaching the truth of winter
To the fallen heart that does not cease to fall.

The Morgue

Each morning when I lit the coke furnace
Unwillingly I passed the locked door,
The room where Death lived. Shadowless infection
Looked from the blind panes, and an open secret
Stained even the red flowers in the rock garden
Flesh-fingered under the sanatorium wall.

And each day the patients coming and going
From light jobs, joking below the sombre pines,

Would pass without looking, their faces leaner
As if the wintry neighbourhood of Death
Would strip the shuddering flesh from bone. They shouted,
Threw clods at one another, and passed on.

But when at length, with stiff broom and bucket,
I opened the door wide – well, there was nothing
To fear. Only the bare close concrete wall,
A slab of stone, and a wheeled canvas stretcher.
For Death had shifted house to his true home
And mansion, ruinous, of the human heart.

The Fallen House

I took the clay track leading
From Black Bridge to Duffy's farm,
In no forefarer's footmark treading,
    Thus free, it would seem, from any harm
That could befall me – the kind of ill-luck charm
    That clings to a once-fair steading –

When South the sky thickened
And rain came pelter on the hill-scurf:
So in a grove (where the wind quickened
    Their young leaves like the mile-off surf)
Of gums I sheltered, whose roots had drained the turf
    Of life till a starved soil sickened.

But an older grief spoke plainly
From the green mound where thistle strewed
Her bearded gossamer. Ungainly
    The sprawled stones fire-blackened could
Recall man; though where the house stood
    Stands ragged thistle only.

It was not Woe that flaunted
Funereal plume and banner there,
Nor an Atridean doom that daunted
    The heart with a lidless gorgon stare;
But darker the cradling bluegums, sombre the air,
    By the wraith of dead joy haunted.

There once the murk was cloven
By hearthlight fondly flaring within:
Adamant seemed their hope and haven.
    O Time, Time takes in a gin
The quick of being! Pale now and gossamer-thin
    The web their lives had woven.

The Homecoming

Odysseus has come home, to the gully farm
Where the macrocarpa windbreak shields a house

Heavy with time's reliques – the brown-filmed photographs
Of ghosts more real than he; the mankind-measuring arm
Of a pendulum clock; and true yet to her vows,
His mother, grief's Penelope. At the blind the sea wind laughs.

The siege more long and terrible than Troy's
Begins again. A love demanding all,
Hypochondriacal, sea-dark and contentless:
This was the sour ground that nurtured a boy's
Dream of freedom; this, in Circe's hall
Drugged him; his homecoming finds this, more relentless.

She does not say, 'You have changed'; nor could she imagine any
Otherwise to the quiet maelstrom spinning
In the circle of their days. Still she would wish to carry
Him folded within her, shut from the wild and many
Voices of life's combat, in the cage of beginning;
She counts it natural that he should never marry.

She will cook his meals; complain of the south weather
That wrings her joints. And he – rebels; and yields
To the old covenant – calms the bleating
Ewe in birth travail. The smell of saddle leather
His sacrament; or the sale day drink; yet hears beyond sparse fields
On reef and cave the sea's hexameter beating.

Lament for Barney Flanagan

Licensee of the Hesperus Hotel

Flanagan got up on a Saturday morning,
Pulled on his pants while the coffee was warming;
He didn't remember the doctor's warning,
   'Your heart's too big, Mr Flanagan.'

Barney Flanagan, sprung like a frog
From a wet root in an Irish bog –
May his soul escape from the tooth of the dog!
   God have mercy on Flanagan.

Barney Flanagan R.I.P.
Rode to his grave on Hennessy's
Like a bottle-cork boat in the Irish Sea.
   The bell-boy rings for Flanagan.

Barney Flanagan, ripe for a coffin,
Eighteen stone and brandy-rotten,
Patted the housemaid's velvet bottom –
   'Oh, is it you, Mr Flanagan?'

The sky was bright as a new milk token.
Bill the Bookie and Shellshock Hogan
Waited outside for the pub to open –
   'Good day, Mr Flanagan.'

At noon he was drinking in the lounge bar corner
With a sergeant of police and a racehorse owner
When the Angel of Death looked over his shoulder –
   'Could you spare a moment, Flanagan?'

Oh the deck was cut; the bets were laid;
But the very last card that Barney played
Was the Deadman's Trump, the bullet of Spades –
   'Would you like more air, Mr Flanagan?'

The priest came running but the priest came late
For Barney was banging at the Pearly Gate.
St Peter said, 'Quiet! You'll have to wait
   For a hundred masses, Flanagan.'

The regular boys and the loud accountants
Left their nips and their seven-ounces
As chickens fly when the buzzard pounces –
   'Have you heard about old Flanagan?'

Cold in the parlour Flanagan lay
Like a bride at the end of her marriage day.
The Waterside Workers' Band will play
   A brass goodbye to Flanagan.

While publicans drink their profits still,
While lawyers flock to be in at the kill,
While Aussie barmen milk the till
   We will remember Flanagan.

For Barney had a send-off and no mistake.
He died like a man for his country's sake;
And the Governor-General came to his wake.
   Drink again to Flanagan!

Despise not, O Lord, the work of Thine own hands
And let light perpetual shine upon him.

My love late walking

My love late walking in the rain's white aisles
I break words for, though many tongues
Of night deride and the moon's boneyard smile

Cuts to the quick our newborn sprig of song.
See and believe, my love, the late yield
Of bright grain, the sparks of harvest wrung

From difficult joy. My heart is an open field.
There you may stray wide or stand at home
Nor dread the giant's bone and broken shield

Or any tendril locked on a thunder stone,
Nor fear, in the forked grain, my hawk who flies
Down to your feathered sleep alone

Striding blood coloured on a wind of sighs.
Let him at the heart of your true dream move,
My love, in the lairs of hope behind your eyes.

I sing, to the rain's harp, of light renewed,
The black tares broken, fresh the phoenix light
I lost among time's rags and burning tombs.

My love walks long in harvest aisles tonight.

Crossing Cook Strait

The night was clear, sea calm; I came on deck
To stretch my legs, find perhaps
Gossip, a girl in green slacks at the rail
Or just the logline feathering a dumb wake.

The ship swung in the elbow of the Strait.
'Dolphins!' I cried – 'let the true sad Venus
Rise riding her shoals, teach me as once to wonder
And wander at ease, be glad and never regret.'

But night increased under the signal stars.
In the dark bows, facing the flat sea,
Stood one I had not expected, yet knew without surprise
As the Janus made formidable by loveless years.

His coat military; his gesture mild –
'Well met,' he said, 'on the terrestrial journey
From chaos into light – what light it is
Contains our peril and purpose, history has not revealed.'

'Sir – ', I began. He spoke with words of steel –
'I am Seddon and Savage, the socialist father.
You have known me only in my mask of Dionysus
Amputated in bar rooms, dismembered among wheels.

'I woke in my civil tomb hearing a shout
For bread and justice. It was not here.
That sound came thinly over the waves from China;
Stones piled on my grave had all but shut it out.

'I walked forth gladly to find the angry poor
Who are my nation; discovered instead
The glutton seagulls squabbling over crusts
And policies made and broken behind locked doors.

'I have watched the poets also at their trade.
I have seen them burning with a wormwood brilliance.

Love was the one thing lacking on their page,
The crushed herb of grief at another's pain.

'Your civil calm breeds inward poverty
That chafes for change. The ghost of Adam
Gibbering demoniac in drawing-rooms
Will drink down hemlock with his sugared tea.

'You feed your paupers concrete. They work well,
Ask for no second meal, vote, pay tribute
Of silence on Anzac Day in the pub urinal;
Expose death only by a mushroom smell.

'My counsel was naïve. Anger is bread
To the poor, their guns more accurate than justice,
Because their love has not decayed to a wintry fungus
And hope to the wish for power among the dead.

'In Kaitangata the miner's falling sweat
Wakes in the coal seam fossil flowers.
The clerk puts down his pen and takes his coat;
He will not be back today or the next day either.'

With an ambiguous salute he left me.
The ship moved into a stronger sea,
Bludgeoned alive by the rough mystery
Of love in the running straits of history.

Perseus

Leaving them, children of the Sun, to their perpetual
Unwearying dance about the ancient Tree,
Perseus flew east, the bird-winged sandals beating
Smooth and monotonous; sauntered above
Fens peopled by the placid watersnake,
Flamingo, crocodile –

And those unfallen creatures, joyful in
Their maze of waters, watched; with reedy voices
Praised the oncoming hero; cried
And coupled in his path. But he felt only
Scorching his shoulders, the shield, Athene's lovegift – and the first
Wind of foreboding blow from Medusa's home.

So entered the stone kingdom where no life
Startled, but brackish water fell
Like tears from solitary beds
Of spaghnum moss, or spray from cataracts
Sprinkled the grey-belled orchid, feathered grass
And spider's coverlet.

Till by the final cleft precipitous
At a blind gorge's end he lighted, stood,
Unslung the heavy shield, drew breath, and waited

As the bright hornet waits and quivers
Hearing within her den the poisonous rustle
And mew, for battle angry, of tarantula.

Fair smote her face upon the burning shield,
Medusa, image of the soul's despair,
Snake-garlanded, child of derisive Chaos
And hateful Night, whom no man may
Look on and live. In horror, pity, loathing,
Perseus looked long, lifted his sword, and struck.

Then empty was the cave. A vulture's taloned body
Headless and huddled, a woman's marble face
With snakes for hair – and in the wide
Thoroughfares of the sky no hint of cloudy fury
Or clanging dread, as homeward he
Trod, the pouched Despair at his girdle hanging,

To earth, Andromeda, the palace garden
His parents bickered in, plainsong of harvest –
To the lawgiver's boredom, rendering
(The task accomplished) back to benignant Hermes
And holy Athene goods not his own, the borrowed
Sandals of courage and the shield of art.

Election 1960

Hot sun. Lizards frolic
Fly-catching on the black ash

That was green rubbish. Tiny dragons,
They dodge among the burnt broom stems

As if the earth belonged to them
Without condition. In the polling booths

A democratic people have elected
King Log, King Stork, King Log, King Stork again.

Because I like a wide and silent pond
I voted Log. That party was defeated.

Now frogs will dive and scuttle to avoid
That poking idiot bill, the iron gullet:

Delinquent frogs! Stork is an active King,
A bird of principle, benevolent,

And Log is Log, an old time-serving post
Hacked from a totara when the land was young.

Ballad of Calvary Street

On Calvary Street are trellises
Where bright as blood the roses bloom,
And gnomes like pagan fetishes
Hang their hats on an empty tomb
Where two old souls go slowly mad,
National Mum and Labour Dad.

Each Saturday when full of smiles
The children come to pay their due,
Mum takes down the family files
And cover to cover she thumbs them through,
Poor Len before he went away
And Mabel on her wedding day.

The meal-brown scones display her knack,
Her polished oven spits with rage,
While in Grunt Grotto at the back
Dad sits and reads the Sporting Page,
Then ambles out in boots of lead
To weed around the parsnip bed.

A giant parsnip sparks his eye,
Majestic as the Tree of Life;
He washes it and rubs it dry
And takes it in to his old wife –
'Look Laura, would that be a fit?
The bastard has a flange on it!'

When both were young she would have laughed,
A goddess in her tartan skirt,
But wisdom, age and mothercraft
Have rubbed it home that men like dirt:
Five children and a fallen womb,
A golden crown beyond the tomb.

Nearer the bone, sin is sin,
And women bear the cross of woe,
And that affair with Mrs Flynn
(It happened thirty years ago)
Though never mentioned, means that he
Will get no sugar in his tea.

The afternoon goes by, goes by,
The angels harp above a cloud;
A son-in-law with spotted tie
And daughter Alice fat and loud
Discuss the virtues of insurance
And stuff their tripes with trained endurance.

Flood-waters hurl upon the dyke
And Dad himself can go to town,
For little Charlie on his trike
Has ploughed another iris down.

His parents rise to chain the beast,
Brush off the last crumbs of their lovefeast.

And so these two old fools are left,
A rosy pair in evening light,
To question Heaven's dubious gift,
To hag and grumble, growl and fight:
The love they kill won't let them rest,
Two birds that peck in one fouled nest.

Why hammer nails? Why give no change?
Habit, habit clogs them dumb.
The Sacred Heart above the range
Will bleed and burn till Kingdom Come,
But Yin and Yang won't ever meet
In Calvary Street, in Calvary Street.

At Taieri Mouth

Flax-pods unload their pollen
Above the steel-bright cauldron

Of Taieri, the old water-dragon
Sliding out from a stone gullet

Below the Maori-ground. Scrub horses
Come down at night to smash the fences

Of the whaler's children. Trypots have rusted
Leaving the oil of anger in the blood

Of those who live in two-roomed houses
Mending nets or watching from a window

The great south sky fill up with curdled snow.
Their cows eat kelp along the beaches.

The purple sailor drowned in thighboots
Drifting where the currents go

Cannot see the flame some girl has lighted
In a glass chimney, but in five days' time

With bladder-weed around his throat
Will ride the drunken breakers in.

Tomcat

This tomcat cuts across the
zones of the respectable
through fences, walls, following

other routes, his own. I see
the sad whiskered skull-mouth fall
wide, complainingly, asking

to be picked up and fed, when
I thump up the steps through bush
at 4 p.m. He has no
dignity, thank God! has grown
older, scruffier, the ash-
black coat sporting one or two

flowers like round stars, badges
of bouts and fights. The snake head
is seamed on top with rough scars:
old Samurai! He lodges
in cellars, and the tight furred
scrotum drives him into wars

as if mad, yet tumbling on
the rug looks female, Turkish-
trousered. His bagpipe shriek at
sluggish dawn dragged me out in
pyjamas to comb the bush
(he being under the vet

for septic bites): the old fool
stood, body hard as a board,
heart thudding, hair on end, at
the house corner, terrible,
yelling at something. They said,
'Get him doctored.' I think not.

The Lion Skin

The old man with a yellow flower on his coat
Came to my office, climbing twenty-eight steps,
With a strong smell of death about his person
From the caves of the underworld.
The receptionist was troubled by his breath
Understandably.
                    Not every morning tea break
Does Baron Saturday visit his parishioners
Walking stiffly, strutting almost,
With a cigar in his teeth – she might have remembered
Lying awake as if nailed by a spear
Two nights ago, with the void of her life
Glassed in a dark window – but suitably enough
She preferred to forget it.
                    'I welcomed him
And poured him a glass of cherry brandy,
Talked with him for half an hour or so,
Having need of his strength, the skin of a dead lion,
In the town whose ladders are made of coffin wood.

The flower on his coat blazed like a dark sun.

From *Jerusalem Sonnets*

(Poems for Colin Durning)

1

The small grey cloudy louse that nests in my beard
Is not, as some have called it, 'a pearl of God' –

No, it is a fiery tormentor
Waking me at two a.m.

Or thereabouts, when the lights are still on
In the houses in the pa, to go across thick grass

Wet with rain, feet cold, to kneel
For an hour or two in front of the red flickering

Tabernacle light – what He sees inside
My meandering mind I can only guess –

A madman, a nobody, a raconteur
Whom He can joke with – 'Lord,' I ask Him,

'Do You or don't You expect me to put up with lice?'
His silent laugh still shakes the hills at dawn.

2

The bees that have been hiving above the church porch
Are some of them killed by the rain –

I see their dark bodies on the step
As I go in – but later on I hear

Plenty of them singing with what seems a virile joy
In the apple tree whose reddish blossoms fall

At the centre of the paddock – there's an old springcart,
Or at least two wheels and the shafts, upended

Below the tree – Elijah's chariot it could be, Colin,
Because my mind takes fire a little there

Thinking of the woman who is like a tree
Whom I need not name – clumsily gripping my beads,

While the bees drum overhead and the bouncing calves look at
A leather-jacketed madman set on fire by the wind.

18

Yesterday I planted garlic,
Today, sunflowers – 'the non-essentials first'

Is a good motto – but these I planted in honour of
The Archangel Michael and my earthly friend,

Illingworth, Michael also, who gave me the seeds –
And they will turn their wild pure golden discs

Outside my bedroom, following Te Ra
Who carries fire for us in His terrible wings

(Heresy, man!) – and if He wanted only
For me to live and die in this old cottage,

It would be enough, for the angels who keep
The very stars in place resemble most

These green brides of the sun, hopelessly in love with
Their Master and Maker, drunkards of the sky.

27

Three dark buds for the Trinity
On one twig I found in the lining of my coat

Forgotten since I broke them from the tree
That grows opposite the RSA building

At the top of Vulcan Lane – there I would lay down my parka
On the grass and meditate, cross-legged; there was a girl

Who sat beside me there;
She would hold a blue flower at the centre of the bullring

While the twigs on the tree became black
And then slowly green again – she was young – if I had said,

'Have my coat; have my money' –
She would have gone away; but because I gave her nothing

She came again and again to share that nothing
Like a bird that nests in the open hand.

From *Autumn Testament*

7

To wake up with a back sore from the hard mattress
In a borrowed sleeping bag

Lent me by Anne – it was her way, I think,
Of giving at the same time a daughter's

And a mother's embrace – friend, daughter, mother –
These kids have heart enough to nourish the dead world

Like David in his bed – to wake up and see
The sun, if not the light from behind the sun,

Glittering on the leaves beside the graveyard
Where some of them cleared the bramble and placed on the bare slab

A jam jar full of flowers – to wake is to lift up
Again on one's shoulder this curious world

Whose secret cannot be known by any of us
Until we enter Te Whiro's kingdom.

18

Father Lenin, you understood the moment
When the soul is split clean, as a man with an axe

Will split four posts from one log of dry timber,
But then your muzhiks still had souls

That smelt the holy bread upon the altar
And knew their mother's name. The mask of money

Hides too well the wound we cannot touch,
And guns are no use to a boy with a needle

Whose world is a shrinking dome of glass
A drug from Hong Kong will splinter open

With a charging elephant on a yellow packet
For riding home to deep sleep. The dollar is the point of it,

Old Father Lenin, and your bones in the Red Square
Are clothed in roubles till the Resurrection.

22

To pray for an easy heart is no prayer at all
Because the heart itself is the creaking bridge

On which we cross these Himalayan gorges
From bluff to bluff. To sweat out the soul's blood

Midnight after midnight is the ministry of Jacob,
And Jacob will be healed. This body that shivers

In the foggy cold, tasting the sour fat,
Was made to hang like a sack on its thief's cross,

Counting it better than bread to say the words of Christ,
'*Eli! Eli!*' The Church will be shaken like a

Blanket in the wind, and we are the fleas that fall
To the ground for the dirt to cover. Brother thief,

You who are lodged in my ribcage, do not rail at
The only gate we have to paradise.

32

Life can be a hassle. Are you free of it, Monsignor,
While you dispute the changes of the liturgy

Or polish up your golf style? At one p.m.
Either in your house or my house

The soul may plunge into pain like a child who slides
Through the grass at the lip of a mine-shaft,

Therefore don't ask me, 'What do you mean by that statement
You made to the *Weekly News?*' – or – 'What precisely is

'Your relation to Sally X – ?' A man is a bubble
Sticking to the edge of a mighty big drainpipe!

Let us be content to play one game of chess,
Share a coffee and biscuit, let Christ work out the deficit, –

There were eight souls, they say, with Father Noah;
Neither you nor I might have made it to the gangplank.

42

The rata blooms explode, the bow-legged tomcat
Follows me up the track, nipping at my ankle,

The clematis spreads her trumpet, the grassheads rattle
Ripely, drily, and all this

In fidelity to death. Today when Father Te Awhitu
Put on the black gown with the silver cross,

It was the same story. The hard rind of the ego
Won't ever crack except to the teeth of Te Whiro,

That thin man who'll eat the stars. I can't say
It pleases me. In the corner I can hear now

The high whining of a mason fly
Who carries the spiders home to his house

As refrigerated meat. 'You bugger off,' he tells me,
'Your Christianity won't put an end to death.'

48

The spider crouching on the ledge above the sink
Resembles the tantric goddess,

At least as the Stone Age people saw her
And carved her on their dolmens. Therefore I don't kill her,

Though indeed there is a simpler reason,
Because she is small. Kehua, vampire, eight-eyed watcher

At the gate of the dead, little Arachne, I love you,
Though you hang your cobwebs up like dirty silk in the hall

And scuttle under the mattress. Remember I spared your children
In their cage of white cloth you made as an aerial castle,

And you yourself, today, on the window ledge.
Fear is the only enemy. Therefore when I die,

And you wait for my soul, you hefty as a king crab
At the door of the underworld, let me pass in peace.

From *Te Whiore o te Kuri*

7

To go forward like a man in the dark
Is the meaning of this dark vocation;

So simple, tree, star, the bare cup of the hills,
The lifelong grave of waiting

As indeed it has to be. To ask for Jacob's ladder
Would be to mistake oneself and the dark Master,

Yet at times the road comes down to a place
Where water runs and horses gallop

Behind a hedge. There it is possible to sit,
Light a cigarette, and rub

Your bruised heels on the cold grass. Always because
A man's body is a meeting house,

Ribs, arms, for the tribe to gather under,
And the heart must be their spring of water.

From *Five Sestinas*

1

Winter in Jerusalem

The *I Ching* tells me *T'ai*, the sign of peace,
Is what I venture in. The pungas on the hill,
So lately loaded with snow, are green again
Though some branches were broken. Where many men gather
From need or friendship, truth begins to waken
As eels rise in the dark river.

If Heaven gives me this old house by a river,
It is not for myself, but for the purpose of peace,
As the thunder and rain of spring make green things waken,
A fence of poplar leaves between us and the hill
Who is our mother, or the chestnuts we gather
In autumn when the earth is warm again.

In our dreams it may happen the dead return again,
As if the earth spoke to us, because time is a river
On whose bank in ignorance the tribes gather
With emblems of battle, yet desiring peace.
The fathers instruct us from their holy hill
So that the warrior souls may waken.

In winter with a heavy mind I waken
And wait for the sun to lift the fogs again
That bind Jerusalem. Like a bridegroom above the hill
He touches with hands of fire the waves of the river
Like the body of a woman. Our words are words of peace
In this house where the wounded children gather.

We can go out with Maori kits to gather
Watercress, or some tough lads who waken
Early will break the veil of peace
With gunshots, combing the bush again
For young goats, or lift the eel-trap from the river
As fog shifts from the highest hill.

The times are like some rough and roadless hill
We have to climb. I do not hope to gather
Pears in winter, or halt the flow of the river
That buries in sludge the souls who begin to waken
And know themselves. Our peace can't patch again
The canoe that is broken, yet all men value peace.

Peace is the language of the pungas on the hill
Not growing for any gain. These images I gather
As eels waken in the darkness of the river.

3

The Dark Welcome

In the rains of winter the pa children
Go in gumboots on the wet grass. Two fantails clamber
On stems of bramble and flutter their wings
In front of me, indicating a visit
Or else a death. Below the wet marae
They wait in a transport shelter for the truck to come,

Bringing tobacco, pumpkins, salt. The kai will be welcome
To my hungry wandering children
Who drink at the springs of the marae
And find a Maori ladder to clamber
Up to the light. The cops rarely visit,
Only the fantails flutter their wings

Telling us about the dark angel's wings
Over a house to the north where a man has come
Back from Wellington, to make a quiet visit,
Brother to one of the local children,
Because the boss's scaffolding was too weak to clamber
Up and down, or else he dreamt of the marae

When the car was hitting a bend. Back to the marae
He comes, and the fantails flutter their wings,
And the children at the tangi will shout and clamber
Over trestles, with a noise of welcome,
And tears around the coffin for one of the grown-up children
Who comes to his mother's house on a visit,

Their town cousin, making a longer visit,
To join the old ones on the edge of the marae
Whose arms are bent to cradle their children
Even in death, as the pukeko's wings
Cover her young. The dark song of welcome
Will rise in the meeting house, like a tree where birds clamber,

Or the Jacob's-ladder where angels clamber
Up and down. Thus the dead can visit
The dreams and words of the living, and easily come
Back to shape the deeds of the marae,
Though rain falls to wet the fantail's wings
As if the earth were weeping for her children.

Into the same canoe my children clamber
From the wings of the iron hawk and the Vice Squad's visit
On the knees of the marae to wait for what may come.

CHARLES DOYLE

Starlings and History

It is again time when sleek and glossy starlings
Invade the lawn in their gentlemanly lemon
And black, comical shakos of their beaks
Thrust forward. Under their clamorous murmurations
    Summer has babbled in.

Oblivious, noisy creatures, they have heralded or
Said farewell to all the seasons of all my life.
I too have seen them on a grey slate roof
Or commuting into trees alive with leaf,
    Or dead on the dark road.

And now, now only I mouth to myself and the glass,
'These are alive, too. Everything lives and moves,
Grows and has meaning.' I recall as I grope for meaning
How once, a boy in the slums, I loved those roofs'
    Grey slate in winter sky;

Brick houses underneath, dark-honeycombed
With little rooms; brass bedsteads, pedestals
Of mottled marble, cracked linoleum;
In the yard a shower of orange blossom petals,
    Path of powdery bricks;

Those Friday nights I listened to the one-man band,
Bass drum and barrel organ by the painted house
On the corner, where the old lady gave us sugar;
How for supper we always opened a tin of sardines,
    Were allowed to stay up late.

Such things are history or happiness,
The quarrel with ourselves, self-renewal
Which Amiel demands of the living soul.
Man must embrace all being, both the cruel
    And, what hurts more, the gentle.

Our corner of time and place, of muted sufferings,
Loud enjoyments, decked in lewd, banal
Catchphrases, snapshots, comics and popular songs,
Though it must be, is all that we are, final
    Measure of us and all things,

Man's meaning and the world's. In the dead life of my life
I hear children cry out among the bracken,
The drowned one quiet, her desolate bucket and spade
Unkempt on the shore of our breathing, her parents stricken
    To another death on the pier.

I see priests in their cassocks and the wild honey
On the refectory table when mine was a golden eye;

Later the creaking hawser, eyes of shorelights
Open, I cast adrift on totalitarian sea
    To discover another self.

From all the seas of my selves I wake and wonder
When the torture of knowing shakes my soul from its torpor,
Knowing that all must end in the unknown voyage
Out of the world of bricks and kicking and the lure
    And deviltry of love.

Every eclectic marvellous detail,
Coarse Wiltshire stone under the caring hand,
Giant kauris aching upon the eye, every kind of love,
Even pity and ceremony must end
    Between the quiet poles.

Now I turn, find it is winter. Dreary birds
Make the grey air untidy, their rough-gutted screech
A hubbub that disturbs me. I suddenly know that all worlds
Are chequered and drab like these, that promise of rich
    Permanent summer is false.

Still there are seasons, summers, migrations,
Flowerings and rebirths. Even the hooded candles
Will gleam upon the reviving ceremonial.
Living and dying seem endless; nothing is endless.
    One does not die forever.
                (1955)

For My Father

(Buried at sea off the West African Coast, Christmas Day, 1947)

Amorphous, ceaseless, slow,
compulsive, slides
the long wave over
what were your dreams; the tides

change to their moons
bearing for you no ill.
Six years have parted us
more than the oceans' swell.

This deft separation
at the waters' head
leaves much between us
though loss to self and pride.

Once, in rain, we crossed
a bridge. You denied,
angry, vehement,
the poet's kind

berth to sleep in,
water, thought, or bread,

knowing more worth
in plough, hammer, spade.

These tools were proved,
like soup kitchens, of use.
What poem could pay
for a bed in your doss-house?

Sworn to the facts
you scorned the howling dog
at his romantic posture
crouched in the fog.

Yet, beyond our merest
words, you had an eye
for the poem of factory smoke
which was your sky.

You rode the wave
heart-high with storm.
Starved solstice, swollen equinox,
charted the way you came

voyaging. We sail for
its peace but, still sea's sport,
wrenched by the waters, limp
for any port.

(1953/1961)

The Journey of Meng Chiao

Who says that the heart of an inch-long plant
Can requite the radiance of full Spring?

My carriage has been waiting at the door
for a long time. I am going
on a far journey. I can't be sure
how well the carriage is appointed
for my purposes. It isn't clear to me
what my purposes are. Returned travellers
report that I must pass through a region of darkness.

Why am I leaving the comforts of this fortress?
I cannot give you a reason. Or perhaps this:
I lie awake at nights in the scent of jasmine
recalling the flowers' opening, the day's sunlight,
conversations of my acquaintances,
the discarding of the straw dogs after ritual,
the affairs of the nine orifices and six viscera.

Demon faces emerge when the petals unfold.
Voices trading in small-talk have tongues of fire.
Every transaction seems a sham to me.
Travelling into the depths of my country, inward
further and further, I shall take no companions.

Maybe there will be many strange seas to cross
but this is a journey I need for myself alone.

Beyond what I have said here I can give you no reasons.
The Country of No Love is full of reasons
and they make nothing clear. I have no reasons.
When the Tao is revealed to me there will be no reasons.
I must leave you here by the pinewoods under the sky.
I must go now. What do I hope to find when I arrive?
If I am lucky, the pinewoods under the sky.

(1970)

ALISTAIR PATERSON

Birds Flying

What am I doing here – in this place where
there are spiders on the white-washed walls
and cryptograms outlined on the ceilings –
what am I doing here? Yes, you saw me
draw my pentagon, set up the phallic symbols
– you know all this – how Tom couldn't manage
it without my help, and how the children –
the children lit their candles every birthday.

FOR CHRIST'S SAKE STOP! It's getting dark
and I can feel the needles, the night-nurse
straightening sheets and smoothing blankets:
what's worse is he could never finish it and
I'd lie there sweating like a horse after the
Derby – PLEASE STOP! Why do the birds fly,
the cranes with their long necks delicately
scaled, and the lizard without ever moving?

And now we are forced to take sides for you
have become puffed up with pride, your hand
stirs the waters and your eyes watch each of
us indifferently: the trout moving by, how
birds build and their unlikely young lift
frailty and bone towards the impassive sky,
the trees choose their random wild canopies
of needle and leaf, bud, flower and berry.

But where were you on the eighth of December
when I turned and looked up from the rice
and the brown water, stared at the sky,
saw the clouds stretch arched and spreading
like small mushrooms after rain, saw how
the quick morning burgeoned into life while
the birds went on flying and the world kept
spinning, dragging after it all the turtles

and the water-buffalo, the fences and gardens,
the village and the road through the village,
the makers of fish-traps, stringers of kites,
all the huts, outhouses, fish, rice, fathers,
mothers and the world's youngest child? Where
were you when the earth flew up and the water
flared like a snake as it straightens and
strikes and there was no earth and no water?

I know it – that each and every last cell
must wither and die – but where were you
yesterday when I knew nothing and had neither
bone, sinew nor belly – when the womb cried
and somewhere in the red darkness the ovum

waited and the tired sperm shrivelled, flesh
had no substance and there was less than nothing
to measure you by – where were you?

They tell me the gardener grows grapes – the
sweet, green kind that are juicy, translucent –
and pomegranites, figs, peaches and apples,
but the grapes are my favourites. They are kind,
they are all kind and say I'll be cured
given time. But they've taken away all the clocks
and I cannot follow the slow flight of their hands
nor the little birds that sweep the hours away.

Livery Stable

This morning I'm sitting in the sun looking at
the livery stable – that building there nobody
seems to notice – the one I know exists
because if I'm absolutely still and squint at it
I can see the horses, the livery attendant,
and the door up top with the suspended block
and tackle that's sometimes used for lifting
bales of hay, sacks of corn to the loft.
It's the traffic makes the watching difficult
mind you – what with the motor-way two miles off
and the cafeteria across the way – but the roan's
certainly there, and the buggy to the left
where that blonde's getting into the convertible
and the tailor's dummy of a business-man pauses
in mid-stride unable to take his eyes off her.

It's the kind of perspective that's suited to canvas,
that has a value could be owned: board
that's weathered almost grey, from which comes
(if you can ignore automobile fumes) the
unmistakable odour of animals, leather, played-out
travellers wearing half the road. Anyone
patient enough and having the time could likely
make out the dark coolness of the building's
insides – blankets, bridles, buckets,
currycombs – the three strangers and the empty
manger in the neighbouring byre. But I'm seeing
the place at its best, in the middle of the morning
with the sun full on it, aware that if I stop squinting
there'll be nothing to look at but the bus-depot
and the traffic's endless, choking miles.

OWEN LEEMING

The Priests of Serrabonne

I

For three sodden miles
The engine howls, scaling a winding stair
Of mud, hauling me up the rugged grade
    Where the past and my past are laid.
Below are olive-trees, veils of rain, tiles
    Of the vanishing cottage where
    The caretaker spits among piles

    Of onions, postcards, rope.
Brown slime and stones give off a poisonous chill
'You're not wanted' feel. The past of sheep
    And villages is fast asleep.
I make this road a trail where neophytes grope
    To their grave, or God's will
    As they would say, whose slope

    Carries them apart, each face
Sour with sweat as they trudge the world behind.
I'm recreating. For history's mild or savage men
    I see today's brethren,
Trappist and Carmelite, filling their empty space;
    And free my apostate mind
    From veracity's saving grace.

II

    Braving the uncivil air,
I come at last to Serrabonne. It transfixes me:
An outline which knifes from mist, such scorn in stone,
    A tower so harshly hewn,
I know I can never forget, with its three square
    Apertures up high, three
    Blanks whose bleak stare

    Dissuades approach. Those eyes
And socket nose, gable, the verticals' hard
Uncompromise, that is the logic of monastic rule,
    Its limit at least, in cruel
Line. Hills, endless, boring, rise
    Like sea-swell. In them is barred
    The priory, whose force supplies

    Resisting force in me.
Grown over with blue-black scrub, scarred by snow,
Scoured by rain, this landscape prompts extreme
    Inhabiting. Its figures seem

Amalgamates of all devotions to their cause. In scree,
   Hardship; snow, the glow
   Of flagellated flesh; monotony

   Of hills, the regular rote-led
Lives. Disputing the cause, I can still admire
   The gritty saints who've built upon this ground,
   The guts of will that bound
Them to self-death during life. Their tower, a head
   Without humour or desire,
   Glares across the lead-

   Coloured, lachrymose skies
Its mission to crush the senses while, here below,
The oblong priory church, a fortress barn,
   Looks imitatively stern,
Repeating in its way the tower's command – to despise
   The world's lures. I go
   To its door. The keyhole cries

   As the corroded foot-long key
Voluptuously inches in. I wonder if they thought
Of that, the monks? It turns with a rusty crash.
   From the creaking door, a gash
Of daylight widens in the dark. Enough to see,
   Be staggered by, a wrought,
   A shadow-fragile filigree

   Of marble, carved in pink!
Riotously carved at that. Vines and palms,
Little bent men, thin pillars alive
   With pattern, defiantly survive
In veined fleshy stone. What can one think?
   Is this rostrum up in arms
   Against the tower, or a link

   With it? Oasis of art
In Serrabonne's Lenten desert, I find
It dares condone the human. Then, looking through
   Its pillars to the altar renews
At once the tower's dominion. Excepting a dart
   Of light thinly outlined
   By an embrasure, no aids start

   From gloom to further the least
Emollient thought. A grey threshold, worn
Hollow by midnight sandals, leads to a stark
   Nave, and on through dark
To an altar of rock that less recalls the Feast
   In the Upper Room than a horn
   Or obsidian knife, a beast

   Bleating before its blood
Is let. Tower, rostrum and altar, are these
The three faces of religion, Christianity above all?

In the thick darkness, tall
Cowled presences gather, their footfalls thud
   To their places, they bend their knees,
   Sing Tenebrae without a sound.

III

   Recreating still. But this
Impinges, spells a history mine not theirs.
These priests are formed on mine: I was taught
   By priests; less strict, but thought
In this dark shell imposes essence – the kiss
   Of celebrant on altar bears
   The weight of my religious

   Past. Contemplatives, nuns,
Brothers, wearers of habits, rattlers of beads,
Office chanters, watchers of Mass behind screens,
   'Brides of Christ' . . . it means
Another Order now. Their vow of silence
   Is made to silence, and leads
   To ending, curt as guns,

   Gas or poleaxe. They kill
Their life and gain a double death; they pray
To space and energy, a witless God. At Serrabonne,
   Where the light has nearly gone,
Augustinians prayed and preached, their will
   Subserving God's, no day
   Their own. And are there still.

   Above the altar, the slit
Of natural light fades and so does hope
Of concord. Another wooden doorway leads
   Outside again, with weeds
Growing under, to a chopped-off cloister, a bit
   Of arch across a slope
   That darkens like the Pit.

   The hard tower stands,
An iron-willed Superior, against the cloud.
Even with faith, I jibbed against monastic Rule.
   Living at boarding-school,
With daily Mass, silence in dorm, our hands
   Knobbed with frost, I bowed
   Uncertainly to all demands

   To conquer private urge.
Impurity, meaning sex, and intellectual pride
Were drummed in as deadliest sins. And yet
   It was not the toughness set
Me riddles, discipline, but aiming to purge
   Oneself of self. Beside
   The fierce ones, monks who scourge

Their backs with little whips,
Our practice was pale enough. No less real.
'Not my will,' we prayed, 'but Thine be done.'
   Human nature was *the* one
Equation for sin. I forced my sprouting lips
   To shape what I could not feel:
   That flesh was bad. Perhaps

   I do my teachers wrong . . .
My final year I won the golden cross
For Doctrine, if that counts. In Doctrine class
   We sometimes tried to pass
The 'asses' bridge' on life enclosed. The long
   Debate would run: 'They're a loss
   To the militant Church. To be strong,

   It needs these mystics here
In the world, active for Christ.' A stock reply
Was dealt: 'By sanctity and prayer they store up grace,
   Provide atonement which pays
In part the debt of sin.' 'Sanctity', I fear,
   Meant self-rejection; as if high
   In heaven God, austere

   Accountant, drew up files
Of good and bad and entered these supreme
Oblations from monks and nuns against impurity and pride.
   All I heard implied
This crude belief. I then believed. The miles
   Of hills have settled, dream-
   Extended, into piles

   Of time, the centuries they hold.
I think of priests who cowed me, tall soutané
Caners who vaunted their humility, their wall
   Of pride hung with a small
Black cross. They are singing now, controlled
   In me. Why do they hand
   Away their vitals, mould

   Themselves to the nothing which is God?
Roughly, I think, insurance: against despair,
The deepest fear; against the yoke of choice,
   Their nagging inward voice;
Against the difficulty of love. For reward, they plod
   Securely, conforming in rare
   Suburban bliss. A rod

   Is always there to make
Their bodies knuckle down. For some, this too
Insures: pain now, not after. So, I explain
   What I abhor, the vain
Denaturing of life. At Serrabonne, they take
   Senses, feelings, true
   Desires, burn at the stake

To leave an anti-man.
From this ledge where monks have shuffled, I look out on France,
I, condemning, admiring, fearing them; because
      I no longer believe there was,
Is, or shall be, the God who approved their plan
      Of suicide. I stake my chance
      On the fading world I scan.

IV

A thousand years ago,
As now, the Church had money, jobs and land,
Affording comfort with salvation. Yet she built
      Her convents, easing guilt
By hiring cells to saints, the ones who go
      Without, who crave to withstand
      Their nature. Rent would flow

In kind: an aureole of grace
On the plaster Body of Christ, a pure tower,
Cut like logic, above this scrubby world.
      Their lives are whole, curled
Without a join about their core. My case
      Denies this core, its power
      Not God but hate. I praise

The wholeness though. With hate
Of self as premise, they build the tower their life
Around and over in flawless logic. Art
      And love have a human heart,
Cherish both self and world, the proper state,
      A greater whole. God's knife
      Cuts cold at me, but cuts too late.

V

Night thickens and rain
Spatters on the stone. I turn through the door. A grey
Pencil marks the altar – altar of sacrifice,
      Mass and men, twice
Over, body and blood. Its horizontals stain
      The dark darker where they pray,
      Those hooded presences of my brain.

Through the night they will pray
And chant their Office, matins and mass, the priests
Of my mind, exalting their release from flesh,
      The fleshly chains that enmesh
A sinning world. I grope to the blur of day
      And leave them at their feasts
      Of conquest. So I stray

To that splendour of chiselled pink
Which warmed me before with its carnal fire. It seems
Now a forest of young trees, rich and dense,
   Embossed like bark with the intense
Humanness of art. My eyes prickle. I think
   More softly. The sculptors' dreams
   Survive; my ascetics shrink

   In a cone of sound. To relate
This rostrum to tower and altar would be, I suppose,
To understand the whole of man. Too much for me.
   But it exists, indisputably,
A wild effusion in the chaste rigour of straight
   Barren surfaces, rose
   Amidst the grey. It is late,

   I must leave, dragging the door
Shut, crash, withdrawing the key inch
By inch, then waiting for quiet to settle. The sky
   Is sullen purple as I,
Holding the key, stand at the lintel. Before
   I leave, I want to clinch
   The union, trying once more

   To bond the lovers of sense,
Illuminators, carvers, with the haters of sense who froze
And whipped and silenced. All for God. All
   For nothing . . . man cannot maul
His nature to complete abstraction! So, instead of tense
   Antipathy, art *might* pose
   With logic without offence.

   Rough guessing that it fits,
I squelch across the grass and pass a very small
Peach tree which flinches in the rain. Planted by man,
   Frail thing, it only can
In this whole wilderness portray those sandalled misfits
   In any human way. For all
   Their praying, they have some bits

   Of gravelly garden in which
They can potter and watch their seeds come up. Yes, again
I'm recreating, with no cause now except a tree.
   The tower, as I look behind me,
Withers my attempt at contact. Letting in the clutch,
   I escape from its gaunt disdain.
   Would a postcard cost too much?

C. K. STEAD

Whether the Will is Free

i

Snow wraps a harsh and gum-grey land,
Slug-blood retreats from the shelled hand

And foot needled for warmth pines
Stamping the hills. Breath-charted air

Caught from a gramophone defines
A girl's mood whose doved hand

Dances. Outside, a bird on the bare
Head of the white-haired day is a stare

At the crop of the sprinkled seed of sleet.
Whether the will is free, the shiver

Runs in me that ruffles the feather;
Whether the will is free, the beat

Of the doved hand, the dove moan,
Chords my mind to the gramophone.

ii

A dog is a hopper on the snow.
Wanting wings, or shoes, he goes

Spring-full as hope, and quivering
An arrow nose at frozen trees.

iii

This loping landscape doesn't care
What falls on it, what freezes there,

Whether the wants are few that house
In the head of a girl, the eye of a stare,

Whether streams have a will, but sends
Them even under ice, to sea.

iv

May be I'm the girl, the bird, the stream,
The hungry dog in this iron time,

Not hell bound or heaven bent,
Willing to get to where I'm sent.

Under its ice my small life crawls
Pecking and snuffing at grey walls.

Whether the will is free or seems
I would be music, doved in snow.

A Natural Grace

Under my eaves untiring all the spring day
Two sparrows have worked with stalks the mowers leave
While I have sat regretting your going away.
All day they've ferried straw and sticks to weave
A wall against the changing moods of air,
And may have worked into that old design
A thread of cloth you wore, a strand of hair,
Since all who make are passionate for line,
Proportion, strength, and take what's near, and serves.
All day I've sat remembering your face,
And watched the sallow stalks, woven in curves
By a blind process, achieve a natural grace.

A Small Registry of Births and Deaths

All night it bullied you.
When it shook you hard enough
They took you away.
I was shaken too. I walked
The frantic corridor praying
Representing
My terror so minutely
It went unnoticed.

The whole place moaned
As it was meant to.
A door flung out a nurse and a scream.
A doctor in a butcher's apron passed
Tying his gauze.
The nurse returned with forceps.

Your door stayed shut. I smoked.
You might have been dead. Or sleeping.

                        *

Bloodshot and drugged you burbled about our boy.
He frothed, mildly confronting whatever it was

Flooded his lungs. I was full of pieties.
We had never been so nearly anonymous.

*

I watch our two-year-old
Among the lawless tribes
Of nursery children.
My skin prickles.
I scan the air for eagles.
It is as if all three of us were born
In that one moment to this one concern.
I lost myself to become
This wary, watchful thing.
I scan the air.
I do not want myself back.

*

Six months ago a Free bomb fell on a school.
Forty-five children were changed.
They became a job for the cleaners.

Villagers carried their bodies
To the southern border, protesting
While in Detroit
Every three seconds
A car was born.

Today America sits at its television.
Its heartbeat rallies with the heartbeat
Of Lyndon Baines Johnson.

Even without his gall
He has a heart that can speak
For a sentimental nation
That loves its cars
As it loves its children.

Lyndon
If ever a missile
Blows one of your Birds to bits
Don't hate it, Lyndon –
It was only misguided.
It wanted to make her free.
Take heart that in Detroit
Every three seconds
A car is born.

*

'To see Life steadily and see it whole.'
Yes. But I wonder what the sideburned sage

Allowed was Life. Where did he see it whole?
Must the Muse eat carrion, and her True Servant
Construct of the small picked bones a White Tower
To see Life steadily and see it whole?

*

All day it has bullied me.
If it shook me hard enough
They'd put me away.
I represent
My terror so minutely
It will pass unnoticed.

I have never been so nearly anonymous.

From *Quesada*

'*Je pense . . .*
            aux vaincus!'

1

All over the plain of the world lovers are being hurt.
The spring wind takes up their cries and scatters them to the clouds.
Juan Quesada hears them. By the world at large they go unheard.
Only those in pain can hear the chorus of pain.
High in the air over winds that shake the leaves
High over traffic, beyond bird call, out of the reach of silence
These lovers are crying out because the spring has hurt them.
No one dies of that pain, some swear by it, a few will live with it always,
No one mistakes it for the lamentations of hell
Because there is a kind of exaltation in it
More eloquent than the tongues of wind and water
More truthful than the sibylline language of the leaves
The cry of the injured whose wounds are dear to them
The howl of the vanquished who cherish their defeat.

4

Dulcinea walks
Through spears of grass
Her feet bare
Leaves embroidered about them
A girl in a dream
Quesada dreamed
How will she live
Outside his tortured sleep?
Hear the cicadas
Using their chain-saws
Listen to those birds
That seem to yap like dogs

Look at the vines
Binding her ankles
See where the spears point.
The spring is mindless
The sun is blind
She's a walking garden
Praise her.

                              5

Quesada dreams: he is walking along a lane
A park à droit, à gauche the backs of houses.
Here is a barn-like building its bricks red in the sun,
Here is a thin hedge, two girls beyond in a garden,
One dark, cross-legged in the grass, seeming to murmur advice,
One pale, kneeling, her eyes cast down as she listens.
Has he passed at last into a world of perfect forms?
Where is the bridge by which the Enchanters cross
To this green pool of silence in which a glance has shown him
Figures of beauty, sun-carved figures of light?

                             10

Odysseus under wet snapping sheets
Quesada in the saddle – all men are travellers
Astride, under sheets, travellers and lovers, they go
To prize the world apart, to learn the spaces
In Circe's cave, on couches of blue satin
In brown grass under summer olives.
As long as seasons change don't look for stillness
Dulcinea, don't ask for kindness or rest –
Only the long reach of the mind always in love.

                             15

Dulcinea, he'd like to show you
A path dropping through ancient trees that shelter
A pool so clear the small fish seem to hang
In sun-shafts over its shingle floor.
You weren't born when he said goodbye to that place.
He'd loved it as he has loved you
With a wild sweet self-consuming passion.
Last night he dreamed you were standing
Beside a dark unruly river.

                             17

That the balls of the lover are not larger than the balls of the priest
That the heart of the miser is not smaller than the heart of Quesada
That the same sun warms the knight and the squire
That the long lance and the short sword open equally the passages to death

That the barber may wear a beard and the hangman have long life
These are the opaque equities of our world.

That the breast of Dulcinea is whiter than the driven snow
That the strength of her knight is as the strength of ten because his heart is
     pure
That the empire of true love is boundless and its battalions unconquerable
These are the translucent hyperboles of art.

Where was Quesada whose grapes fattened uneaten at his door
Whose fields were ripe, whose mill-wheels were always turning?
He was beyond the horizon, riding against the sunspears
Remembering the foot of his lady tentative as a white pennant in the cold
     mountain stream.

Pictures in a gallery in his brain
Were turned facing the wall, his limbs jolted
Coming down into a valley, night coming down
Sun catching flax and pampas along a stream
A church white in the foot-hills, the dead on his mind
The empty world full of their singing ghosts.

Owls in the poplar candles, a pheasant dead on the road
Thunder over the treeless mountain burned brown by summer
Thunder over the flooded fields, thunder over the dunes
Thunder over the darkened ocean shafted with light
Thunder in the long line of the surf breaking against an offshore wind
Thunder in the long line
Exaltation in the defeated heart of Quesada.

Who but a Christian would sing the broken body of love?
Who but a lover would sigh to be a plaything of the gods?

From *Twenty-One Sonnets*

2

Rain, and a flurry of wind shaking the pear's white blossom
Outside our kitchen window and tossing the lassiandra

As it did that morning four-year-old Michele Fox
Sat at our table painting shapes she said were flowers

While we listened to the news: a coaster missing up North,
A flare sighted in the night over Pandora Bank,

Radio contact lost – the ship's name, *Kaitawa*.
That was eight years ago. On the bus north

To Reinga and Spirits' Bay the driver remembers it –
Not a man saved, not even a body recovered,

Only smashed timber scattered down miles of coast
To tell how quickly it can come. I kept that painting –

It was the world she saw believing she had a father –
He was third engineer, a Scotsman, a good neighbour lost.

9

Spring is a recurring astonishment – like poetry.
So suddenly the oaks in Albert Park have assumed

Their bulk of green, so helplessly I find myself
With forty-two years notched up, my birthday presents

Hedge-clippers, screwdrivers, and *The Gulag Archipelago* –
And as I unwrap them a young man with a pack on his back

Knocks at our door wanting breakfast. His name is Blackburn,
Son of the 7th Fleet Admiral who rained down death

For years on North Vietnam – but the boy went to jail
Sooner than fight, and he's here to study mushrooms.

'He who forgets the past becomes blind,' says Solzhenitsyn
In that bookful of Russian blood. 'Cultivate your garden'

Say those Voltairean hedge-clippers. The quarrel of sparrows
Fills the silence of God that has lasted forty-two years.

From *Walking Westward*

Balmoral Intermediate
                1945
learned to spell 'principal'
        (distinct from 'principle')
because it was on the headmaster's door
committed to memory that the chief was chiefly an adjective
(despite his great bulk)
                    not a noun
Pemberton
            who told me to ring the bell
because the War was over
        (50 million dead and half of Europe in ruins)
and ringing the bell I was worried
it had been War so long
        what would Peace be like?

This morning a quartz sky   an opal harbour
        late summer gardens in flower
        city of clean edges
and the little boys in black and the bigger boys and the big ones
gathering in tens in scores converging in hundreds
across the Domain   up from Newmarket   down from Mt Eden
staggering
        their bags full of what might be stones
but are free text books

to learn in English 'the 8 modes of language'

(oracy) $\left\{\begin{array}{l}\text{speaking} \\ \updownarrow \\ \text{listening}\end{array}\right.$ $\left.\begin{array}{r}\text{reading} \\ \updownarrow \\ \text{writing}\end{array}\right\}$ (literacy)

(production) $\left\{\begin{array}{l}\text{moving} \longleftrightarrow \text{watching} \\ \text{shaping} \longleftrightarrow \text{viewing}\end{array}\right\}$ (reception)

confusion of thought enshrined in diagrams from the Government printer
tortured into text-books
small clear brows furrowed with incomprehension
        or ruffled in revolt
to be read as failure.

Peace was Korea
        the Cold War
the CIA
    Vietnam
corruption of action because corruption of thought
corruption of thought because corruption of language

a white butterfly drifts across the tomatoes
a bell rings
      50 million.

GORDON CHALLIS

The Iceman

What happened to the iceman after all?
Amazing how we waited for his call
and ran across to pick up chips of light
as the iceman's hook would beak-like bite
deep into ice, which he shouldered on a sack
and carried to our verandah at the back,
invisible the winter halo round his head.

We have other means of freezing now instead
of ice; it only lasted half a day
unwinding summer's waterclock away,
filling the tank, falling on zinc
under the icebox.

                    Nowadays I think
the nameless birds outside have hauled
some massive block of silence called
the morning to my door; with beaks well-ground
have started chipping splinters made of sound,
have sung me almost unaware how sick
I felt one childhood day, the embryonic
pain of seeing yolk and shell all splashed
together yellow where a bird's egg smashed;
yet pain evolves, perception grows more keen
as fits the many-coloured bird that might have been.

What happened to the iceman after all?
Amazing, how we waited for his call.

The Shadowless Man

You have to be quick to stamp out your own shadow.

So first I got to know my shadow's ductile tricks
of transformation: jet-black dwarf, diluted giant
– sometimes both at once – rotated slowly
like clock-hands as I passed
beyond the last street-lamp toward the next one,
keeping double reckoning. Every time I pounced
my shadow dodged adroitly, ducked or swerved aside.
If only I could work one jump ahead, if only
I could beat his perfect sense of timing!

Then one day I used my lethal steel-stud boots
and caught him napping, flat-footed in full sunlight,
got him good and hard right in the guts. He disappeared,
went underground a goner and good riddance.

People said: 'See here this man without a shadow,
a man through whom light shines, lies all around him,
a man more pure than rain and more transparent.'

I, however, fear another explanation:
What if I have not fully stamped him out?
(Perhaps his absence is a mere delaying)
What if the lakes are low, the power failing,
and it is my own night that keeps him waiting?

Thin Partition

Someone next door is moving things about –
dusting the shelves which don't need dusting
making changes simply for the sake of change
or hoping that new order in the room will rout
those evil demons who resent what's new and strange.

Someone next door is singing as she moves –
maybe this tune will mark the turning,
work the trick for years-old resolutions
really to come true; but then she leaves
a word amiss and spoils the spell's relations.

Someone next door is thinking what to do –
wondering what meat to buy for Sunday
or shall she go back home and try again
to hide the fact that there she feels more lonely
and knows the reason yet cannot explain.

Someone is talking to us in her way –
her shadow gestures windlike through the scrim;
my wife and I are hurried, we are going out;
someone next door is asking us to stay,
someone next door is moving things about.

The Black One

Ask of the black one; leave the others be –
their gifts of gold and frankincense are rich
but not so lasting. Ask of the black one – he
is not so sought for; children fear to touch

his robe because he looks so fierce, because he hides
a bitter gum to seal all speech and make opaque
those eyes where they saw sunlight stored inside.
Do not heed these tales but ask him quick

before he rides away. He'll bring the star you want
to stay forever reigning on the Christmas tree
so no-one can take down. He'll bring the toy you can't
destroy, which broken, bent, reforms repeatedly.

Ask of the black one. Close your eyelids tightly,
lock inside the precious sunlight stored all day:
you may dream his journey further nightly,
you may give him sight enough to find the way.

Dream of the black one; dream of him coming blind
till lightning spreads its roots and trees of thunder
open their leaves as if they stored the sound
of twelfth night drummers sent proclaiming wonder

to wake a sleeping town. Dream of the black one
who only comes if you are really sleeping,
whose robe is ample; he won't mind you keeping
the tatter from the window sash where he has gone,
dark with the colour of blood, strong with the scent of gum.

The Thermostatic Man

The world could fall to pieces any moment now;
with luck it won't,
mainly because it hasn't yet. Though cracks appear,
I'll merely count
them leeway spaces left so masses may expand
to meet and don't.

But I, who used to walk bolt upright, this day bow
as meek as wheat:
how can I be sure I shall not always fear
to face fierce heat,
to face the sun, not watch my shadow lagging back behind,
and feel complete?

From strips of many metals am I made. I grow
beneath the sun
unevenly. I cannot cry lest the least tear
should cool down one
soft element and strain the others. I am bland,
bend to become

the thermostat which keeps my spirit burning low.
One day I shall
perhaps be tried by a more humble, human fire
which, blending all
my elements in one alloy, will let me stand
upright, ready to fall.

The Sinful Man

You cannot see it now, of course,
but if you ever went to Sunday-school
and got those prints they give for good behaviour
you might have met a case quite similar to mine:

I mean that picture of a man who toils
toward a green hill with his hoisted sack of sin.

You cannot even touch it, nor can I,
and yet you cannot say it isn't there,
for you don't have to carry it . . . I do.
And I've begun, these past few days, to wonder
what this sack contains. Coming across the stream
it grew much heavier; this fact suggests

the stuff that sins are made of may be
dehydrated, crystal-forming, or absorbs
its water by osmosis. If you prefer
a mythical account then call me Christopher
and say I save my master who could walk the waves
though in the process I go deathwards down.

I do not think, however, Christ would ride
any man that hard. The only handicaps
are heaven-set and judged on past performance;
mine was never good, but people sometimes bet
heavily on rank outsiders, try to beat
the tote by backing me at odds against myself.

So now I'm only fit for packhorse duties
bearing this black old sack, not knowing what
material is here. Is it the sand on which
the random seed was scattered to be gleaned by birds?
Is it the seed itself which, moistened now, would grow
but burst holds open, break my back in two?

Sometimes I like to think I stumble
under a load of roses, spilling on the stream
for someone else to gather, a load I might
see for myself if only I could go
back to where I started, right back to the bank,
before I shouldered them forever out of sight.

The Oracle

One-time liaison officer in Babel's tower,
I prophesy in any tongue; and in your voice
I hear both answers – one your question craves,
the other unacceptable. The prophets truer
to their trade would not shirk words that grieve,
nor care to be believed. However, their advice

is hard to come by and, when sought, neglected
like disused diamond mines where they retire.
They offer truth, more hard than any stone,
which trimmed to shape traps light within refracted
but when reduced to crystal thin-ness shows its own
extinction angle, just like any stone; its fire

is swampwards lost back in the lairs of time.
Meanwhile a lesser substance came from those swamp trees:
here I inhabit galleries where coal was mined
and, though the pit's redundant, people climb
down these shafts, like shifts of miners, bent to find
some little fuel for their dreams before they freeze.

Yet my advice is neither coloured black as coal
nor white as ash; the truth half-told suffices,
being the only kind that calls for full belief.
And if I say that you must seek your soul
where waves begin, beyond the hidden reef,
you still may choose to put away the crisis

of choosing till another day, the weather
being unpropitious and the route through pain.
Or, like most, you may interpret me to mean
'go such a way, seek this sign or that other,'
and then you'll thank me, ask what sacrifice has been
ordained. There was a sacrifice . . . You came.

KEVIN IRELAND

Parade: Liberation Day

Think of a tree-lined city street
on an early autumn day;
fashion placards and bunting;
imagine a display
of dripping clothes
drying among the flags and signs
hung from the balconies;
think flags onto washing-lines.

People this street;
create language and breed.
Then think of, say, twenty tanks,
cornering at a terrifying speed,
powdering the paving-bricks;
imagine parachutes, drifting like thistle seed
through the gusts of autumn leaves and sticks.

Now picture the infantry,
young, strong,
measuring with hobnails
their heroic song.
Yet make this song trail from the distance,
though the soldiers are near:
the rhythm is significant,
the words need not be clear.

Think of a happy street
on an early autumn night;
imagine tables and chairs beneath the trees,
and the gay light
of coloured globes,
swaying with flag and sign.

People this street;
create chatter and wine.
Then think of, say, a billion stars,
and a moon darting at a terrifying speed
from darkness, to darkness again.
Erase it all
with sudden drenching rain.

Now picture the infantry,
cold, damp,
measuring with hobnails
the way back to camp.
Yet make their tread trail from the distance,
though they are near:
gently imagine them,
their future is not clear.

The Man in the Pool

Narcissus would look into a mirror
and see right through
he obviously could not shave or comb
he could not do
ordinary things with his face
he had no way
of knowing how he looked
but folk would say
that a man was much more natural
when not self-seen
that a man was then unspoilt
they did not mean
that they were thus Narcissus
became well liked
nymphs sang to him swam with him
they even hiked
into the faraway hills with him but he
was searching for
the other side of a mirror and kept cool
one day he saw
a large pool full of lilies
he felt impelled
to gaze on it to find
all that it held
and there at last he saw his face or anyway
he thought he knew
it was and not another's surfacing
drowned swollen blue
remember he could not shave or comb
he could not deal
with the mystery of obviously mirrored opposites
nor with the real.

Running a Risk

I laid both hands
upon her heart:
I staked my life
against that part

by risking all
sly lovers thrive:
my hands are full
I'm still alive

Striking a Pose

we'll stock up books
and wine and pie
then stop the clocks
and never die

we'll nail the windows
brick up the door
and live on a mattress
on the floor

if death still comes
we'll strike a pose
and hold our breath
until he goes

Threnody

for Bob Lowry

the dinghies
have been dragged
high above
the weed-mark
of full tide
their keel lines gash
the dead-grey beach

the yachts
have been bundled
in canvas and stacked
at the slipway
like mortal remains
ready to go
down through the deep

the drum
of the sea
has been muffled
and the hunched gulls
lament
motionlessly
on the sandbanks

the sun
has gone out
and the cold pale face
of the sky
is scratched
by the black fingernails
of the coming rain

Caroline beside the Sundial

for a fraction
everything was stilled

camera-lens and water-lily

a droplet hanging from a leaf
undropped

the gnomon
idled in the sun

thistledown bristled

you said the dial
said one

for five-hundredths of a second
the shutter gaped

riplets pitched the lily-pond

droplets plopped
thistledown swarmed off

in that tripped moment
daylight blinked

time lay in a tray of fixative

Caroline and Eternity
are linked

A Signal to the Past

when I stooped
to look past you at someone else
you thought the gesture meant to kiss

you raised your chin
half-shut your eyes
face wrinkled in a smiling frown

yet there had been no word
no prior move to show that if I bent
just so you'd bring your lips to mine

quickly we both drew back
wakened not by desire but amazement
then we began to laugh

you had been tricked by a chance tilting
of my head a familiar inclination
that tripped a signal to the past

or so it is less clumsy to suppose
not wishing to distort the matter
or regret not kissing you

Auto-Da-Fe

yesterday you burnt your olden times:
proposals snapshots invitations declarations

your years of real and fake and flash affection
gusted into blushing flame

your lovers' hands across your shoulders
baked and blistered cracked then peeled away

your grinning moments at the horn-mad beach
fanned hot crackles then twisted into ash

yesterday you gave cruel riddance to the lot
and sent your past loves to the stake

but though I am impressed by ways or codes
so drawn to irreversible convictions

yet I am of that self-same faith which brought
these luckless men to their ordeal by fire

thus should I fear for our remembrance:
confess new fuel to a later blaze?

From *Literary Cartoons*

15 A Literary Tag

those Romans tagged it right
he thought:
art is long
[and] life is short

but having neatly versed
the nouns
he turned their bearing
upside-down

and compared the brief
effects of art
to the endless torments
of his heart

18 The Literary Exile

he remembers more than twenty years ago
lying embedded to the thighs in sand
on a beach curved at the end like a hook

wishing to catch poems he could salt
and peg out on a line in the wind
to dry like Dally fish

but all he brought in that day was: Rangitoto
rises like an upper lip . . . its teeth sink
into the sea's rim . . . it gnashes the sun-scaled waves

images he keeps for good luck in his exile:
little nets of words to hold a moment and a view
as he grows older and closer to his past

21 A Serious Literary Slip

when the literary man
went soaring through the evening air
at a legal thirty miles an hour
(or very slightly more)

he had all the slow-motion time
in the world to formulate
a famous well-phrased
final thought

so imagine his embarrassed rage
not at the homicidal motorist
the broken motorbike torn shoulder
bruised wrist

but at the clown inside him
who suppressed his perfect set
of valedictory words and substituted
Jesus, this is it!

30 The Literary Man Observes a Window to the Sky

he remembered the street he walked along
but without being able to tell how or why
until he recognized the place where he had stayed:

first he noticed that the brickwork scored his absence:
it was cracked soot-dribbled grey: then – more disturbing –
saw how the windows seemed to contain no interiors:

they reflected the sky – as though they outlined gaps
gazing through the walls at outer space: no longer
could he place himself inside – his talk his bed

his books: yet where had they all gone?
that part of memory which recollected his old rooms
had become a sky-blue window full of shapeless cloud

a two-dimensional illusion – like a film set –
a false-front a prop an uninhabited sham:
it had become a frame for trick-effects and ghosts:

how could he foresee that it would come to this:
that time would disembowel the structures of this town
and his dwelling would become but windows in the sky?

PETER BLAND

The Parental Bedroom

A tomb or chapel smell about it. Always
So largely quiet – something unforgiven
About such silence. Looking in
At that huge slab of smoothed-down linen,
The bedside gadgets, rows of pills, the thin
Smooth silky stuff that crammed out cupboards,
I sensed some house-worn secret hidden
Beneath the camphored holiness. So

Often when guarding my parents' absence
I'd dare that toe-deep silence, creep
Consciously alone along the landing,
Enter sidewise like a crab; within,
Grab at the tattered *Mastery of Sex*,
Drink brandy from a glass empty of teeth,
And breathe my medicinal breath in mirrors;
My blood, loud as a clock; my feet

Cold as the odd abstractions I could finger
But never quite believe. Those mirrors,
Those blood-loud clocks and thieving fingers
Chasing me to the shed downstairs
Where, page by page, I'd probe by heart
That guide-book to Love's working parts.
They must have guessed, yet never barred the way
Between their chapel and my hermit's cave.

Past the Tin Butterflies and
Plaster Gnomes

Past the tin butterflies and plaster gnomes,
The home-made garages, the weekend roasts,
The cats' paws delicate in new-laid concrete,
The cast-off sheaths and ice-cream cones
Outside the phone-box, and a mist of screams
Clouding the blue above the net-ball courts,
Past pastel avenues and rainbow houses,
Past father fuelling at the Bottle Store,
Past the Chemist Shop and the Corner Dairy
And the family photos on the kitchen walls,
Past clocks and mirrors and the coloured pictures
of *Nature's Wonderland* – all sheep and snow,
And home in time to switch the radio over
From *This is New Zealand* to *My Orphaned Soul*.

Lines on Leaving the Last Reservation

State Housing Area – Hutt Valley

The truck grinds off with all our debts
packed arabwise . . .
                              disturbed, the air
sinks back on waking kitchen-stirs
and plugged cot-cries
                              A neighbourly
suburban cock
                    rust red
flames from a garage roof. He bangs
his voice against our newly
naked panes . . .
                    The sky's a mineral blue.

I'm barely sane . . .
                              Three years of cramped
good living leave me squat in spirit.

I'd like to think we're getting out
in the nick of time
                              but
                                    looking round
my sense of mild fatality comes through.

The spirit here has learnt a shrewd
backgarden whimsy . . .
                                    crushed, it curls
still smirking in dog-kennel warmth:
such arse-sniffing could go on for years.

Thank God we're off!
                              That Absolute
of public peace called *Home*
leaves me so insecure . . .
                              'Man *must* grow roots'
is such a vegetable rule.
                              I dream
of hatchets gleaming at my neighbour's
grim approach . . . his backhand chop
would fell me like a fencing post.

The taxi clarions . . .
                              and the cock
sinks back into his feathered roost
                              (I feel
the stare of watching eyes
uncurl like bulbs beneath warm roofs.)

It's not enough!
                    When said and done

our leaving celebrates some cause
                                      leaves us
some differences in common
                                Someone
should at least appear
                         if only
to fill a vacancy we all approve.

Squint back!
                In shrinking taxi-glass
look how peace like dust descends
on no one . . .
                   how . . .
                                alone at last
that Absolute we rented
starts to settle down
                            (It looks
almost at home now)
                           Ahead
                                 the road
gathers up our swaying truck
carved like a camel against the void.

House with Cat or Sun

(A drawing by Jo, aged 4)

An idiot sun, cross-eyed, smiles down
benevolence on a fist-full of windows
crammed into a house . . . A huge
three-legged cat is trying
to squeeze in through a floating door.

Or perhaps a malevolent cross-eyed cat
is jumping onto the roof-top, while
a huge, three-legged, idiot sun
is floating out of the open door.

Or it could be a helicopter taking off
that has nothing at all to do
with either cat or sun – while a three-legged flower
grows outside the only window
in an idiot house crammed full of doors.

The Building

I'd like to live in your lap, said
my daughter. *And that* (my pocket)
is a door. She stepped
up from the ground floor of my toes, and began
the bony climb to where my backside spread
big as a boardroom on the sofa. Curiously
I was feeling about as bare as a public

building after work – that time
of being when light falls streaming
on to dust and detergents, when foreign women
slop out hidden mops. Chest-
high, she stopped, knocked twice, and entered
ignoring the huge KEEP OUT sign. (Not
that she would lose her step
in that blackened inner smoke-room.) It
wasn't guilt made me want to push
the stale jokes and doctored pin-ups
out of her way, they just seemed dull – so
unforgivably monotonous when faced
by a true professional. *Go away*,
I said. And she took the lift
back to the basement. She wasn't hurt
just bored with one so full of doors. These
days, public buildings are all the same.

Kumara God

Three days and still the slow fogged rain
Drifts inland – all along the valley
Light melts to clusters of steamed-up panes.
All's formlessness – a sharpened will
Won't chip us free of it. It is
A melting back, an elemental drift
Beyond time or season . . .

                              And so I bring
The little stone cramped kumara god
In from the garden . . . Take down the clock
And set him there, upon the mantelpiece,
To be my curled-in self, grown
Old in embryo, slightly sardonic . . .
Feeling around me this slow retreat
Of lives gone underground, of sleep turned solid.

So Many Cenotaphs

So many cenotaphs! As though a people
Had come here just to be remembered;
Finding no other future but to fall
Somewhere else and for some other quarrel
Than that which brought them. So,
To atone for leaving . . . to leave again;
And for that Fall . . . to Fall.

                              So much dead stone!
As though a people, turning back to wave,
Stepped out into their own memorials.

The Happy Army

The child has a vision of the happy army. He
has carefully sketched in my appointment book
the smiles, the fingers, the boots and guns
his happy army wave like rattles. No
one is dying, no one's bad or good,
and even the one at the back has a medal
while the generals beam pure love. The sun
has rolled to the ground, has been caught up
in a growing air of excitement that runs
riot, filling the sky with faces, arms, legs
and bits of old tanks. It is natural
that everyone, everywhere, faces the front,
not out of discipline or to scare the enemy
but in frank expectancy of applause. And
of course this is why this particular army
is happy, why no one dies, why the sun
shares in the happy army's happiness
and rolls down to earth. It is why I run
towards the boots and guns, why I come
as far as I dare to the edge of the paper
to stare . . . to stare and to cheer them on.

Lament for a Lost Generation

Between V-J Day and 1951
we wore our first grey longs.
Drab, insular, short of vitamin C,
much given to fags and the fumbled grope

we became – like prefabs
or the last steam train –
something slightly embarrassing
that goes on and on: fodder for talks like

The Ration-Book Age or
The Wartime Growth of the Working Mum.
We were few; conceived in the slump;
brought up in shelters and under the stairs;

eleven-plus boys; post-war conscripts
who lowered the flag on better days.
What we lacked was a style! We
were make-do-and-menders, utility-

grey men, the last of a line. You
can tell us a mile off, even now;
there's a touch of austerity
under the eyes; a hint of carbolic

in our after-shave; a lasting doubt
about the next good time.

FLEUR ADCOCK

Note on Propertius I.3

Among the Roman love-poets, possession
Is a rare theme. The locked and flower-hung door,
The shivering lover, are allowed. To more
Buoyant moods, the canons of expression
Gave grudging sanction. Do we, then, assume,
Finding Propertius tear-sodden and jealous,
That Cynthia was inexorably callous?
Plenty of moonlight entered that high room
Whose doors had met his Alexandrine battles;
And she, so gay a lutanist, was known
To stitch and doze a night away, alone,
Until the poet tumbled in with apples
For penitence and for her head his wreath,
Brought from a party, of wine-scented roses –
(The garland's aptness lying, one supposes,
Less in the flowers than in the thorns beneath:
Her waking could, he knew, provide his verses
With less idyllic themes). Onto her bed
He rolled the round fruit, and adorned her head;
Then gently roused her sleeping mouth to curses.
Here the conventions reassert their power:
The apples fall and bruise, the roses wither,
Touched by a sallowed moon. But there were other
Luminous nights – (even the cactus flower
Glows briefly golden, fed by spiny flesh) –
And once, as he acknowledged, all was singing:
The moonlight musical, the darkness clinging,
And she compliant to his every wish.

Incident

When you were lying on the white sand,
A rock under your head, and smiling,
(Circled by dead shells), I came to you
And you said, reaching to take my hand,
'Lie down'. So for a time we lay
Warm on the sand, talking and smoking,
Easy; while the grovelling sea behind
Sucked at the rocks and measured the day.
Lightly I fell asleep then, and fell
Into a cavernous dream of falling.
It was all the cave-myths, it was all
The myths of tunnel or tower or well –
Alice's rabbit-hole into the ground,
Or the path of Orpheus: a spiral staircase
To hell, furnished with danger and doubt.
Stumbling, I suddenly woke; and found
Water about me. My hair was wet,
And you were sitting on the grey sand,

Waiting for the lapping tide to take me:
Watching, and lighting a cigarette.

Wife to Husband

From anger into the pit of sleep
You go with a sudden skid. On me
Stillness falls gradually, a soft
Snowfall, a light cover to keep
Numb for a time the twitching nerves.

Your head on the pillow is turned away;
My face is hidden. But under snow
Shoots uncurl, the green thread curves
Instinctively upwards. Do not doubt
That sense of purpose in mindless flesh:
Between our bodies a warmth grows;
Under the blankets hands move out,
Your back touches my breast, our thighs
Turn to find their accustomed place.

Your mouth is moving over my face:
Do we dare, now, to open our eyes?

For a Five-Year-Old

A snail is climbing up the window-sill
Into your room, after a night of rain.
You call me in to see, and I explain
That it would be unkind to leave it there:
It might crawl to the floor; we must take care
That no one squashes it. You understand,
And carry it outside, with careful hand,
To eat a daffodil.

I see, then, that a kind of faith prevails:
Your gentleness is moulded still by words
From me, who have trapped mice and shot wild birds,
From me, who drowned your kittens, who betrayed
Your closest relatives, and who purveyed
The harshest kind of truth to many another.
But that is how things are: I am your mother,
And we are kind to snails.

A Game

They are throwing the ball
to and fro between them,
in and out of the picture.
She is in the painting
hung on the wall

in a narrow gold frame.
He stands on the floor
catching and tossing
at the right distance.
She wears a white dress,
black boots and stockings,
and a flowered straw hat.
She moves in silence
but it seems from her face
that she must be laughing.
Behind her is sunlight
and a tree-filled garden;
you might think to hear
birds or running water,
but no, there is nothing.
Once or twice he has spoken
but does so no more,
for she cannot answer.
So he stands smiling,
playing her game
(she is almost a child),
not daring to go,
intent on the ball.
And she is the same.
For what would result
neither wishes to know
if it should fall.

From *Night-Piece*

2

Before Sleep

Lying close to your heart-beat, my lips
Touching the pulse in your neck, my head on your arm,
I listen to your hidden blood as it slips
With a small furry sound along the warm
Veins; and my slowly-flowering dream
Of Chinese landscapes, river-banks and flying
Splits into sudden shapes – children who scream
By a roadside, blinded men, a woman lying
In a bed filled with blood: the broken ones.
We are so vulnerable. I curl towards
That intricate machine of nerves and bones
With its built-in life: your body. And to your words
I whisper 'Yes' and 'Always', as I lie
Waiting for thunder from a stony sky.

Statues

'I daren't love you any more.'
Because he whispered, and because

it was so odd, I thought he said
'I don't love you. . . .' I held him close,
his face hidden in my shoulder,
and shivered, once. It was perfect.
We lay like stone tomb-figures.
                              Then
the words resaid themselves, inside
my head: 'I dare not . . . any more
than I do now.' It was all right:
likely, normal. We became warm
again; but no longer sculptured.

Afterwards

We weave haunted circles about each other,
advance and retreat in turn, like witchdoctors
before a fetish. Yes, you are right to fear
me now, and I you. But love, this ritual
will exhaust us. Come closer. Listen. Be brave.
I am going to talk to you quietly
as sometimes, in the long past (you remember?),
we made love. Let us be intent, and still. Still.
There are ways of approaching it. This is one:
this gentle talk, with no pause for suspicion,
no hesitation, because you do not know
the thing is upon you, until it has come –
now, and you did not even hear it.
                              Silence
is what I am trying to achieve for us.
A nothingness, a non-relatedness, this
unknowing into which we are sliding now
together: this will have to be our kingdom.

Rain is falling. Listen to the gentle rain.

Against Coupling

I write in praise of the solitary act:
of not feeling a trespassing tongue
forced into one's mouth, one's breath
smothered, nipples crushed against the
ribcage, and that metallic tingling
in the chin set off by a certain odd nerve:

unpleasure. Just to avoid those eyes would help –
such eyes as a young girl draws life from,
listening to the vegetal
rustle within her, as his gaze
stirs polypal fronds in the obscure
sea-bed of her body, and her own eyes blur.

There is much to be said for abandoning
this no longer novel exercise –

for not 'participating in
a total experience' – when
one feels like the lady in Leeds who
had seen *The Sound of Music* eighty-six times;

or more, perhaps, like the school drama mistress
producing *A Midsummer Night's Dream*
for the seventh year running, with
yet another cast from 5B.
Pyramus and Thisbe are dead, but
the hole in the wall can still be troublesome.

I advise you, then, to embrace it without
encumbrance. No need to set the scene,
dress up (or undress), make speeches.
Five minutes of solitude are
enough – in the bath, or to fill
that gap between the Sunday papers and lunch.

Please Identify Yourself

British, more or less; Anglican, of a kind.
In Cookstown I dodge the less urgent question
when a friendly Ulster bus driver raises it;
'You're not a Moneymore girl yourself?' he asks,
deadpan. I make a cowardly retrogression,
slip ten years back. 'No, I'm from New Zealand.'
'Are you now? Well, that's a coincidence:
the priest at Moneymore's a New Zealander.'
And there's the second question, unspoken.
Unanswered.
              I go to Moneymore
anonymously, and stare at all three churches.

In Belfast, though, where sides have to be taken,
I stop compromising – not that you'd guess,
seeing me hatless there among the hatted,
neutral voyeur among the shining faces
in the glossy Martyrs' Memorial Free Church.
The man himself is cheerleader in the pulpit
for crusader choruses: we're laved in blood,
marshalled in ranks. I chant the nursery tunes
and mentally cross myself. You can't stir me
with evangelistic hymns, Dr Paisley:
I know them. Nor with your computer-planned
sermon – Babylon, Revelation, whispers
of popery, slams at the IRA, more blood.
I scrawl incredulous notes under my hymnbook
and burn with Catholicism.
                           Later
hacking along the Lower Falls Road
against a gale, in my clerical black coat,
I meet a bright gust of tinselly children
in beads and lipstick and their mother's dresses

for Hallowe'en; who chatter and surround me.
Overreacting once again (a custom
of the country, not mine alone) I give them
all my loose change for their rattling tin
and my blessing – little enough. But now
to my tough Presbyterian ancestors,
Brooks and Hamilton, lying in the graves
I couldn't find at Moneymore and Cookstown
among so many unlabelled bones, I say:
I embrace you also, my dears.

Script

'Wet the tea, Jinny, the men are back:
I can hear them out there, talking, with the horses',
my mother's grandmother said. They both heard it,
she and her daughter – the wagon bumpily halted,
a rattle of harness, two familiar voices
in sentences to be identified later
and quoted endlessly. But the tea was cold
when the men came in. They'd been six miles away,
pausing to rest on Manurewa Hill
in a grove of trees – whence 'Fetch the nosebags, Dickie'
came clearly over. A freak wind, maybe:
soundwaves carrying, their words lifted up
and dropped on Drury. Eighty years ago,
long before the wireless was invented,
Grandma told us. It made a good story:
baffling. But then, so was the real thing –
radio.
           My father understood it.
Out on the bush farm at Te Rau a Moa
as a teenager he patiently constructed
little fiddly devices, sat for hours
every day adjusting a cat's whisker,
filtering morse through headphones. Later came
loudspeakers, and the whole family could gather
to hear the creaky music of 1YA.
So my father's people were technicians, is that it?
And my mother's were communicators, yes? –
Who worked as a barber in the evenings
for the talking's sake? Who became a teacher –
and who was in love with tractors? No prizes.
Don't classify. Leave the air-waves open.

We each extract what we most need. My sons
rig out their rooms with stereo equipment.
I walk dozily through the house
in the mornings with a neat black box,
audible newspaper, timekeeper and -saver,
sufficient for days like that.
                           On days like this
I sit in my own high borrowed grove
and let the leafy air clear my mind

for reception. The slow pigeon-flight,
the scraped-wire pipping of some bird,
the loamy scent, offer themselves to me
as little presents, part of an exchange
to be continued and continually
(is this a rondo? that professor asked)
perpetuated. It is not like music,
though the effects can strike as music does:
it is more like agriculture, a nourishing
of the growth-mechanisms, a taking-in
of food for what will flower and seed and sprout.

On a path in the wood two white-haired women
are marching arm in arm, singing a hymn.
A girl stops me to ask where I bought my sandals.
I say 'In Italy, I think' and we laugh.
I am astonished several times a day.
When I get home I shall make tea or coffee
for whoever is there, talk and listen to talk,
share food and living-space. There will always
be time to reassemble the frail components
of this afternoon, to winnow the scattered sounds
dropped into my range, and rescue from them
a seed-hoard for transmission. There will be
always the taking-in and the sending-out.

Kilpeck

We are dried and brittle this morning,
fragile with continence, quiet.
You have brought me to see a church.
I stare at a Celtic arch in red sandstone
carved like a Mayan temple-gate;
at serpents writhing up the doorposts
and squat saints with South-American features
who stare back over our heads
from a panel of beasts and fishes.
The gargoyles jutting from under the eaves
are the colour of newborn children.

Last night you asked me
if poetry was the most important thing.

We walk on around the building
craning our heads back to look up
at lions, griffins, fat-faced bears.
The Victorians broke some of these figures
as being too obscene for a church;
but they missed the Whore of Kilpeck.
She leans out under the roof
holding her pink stony cleft agape
with her ancient little hands.
There was always witchcraft here, you say.

The sheep-track up to the fragments
of castle-wall is fringed with bright bushes.
We clamber awkwardly, separate.
Hawthorn and dogrose offer hips and haws,
orange and crimson capsules, pretending
harvest. I taste a blackberry.
The soil here is coloured like brick-dust,
like the warm sandstone. A fruitful county.
We regard it uneasily.

There is little left to say
after all the talk we had last night
instead of going to bed –
fearful for our originality,
avoiding the sweet obvious act
as if it were the only kind of indulgence.
Silly, perhaps.
               We have our reward.
We are languorous now, heavy
with whatever we were conserving,
carrying each a delicate burden
of choices made or about to be made.
Words whisper hopefully in our heads.

Slithering down the track we hold hands
to keep a necessary balance.
The gargoyles extend their feral faces,
rosy, less lined than ours.
We are wearing out our identities.

An Illustration to Dante

Here are Paolo and Francesca
whirled around in the circle of Hell
clipped serenely together
her dead face raised against his.
I can feel the pressure of his arms
like yours about me, locking.

They float in a sea of whitish blobs –
fire, is it? It could have been
hail, said Ruskin, but Rossetti
'didn't know how to do hail'.
Well, he could do tenderness.
My spine trickles with little white flames.

Things

There are worse things than having behaved foolishly in public.
There are worse things than these miniature betrayals,
committed or endured or suspected; there are worse things

than not being able to sleep for thinking about them.
It is 5 a.m. All the worse things come stalking in
and stand icily about the bed looking worse and worse
and worse.

The Soho Hospital for Women

I

Strange room, from this angle:
white door open before me,
strange bed, mechanical hum, white lights.
There will be stranger rooms to come.

As I almost slept I saw the deep flower opening
and leaned over into it, gratefully.
It swimmingly closed in my face. I was not ready.
It was not death, it was acceptance.

*

Our thin patient cat died purring,
her small triangular head tilted back,
the nurse's fingers caressing her throat,
my hand on her shrunken spine; the quick needle.

That was the second death by cancer.
The first is not for me to speak of.
It was telephone calls and brave letters
and a friend's hand bleeding under the coffin.

*

Doctor, I am not afraid of a word.
But neither do I wish to embrace that visitor,
to engulf it as Hine-Nui-te-Po
engulfed Maui; that would be the way of it.

And she was the winner there: her womb crushed him.
Goddesses can do these things.
But I have admitted the gloved hands and the speculum
and must part my ordinary legs to the surgeon's knife.

II

Nellie has only one breast
ample enough to make several.
Her quilted dressing-gown softens
to semi-doubtful this imbalance
and there's no starched vanity
in our abundant ward-mother:
her silvery hair's in braids, her slippers
loll, her weathered smile holds true.

When she dresses up in her black
with her glittering marcasite brooch on
to go for the weekly radium treatment
she's the bright star of the taxi-party –
whatever may be growing under her ribs.

*

Doris hardly smokes in the ward –
and hardly eats more than a dreamy spoonful –
but the corridors and bathrooms
reek of her Players Number 10,
and the drug-trolley pauses
for long minutes by her bed.
Each week for the taxi-outing
she puts on her skirt again
and has to pin the slack waistband
more tightly over her scarlet sweater.
Her face, a white shadow through smoked glass,
lets Soho display itself unregarded.

*

Third in the car is Mrs Golding
who never smiles. And why should she?

III

The senior consultant on his rounds
murmurs in so subdued a voice
to the students marshalled behind
that they gather in, forming a cell,
a cluster, a rosette around him
as he stands at the foot of my bed
going through my notes with them,
half-audibly instructive, grave.

The slight ache as I strain forward
to listen still seems imagined.

Then he turns his practised smile on me:
'How are you this morning?' 'Fine,
very well, thank you.' I smile too.
And possibly all that murmurs within me
is the slow dissolving of stitches.

IV

I am out in the supermarket choosing –
this very afternoon, this day –
picking up tomatoes, cheese, bread,

things I want and shall be using
to make myself a meal, while they
eat their stodgy suppers in bed:

Janet with her big freckled breasts,
her prim Scots voice, her one friend,
and never in hospital before,

who came in to have a few tests
and now can't see where they'll end;
and Coral in the bed by the door

who whimpered and gasped behind a screen
with nurses to and fro all night
and far too much of the day;

pallid, bewildered, nineteen.
And Mary, who will be all right
but gradually. And Alice, who may.

Whereas I stand almost intact,
giddy with freedom, not with pain.
I lift my light basket, observing

how little I needed in fact;
and move to the checkout, to the rain,
to the lights and the long street curving.

VINCENT O'SULLIVAN

Medusa

Sits at the window, waits the threatened steel
as any common housewife waits near dark
for groceries that should have come at four,
when it's too late to 'phone to hear they're certain,
to know the boy is pedalling up the hill
and not gone home. A boy who's late –
it could be simply that, so still her hands.

Two or three birds. Bare branches.
A thrush taps on the gravel, tilts its head.
Her eyes, she thinks, could hold it if she wanted,
could make it come up close, think this is home.
Sits there, her hands folded, her lips cold,
the expected blade already on her skin.
A piece of wind no bigger than a man
moves the dead leaves, bends the sopping grass.
A blind cord knocks the window like a drum.
'Perseus, stalwart, honest, comes his way,
his footstep nicks the corners of the day
like something hard against a grey, chipped stone.'
The stone he says she makes with those grey eyes.
Jade in the dusk. Heavier than grey.

And when he comes, how talk moves like a mirror,
a polished shield, in shadows, then in light,
always his care to stay behind its hurt.
Talks of her greatest gift – to deck out men
in stone: stone heart, stone limbs, the lot.
Turns men to stone, turns them to herself.
'The only way to end, for both our good.'
And like a man who shows off coins or gems
he lets his words fall in the room by ones,
and twos, or if in piles, it's when
their rushing sounds and feels a streaming sword.
Edges in close with that, to do his work.
And all her strength, to keep her eyes from his.

Interview with Theseus

Well – after congratulations –
You're glad to be back?
    That's hardly a question, is it?
    That says blood, says bone,
    or the essence of what I am,
    may at least continue.

Can I rephrase it?
The labyrinth is now like a bad dream?
    If you want it that way.

But as for that fine line
where day begins to edge
the nightmare out,
the fine line like a cut
where your flesh held smoothly . . .

Your fiancée says to make it
more specific.
                    The walls, for instance.
The first thing to strike one.
That's where all our talk,
all preparation, shrinks like a fog
into a tattered ball,
a mechanic's rag.
Its walls are curtains.

Curtains?
    The opposite to hard, or absolute.
    It's no good beating your head there
    if you're lost.

Then you weren't scared?
    Each next corner's coming
    was smooth as oil.
    The crushed maze of oil on a road
    flared up to wall size, round you.
    Understand?

She says you now sit here
And hardly speak.
                    Relief, perhaps,
or shock? But you're over fear?
    Of walls? of oil? which?

I mean, the very centre.
    There was nothing in its hulk
    not waiting here.
    Its eyes were mirrors catching
    all sides at once.

But you were quicker?
    Its speed was as I chose it.
    It would have sat all day
    and even yawned when I yawned,
    slept beside me, snorted me in
    to truffle at its trough.
    The minotaur's too devious for fear.

Then how escape?
    I came away on terms.
    I brought it with me.

I beg your pardon?
    That great beast I'm said
    to be so smart with –

you needn't move aside –
it's here between us.
It's crammed under my shoe
like another sole.
                    It rides
the scented waters
she rigs to bathe me.

She? Your betrothed?
When I hear the cool splashing
from her jugs on marble,
see the mosaics pale
under rising water,
the curious play of that element,
well, yes, I'm grateful.
But I also know the code.
I hear the black perfection
of its hooves;
I see the tongue unroll
like a burning carpet;
I feel the rugs of its breath.

Perhaps you're tiring, are you?
You'd like to rest?
My point, if you care to listen –
fear, and talk of courage,
of gratitude or luck,
the showground melodrama of one's pulse –
these are the coloured chalks
for drawing squares,
squares for a child's game
that says here, yes, or here, no,
because you've said that colour
is this and will mean this
while the game keeps on.
Yet once it rains . . .

But the labyrinth? the maze?
Squares without chalk.
Or squareless colours.
I mean our talk of form,
of conduct, love, proportion,
– talk, in other words, of talk –
have shrunk like burned peas
on a too hot stove.

But why, sir? Surely . . .
There is no more *surely*.

Madre de la Vida

The great Aztec statue of Life and Death.

I

There is a Virgin perhaps for every heartache,
santissima or *dolorosa*,
          for the day of abscess, the eve of childbirth,
for the hour of truth which was always doubted
yet commended to her as a child
          places its doll to catch early shade,
as the bull is offered merely by laying
the cape across a rail, which says *here, yours*.

Mistress of swords, of roses,
          share like any mother
the ways of blight or hunger,
the graze of rice at the bride's throat.

          With two heads
   pouring from hacked arteries
   with a necklace of severed hands
   with her cincture of skulls for baubles
   her feet the claws of jaguars or eagles
   the older rival towers,
          patient as plague.

Indifferent as fire, gifted
   with her thousand skills in snarling hope,
she hears with the strength of stone
   the gossip of water.
          Knows how sun will choose.

II

The female spider with distended belly,
the bride turning from the wall to show her skull,
the queen bee embracing her succession of cadavers –
these are trove from one pocket
          of the Lady Mountain,
madonna of rape, of honed edges,
of guts melting at her threatened service.
She is nature without our classical clutter,
without mind's ambitious tinkering
at her dropped dugs, pouched belly,
          inconsolable maw.
She slips over talk of love like a cobra's hood.
She is time making of Christ what she made of Tammuz,
Of Maui, Cuchuláin, Quetzalcoatl, Baal.
She is dark packed close as brick
          with the ash of suns.

Telling the Neighbours

Back on green sward and Anchor butter
I can afford to think 'culture shock'
when my friends ask me and I tell them
of San Cristóbal, of Quezaltenango,
the names like tail-feathers
            on the famous bird I never saw.
I avoid that pretentious phrase
as too close to home, and so speak of contrast,
colour, pick out images most vivid
for those who wait to hear them,
let the sequins of the bull-killers wink in the sun.
But the fact is too awkward to hand across
with the gems from Queretero, or the silver rings.
It is daylight here to begin with, and there, night,
there the stone hill who appals us, the composite
goddess.
       When my neighbour asks
'How was it?' I think of ten this evening,
of early morning at the world's sharper edge –
when the light there stretches a yellow whip
that may touch, to begin with, her taloned feet,
rise to her serpent skirt, her feathered knees,
strike the skull she wears like a buckle,
the human thing about her – when we wind the clock,
drop coins in bottles, run our baths,
about then, you might see the answer.
                        That's how it is.

Resthaven

This morning we have opened
the Home for the Elderly
and Vogel Street did itself proud.

The Minister spoke
and the Rotarians applauded
and all in all it was pretty impressive.

The public stood at the bedroom doorways
approved of the deep-pile carpet
remarked on the comfy lounge and the widescreen telly.

It was beautiful Waikato morning
a top-dresser flew over the macrocarpa
the loudspeaker blared from the junior athletics

and the truth of yellow earth was never touched on.
The old woman with a silver-tipped cane
the man whose wife

must sleep in a different wing
smile shakily at us
their eyes crinkle against the sunlight,

say Thank you so much
for coming to see us off,
thank you for good wishes and applause

as they step inside
to the lobbyful of gladioli
and decorative fern,

where they keep smiling
at their families on the other side
like astronauts just before the countdown.

Only Natural Things

Here are garden things she loved,
For her eyes we look
At wisteria in her birthday's month
That falls across pine and back
Towards the house and the shaded room
Where I and my children take

Not a sprig of that blue flare
For our grieving's badge,
Not a branch where it leans on the pine
Or at the path's rough edge,
But the lift of the sky it seems, from here,
The crammed sky, as pledge.

There is no day among September days
Not that vine's natural
Stage between scarcely hinted
And immeasurably full,
Hail at month's far beginning,
At month's end, *Farewell*.

From *Butcher, Baldy, Related Matters*

Butcher Talks on Time

'Well' Butcher says 'they're all in for an end
the old stuff with its tall columns
the middle stuff with its pointy arches
the jumble of all the others
stations palaces airports racetracks.
That's the only vision *I* know.
Dust to dust.'
        His cleaver glints
up and down through the ribs. He breaks
the cage, there's nothing to fly out.

(A small blob of kidney in the sawdust
could though be canary's head, gone ruffly.)
Time's the sweat under his armpit
Sheila's quick grunt (lovely!)
it's the thin needle white as God
knocking the figures back
when your foot's right down.

'Well' says B. again 'we're all in for an end.'

From *Brother Jonathan, Brother Kafka*

8

On the day my father died a flame-tree
with its stiff immaculate flares cupped over
the leafless branches outside the hospital window
said for us several things voice could not get round to,

yet not only and not foremost the riding of life
above the stark branches nor the perfect *Fin*
once the work is done, as though time's shining
is when the match is struck and is over, so.

It spoke, each opening red fist only feet from dying,
of small errors, of mornings forgotten by afternoon,
of words taken or words put down lightly
as a glass, or laid like a single log on a fire,

or touched as the head of a child absently
while other words moved on; the looks,
brushings, immediate treasure, the cusps of morning
lifting as sky lightens the withholding tree.

25

We stood by the children's playground in a famous square,
remember, by a sandpit, where you saw your first squirrel?
You leaned forward like a woman over a bassinet,
your hands together more or less as the squirrel's.

And a week later we sat on a lawn
in Richmond, Virginia, under longstanding oaks
where half-a-dozen, larger, better-fed, moved out
and glanced us over and went about their scuffing

or chafed the midsummer leaves a few feet above us.
We talked about how their Greek name means 'shadow-tail'
then tried to close our eyes till the giant ants
drove us to haunt the streets in Edgar Poe's town –

and since then no shortage of ravens, to put it cutely.
And I liked seeing a squirrel today, so long after,

because bitterness was not possible, nor regret, nor pondering
time and change and the rest – not while he looked and dabbled.

32

A young bee falls between my window
and the wire screen. It slips as it climbs at one,
is caught with legs and rough belly against the mesh
of the other. I raise the screen slightly and it shoots

across to sunlight, a small furred bullet.
So another, five years ago, I remember, catching
beneath an infant's singlet and stinging his chest.
The child clutched his breath, looked it seemed with appalling

wisdom at those who fussed about him, who
rubbed ointment on the red welt, carried
the bee to the porch in a scrap of paper
and stamped it on the boards.
                    The boy looked and moved

his head to take in the kitchen, the relations,
the afternoon of his first summer, the pain rising
on his body while he still forbore crying . . .
                    On, on through endless summers,
the look of the boy looking, the bee never crushed.

43

There is a day when elaborate weathers ease down
to a harbour held so simply in the meeting of hills
as water cupped by the two hands of a child
who then stands, surprised that his hands hold it.

And so today: the air, the mild edging stumble
of sea beneath the highway, along the sand
which is unwalked on since the last tide smoothed it,
a few men leaning or sitting on the rail,

who spit across their shoulders or grab the bar
beneath them as gymnasts about to swing themselves outward.
A morning of intimations, on the point of mornings
when the backyard leaves may be suddenly yellow

and the cold grains of frost are on the steps like salt.
There is this delicate pause which is intricate, turning,
the day which is pivot to commissioned seasons.
I write it to let you know why I cup my hands.

In Parliament Grounds

The sparrows are taking Seddon
seriously enough to try

making a nest between his feet
that can't – not in this town,
its winds, its preordinations –
last beyond tomorrow noon,
or Friday at latest.

Even the trouser cuffs of the great
can't protect past that.
Yet being sparrows they persist,
they get on with living
between the very feet
of big bronze death,
they work at perdurable shacking

against season,
against weather,
against the choler of experts.
With sparrows, again, perspective
is with means, as ends:
their squabble is with a straw
that almost gets away.

On Sunny Days, a Thinker

He prefers to think of insubstantial rock,
of tangible sky, while he sits, his senses eased
into paradox, completion, above

the actual glint of crystal in the razzled
quartz, beneath the blue expanse
his fingers dream to tap at as a thrush's egg.

There is no point (he instructs) in the mere fact
without mind's regular trimwork
fitting, fattening it, thus; nor in mind's attending

on tendencies, directions, the depths
and heights, the invariable measures,
without actual axe to chip it, without lucre's ring.

So he tos and fros.
His thinking hutches out, it nibbles,
dashes among stalking things, among tall terrors;

at *see it! touch!* he is hived inward,
broods thick richness the colour of painted sunlight
in a room buzzing behind drawn curtains.

Neither Platonist proper then, nor true believer
in his own corner's intrinsic squareness,
his eyes open, close, open, on worlds never there.

K. O. ARVIDSON

The Tall Wind

He said to them, Look at this: you see
where the tall wind leans against your window-pane?
And they said Yes; the cold has come again.
Which being true, he dared not disagree.

Instead he said, If that wind once more blows
like that, your house will fly away like straw.
But they, of course, had thought of that before.
And also, though he did not dare suppose

they might have done, they'd seen a dead man lain
for laundering on half a fallen tree.
He thought, How strangely that man looks like me;
and said aloud, With luck there'll be no rain . . .

and just as he spoke, it started in to pour.
One of them laughed, and one said, Thar she blows:
we'll find out now what this young charlie knows.
There's a tall wind out there, leaning on our door.

Fish and Chips on the Merry-Go-Round

In caves with a single purpose
fish were drawn deliberately
from room to room.
Pallid Romans employed them
in a kind of masonry.
They even had their own day of the week.
Before that, though,
presumably,
before the nails from Calvary went back
like bullets into the dove on Ararat,
there must have been a fish or two
sharked many a household bare,
great bloated sunfish, ogling octopi,
between the bedstead and the hearth with relish
tearing apart all shining, arkless men,
competing for the viscous eyeballs loose
like opals on the suffocated floor.

A seasonable peripety assures
contemporary hygiene,
symbol and ancestor alike
hosed out, or splintered off.
Little, or large as eels, fish
fodder us; best of all
on the six days in between.
They build us up.

Still,
on a slow wheel, sharpening fins
give glints.

The Four Last Songs of Richard
Strauss at Takahe Creek above
the Kaipara

1. Frühling

(Hesse)

Waking's urgency, that sets
the day's track of desire, I deem
instinctive, right as the opening flower.
It surely leads me. Newer the sense of sky,
of skittering cloud, of new winds in the marram
murmuring. Gulls go blithely. And on the terrace,
north, and over the formal lawn,
the air itself sings freshly of my love,
its sweet betokenings, its fierce and morning
certainty.
          In what sense is it I regret
the harbour's tranquillity? Sun upon water,
and small lights murderously encroach
of elements at ease, in subtle harmony.
Eyes against eyes. And my eyes briefly wish
the whips of wind back, and the speed of rain,
the water's winter trepidation. Peace,
and the promise of this rising tide,
betray me; even in such a morning;
even in all this complement I find
to my conviction, fixity of dear pain,
anguish of the rose unfolding
in beauty once again.
          But the time
does lead me; and I breathe
consuming fragrances.

2. September

(Hesse)

I am assembled here, at ease
in foreboding. I have measured the shadow
dying, and the brilliant wind
is alive with new things, lambs and petals and light,
asserting permanence. And yet,
this little thrush, that madly
flew through the scents of newness, now
grows cold within my hand. Strange noon,
to smite so casually, to freeze so small a thing
and drop it on warm grass!

I watched this little bird. It sped like a thistle
recklessly, bucketing on the air,
and very loud: implying, I think,
mortality, because I watched it all the way
from the long soft grass through that abandonment
to the tree so landmark-large, to the last and sudden
blindness, staggering ecstasy, light
singing
        death.
              I am assembled here, at ease
in foreboding. And my desire?
My love should bury this with love.

My love would not. My love would
toss it in the air.

3. *Im Abendrot*

(von Eichendorff)

The far Brynderwyns heave across the harbour,
rising upon the second tide, mountains
in mangrove moving, weaving
the last complexities of the sun. These
are a tangle of reflections. Over them,
the next peninsula shines yellow,
pastoral century of slow change,
and the roofs of pioneers, like beacons, prophesy
the imminence of fishermen, their lights
alive and casting, quick
to be out before the strong tide sucks and runs.

    I sing of our long voyaging,
    and you who led me, at my side;
    I sing the saddest of all things;
    I sing the unaccomplished bride.

The hills will cease to float soon, and the mangroves.
ripple themselves away.
The wandering flames of grass will calm, and the cattle
boom night's gullies up and down. My lights
will anchor a headland. Boats will take bearings,
seeking the channel; and then,
the Kaipara will move out.
A shag clap-claps in shallows.
I point the way to an open sea,
though all my doors are closed,
and I within.

    Go slowly, sun. A gentle death
    of day is in the birds that wheel
    in clouds to their accustomed rest,
    and in the racing of the keel

before the racing of the tide,
and in the crowding of dark trees.
I sing the unaccomplished bride.
I sing my death in all of these.

There Was a Day

There was a day. There was a day
I gave her daffodils. That
was an August day, and I who gave
took beauty. She is older now,
but her age for me is still of that fine spring.
I do her injustices with daffodils
to keep it that way. Light of the blooms,
                    susurrus of their almost
paper trumpets,
                    wince of fingers folding
the florist's waxed bedeckings;
                    memory,
                    fugue,
                    effigy;
memory only,
fugue in manuscript only,
effigy only,
                    these she knows;
the memory of what was possible weighted down,
crushed corms of conversation, the prothalamium
scored on a priceless vellum silent. Silence.
Daffodils. White limbs in the moon. Pavan.
I do her injustices.
There was an August day.
She is older now.

MICHAEL JACKSON

Return from Luluabourg

My report is not of schools
we built out there, or market gardens
planted to help the poor
but of an evening after work
when through a ruined iron gate I saw
a garden overgrown with weeds
and entered it.

Before me rusted boats, swings
dislodged like giants on a dungeon rack,
seesaws split, unpainted, thrown aside,
a wall from which I could not turn my back,
my own hands tied.

That concrete prison drop was set
with broken glass along the top,
bottles once put to European lips
at evening on a patio.
I climbed a metal staircase,
looked across a land scarred red,
huts roofed with grass on which
bone-like manioc roots were dried
to rid them of their arsenic.

But poisons which had touched that place
still kept it out of bounds;
pleasures were gone, children's voices
were not heard
except beyond that wall, in villages
or in the dusk, the garden, one night bird.

Fille de Joie: Congo

Lips caked with lipstick
And the smell of booze
You dance with the man of ten thousand francs
Until the music moves him to
Take you to the room where the rite will be.

Preferring him not
To put out the light
You remove a bonnet of dead women's hair
Beneath which you jealously preserve
Stiff twirls of the African coiffure.

Down to your silken underthings
Breasts astir
And his own undoing scarcely seen
You are the cur under midnight heat

Of a mad dog doing it
For what in Europe would have been love.

A Marriage

In a room of black enamel, gold
filigree, two schemed to love;
often must they have been like us,
one stood at this window looking down
into a maze, the clouded waters of
the moat, the other recollected
something of that first far meeting,
a hunting party in the White Chateau
and the cold hills near Orleans.

Now it is all embellishment, grace
of swans, eglantine under snow
and barking hounds, is woven on
the legendary cloth that hangs
upon the spontaneity of dawn;
by a lucid river, how could our love
go on? I turn from reverie
to welcome you, in whom the sound
of hunting in the forest ends
a pale fox dead on a green lawn.

Pioneers

Someone took a photograph of them
standing in a clay track,
a winter frontier town
a hundred years ago.

Surrounded by forest
in an archive of silences
I cannot believe them gone.

I have imagined a grave
marked by a pine slab
and run my fingers over the rain blurred
braille of their origins.

I have woken to the traffic
of the rain, pine branches
waved like river water
and a workman shovelling in the dark

And I have seen them again
the sepia of their expressionless faces
in the bush they cleared.

What do they want me for?

I am theirs and of them and for them speak.
My hands have gone over the roofs and gullies
of their names.
These hills I live under are their doing.
I have been given what they got,
I am what they became.

River Man

Should have a name
months drowned
should be known by now
this pilfered remnant of a man
they pulled from the river

Should have a wife a girl a
mother who has listed him missing
this sack in its cold cabinet
they joke about in the morgue,
that the eels enjoyed
that snags held up to ridicule
in the tow
that gravel by the bridge scoured
of fingerprint and finger,
whose mushroom skin
was the worms' home

Should have a name by now

But only this stretch of pebbled
water that yielded him,
all night and daylong
elbowing the shore
where tractors haul the eel traps out
in winter, and horses shy.

And his trade,
this lout of the weed and silt?
Scrubbing the stone
steps of the hill,
paving the sky
with the cement of his stare,
and with his pumice hands
rummaging through our lives
for a name.

The Moths

Our house had filled with moths,
a slow silting of lintel and architrave
a cupboard dust,
until I looked much closer
and found the wood-grain one,

the white quill paperbark, the blotched
shadow of a patch of bush,
an elbowing riverbank that had gone deep blue.

The soft perimeter of forests
had entered our house
fluttering around the moon.

Then for five days they drowned
in sinks and pools or seemed to wane
into sanded wood or ash on windowsills
until they became
what they were when I first noticed them;
fragments of a dull interior.

RACHEL McALPINE

Zig-zag up a thistle

i

A lot has changed here since the day
he left.
Fig trees have thrust up
their chubby fists,
tiny thumbs are dangling
from the sycamores,
cabbage tree rococo
in her blonde embroidered plaits,
fuschia bleeding pointedly
from every joint.

Some things remain the same:
the cat is happy.

And my fridge is over-full
of half-forgotten love,
marbled with islands of mould.

ii

It's hard to fix your pronouns.
I was happy with 'me'.
Then we made an effort to be 'us'.
He retreated, I had to learn
'you' and 'him'.

I still say 'There are fig trees
in our street.'
I belong to many an us:
the family long and wide,
the human race.
Nobody lives alone.

Romans began their verbs incognito.
I (a part of us) got
two Christmas presents.
A Latin grammar once belonging
to my mother's grandmother.
A four leafed clover
which I keep between
'idem, alius, alter, ceteri'
and 'hic, iste, ille, is'.

iii

I used to have a friend and people said
how strong she was. I sanded
the banisters yesterday.
If only she were here! Her eyes
are nimble and her fingers slick
with putty, brush, plaster.

Today you touched my breast and so
I must be near. Thank you, thank you.
If I could find my friend
I might supervise your loving.

A final decision every day.
I check the calendar:
so far, thirty-two – nil.
Poetry's algebra,
love is arithmetic.
Some people say we are living
lives with a shape.

iv

Sometimes you forget your lines
and have to act them out
again. This time,
should I flatter him, or cringe?

I have had such an urge to tidy up.
But I can work in a mess
and I usually do.

There is no
single perfect gesture,
and there is no amen.
The world will ad lib without end.

v

My children call me Mum.
I see the damn sun
jump off the hills
and fork the clouds again.
And Reagan's let me down:
where's his nerve?

I submit to the children
and the sun
and prod my black words
to grudging margins.

vi

Suddenly there are the words
I want to hear.
Sleep comes slopping,
belly's off the boil.
Please God let me think
like this tomorrow!

But others have also hosed me
with their insights:
Be firm. Be passive.
Be frank. Be quiet.
Be glad.
Each one dirties the one before.

The self-adjusting law of Lauris:
you may not have what you long for
till you cease to crave.

vii

On a dry hill I look
at small brave lives

A lark aspires to the orgasm
of a Pegasus. A ladybird
uses cocksfoot
for tightrope and trapeze.
Spiders zig-zag up a thistle.
Butterflies rely entirely
on their buoyant colours.

No one but the skylark travels
in a straight line.
The rest of us polka and pussyfoot.

viii

The dandelion opens twice,
first to a dominant gold.
Then discarding petals
it clamps up tight,
and leggy seeds develop
in its grip.
And later – froth.

Love must change or die.
The future needs no feeding,
no permission.
It is white.
It happens somewhere else.

Love, work, children.
Angels fly on
two wings.

                    ix

A good decision, that,
deciding to live, and properly.
Down on the beach it's hard to play
the tragedy queen for long.

Fathers watch their toddlers waddle,
lollipops laze in candy togs,
the sea explodes
with kids and yellow canoes.

You popping seed-pod of a world,
I love you, I love you,
let me come in!

        Surprise surprise

I expected Sydney women
to be warm, lovely, sensible, lovely,
generous, lovely, and lovely,
lovely,
the way women are.

I expected the men
to have bristly necks
to leave me outside the pub
with the dogs
and to shout me an apron
for a real good time.

I was right about the women.
I was wrong about the men.

Now isn't that always the way?

DAVID MITCHELL

ponsonby/remuera/my lai

th warrior's come home
there he goes!
right
  here
    & now

up queen street
in a gun carrier

palm to th clear brow
in th oldest, most obscene
salute
  & in th eyes
th mandrake root –

th blackened bone.

2 million years
have proved nothing
he did not already know
ah! there he goes!

th kiwi's come home.

he
sits in th barber's chair
'short back & sides'
& he
lingers in th chemist
buying coloured slides
& he
ponders on time / yeah. &
destiny; /
   also th fates . . .
& he
sits in th kitchen
playing poker with his mates
& he
contemplates his hand
& he
holds a king
    to each soft lip
in turn

& th others pass
(& he waits his turn)

& 30 seconds pass
& he
    plays his hand
&
    children burn.

        yellow room

he is sitting in th cafe lebanon
& his legs are crossed beneath th balls
& th traffic in th street is slow . . .
&
he is waiting, while he is sitting in th cafe lebanon
fr something GREAT to happen . . .
&
her face, in the mirror on th wall
reflects her boredom . . .
&
his face, is in th mirror, too
looking 'deep'

but all he's thinking is:
'that waitress is asleep'
&
there comes a curious palpitation in th traffic
& th green bus goes by. there it goes!
      (it has gone)
&
his balls ache
while he is sitting in th cafe lebanon
waiting fr something GREAT to happen
(his balls are waiting, too)
yet
he cannot bring himself to uncross his legs –
his balls . . .
&
he is smoking
while he is sitting in th cafe lebanon
waiting fr something GREAT to happen

. . .

now
outside th traffic has jammed up; stopped
completely
&
his cigarette burns down; goes out
&
she scratches her wrist; absent minded
glazed eyes gone yellow with winter
&
now she is scratching with th other hand
& outside th bus driver cuts his idling engine
&

they are still
                    sitting in th cafe lebanon
waiting for something GREAT to happen

&
that seems to be all –

o yeah.

&

A FINE RAIN BEGINS T'FALL.

lullaby/blazing house

(for sara)

child's painting; devonport naval dockyards
harbour sunset; tree; man; princess; long
jet aeroplane; blazing house; angel; etc.

hey, little chicken legs, how come you cry?
red is a find / do not fear red
though mars shine baleful through this evening
sky . . .
        th gone sun / like old father time
will tell you / tomorrow
                        tomorrow belongs
to no tradition you cannot create; hey . . .
red is not final / do not fear red
                        red is a find / red
                    is a fine
                                tomorrow

ah! my pisces child! I cannot snare th moon
though I have tried / throw you instead
a small & falling star . . .
let it be green / let it be blue
let yr first wish be for peace / also th others
too; th other 2 . . . peace
& a quiet time to dream
(row gently down th stream.)

tomorrow /   th navy disbands & sailors dig pipis
tomorrow /   th air force fails & well, ah; we teach
             them bomber flyboys how to walk . . .
tomorrow /   th army breaks up altogether & soldiers plant grass . . .
tomorrow /   th screaming captains are kind old kings
             again / & they remember how to talk . . .

tomorrow /   th mad butcher goes from our street
tomorrow /   each of th 4 black horses dies˙
tomorrow /   there will be born; th fabulous white
             unicorn!

tomorrow /   flowers spring up through steel & concrete
              & th dancing girl flies . . .

tomorrow /   NO HOUSES BURN! / tomorrow there will be
              a feast! & a journey! / &
              a return . . .

red is not final / do not fear red / no; & black likewise.

                    a last word / now
fr yr masters & princes
fr yr madames & fools
                    a last word / now fr yr
teachers & strangers . . .
                    you! who throw switches
                    will never ring changes!
                    voluntary machines!

money / power / comfort / discipline / timetables / uniforms
         THESE ARE TH DANGERS!
& you are to be enlightened / by way of dreams . . .

ah! my pisces child! I cannot snare th moon
though I have tried / throw you instead
a small & falling star . . .
let it be green / let it be blue
let yr first wish be for peace / also th others
too; th other 2 . . . peace
& a quiet time to dream
(row gently down th stream.)

dream on / dream
a silver dream
sally serene . . . (hush now) tomorrow / no body weeps
     . . .   wind in th pines . . .
              a steamer's whistle . . .
                    ah! voyages
                          voyages!

dream on / dream
a silver dream
         sally serene . . . (hush now) . . . she sleeps.

ELIZABETH SMITHER

Mission Impossible

He had been in paradise
Surrounded by a whole flotilla of angels
Each reflecting like mirrors
The warmth of the father;
We'll talk of this later. Well done,
My son. Stand back, to the angels
Their hot wings pressing like a feather
Mattress. Rest tonight and tomorrow
In the room next to mine
Tomorrow when you're feeling recovered
I have a proposition to put to you –
It involves going back. A spasm crossed
The wounds, a few drops of blood fell
On the floor. No not that, my son
But to show there's no misunderstanding between us
Remember the last dark words and the sky
The angels gagged me then by my orders in case
I intervened. Just to see a few friends
Walk round a bit like happier times
Be in their rooms without locks. Console them
Show yourself to the ones who seemed sorry.
The angels will take care of the stone.

Did he smile early on Sunday
Smelling the spices in his wounds
Tasting the white walls of the tomb
With his eyes, the fresh air of morning?

Man watching his wife in a play

In the second scene she has to strip
To underthings. It shocks a bit:
The bedroom scene he ignores each day
Sending a ripple through the audience.
Those gestures that used to captivate
Captivate now a wider span
The indrawn breath sucks in his ear
He angrily searches out the sound
He's blasé by the curtain fall
Damn it all, he owns the lingerie!
No acting on the stage compares to his
As he meets her by the dressing room.

Temptations of St Antony by his housekeeper

Once or twice he eyed me oddly. Once
He said Thank God you're a normal woman
As though he meant a wardrobe and went off

Humming to tell his beads. He keeps
A notebook, full of squiggles I thought, some
Symbolism for something, I think I've seen
It on lavatory walls, objects like chickens' necks
Wrung but not dead, the squawking
Still in the design, the murderer running.
He's harmless, God knows. I could tell him
If he asked, he terrifies himself.
I think it makes him pray better, or at least
He spends longer and longer on his knees.

Visiting Juliet Street

All the streets are named after Shakespeare.
Hamlet and Juliet are separated by an intersection
Down which floats Ophelia Street, very sleepy.
They are all such demanding people
Which lends the town an air of tragedy
As though Mercutio coming home after a party
Failed to dip his lights and ran over
Polonius Street right up onto the sidewalk.
Even Shakespeare thought it best to keep them separated.
At the end of long girlish Juliet Street
With limbs like Twiggy the air grows
Sleepier and sleepier as though
Juliet had anorexia nervosa and could hardly bear
A morsel of blossoms or any sap.

*Fr Anselm Williams and Br Leander Neville hanged
by Lutheran mercenaries in 1636 while out of their
monastery on a local errand of charity – from the
guidebook to Ampleforth Abbey and College.*

'We'll see who can stick
Their tongue out first for God
Out of you two,' binding the hands
The flowers in the hedgerows starting
The sky turning over with a lurch
As when Brother Leander dropped the eggs.
They wouldn't be back to Compline
The hedgeroses looked askance now.
A swallow passed. Their hands touched
Just the fingertips like passing a note.
The tongues would come out later
Into an air gone blue, a world.

From *Casanova's Ankle*

Casanova's ankle

Casanova was turned by an ankle
Over and over. His glance ascended

To towers of conquest, snares set
In the shade of trees. Too bad
He had to toil as well in the trap
To free the booty used
And stained by capture. Distasteful
Somehow what he possessed
When the time for possession came.
It was better in the stalking light
With the moon half-hid
Following the scented glove, the ankle.

Casanova the technician

Call me in like a mechanic. I can fix
All malfunctions of the flesh
Who cares for love when I subdue
The will to an ache and a place?

Love is for time and I cannot spare
Longer than a ribbon or a song
But am I not more in tune
With the comings and goings of birds?

I was born a technician. Some might call in
A doctor, a quack or a surgeon
Only at love can they call me charlatan
My technique was perfection.

Casanova's pied-à-terre

Time to take off the dust sheets and go through
The list of black addresses, code
The letters and file them, burn some
Wash the hands in ashes, hope the heart
Plucked from the fire will endure
In someone's pocket. Endure in a laboratory more like
Unless I sleep some nights single
On a camp bed, lamp lowered, diary gutted.

Casanova and the shop dummy

Yesterday I saw your torso
Carried by a clerk in a waistcoat
Levitating between alleys and dustbins.
I followed scenting a fish head.
Today behind a screen he dresses you
A tape over his shoulder divides the dandruff
His hands nervous and I observe
A pair of scuffed patent leather shoes.

Madam, I salute you.
So often was the process reversed

But this is proper, your deserts
Nakedness deserves covering in any case.

Casanova and the residues of indifference

At the amusement parlour
The fellatio clowns
Taking balls into their mouths
With the o of choirboys
Singing Palestrina

Remind me of calendars
Circled around and dropped clothes
Satin lamps, the latest books
And the night turned back
Like a quilt.

PETER OLDS

'Before the Wandering Wind Finally Dies'

I was looking to find a cup of tea
to drop my head into, to change the perspective
of my dreams and the reality of the morning
when you screamed 'Don't throw me anymore questions –
I've had enough of your insane bedroom shithouse!'

Then you, sick in the guts from chemicals and 22 years
membership in the club for unwanted mothers,
abort yourself by climbing the wall looking for Fred
the dizzy needle freak . . .

He enters, swinging from
a 3 A.M. powerline, screaming 'Today I have stopped
inventing words until further notice.'

Seeing you, he yells blindly
'Are you the one who is hooked to the twisted
man who dreams of incredible Fame?'
'Yes,' she says pointing a bleeding finger at me.
'No,' I protest, 'I write poems under the influence of shit.'

Fred had no strength to argue, so
taking with him, Lady Moss, Midnight Queen,
(the 2 motorcycle nuts) they vanish down the road.

I climb up from the floorboards to write my last bedroom
words to submit to psychiatric editors –
to the also-switched-in-know-it-all powerline
by the name of Civilized Shocktreatment.

Alone at last with my friendly friend Paranoia,
we dance
before the wandering wind finally dies.

My Mother Spinning

Sit too close
& the spinning bobbin cools you.
Leave the room
& the foot pedal beats
on a raw nerve.
Leave the house

& a thread of wool follows.

The Nightman

Once a week he came
whispering past my six year old cot,
his grey horse snorting in the frost
gravel moonlit road
while my parents and brothers and sister slept
in their hotwaterbottle beds.

Like a black ghost he coughed
his shadowed way
to the whitewashed outhouse
to collect our limetopped deposit,
and like a demon perfected
hoisted the can without spilling a drop
on a shoulder as big as hell.

From the depths of my pillow
I feared him the outcast uncle.
But in the morning, Mother wouldn't
hear of it. Denied knowledge of him
in the face of our breakfast porridge.
So it seemed, his job was an act of God,
not that of giving new turds more freedom.

Still, week after week his faceless frame
came – shining his lamp
on the private parts of man,
without a grumble, whipping through
the drunken clouds and gone . . .

Then came the age of septic tanks.
I remember the day ours got blocked
and a specialist was called. Bentbacked
and black he plunged the problem away.
'These things have clogged the brightest of brains,'
he grinned
wiping his hands on a grubby piece of sack –

and like a ghost was gone.

Thoughts of Jack Kerouac – & Other Things

I work nights at the University Bookshop:
Junior, Intermediate, Headman, Honorary Caretaker,
Master Cleaner. I work in every conceivable position
from toilets, Foreign Language to Herbal Cookery,

sometimes singing 'Oh What a Beautiful Evening' and
sometimes not. Mostly, I just race about like
Neal Cassady with an overstuffed vacuum
cleaner snarling on my tail, cornering fast on one

sneaker past SUPERWOMAN and gassing like a madman up the BIOGRAPHY Oneway Section – chewing-gum,
cigarette-butts, paper-clips and brains dissolving before
my foaming fury . . . Zap, out the back, empty a tin,

grab a bucket one mop one broom, flash back
past LAW, Modern PSYCHOLOGICAL Medicine, Heavy
Granite Colour-filled Graffito ART, Sex Cornered
PAMPHLETS, miles of wrapping paper and up the stairs

to the staff room for a coffee break at 8. Ten
minutes only. Into the toilets, scrub shine wipe
on hands and knees, sometimes thinking 'The Closest
I Come To God and Other Things' and sometimes not.

Mostly, I just thank the Lord for the Detention
Centre Experience many Rocky Youthful Years back
and get the hell out of there down the stairs (4 at
a time), jump over a hot PAN Paperback, switch off

the lights (5 second silence by the NZ POETRY
Section), scratch my backside, straighten the doormat,
lock up, slam the outside door tight, run to the pub
(9 PM), sweat, feel proud, get half drunk,

crawl home, sit down, try to write a love poem
to a girl who works in the Bookshop Office . . .
Her typewriter and hairpin, her mystery yoghurt con-
tainers, her tiny footscuffed secrets and solitary chair.

E Flat

I've got this flat, see,
& it's got in it this piano
which I don't play,
but I've got a guitar –
you know, the lonely instrument –
& I use the piano's E Flat string
(which happens to be the only one that works)
to E Flat tune the guitar's 6th string.

Now, a guitar's got 6 strings
& a piano's got about one thousand & two,
while, on the other hand, this room
in this flat has no strings,
not even semi-attached.

I guess the E Flat string
must be the loneliest note I know . . .
But I'm not silly, see –
when I play the guitar
I always pick the chord of D –

well, D Sharp, actually.

BRIAN TURNER

The Stopover

When the trout rise like compassion
it is worth watching

when the hinds come down
from the hills
with a new message

it will be as well to listen

Late Winter Snow

(for Phil and Steve)

The child has never been older
than in August
snow blanketing the countryside
and we never to be younger
greet the misty morning
sunlight spraying iridescent mountains
across the lake . . .
                 the birch trees sway
like frail dancers,
strings of light merge
and the violas of night put down their bows
as feet move in search of hands to clasp
and I say
        Lead me not into harsh ministrations
of cruellest spring
or the wells of inconsolable days
but down pathways leaf-lined to summer
in the absence of fog,
ladders of rain.

The Initiation

Use a decent length of no. 8:

make sure you get it in deep, right
to the back of the burrow
if you have to.

Push and probe
until you feel the bastard
trying to squirm out of the way

then when you feel you've got it cornered
shove it in
and twist like hell

until you've got the bastard
really wound up
tight (it'll

squeal a bit) then
pull it out slowly
like you were pulling a lamb
from an old ewe's cunt,

then grab it
and break the bastard's neck,

the foreman said.

It wasn't *that* easy.

Trout

The river runs over
and under him slickly.
The bottom is green
and black and dull yellow.

You can hardly see him
for nature's camouflage; trout,
magnificent trout, darkly
speckled, toffee brown.

He lies and swings
with the current. He
pumps like a bellow, slowly.
The water swirls
and purrs over him.

He edges upstream
till his belly rubs gravel,
then he drifts back
and swings turning
downstream, returning
and sinking to nose
among mottle green and white
stones; then

he floats upward,
pouts, takes the fly
from the puckered surface.

Look out, trout.

A Drive on the Peninsula

Sunlight quivers on crater and cone
and shadows reach across the bays

where a sniping wind sweeps
over turbid water. The children

do not count species of birds
or notice sagging fences and derelict houses,

seem unmoved by what is past and passing
and the freedom of gulls

banking high in an empty sky.
The wind tinkers among flax

by the roadside; gravel squirts
from under the wheels; a kingfisher

flies ahead in spurts from wire to wire.
In the carpark at Allans Beach

I stand by the stile
cold as a nail in ice

forehead wrinkling in the shimmering air
while the sea booms beyond the dunes.

Country Hotel

One man with a frown ruining
his once-young features, one woman
by his side and yet, one hopes,
by herself sometimes,
her body collapsing slowly, partly
because of the ravages of duty,
and partly through simple neglect,
her spirit not-quite-devastated
with weary camaraderie . . .
What use to ask or wonder
Where have they been; what do,
and did, their lives mean
to each and one another.

Not that we should grow morose
and feel a swift *frisson*
at the sight of such ordinariness,
two people who happened to touch,
one day, for one moment
when something exciting broke
and left them reeling.

I can tell you this
because it happens to many of us,
because I know how random
whim and randomness are,
how opaque emotion conspires
to drive insight out the door.

Why, only the other day
I held two ducks who were
not quite ready to fly.
A friend had run them down
on the river bed, and rather
than killing and eating them,
decided on photographs instead.

I do not know, entirely,
what this tells of us, of ducks,
of what it *means*, but what I do know is,
that had it been the day before,
or the one after,
things might have been different.

Coming Home

Coming home late through the smoky
fuzz of late autumn, winter rackety
on the elbows of birch trees,
a storm of finches pecking an apple,

I feel some things are never
lost in the conspiracy of the evening,
the garnered and gathered
puddling silences of chill air.

I find you, wet hair glistering,
lying in a bath of foam, so I soap
your back, my hands revived
by your smooth skin, its perfect slither,

and then I go in my dubious mind
to stand in the damp and addling
dark beside the beetle-browed barn
and wait for tribulation to pass, music to begin.

SAM HUNT

A White Gentian

Remember Ruapehu,
that mountain, six months ago?
You sat in an alpine hut
sketching scoria, red
rusted outcrops in the snow.

I climbed some southern peak
and made up the sort of song
men climbing mountains sing:
how, no longer your lover,
I knew it was over.

I thought I'd try out my song
when I returned that evening
as though there were nothing wrong.
Instead I brought a flower down
smelling of the mountain.

A Valley Called Moonshine

(for Josh Andersen)

The lights in the farmhouses
go out. The inlet is out.

An iron shack on the shoreline
floats its light on the water.

A grandfather up Moonshine
remembers the first daughter.

Dreams are easy. Wild horses.

School Policy on Stickmen

It's said that children should not use
stick figures when they draw!
And yet I've lain all night awake
looking at this drawing here
of orange men, stick figures every one of them,
walking up a crayon mountain hand in hand
walking up my wall.

They're edging up a ridge
their backs against the mountain
pinned against my wall.
And every one is smiling.
They know the way a mountain laughs,

especially crayon mountains made of brown.
They know they're not allowed,
these orange men.

I Cried for This Man

It is never before I have cried at
The death of a man I never met –
Nothing at all to do with sentiment

I knew no one who knew him to set
Tears flowing with some whisky anecdote –
The sort of story you hear of the great

How he kept his old mother in comfort
Kept a great mansion for the down-and-out –
I knew no touching stories like that

The reason, pure and simple, was the thought
That when a man dies, then, man, that's it –
I cried for this man, quite by accident

Stabat Mater

My mother called my father 'Mr Hunt'
For the first few years of married life.
I learned this from a book she had inscribed:
'To dear Mr Hunt, from his loving wife.'

She was embarrassed when I asked her why
But later on explained how hard it had been
To call him any other name at first, when he –
Her father's elder – made her seem so small.

Now in a different way, still like a girl,
She calls my father every other sort of name;
And guiding him as he roams old age
Sometimes turns to me as if it were a game . . .

That once I stand up straight, I too must learn
To walk away and know there's no return.

Every Time It Rains Like This

Every time it rains like this:
rain from early morning falling
thick with light: the whole
wide world of our bay
has given in: rain: and nothing any
friend or fisherman can do

Every time it rains like this:
oilskins sweat in boatsheds:
well indoors: all's gone on for
far too long. . . . I am
one with rain, no longer to
that woman there; we're through

Every time it rains like this:
I walk hangover beaches, make
no more sense of it:
in love with a winter woman,
a woman when she steams, I kiss
wet winter lips, return to you

Every time it rains like this

Up Battle Hill

Trees move because the wind
moves them. They rock asleep.
The wind does not let up.
This moment has no end.

Light on the river moves
as if to move away.
Trees, wind, light, river, stay.
As you do too, far loves.

My Father Today

They buried him today
up Schnapper Rock Road,
my father in cold clay.

A heavy south wind towed
the drape of light away.
Friends, men met on the road,

stood round in that dumb way
men stand when lost for words.
There was nothing to say.

I heard the bitchy chords
of magpies in an old-man
pine . . . 'My old man, he's worlds

away – call it Heaven –
no men so elegantly
dressed. His last afternoon,

staring out to sea,
he nods off in his chair.
He wonders what the

yelling's all about up there.
They just about explode!
And now, these magpies here

up Schnapper Rock Road. . . .'
They buried him in clay.
He was a heavy load,

my dead father today.

Birth of a Son

My father died nine months before
My first son, Tom, was born:
Those nine months when my woman bore
Our child in her womb, my dad
Kept me awake until the dawn.
He did not like it dead.

Those dreams of him, his crying
'Please let me out love, let me go!'
And then again, of his dying. . . .

I am a man who lives each breath
Until the next: not much I know
Of life or death; life-after-death:

Except to say, that when this son
Was born into my arms, his weight
Was my old man's, a bloody ton:

A moment there – it could not stay –
I held them both. Then, worth the wait,
Content long last, my father moved away.

BILL MANHIRE

The Elaboration

there was a way out of here:
it went off in the night
licking its lips

the door flaps like a great wing:
I make fists at the air
and long to weaken

ah, to visit you
is the plain thing,
and I shall not come to it

A Death in the Family

His face is gone golden with the dusk
You would think he burned, he burned

We came without invitation
We did not follow the highways

Trees we went beneath, bending
Then climbed the stone walls

Golden, golden, and he.has not spoken
We sent so many missives

Let us go brother, let us go sister
Open the gates, how can we remain?

He will not answer us
His eyes blaze out beyond us

His face is gone golden with the dusk
You would think he burned, he burned

The Old Man's Example

These drifting leaves, for instance
That tap my shoulder
Come along with us, they say
There are one or two questions
We should like to ask you

The snow

Men are singing by the willows
as your boat passes upstream,

drawn by other men, waist-
deep in water. You pass as clearly
over: hands of
the wind, the solemn parting.

In the dream, you fell into
the story, a light
in the mountains, and the people
seeking it. High up, snow
kept falling: its small wings rose
to shake the darkness.

Movement in and out of sleep,
you tell the simple pattern.
Each minute it will soon be evening:
a scarf of earth,
your wrist in earth,
the old sad planet's voices.

The proposition

the week it
snowed, the day the
footpaths didn't matter,
I wanted to get

a number of things
straight, but didn't:
and the next day, when
people were out

again, driving, you said
let's take ourselves
off, into the country,
to a cave, or that

kind of expedition: I bent,
tentative, over the
table, and cracked my
knuckles: would you

care to be more
precise about whatever
it is you are
saying, I said

The pickpocket

We get on well together.
We vie with each other in politeness,
promising no special treatment.
We contradict ourselves constantly.

Look at those people. She leads him
round by the nose, they are always bickering.
He is nurturing a viper in his bosom:
she must have applied for the post.

But, what a day! The favourite lost
by a neck. We lost everything but the clothes
we stood up in! I wish you
good fortune with all my heart.

The song

My body as an act of derision,
eating up the answers to life.
There is the bird-song, now,
elbowing through berries while
the hairs in my nose catch
at the little bits of existence.

And I know you go on living
because you need to be cared for.
I embrace you, I kiss you,
trusting in an ordered development,
watching the small explosions
under your wrists.

Oh we survive merely by good fortune,
by random appetite: going
outside to lie on our stomachs
as if we meant to swim in the earth,
floating near the dazed horizon,
giving this music into the light.

A Song About the Moon

The moon lives by damaging the ocean
The moon lives in its nest of feathers
The moon lives in its nest of clamps
The moon lives by aching for marriage
The moon is dead, it has nothing to live for

The bodies are dangerous, you should not touch them
The bodies resemble our own, they belong together
The bodies are weapons, someone will die of them
The bodies will not lack for wings, someone will find them
The bodies are maimed but you will not remember

Do you still suffer terribly?
Do you always speak French?
Do you stare at the moon for you cannot forget it?
Do you long to be emptied of nothing but feathers?
Do you want to go on like this almost forever?

You must abandon everything after all
You must abandon nothing at least not yet
You must abandon hilarity
You must abandon your flags
You must abandon your pain, it is someone else's

You must abandon poetry for you cannot forget it
You must abandon poetry, it never existed
You must abandon poetry, it has always been fatal
It is like the moon, it is like your body
It is like the ocean, it is like your face

Children

The likelihood is
the children will die
without you to help them do it.
It will be spring,
the light on the water,
or not.

And though at present
they live together
they will not die together.
They will die one by one
and not think to call you:
they will be old

and you will be gone.
It will be spring,
or not. They may be crossing
the road,
not looking left,
not looking right,

or may simply be afloat at evening
like clouds unable
to make repairs. That
one talks too much, that one
hardly at all: and they both enjoy
the light on the water

much as we enjoy
the sense
of indefinite postponement. Yes
it's a tall story but don't you think
full of promise, and he's just a kid
but watch him grow.

An Outline

First we disowned parents
because they always said *after*;
and friends promised to be around
but were not. Our teachers gave
encouragement and then prescribed
the lonely flower inside the brain.
One showed a picture
but soon would kick the bucket.

At home, away from home, but mostly
nowhere special, we took our own advice.
We got in the car and then just drove
along the road past cliffs and river,
and when we stopped
we slept on the parchment floor,
taking it for the real thing.
We wrote out the poem and slept on it.

Still, there was nothing good for us in words,
or nothing couched in formal English,
while being good itself was good for nothing,
and then again there was always something
coming next, though no particular direction.
The baby lay in its cot and cooed
or it lay afloat in water inside mother.
When once that baby grows, we said.

and put away the car. We built the house then
by the side of the road
at the end of the road beside the river.
Friends came and were welcome
though many failed to make sense
except in pieces, and others
had only rested quietly by mistake.
All day they took their boats

upon the water. We felt alone
perhaps, but full of promise.
We still possessed the poem in outline,
we had kept some image of the flower in mind.
Now, too, there were provisions, jars of preserves
against the future, photographs to remind
that nothing entered the picture
save cats and children; and the telephone rang

to tell of father's death or just
in other words to ask who's speaking.
We sat by the road and watched

the water tremble as it still stayed perfect.
We woke and slept and that is how
we kept in touch. The children woke in the night
and cried and we sang words to cure.
One crashed the car

and the others soon shot through.
We were young too: we thought
that every goodbye was the last goodbye
and that every last word was made to be careful.
We waved and we waved of course, and now
we find we don't stop waving: believing we see
our life at last, and thinking it over,
knowing how far the road goes home.

IAN WEDDE

From *Earthly: Sonnets for Carlos*

2 for Rose

9

'If thy wife is small bend down to her &
whisper in her ear' (Talmud)

.– what shall I
whisper?   that I dream it's no use any
more trying to hide my follies. If trees &

suchlike don't tell on me I understand
my son will & soon, too. His new blue eyes
see everything. Soon he'll learn to see
less. O the whole great foundation is sand.

But the drought has broken today, this rain!
pecks neat holes in the world's salty fabulous diamond-backed carapace & doubt comes
out, a swampy stink of old terrapin.

What shall I say? 'I hid nothing from you,
but from myself. That I dream, little one,

10

by day & also by night & you are
always in the dream . . .' Oh you can get no
peace, will get none from me. The flower smells so
sweet who needs the beans? We should move house there
into the middle of the bean-patch: a
green & fragrant mansion, why not! Let's do
it all this summer & eat next year. O

let's tear off a piece. It's too hard & far
to any other dreamt-of paradise
& paradise is earthly anyway,
earthly & difficult & full of doubt.

I'm not good I'm not peaceful I'm not wise
but I love you. What more is there to say.
My fumbling voices clap their hands & shout.

Pathway to the Sea

to A. R. Ammons

I started late summer-before-last
    digging for a
        field-tile drain
at the bottom of the garden
    where below
        topsoil that leached away
as fast as I mulched &
    fed it was
        a puggy clay

slick turning rainwater
    frost dew snow sparrow-
        piss & other seepage & drainage down
under an old shed
    in the lower adjoining
        section: here the water
bogged foundations & floorboards
    till the whole crazy
        edifice began to

settle sideways &
    slide on greased clay
        downward
taking a fouldrain with it:
    visions of 'faecal matter'
        bubbling up from clogged
overflow traps bothered
    me & some
        others too: it was time

to act! especially since
    in addition to ordure getting
        spread around &
putting its soft mouths in
    deep cloacal
        kisses to our
livers any obvious
    breakdown in the system for
        disposal of this shit

(our shit) would
    bring the council inspectors round
        like flies
aptly, & *that* would mean
    they'd get to look at
        other aspects of how
we choose to
    live which might strike them as
        unorthodox or even

illegal: for example there's
    lots being done round here
        with demolition
timber, & that's illegal, you gotta
    use *new* timber,
        citizen, the old stuff
which was once forests of kauri &
    totara & rimu took oh
        hundreds of years to get to

where it was when it was
    milled, the house it knit
        together stood & with-
stood 'better' than the forests
    I suppose: the timber
        served, anyway, it
did that for whoever watched
    the process through, &
        now that the houses're out

of phase much as the forests once
    were, though like the
        forests the fibre of the brittle
timber can still spring
    & ring . . . anyhow,
        now it's time
to go, it has to be stamped down, splintered
    by a dozer's tracks & what's
        left of fibre knot

& resin has a match
    put to
        it: it goes 'up
in smoke' – but round
    here we hoard the stuff &
        use it, it easily bends
nails, it splits & you
    belt your thumb often enough
        to know all about that

but the structures
    stay put! & the inspectors
        would say 'Down
with them' – well, down with
    them! . . . I like the way you
        have to compromise with brittle
demolition timber: what gets
    built has bent the
        builder as well as his

nails & nerves: he's
    learnt something about
        service, the toughness of the
medium may have taught him
    that ease is no grateful

              index to dispensability
or availability: like
       who wants a companion for
              life or whatever span

you fancy (they're all 'for life') who can't
       put some juice
              back in your
systems? – ah how you value
       the tough lover who
              keeps you up
to the mark, whose head
       eyes language hands
              loins *en-*

gage you, give you
       elevation, a prospect, with whom you ride
              up the up &
up like birds beating on in
       the mutual updraughts of
              each other's wings – *birds*, a
subject I'll come back to later
       when I'm through with this
              drain: what needs

to be noted here, though, is that even if
       some things don't fight
              back at once or
obviously, you can still
       bet your 'sweet' (for)
              'life'
they fight back all right & your children & children's
       children will be paying *your*
              blood-money; citizen –

well, meanwhile, we agreed, let's
       keep our shit out
              of the public eye & let's
keep our friendly sheds, our lovely slums,
       our righteous brittle screwy
              inspired constructs
up: & then
       let's add some
              flourishes, decoration in this kind

of setting doesn't coddle
       anyone, least of all the chickens
              whose coop's
included in the drainage
       problem threatening to
              overwhelm us
all: besides, we'll all
       benefit: chickens with dry
              feet lay more eggs

because they're happy: happiness
        as a concept may be
            about as brittle as
demolition timber when the latter's traced
        back to its
            forest & the former
to its causes, but it
        serves likewise, it teaches us
            'for life': if you're

for life you're for its crazy outhouses,
        the corners of happiness that don't
            square: right,
there were lots
        of reasons, the practical & the
            ideal didn't separate out,
the forests & the brittle planks
        were one, we
            were *engaged*, we wanted

to convert our drainage problem,
        transform it, *tran-*
            substantiate it, assume it into
the causes of our happiness & the
        happiness of our
            chickens whose wet feet
& poor laying rates
        rebuked us daily – we picked
            up shovels, backed off somewhat,

then we started digging fast, we went at it, we went
        down four feet & then
            two more, there was
all kinds of trash, bottles & old
        sofa springs & broken
            masonry & bricks
& unusual quantities of bones dating
        from a previous owner who'd bred
            dogs, Dobermans (-men?) I

heard, then we began to get
        into the clay
            pug, we were out of
sight by now, the shovels hove
        into view at
            rare intervals,
shaken by
        buried handlers
            to loose the sticky glup:

a comic & as time went by
        popular spectacle: for those
            down in the drain
the strain began to
        tell: some quit, some

    hid, some developed rheums
blisters & trenchfoot, streptococci
    swarmed upon their tonsils,
        they pissed

chills straight from the kidney (it was
    now winter, autumn had
        dallied by among
the easy wreckage of an
    earlier level)
        they defected, deserted,
they offered their apologies, they
    fucked off, the practical &
        the ideal

sprang apart like
    warping unseasoned
        timber, boiiiinngg-
ggg . . . a sound, I
    thought, not
        unlike a drop
on a long rope: what
    deserters got once, & I found myself
        wishing it on them

again as I
    plied my lone shovel, bucket,
        grout, mattock, axe & spade,
baling out the boggy trench
    as the 'drainage problem' halted
        right there, hacking
through roots (that deep!) shoring
    up avalanching walls (the drain – huh! – was
        by now fifty yards

long & in some
    places twelve feet
        deep! impressive even
if left at that) & shaving
    out gummy scoops
        of clay which grunting
I then flicked heaven-
    ward into the blue
        icy sky or

alternatively into the sky
    the low colour
        of clay: clay
anyway, clay & more
    clay, the gobs landed up
        there pretty
randomly after a while, & sometimes
    they got washed
        down again by the late winter

rain, heavy rain, which the
    roots of trees were
        sucking at, sap
beginning to rise in them,
    refreshed by those
        surface-feeding tendrils, those deep
tap-roots, & it's here the
    story really
        starts: not

that what's been said so far's
    irrelevant, though I apologise for its
        disorderly development &
the large number of
    seeming non-sequiturs – things
        do
follow I assure you, they
    proceed, citizen, they practically hunt
        you down, & me, who've

just been enjoying the way
    these lines unfold, much
        more easily than how the pug
& clodded
    marl left that
        drain, landing up there
out of sight & almost
    burying one
        of three baby

fruit trees (we're here) which
    therefore didn't get its tiny
        branches cut
back before the
    sap rose in them as spring came
        on gravely, gaily, with me still down
there in the trench
    still chucking the odd
        clod up & still

covering that pear tree: finally
    a retaining wall
        got built (use
was made of
    used materials) & then a truck
        came with field tiles
& another with shingle & we got
    together some
        used roofing-iron

& we had a drain! Yeah! there
    was enough fall in it to get
        'the problem' drainage
away & out of our way, the chickens
    basked & laid, the clammy surfaces

of seeping banks
dried up, the rotting
    structures with their feet in
        clay delayed their

inevitable demise, miasmal
    damps & soaks breathed
        out their last stinks of mould
& fungus, artesian
    cheeps & kisses of surfacing
        wet were drowned in
birdsong, when the sun shone it
    dried & when the rain fell it ran away
        the way

we wanted: it was
    summer, the leaf
        uncrinkled from the bud
blossom fell, fruit
    spurs plumped out,
        sap circulated with its natural zest,
& one small
    pear tree, un-
        pruned, went

crazy! was a mares-nest
    of wild growth, capillary
        maze of shoots & tangled
twigs gobbling the provisions
    of root & leaf, starch
        & water, sweet open
sandwiches of rotted
    stackbottom & whatnot,
        bonbons

& snacks broken & tasted
    by those bon-vivants the
        earthworms: the whole gusty
catering-service
    served
        that tree whose clusters
congested & grew
    together with ungainly health
        while nearby

the other two grew
    straight sturdy
        & slim, sunlight
entered their hearts,
    they reached up
        heavenwards: 'benighted' is
a word we should have
    the use of
        more often: oh pear tree! in

that condition you'd never
score a single
shrivelled product: well
come autumn I cut you
back till there was almost
nothing left: the lesson
is, effort's got to be directed . . .
yeah, I heard
they wanted to build an

ALUMINIUM
SMELTER
at
Aramoana, the sea-gate, & someone's bound to direct
more effort that
way soon: listen, there's
birds out there, we're
back with those lovers, the buoyancy
& updraught of some kind of

mutual understanding of what
service is, of the fact that
a thing being easy doesn't
make it available or passive:
listen, effort's got to be right
directed, that's
all, the catering's amazing, everything
proceeds, citizen, sometimes
it's hard work, but you're

engaged, you want
to keep practical & ideal
together, you're
for life, you know that happiness
has to do with yes
drains & that nature
like a pear tree
must be served before
it'll serve you, you

don't want your children's
children paying
your blood-
money, citizen, you're
for a different sort
of continuity, you want
to live the way
you want
to, you want to keep

your structures up, you
want elevation,
you're ready to do
your share, you'll dig your field-
drain & you'll

            keep your shit out
of the water supply:
      you want to
            serve & to be left alone

to serve & be served,
      understanding tough
            materials, marl & old timber,
the rich claggy rind
      of the world where
            dinosaurs once
were kings: well they're gone now though
      they survived longer
            than we have

yet, but then we know, don't we,
      citizen, that there's nowhere
            to defect to, & that
living in the
      universe doesn't
            leave you
any place to chuck
      stuff off
            of.

MURRAY EDMOND

My Return to Czechoslovakia

1

This is my return to Czechoslovakia.
Twice in my life I have felt utterly
foreign, staying in a place.
The first was in Prague.
I felt the need to leave behind me
a book I had written myself
– a present for the people I stayed with.
It was as though time stopped
and I needed to rest, and in their house
I rested. At night I rested
and listened to the one cold water tap
running all night in Prague,
running on and on like silence.
By day they took me by the hand
and showed me the churches, the palace,
the cathedral with the tiny window
up high where Kafka wrote and looked down
and saw the drama of K. and the priest.
They took me in hand and led me
down that long side street by the Vlatva
to a place where on a brick
at the corner of a building
at the height of my eye
some one had scratched the name Dubček.
Because nothing seemed to correspond
I needed to leave something complete
that would stay there,
that would live its own life there.
This is my return to Czechoslovakia.

2

The second place I left a book behind me
was Christchurch, night of a lunar eclipse,
and I sat alone in the middle of a garden
perched on a chair, a singular point
in the whole of the Canterbury Plains.
I watched the moon disappear
and thought of myself as the sum
of all the people who went into my making
– my father's stoop, my mother's hands,
grandmother's hips, my Scottish soul,
doctor, preacher, grocer, weaver,
silent, dead, mad and drowned,
and not one present beside me
to watch the moon turn black.
The tide of everything being born and dying

stopped for a time in the eclipse
and I looked right through the window of the moon
– right through into Czechoslovakia.

From *Poems of the End Wall*

House

Last night as I lay beside you all the desire had gone out of me
and I was cast up like a heap of sand, porous, shapeless, shifting,
a thing of shape, an entity, only by virtue of its million parts.

Here I live on a cliff in a tiny house at the end of the island
and in the face of the wind from the north and the wind from the south
I surround myself with this thin wall of wood, this shape in space

and you are there asleep in the bed, curled to the end wall of the house,
your breathing blowing shapes in the cold air, your dreams dreaming,
your dreaming holding up the whole fabric of paint and wood and tin.

If you stop wanting to dream it will collapse. Your desire to dream holds it
        up,
all the bare longing of the imagination holds it up, the desire of the nail
to enter the wood, the desire of the wood to embrace the nail,

the desire of the paint to hide the wood and reflect the light,
the desire of the roof to contain a secret shape of darkness,
the desire of the glass to shine like the sun in the face of the sun.

And the earth desires to lie asleep under the house and dream,
it dreams the very shape of the house as though it was something organic,
whole as a body, breathing and seeing and standing cold in the wind.

The house is the container and you are the thing contained.
Its membrane protects you and your life gives it energy
and stops the walls from collapse. And the moment of seeing this

and the moment of saying this are two separate moments:
the first, the moment of seeing is a moment without desire,
at night, by the bed watching you sleep, alone, still, chill,

but not cold, watching, as the silence of space watches the grinding earth,
when all the desire has gone out of me and I get up,
get up out of the bed, go out the door, out through the end wall,

and grasp hold of the string on the balloon and rise slowly, steadily,
shimmering like a giant eye over the house, the whole town, the capital city,
rising over the island and the ocean, the earth opening like a flower.

But the second, the moment of saying, involves me in the grammar of
        desire.
I have to touch you with my speech to be heard.
And grammar itself is a thing of desire, announcing its capacity

to evolve infinitely more complex systems out of bits of nothing,
to put together the grains of sand to make rock and the rock to build
a cliff and the cliff to hold a house, many houses, a city

to stand at the end wall of the island, the end wall of the land
turned like smooth wood in the yielding shape of the bay
to embrace the random desiring waves of the sea.

Somewhere a child is sacrificed and buried at the foot of the posthole
which comes to hold up the whole house. Building walls for the compost
    heap
I smash a post in half and in its rotted core a weta lies, soft and sleepy,

hiding until its new exoskeleton hardens enough to let it safely live,
to let it grow vulnerable, as earth to light, as sand to sea.
Tonight I embrace you and trust the roof will hold up till morning.

FRANK SARGESON

The Undertaker's Story

A stocky powerful man somewhat gone to seed, he was thrown out of a seaside pub one fine Saturday afternoon when I was sitting on the verandah.

The bar had been too crowded and noisy, too intolerably hot and sticky, and I had taken my beer outside, where the sun would be some time yet before it hit the bench against the front wall. A breeze off the harbour kept the high tide slapping at the sand, which sloped up until it met the concrete verandah flooring, but the glare and glitter was too trying on my eyes and I turned sideways on. The noise from within was a babble and roar, but the moment my ears began to pick out the sounds of a quarrel, it was strange to see how the backs that curved from the wide-open windows began to straighten. As the moment of climax approached they all disappeared.

Spluttering and blowing, his face red unshaved and swollen, he braked with his feet and grabbed at the jamb of the doorway, but so many were pulling and shoving he hadn't a chance. He went limp as they heaved him down the slope, and he lay like something washed up by the tide. It was as though he knew himself to have been defeated beyond all question.

They all turned and went inside again, dusting and straightening their clothes. There was no fuss, no sign of either malice or sympathy. A quarrelsome drunk had been dealt with. The faces at the windows looked the other way, and the backs curved out again.

There were two of us outside now, and while I was trying to work out the problem the incident had presented me with, there appeared in the doorway an elderly under-sized man, very tidy in a panama hat, a maroon blazer and flat rubber-soled shoes. With his white tooth-brush moustache as well, he looked as though he had by some mistake dropped in instead of going to bowls. He had with him an old felt hat, which he dusted with his handkerchief as he went down the beach, and for quite some time he kept turning it in his hands as he sat beside the heap of discarded humanity. When he began to speak I could not hear what he said, but the heap immediately came to life. The hat was accepted, and soon they were sitting side by side with their backs to the pub as they talked. Or rather, while the older man went on talking.

I was moved, but perhaps my strongest feeling was one of gratitude that my problem hadn't had to be solved.

When they at last stood up and parted, it seemed that the drunk was perhaps not so drunk. Quite steady on his feet, he returned from along the beach for the ceremony of trust and friendship. Hands were gripped and held, placed on shoulders and left there. It was a sort of tableau, or they might have been figures on a frieze. Beyond them the sea's dark blue suggested melancholy, and the unceasing movement seemed not to hold out any promise of permanency for their bond, but at least they stood on sand that was solid and clean after the high tide, and there was the sunlight for an impartial golden blessing.

The elderly man gave me a nod when he re-entered the pub, and I was not surprised when he brought out his own beer.

Ay, he said, quite without any preliminaries as he sat down alongside, ay. It is a sad thing when a man cannot forgive himself for his own failure.

This was direct and intelligent, somewhat unusual. Also, he spoke with a slight Scottish burr, which is often supposed to go with reticence.

I said I thought I understood.

Duncan, he said. I knew him when he was a Highland lad, a sturdy young bull of a lad that lived his days on the hills with the sheep. I remember well I saw few lads of his like when I went on my rounds to those Highland places.

Ay, he said – and it seemed not unlikely that the hills he looked at across the harbour, were re-shaping themselves into something rather different.

You're not a Highland man yourself? I asked.

No. I was a Paisley boy. My people settled from Lancashire, Manchester. I grew up a Lowland Scot, but except for a manner of speaking there's not all that difference. The Lowland Scot is Anglo-Saxon as you may remember from your schoolbooks, and much the same by nature according to the way I figure it out. But there is much to separate him from the Highlander.

You visited the Highlands? I prompted him.

I was a young man travelling with a line of knick-knacks. For the most part it was jewellery, cheapjack stuff. There was money to be had by my boss in Glasgow, but nothing much for a young fellow working on commission. The Highlanders were hard folk to persuade, and if it had not been for the lassies, with their liking to deck themselves out with a bit of finery – well, the order sheets I sent back to my boss would never have added up to much of a turnover.

But this Duncan? I prompted again.

Duncan, he said. I remember well I said to his mother, a Mrs McGowan – I said the land's poor and the season is bad, and I don't forget there is always the landlord, but remember Mrs McGowan I said, it's the townsman in the big city that's first to go without his supper when times are bad. I said it was goodbye to Scotland, for I was off to New Zealand, where by God's help and good luck I would make my fortune.

It must have been a long time ago, I said. How is it you remember so exactly?

Duncan, he said. It was Duncan. The boy was there in the yard, feeding a handful of grain to his mother's hens while I talked at the doorstep. He heard me say the name of this country.

How could I know, he continued, how could I know that name would never shift from the boy's memory?

So he followed you out here? I questioned, thinking I might cut down some of the story's trimmings.

It would be wrong to say that. He never remembered my face, and I did not recognise him until I heard his name called out and took stock of him. You see, I had not made my fortune after near on twenty years, and I had trouble enough to put thoughts of Scotland far from my mind. It was bad luck I took up with my old line of commercial travelling, although it did not look like bad luck at the time. I was employed by a grocery warehouse, and glad of my opportunity to see the country, but there is temptation for a young man when it is rare for him to sleep in any bed except what he can get at the country pubs. I don't mean to say I went to the bad with the drink, because your Scot is canny as a rule, and he has a great respect for book-learning. Many a night when there was drinking it would be no attraction for me, because I was lying on my bed with a book, and to this day I am a great reader of good books. But there is the temptation of women, and that our Maker has decreed for the population of the world. No man may refrain, as you a young man will understand. But no great amount of looseness was ever in my nature, and I took my wife from a pub where I was in the habit of staying, a grand girl with a good hand for cooking, and a full bosom where any man might wish to pillow his head for his contentment.

Yes yes, I said, but what about Duncan?

Duncan, he said. If you are not in a hurry there is time to tell you about Duncan – and he was silent a moment while he appeared to gather up his threads.

My wife left me, and she took away the wee boy. I had never settled in this country, do you see? – even though it was ten or twelve years since I landed. I was still on the road, and it was no life for my wife. A woman should not be exposed to temptation when she has a husband to tend her. I tried, but I could not mend my situation, so I swore by God's help I would mend my ways in case I had another opportunity for settling. I thought hard and deep, and I decided to give up the road. I sat and looked at my soft hands, and I remembered about my grandfather. He was a master spinner, and he settled in the North because he hoped to better himself at the fine Paisley work. There was none of that sort of thing in New Zealand, but I remembered my bachelor uncle gave me a cardboard box of carpenter's tools for my birthday when I was ten. It was because I had said I was going to be a carpenter. The tools were toys, which I was proud to bring out to show the visitors, but although there was a book of directions, and my uncle brought me pieces of wood, I was never known to try to use those tools. It all came back to me in my distress, and I decided (when I was near to turning forty, mind you), I decided I would make myself into the carpenter I said I was going to be.

And? I had to prompt.

Did you not see the big sign as you came through the town?

I thought a moment, and replied that apart from the hoardings, the only sign I could remember was the undertaker's.

That's it, he said. Robert Wilson is my name.

But, I was about to say, when he continued.

You see, I was a very determined man and I had made my decision. I learned the carpentry, and I did more by learning the joinery and cabinet-making. I discovered I had nimble hands when a delicate job was called for. I came over to the coast here, and I set myself up in the furniture line of business, but it would be untruthful to say I prospered. I made none of your cheapjack stuff, which the public preferred because of my prices. I remember well a customer said when I showed him a kitchen cupboard – he said I had put in enough work to make it watertight. He said I should have been a boatbuilder. Ah, but it was about that same time my opportunity came to me. There was just one other furniture-maker in the township as it was then, and he was the undertaker. He died, he was undertaken himself as you might say, and I made my arrangements to take over his business. Now wasn't that a strange thing? – it was honest work for living folk I had done, but the public wouldn't have it on account of the prices. I did not prosper until I worked for the dead man that could have no argument about the price, and no say about what I provided.

He paused, but he held up his hand when I opened my mouth to speak.

Duncan, he said. It was about that same time when I began the undertaking. It was unbeknown to me that Duncan was living behind the hills you see eastwards yonder as you come up the coast. He had taken up a bit of land in a ballot. It was O.R.P. if you understand, occupation with right of purchase, what is reckoned third-class land. But alongside of him being hampered for lack of ready money, the floods washed out his fences, and the wind blew a gale that carried away his cowshed, and the lean-to where he lived until he could prosper. I learned the story of his misfortunes one day when I had business at the Courthouse, and heard his name called out before the Justices for sheep-stealing. Duncan, I said, when they allowed me to talk with him, before he was taken away to be tried at the Supreme Court – Duncan, I said, do your time as you must if the judgment of the law goes against you, but don't lose heart man. Stand up on your two feet and look folks in the face, for it is in the nature of man to fall according to the law of God. But all may hope to raise themselves by the help of God and man, and if the Almighty does his share so will I too.

You see, I am none of your strict Calvinists in my belief, he broke off to say.

I told Duncan I had not made my fortune, but I stood in a fair way to prosper, and if he would return to the district I would do everything on his behalf that lay in my ability.

And he did return, I said.

Yes. But not before I had lost sight of him for close on ten years. He was not much changed in his appearance, but I never knew a man so reluctant to speak. He scarce spoke a word to me as a boy, and I forced the answers from him that sad day he was brought to the Court, but now he spoke up only one answer when ten might be required. And not to hear his wife answer at all was very aggravating.

You see, he said after a pause, he had taken a wife, and the pair were like foreign immigrants to America that have not learned to speak the English language. But what was the more strange, it was rare you heard them say a word to each other – no, not even upon an occasion of importance as you will hear.

Now do you see? he went on, I had my doubts about them being married. They were matched like to like if you understand, and in the marriage state it is best for the dark to be set against the fair, and the light and merry against what is more sober. But I did an injustice. Duncan had his bit of money saved up, and wished me to help him on to the land according to the word I had promised. I had prospered and I was willing to honour my bond, and indeed it suited me well, because I had bought up sixteen acres of good dairy country going cheap beyond the town boundary. If Duncan would settle, he and his wife could milk for the town supply, and by delivering to the householder as well the profit would be increased. So we made an arrangement, but first I told Duncan there was just one matter. He was a man with a conviction, but that would never be held against him with me supporting him – and I explained how I now had the honour of sitting as a JP. But there must be nothing irregular in addition that might cause people to talk, and if he would pardon me for mentioning it I would be favoured if he would show his marriage certificate.

Good Lord! I couldn't help exclaiming. And did he crack you?

I was aware of the risk, he went on. But do you see? – I knew if the marriage lines were shown swiftly, I could fairly reckon it was because they were in the possession of Mrs McGowan, and instead of free choice, I could infer the probability of what the young people nowadays speak of as a shotgun marriage. And in the event, it turned out that Duncan's wife visited me immediately with the document I wished to see.

But there was no child, I said.

Ah, I'm coming to that. I supposed the child had miscarried, and there I had the explanation of two people, man and woman, bound up together as man and wife for no reason but the child. There was no child, but they were still bound. Duncan, a fine strong handsome man, was bound to a poor creature that carried scarce a hint of feminine flesh anywhere on her bones.

His pause was so long I had to say, And?

And I was deceived. They settled nicely, putting heart and soul and all the strength of their two bodies into the work on the land. But I confess I was very surprised to hear there was to be seen a wee boy running about the place, and sometimes riding on the float when Duncan came to town for the early delivery. I inquired, and I found he had been left with his grandmother, Duncan's mother-in-law, until they were settled. Not that I counted the circumstance against them, but it irked me to be deceived when I was right in my reckoning. And I still could not understand why they did not speak to each other, whatever the wrong that had been done, when they had the boy to compensate them for being bound. He was a merry lad, too young for his schooling, but fine strong and healthy. And he was equally fond of Duncan and his mother. He would run from one to the other, and although his frolics never persuaded either to speak except perhaps a syllable, I marked it one day when Duncan placed his hand on the child's head – because Duncan smiled, and that was a thing I had never known him to do.

Ah, but then it all happened, and it was sudden like the plagues visited on the Egyptians by the God of Israel. I have no evidence that Duncan was in the habit of taking liquor privately, but occasionally of an afternoon, perhaps one day a fortnight, he would ride into town and drink until closing time. It was never reported to me he drank to excess, and indeed it was complained by the barmen that he was the slowest drinker on record. But it did not matter how much he drank, he would never seek company in the bar. For my own satisfaction I ascertained that his wife did not sit wringing her hands waiting on his return, on the contrary she would have the milking done and everything washed up ready for the morning, so I did not consider I had any grounds for complaint. But so far as I can piece together the happenings, one late winter evening Duncan rode home and heard the cows bellowing on account of not being milked. His wife's excuse was Jock, the laddie – he had been taken ill with a bad stomach pain in the afternoon. He was tossing and delirious with fever, and the wife dared not leave him to walk some considerable distance where she could ring up the doctor. She asked Duncan to go and ring, but he was obstinate and said the boy would be well by the morning. He went to milk the cows, first forbidding his wife to leave the house, and swearing he would have no doctor calling, with authority to poison the boy with his medicines. The poor creature was distracted, but she obeyed her husband, and Duncan delayed returning to the house until the evening was well spent. She thought from the delay he had been for the doctor after all, but it was not so, and immediately he returned she risked disobedience, because although the boy had turned quiet he lay cold in a sweat – and when the doctor came at last, husband and wife were sitting each side of the bed, not speaking, but each clasping upon the boy's hands. And the boy was dead.

He was silent a moment, and the noise from inside the bar seemed suddenly very loud. I did not know what to say and said, I see.

But, he went on, there was more happened that winter night. The doctor got me out of bed to notify me on the phone. I could not sleep after such news, accustomed though I was to notifications of the kind, so I dressed myself and drove out to the farm. I shut off the engine to coast down the hill to the gate, and I considered returning to town, because there was no glimmer of light to indicate they were not in their bed. But a light commenced to shine beneath the macrocarpas that separated the garden from the paddocks, so I walked up the track and rounded the house but I went no further. There was toi-toi I could stand behind, and I could see well that Duncan's wife was holding a storm lantern while Duncan dug and chopped at the roots of the biggest tree. I heard him grunt at his work but he never spoke, and he worked hard and fast until there was a big hole tucked well in under the tree. Then I had to hold in my breath as they passed near returning into the house, but immediately they came again, Mrs McGowan still carrying the lantern but Duncan bearing a rough timber box. He placed it well in the hole, and when he had finished throwing back the earth and was stamping it with his feet, then his wife placed the lantern on the ground and returned into the house. Neither had spoke a word, but as for Duncan, when he had finished stamping he picked up the lantern and stood before he returned into the house. And I heard him say, Jock! my Jock.

For quite some time we were both silent, but the spell was broken when he had to respond to greetings from a group which came round the side of the pub to enter by the front door. It was in any case high time for me to be out on the road, to wait for the bus that would take me further up the coast.

I shouldered my rucksack.

Are they still living together? I asked.

Never. She left him after the inquiry.

And is Duncan still on the farm?

Never, never. He earns his bit of money here and there. He is tipped for marking the scores in the billiard saloon.

Tell me, I said, did you ever marry again?

Ay, he replied. I married my housekeeper. It was in keeping with my position when I was appointed a Justice of the Peace. My wife is a fine figure of a woman.

There was an indefinable something about his eyes – what is called a twinkle, I suppose.

And she has an excellent hand for cooking.

Yes, I said as I raised my hand for a goodbye. I'd expect that.

A Final Cure

When he had at last put his name to the separation agreement his wife refused to help him find suitable lodgings. It was her excuse that she was exhausted by the worry of his irresponsible behaviour, and the more especially his bad influence upon the younger children.

It was fortunate for him that he had the affection of his eldest son Roger, who rang up advertised numbers and went looking for likely rooms. The boy wished when he had finished school to follow his father and become a doctor. Stubbornly sure of himself, determined about what he wanted, he in most other matters resembled his mother: he resembled what she had once been in being fond of his father.

When he was confident that he had found the right room Roger assured his father a preliminary inspection wasn't necessary.

We've only got to pack up your things dad, he said, then I can run you over.

There was nothing to be done. There were no patients to speak of any more, he had signed the document and must get off his wife's premises. And they were indeed hers – she had married him with property and money of her own. It was fortunate for the boy and his career, and for the younger children – upon whose account she had pressed for the separation. Since he would be living in lodgings paid for by a wife-in-name it was also his own good fortune.

And he agreed with Roger that the room would serve. Ground-floor, a large front room with wide windows, with a couch, a table and an easy chair, all was run-down and faded though not yet frayed and torn; and the sheets on the bed were clean. And he was reassured about having to prepare his own meals when he inspected the kitchen – also run-down, but spacious, with a row of gas stoves to suggest that any serious jockeying for position among lodgers must surely be unlikely.

I'll manage, my boy, he said. In any case, people. I want to keep in touch.

His approval of Roger's judgment was clinched by an air of spaciousness about the entire double-storeyed run-down house, an elaborate wooden structure which dated from beyond the beginning of the century. It was miraculous that a house with a balcony of wooden fretwork and a slate roof nicely pitched had survived among all the factories and warehouses. And he

decided that the best of its indoor attractions was the staircase, which
descended in a progressively widening, pleasing curve.

Dignity, my boy; he said. Most attractive.

Roger mentioned that he had inquired, and actually (he hoped dad wouldn't
mind if he said so), the house had been in the old days the home of a doctor.
There was what remained of a stable at the end of the backyard.

Ah! his father said. Style! In those days a professional man would never be a
moment in doubt how he stood.

According to his self-diagnosis, it was his recognition of the human need to
know exactly how one stood that had been at the bottom of his domestic
trouble. He could recognize this unsatisfied need in his patients – people who
suffered (he remembered his Latin): they were diseased (and it should always
be stressed that the word was more properly dis-eased) by their isolation.
'Patients' was just another word for humanity.

Long years ago he had begun to practise as a conventional bottle-doctor –
and moved with the times until the writing of a prescription began to prompt
him to pause over some curious thoughts. Shouldn't he by rights recommend a
chemist who was certified to be neither colour-blind nor unable to count? And
before very long he had begun to exhibit the unusual characteristic of moving
according to his own time. Disease – it was isolation – being out of touch, with all
the uncertainty of not knowing how one stood. Why prescribe when the
physician was himself, or should be, the cure? – *not* the modern substance,
sometimes unstable, and probably always poisonous, which was concealed in
the pretty technicoloured capsule. The time he devoted to his consultations was
much increased. People who suffered were not to be rapidly got rid of with the
pseudo-magic formula illegibly scribbled. And once he had decided that time
was of no importance in matters of such urgency (he repeated to himself the
illuminating words and relished the contradiction), nobody saw much of him
any more except his patients. Some of these unfortunate people might well
deserve from him an entire day. And when not closely engaged with his
consultations many hours were consumed by a footling correspondence with
the Department. The subsidy was most inadequate – he was providing what
amounted to a specialist service and should be subsidized accordingly. No? But
surely the sum he saved the Department in chemists' bills should be taken into
account? No? Very well then, was it the Department's policy to coerce him into
again becoming a bottle-cum-capsule doctor?

But a doctor who never wrote a prescription! It was talked about around the
suburb. Apart from a handful of eccentrics (and that included prolonged daily
visits from a deaf old lady), nobody could be bothered with him any more. And
the crisis came soon after his wife had decided that since he had ceased to earn
enough to keep the house in cats' meat he must certainly be mad. She was not
comforted when he begged for understanding *please*!

My dear, it's a truism – the more we *have* the less we can *be*.

His wife also suspected some kind of impropriety, and irritated him by her
sudden and frequent incursions to suggest a cup of tea – including one for the
patient (usually the old lady), with whom he had been secluded for so many
hours. She was inclined to be convinced that he was being as bad as he was mad
when she discovered the disturbing nature and number of the doodles daily
discarded in his wastepaper basket.

To be alone in his lodgings was at first a delight, the kind of quiet holiday he
had never enjoyed over so many overworked years. Disengaged from every
demand of daily obligation, and free to occupy his mind as he wished he read
no newspapers – time was now much too precious to waste on appearances that
were so absurdly contingent; and he vowed that he would not be deflected from

his purpose of dedicating himself wholly to what was permanent. It was a surprise to apply himself so readily to the books he had put off reading for a lifetime – and he relaxed by relishing his opportunity for an attempt at recapturing a little of his thirty-year-old and now somewhat rusty promise for playing the 'cello. He avoided too the mistake of rushing headlong and heedlessly at establishing his contacts. In the kitchen he spoke the greetings appropriate for the time of day and left it at that. If the response came he would respond. The core of it all was his sure conviction that the permanent stuff of human nature was something neither he nor anyone else could ever get past. In one of his books he discovered the forgotten formula: nothing human is to me alien – and he began to believe that all government in the world had so far failed because human nature had never been properly discovered and understood. It was without question what you started off with – wonderful things might follow, but they must be surely grounded on the permanent truths of human necessity. All had changed in worldly affairs since Galileo had put his eye to that fatal telescope: it was not a man-centred universe – on the contrary, humanity was right out on a limb. And that was why all things human would always demand every scrap of humble reverence which every sane man would always and naturally want to muster.

But in the kitchen signs of response were not encouraging. He was smiling and benign, but when he one morning inquired, And what might your name be? from the tired and taciturn hotel night-porter (a part-time worker crippled by age and arthritis, he occupied the outdoor room in the backyard beyond the wash-house), he was answered by a look that surprised by being as contemptuous as it was sour. His landlady was polite and mentioned the weather – but she also remarked about the fiddle he played. What a pity it didn't sound a bit more cheerful! He would understand she was speaking in the interests of her lodgers in asking him not to play of an evening later than eight o'clock. But he failed to register her request since he had already begun to say:

How very right you are, Mrs Hinchinghorn! A sombre instrument indeed!

It touched him that in her room off the kitchen she that same day began to compete with him by thumping out tunes on her untuned piano.

A tall Dutchman spoke only (although frequently) to say he intended to see the landlady and lodge a complaint; and there were the two Miss Cooneys, not young, red-haired and perhaps twins (that was to say, if they were sisters at all), who occupied a room together and smiled but never spoke (he did not know that they had lately retired from the telephone exchange – and after forty years of listening without any right of participation were not much interested in participating now). His one cheerful and promising kitchen companion was a freezing-works chain slaughter-man (with appropriate gestures he explained about his job as a brisket-puncher), who watched the clock while he scurried about the kitchen, and belched over the food he bolted standing immediately it was removed from the stove.

And then, late one evening when the doctor was making himself toast, the kitchen door was booted open by a very large Maori in a torn jersey and bursting trousers, his arms enclosing two large and bursting bags of mussels: the ukulele slung around his neck was made to look like a child's toy by the size of the vast old iron pot which was likewise suspended. He politely greeted the doctor, and made his excuses as he departed for his room upstairs after putting mussels and water to heat. The sound and thought of gumboots stamping up the stairway made the doctor smile – but soon after he had taken the toast to his room he was frowning instead. The chords strummed overhead and the voice that accompanied them were interrupted by the rumpus which had developed in the kitchen. It was no doubt the persuasive odour of cooking mussels which had brought there the landlady and the Misses Cooney. Unpleasant words were loudly and unpleasantly repeated. A Miss Cooney was heard to threaten, If you don't get rid of him this instant! . . .

The doctor never saw the Maori again.

But although troubled, he was not all that much discouraged by these unfavourable manifestations of human nature. People were to be taken as you found them. It was all genuine and valuable experience – and he reminded himself that it had for many years been his habit to evade much experience taken for granted in his student days: a busy doctor could rely too much on the laboratory to handle many a raw and disagreeable task. One day entering the bathroom, he was sharply reminded how seriously he had slipped. Answering the phone, his landlady had apparently been interrupted while her false teeth were removed – and the sight of two unpalatable-looking plates would not normally have disturbed him, but the occasion had unfortunately been improved upon by a bluebottle and a gang of houseflies. It surprised him to be affected by nausea; and he was afterwards tempted to suppose that he had only to announce himself a qualified practitioner, and his chances of being distressed over encountering any such human contact would immediately be reduced. He resisted the temptation, which succumbed to would have branded him a cheat. Contacts between individuals were two-way working: he hoped he might be accepted upon his naked merits as a human being even as he hoped to accept.

But there were many bad days when he was so much troubled by his doubts that he would emerge from his room only very briefly to satisfy animal necessities: feeling keenly his own isolation, he consumed the hours by relaxing over his doodles, drawing cornucopias which proliferated over sheet after sheet of scrap paper – integrated satisfying patterns of unimaginable yet meticulously detailed fruits, all of them tumbling out from curling goats' horns in a various and bewildering profusion: some, and some of the horns too, were so oddly shaped (what his wife had thought of as so 'suggestive'), that others too might have had their doubts about his sanity and moral health.

It was Roger who called one afternoon when his father was out buying his provisions, and without thinking inquired the whereabouts of Doctor Dudley. Soon after he had returned there came the first knock on his door; it was the night-porter, introducing himself as Clarrie.

Rheumatism! Well Clarrie, we know next to nothing about that one – in fact you could say nothing at all. He laid his hand on the man's shoulder. I think it helps, Clarrie, if each man will learn to live with his mortality – it's a shame we don't make that the first lesson we teach our schoolchildren.

Clarrie would have again mentioned his pain, but the doctor continued.

Yes, yes, I know – but we're all of us nagged by our aches and pains, Clarrie. Here! He took the man's hand and pressed it against his own side. Feel! There – that's it. Where I've had a pain for the last eighteen months. I wake up in the night – in a father of a fright, Clarrie. I say to myself – Doctor Dudley, you've had it!

Clarrie looked worried. All was a mistake – a doctor who told you he had a pain!

What about bee stings, doctor? Do you reckon it's worth a try?

The doctor smiled and put his hand in his pocket.

Buy yourself a new hot-water bottle, Clarrie. I know something about you people – you make do with some old thing worn out and leaking.

Bewildered and suspicious Clarrie backed out. He had *meant* to leave ten shillings in silver on the doctor's table. He was not ungrateful, but he disapproved. It was no way for a doctor to behave.

There were other knockings on the doctor's door – although a Miss Cooney smiled on him in the kitchen and apologized: If you will excuse us, doctor – it has long been our custom to consult a lady physician.

But although he welcomed each visitor into his room he contrived to evade any admission that he was available for formal consultations. Mrs Hinchinghorn wanted a prescription for aspirin, and he could fortunately 'tide her over' from a supply discovered among the odds and ends that Roger had packed. And in the same way he obliged with alkaline tablets sought by the Dutchman and also the slaughter-man.

Samples, my friend. You're welcome – I don't imagine they can do you any great amount of harm.

There were however several lodgers never seen in the kitchen, who even more mysteriously appeared only very seldom to have any use for the house's other conveniences. Across from the doctor's room there lived a little old man who with his head down appeared to be greeting the ground with a smile of affection, whenever he might be seen getting off smartly along the street on short chubby legs and a pair of little round feet. It had become the doctor's practice never to lower his blind or hide behind his curtain (he had read about the humanists of the Renaissance who hoped for self-protection and a quiet life by consistently allowing their private lives to be publicly inspected), so he was in no doubt that his little neighbour's disregard for the kitchen was explained by the regular midday arrival of a lady social worker in a shining car loaded with meals on wheels. But this service was limited to five days a week. On Saturdays and Sundays the little man seemed never to emerge from behind his closed door – although it was clear from the sounds of a broom that he swept his floor: occasionally he would lean from his window to shake his square of carpet. It was therefore perhaps a little contradictory that during one entire weekend when the doctor could not afterwards recollect hearing any sounds at all, he should also fail to notice that his neighbour's door had remained consistently not quite shut. Afterwards too, it was a Miss Cooney who was quick to claim that *she* had noticed. Yes, several times! Nor had it escaped her that on the last occasion several large blowflies had been in one great buzzing hurry to enter through the doorway. It was nonetheless the social worker who discovered that the doctor's neighbour was dead when she delivered his Monday meal on wheels. Fully dressed and face down, he lay on his square of carpet with his hands clasped in advance of his head. It was as though the ground on which he had smiled for so long had at last consented to an embrace.

There was immediately a gathering – the two Miss Cooneys, Mrs Hinchinghorn, the slaughter-man who was on strike that day. The last to join in was the doctor, and it was upon him that all eyes focused. Could something marvellous be expected? – the newspapers were these days reporting many instances of 'the kiss of life'. But the doctor simply looked as they did, and had nothing to say except, He's dead, you must ring the police. There was silence. The simple functional words were somehow offensive. The slaughter-man withdrew – he was very familiar with death, but this was no occasion for brisket-punching. Nor did the doctor stay – after he had invited more disapproval. He did nothing, but it was judged from his use of his handkerchief that he was affected. A display of feeling was hardly the sort of thing anyone would expect from a man in his profession.

The news item included the unusual announcement, 'no suspicious circumstances'. But that view of the matter did not wholly satisfy the plainclothes men who made some formal inquiries after taking over from the uniformed branch. What the devil was a properly qualified although it seemed non-practising doctor up to living in such a place? What was the story? But the answers were nothing unusual: some kind of emotional trauma – you could say a bit dopey: yes, a crank but quite probably harmless: no prosecutions: no history of drink, drugs or violence: abortions no, not thought to be likely: not a pervert: his wife had money – that could be the story.

The doctor was not required to appear at the inquest, but Mrs Hinchinghorn's mention of him as a lodger was reported – with the unfortunate result that several of his former patients were enabled to discover his whereabouts. And he was soon so much occupied with familiar re-visitings that it virtually escaped his attention there were no more knockings on his door from his landlady and her lodgers. (His failure to notice his deceased neighbour's unclosed door over an entire weekend had been much discussed and held to be against him – after all, you would suppose a properly qualified doctor to be trained to notice things it might be important to notice; and in any case, what was one to think of a doctor who had for several days repeatedly passed up and down within a few yards of a dead body and never had an inkling! Who could have faith in a doctor without a nose for the very thing it was the whole aim and purpose of his profession to prevent?) A regular arrival each morning was the deaf old lady, and she would remain until he sent her home in the taxi he paid for; but it was one of his elderly eccentrics who arrived with a disturbing story. The man insisted that his health was much improved now that he had begun the practice of smoking reefer cigarettes, and he wished for the doctor's co-operation in buying up a large supply which was in danger of failing as police suspicions were thought to be growing uncomfortably warm.

Now the doctor was aware that the use of this drug was in itself agreeable and harmless: it could however prompt one into becoming addicted to the really dangerous drugs and was in any case forbidden by the law. He was shocked by his patient's cynicism and his indifference to the chances of corruption – and the more so as he was a man with a background of education who had at one time been prominent as a Church of England clergyman. It became his long and delicate task to induce his patient to admit the light of reason, and one that was successfully completed at last only by the use of a stratagem. Yes, he would assist in buying up the supply of cigarettes (by an ancillary stratagem his wife was persuaded into financing the transaction), but only so long as it was clearly understood that he was aiming at bringing that particular supply of the drug under proper control: that was to say, the reefers would be surrendered to the doctor, and his patient would be rationed and reduced until he ceased to make any more use of the drug.

The plainclothes men had in the meantime decided after much chewing matters over that a try-out on abortion was as good a tack as any; and the doctor was one evening called upon by a handsome well-set-up and powerfully-built young woman, a member of the uniformed branch clad at the moment in off-duty clothes (which only by an abuse of language could have been described as plain). After a competent show of hesitation and embarrassment, together with a plea that her confidence would be respected, she explained the purpose of her visit, intimating that she could immediately put down a five pound note as a pledge of her good faith. And then she began to feel herself genuinely embarrassed, because despite his appearance of sympathetic interest the doctor made no move to lower his blinds (although the circumstance was in fact no disadvantage, ensuring as it did that all transactions could be readily viewed by her male colleagues stationed on the far side of the street with night-glasses). There were however no transactions of any kind, and the doctor although he remained sympathetic appeared rapidly to lose interest.

My dear young woman, he said, my advice to you is that you have your baby – and may it be your blessing and happiness to bring healthy new life into our sick and sorry world.

As he reached for the doorhandle he withdrew from his pocket a pound note which he pressed upon his caller.

It's nothing, he said, simply a little something to help you with your baby.

A handy Justice of the Peace was located after the two plainclothes men had received their colleague's report; and provided with their warrant they were soon at the doctor's door. Through the night-glasses they had seen the doctor provide their young woman with money – without much doubt intending to assist her to achieve an illegal aim. But there was a good deal more to it than that – the young policewoman, trained to notice what might be important, had informed them about the many rude drawings which lay about the doctor's table, yes, very rude definitely! It was satisfactory to search a cupboard and discover stacks of pencilled filth – but a very great satisfaction indeed to uncover what they had all along more than half suspected, a large haul of reefers, all neatly packed in cigar-boxes.

The publicity was all very painful and bad for his innocent wife and children: poor Roger was obliged to begin his professional career under a cloud. But there *was* the compensation that his professional colleagues most generously rallied round. You could say, to a man: there were some very eminent names among those who testified. Doctor Dudley readily agreed to retire to an approved Rest Home – but after some years there is still no prospect that he would want to emerge out into the world again. It had all cost his wife a large slice out of her fortune. On most days he prefers to remain in bed – and yet when his health is inquired about he consistently replies that he is confident of moving steadily towards a final cure.

RODERICK FINLAYSON

A Little Gift for Harry

That crisp morning, soon after the sun was up, Maori horsemen were ambling along the Tairua road to the village. Faraway puffs of dust showed where cars and buggies loaded with people were on the move too. All these travellers sooner or later converged upon the meeting-house by the bare poplar trees where, after every new arrival, the keening of the tangi for the dead broke out afresh.

The funny grubby little bus from the Bentville railway station pulled in with more country visitors at about ten o'clock, and just before mid-day a big sleek bus, all chromium and gleaming blue enamel, hired specially by a party of city Maoris, arrived all the way from Auckland. The driver blew his musical horn loudly to clear some of the village kids out of his way, but that only brought hordes more running and shouting, 'Hey! See the new pakeha bus! What about a ride mister?'

'Such behaviour at a tangi nowadays!' Mrs Tamahana, a stickler for solemnity, exclaimed.

Men and women, most of the latter in the latest city fashions, piled out of the bus to join those already congregating in front of the meeting-house. It was winter, but the weather was beautiful – clear warm sunny days with crisp still nights – so that people loitered in the sun instead of hurrying to shelter. The village seemed to be crammed with men, women, children, babies, dogs, horses, and every kind of conveyance. No wonder such a crowd! The dead man was the last of the old chiefs of that coast. There were even paragraphs in his honour in the big city papers.

In the bus with the city people came Harry Rose who didn't look much of a Maori. He had curly red hair and light grey eyes and a round pale face, rather freckly. As if he thought himself a cut above the others he narrowed his eyes and kept a little aloof in his expensive clothes, very sporty but nothing loud, nothing vulgar. Harry had a drop of the blood though – a Maori great-grandmother or something like that. He laughed it off as a joke if the fact accidentally came to light. Although sometimes, as when the Maori Battalion was in the limelight, he would boast in company where he couldn't be contradicted, that he could be a chief in such-and-such a tribe.

He had been talked into this trip by his cousins, the Taunga boys, who worked in an Auckland foundry. He had no time for the bad old ways, tangis and all that, he said. But, although at first he was sulky at being dragged off to just such a show, now, strolling in the sun while the Taunga boys greeted relatives, he told himself that it wasn't too bad after all. A few days' spell from the dry cleaners delivery too.

Already the village kids were scrawling in the dust on the parked bus such legends as: Don't fence me in; and, Stick em up Cowboy. Just across the courtyard was the meeting-house with its splendidly carved posts and panels. And on its sunny porch lay the old dead man, his coffin surrounded by flowers and feather cloaks and family photos, and lean old women in long black skirts and black head scarves who suddenly took up their wail again. They seemed to eye the elaborately made-up city girls with some distaste.

Near the poplars were two marquees, one old, leaky as a sieve, but nice and roomy for the men, and the other new but dreadfully overcrowded for the women. All agreed it was a fair arrangement – if it rained . . . . The weather continued fine however.

Beyond the weatherbeaten old Tairua village, on the river flats amid newly broken-in land, were neat new houses, large glass windows and aluminium roofs reflecting the sun. 'The big land scheme for the Maori Battalion men,' a friendly chap told Harry.

In spite of the gossiping of the crowd and the bright hard sunlight it all seemed to Harry very remote. 'Almost as good as a movie,' he thought.

'Here's young Hira!'

Jack Taunga's voice roused him and he turned to find a good-looking young fellow talking to his cousins.

'Oh no, you don't sleep in the tent,' Hira said. 'My old man says you got to put up at our place. All in the family, eh?'

Harry felt relieved that he wouldn't have to push in with the noisy crowd in the tent. They walked to one of the larger of the houses on the slope above the meeting-house, a place with a long verandah facing the sun, some old peach trees, and a garden of turnips in front. In the big dark kitchen they met Hira's good-natured mother, and Henare his father, a sharp-featured dignified man. Harry found he was to share Hira's room off the verandah. There was a spare bed covered with a tartan rug. It would be O.K. there, he decided.

They trooped into the kitchen again for a bite of lunch – cold sausage, bread, and tea.

Harry was so busy impressing Hira with the advantages of his city job that at first he didn't notice the girl who put his cup of tea in front of him. But when she moved over to his cousins he saw her properly. Then he didn't hear Hira offering him the sugar.

'Sorry, it's only rough and ready here,' Hira apologized, thinking that Harry hadn't noticed the sugar in the old treacle tin.

'Gosh! that's all right,' Harry said, dipping into the tin at last. 'Sugar is sugar any old way,' he said looking at that girl again.

Of all the hundreds of girls he'd met, many real dazzlers, why had none knocked him silly like this? This girl now was rather thin. And she wore only an old blue dress, and no make-up. But she was different; gosh, she was different! It must have been her sort of freshness and her downright simplicity, he decided.

And then she smiled at Harry. In the way that such affairs go it was plain from the very first that she liked him. He guessed it was his superior manner that did the trick. Yes, she liked him all right.

You could still hear the faint keening of the women in the distance, but for Harry from that moment the old dead man was forgotten. And it wasn't quite like a movie show now. It wasn't remote and meaningless. Here I am, he thought, out to get this girl. No fooling. He guessed he'd never be satisfied with any other girl. He heard them say her name – Meri.

Out on the verandah that afternoon, sitting on the sun-warped boards, they had a chance to talk.

'Hello, Meri.'

'Hello, you. You come from Auckland, Harry?'

'You'd like the city, Meri. You should come to Auckland. Look, you could get a job in a clothing factory. Lots of Maori girls do. Good pay, good times. You just ought to be there at some of the dances I go to.'

She looked over the lonely river flat, over the raw new farms with the new Maori Battalion houses, all fresh paint and aluminium roofs shining in the sun.

'Look, what about driving with me tonight to the movies at Bentville?'

She had to remind him that it was her grandfather who was dead.

'Sorry . . . . Never mind, wait till you come up to Auckland.'

They became silent, thoughtful. Around the old village the poplars and wild fruit trees were bare against the blue sky. Along the river banks the tufty heads of the cabbage palms glistened in the setting sun, and on the far hills the bush was mottled in varied shades of green.

'You two talk like old pals,' Hira remarked with mock surprise as he came to take Harry down to the chief's family at the meeting-house.

It was that night that Harry first saw Tiki. Tiki was one of the returned soldiers now working on the new land settlement scheme, a big slow good-humoured chap some years older than Harry. Wearing a bright check shirt and khaki trousers he came over to the tangi after his day's work. He walked into Henare's kitchen with a slight limp. They introduced Harry and he seemed very pleased to meet this young visitor from the city. Some other returned men came in and began talking of war adventures; but Tiki had little to say of the war. And Harry was narked because he had done only home service and couldn't make a big impression.

He was glad when they turned the talk to the life of the old chief.

'Hope I have such a long contented life. I've had enough adventures,' Tiki said.

The old man was nearly ninety, Hira told Harry, and had never travelled far beyond his own district. 'Boy, I wish I see the big cities sometime!' Hira said.

'Ah, they settled down to life, those old people,' the father said. 'Look at his wife, down there at his side still, near eighty and faithful all the time. They marry young in those days,' he told Harry with something like deliberate emphasis, 'boys and girls in their own district. No need to go roaming looking for God knows what.'

As they were going to bed by candlelight in their little room Hira said to Harry, 'You know Tiki is going to marry Meri soon as he finish build his house.'

'But Meri . . . . I didn't think she was his girl.' Harry was confused, didn't know what to say.

'Oh, it's not a case of sweet fall in love right now. You know, it was all fixed more or less by the old folk, before the war.'

'But how does Meri look at it now?'

'Oh, she's a girl. You know, they're all a bit silly sometimes. But you don't want to take too much notice of that. Girls settle down you know, Harry.'

He had a feeling that Hira was trying to drop him a friendly hint perhaps. Anyway, it was a bit of a shock. Harry began to dislike the look of the big slow unromantic Tiki.

But Meri likes me, he thought to reassure himself. Why shouldn't I have her?

The following morning he drew the girl away from the others after a late breakfast when she had waited upon the men at the table. They walked down toward the river where the cowshed and willow trees hid them from view. He wasted no time.

'I know about Tiki,' he said. 'Hira told me. What are you going to do about it?'

'Oh, I do not know, Harry.'

'So you don't *want* to marry him, Meri?'

'Oh, do not ask me that. I never met you then.'

'You would be stuck here for good. You wanted to see the city; get some fun out of life, didn't you?'

'Yes, I wanted.'

He went on to tell her what they could make of life in Auckland together. He let himself become quite carried away.

The girl, who had longed for a change from the unexciting monotonous life, could only shake her head sadly. 'This place awful lonely sometimes,' she said.

'Look here, Meri, come with me and let the rest rip.'

'Oh, but how? You don't know how these things are, Harry. Let me think it over.'

But for Harry a decision was urgent. Two more days and the old man would be buried and the visitors on the way home. He lay awake that night thinking how much he needed Meri. He wouldn't admit the doubts that arose. Would Meri be happy, friendless, far from relatives in a strange city? In the smart haunts where Harry spent his time would Meri still look as lovely as she did here in the backblocks? Would he be proud to own this ordinary Maori girl? What would his friends say?

'You pretty restless last night, Harry. Must be the old fleas,' Hira laughed next morning.

Harry shook his head and pulled a wry smile. 'No fleas, Hira. If only there was nothing worse than fleas to worry a man . . .!'

Hira laughed again and went off singing, 'Murder in de market . . . .'

As soon as he got a chance Harry had a word with Meri alone.

'This can't go on. No use me pretending. There's only one thing to do, Meri – you and me clear out together.'

Although this was the tangi for Meri's grandfather and they would be burying the old chief after the solemn funeral service early next morning, and although she had been happy with her parents, Meri now had only one thought – to go away with Harry.

Harry said he would get hold of a car; borrow or take one. So they planned to meet in the early hours and get away before dawn.

That night Harry would rather have kept away from the others at Henare's place, but he was drawn into a group around the kitchen fire and before he could make up an excuse to leave them in came Tiki.

'Oh hell!' thought Harry, 'how can I look that fellow in the face tonight?' But there he was.

'Tell us something about life and death in the desert, Tiki,' some young fellows from down the coast urged him.

He was reluctant. 'Gosh! All that! I'm a farmer now, you fellows.'

They persisted.

'I tell you one thing then that I tell no one ever before. Now I can tell it because it has come to a good end.'

And he went on to tell about the wounded prisoner in the desert, an Itie, sick, starving, and in rags, and yet with such a childishly cheerful smile because he was sure he was safe – no more war for him.

'I thought, heck!' Tiki said, 'with all that the poor devil can still smile. So I give him a packet of smokes. You should see the way he act. As if I give him everything I got, eh? Well, after a while he says, "You have this. She keep you safe for home, like me." What you think it was? A holy medal, eh? Those jokers all doolans you know. It was on a string to hang round the neck but I put it in my paybook, because I never want the boys to see it. They joke me, eh? They all know I'm not the religious man. But I say to myself, well, anyway I make *one* prayer: Keep me safe for my girl waiting home for me; keep my girl safe too. No harm in that, eh?'

They nodded solemn agreement; it was a good prayer. But Harry, hot with discomfiture, edged away from the fire. He'd have to get the hell out of this! Looking toward the door to escape he was horrified to see that Meri had come in with some of the women and had been listening to Tiki's story.

Something made Tiki turn, too. 'Hello, Meri! . . . You see, you people, my prayer answered, eh?' His big honest face shone with simple pleasure. 'Now I never need keep that holy medal no more. Perhaps it not so good for a fellow like me to keep it now and never go to church. I don't know.'

He fumbled in his hip pocket and brought out a wallet, and from the wallet he fished out the medal. 'I think I give it away sometime.' He held it up in the firelight, a small silver disc dangling from a black cord. 'Bit battered and war scarred, but good all right. Who would like . . . ?' Tiki began to ask.

Quickly the father spoke. 'We have our guest of honour here. All the way from the big city. I think he should have a little gift. What about a gift for Harry here? What you say, Tiki?'

'O.K. Henare! Harry sure must have this little holy medal. Now a young chap like him need it more than me, I guess.' Tiki laughed with pleasure. They all clapped and joined in the laugh. Beaming with goodwill Tiki held out the medal for Harry.

'No,' Harry protested, 'I don't believe in such things. No,' he said, 'perhaps your family would like to have it.' He caught Meri watching him and looked away embarrassed. He tried to turn his back on Tiki.

But Tiki insisted. He got up slowly and pressed the medal into Harry's hand. 'You read the words, Harry. An educated fellow like you, Harry, you know what it means.'

With them all watching him Harry was forced to look at the thing. He saw a woman's head, tried to spell out the worn inscription. But in his gloomy corner with only the flickering firelight he couldn't make out a word. He mumbled some vague expression of thanks and stuffed the unwanted gift into his coat pocket.

'That will keep your girl safe for you, eh Harry?'

Hira gave a short nervous laugh. Harry forced a sickly grin.

They were calling the women to hand round some drinks. Harry was thankful for this diversion. But before Meri turned away to help the other women he saw her face full in the firelight, and he knew it was all up. No need now to ask her about tomorrow.

The women were handing the men glasses of wine. Henare said that the Dally from the vineyard up the road had given him a gallon of wine. A good fellow that. He gave good wine for the tangi.

Harry looked up. Meri was in front of him, offering him a glass of wine. She avoided his eyes until his persistent gaze made her look at him. Then she smiled, but it was a poor weak smile.

He took the glass, held it eagerly up to her lips. 'Come on, Meri you have a drink.' In spite of his jesting tone he was tense, his hand shaking, spilling wine on the floor.

The girl turned her head slightly. 'No, Harry, don't . . . .'

So it was no use, eh? He put the glass to his lips and drained it.

He didn't go to bed that night. In a mockery of his plans he set out for the railway – alone, no goodbyes said. He walked. There was plenty of time for walking. Even then he had a long wait at the lonely backblocks station, stamping up and down the platform in the bitter cold of dawn, before the Auckland train pulled in.

In a second-class smoker he found a seat beside an elderly, dozing man; and with the clatter of the wheels in his ears he thought bitterly over his failure. He knew that it wouldn't have worked, of course, with Meri in the city; he knew that she would soon settle down and be quite happy with her man; that with the young, in two or three days nothing goes very deep; that it won't be long before he gets over it. But gosh! he guesses he will always remember her face whenever he sees a glass of wine.

Suddenly he felt an intense curiosity to examine the holy medal, and not wishing to let the stranger see it he went out to the compartment where the water-filter was, and took it from his pocket. It was battered all right. On one side the inscription was too worn and defaced to be decipherable. The other side was easier to make out, though. Around the woman's head was the word LIBERTY, and, in smaller letters below, IN GOD WE TRUST. Harry recognized it straight away. He'd seen plenty of them in Auckland around about 1942 – a United States dime.

He heard someone coming through from the next carriage. Hurriedly he pocketed the coin again, took one of the paper cups, filled it from the filter, and pretended to drink, although the cold water almost choked him.

Watching in the mirror the man pass by he caught sight of his own strained unhappy face, the eyes bloodshot with fatigue – so comically tragic in fact that a hint of the irony of things broke through in the form of a rather twisted smile.

He had been going to chuck the coin under the wheels of the train before going back to his seat. Now he thought, 'Well, perhaps someday I'll look on it as lucky.' He fingered the smooth roundness of the coin in his pocket. 'Someday, eh? In my own home eh? Picture old Harry saying to Someone, Look, old girl, here's that phoney holy medal. *Real* lucky, wasn't it?'

Another Kind of Life

Let me tell you about going down to the old people's place at Waiari to look up some of the family, especially uncle Tu. You remember, he was one of old Hone Tawa's grandsons who was living there at Waiari just before Hemi died in that motor accident. When he was up in Auckland for the Queen's Birthday races he talked a lot to me about his young days. 'Charlie,' he said, 'you should come down where you people belong. You young fellers don't keep in touch with the old folk.' But you know how it is with a job like driving the buses, you don't get anywhere.

This stopwork in the city give me the chance, so I think now's the time to go and visit uncle and auntie at Waiari. But it was all wrong from the kick-off. I say to the wife, 'The long distance buses are still running and one takes off down the coast early. Grab the baby and let's go.' Well you know, she says there's the two school kids she can't leave and she promised help with the school lunches this week and so on and so on. She's half a Pakeha in more ways than one, if you see what I mean.

In the end I'm so mad I go alone. That's not the Maori way where you take the family too. But that the way it goes now. I got down to Waiari pretty early in the day. Nice sunny morning and the sea looked good and I began wondering about the chance of a load of pipis and mussels, it was a great place for those. But when I tried to get my bearing, golly, it all looked somehow different. I nearly forget where the people live because the last time I was down there was grandpa's tangi, old Hone Tawa's youngest son, and I was only a bit of a kid then. Lots of places seemed to have gone and there were a lot of new places like Pakehas live there. Looked like someone was trying to turn it into a holiday place. All used to be Maori land round the old marae.

At last I see on the little hill above the beach the old place I remember where uncle lived. Only now when I look at it it's somehow different too, newer looking, and I see that it's a newer place with a bit of a garden around it. Anyway, up I go and there's a two or three year old playing on the door step and he says hullo, and then he calls out, 'Mummy, there's a man to see you.' And this young woman comes to the door.

Now as for me I can't speak Maori, can't even understand what they say, the old people. But there was me in the old home kainga, in the middle of Maori country, and there was this young woman that looked real Maori, so the words just came naturally. 'Tenaa koe, e hine,' I said to her. I do know that greeting and a few of the old words, you see, not that I'd ever come at old Maori greetings to anyone anywhere in Auckland. But there at Waiari, my people's kainga, it just came natural. And what do you think that young woman said, eh?

She looked puzzled. 'Pardon, what did you say?' she asked, a real Kiwi accent too, not a trace of Maori. But she looked more Maori than me, and I think she don't know one word of Maori. There was me, I look near enough Maori allowing for one or two Pakeha ancestors, and I know how to say tenaa koe and so on. She surely must have heard those Maori words sometime. It got me wondering. Anyhow, I quickly kept to good old plain English from that on.

She turns out to be the girl young nephew Henare married. She wouldn't know me of course. But where was uncle Tu, I asked. Didn't he live there anymore? Oh yes, she says except when he was away at his cousins' place in Rotorua. But today he was away at work. 'Not the work on the farm here, eh?' 'No,' she says, 'the bus comes every morning at six-thirty and take the men to the Metal Industries factory in Pinewood.' He wouldn't be home till late – overtime.

I looked around and think well, well, well! 'Tu must be getting on in years now,' I say. 'Getting a bit old for hard work, eh?' 'He'll get the pension next year,' she tells me, 'but now he's got no land or anything– well, he does what he can.' I remember when I was a kid, uncle talking about his farm, I could think of him happy on the land, his own boss, eh. It's turned out a bit tough for him.

Was I staying? Well, things weren't the same with uncle not there, and one thing and another. 'I better get back to Auckland tonight,' I said. 'The stopwork's over tomorrow and I might lose my job.'

'Oh yes,' she said, 'the job. What do you do in Auckland?'

'Oh, I drive the city bus.'

'Oh,' she says, 'lots of Islanders, aren't there, driving the buses in Auckland? Lots of Islanders. The Islanders might grab your job.'

'Yes, the stopwork ends tomorrow, I better get back.'

'It's last year since Tu had a stopwork. He might have been here to meet you if only he had a stopwork now. But he goes to work every day.'

So I just had a few more words before I go, about how things changed.

'The Pakehas want to get the seaside places,' she tells me, as I noticed. 'And the government people took Tu's land for the big tourist hotels sometime. It isn't the same here anymore.'

Ae, it isn't the same anymore.

So at last I said so long, maybe see you some more. And the kid shouted goodbye as I go out the yard.

Maybe you should never go back. I felt sort of sad and lonely. Down in the settlement by the beach I wondered where the old people were. Not a soul! Surely not all at factory work, or shut up in the house like Pakehas. But I see a big sprawling new motor camp where the old-timers used to sit in the sun and yarn. A cool breeze sprang up, south-east right off the sea and the sun disappeared behind clouds. There was the meeting-house where I remembered being taken at the time of grandpa's tangi, but of course it was shut up now, and it looked a bit more dilapidated. I felt quite cold. There was time before the bus back to Auckland so I think I'll have a drink or two to warm me and cheer me up.

The old wooden pub's gone and there's this new fancy brick place for the tourist. Anyway, I go in the public bar and get me a beer. There was two middle-age Maori men at the far end of the bar and I hear them talking in Maori, but I don't try that trick and make me feel the fool again. And there's one or two Pakehas together. But anyway, I don't feel much like talking to anyone. And the beer don't cheer me or warm me. I knock back a whisky or two. But I still feel chilled and sickly. Not sick, mind you, just sickly, like I might have got on the wrong side of tapu or something like that. But cut that out, I say to myself, don't you go getting like the old people. And anyway, bloody lot you know about tapu.

I listen to the Maori voices of the two men at the other end of the bar and try to make out what they say. But it's no use, I understand only one or two words here and there. What it is, the sad beer or something, I don't know, but it makes me mad when I cannot understand. In Auckland, in the big city, I never get mad when a few times I hear some man speak Maori, but here in my own home kainga, in this Maori place, in all this Maori country I am shamed that I cannot speak my people's language, that I cannot even understand, and it makes me mad. It is because of what the Pakeha did to my father, and to all the other kids' fathers, when they were youngsters. My father told me the teacher strapped him when he was a little boy going to school the first time, and how could he know better. The teacher strapped him, a little Maori boy, for speaking Maori, and then he made him wash out his mouth with soap and water, wash the dirty Maori off his tongue. So my father stopped speaking the Maori. And I never learn.

Golly, that cold pub give me the shivers. I stretch my nerves to understand the words of the two Maori men at the other end of the bar. What the heck! Their words flowed around and about them with a big warm friendly sound. The men look into each other's eyes, and they laugh a bit and they put an arm around the other's shoulder. You can tell they're never alone and cold there in that place where the words warm the heart. Then I think of the busload of young Maoris I drive up to a marae way up north to talk about the treaty of Waitangi – was it for good or the saddest day ever. And I begin to see what they mean. One time I never had much patience with such people, but I begin to see. They're mad because of what they've lost, everyone pushing them around to turn them Pakeha, and they wake up to find what they've lost. And they get mad. Some things you lose, you can find them again, but other things you lose you know it's for ever, and you mourn, you tangi. And for them that's Waitangi. And for me, the day of uncle Tu and the things dear to his heart, all lost. What the use me coming back to my people that I cannot speak to? And the young woman and her husband and kids lead another kind of life in that old place, something I don't know of. But their talk is what I hope I'd left behind – the stopwork, factory shift, the overtime, the sack.

I wished the Auckland bus comes soon. It was all wrong the way I came down to see uncle. It was because of the stopwork, a Pakeha thing. When a man goes back to his people's old kainga it ought to be because of a Maori thing, he mea Maori, if those the right words – you see, somewhere in the back of my head or my heart the old words kind of whisper, they keep coming up trying to get out, and give me no peace. Anyway, coming back should be because of a Maori happening – such as a tangi. Ae, a tangi for one of us departed, like grandpa when I was a little kid. Maybe it's only death that can bring us city horis back to the heart of our people now.

Then the bus comes. I know I never see my uncle Tu again.

JAMES COURAGE

Scusi

At this end of the Promenade you could hardly hear the sea: gently, in the vacant autumn evening, it lapped on the pebbles of the civilized beach as though it too were tamed by the white stucco face of the town above. Only its raw salty smell eddied with the shoreward breeze across the pleasure-boats drawn up under the sea-wall, the strips of marine garden explosive with red zinnias, the balustrade of the road, the dark liquorice of the roadway, and reached the first-floor balcony and open windows of the Commander's narrow Regency house. Here the long net curtains rippled; petals fell from the roses on an elegant table in the beautiful room.

It was just after six o'clock of a warm day. Among the Commander's guests the Italian manservant was handing a tray of sherry glasses. His starched mess-jacket came just below the belt of his taut black trousers as he leaned forward. His young eyes, mournful, were bent on the tray. He did not look at the Commander, who stood drawing on a cigarette by the fireplace and watching the man's black shoes as they shuffled over the Aubusson carpet between the chairs.

'That's settled then, Francis,' said Mrs Lanfrank to her host. 'We'll pick you up in the car tomorrow. About twelve-thirty? We can lunch on the Course.'

'Thank you, Myra.' The Commander assembled his eyes, his long pink face, his deep voice, with an effort. 'I see Oakim is entered for the Cup,' he said. 'I shall certainly try a flutter there.'

'Depends who's in the saddle.' Geoffrey Lanfrank, Myra's husband, spoke. He lit a match for his wife's cigarette, his leathery golfer's hands shielding the flame. 'The other end, my dear,' he admonished her. 'Not even you would enjoy a drag on a cork tip.'

'Oh, sorry.' Myra reversed the cigarette. 'I wasn't thinking.' She drew smoke into her plump little mouth and puffed it out through her nose. 'I'll wait till I see the card before I do any plunging myself,' she said to Francis Wood, the Commander.

The Italian manservant edged the tray on to a side-table, looked at the Commander for orders and, receiving a nod, went out, closing the door. Some warmth seemed to leave the room with him. Myra Lanfrank's geranium-painted lips went slack, then tightened with curiosity. She brushed a hand over the tweed of her skirt. 'Goodness, Francis,' she said to the Commander, 'where did you get him?'

Sometimes he seemed slightly deaf. 'Get – ?'

'Him, it, that.' She stabbed with her cigarette after the closed door. 'Or is he a relic of your Naval career?'

'Far from it.' The Commander smiled, his lips arching above uneven teeth. 'He came to me through an employment agency in London – or rather, they suggested him and I had to sign a chit before they'd let him into the country. He's a northern Italian – was a German P.O.W.'

'These Eyeties,' said Geoffrey Lanfrank who had fought in Sicily, 'they think they can simply barge over here –'

'He had no job in Italy,' the Commander said shortly. 'I said I'd try him here, anyway.'

'And?' Myra Lanfrank glanced into her sherry glass: she could never keep servants herself and suspected her own bossiness. She modified her question. 'Your house looks spotless as usual, Francis,' she said. 'What's this man's name?'

'Giovanni, I believe,' the Commander replied, distantly, 'though when I first asked him he said "Scusi"; so, not speaking much Italian myself, I call him Scusi.'

'But how delightful. Just "Scusi"!'

Geoffrey Lanfrank broke in: 'There's a nag of that name running tomorrow, Francis.' He twirled the end of his moustache, chuckling. 'You might back that, too. He's from this bloke Magnani's stable.'

And they were back on the subject of the Brighton Meeting, on the following day. The Commander occupied his time, his leisure, with golf, bridge, the theatre, books and race-meetings. He was a man of forty-eight, retired now from the Navy though still on the Reserve List: he was well-off, rich through an inheritance from a family of cotton-millers. His wife was dead. It was she who had bought this fine little Regency house on a South Coast Promenade, just before the war: she too who had furnished it to her own safe taste, in period, though with some help from Francis, who had his own itch for perfection, for an elegant upholstery in life. There were no children of the marriage. Francis was now what he fancied he had always been at heart, a celibate. He preferred his bachelor ease: he was not particularly lonely. He had his car, he had his friends – retired people mostly, good sorts like himself. His long face, his long body, were bonily handsome: he had not put on flesh, only the lines between his nose and chin had deepened, as though knife-carved. He did not regret having left the Navy: its order, its male cleanliness were safely about him in his smart, polished little seaside house. The one person he loved now was his mother: he wrote to her every few days, he telephoned to her frequently, every Christmas he went north to visit her in Edinburgh in his small polished car. There was a deep bond of affection between them. Francis's father, who had left him so much money, lay under a granite slab in Edinburgh.

'And does he cook?' asked Myra Lanfrank, who was still thinking of the young Italian in the white mess-jacket. 'Does he make you wonderful meals, Francis?'

'Unfortunately, no.' The Commander took up the sherry decanter, inspected the level of the very dry Amontillado he favoured, took out the stopper and stood still, in thought. 'A rather poor cook,' he said. 'Never been taught. But he's handy enough in the house.' He held the lip of the decanter over Mrs Lanfrank's glass. 'Fill up?'

'No,' she said. Her ringed hand went over the rim of her glass. 'I've got to remain sober enough to cook Geoffrey's dinner when we get home. But oh,' she went on, 'you men have all the luck with servants.'

'I wouldn't say that,' said Francis judicially, 'I wouldn't say that at all, you know. Scusi's only a stop-gap – in fact I find that he only came to England in the hope of becoming a lorry-driver. He was oddly misled.'

Myra giggled. 'How very peculiar.'

'Wops,' said her husband to Francis, 'have no mechanical sense whatever, I can tell you that. When their tanks ran out of oil they just left the damn things in a ditch and skedaddled. No sort of nous with engines.' He got up. He was nearly as pudgy as his vivacious little bun of a wife. 'Come along, old girl,' he nagged her, 'time we made tracks for the nest. Thanks for the drinks, Francis.'

'We'll pick you up tomorrow,' Myra reminded the Commander. 'Your Scusi will have your dinner ready now,' she added, playfully mocking. 'You mustn't keep him waiting.'

The Commander showed them down the stairs he called his escape-hatch – a spiral iron stair that had once, when the house had been split into a couple of maisonettes, formed an interior ladder, so to speak, between the ground- and first-floors. Now it was rather a joke, a surprise, like a fun-fair contraption – this narrow, vertical twist of iron steps that was as constricted as though inside a submarine. Women's heels clattered and skidded on it, men's boots made a hollow clank. The Commander himself, when he used it, negotiated the treads with great dexterity, one hand on a silken rope dangling beside the wall. Now the Lanfranks hopped down this stair like fat, cheerful monkeys. It was one of dear old Francis's little tests – a joky sort of inheritance from his naval past, they told him as he saw them out, grinning, into the salt-smelling air of the Promenade. They waved goodnight in a high humour and were gone.

Francis took himself back upstairs to the empty Regency room, to the vacancy of drifting smoke and drained sherry glasses. He pressed the bell-push beside the marble fireplace.

The Italian servant did not often use the iron 'escape-hatch'. Now he came loping silently up the ordinary staircase in the well of the house, from the basement.

'Commendatore?'

The Commander hid away a little Italian dictionary he carried in the hip-pocket of his blue pin-striped suit. 'The glasses, Scusi,' he said, and pointed. 'I bicchieri. Take them.' When he could not cope with the Italian words he used a half-forgotten French. 'Prenez,' he directed now, faltering.

'Si, Commendatore. Pronto.'

The Italian moved about the room, surely yet rather clumsily, a well-meaning country youth in a white coat. The Commander took up a newspaper, annoyed at the man's gusty breathing after the stairs, his intrusion on the silent room. The man was a clod, undisciplined.

'Why don't you try to learn English properly?' the Commander asked, not looking at him.

'Scusi, signore?'

'Learn more English,' the master said loudly. 'It's your job.'

The Italian paused, his black eyes blank, his rich mouth smiling as though snatched from melancholy. 'Si, Commendatore,' he hazarded.

'Not a single word do you understand,' shrugged the Commander. 'Well, it doesn't matter, I suppose. You're probably a fool, anyway.'

'The Commendatore wants dinner – ' the man grinned, holding the tray of glasses. 'Down the stairs,' he said in hesitant English. 'Ecco! All set.'

'All set?' Francis laughed, oddly pleased. 'You've picked that up, anyway. All right. Allez now.'

'Scusi, signore?'

'No matter. I'm coming down. Vengo.'

The man departed, puzzled, his eyes mournfully lowered. Francis went down to dinner. Everything was placed close together in the centre of the round table – dishes, glasses, flowers, plates, all in a careful but parsimonious order, as though on parade. The manservant waited.

'For God's sake,' said the Commander, 'do you think I'm a bird, to reach all that?' He stood beside the table.

'Scusi, signore?'

'Look,' and Francis re-set the table. 'Look, you bloody young fool. Like this, always. Sempre.'

The man nodded, his moist young face studying the effect. 'Si, mio Commendatore. I under-stand.' His eyes switched sadly to the master's. 'Sempre,' he repeated. 'I do forget not.'

'All right,' said Francis, sitting. 'Go back to the kitchen now.' And, irritated, he began his dinner. Afterwards, because he thought he had been harsh with the young Italian, he sat upstairs drinking whisky, his eyes staring across the dark Promenade outside, at the civilized, lapping sea. At ten o'clock he rang up his mother in Edinburgh and for a quarter of an hour they chattered on long-distance. His mother had not been well – 'Old age,' she said, telling him not to worry about her. Nothing more of consequence was said, but the

Commander felt happier, more humane, for the talk. He could forget that he had shown bad temper to the Italian servant.

The following evening, after his day at the races, the Commander came home alone. He had told the manservant that he could have the evening off, since he himself would go out for dinner. But he did not go out for dinner. And he watched the Italian leave the house dressed in a tight black suit and yellow – deplorably yellow – shoes and wander off along the Promenade, alone, his shoulders drooping, his hair smarmed back. Where did the fellow go? Francis supposed, with irritation, that he drifted about on the pier, whistling after girls. Oh, well, it was no concern of his.

He poured himself out four fingers of gin, added a dash of limejuice and sat among his Regency furniture, a novel on his knees. But the feeling of annoyance persisted, only sharpened by the taste of liquor. He had won much canny money during the afternoon – had seen each runner of his choice placed, save one. The exception was the horse named Scusi: this animal had made a mess of the race from the start and had finished indistinguishable among the rabble down the course. The Commander had cursed himself for a mug: he, an able studier of form, had this time ridiculously put his money on a name. And what a name! The chance sobriquet of an incompetent Italian servant. He had carefully not mentioned his bet to the Lanfranks: he had even denied, to Myra, that he had laid out a penny piece on the race. Yet now the horse's failure rankled. Scusi, he felt, had let him down.

Francis put aside his book. The room was growing too dusky for him to read. He lit a cigarette, brisked his hair at the oval mirror above the mantelpiece, and swung himself down the spiral stairway to the dining-room. Thence he went into the hall and, by the ordinary stairs, to the basement. In the white kitchen an alarm-clock ticked blankly; the refrigerator purred; a string of onions hung like a swollen rosary beside the sink. On the table a grubby English phrase-book lay open. The Commander turned the signet ring on his finger, pensively, and let the book lie. He opened the refrigerator: a couple of eggs bald on a plate, a jug of milk, a saucer of dank boiled potatoes. The Commander shut them back into darkness and stood still in the impersonal room. Why had he come downstairs? He had not entered this part of the house since before the Italian's arrival, a fortnight earlier. Mrs Hame, the woman who came in twice weekly to scrub and sweep for a few hours, had shown the manservant his quarters and agreed to help him with the shopping. The Commander left the household's running to the two of them. The woman was elderly, a carpenter's wife from the town.

The Italian's room was behind the kitchen, at the end of a stone-floored passage. Now the Commander went along this passage, opened the door of the room and strolled in. Under the crude glitter of a single bulb the floor was clean, rugless; a pink-striped tie hung behind the door; a suitcase of tan cardboard, roughly tied with twine, sat in a corner; the bed was unmade, with crumpled blankets. But what struck the Commander most, offending his senses as an outrage, was the room's smell: a barracky fug of unaired bedding, sweat, the tang of a peasant's body, warmth conserved only to stale in chilliness. The smell was really unforgivable. The Commander, holding back the breath in his chest, stalked across and pushed up the window. Outside were black iron bars, then a little prison-like cage of a yard. He drew the fresher air into his lungs, frowned, and again faced the room. It was extraordinary, how angry he felt that anyone should brew such an animal smell in his house. Not even below-deck in a ship would he have forgiven such a stink: he would have had the responsible man up before him at once.

He went back upstairs, snatched his hat and mackintosh from the hall, and walked off into the town, with long precise strides. The lamps were lit, high along the Promenade, distantly twinkling in front of the cream stucco houses. He took himself into a narrow street, into a bar behind the theatre. Here he had an old respectful acquaintance with the publican and his pretty wife. The bar, between theatre intervals, was almost empty: overlit photographs of actors and actresses on the walls grinned and ogled at nothing.

'Well, Commander,' the man greeted him, 'win anything on the hosses?'

'No,' said Francis shortly, 'a rotten day.'

'Uh-huh? You're usually well in.'

The Commander took his beer and a couple of sandwiches and sat himself apart. The publican and his wife polished glasses behind the bar.

'Some sort of a foreigner was here, earlier,' said the wife presently. 'An Italian, I suppose.'

'Ah.' Francis stared at her, hostile.

'Poor lad, I think he wanted wine— I didn't understand him properly— but we don't sell wine, not by the glass. He went off.'

'Ah,' said Francis again.

'He'd be lonely,' the publican's wife remarked. 'Away from his own country, like that, and not speaking English.'

The Commander sat on, smoking, until the bar closed. Then he strolled back along the Promenade to his Regency house. There was a light in the basement. He let himself in to the hall and went down the stairs, quietly.

The manservant sat at the table in the kitchen, his face propped by his hands, his eyes on the grubby phrase-book, his hair like greased plumage under the light. He looked up as the master appeared.

'Commendatore?' He rose.

'Giovanni,' said Francis, almost softly, 'I want a word with you about your room.'

'Scusi, signore?'

'Your room,' repeated the Commander. 'Your bed-room.'

The man looked down helplessly at his book. 'Your room,' he echoed, in phonetic imitation. 'Si, signore.'

'Not mine. Yours.' The Commander took up the phrase-book. 'Vostra camera,' he said at last, finding the words.

'La mia camera?'

'That's it. You must open your windows.' And again he turned the pages. 'Non chiuda le finestre, sempre,' he pronounced in his clipped officer-accents. 'Non sempre.'

The manservant's mournful eyes narrowed. 'Si, signore.'

'The room stinks,' said the Commander, with sudden anger. 'Stinks, understand?' And he broke out, in French: 'Ça pue,' and touched his nose. 'Stinks.'

The servant's face surprisingly smiled. 'Stinks,' he said. 'I under-stand.'

'It's no laughing matter, damn you. I won't have such a smell in my house.' He threw the phrase-book on the table, furiously.

'Scusi, signore?'

The Commander found himself looking down at the man's bowed head, the rounded tops of his neat ears. 'I won't have it,' he said again, as though to a child. 'If you're cold at nights you can have as many blankets as you need.'

The Italian stood to attention, stiffened by the master's tone. And he said, in a surly voice, deeply offended: 'Si, mio Commendatore.'

For a moment there was a pause, with both men breathing roughly. Then:

'All right,' said Francis. 'Don't take it too hardly. You've got to learn. . . . Did you enjoy your evening out?'

'Scusi, signore?'

'No matter. I'm afraid the place is lonely for you. Go to bed now.' And he himself left the kitchen, his hands shaking, and went upstairs. He felt ashamed of himself, a bully: yet undoubtedly the Italian wanted discipline if he were to make a good servant. And he, Scusi, must learn English: this semi-pidgin nattering between them was absurd. All the same, Francis felt ashamed of himself: he had a liking and twisted pity for the young Italian. He could not dismiss him.

The next day, early, the manservant set upon the house with a vacuum-cleaner: in a sort of trance he careered behind the machine as though his job depended on it. He loved any mechanical contraption, anything workable, tendable.

'Buon giorno, Commendatore.'

'Morning,' said Francis on his way to the bathroom. The zoom-zoom of the cleaner had wakened him earlier than usual. Now he asked gruffly about breakfast: 'Colazione non pronta?'

'Adesso, signore.'

Later, Francis fetched his car from its garage: he was off for a day of golf behind the town. But first he told the Italian, with gestures, to polish the car. And Scusi descended on the car with absolute delight, singing. Dusters and leathers flew over the paintwork, the windscreen, the lamps. The Commander, behind his *Telegraph*, watched him from the window above – the man cherishing the varnish of the car, skimming his hands over its expensive beauty in sensual pleasure.

Once, the Italian looked up, grinning. He pursed his broad lips forward into a word which the Commander took to be 'Bella'. Francis drew back from the window. He was pleased, nevertheless, by Scusi's liking for machinery: it made up for his hit-or-miss cooking, the stink of his room, the awful tenor-ness of his singing. Presently Francis went downstairs, collected his golf-clubs, and descended the steps to the car. Autumnal sunlight lay as gently as gossamer on the Promenade, on the morning sea beyond.

The Italian displayed the car. 'You like, Commendatore?'

'I like,' nodded Francis, and smiled. 'Thank you, Scusi.'

The manservant, in his waistcoat, stood on the steps; waved him a goodbye. The Commander did not wave or look back. He went off for a serious day's golf.

In the evening he was back for dinner, his body rich-feeling from its exercise as he took his before-dinner bath and drink. Then he heard voices, a murmur below him in the basement. Ordinarily he would have paid no attention to kitchen-chatter; now he hesitated. Mrs Hame would not be in the house so late; Scusi was supposed to be alone, preparing the dinner. The Commander's hand stretched out to the bell-push but he did not ring. Instead, he went down to the kitchen.

The first thing he noticed was an open bottle of red wine on the table; then, behind it, two strangers, a man and a woman. Scusi bent by the stove. He straightened at the Commander's entrance.

'Commendatore?'

Francis said bluntly: 'I am ready for dinner.'

'Friends,' grinned Scusi, and pointed at the strangers. 'Friends from Londra, signore. My friends.'

And now the woman spoke. 'Forgive us, sir. But Giovanni wrote us a sad letter so we came to see him.' She was smallish, closely dressed in brown and had an almost Cockney voice. 'This is my husband,' she said, introducing the second stranger. 'The only Italian man Giovanni knows in England. . . . So we came down from London for two hours.'

'I see,' said Francis. 'Of course.' With his natural good manners he felt he had intruded, but he did not move.

The woman's dark husband spoke: 'Will you take a little wine, sir? It was to cheer him up.' And he nodded towards the static, smiling Scusi. 'I knew his brother in the war, in Genoa.'

'I won't drink, thank you,' said the Commander. The male amiability, out of his class, had nonplussed him, but now he heard himself saying: 'You'd both better have some food with Sc— with Giovanni.'

'Oh no, sir,' the woman broke in, alarmed. 'We're just leaving. The 'bus goes at seven. My husband must get back to his restaurant.'

Francis, with a show of well-bred ease, took himself off to the dining-room and sat staring at his eighteenth-century engravings on the walls. The room was as neat and as becalmed as a shop-window. Presently he heard the guests leave by the steps from the basement-area. There was a clatter and bustle below, then Scusi brought in his dinner: all together, piled on a tray, were soup, a chop, potatoes, and a collapsed castle of blancmange.

'Gone, Commendatore.' The man was vinously cheerful.

'Your friends?'

'Si. Gone.' He laid out the dishes. 'Il pranzo for the Commendatore.'

The dinner, however, was almost uneatable: over-cooked, tasteless. Francis sighed, but he was angry. The man was impossible. And what was that remark the woman had made – 'a sad letter'? Francis was uneasy, remembering. What right had this Italian youth, to whom he'd given a job in a good house, to write sad letters? Wasn't he contented? What more did he want? A brooding fuse of indignation seemed to break into sparks in the Commander's mind. He forked over his filthy dinner without appetite. He'd have to have another talk with Scusi. And he produced his pocket dictionary and, coldly furious, looked out a few words in readiness, noting them on the flyleaf in his delicate Gothic writing. Then he left the dining-room and the fallen blancmange.

Upstairs he switched on the wireless and listened for an hour to a symphony-concert, to calm himself. But the exquisite formality of Mozart, the experience of controlled poetry in sound, did not calm him. At nine o'clock he lit all the lamps in the room and pushed the bell-push to summon the Italian. He had always disliked having to interview servants.

'Commendatore?'

'Yes,' said Francis, his blue eyes holding the man's dark gaze. 'I wanted to ask you a thing or two. Aren't you – '

'Scusi, signore?'

'Listen – don't interrupt. . . . Are you not happy here? . . . Non contento?' he amended.

'Qui, signore?'

'Yes, here. With me.'

The man hung his head, reproved, stroking his white jacket. The effects of the wine were still with him. The flesh of his cheeks shone with a moist sadness like tears, though he was not weeping. And he said slowly, in his throat: 'I do not know, mio Commendatore.'

'Do you want to go to Londra?'

'Londra?' The youth struggled in silence. 'No work,' he shook his head. 'Non Londra.' A rich melancholy troubled his mouth. 'Here I work,' he gulped.

'Ah,' Francis nodded. His anger had vanished, but he fought against looking at the man and kept his eyes on his own well-brushed shoes. 'But what you really want to do is to drive a cambio – a truck?'

The man gave a spasm of a smile. 'Si, signore.' He looked at Francis, it seemed, with such love and hope that the older man fiercely turned aside. Even without meeting it, he could not stand that undefended look: it struck him in his lonely soul.

'If you could only speak English better,' he said, 'I might use you as a chauffeur. But, as it is, there'd be licence difficulties.'

The Italian waited, not understanding, his face drooping into sleepy stupidity. The sea, sounding on the pebbles of the beach beyond the Promenade, was not more vacant than he. The Commander felt him standing there: the man's breathing and vulnerable flesh, in this fastidious upper room of his house, was a liability he could not meet. He must make some move to extricate himself.

'All right,' he said at last. 'Go now. . . . And keep your windows open, downstairs.'

The Italian turned in the doorway. He had caught the word 'windows' and now he smiled with all his white teeth, implying an obedience that was an affectionate mockery of his employer's power. The wine inside him was still warm: if this high-minded Englishman insisted on the malarial airs of night sweeping into the house, then sweep they must. He would open every crack of a window, everywhere.

'Ecco Commendatore.'

He pivoted round and, with a clatter of his boots, attacked the descent of the iron stair to the floor below. But the wine in his head had altered his balance. He slipped, made a grab at the silk rope, missed it, and fell, bump after bump, down the iron spiral, his white jacket rucked up to his arm-pits. For a moment, stunned, he lay on the green carpet of the passage, his mouth open. The Commander, meanwhile, hearing the commotion, hurried down the escape-hatch behind him. At first he thought the Italian was dead. All his muscles tightened with fear, then he spoke softly:

'Christ, man – what have you done?'

The servant's eyelids fluttered, confused. 'Signore . . . signore. . . .' Childish contortions of shock made his mouth tremble. And he babbled excuses in Italian, struggling to pull himself up and his coat down. 'Signore . . . signore. . . .'

'All right,' said Francis, 'keep calm.' He helped the man to his feet, brushed back his tumbled hair, and carried him down to the basement and his room. The place was as stuffy as ever, the windows utterly shut. Francis laid the man on the bed: the thick body had been hot and heavy to carry.

'Do you want a doctor, Scusi? A medico?'

'No, Commendatore.' The man began to explore the joints of his arms, his knees, his back – particularly his back. 'Niente,' he said presently, and sat up. He touched his forehead and grinned up at the master meaningfully.

'I know,' said Francis, 'too much vino.' He opened the window. 'Far too much vino.' For some reason now he felt a dread of being so close to the Italian. 'Still, you might have broken your neck,' he observed, distantly.

The servant nodded, though he did not understand the words. Nevertheless he said in English, wiping his eyes and his smooth face: 'Thank you, signore. Thank you. You are good.' And he cradled his arms to imply the Commander's carrying him downstairs. 'Good to me.'

'All right,' said Francis in his officer's voice. 'There's not much wrong with you. You'll be up in the morning.' He left the room.

In the morning the servant was stiff, but well, and careering round the house with the vacuum-cleaner. The Commander, seized with intolerable impatience, fetched his car and drove himself up to London, where he was a member of an officers' club. Here he took a room for a week. It soothed him to be among men who remembered him or whom he remembered. The atmosphere of the wardroom was strong in the club – Hitler's war had, as it were, been an exclusive school which had fostered the manhood of these ex-Navy men. But, between drinks, Francis was worried: he had pains in his back, possibly lumbago. So he took his elegant bony body to a doctor. The doctor found nothing wrong, nothing whatever – the Commander had been playing too much golf perhaps. Francis pooh-poohed the idea. And the following evening he rang up his mother. How was she? Her frail, faraway voice sounded cheerful, but she wandered a little – she had been thinking of a pet cat that had been run over, long ago. Francis, hanging up after ten minutes of the cat, thought of flying north to see her, then decided – in words that surprised him – that he 'wasn't going to be driven out of his own house by a confounded Italian manservant', and sped himself and his car back to the coast.

Scusi met him at the door. 'Commendatore!' His dark eyes warmed into welcome; he broke into gusts of Italian as he carried in the master's cream-hide suitcase. 'Good, good! I fetch.'

The house was clean, everything in order, but strangely empty. Francis promptly rang up several golf- and racing-cronies, inviting them in for a drink. He felt he could not be alone with the Italian. And the cronies came; most of them, in their laconic way, admired the Commander's house, his taste, his monied bachelorhood, his Naval record. They drank his gin and his whisky and treated the Italian servant as though he were not there. But Francis knew he was there and was irritated when, after the visitors' cars had rolled away, Scusi came to speak to him.

'Very well, what is it?'

The servant stood at attention, stocky in his white jacket, his face shining in the apricot glow of the lamps. He made his master understand that the signore and signora from Londra – his friends of a week or so back – would be coming again on the morrow, and might the signora have a talk with the Commander?

'Yes, if she wants to. And if she leaves the vino at home.'

Francis dismissed the man and went to bed early. His touch of lumbago came back: he lay, stretched out, thinking of his solitary life and finding its drawbacks sharpened by this pain which might or might not be imaginary. And why should the 'signora' want to talk to him? Had Scusi decided to claim damages for his fall on the iron stairs? The Commander groaned, got out of bed, and stood at his window looking at the dark sea. It was late September, an Indian summer on the coast, the stars bright without frost, the Promenade as empty as a road in a dream. He lit a cigarette, then stubbed it out, shivering, listening to the silent house below him as though fearful of footsteps, a criminal entry. . . . And for the first time for years he thought of his dead wife with emotion: she had, after all, been his friend, his companion; they had lain awake together in this room, talking, talking. True, they had been lovers only with shame, but in retrospect that did not seem to matter: time had absorbed the stress of such a disturbing mutual discovery. Now he missed her.

'I might marry again,' he smiled to himself, getting back to bed. 'I must look round. . . .' His lumbago seemed relieved and he slept.

The following afternoon, about five, he heard Scusi's visitors arrive down the area steps. Francis sat reading. He had put off an afternoon's bridge, to be at home to the Cockney signora. And presently the manservant, after some whispering on the stairs, ushered her in to his master. She was dressed as before, in brown, with a coat-collar of fox-tawny fur. Scusi himself waited erect by the door with a hovering grin of indecision. The signora's husband, it appeared, had been jettisoned in the basement.

'Ah yes,' said Francis stiffly to the young woman. 'Sit down.'

'No, sir. I will stand, thank you.' Her voice was decent: a parlour-maid's trained tones overlaying the Cockney. And she went on: 'Giovanni's English is so bad, sir, he has asked me to speak to you for him.' She wiped her pale lips.

'Giovanni is learning,' the Commander said, moved to defend his servant. 'I'm teaching him.'

The Italian, hearing his own name, bobbed his head like a good dog, smiling. 'Si, signore.'

'But he can't explain himself,' the woman said with dignity. 'No, sir.'

'Very well. Go ahead.'

'He is grateful to you, sir, but it is too quiet here. My husband has found him a place with an Italian firm in Soho. He will drive a van for them. The Italians in London, Sir, all help one another.'

'You mean Giovanni wants to leave me?'

'He is an unhappy boy, sir. And he did not mean to be a cook.'

'No,' said Francis, 'I'm afraid that's obvious. But, again, he is learning here.' He did not look at Scusi. His tongue felt thin and cold in his mouth.

'All the same, sir,' said the woman, 'he wishes to go, though you have been kind to him. He wants to give his week's notice now.'

The Commander glanced across at his servant. 'Ask him in Italian,' he said to the young woman.

She spoke for a long time, a minute, to Scusi, in his own language.

'Si, Commendatore,' said Scusi at length, 'è vero. It is true.'

'Very well,' Francis brought out obliquely. 'Then I cannot stop him. But he must fix it with the employment authorities – '

'My husband will do that, sir.'

And presently the woman and Scusi went below. A door closed in the basement. Francis sat alone, his long hands on the arms of his chair. 'Perhaps,' he thought, with a nagging pain that surprised him, 'this is for the best, though I don't want it . . . I don't.' And it seemed to him that he felt a weight in his arms and back, bowing him down towards the floor.

For the next few days he was coldly polite to the manservant. He no longer cursed him for his lack of English, his shut windows, his atrocious cooking. What did it matter? He went off, out of the house, to play golf; he accepted invitations to bridge; he drove to Myra and Geoffrey Lanfrank's bungalow and talked of the remaining race-meetings of the season. He tried not to look at Scusi; he even wrote down his few household instructions to the man, in English, and left him to worry them out with Mrs Hame's help. Scusi, for his part, after a day or so of fruity singing round the house with the vacuum-cleaner, showed mournful signs of offence. The Commander was behaving as no Italian would behave save in vendetta: the bond between man and man was being insulted. Only the Germans in the prison-camp had treated Scusi in this fashion, and he could not, ever, hate the Commander as he had hated the Germans. So he was puzzled and hurt by Francis's exhibition of integrity. An admiration for the Commander was genuine in his heart. Now he even kept his windows open to please the master, but the master did not care.

And then something happened in the tense little house on the Promenade. On the evening of the day before the Italian was due to leave, the Commander had a telegram. His mother had died that morning in Scotland. He read the message at dinner and was stung with remorse: he should – yes, yes – have gone north from London to see the old lady, not rushed back to his house. Now it was too late. And his mind, his carefully controlled will, was torn in two. The manservant, who had brought him the telegram and remained to clear the table, moved clumsily about the room beside him.

'Scusi,' said Francis.

'Commendatore?'

'You are going tomorrow,' Francis said in Italian.

'Si signore. To Londra.'

The Commander folded the telegram with taut fingers. And he heard his voice say: 'Very well. Will you bring my coffee upstairs now, please?'

With the telegram in his pocket he walked slowly into the lit passage behind the dining-room, to the foot of the iron spiral stairway, while Scusi departed to the basement. Francis halted before the lower of the iron treads. And suddenly he felt he could not move or mount; the pain in his back was not more paralysing than that other pain in his mind – the spasms in the lumbar muscles below his ribs and the spears of desolate grief in his heart. He stood without moving, his hand as though lifeless on the silken rope of the stair, his eyes staring down at the green carpet. He felt his life had split apart in confusion.

The Italian, bearing the coffee-tray high, appeared behind him and waited, his eyes on the Commander's lowered nape in surprise. He said, gently: 'Commendatore?'

Francis raised his chin, without turning. The man's voice only added an edge to his sorrow, his pain.

'Listen,' he said presently, 'I must go away tonight, I must go to Scotland. Do you hear?'

'Signore?' The man had not followed.

'I must go away,' said Francis. He let the rope swing aside from his hand as he turned. 'And I have this pain.'

Again the Italian did not understand. But he sensed from the master's tone that he was suffering, and he put the coffee-tray aside – on the floor – and stood anxiously ready to help, his eyes blinking. 'Signore?' he whispered.

The Commander looked at the youth, looked him up and down, fighting to destroy the intensity of his grief as though it were another man, a stranger inside his own body. 'I must go,' he said. 'We don't even speak the same language, but my mother is dead.' And he repeated the last words in Italian. 'Do you understand?'

Like a light, understanding switched on in the man's face. His own mother was dead and the words went straight to his emotions, so that he took a step forward to support his master. 'My pity, Commendatore,' he brought out.

Francis had seldom cried in his life. Now tears to which he was utterly hostile came chokingly into his throat, his eyes. He put his hands on his back. 'I'm in pain, Scusi. Help me to sit down.'

'Your mother – ' the Italian said.

'Yes. Help me.'

The manservant, uncomprehending, took Francis's arm and bending forward as though to solace one of his own countrymen, kissed him on the cheek. 'My pity, Commendatore,' he repeated in English.

Francis drew back. The gesture had touched so deep a nerve of horror and shock in him that the blow with which he answered the Italian was beyond his will, automatic. It went off like an explosion. He hit the man hard in the chest, feeling all the pain in his back rush upward in a steel tension. 'I didn't ask for your pity,' he said.

'No, signore.' The man was crushed, but not angry.

They stood in silence, panting. 'Very well,' said Francis at last, 'now I shall go upstairs.' He swung himself slowly up the iron spiral. 'And if I hurt you just now you will say no more about it.'

'Si, Commendatore.'

'I shall go to Scotland tonight, by train, and you will go to London tomorrow.'

'Suo caffè, signore?' the man called from below, after a pause.

'Yes, yes, bring it up. I must pack.'

Francis began to sort out the clothes for his journey. Astonishing, but the pain in his back had vanished. Now it was only his mind that hurt him – in this grief that he knew now was not wholly grief on his mother's death. His mind hurt him very much. Meanwhile, the Italian manservant had put down the tray and had turned to leave the room: something was ending.

'Scusi,' the Commander called him back: then he did not know how to go on. He had hit the man, but he had struck himself harder. 'Giovanni,' he said in his officer's voice, 'I wish you luck in your future.'

'Scusi, signore?'

The Commander began to pour his coffee. His feelings were not equal to the words he wanted. 'You must learn to speak English,' he said in their place. 'You ought to get out of this habit of always saying "Scusi". It's a vice.'

The winds of late October hurried in from the sea, across the cold pebbles of the beach, and harried the fronts of the houses facing the Promenade. The red zinnias in the marine gardens were burnt up, gone. Gulls flickered above the balustrades, looking for scraps in the last light of the dusk.

'How I dislike the winter,' Myra Lanfrank cried as the Commander drew the curtains on the evening. 'I'm not really built for the cold.' She sipped at her sherry as at a cordial, her little fat ankles crossed before her. 'Besides,' she said, 'both Geoffrey and I get rheumatism in that hovel of ours.'

'It's all that beer you drink,' her husband remarked.

'I? Nonsense.' And she turned to their host. 'Francis, you had lumbago lately, didn't you? How is it?'

'It went, Myra.' The Commander stood before the fire, a cigarette in his bony, long fingers. 'I must have ricked my back somehow, carrying something too heavy for me.' He straightened himself and took his glass from the mantelpiece. 'The pain disappeared before I went to Scotland.'

'The funeral,' Geoffrey Lanfrank nodded stolidly. 'Well, we have to lose our Mammas some time.'

'Geoffrey mislaid *his* early, thank God,' said Myra. She peered round the elegant little room, as though something were missing. 'By the way, Francis, where's your Wop? The good-looker with the silly name?'

The Commander was listening to the wind shaking the house, the onset of winter. 'Giovanni's delivering spaghetti in Soho, I believe,' he said, but he did not smile. 'I've replaced him here with a housekeeper who fills the basement with cheap scent.' He roused himself from a melancholy he had conquered. 'She's more satisfactory as a cook,' he added.

'You ought to marry again, Francis,' Myra remarked.

The Commander shook his head. 'One day, perhaps. You must find me somebody, Myra.' He stared for a moment at his own reflection over the mantelpiece, then turned away.

There was a silence. And presently Geoffrey Lanfrank said: 'Incidentally, Francis, I meant to tell you – I see that horse with the Eyetie name – Scusi, was it? – won one of the season's last races at Kempton Park. You may have noticed.'

'No,' said the Commander. And it seemed to him that he overheard his own word No cross the borders of all this trivial conversation with the Lanfranks and echo throughout some vast hollow space within him that he had never, until this moment, acknowledged to be his own life. He closed his eyes. And 'No,' he said again, with fear.

An Evening for a Fish

The day had been very warm, with a nor'-wester threshing at the tops of the firs and blue-gums behind the Blakiston homestead and, indoors, a fine greyish dust settling like fur on floors and tables. The heat and the wind had made everyone irritable. When Mr Blakiston came in from the farm to a late tea with his wife and young son he was in one of those explosive nor'-west tempers dreaded by the boy. His wind-burnt face, with its blue eyes and long upper lip, looked surly and accusing. After tea he tapped with the back of a knuckle against the glass of the barometer in the dining-room and growled towards his wife:

'We're in for a calmer evening, thank God.' He waited a moment. 'I thought I might try for a trout, at the river.'

'That means you'll be late for dinner.' She spoke mildly, turning the wedding-ring reflectively on her finger. 'In any case, you never seem to catch these wretched fish – if they're really in the river at all.'

'They're there all right. The trouble is they won't rise to a fly. I'll try with a spear this time.'

The boy Walter, who had been scratching the mosquito-welts on his ankles and cooling them with spit and tea under the table, looked up. At seven years old you hear a word like *spear* extra loudly. He was excited, but doubtful.

'Spearing fish isn't allowed,' he said to his father. 'I've heard you say it isn't.'

'You keep quiet,' his father said. He put a lit match over the bowl of his pipe and sucked in the smoke for a moment. 'You hear too much.'

Walter looked down at the table. 'Could I come with you to the river?' he asked, subdued.

'You?' And his father pointed the stem of his pipe at him. 'Who left the gate of the cow-paddock open?'

'I did,' Walter admitted. He had already had a whipping for the offence, some days past. 'I've said I'm sorry.'

'You're always saying that,' Mr Blakiston grumbled. He frowned away from his son. 'All right,' he said reluctantly, 'I suppose you can come along, if your mother lets you.'

'Can I go, Mum?'

'So long as you don't drown yourself, yes. You've certainly been a nuisance about the house all day.'

'I'll wear my gum-boots. I promise.'

'Very well, dear.'

Walter's father rose, patted the pockets of his Norfolk jacket, and chose a felt hat from the collection of sweat-stained horrors in the hall. 'If he's drowned you'll be the first to know,' he called back to his wife.

'That's all very well, George –' she sighed and gave up the argument: the day had been too hot and she had a headache. Leisurely, smoothing down her white cotton dress, she began to raise the rattan blinds that had been lowered against the glare of the afternoon. From the windows she could see across the long descending miles of the farm's paddocks as far as the blue waters of the bay and the horizon. She sighed again and looked at the garden directly in front of the verandah: even the fuchsias and laurustinus had drooped in the wind, and the wallflowers she had planted lay flat on the dust. Later on, she decided, she would take out a watering-can, before cooking the dinner.

Walter meanwhile followed his father from the house to the stables. Mr Blakiston led out the mare he had ridden that afternoon and harnessed her into the shafts of a small spring-cart with wheels higher than the seat. Then, leaving Walter with the reins, he crossed the yard to the apple-shed and brought out a fish-spear, a short gaff and a rolled-up grain-sack. The spear had whisky-corks stuck on the sharp points of the tines, and looked like a hay-fork. He laid it on the floor of the cart, telling the boy to keep a foot on the handle to hold it steady. Walter's feet were bare and hard-soled. He had forgotten his gum-boots.

'Now,' said Mr Blakiston at last, 'I think we're all ship-shape.' He took the reins from Walter.

'It's like a pirate's expedition,' the boy remarked as they started. 'Dangerous.'

His father grunted but did not answer, his temper still uncertain. He pulled his hat down over his eyes.

They drove past the plantations and into the open airy paddocks. The wind had dropped. Sheep grazed among the tussocks. Larks sang overhead, in the slanting sunlight. The river lay a couple of miles from the homestead and formed one of the boundaries of the Blakiston land, before the country rose into coastal hills to the north. The fish – a very few rainbow trout – occasionally came up the river from the sea when floods had broken the shingle-barrier of the lagoon at the mouth. But to spear trout was, as Walter knew, not allowed by the law.

'Would it be fun in a lock-up at night?' he asked his father now.

'It's not the *offence* that counts so much,' Mr Blakiston said at last testily. 'It's the *principle*. Poaching is poaching. And, generally speaking, Walter, spearing is no way for a man to catch a trout.'

Walter was silent. He had been shy of his father for a long time, and desperately wanted to please him. Perhaps if he said something hopeful it would help.

'We might be able to take the fish with us into the lock-up,' he suggested. 'If we're caught.'

'Enough of that,' said his father shortly. 'We may not find a fish anyway, so keep quiet.'

'All right,' said Walter. But the fact that his father, a man who could be so strict about leaving gates open, might knowingly break the law was downright puzzling.

They left the paddocks behind and the wheels of the cart ground along the gravelled road between fences. After half an hour they came to the cutting that led down to the river-bed. Tall manuka bushes on either side made the cutting almost dark, though presently Walter could see the river below. The river wound seawards between high cliffs and bluffs of limestone and yellow clay, and its bed of pale shingle, with the main stream isolated like a vein near the middle, looked very broad and blue-grey in the late afternoon light. The whole wide river-ravine was deserted and silent save for the curious sweeping whisper of the water on the stones.

'Nobody about, anyway,' Mr Blakiston declared aloud when they had halted on the strip of level ground leading to the ford. He pushed back his hat, looked about him cautiously for a minute, then jumped nimbly from the cart. Walter helped him to tether the mare among the manuka bushes, the leaves of which gave out a sweet dry scent like tea. Then Mr Blakiston took the fish-spear and the gaff from the floor of the cart. Walter was given the rolled-up sack to carry.

'Right,' said his father when they were both ready. With the spear over his shoulder he paused to glance at the sky. 'Another hour or so of good light if we're lucky.' His temper was improving; he was almost larkish. 'Come along, son, we'll try the pools downstream for a start.'

They set off along the bank, between clumps of gorse and stringy wind-bent willows, Walter following his father. The air was cooler than in the country above the cutting. Rabbits scuttered away into the grass, across the sandy turf between the bushes.

'Keep to the side of me, Walter,' Mr Blakiston warned. 'If you're behind you might get the spear in your face.'

After a few hundred yards the bank became a broken series of limestone bluffs which overhung scooped-out pools joined to the river's main stream only by rivulets and freshes across the pale stones. The pool-water was deep: the coarse flood-sand could be seen clearly through it for ten feet down. A few branches of green duckweed wavered near the bottom. The water looked beautifully limpid, powerful and full-flowing, though it moved slackly.

'Keep close now, Walter. Don't show yourself,' Mr Blakiston whispered. He crawled out along a reef of rock above the main pool and for a long time slowly and cannily inspected the water close under the bluff. He had taken off his jacket and hat. Walter crouched behind him, scared to move, clutching the sack to his chest. After five minutes he broke the silence with a cracked whisper: 'See anything?'

His father straightened himself, shaking his head. 'Nothing here. Or they're lying too close.'

They passed to further pools. The water seemed to sleep against the rocks; the underwater stones and weeds had a swollen look as though caught below huge lenses of clear liquid. But there were no trout. The pools were fishless.

Mr Blakiston rubbed his forehead and put on his coat. 'You'd think they'd be rising to feed at this time of the day,' he complained. He glanced up-river. 'Come on, we'll try above the ford. Not getting cold, are you?'

'No.' Walter was shivering but the shivers came from excitement and from a feeling that his father mustn't be disappointed in this quest for fish or the fault would be his, Walter's, and his father's bad temper would start again. 'I'm not cold,' he said loudly.

'You'll never make a proper man of yourself if you shiver in this weather.'

'I wasn't shivering. It was my mosquito-bites making me sort of twitch.'

Mr Blakiston shouldered the spear, gripped the gaff and led off up-river towards the ford. Oh God, Walter prayed below his breath, please let there be a trout, a big one, to keep the temper at bay.

'There must be a fish somewhere, dad,' he said vaguely and cheerfully. 'I can feel there must be.'

His father snorted. 'You're like your mother, Walter. You rely on feelings, emotions. It's a woman's failing. Half the troubles of the universe arise out of that.'

'Out of what?'

'You don't listen properly either – another of your mother's tricks. God knows what you'll use for ears when we get you to school.'

They reached the road and the ford and heard the mare utter a snuffling whinny among the trees as her ears caught the passing footsteps. The river-bank above the ford lay under steep scarps of clay and shale, with only a narrow shore of cocksfoot grass and willows shelving to the floodpools. The water here was less deep than that further down: the bottom was limestone, giving the pools a pearly light above the rock. Gnats and mosquitoes moved close to the surface of the water.

And now Mr Blakiston took off his hat and again began to lower his head, tautly and unbreathingly, over those pools that might hold a fish. Walter noticed that his father's hair grew very like his own, tufty and fair, though most of his father's crop had retreated far back from his forehead.

After five minutes Mr Blakiston stood upright. 'Nary a sign of a damned fish,' he said softly and sourly towards his son.

'Perhaps somebody else has speared them all,' Walter said.

'I shouldn't wonder,' his father grumbled. 'Too many thieves and blackguards in this country. No respect for law or property.' He spat into the water. 'The natural result of government by mugs and fatheads, if you ask me.'

He laid down the spear and gaff, strode a few paces under the willows and began to urinate in the grass, his hips thrust forward, his back turned to Walter. Surprised, the boy glanced up at the summit of the bluff above: a policeman might be on the watch against men easing themselves beside rivers. A policeman might also be patrolling on the watch for blackguards who took trout with spears on a fine evening. But no head in a helmet appeared against the sky.

'Anarchy,' said Mr Blakiston, turning and doing up his buttons with one hand. 'Anarchy's where we're heading the ship if we're not careful, Walter.'

In the act of looking away, embarrassed, the boy saw a lazy stir and dimple appear on the surface of the long pool, twenty yards up-river. A velvety spat of sound followed. Walter turned instantly to his father.

'Did you see?' His whole body grew tense. 'Did you see, Dad?'

But already Mr Blakiston had run quickly along the bank. 'You stay where you are, Walter. No wait – hand the spear to me. Look sharp now.'

Walter handed him the spear. He saw his father peer downwards in the place where the trout had risen; he saw his neck moving cautiously in the search. A moment later his father had beckoned to him, gently.

'Quiet now. You'll see him on the bottom.'

At first Walter could see only ledges of grey limestone, a stick or two and a few trailings of green weed. Then he made out the fish – a laurel-dark back, long, and as smoothly tapered as though cast in metal. The tail fins and the gills were almost idle; the shoulders lay markedly over the pale bed of limestone.

Mr Blakiston drew his son back, took another cautious glance over the edge, sought with his boots for a securer hold in the grass, and with the shaft of the spear tightly grasped lowered the arrowed prongs softly until, with the slowness of motion of a clock-hand, they had reached the surface. The trout gave a slight wriggle but did not stir from his place over the rock. Mr Blakiston braced his back, he sucked in his breath, then in a single motion leant over and launched the spear with his whole strength and aim upon the form of the fish below. At the same moment Walter, craning to see, slipped, caught at the bank and landed sideways in the water. The splash took him under, gasping. He lost sight of his father, hearing only an immense curse as he floundered to the surface:

'You damn young fool!'

But the boy was forgotten. His father began to haul up the spear. And with it came the trout – a fish convulsed, plunging, his flesh-white belly flashing as he reached the air. Mr Blakiston swung both spear and fish as far as the base of the bluff behind him, among the grass and shingle, before he turned to rescue his son.

'Hold on, old chap. I'll get the gaff to you.'

Two minutes later, disentangling the gaff from his shirt, Walter lay alongside the convulsions of the trout. Through the hair over his eyes he saw, now and forever, what was certainly the most beautiful fish he had ever imagined.

'A ten-pounder or I'm a Dutchman,' said Mr Blakiston and hit the trout a blow on the head with the base of the gaff. 'And speared as clean as a whistle,' he added, beginning to work the tines of the spear clear of the still-struggling green shoulders of the fish.

'Is he a rainbow?' Walter inspected the freckling of pink, pale blue and gold along the trout's flanks, among the trickles of blood. 'Is he a rainbow trout, Dad?'

Mr Blakiston nodded. He was very pleased about almost everything in the world. 'You'd better rub yourself dry on the sack, Walter,' he said softly. 'Strip off your wet duds and rub yourself hard.'

'I'm sorry I fell in.'

'I think we'll forget about that.' And, grinning, he helped the boy to scrub his naked body dry and warm, humming tenderly to himself as though he were curry-combing a young horse. 'I hope your mother won't blast the daylights out of us both, Walter,' he confided after a moment. 'She can be a terrible fierce woman about wet duds.'

'Well, we can show her the trout.' Walter kept twisting aside to glance at the fish, now still. 'It must be the biggest fish that was ever in the river.'

When he was dry his father gave him his own jacket to wear. It came down to his knees and was warmer than his shirt and pants together. Wearing the jacket gave him a strange glow and made him lose all fear of his father, as though the fish and the jacket were shared between them like secrets. And now Mr Blakiston held open the mouth of the hard wet sack and let Walter lay the heavy fish inside, delicately, so as not to break the fins.

'The mugs and blackguards didn't catch that one,' said Walter, with satisfaction.

'Too many of their ilk about, all the same,' laughed his father and led the way back to the spring-cart and the waiting mare. 'Not enough honest men, Walter.'

'Are we going home now?'

'Yes, we're going home.' And Mr Blakiston began to sing a verse of 'John Peel' as they started up the cutting, his voice lazy and relaxed, his head back.

Walter curled up his toes against the roll of his soaked clothing on the floor of the cart, and listened. His father did not often sing, not even to his mother. The trout, meanwhile, wrapped in the sack and looking as big as a cat, gave out a fresh fish-smell under the seat. Overhead the stars came out above the open dark country.

At the homestead there were lights in the kitchen and dining-room. Mrs Blakiston, who had long ago put the dinner back in the oven, sat darning her husband's knitted socks under the kitchen lamp.

'Walter', she cried out in panic when the boy arrived draped in his father's coat. 'What on earth – '

'I'm not drowned, Mum. Honestly. Or cold.'

'As warm as a bug in a rug,' said Mr Blakiston, coming in behind him. 'Aren't you, son.' Playfully he bent to kiss his wife on the ear.

'It's no use trying to be funny, George.' She avoided him crossly, jumping up from her chair. 'You're just a fool, letting the child fall in. It's I who'll have to nurse him if he gets pneumonia.'

'Well, for God's sake!' Mr Blakiston snorted. 'As though I'd promised to wrap the kid in tissue-paper. . . .' Affronted, he threw the fish on the table. 'You women,' he exclaimed, 'always grousing and being so damned unfair – '

'I'm not in the least unfair, and you know it. You're an utter idiot. Come, Walter, straight to bed, this instant.'

'Not till dad's weighed the fish.'

The magnificent trout, speckled and faintly luminous, lay heavily in the pan of the kitchen scales.

'Eleven pounds and an ounce,' Mr Blakiston told his wife. 'Cast your eye on that and be grateful.'

'I don't care one rap about your wretched fish!' She hauled at Walter's sleeve. 'You oughtn't to take them with a spear in any case.'

'No policeman saw us,' cried Walter. 'Honestly Mum.' In his excitement he threw off the coat and stood naked before them, his eyes on the fish. 'Anybody can do anything and never get put in the lock-up – or be caught.'

'You try it and see,' said his father explosively, not looking at his wife. And he banged the fish off the scales. 'You just try it and see.'

A. P. GASKELL

All Part of the Game

The Sockburn tram clanked away. I picked up my suitcase and walked along to their gate.

Well, there it was again, all just the same as I'd remembered it from last year; the long straight gravelled drive, the brick and roughcast house with the rose bushes over on the left, and down at the end of the drive the high brick stables with the loft above. Somebody led a horse out of the stable doorway as I watched, and took it round to the paddocks at the side. I couldn't see who he was. He didn't look like Cliff, but the shed under the windmill stopped my view before I had a good look at him. Perhaps he was a stable-boy. He looked small leading that high green-covered horse. Perhaps he'd been rubbing it down and was just going to turn it out. I couldn't see properly at that distance.

Down right at the back was the row of poplars beside the water-race. The ground was flat for miles and miles, the soil was grey and glittered in the sun, the grass in the paddocks behind the gorse fence was burnt brown, people rode their bikes on the footpath, everybody had a windmill, and in town, the trams were green and white, the pictures kept open continuously all day, clear water ran along in the gutters, and, of course, there was the Avon. It was all so different from New Plymouth. We had hills all around there, and the Mountain too, but here I could look across flat country, away beyond the rows of trees, and see the Southern Alps right over by the sky. I liked holidays in Christchurch very much, even the air smelled different, and nearly always I used to cry on my last morning before I got up, because I didn't want to go home again. Of course other times Mum had come with me, but this time I had come the whole way by myself, except that Dad's cousin had seen me from the train to the boat in Wellington.

I opened the gate, picked up my bag, and went in. I started to walk along the drive, but someone in the shadow down by the stables yelled, 'Get off the drive.' I saw that the drive had just been raked so I walked on the strip of grass along the side. That sounded like Cliff who shouted, though I wasn't sure of his voice after a year. I suppose he'd just raked the drive. I couldn't help smiling as I walked along. It felt so good to be coming here again.

I went up the steps to the back porch and knocked. 'It's me, Auntie,' I called.

'Is that you Gordon? Step over the step.' My auntie always kept the doorstep scrubbed very clean. I went in, and there was the smell of their place again, quite different from at home. My uncle kept a cow, and I could smell the big basin of milk that would be sitting in the pantry, and scrubbed wood, and cooking, and their own warm smell that came from the people who lived in the kitchen. My auntie was down on her knees polishing the range. She smiled up at me. 'Hello Gordon. My word you've grown. Give us a kiss, you're not too big for that are you?'

I bent and kissed the faint dark moustache above her mouth. She was very dark and good-looking, and her eyebrows met faintly above her thin straight nose. She had dark brown eyes like Mum's. I noticed she had her hair short in a buster-cut.

'Mum told me you'd got your hair cut,' I said.

'Do you like it? It's the latest. Hasn't she got hers done yet?'

'No. She says she will if many more people do.'

She told me to take my coat off and sit down, then she asked me all about the trip and about Mum and Dad, and told me about the wins they'd had lately with Red Wing, and about the nor'-wester they'd had that she was still cleaning up

after. She kept rubbing at the range until it shone. She was very particular
about her house. All the time I was wanting to get away down to the stables to
see Cliff and the horses and my uncle and Mary.

'Would you like a cup of tea?' auntie asked. 'They always want one after
they've finished mucking out. They'll be up soon.'

'I think I'll go down and say hello to them.'

'Well you can take your things down. I've put you in the whare with Cliff and
Norman.'

'Who's Norman?'

'He's the new boy working for your uncle. He's a steeplechase jockey.'

'I think I saw him. Does he get many wins?'

'He used to be very good, but he had a bad fall last year and he's just getting
his nerve back. Your uncle thinks he'll be good again if he just has a win or two.
He's a nice wee chap.' I picked up my bag and coat. 'If you want a wash, you
know where the wash-house is. Or you can wash in the sink if you don't make a
mess. I don't want you mucking up my bathroom. I've just cleaned it out.'

'Righto,' I said. I had looked in her bathroom once the last time I was there. It
was corker and clean and shiny. But last year, when Mum was there I used to
roll up my pants and sit on the bench and wash my legs in the sink. Some of the
water would run down under my pants and not get dried properly and make
my legs sore.

I took my stuff and went smiling down to the stables.

I looked in at the whare door and sniffed the familiar smell of tobacco smoke
and grey blankets. Someone was lying on one of the bunks reading. My shadow
on the floor made him look up. 'Hello,' he said. He had a smooth round little
face.

'Hello.' This would be Norman, the steeplechase jockey. 'Where's Cliff?'

'He's mucking out. In the stable.'

I went through the big doorway on to the concrete floor. The air was full of
the smell of straw and horses and leather. Someone was hissing through his
teeth, and a horse stamped with a hollow sound on the packed earth in the
loosebox. 'Stand still, blast you,' said a voice. I looked in over the lower half of
the door, and there was Cliff, hissing as he brushed down the horse's legs. The
horse was flicking his tail and gnawing the edge of his manger and stamping.
'Oh, you bad-tempered bastard,' said Cliff. He was thin-faced and dark, and a
few years older than me.

'Good-day there,' I said. I could feel my face cracking, I was so pleased.

He smiled up at me with his cheeky sort of smile, and came reaching over the
door to shake hands. I was too slow and he got the grip on me and squeezed.
'Hello Gordon,' he smiled, squeezing, 'how are you?'

'Ow, Cliff,' I said. 'Cut it out. You're hurting. Oo. Dicken.'

He let me go. 'I've just got to wash his face,' he said. 'Like to come in and do
it?'

'What's his name?'

'Gloaming,' he grinned at me. He had dust caked round his mouth and it
made his teeth look white. 'I'll just finish him and then I'm set. How about
getting me some water in that bucket.'

'How many horses have you got now?' I asked, handing him the bucket.

'Five. There's this one, he's Scallywag, and you know old Red Wing, and
three others.'

'They're not all yours though?'

'Oh no. Only Red Wing. Scallywag's running at the next meeting. Haven't I
got him looking good?'

When he had finished we went into the whare at the end of the stables.
'Norm, this is Gordon.' Norman got off the bunk to shake hands. He was just

about the same height as me and he was a grown man. He had funny little legs. 'Pleased to meet you,' he said, and he didn't squeeze my hand. When he smiled he looked like a little round-faced boy and he had a high sort of voice.

'See what happens to you if you start smoking too soon,' said Cliff. He was a good bit taller than Norman.

'Pity you didn't start a bit sooner,' said Norman bitterly. 'You've grown out of a job.'

'Don't worry about me, I can get a job all right.' Cliff took out a packet of Yellows. 'Have one?' He held them out to me.

'Have you started smoking?' I asked. 'Does auntie let you?'

Norman laughed. 'She makes him. He's nearly ten stone now.'

'Some people never grow up,' said Cliff airily.

'Not in the head they don't.' Norman went and lay down again.

'I had a cigarette the other day after school,' I said. 'Another kid and I smoked one in the woodshed.'

'Did it make you sick?'

'No, but afterwards we ate all sorts of things to take the smell away, cabbage leaves and raw onion.'

'Chewing gum's best,' said Cliff. 'Or Smokers.'

'Where's uncle and Mary?'

'They've gone down to the store,' said Norman. 'Hang up your coat. There's a hook.'

'Which will be my bunk?' I asked.

'Do you wet the bed?' Cliff asked. 'Well you can sleep above me.' Cliff was a hard case. He knew lots of yarns too. He'd always start by saying 'Did you ever hear the one about . . .?' He didn't seem to like telling them when Norman was there, but he told me some corkers after. He was a real wag. It was good fun going round with him.

By and by, we went up for a cup of tea. Uncle had been a jockey once and he was short too, only he had got a lot thicker now. He was fair and red-faced with little veins on his cheeks, and he always had to wear a hat outside because he sunburned very easily. He never used to talk much to me because I didn't know about horses, so he kept asking 'How's your Mum and Dad?' and 'What class are you in now?' When Mary came in from the front, I noticed straight away that she had her hair up. She looked just about grown-up like that. I thought she was very pretty too, because she took after uncle and her face was fair and smooth and she looked corker when she smiled.

'Hello Gordie,' she cried, and grabbed hold of me and started hugging and kissing me a lot before I could get away. It was hard to know how to struggle with her because Mum had told me never to punch girls in the chest. It was funny too because when she kissed me she would look over at Norman to see if he was watching, and he turned very red.

'Here here here,' said auntie. 'That's enough of that in my clean kitchen. Mary, don't be such a damn fool. It's just as well for you my lady you didn't bump the table.'

'Yah, you big sissy,' said Cliff. 'Always kissing the girls.'

'You'll change your tune one of these days, smarty,' said Mary. 'What about Doreen?'

'Her!' said Cliff. 'Why I – '

'That's enough,' said auntie. 'Gordon you get round there behind the table. Sit in your usual place Norman.' .

Gee it was good fun there with them all, talking about the horses and everything. I thought I'd better remember later on to ask Cliff about Doreen. He was a hard case with girls.

Afterwards, auntie told me I'd better go and change my clothes. 'Can you unpack your own things?'

'I'll come down and do them for him,' said Mary. 'I'll be his mother while he's here and make him wash his neck.'

'You'll do these dishes first. You haven't done a hand's turn all morning. Plenty girls are out working long before your age.'

'Now now,' said uncle. 'We've been over all that. Mary's work is around here, helping me with the horses. Isn't it, Mary?'

'Too right. Gordon, did you know I ride work now in the mornings?'

'Yes, on Red Wing,' Cliff broke in. 'That old thing. You try it on Scallywag. I bet you wouldn't stay long on him.'

'Cliff sometimes doesn't stay very long on him either,' said Norman in his soft little voice, smiling.

'Cliff got dumped the other morning,' said auntie. 'He's getting too long in the legs. We might have to find another job for him.'

'He won't dump me again,' said Cliff darkly. 'I made him feel sorry for it.' He took out his packet and lit a cigarette.

'Started smoking yet Gordon?' asked uncle. He took out a wooden match, split it with his thumbnail and started picking a place in his teeth. He opened the paper at the racing page.

'I've got to go to High School after I finish primary,' I said. 'You can't smoke there either, though some of the boys do.'

'More school yet!' Cliff blew a smoke ring. 'Don't you get sick of it? You wouldn't catch me going there.'

'Everybody isn't –' Norman started to say, then he stopped and went red. 'I'll dry the dishes for you Mary.'

'See if you can put them away in the right places this time.' Auntie was smiling at him. She liked anyone who did things for her. Last time, she asked me to pluck and clean a fowl for her. It was a hell of a job, and I got in an awful mess. Mum was very annoyed with auntie over that, but auntie just laughed. I suppose Norman was doing things for her now. I didn't mind doing them really because if she was around she would talk about people and crack jokes about them and make the time pass. She knew some yarns too, but she didn't tell very bad ones. She did enjoy a bit of fun though, like the time years ago when she was staying at our place and she came out all dressed up in Dad's clothes and bowler hat that he wore on Sundays, with a wee mou drawn with chalk, and said she was going down to work with him. She went right out the gate and along the street a bit. Dad didn't like it much, but Mum and I nearly died laughing at her the tricks she got up to. Mum used to say it was a different story in her own place though.

Down in the whare again, Cliff stretched out on the bunk while I took the things out of my bag and changed my clothes.

'That little runt. He's always hanging round Mary these days. Mum lets him take her to dances, too.'

'Who?'

'Norman. If I catch him up to any monkey business with my sister I'll bash him.'

'Could you fight him? He must be pretty strong.'

'Him? Course I could. That little squirt. You just let him try anything on and you'll see. I don't like Mary going out with the stable-boy.'

'But isn't he a jockey?'

'He's a jockey when anyone gives him a mount, but he's our stable-boy most of the time. He's half crazy too.'

'Crazy? He looks all right to me.' I began to feel a bit uneasy.

'Course he's crazy. He got dumped at the board fence last year and kicked on the head. You never know what he's going to do. He's moody as hell. If I was Dad I'd give him the sack. I could work Red Wing out over the jumps. I'm a damn sight better rider than he is. It's only that they skite him up, and he's a bit smaller.'

I didn't like to say what about getting dumped off Scallywag the other morning because Cliff knew some corker tortures. One of them he tried last time was to stick his finger in under your ears, or he'd get you down on the floor and kneel on your arm and roll back and forth.

'What books have you got there?' I asked.

'I'm reading a beaut now, *Drag Harlan*. Just when he's going to draw he stops and lets the other joker draw first, and then he flashes it out. There's another one there by the same author, *Square Deal Sanderson*. Have you read it?'

'I've read *Bar 20*,' I said, 'and *Bar 20 Days* and *The Bar 20 Three* and *Johnny Nelson*.'

'He's a wag,' said Cliff, 'that Johnny Nelson. He's like Hoot Gibson in the pictures.'

'He gets married in the last book,' I said.

'Does he? Aw hell, I hate that mushy stuff.'

'Have you read *The Three Musketeers*?' I asked. 'It's a corker, all sword fights. Like Doug Fairbanks.'

'No, I don't like that old-fashioned stuff. Give me quick on the draw.'

After dinner, everybody had a lie-down. They said it was because they got up so early in the morning to ride work. Norm was there reading a book called *My Man Jeeves*. He said he hadn't read any cowboy books for years. Sometimes he read Nat Gould, but he liked adventure stories best, or funny ones. Cliff had just put down his book and was going to have a doss when there was the sound of wheels on the drive. From the window you could see right up the drive past the house. It was a big two-horse wagon loaded with bales of straw.

'It's Charlie,' said Cliff. 'Blast him. What's he want to come now for? We only ordered the bloody stuff this morning. A man never gets any peace round this place.' He began slipping on his shoes.

The two big heavy horses stopped just outside the door, and threw out their heads to loosen the reins. You could hear their teeth chewing on their bits. One of them lifted his tail and dropped some dung. Charlie, high on his seat, leaned away down to look under the doorway. 'Anyone home?' He wore a waistcoat and his shirtsleeves were rolled up showing freckly forearms. It was hard to tell what his face was like because it was almost upside-down looking under the doorway. I went out to see him. He was thin with a big sandy moustache and big eyebrows, and was wearing an old bun hat. 'I drove 'em nice and straight down the drive,' he said to Cliff. 'Look at it. Two nice straight marks down the middle. Decorate it for you. Bet you I can drive back on the same marks. Couldn't I girls?' he said to the horses. 'I could draw flowers for you along the edge with this pair.'

'One of them's not very well-behaved,' I said.

'Haw, haw, haw,' he went, 'that Bessie, she just don't like the job Cliff made of the drive, do you Bess?' He put his hand on her rump and jumped down.

'You can bloody well clear up that mess before you go,' said Cliff.

'Haw, haw, haw. He's a hard case our Cliff. She's thinking your skinny racehorses don't do much of a job so she's giving you some good manure.' He became very businesslike. 'Where will you have it? Up aloft?' He backed the wagon to the doorway of the stables. The horses moved stiffly backwards, chipping their shoes down on to the drive and scattering the gravel.

I went with Cliff up the steep narrow stairs into the loft. It was warm and dusty up there under the roof. There were some bales of hay and straw, and sacks of chaff, and some horse covers, and dry-looking cobwebby bits of harness hanging from nails. Three or four cats scampered out of sight. Cliff opened the door at the front and the light poured in. There was a little platform, and a beam above it with a pulley. Cliff fed a rope through, with a hook on the end, and we hauled the bales up, swung them in to the platform, and rolled them over into the loft.

'That's the lot,' called Charlie. 'See you some more. Tell your Dad I got a good line of oats now. Come on girls. Giddap.' We watched him go away down the drive.

'I'll tell you what,' I said to Cliff. 'I'll go down and you haul me up?'

'To hell with that for a joke. Do you think I like work? I'll tell you what,' he said. 'I'll tie this end and you can slide down the rope.'

'I don't know how to hold it with my legs.'

'What, aren't you game? Go on. Look, I'll tie it here.'

'You go first.'

'Me? I could do it easy. I often do it. I'm sick of it.'

I went out on the platform, leaned out, and grabbed the rope, but it looked a long way down and the stones were sharp. Cliff gave me a push and before I knew where I was the rope was burning through my hands and I was waving with my legs to grab it, and just when I was getting it the ground hit under my feet and I went down on my knees on the gravel. There was Cliff's head sticking out over the platform, laughing, 'I knew you could do it. Easy, isn't it?'

I gulped a bit before I could smile back at him. It didn't look very high from the ground, but from up there the ground looked an awful long way down. I'd got a bit of a fright and felt shaky so I went to sit on the whare step and look at my knees. One was bleeding.

Norman came over to me. 'You be careful with him or he'll hurt you,' he said. 'He's got no common sense at all, especially when it doesn't concern himself. He's just at the awkward age.'

'I'm all right,' I said. 'I just wasn't expecting it that's all.'

Cliff came in. 'Well, now you know how it's done.'

'I thought you'd have more sense than let Gordon do that,' said Norman.

'You mind your own bloody business,' Cliff blazed at him.

'This is my business. I'm in charge of the stables when your father's not here.'

'Then why weren't you hauling up that straw?'

'Oh, I let the stropper do jobs like that. I'm a jockey. And I don't want anyone hurt around here. You be more careful.' He stood there with his round little face looking up at Cliff, standing up straight, looking very light and quick. His eyes didn't blink at all but his face got red. I thought Cliff was going to hit him, but Norman smiled and said, 'There's enough mess to clear up as it is.' He got a shovel and a handful of straw and picked up the dung.

Cliff came back from the dressing-table with some ointment. 'Here rub this on.' It had a corker clean smell. Then he lay down on his bunk and didn't say anything for a long time.

That night after tea, uncle got up with the match between his teeth and took his hat. 'Better see Harry about those acceptances,' he said and went out.

'Are there races soon?' I asked.

'Too right,' said Mary. 'Red Wing's going to win the steeplechase, isn't he Norman?'

'He's getting a bit old now.' Norman was smiling at her. 'He might win if I get off and lift him over some of those fences.'

'I'll lift you,' said Mary, returning his smile, 'right under the ear. If he doesn't win it's because his rider's no good.'

'He won't win then,' said Cliff, lying back on the sofa.

'Are you going to ride him, Norman?' I asked.

'If Mary'll let me. I'll tell you where I'd like to ride him, and that's down to the glue factory.' Norman looked corker with that wee cheeky smile. You couldn't help liking him, though sometimes it seemed funny for him to be acting like a grown man when he was so small.

'What are your colours?' I asked.

'Sky blue. A nice clear colour. Like Mary's eyes.' Norman and Mary both went red when he said that, but I thought Mary was quite pleased about it.

Cliff snorted and auntie looked up. 'Here here you two. That's enough of that damn silly nonsense. Just as well your father's not here my lady.' They were both uncomfortable, looking down at the table. 'Well, what about these dishes?' said auntie. 'A woman's work is never done.' She was looking at Norman but he didn't move. 'Norman, will you give me a hand?' She was smiling nicely at him, but his face had a funny closed look.

'Not tonight,' he said. 'I want to take some books back to the Ellis's.' He started to get up.

'You men are all the same,' said auntie. 'Big ones and small ones you're all the same. Who'd be a woman?'

'You've got a big one lying there on the sofa doing nothing.'

'Never you mind about him,' said auntie sharply. 'I'll see he does his share.'

'If it goes according to size,' said Norman, 'he ought to do them a good bit more often than I do.'

'Leave his size out of it. We can't all be as small as you.' Auntie did look fierce when she was angry. She was so dark.

'I suppose it's just as well,' said Norman. 'Quality before quantity.' He stood leaning his hands on the table as though he wanted to get away but was making himself stand and face her.

'You leave him out of it,' said auntie. 'Just leave my family out of it. When you get a family of your own you can start bossing them around. Poor little beggars.' Then she seemed to realize she'd said too much because Norman was looking awful. His face had gone pale and thin-looking, as though he was very cold.

'Now Norman, let's not quarrel again,' she said. 'My tongue runs away with me. Sit down for a while and we'll have a game of cards.'

'It's all right,' he said stiffly, and went out, looking very small.

'Mum, you've hurt him. You are a devil,' said Mary. 'You know he's awfully sensitive about being so small.'

'You needn't start telling me what's right and what's wrong. I've got along so far without your advice, thank you.'

'But Mum, you must remember he's not right yet. Just when he's getting along nicely you have to go and upset him again.'

'I go and upset him. I like that. If he's so damned thin-skinned he can't take a bit of a joke he deserves to be upset. What he needs is a good hard kick on the backside to wake him up a bit.'

'Oh don't be so childish. He's not a little boy. You can't smack him to make him better.'

'I can still smack you, my lady. Not so much of your backchat. It's all your fault anyway. If you didn't encourage him, he wouldn't – '

'I don't encourage him. I like him, that's all, and I feel sorry for him.'

'Oh, you feel sorry for him. So that's why you're always down at the stables instead of doing your room out. That's why you're off to dances with him every night of the week. That's why you're always talking about him. You better watch your step my lady. He's not your class and you better let him know it, the sooner the better.'

'There's nothing the matter with him. He's always perfectly all right with me. I know how to treat him. And I like him. So there.' Mary stood up and started clearing the table. She didn't look like a girl at all. She'd grown up a lot in the last year. Auntie was glaring at her.

'You watch yourself,' said Cliff from the sofa. 'I don't want any half-wits in our family.'

Auntie rushed across to him and gave him such a box on the ear that his cigarette went flying out of his mouth. 'If you don't get up off your backside and help your sister this minute and stop smoking those damned cigarettes I'll knock you into the middle of next week,' she yelled.

Cliff got up, whimpering. I was too scared to do anything. I didn't know what to do. If I went down to the whare Norman would be there. I just sat and shivered.

The other three got busy on the dishes. After a time, auntie turned and smiled at me. 'Well Gordon, you'll be able to tell your mother I'm having trouble with my family.' I tried to smile back. That was one good thing about auntie, she would flare up suddenly, but she got over it just as quickly. She was right back to ordinary things again now. 'Has your mother got any new hats lately?' she asked.

'She's got a wee one,' I said. 'A high sort of a one with a narrow brim. She says she'll have to have her hair cut before she can wear it properly. It's not round, it's – you know – oval.'

'Mary and I are going to get new ones like that if Red Wing wins this race. They're the latest.'

'You won't know me if we have a win,' said Mary. 'I'm getting a new dress, very short, nearly up to my knees, with a low waist, and some new gloves, and a new coat, aren't I Mum? I'll be really coming out in all the latest. And Mum and I might go up to Wellington for the races. Gee, I'm looking forward to that. I hope we get a win.'

'You better keep Norman sweet then,' said Cliff. 'Shall I go and see if he's there?'

'No, I'll go.' And Mary was out the door before anyone could say a word.

Auntie put the red cloth on the table and we sat down. Cliff handed me the cards. 'Let's see if you can shuffle any better than last time you were here.' I tried it, but we didn't play cards much at home, and my fingers were too short and stiff. Bits of the pack kept falling on the floor. 'Look, I'll show you,' said Cliff. He took them and did it easily, and then put two lots down on the table and flipped their corners in together.

Auntie started laughing. 'Gordon, do you remember that time years ago at your place – perhaps you wouldn't remember it – we played strip poker and we had your father sitting with only his pants and socks on?'

'He doesn't play cards as a rule,' I said. 'I suppose that's why he wasn't much good.'

They were both laughing. 'I'll never forget that as long as I live. It was a cold night and he was sitting there shivering and looking miserable and he couldn't win anything back to put on.'

'And that Christmas a long time ago when we were staying at your place,' said Cliff, 'and we hopped out the bedroom window and sneaked round and looked in the sitting-room window and saw all the presents waiting to go in our stockings.'

'Yes, you little devils,' said auntie. 'You didn't deserve any presents after that.'

'Do you remember the time the pony chased you when you were eating a carrot?' Cliff was always reminding me about that. Cliff and Mary used to have a pony when they were in the old place, and it was dead keen on carrots. One day it followed me, trying to snatch one out of my hand. I ran inside and locked the door. I was small at the time of course, and not used to horses.

'Mary is a long time,' I said. 'Shall I go and tell her to hurry?'

Auntie nodded so I went out into the dark. I knew there was a clothes-prop leaning across the path so I was walking on the grass and not making any noise and I almost bumped into them. They were very close together, perhaps they were hugging, and Norman was saying, 'Please Mary. Will you? Please.' But she said, 'Not now Norman. Perhaps if Red Wing wins.'

I said, 'Are you two going to play cards?'

They got a fright and stepped back. Norman said, 'Why, it's Gordon. How are you Gordon?'

'I'm all right thanks. Are you coming to play cards?'

'Not me,' said Norman. 'I've got to take these books back. You'd better go, Mary.'

As we walked back, Mary put her arm round my shoulders and took hold of my ear. 'I don't know what you saw. But not a word of this inside or Mum will hit the roof. It's our secret, eh?' She squeezed my ear. I wanted to ask why auntie would hit the roof, but I forgot because I was measuring myself against her to see if she would be much taller than Norman. My head came up to her ear.

Gee, we had some fun that night. After we had played cards, we got to talking and laughing about things, and auntie took her teeth out, pulled her hair down over her face, and acted old mother Kennedy going into the store and trying to say, 'Three fresh sausages please.' Then Cliff put on some of auntie's old clothes, and Mary dressed me up in some of her things with a hat and powder and everything, and we pretended to be two girls. Mary got her father's suit and hat and then came out and pretended to be courting me. She took off her hat and asked me for a dance and wondered if she could see me home afterwards. She asked me to marry her, and auntie put some white paper round her neck and hung her top teeth down as though she was buck-toothed and pretended to be the parson. Gee, it was great fun. I nearly died laughing. We never had fun like that at home.

Uncle came in and said what a skinny girl I was, but he said Mary had a good backside on her for a man. He said to be careful she didn't bend or she'd burst his pants for him and then he'd have to wear hers. I think it was the best evening's fun I ever had. Norman came in later for a cup of tea, and he seemed all right again too. I always had corker fun at Christchurch.

Next morning I was tired and had a good sleep in, but later on in my stay I'd get up early and go over to the course to watch the horses working and rolling in the sand. I wasn't game to ride any of them. Cliff kept asking me to try, but they looked too tall. I used to help Cliff with the mucking-out. I could carry two buckets of water. Last time I was there I couldn't do that. Of course I slopped a bit, but still it showed I was getting stronger. Uncle wanted me to come and learn how to milk, but I liked the horses better. Besides there were plenty cows just over the road from our place at home, so I stayed in the stable. Up in the loft, there were bags of oats to dip your hands and arms down into and feel them dry and cold and slithery. One of the cats had kittens and they were a lot tamer than the mother, though the old mother didn't like you touching them, and she kept handy all the time. Sometimes uncle would let me sieve the chaff, but I couldn't make it curve up in the air the way he did. Sometimes in the mornings I'd take a book up in the loft and sit on the wee platform in the sun and hang my legs down. I could look down between my knees and there was the gravel away down below. I always took care Cliff wasn't in the loft when I sat there.

One morning when I was there, Mary came up and then called Norman to come and shift a bag of chaff for her. I don't think they knew I was there because they were talking quietly for a long time, and then there was a clatter and Mary said, 'You devil, you're stronger than I thought you were.' She didn't sound very annoyed though and Norman was laughing as they went down. I suppose he had hugged her or kissed her. I wondered for a while whether I should tell Cliff about it but I thought there might be a row, and anyway Mary hadn't seemed to mind. If it had been anything much Mary would have made a fuss. Besides, Norman was jolly nice to me. For a while I had been a bit nervous with him, and didn't like to say anything was very small or little in case he got offended, but I soon forgot about that. Sometimes he did get a bit moody and hard to please, and then he wouldn't answer and ask you to leave him alone and sit and look as though he was thinking of something unpleasant, but he never got as crabby as our school-teacher, although I suppose they're different. Most of the time he was corker and friendly, and he didn't try to play tricks on me at all.

One afternoon, Cliff and I went over to the water-race and caught some tadpoles. Cliff splashed me a bit of course, but I got him a beauty just at the end. He couldn't catch me either. I suppose the cigarettes made him short-winded.

Another day, I went into town with auntie and Mary, and we had a good look round the shops and the Square, and then Mary and I came home on the top deck of the trailer. That was corker and breezy. Another afternoon, Cliff and I went in to the pictures to see Doug Fairbanks in *The Mark of Zorro*. He was a stunner sword-fighter and he cut a Z on their faces. Cliff liked it too because Doug Fairbanks could ride so well. The girl in the picture said to him, 'You ride like a part of the horse.'

The next morning, when they all came riding back from the course, before they got off at the stables, Cliff called out to me, 'Look at me Gordon. I ride like a part of the horse.'

Norman started laughing so much he could hardly speak. 'Which part?' he said. 'When that tram passed and Scallywag started to play up, you were riding like a part of his neck.' He was laughing so much he could hardly get down. Poor Cliff just glared at him and moved his mouth, but he couldn't think of anything to say at all. It was funny, and good too, to see Cliff without an answer. He was still pretty wild afterwards, and kept swearing and muttering that he would get even with Norman if it was the last thing he did. I felt like laughing, but if I had it would have meant a long run so I kept quiet.

Well, by this time the races were only a day or two off, and we were all busy getting ready. Norman had washed his colours himself and Mary ironed them for him and they looked stunner. He was sitting in the sun on the doorstep of the whare cleaning his racing boots. They were very light and soft. I tried one on, but it was a little too small for me.

'Gee, I'm excited about these races Norman,' I said. 'Are you getting excited?'

'Not yet,' he said, 'but I will. I always get a bit windy just before a race starts. It's so long-drawn-out, you know, the way you have to hang about before you line up at the barrier. Most of the jocks get the wind up a bit.'

'Is Red Wing good at the barrier?'

'Oh yes. Most steeplechasers are pretty quiet. It's the sprints where they play up.'

'Do you think you'll win? Honestly, do you?' I asked.

'I hope so. Your uncle and auntie will be very pleased if I do. Your uncle's got old Red Wing in great nick.' He went on rubbing away at his boot. 'Do you want us to win?'

'Of course I do. If you win it'll be a sort of – you know the word, what it all works up to.'

'A climax?'

'Yes. It'll be the climax of my holiday. I'm going home next week.'

He asked me about home, and would I be sorry to go, and then he said, 'What about Mary? Does she want us to win?' I was surprised at that. I thought she would have told him. They were always talking about things and riding to the track together. She must have told him plenty times. It seemed funny he should ask me. But perhaps he didn't believe her.

'Too right she does,' I said. 'If you win she's going to do all sorts of things, get a lot of new dresses and gloves and things. She's going up to Wellington, too. She's dead keen on it. And she and auntie are going to get new hats.'

He looked a bit funny as though he was disappointed, and kept rubbing at a shiny place on his boot. 'I might get a new hat myself,' he said, and got up and went inside, leaving me wondering what was the matter.

'Yoo-hoo,' auntie was standing on the porch and waving. 'Yoo-hoo, Gordon.' When I got there, she had on her nice smile. 'Gordon, would you like to turn the wringer for me? It makes the job such a lot quicker.' The wash-house was full of steam, and the smell of soap and wet clothes. She was getting our things ready for the races.

When I started to turn the wringer, it squeaked a bit. 'Shall I get some oil? There's some down in the stables.'

'I'll oil you. Do you think I want oil on these clothes? Leave it just now.'

I remembered Mum telling me how particular auntie was. One time, when auntie had been away, uncle did all the washing just before she came back, but auntie said that it wasn't clean enough for her, and she did it all again. But that wasn't really what I was thinking about as I turned the wringer.

'Auntie, do you want Norman to win?' I asked.

'What a damn silly question. Would you like £800?'

'You bet. I'd get a motor-bike. We have motor-bike races on the race-course up home.'

'If we win,' said auntie, 'we get £800. And then there are our bets too. Besides, if your uncle wins, he'll get more horses to train.'

'What about Norman?' I asked. Auntie was sloshing the clothes in clean water. Her hands were all pale and wrinkled and very clean from the suds.

'It would do him good too,' she said. 'Not only his share of the money, but he'd get more mounts too. He's had rather a lean time since his spill. He used to be very good.'

'Auntie – '

'What?'

I was going to ask her if she'd let Mary marry Norman if he won, but she was looking at me and I wasn't game. I started to turn the wringer. 'He thinks an awful lot of Mary, doesn't he?'

'Who told you that tale? Did he?'

'No, but I mean – they go round a lot together, don't they?'

'Mary's a mile too young to think of settling down yet. She'll have plenty more boys before she strikes the right one. It's too risky marrying a jockey. You never know when they'll get hurt. Besides Norman's not her class.'

'But wasn't uncle a jockey when you married him?'

'That was quite a different matter. A flat jockey's quite a different matter. Your uncle was one of the leading jockeys. Come on, turn a bit faster.' She pushed the clothes in between the rollers. 'Has Norman been having any more of his moods lately?'

'No, he's corker. I think he only has the really bad ones about Mary. I've never seen him really bad. Cliff makes him wild sometimes but he doesn't get any moods over it. He just gets angry.'

'Cliff's just at the awkward age,' she said. 'He thinks he knows more about training horses than his own father. Your uncle's thinking of sending him away somewhere else to work for a while to see if he'll steady up a bit.'

That sank in. 'Won't he be here if I come another time?' That did knock the bottom out of things.

'Come on, turn the handle. We'll see about that.'

'But auntie, fair go, will he be here next year?'

'I suppose he will. Turn a bit faster or we'll never get to the races at this rate.'

That was news indeed. I wandered down to the stables to ask Cliff about it. Mary was there, cleaning Red Wing's bridle. 'Hello, sweetheart. Come to give me a kiss?'

'Don't be silly. Tarts are always silly when you're thinking about something.'

'None of your cheek now, young Gordon, or I'll rub my hands all over your face. Look at them.' She held them out for me to see.

'You'd have to catch me first. Where's Cliff?'

'He and Dad have taken the horses down to have their racing plates put on. They were looking for you. You could have gone on the bike.' I stood watching her for a while. 'The winner must have a clean bridle,' she said. 'What have you been doing to Norman? He's as miserable as a bandicoot. I'll have to go in and sweeten him up as soon as I finish this. Shall I give him a nice big kiss. Like this?' She went to grab me but I ducked out.

'Couldn't catch a flea,' I said. I went into the whare to ask Norman if it was all right for me to take the bike. He was standing looking at his face in the mirror, not doing his hair, or shaving, or anything, just looking at himself. His reflection had a sad sort of expression as though it was looking out and seeing Norman and not liking the sight of him very much. 'Norman,' I said. After a while he turned towards me, and his reflection looked away. 'Norman, can I have the bike?'

'Don't bother me,' he said as though he hadn't really listened to what I said. He went and lay down on his bunk, still with that same expression on his face.

I went to the shed under the windmill and got the bike and rode off to the blacksmith's. It was uncle's bike and I could reach the pedals by just stretching a little bit, and of course I rode on the footpath all the way. There were lots of horses and jockeys round the smithy, and there was the smell like burning toe-nails, and the hammering red-hot iron, and the smoke when they tried the shoes on. It was such good fun watching and listening to the talk that I forgot to ask Cliff.

When race morning came, I can tell you we did bustle round to get there for the first race. Gee, it was great. There were crowds and crowds of people, and cars going in one gate all the time, and trams with two trailers, and as soon as they stopped the people all made a rush for the gates. There were wee jockeys leading in horses, and some of the horses had covers right over their faces with just holes for their eyes and pointed things to fit their ears into. Men were yelling and trying to sell race-books, and round the back of the stand there were refreshment tents and places for hot water, and people carrying teapots, and the smell of hot pies and beer. It was a stunner day and the place was packed with people. I thought when we left auntie's place that she and Mary were all dolled up, but gosh, they were nothing to some of the sights. The men were just ordinary though.

We went down to the birdcage to see the horses. It was funny too. The birdcage had white iron posts all round, on this side and on the far side too, and when you walked past them they looked as though they were going backwards. Mary said it was like the wheels in the pictures. We got a good possie just as the horses were coming in. Auntie and uncle kept talking about their names and weights and riders, and how they ran at the last meeting, but I just watched them walking round. Gosh, they looked stunner when they had their covers off. So tall and shiny and proud, and they just sort of drifted round as though the grass was springy and they didn't need to touch it hard at all, and their skins fitted them perfectly without any wrinkles or baggy places, all just smooth and ripply and neat.

Uncle went away to have a bet, and Mary, auntie, and I went up to the stand. We had to go away up to the back to get a seat. It was high up and you could see for miles and miles right away over the smoky part of Christchurch. I could see auntie's place too. I could tell it by the loft above the stables. The horses started away over at the back of the course and when they got away it looked as though all the bright colours of the jockeys were sliding round on the railings. They soon swung into the straight and everybody stood up. I couldn't see very well, but auntie was yelling 'You beauty. You beauty,' and hammering my shoulder, and Mary rubbed her cheek against mine, so we were on a winner all right.

That made us all happy, it was such a good start. Mary kept saying, 'I've got a feeling this is going to be our lucky day. Don't you feel lucky, Gordon?' She looked lucky. She was smiling all the time and her eyes were bright, and when we met Norman at the corner of the stand, he couldn't help looking at her. He was all dressed up in a wee suit with his collar and tie and hat on, and he looked smaller than ever. I noticed that he went and stood on the uphill side of us, so that he could look down to us. Cliff and uncle were busy with the horses, so we went in for a cup of tea. When we found a table in all the crowd, Norman wouldn't have anything to eat, but he came and sat with us.

'Well Norman,' said auntie, 'how do you feel about it?'

'I'm beginning to feel a bit weak about the knees,' he said. Then he smiled. 'But Mary's my lucky charm. She says we'll be all right.'

'Too right you will. I'm sure you're going to win.' Mary patted his hand. I looked at auntie, but she was all smiles too. I was beginning to think they were a bit silly, and I wished Cliff was there. He'd lucky-charm them. I wanted to go and see him, but auntie said she couldn't be sure where he'd be, so I'd better stay with them or I'd get lost in the crowd.

When the steeplechase came on, we went to the birdcage to see the horses, and there was Norman in his sky-blue blouse and cap and clean boots perched away up high with his knees up. Old Red Wing was looking quite used to all this and not making any fuss at all. Norman looked pale. Auntie said the others did too. They were nervous because a steeplechase was a big risk.

'I can't bear to watch this all the way round,' said Mary. 'Let's go down by the rails and see the finish.'

Just as we got down there, a man in a blue suit began to stagger backwards and fell over, wallop. He just lay there. I was going over to look at him, but auntie caught my arm and dragged me up to the rails.

'Stay here,' she said. 'He's probably drunk or something.'

He was lying there on his back just a few yards away. His hat was off and his face was a funny purply colour, he still had a dead cigarette butt in his mouth, and he was making noises in his throat as he breathed. Lots of people were turning round to look at him, and then they'd look away as though they hadn't noticed him.

There was a roar, 'They're off,' from the crowd up in the stand. I couldn't see very well except when they went over the jumps, but blue seemed to be near the front, and auntie and Mary got over their fright about the man falling over and began to get excited. While we were waiting for the horses to come round for the first time, I had another look at the man. I could just see his legs between the people behind us. Nobody seemed to be helping him. They should have loosened his collar. Just then there was a beating sound and people began to shout. I leaned over the fence in front of Mary. I had a great view. And Red Wing was first over the hurdle into the straight. He was. He stuck his head and neck out and stretched out his front legs and there was Norman in blue and they were over the hurdle. 'Norman,' we yelled, 'Go it Norman,' and old Red Wing came striding past, nice and easy with about four others fairly close behind. Norman was very serious and he didn't look when we yelled. I suppose he couldn't hear us. He told me the wind roars in your ears so that you can't hear anything. Besides, there was the crowd.

Well, you can imagine how we felt after that. We couldn't see them after they'd gone round the turn. We could see little bits of colour hopping up and down over the jumps away at the back, and it looked as though blue was still in front. It took ages for them to go round the back stretch. My mouth got dry. I was holding tight to the railings. If I let them go, I felt Norman would get beaten. Mary was leaning on me all soft and hot and squashing me against the fence. 'What the hell's the matter with them,' said auntie. 'Have they fallen?' 'Mum, stop it,' said Mary, right beside my ear. 'Keep your fingers crossed.' I thought they were never going to come round again.

Then the crowd at the back began to roar so loud you could tell it was going to be a close finish, and the yell got louder and more excited, and underneath it came that beating sound again. Over the top of the hurdle you could see heads bobbing, and then the first horse came up and over and it was Red Wing still. He landed with a jolt and Norman bounced in the saddle. The others poured over just behind him. Norman had lost his cap and he seemed to be riding lopsided. 'He's lost a stirrup. He's lost a stirrup,' Mary yelled. 'Norman, Norman,' we screamed, but the whips were out and two or three others lashed their way past him just in front of us. The horses were running heavily with no spring, stretching out hard.

I felt like crying. I didn't want to turn round in case the others should see. I suddenly noticed the crowd was still cheering. Someone was pleased at any rate. My hands were stiff and I could hardly let go the rails. Mary leaned away and my back felt cold.

We watched the Clerk of the Course bring in the winner. Norman was fourth. Poor old Red Wing looked very tired. Norman had both feet in the stirrups now. 'Well that's that,' said auntie. We turned away and there was the man in the blue suit still lying there with the blackened cigarette butt still in his mouth. It seemed ages since he'd fallen over. His eyes had only the whites showing. The people all streamed round him, leaving a gap where he was lying. They looked away from him as though they were ashamed of him. One man stepped over and winked at me.

We just wandered along without saying much. We met uncle and he didn't seem to mind much. He said it was jolly hard luck Norman losing his iron like that. It was Red Wing landing with such a jolt over the last fence that did it. Norman did jolly well to stick on. He said Norman was very upset about it all.

Well, the rest of the afternoon I couldn't get excited. Norman didn't come to see us. There was some fun at the last race though. Scallywag came second. He wasn't really second, he was third, but there was a protest, and the winner was disqualified. When the winner came in, some of the crowd started to boo and others took it up. A fat old lady just in front of me was boo-ing away, pushing out her mouth and saying, 'Boo-o-o-o.' Then she turned to me and said, 'What are they boo-ing for son? What's it for? Boo-o-o-o.' Anyway they made Scallywag second. I don't know how uncle got on with the betting.

As we walked home, auntie was talking to people she knew. 'It would have been very nice if we'd won,' she said, 'but it's all part of the game. We'll be lucky some other time.' I was glad to get home again, I was tired of all the crowds and the pushing. Mary had hardly said a word since the steeplechase. She didn't seem to hear if I spoke to her. I suppose she was very disappointed at not getting the new clothes or the trip to Wellington or anything. And then she used to ride Red Wing to work, and she was fond of Norman, so I suppose just about everything had gone wrong.

Well, when we got home, there was Cliff looking as pleased as Punch. 'What about Scallywag now,' he said. 'Eh? Who's the best trainer in this house?' He pushed his hat on to the back of his head and stuck his thumbs in the armholes of his waistcoat. 'Cleaned up the old man,' he said. 'The only one in the money all day. Think I'll leave you and set up as a trainer on my own. Got a second with my first start. Not bad, eh?' He was showing off in great style. 'How did you like him, Gordon? Didn't he finish well? Didn't I have him fit?'

Auntie was laughing at him. 'Oh, you were wonderful,' she said. 'We all thought that.'

'Except that you didn't really train him, and you didn't ride him,' said Mary. She was still in a bad mood. 'And it looks as if you've left Dad to bring him home.'

'I did a damn sight better than your wee joker,' said Cliff. 'Calls himself a jockey. Hell! Wait till I have a piece of him. Talk about riding like a part of the horse. Where is he? There's a few things I'd like to tell him about riding.'

But we didn't know where Norman was. Uncle came down the drive riding Scallywag and leading Red Wing, but he hadn't seen Norman either.

We all changed into our old clothes again except Mary. There was going to be a dance that night and she didn't know whether to go or not. She said she'd see how she felt after tea. She didn't feel much like going.

'Go along, Mary,' said auntie. 'It'll do you good. It might cheer you up a bit. You took this race too damned seriously. There'll be plenty more you know.'

'I'll see how I feel,' she said. I was just going out the door when I think she said, 'I won't go with Norman.' I think it was that. It sounded as though she was going to rub it in a bit. Poor old Norman.

'Where do you think Norman is?' I asked Cliff. We were down at the stables. Cliff was feeding the horses and uncle was out the back, milking.

'Blowed if I know.' Cliff was sieving chaff and hissing so the dust wouldn't get in his mouth. 'Here you are,' he said. 'No, wait on.' He put some oats in with it. 'Put that in Red Wing's manger.' Old Red Wing was waiting for it, and leaned down over my shoulder to eat before I had it all poured out. He kept snorting down his nose to blow the chaff away so that he could get at the oats.

'I should think most likely he's gone to the pub,' said Cliff.

'Who, Norman?'

'Yes. I thought I might drop in myself and celebrate, but old Harry knows I'm not near twenty-one. There'd be too many cops about there today.'

'Does Norman drink?'

'Does he what! I've seen him shickered two or three times since he's been here. He gets one of his moods, then off to the pub.'

'Why?'

'To get drunk of course. It cheers him up. You ought to see him trying to get to bed. He thinks he's hung his clothes up and they fall down and he just stands and looks at them as though he doesn't believe it. It's hellashin funny. One night I made his bed up on the top bunk for him, stripped everything off his bottom one. Laugh. I nearly burst trying to keep quiet. He couldn't climb up and in the end he just lay down on the wire mattress. Jesus I laughed.'

Well that was how Norman came home all right. We were all having tea and there was a knock at the door. Mary went and we heard Norman speaking. Auntie called out for Mary to tell him to come in and have his tea, but he said he didn't want any tea, he just wanted to talk to Mary. He'd only be a minute, he wouldn't keep her, he just wanted to talk to Mary.

Cliff winked at me, and I was going to go and see him but auntie made me stay in my place. It was a good while before Mary came back.

'He wants me to go to the dance with him,' she said. 'He's been pestering the life out of me. He's drunk too, and you can smell it a mile off.'

'Are you going?' asked auntie.

'Not with him like that. Not on your life. I think it's a damned insult him coming like that and expecting me to go with him. I thought he was a decent sort of a chap.'

'So he is,' said uncle. 'He's all right. Just had a few too many.'

'One over the eight,' said Cliff.

'I'm not going with him,' said Mary. 'He's just being damned silly, coming here like that and expecting me to go with him.'

'I thought I heard you a couple of days ago saying you'd go,' said auntie.

'I said I'd go if he won. I didn't say I'd go if he lost. I wouldn't have minded so much, but for him to come here stinking like that, and he's all untidy, it's a damned insult.'

'You're too touchy,' said uncle. 'Where is he? I'll get him to have a sleep for a couple of hours, and then a good wash and a cup of tea and he'll be all right.' He went out.

'You don't have to go out with him,' auntie told Mary. 'There's plenty more boys. As far as that goes, you could go with Mabel and get a partner there.'

'Go with Fred,' said Cliff. 'That'll teach his nibs a lesson. You've hardly looked at Fred for months. Show Norman he's not the only pebble on the beach. Fred rode a winner today too, and he's more your size.'

'I know that,' said Mary. 'You don't have to tell me.'

Uncle came in and said he couldn't find Norman.

Well in the end, both Cliff and Mary went to the dance. There wasn't much for me to do with Cliff away. Auntie and uncle talked about the races for a long time, and then auntie started to teach me how to play crib. We were all pretty tired and went to bed early. I wasn't very scared at going down to the whare by myself. Of course I was a bit nervous at the noises, but I knew they were only the horses stamping and moving about.

Cliff came in, I don't know what time it was, and woke me up when he put the light on. He said he had a hell of a lot of fun. She was a great show. He said if it hadn't of been for bringing Mary home he'd of been on to a good thing. He had a promise for another night.

'And you should of seen Norman,' he said. 'Did I rub it in to him. I paid him back for that "part of the horse" the other morning. I put a beaut across him.'

'How?' I said, struggling up in bed so that the light wouldn't get in my eyes. 'What did you do?'

'Well he came in about halfway through. He'd been drinking again and his coat was all dust. Mary was dancing with Fred and I said, "Mary only dances with jockeys who win," I said, "it's all over with you now. Especially coming along shickered like this," I said, "she's very offended over that. And who rides like part of the horse now," I said. He didn't like that a bit.'

'Did Mary speak to him?'

'No, I don't think she saw him. We were just by the door. "Mary only likes big jokers," I said, and then I went away for a dance. He was standing there for a good while watching her. He looked pretty rough with his clothes all untidy and his face red and puffy. He didn't say a word after he saw she was dancing with Fred, he just stood there looking miserable as hell. I got my own back on him all right. "Who rides like part of the horse now?" I said.'

Cliff got into bed and I didn't hear Norman come in. In fact the next thing I knew it was morning and the sun was up. I was a bit dopey from waking up, but I thought I heard the lock rattling and uncle calling, 'Don't come out, Cliff, stay where you are.' Then the door opened and uncle reached round, took the key out and locked the door on the outside. That was so strange I thought I must have been dreaming because usually uncle had to yell at Cliff to get him up, and often Norman would call him too. Then there were quick steps scrunching on the gravel outside, and I twisted round and looked out the window. Uncle was running up the drive, taking fast little steps with his funny little jockey's legs. I heard the bunk below me squeaking, and Cliff said 'What the hell's all the fuss?' I peered down over the edge of my bunk at him and he was looking out the window too. 'Well, I'll be – . Look.' Uncle must have been in the shed under the windmill to get his bike, and now he was pedalling flat out up the drive. He skidded on the gravel, just about fell off at the gate, dragged his bike through, left the gate open and disappeared.

'What the hell do you make of that?' Cliff looked up at me with his mouth open. His hair was all over the place.

'Search me.'

Cliff got up and tried the door. 'He's locked us in,' he said. He scratched his chest, and rubbed one foot over the other. 'This floor is cold. Where's Norman?' Norman's bunk hadn't been slept in. His coat and hat were not on their pegs. 'Hell, he has had a bash,' said Cliff. 'Spent the whole night on the tiles, eh? I suppose he'll be asleep in a loosebox somewhere.' He tried the door again. 'I wonder why he locked us in?'

'I don't know. And where would he go on the bike?'

'I'm going to have a look.' He opened the window, jumped out, and went round to the door. 'He's got the key,' he called. 'You'll have to get out the window.'

I climbed down and jumped out. The gravel hurt on my bare feet. It was cold too. I hobbled round the front. 'Jesus Christ,' said Cliff in a funny voice. 'Oo-o-o-o.' He was looking up at the loft.

Norman was hanging from the beam above the platform. He had his overcoat on. His feet hung down pigeon-toed. The rope round his neck must have been very tight for his face was all blue and swollen and twisted. You could see his teeth. His neck seemed to twist up out of his coat collar and his face was round to one side. He was just swaying a little bit. His hat was down on the gravel in front of us.

I started to shiver and I couldn't get my breath. Cliff gulped and turned and pushed past me and got in the window. I followed. I didn't feel the gravel at all. We got back into bed, but I couldn't stop shivering. Cliff said 'Oo-o-o-o' again like a moan and started to cry. I was very frightened but I didn't cry.

Well of course the policeman came back with uncle, and a doctor came, and they got him down. They were talking and moving about just outside, but Cliff and I stayed in bed and pretended we didn't hear anything at all. We didn't know what to do. We didn't even talk to each other.

There were people coming and going all morning, and I didn't know what to do. I seemed to be getting in the way all the time and nobody wanted to talk to me. Cliff didn't get up, and kept crying when they asked him to. I didn't see Mary either. Auntie didn't know what to do about me. I didn't want to go down to the whare again once I got in the house. I kept shivering.

In the end uncle brought my clothes up, and auntie took me into town and managed to get me a berth on the boat for that night. She came right to Lyttelton to see me off. It was the first time she'd ever done that for any of us. She sent telegrams too, to Dad's cousin in Wellington, and to Mum. But it wasn't until the boat had pulled out and I was in my bunk, feeling it press up underneath my back and sink away again that I started to cry. I liked Norman, and it seemed so awfully sad to think that someone always had to be the loser.

DAN DAVIN

The Quiet One

The band concert was over and three of us came out of the Regent into Dee Street with the rest of the crowd.

'I could swear she gave me the eye,' Sid said.

'I'll bet she did,' Wally said. 'One look'd be all she'd need, too. Who did, anyway?'

'That sheila with the black hat on that was in front of us about two seats away. You'd be too busy looking at the statue of the naked Greek dame to notice, I expect. Anyhow she was just in front of me when we were coming out and when I pushed the swing door open for her she turned round and gave me a real grin. Look, there she goes.'

He pointed the way we were going, and, sure enough, we could see a black hat bobbing along a bit in front where the crowd wasn't so thick.

'Come on, boys,' said Wally, 'Here we go.'

'But, look here,' I said, 'I thought we were going to the Greek's.' All the same, I changed my pace to keep up with theirs.

'To hell with the Greek's. Who wants to be sitting down to eggs and chips when there's a chance of picking up a sheila, eh, Sid?'

Sid just grunted. You couldn't see the girl because of the crowd and he was staring straight down the footpath, towards where we'd last seen her. You wouldn't have needed to know him as well as I did to guess from the sour way his mouth was closed that he didn't fancy the shape things were taking much. Wally was a tiger for the girls, and a good-looking joker, too. And old Sid hadn't had the same confidence in himself since the dentist made him have all his top teeth out. Wally didn't give him much chance to forget about it, either, calling him Gummy all the evening.

Not that there was anything in it for me, anyway. If there was only one girl I wouldn't be the chap who got her, that was certain. And, as a matter of fact, though I'd have been the last to say so, I'd have been scared stiff if there'd been the least danger of me being the one. I never really knew why I tagged along with them those Sunday evenings. I must have hoped some sort of miracle would happen, I suppose, and that some sheila or other would fall for me and put me into a position where one move had to follow the other in such a way that my mind'd be made up for me. At the same time I was terrified that just that would happen, knowing in advance that at close quarters with a girl I'd be like a cow with a musket. Anyhow, I needn't have worried. Nothing ever did happen and by this time I think I was getting to realize, only I wouldn't admit it, that nothing ever would.

That didn't stop me, though, from putting off going home till the last possible moment in case some sort of miracle turned up and when I finally left Wally or Sid at Rugby Park corner of a Saturday or Sunday night I'd trudge the rest of the way home in the rain or the moonlight, cursing myself and the town and everything in it and wondering what the hell was the matter with me, whether I was a different breed or what, and why it was always me that was left, and thinking that in some other country somewhere things mightn't be like that at all and people would see what I really was instead of what I'd always been.

So, with all that at the back of my mind, and Wally rampaging alongside with about as many afterthoughts as a dog has after a rabbit, and Sid on the other side getting down in the mouth already at the thought that Wally was going to pinch his girl, I didn't think much of the night's prospects. The upshot'd be that Wally would get her all right and I'd have to spend what was left of the evening at the Greek's trying to cheer Sid up by encouraging him to skite about all the girls that had fallen for him and pretending not to notice how much Wally going off with this one had got under his skin.

Well, after a bit the crowd got thinner and most of them started to cross over to where the last tram was waiting, towards the Majestic side. So we could see better what was in front of us. And there was the girl all right, about twenty yards ahead, all by herself into the bargain, and pacing along at a fair bat. Good legs she had, too.

'I reckon she knows we're following her,' Wally said. 'The trouble is, there's too many of us.'

'That's right, Wally.'

It was very sarcastic the way Sid said it but that didn't worry Wally.

'Go on, Sid,' he said, 'don't be a dog in the manger. A fair fight and let the best man win, eh?'

Of course, that was just the trouble, the way Sid looked at it. It's always the best man who says these things.

Anyhow, before Sid could think of an answer, or before he could think of something that wouldn't have given away he knew he hadn't a hope against Wally whatever kind of fight it was, the girl started to cross the road and so, us too, we changed course like a school of sprats and over the road after her, only about ten yards behind by this time.

She stepped up on to the footpath on the opposite side of the road, us tagging behind like three balloons on a string. She looked behind just then and saw us.

'Now's our chance,' Sid said, getting quite excited and nervous, I could tell.

Wally didn't say anything but he took advantage of his long legs and he was up on the pavement a good yard in front of us.

It was darker on the footpath because of the shop verandahs and because the nearest street-lamp was a good distance away. At first I couldn't see what was happening, owing to the notion I had that if I wore my glasses when we were out on the pick up on nights like this I'd spoil my chances, such as they were; but I felt both Wally and Sid check. And then I saw what it was. The girl had stepped into a shop doorway and there was a chap there waiting for her.

The girl and her bloke came out of the doorway and walked off towards the other end of Dee Street, her hanging on his arm and talking a blue streak and laughing the way we could tell the joke was on us. And the bloke looked back, once as if he'd like to have come at us. But, seeing Wally and thinking he had the trumps anyway, I suppose, he turned round again and kept on going.

'Well, I'm damned,' Wally said.

'Foiled again,' Sid said. But he didn't sound narked at all, really, and I knew by his voice he'd sooner have had it that way so that the laugh was on Wally instead of on himself as it would have been if things had gone differently.

I was pleased, too, for that matter, though I couldn't help envying that bloke a bit with a good-looking girl on his arm and a nice new blue overcoat and Borsalino and never a doubt in his head as to where he was going and what he'd do when he got there.

Still, envying him made it easier to pretend I meant it when I cursed the girl up hill and down dale like the others. For it wouldn't have done for me to show I was really relieved. It was sort of understood that even if I didn't mean business like Wally and Sid I had to go through the motions just the same. They really weren't bad blokes in a way, Wally and Sid, because they knew all the time I wasn't a serious competitor and yet they always treated me as if I was, thinking I'd be hurt if they didn't, I suppose.

And I would have been hurt, too. Somehow, if there hadn't been this kind of agreement about the way we were all to behave, I'd have had to drop the game altogether. I could tell that, because when, as happened sometimes, other blokes joined us who didn't know the rules or didn't care if there were any and they began to pull my leg, I always pushed off after a while. Which was what these other chaps wanted, I expect. 'The Wet Napkin', I heard one of them, Ginger Foyle it was, say once after I'd gone and he didn't think I could hear him, because I hadn't got my glasses on, perhaps.

No, Wally and Sid weren't like that, especially Wally. They knew I was all right once you got to know me and, besides, I used to be able to make them laugh when we were by ourselves and get them to see the funny side of things they'd never have noticed if it hadn't been for me.

Well, anyway, there we were left standing in the middle of Dee Street and all cursing our heads off in the same way.

'Nothing for it but to go over to the Greek's,' I said.

'Listen to him, will you, Sid,' Wally said. 'Him and his bloody Greek's. And us all whetted up for a bite of something tastier than old Harry could ever put under our noses.'

I felt a fool immediately, because I might have known that was the wrong thing to say, the way they were feeling. Once Wally had got the idea of skirt into his head it wasn't easy to put him off. And Sid, for all I don't think he really liked Wally, would trail along with him all right, knowing that was his best chance. That was what fascinated him about Wally, he could always have what Wally didn't want. But it was what made him hate Wally's guts, too.

Besides, I suppose they felt I'd sort of broken the rules by not being keen enough and waiting a bit longer before giving up what we all knew was a bad job.

'Well, what'll we do now, Wally?' Sid said.

'Let's take a stroll as far as the Civic and back,' I chipped in, trying to establish myself again. 'You never know, we might pick up something.'

'That's more like it,' Wally said. And then, because he wasn't a bad bloke, a better chap in many ways than Sid would ever be, he added: 'After all, if there's nothing doing, we can always go over to have a feed at the Greek's later on.' Which showed he wasn't really fooled by what I'd said.

So away we went, down past the Majestic where Len Parry and Alec Haynes and all that bunch were as usual, pretending they were talking about who was going to win the Ranfurly Shield when all they were interested in really was the girls who kept scuttling by on their way back from the band concert. I took a look at the Town Clock on the other side as we went by and there it was, half-past ten already, one more Sunday evening just about over and nothing happening, only the same old thing. Already everyone who had anywhere to go was going there and soon the only people left in the streets would be chaps like us who couldn't think of anything better to do and soon we'd be gone home too and the streets would be empty and another night would be gone out of a man's life and him none the wiser one way or the other.

'Was that your cousin Marty I saw all by himself in the doorway next that bloke who met the sheila, Ned?' Sid suddenly asked.

'I didn't notice.'

'It was him all right, poor bastard,' Wally said.

I pricked up my ears at that. My cousin Marty wasn't the sort of chap you talked about with that particular tone in your voice. He was rather a big shot in the eyes of our crowd. A good five or six years older than any of us, he must have been twenty-two or twenty-three, and he used to earn good money before the slump. A plasterer he was, by trade. But he'd been one of the first to be turned off when things got tough because, though he was good at his job, he had a terrible temper and was too handy with his fists. A big joker, he was, with reach and height, and they used to say that if only he'd do a bit more training there wasn't a pro in the business he couldn't have put on his back for the count.

As it was he'd made quite a name for himself round the town as a fighter and once when I was at the barber's and got fed up with the way slick little Basset kept taking me for granted because I didn't know what was going to win the Gore Cup I'd managed to get in casually that Marty was my cousin and after that Basset could never do enough for me.

'What do you mean, "poor bastard"?' Sid was saying.

'Didn't you hear? The trouble with you, Sid, is you never hear anything now you've got your teeth out.'

'Come on, come on, know-all. What's it all about?'

'Yes, what was it, Wally?' I asked; for I could tell Wally was wishing he'd kept his mouth shut, knowing Marty was my cousin.

'Well, it's only what they're saying, Ned, and there mightn't be anything in it, though I have noticed Marty hasn't been about much lately. You know how you'd always see him and Dulcie Moore round together of a Saturday and Sunday night?'

'That's right,' Sid said, glad to get in on the inside again. 'I saw them coming out of the Rose Gardens about two in the morning the night of Ginger Foyle's keg-party and they were always at the Waikiwi dances together.'

'Well, they say he put her up the spout. And then he got some old dame who hangs out in Georgetown to fix her up. Of course, that's happening all the time all over the place, you know, and nobody ever thinks a thing about it as long as no one gets caught.' This was for me. 'But the trouble this time was that something went wrong and she got blood-poisoning or something, and now she's in hospital and they say the johns have been at her all the time beside her bed trying to find out who did it and who was the man. But so far she won't say and the odds are she won't pull through.'

'Jesus,' said Sid. 'I thought he looked a bit down in the mouth.'

'Wouldn't you be?'

'But, look here, Wally,' I said, 'who told you all this?'

'I heard Marty's crowd, Jim Fergus and all that lot, talking about it yesterday after the game. And when I was shaving in the bathroom this morning and they didn't know I was there, I heard Mum telling the old man about it. It was her that told that bit about her not being expected to live.'

We'd got as far as the Civic and turned back by this time and the crowd was getting very thin by now, everybody making for home, feeling much the way I'd been feeling, I expect, that they might as well be in bed as hanging round. Only I didn't feel like that any more. Things happened, sure enough, and even to people you knew, even to your own family, near enough.

Sid and Wally kept talking about it all the way back up Tay Street. It was queer the way they seemed to get a sort of pleasure out of discussing it. And what was queerer still was that I liked hearing them talk about it. It must have been partly how old we were and partly the town we lived in. You felt the place wasn't quite such a dead-alive hole, after all, and you felt you really were grown up when things like that, terrible things but things all the same, happened to people you even knew.

Anyhow, just as we got to the Bank corner, two girls came round it the opposite way and we almost banged into them. While we were dodging around them to let them pass and show what gentlemen we were they cut through between me and Wally and we could hear them giggling as they went on.

'Sorry,' Wally called back in an extra-polite voice I hardly recognized, he could put on the gyver so well when he wanted to.

'Don't mention it,' one of the girls said and giggled again.

We stopped at that and Sid made a great show of lighting cigarettes for us while we all had a good dekko back to see what the girls were up to.

'They've stopped in the doorway next the jewellers,' Wally said. 'Come on,

Sid, here we go. We're home and dry.' He was so excited he forgot to pretend I was in on it, too.

The two of them cut back the way we'd come, like a couple of whippets at first and then as they got closer with a sort of elaborate stroll as if they might just as well be walking that way as any other. I followed after them, trying to catch up and yet not to catch up. I knew I ought to have gone away. There was no good just tagging on, being a nuisance. But I kept following, all the same.

'Hello,' Wally was saying as I came up to the doorway. 'Going anywhere?'

'What's that got to do with you?' the girl who had called back to us said.

'Well,' Sid said, 'it's getting late for girls to be out by themselves with all the roughs there are about this time of night and we thought you might like to have an escort on the way home.'

Sid could always talk well when it came to the pinch, especially if he had Wally with him. I of course couldn't say a thing, being as nervous as a cat, although I knew already that it didn't matter much what I did, me being only the spare part.

'You know what thought did,' the girl said.

'Come on, Isobel,' the other girl said. 'It's getting late.'

'Will you have a cigarette, Isobel?' Wally said. And he took out his case. It was the one he kept his tailor-mades in, not the one he used for home-rolled ones and butts. In that light you'd have taken it for silver.

'Don't mind if I do.'

'Come on, Isobel,' the other girl said again.

'Now, Jean, don't be an old fusspot. There's heaps of time really. Why don't you have a cigarette, too.'

'That's right,' Wally said, and so Jean took one from the case, a bit nervously, I thought.

'We don't even know your names, do we, Jean?' said Isobel when Sid had flourished his lighter for them. You could see them trying to get a look at us while the flame was there. But of course we had our backs to the street-lights and they couldn't have made out much what we looked like.

'That's easy,' Wally said then. 'I'll introduce us. My name's Wally Radford and this is my friend Sid, Sid Cable. And this is Ned.'

'He's a quiet one, isn't he?' Isobel gave Jean a nudge and giggled at me.

I tried to think of something very witty to say, the sort of thing that would have come to Wally or Sid in a flash. But I couldn't think of anything at all and I could feel myself blushing. I hated that Isobel then. It was always the good-looking ones that made me feel most of a fool. The other one, Jean, I didn't mind so much because I could tell by her way of giggling that she was nervous, too. She wasn't anything like such a good-looker, though.

There was a bit of a silence then. They were all waiting for me to say something. When I still didn't say anything I felt them all just give me up. Wally got into the doorway close to Isobel and tried to get his arm round her. She kept fending him off and looking at him and then at Jean in a way that said as plain as a pikestaff: Wait till afterwards when we can get away by ourselves.

Sid was talking a blue streak to Jean so as to give her a chance to get over her shyness, I suppose, and to shut me out of it and make me see I was being the gooseberry, in case I didn't see it already.

There was nothing to do but leave them to it. I was only holding Wally and Sid back from doing their stuff, hanging round like that.

'Well, I must be getting along,' I said.

'Why don't you come with us?' Jean said. Her voice sounded quite scared. But I could tell Sid wasn't going to get anywhere with her and I wasn't going to have her use me as an excuse to keep him off and then have him putting the blame on me next day.

'I'd like to,' I said, 'but I live up the other end of the town.'

'OK, Ned, good night,' Wally said in an offhand sort of way and Sid said good night too, in the friendly voice he always used when you were doing something he wanted you to do. That was one of the things Sid liked about me, that I always did the expected thing. It wasn't one of the things I liked about him.

So I set off by myself up towards the Bank corner again, feeling like a motherless foal, as the old man would have said. I thought I'd better give them plenty of time to get clear and so I decided I'd walk a few blocks up Dee Street and back again.

The Town Clock was pointing to nearly eleven by now. All the crowd that'd been in front of the Majestic was gone and Dee Street was as empty as the tomb except for a bobby standing in the library doorway over the other side, just in case there should be a row at the Greek's, I expect.

Seeing the Greek's lighted windows gave me the idea of going in for a feed, after all. But it was pretty late and I couldn't face going in there all by myself, with the blokes eyeing me and guessing what had happened. So I crossed Esk Street and went straight on up.

But it wasn't nearly so bad being by yourself when the whole street was empty like that and you didn't have to wonder what people were thinking about you. I quite liked striding along under the shop verandahs as if I were going nowhere in a hurry and listening to my heels hammer on the asphalt and seeing my reflection pass dark on the windows. It was better feeling miserable by yourself and not having to put up a show any more. Or else the kind of show you put up when there was no one but yourself to watch was more convincing.

'Hullo, Ned.'

I stopped in my tracks and looked round to see where the voice came from. Then I saw him. He was in the same doorway that the sheila had met her bloke in earlier on. He was standing there, all stiff like a sentry, and in that light you'd have thought his eyes were black they were so dark. A Spaniard, he might have been, with the long sideboards halfway down his cheeks and his straight, thin nose, that had never been broken for all the boxing he'd done.

'Hullo, Marty,' I said.

He didn't say any more, just went on looking at me. I didn't know quite what to do because it struck me it was probably only the suddenness of seeing someone he knew that had made him call out and probably he wished he hadn't now. Besides, knowing what I did, I felt uncomfortable.

I went up to him all the same, not knowing how to get away without it looking awkward and as if I'd heard about his trouble and was dodging off so as not to be seen with him.

'Have a cigarette,' I said and I produced a packet of ten Capstan.

'Thanks.'

I lit them for us both and when that was over there I was still stuck and unable to think of anything else to say. The only things that came into my head sounded quite hopeless compared with the things he must have on his mind.

'All the crowd gone home?' I said in the end, for lack of anything better.

'Suppose so,' he answered and took a puff of the cigarette. Then he added in a voice so savage that it gave me a real fright. 'Who the hell cares what they've done? Pack of bastards.'

I didn't say anything. I was trying to work out what he meant by that. Had they done the dirty on him and talked to the johns? Or was he just fed up with them?

He gave me a look just then, the first time he'd really looked at me since I stopped.

'You've heard all about it, I suppose?'

That stumped me properly. I didn't want him to get the idea the whole town was talking about him. Especially as that was what they were probably doing. I was scared of him, too. He'd be a bad bloke to say the wrong thing to.

'Heard about what?'

'You know.' He'd guessed by the time I took to answer. 'About Dulcie.'

There was no good pretending. 'Yes,' I said. 'How is she?'

He didn't answer but he kept on looking at me in the same queer way that he had been looking at me before. And then, as if he'd been sizing me up, he got down to what was on his mind.

'Look here, Ned,' he said. 'What about doing something for me?'

'All right,' I said. 'What do you want me to do?' My heart was in my boots because I didn't know much about the law but I felt sure this was going to be something against it.

'It's like this. I can't ring the hospital to see how she is because the johns are there and they keep asking me my name and they know my voice, too. What about you ringing for me?'

'All right, Marty,' I said. 'But what'll I say if they ask who I am? If I give my name they might come poking about home trying to find out what I know about it.'

'Say your name's Eddie Sharp. That's a friend of her young brother's and it'd be quite natural for him to ring. Will you do it?'

'I'll just see if I've got any pennies.'

We walked back towards the Post Office square. But the john was still in the library doorway and so I told Marty to go back to the place where I'd met him and wait for me there.

The john gave me that hard look that policemen give you but I went straight past him without giving a sign of how nervous I was. It was being so sorry for Marty that made me able to do it, I think.

'Southland Hospital,' a woman's voice answered when I'd got the number.

'I want to inquire about a patient, Miss Moore, Miss Dulcie Moore.'

'Will you hold on, please?'

There was a lot of clicking at the other end and I could hear whispering. Then a man's voice answered.

'The patient died an hour ago. Who is that speaking?'

I didn't answer. I just rang off and came out of the phone box.

How was I going to tell him, I kept asking myself as I went back past the john, hardly noticing him this time.

Marty was standing in the doorway, just as he had been the first time.

'How was she?'

There was nothing else I could do. I out with it.

'She died an hour ago.'

He stood there without saying a thing, just looking at me and yet not seeing me. Then he took a deep breath and his chest came out and he stood even straighter.

'So that's how it is,' he said. 'She's dead.'

I didn't say anything. I just stood there, wishing I was anywhere else in the world.

'If only I'd known,' he said. 'Christ, man. I'd have married her a hundred times, kid and all.'

He stopped. His mind must have been going over and over this ground for days.

He gave a laugh suddenly, such a queer, savage sort of a laugh that I jumped.

'If it'd been twins, even,' he said.

I had enough sense not to think that I was meant to laugh at that one.

'And those bloody johns sitting by the bed.'

'Did she come to?' I asked.

'Yes, she was conscious a lot of the time. But she wouldn't talk, not Dulcie. Not her. She was all right, Dulcie.'

Then there was silence again. I didn't know what to do or say. It was getting late. They'd have locked the door at home and there'd be a rumpus if they knew what time it was when I came in. How queer it was: here I was in the middle of something that really mattered and worrying about what my mother would say if she heard me climbing in the window.

All the same I wanted to get home. And then I had to admit to myself it wasn't really that. It was that I wanted to get away from Marty. I think it must have been the first time I was ever with someone who felt as badly as he was feeling.

'I remember her,' I said. 'She was a stunner to look at.'

'Wasn't she?' Marty said. And the way he said it made the tears come into my eyes.

'Why don't you walk my way?' I asked him. If he did that I could be making towards home and at the same time wouldn't feel I was ratting on him.

'No, I'm not going home yet,' he said.

I shuffled from one foot to the other, wondering what to do next and a bit worried what he would do after I'd gone.

'We always used to meet here,' he said. 'In this doorway.'

'Oh,' I said. 'Well, look here, Marty, I've got to be getting home now.'

'That's all right.'

I tried to think of some way of saying how sorry I was. But there was no way of saying it.

'Good night, Ned,' he said, and then, as I began to walk away, he called out: 'Thanks for doing that for me.'

So that's how it is, I was saying to myself all the way home. That's the sort of thing that happens once the gloves are off. And by the time I'd got to the front gate and opened it with one hand on the latch to stop it clicking and sat on the front verandah to take my shoes off I think I'd taken it all into myself and begun to wake up to how we only kid ourselves we can tell the good things from the bad things when really they're so mixed up that half the time we're thinking one thing, feeling another, and doing something else altogether.

Coming and Going

By the time I'd got myself marched into Base Camp at Maadi and fixed up with a bed I could see it was too late that night for the spree I'd been counting on having in Cairo. Too late to bludge a lift in and rouse up a few old pals. They'd all be out taking their snakes for a walk before I could get there. Still, there was bound to be someone I knew at the Mess. If the worst came to the worst there was always the duty officer.

'Where's everyone, Jack?' I said after I'd scoured the ante-room and the bar.

'They've all gone off to the show at Shafto's, sir. I expect you could do with some scran if you've only just got in?'

'It's a bit late for that, isn't it?'

'Well, the bar's not busy, you can see that. If you'll just sit on that drink for a bit, I'll soon jack you up something. Where'd you like to have it? In the dining-hut?'

'Here'll do just as well if that's OK with you.'

'Right. It'll have to have a bully beef base, though.'

So Jack scratched round in the kitchen and before long I had my entrenching tools into a fine binder of bully fritters and fried tinned potatoes, with any amount of marge and that fig jam we used to get that's all right if you're hungry enough. I was, what with the long trip up from the rest camp and only the unexpended portion of the day's ration for company.

And then Jack fetched over a big pot of tea and two cups and we settled down to a good natter about old times. He used to cook for A Company in the early days. But then he stopped one, I forget where it was, one of the Sidi Rizegh battles I think, and they found out about his age – he'd joined up to keep an eye on his grandsons, some of the blokes used to say. So they dumped him in this job at the depot until his turn came to go back home.

'Who's all here now, Jack?' I asked him when we'd chewed the rag for a bit about the end of the war and all that.

'No one much you'd know, sir. There aren't many left out of the old crowd now. Jimmy Larsen's here on his way back to the unit, he's a captain now. He got a bad one at Ruweisat. Tiger Smith's been on leave and he's going back, too. And there's Ted Tarrant just out of OCTU, you'll remember him, he used to be QM in the November '41 show. And there's Colonel Maitland, he's OC. And Bill Adair.'

'Yes, I saw him on duty when I clocked in.'

'Well, that's about all you'd know. The rest are reinforcements. It's a here today and gone tomorrow sort of place, this. Nothing much for the officers to do except take a parade or two for the look of the thing and censor a few letters.'

'Thank Christ I'll be out of it tomorrow. It sounds worse than death.'

'I suppose that's the idea. I used to think it was Christmas, having a good bludger's job, when I first got here. Now if I hear a Bren go off on the range I get homesick for the unit. And Rommel would be a relief after the sergeant-major.'

There was a banging against the wooden slide in the bar.

'Someone wants a drink,' I said.

'Always some bastard wanting something.' He was out quite a while.

'Anyone I know?' I asked when he was back in the kitchen.

'You'll know him all right.'

'Who, then?'

'Major Reading.'

'What's he doing here? I thought he had A Company.'

'So he did.' Jack got up and began to put the gear away.

I didn't take much notice, beyond spotting he didn't seem to have much time for Reading. But then none of us, men or officers, ever did and I thought it was just this that had made him dry up on me. Anyway, it was a long time since I'd seen Reading. In a long spell on your back you usually see only the chaps in the same ward with you and any of your cobbers who happen to be back from the sharp end. And I was too glad of a bit of company over a few drinks to remember that the last time I'd seen him was when we had the run-in over company boundaries the night before I got knocked at El Mreir.

'I think I'll go round and have a yarn with him.'

Jack said nothing but just gave me a sort of look.

'Thanks very much for the feed, Jack,' I added.

'That's all right, sir. It was nice seeing one of the old faces and talking about old times.'

'I liked it, too, Jack.'

Then I went out through the bar to the ante-room.

Reading didn't look up from the old *Free Lance* he was turning over. But he must have heard me and I fancy he could see me out of the corner of his eye anyhow. He was sitting on the other side of the room from the Mess piano. The wireless was on low and someone was drivelling away in Arabic.

'You don't want to listen to that, do you?' I said and I turned it off. 'Just someone telling the poor wogs about democracy.'

'Oh, it's you, Andy.' He gave me a quick look. I grinned back at him. We were from the same battalion, after all. 'Where've you sprung from?'

'Just back from sick leave. Guaranteed a new man. I've been eating so much white fish and milk pudding it was a waste not having an ulcer. What about a drink?'

He emptied his glass. 'Gin and lemon.'

I went back and knocked on the slide.

'Might as well keep the hatch open now, Jack,' I said. 'One gin and lemon, one whisky and water. Make them doubles. Have one yourself?'

'No, thanks all the same, sir,' he said.

I brought them over to Reading's table and pulled up a chair.

'Here's looking at you,' I said.

'Cheers.'

I was just going to ask him what he was doing. But he got in first.

'Seen any of the others?'

'No, I've only just got in.'

He took his glass in his hand and sat back. The cane chair gave a creak as he relaxed.

'Any of the boys back from the battle in Number One General when you were there?' he asked.

'One or two I didn't know came in just as I was leaving for rest camp. There were a few from our lot in Number Two, they said. These chaps looked pretty bashed about. A bit of an MFU, I gather. But I ought to be asking you. When did you leave them?'.

'Oh, I left after the first night on Miteiriya. Have another?'

I watched him go up to the bar. He could have been back on leave, of course. But it seemed queer. After all, you didn't usually swop company commanders on the first night of a battle. Unless you had to.

There were still two wet rings where the last glasses had been. Reading fitted the two new ones in as carefully as if he was playing some kind of game, fiddling with them this way and that until he'd got them exactly right.

'You'd miss the main part of the scrap, then? There was some pretty heavy going, after that.'

'Yes,' he said.

Neither of us spoke for a while. It wasn't a comfortable sort of silence. I ransacked my mind for something to say but I couldn't think of anything. Not my usual trouble.

'Good luck,' I said, picking up my glass. It was the best I could do.

'Good luck,' he said and picked up his.

Then we said nothing again. And I caught myself planting the glass exactly in the ring, the way he had done. This wasn't my idea of an evening. It wasn't even my idea of Reading. In the old days he'd have been shooting some line about what he did in peacetime – he used to be a stock agent I think it was and he'd got mixed up with some of the big station families.

I began to wonder when the others were coming back. It must be getting on towards the end of the film at Shafto's. Reading was breaking a little thread off the left sleeve of his battledress jacket. Well, he hadn't changed that way. He was always very fussy about his togs. It used to annoy the jokers, I remembered. And he was a terrible man to fuss before ceremonial parades and all that kind of thing. Used to do his scone completely if everything wasn't just so. 'A very smart officer,' our first CO used to say before we left him behind in Trentham. The new CO wasn't so quick to make up his mind.

'I'm off back tomorrow,' he said suddenly.

'So am I.'

'No, not back to the battalion. Back to New Zealand.'

'The hell you are? Jesus, that's a bit of luck, isn't it?'

'Luck? Yes, I suppose it is, in a way.'

'Give my best to anyone I know.'

Not that it was likely he knew anyone I knew outside the army. He came from Christchurch and was the sort of chap who, when he wasn't spending week-ends up on some sheepstation, would take an interest in the territorials and all that. Chaps like him had got off to a flying start when the war broke out. Still, you had to be fair, there were some quite good blokes among them, though I'd never have believed it in peace time and took a bit of convincing when the war came too.

He didn't seem as cheerful as you'd expect, though. After all, we'd been away three years then. And if a man had a piece of luck like this thrown at him, there was more than an even chance the war would be over before he heard shots fired in anger again. What more did he want?

Still, I thought, I suppose even old Reading feels it a bit, clearing out and leaving the boys to it like this. It'd be better to be going home when everyone else did, with the feeling that you'd taken your chance right up to the last like the rest of them. Provided you weren't being left behind for good, like so many who'd had it already; Buck Travers, for instance, who got his the night I was hit.

'I expect you take it a bit hard, though,' I said, 'leaving the old battalion.'

'Yes,' he said. And bugger me if I didn't suddenly get a horrible feeling he was going to let go and bloody well cry. Why not, anyway? Just because they didn't like him much it didn't mean he mightn't like them.

'I'll fill them up again,' I said.

It's probably the gin, I said to myself as Jack poured them out. They always say it does that to you. It never did to me, though, and I've had a power of it in my time.

Where the hell were all the blokes? I could have done with someone knocking out a tune on the old piano and a bit of a sing-song with plenty of drinks on the table and the boys letting themselves go with Samuel Hall or The Harlot of Jerusalem or, when they'd got sentimental, 'To you, sweetheart, Aloah'.

Reading seemed to have pulled himself together a bit by the time I brought the drinks back.

'You work the racket all right,' I said, the way we used to talk in those days half-thinking we meant it, 'and you should be jake sitting out the rest of the war in some bludger's job in Trentham.'

He didn't seem to like this much. We never really talked the same language, anyhow.

'I don't know,' he said and his accent seemed to have gone a bit pommier than usual, or what he thought was pommy, only that was another thing that meeting a lot of pommies had made some of us wise to.

'I might ask for my discharge,' he said.

I was a bit surprised, even a bit shocked. Everyone says these things from time to time. But he sounded as if he meant it.

Just then, though, you could hear the trucks pulling up outside.

'Here they come,' I said, 'the dirty stop outs.'

'It's time I was off to bed. An early start in the morning.'

'Come off it,' I said, 'you might as well stay till you finish your drink, at any rate.'

'Yes, why not?' But when he said it he set his jaw the way you'd think he was sitting on one end of a tug-of-war.

Well, the door opened and a lot of the blokes came in. I didn't know any of this first lot and so I didn't take much notice when, after one look at us, they went straight to the bar without saying anything to either of us. I did think it a bit funny, though, the way they all quietened down suddenly when they'd been talking their heads off outside.

Then in came Jimmy Larsen, Ted Tarrant, Tiger Smith and several others I more or less knew. They glanced over our way. Tiger called out 'Hello, Andy,' and the others waved. They joined the rest at the bar.

This struck me as a pretty queer way of going on. And, of course, dumb as I was, it wasn't hard to guess there was something the matter and the something was Reading. I looked at him. He'd gone white in the face and as I watched him he slowly went red again, red all over.

Now I'm not a joker to kick another bloke when he's down but I'd sooner have been back in hospital, back in El Mreir for that matter, than where I was then. I couldn't think of anything to say to Reading and I don't think he was even trying to think of anything to say to me. He was just staring into his glass where there were a few little husks of lemon floating about on a thin wash of drink.

How the bloody hell was I going to get out of this one? Say what you like nobody much wants to be with someone everyone else seemed to think lower than a snake's testicles. If it was a cobber that might be a different thing. But Reading was a bloke I wouldn't have given you two knobs of goatshit for, even in ordinary times. Not my kind of chap at all. Yet I couldn't very well clear out and leave him flat, all on his lonesome like that.

'Good night, Andy,' he suddenly said.

I was relieved, I've got to admit. But at the same time I felt ashamed at feeling relieved. So I asked him to have another drink, though I must say I was pretty sure he wouldn't.

He didn't seem to hear but just got to his feet and walked straight out of the room. The other blokes didn't look at him and he didn't look at them.

I didn't like to get up and join them even then. Too much like a rat leaving a sunk ship. I felt in a way as if Reading was still there. Besides, I was damned if I was going to start explaining myself to all these jokers, a lot of them I'd never even seen before, just new chums and red-arses.

'You know I don't like to see my little Andy boy in bad company.'

It was Tiger Smith and by God I was glad to see him standing there and grinning down at me. He was the sort of joker everybody likes and if a thing or a chap's all right with him then it's got to be all right with everyone or he'll know the reason why.

'What's he done?' I said.

'What I always thought he'd do some day. Cleared out. Ratted. Buggered off. Said he had to report back to battalion. There was a counter-attack coming in. You know, just when the light was right for them. With tanks, too. Luckily the sergeant-major, old Dick Coster, was on the job. But it's mafish for Reading. The high jump. Of course, no one could prove anything. But Dick got killed and later on when Larry took over he got killed too.'

'Court martial?'

'No, no court martial. As I say, you couldn't prove anything. I don't suppose anybody'd want to. Nothing like that ever happened before in the battalion.'

'No,' I said. 'Not in the battalion. The bastard.'

Jim Larsen and Ted Tarrant had come over by this time. 'Come on, Tiger,' Jim said. 'We're all going back tomorrow. Let's make a night of it before the flies wake up and get us. Get cracking on the old piano, Andy.'

It was late when we broke up. I was still clear in the head but pretty shaky on my pins when I left the others and cut across the parade ground for my hut. You know what those huts were like, all the same size and all alike.

Anyhow, I found mine at last. I thought I was the only joker there but as I passed the end room I noticed a light coming under the door. Naturally, I thought it was one of the boys, so I knocked and went in.

'Hello, Andy,' Reading said.

He was sitting on the edge of the bed. All his kit except what he'd need in the morning was packed up. On top of his tin trunk there was a hurricane lamp and a bottle of gin and a mug.

'Sorry,' I said, 'I thought you were Bill Adair.'

'Sorry to disappoint you. Sorry to disappoint everybody. Have a drink.'

I didn't see how I could get out of it. And anyhow I felt sorry for him sitting there drinking with the flies when all the rest of us had been over in the Mess singing and wrestling and slapping one another on the back, the way we used to in those days.

I sat down. He fished out another mug from his kit, rinsed it with some water out of the seir, and poured me a stiffish gin.

'No, I'm not Bill Adair,' he said. 'I'm not Tiger Smith, either, or Ted Tarrant. And I'm not sorry I'm not. I'm damned glad.'

'You're glad you're not Dick Coster, too?' I couldn't help saying.

'They've told you all about it, of course.'

'Yes.'

'Self-satisfied bastards. Anyone'd think they'd never thought of doing the same. A hundred times, every one of them.'

'They never did it, though.' And I remembered all the times I'd had that feeling in my own guts as we went forward under the barrage, or waited shivering in the half-light for the counter-attack to come in.

'No, they never did it. Brutes, clods, that's all they are. You think it's guts. But it isn't, I tell you. It's only that they're afraid of what people'll say.'

I said nothing. But I was remembering how on mornings before a big parade he'd be nagging at his batman because his trousers weren't properly pressed and giving his platoon commanders hell if the men's gaiters weren't blancoed and every other bloody thing just exactly so.

'And anyhow I wasn't well, I tell you. I hadn't slept for nights before that.'

I still didn't say anything but that didn't worry him. He just went on and on, in a mixed up kind of way, sometimes saying he hadn't done anything and other times saying he couldn't help doing it, anyone else would have done the same and anyhow he was sick. I felt very embarrassed. At the same time I'd sobered up and I was tired and sleepy. I remembered the batman was to give me a call at first light.

From time to time he'd pour himself another but after the first one or two he forgot to offer me any – it wasn't really me he was talking to but himself. And I didn't tell him I could do with another because I knew I was too tired for any amount of gin to jack me up and besides I was looking for an excuse to get away. In fact I was so busy trying to find one that I almost missed it at first when he started off on a new track.

'I suppose they think that the only thing for a chap in my position to do is bump himself off. I suppose that's what you think too. You think I won't be able to go back to my old job because the blokes'll be back sooner or later and they'll tell the story round and people'll begin to pretend they don't see me there either. You all think that's what I ought to do, don't you?'

He wasn't shouting at all, but the way he was staring at me I could see he was looking for some kind of an answer. I felt all dopey with a hangover coming on and being in need of a bit of sleep and I didn't know what to say. And as a matter of fact I couldn't help feeling he could do worse. But I didn't say anything. Only I thought it really was time I cleared out. So I got up.

'Yes, that's what you think, the whole bloody lot of you,' he said, sitting there with the mug in one hand and the other hanging down the way you could see he was up to the eyes in booze.

'But you're bloody well mistaken,' he suddenly shouted at me and his hand came up so hard that the gin splashed out of the mug. 'You needn't think I'm going to do anything of the kind.'

'I don't,' I said. 'But look here, I've got to get to bed. I'm off back in the morning, remember.'

'That's right,' he said. 'And I'm off back, too.'

He said this so quietly I thought this was my chance.

'Good night,' I said.

He said nothing, didn't even look at me. I felt bad somehow, so I said, 'I'll look in before I go.'

'You needn't bother.'

So I left him sitting there, staring at the floor.

After I'd put my light out and was just getting off to sleep I heard someone trip over my shoes.

'It's only me, Andy,' Reading said. 'I just came to say good night. And good luck.'

'Thanks, Cliff, and good luck to you.' It was a bit of an effort but I managed to call him by his first name.

I heard him stumble back in the dark towards the door.

But I must have slept very heavily after that because I didn't hear the shot and it wasn't till the batman rushed in and told me at first light that I knew anything about it. And the Adj insisted on me staying for the court of inquiry though what the hell there was to inquire into I don't know. It all seemed plain enough to me. Anyhow by the time I got back the Div was getting ready for the left hook round Agheila and before we had time to stop and think again no one felt much interest in what had happened to Reading.

Under the Bridge

Black, opaque and in hundreds they interposed their darkness between us and the smiling Cretan sky, shattered the summer's peace with the death they carried, slew its silence with the roar of their engines and the punctuated thunder of the bombs. Each explosion overtook its predecessor's echo, and merged with it to make a perpetual rumble in the hills.

Sometimes a shadow would pass directly over us, swiftly, flitting and bat-like. The drone increased to a roar and the plane would follow, bullets streaming with the undiscriminating prodigality of rain. Like rain on a gusty day. How long since I had seen and felt rain, refreshing rain not deadly, from grey, unhurrying homely skies, not this lethal metallic rain.

Our hill overlooked the village on its left, on the right front the sea. The sea, smooth and untroubled, its calm a promise of permanence when this tumult should be silent, road home to the lands of rain. Crouched under the lee of the rock, nostalgia gripped me like a cramp, nostalgia for the past or for the future. Anything to be out of this moment where we were held by the slow, maddening pace of time. But not for long this mutiny of the heart. Madness to venture hopes on such a sea, to commit oneself to anything but a prudent despair. Try to save your life certainly, but within the bounds of decency and dignity. And not expect to save it. Fighting was easier, dourer in despair.

Nothing much to do till the air quietened down a bit. There might be more parachutists to follow soon, the concentration was so fierce. But no; it was the town that was getting it this time. Our share was only the overflow. They were solacing themselves for their reverses on the ground in an orgy of undirected destruction, an orgasm of rage and inflicted terror. Clouds of dust and smoke rose tranquilly, unfolding and expanding with the leisure of time itself from crumpled homes and ruined walls. Flames groped up into the afternoon, their red transparent to the day and then, as their mounting impetus declined, filmy and water-coloured but still bloodshot.

Just outside the village where the last houses straggled like lost children, the road bridged a gully. I was watching the bridge. During raids the people sheltered under it. We had warned them to go away, not to wait. They were obstinate, they would not leave their homes. We told them the bridge would probably be hit, was a military objective, but the mere physical fact of its shelter, its mere bulk blinded them to its danger. They continued to go there.

That would have been bad enough. But now we all had a personal interest there as well. Angela and her grandmother would be there too. And Angela had somehow succeeded in making herself real to us in a way civilians are not usually real. The two didn't even belong to the town but had come down from their village in the hills. They used to help us with food sometimes and do the washing. There was something about Angela's smiling freshness, the beauty of her teeth and hands which made everything she did for us seem better than if someone else had done it. Seeing her made you notice how good the weather was and when you looked at the sea you would see how blue it was and the snow on the mountains inland would strike you in all its cold remote whiteness for it seemed the first time. On the old, leisurely standard I would have had time to fancy myself in love with Angela.

From where I was I could see the bridge perfectly. The gully ran out from the foot of our hill and in a straight line away from us till it passed under the road. You could not distinguish individuals. But you could see them praying. They were all kneeling under it, the women and the children and the very old men. You could see them praying, making the sign of the cross over and over again. Their fear was erect and dignified. For the hundredth time I admired the bravery of these Cretans, their steadfastness. Angela and her grandmother would be there too, like the others afraid, as who would not be, like them calm and accepting with a proviso of reserved revenge.

I felt so close to them that I was with them. I almost blessed myself too when they did. It was like the family rosary of long ago. But the devil 'who wanders through the world to the ruin of souls' sought bodies too. He was real and present. He was death, travelling with every bullet now broadcast from the air and guiding, too, haphazard chance, and the cool selection of the sniper's eye.

In spite of the intenseness of my presence with them I was aware too of the planes, could see them as one after another detached from the intricately weaving group and swept low with a rising roar over the prostrate village.

They would have been better off spread along the gully. But they might have a chance. The German hadn't yet bombed any bridges to my knowledge. Saving them for himself. But this was a side road. It wouldn't matter much to him. And today he didn't seem to care greatly where he dropped them: he was out to terrorize. By now the town couldn't be much more than a chaff of mortar and rubble among drunken walls.

From over the centre of the town a bomber came sailing out towards the bridge. Slowly, very slowly. Above the outskirts they began to drop, swift and glistening where the light caught them. I watched them. The first struck the edge of the town. A series of explosions among the scattered houses. I heard them only. I was watching the last. I don't think he particularly meant to hit the bridge. But it disappeared. The whole scene disappeared. It was as if I had become blind with smoke and dust instead of darkness.

I waited for it to clear. For reality to reassemble. The cloud settled into the grey-green olives in either side of the gully. The bridge was still standing. The bomb had fallen in the gully, on the far side. I began to breathe again. And then I saw that the group had changed. They were no longer kneeling. Their small dark knot had opened out like a flower. There were shapes scattered in a semi-circle this side of the bridge, still. The bomb blast must have travelled along the gully like an express train through a cutting. Still, I thought at first; but after a while I seemed to discern movement. It was not a movement of whole bodies, a stirring of limbs rather, of extremities, faint and painful like the movements of a crushed insect whose antennae still grope out pitifully with a hopeless, gallant wavering to life.

This was the bare slope of the hill. The red clay showed through the thin soil and the olives were few, thickening only at the bottom. And the planes were as active as ever. It was impossible to get down. And anyhow we had a position to hold.

Afternoon became evening, since time moved even in that eternity. And day diminished into dusk. The racket slackened. Only an occasional rifle shot or burst of machine-gun reminded the twilight silence of its brief tenure. Silence like us and them was mortal.

I told the others I was going down. They were to cover me across the open patch. I slipped out from cover and holding the tommy-gun bolted for the olives. No firing, no vicious swish of bullets. I made my way through the olives, along the lip of the gully. The dusk was deeper in the olives. The hill held its bulk before the sun.

As I approached the bridge I hesitated. I knew what I was going to see. And there had been so much of it in these last days. I stopped and listened. Not a sound. That eternal, suffering grey of the olives, the agony immobilized of their gnarled trunks anticipated and accentuated what must be in the gully. The silence, the patient silence and the dusk, but mostly the silence, were too much. It was silence of mangled bodies, a silence of negation and death. There was no life in the gully. Pain, perhaps, frozen into immobility, but no life. If I should see it as well, bodies caparisoned in all the bloody trappings of a violent death, blood and grotesque distortions of the body's familiar pattern, it would be too much. Not as if it were new. The very familiarity of the distortion, the blasphemy of it, would prove final. I did not want to see any more. I did not want to see Angela, her grandmother, others I had known. Or supposing I did see them and did not recognize them?

But perhaps there was something one could do. I listened again. Not a groan or sigh. There was much to do, much fighting yet. One must fight for one's sanity as well as one's life. I hesitated. In sudden horror I knew there was something else dragging me to the edge. Appetite for frightfulness as well as revulsion. Death squatted within the hollow like a presence, its emanation came up, grisly, dragging at me. I felt the hair on the back of my head stiffen. I took two steps forward. My eyes saw but my brain would not see. I turned and ran.

At the edge of the olives I halted. My knees were like jelly, with a hot trembling I waited. Then ran again across up over the bare slope. It was with relief I heard the bullets searing their tunnel through the air. At the rock I turned and dropped into cover, a soldier again. And the bridge and the gully of bodies waited in my memory.

JOHN REECE COLE

She's all yours

The instructor pulled the pin out of his safety harness and eased himself out of the cockpit. In his flying suit his movements seemed cumbrous as he turned and leaned into the cockpit to remove the front stick.

'She's all yours!' he said and smiled. He affected not to notice how the head and shoulders of the pupil became even more tense. Keen as blazes, he thought, but too sensitive. Yet he appeared to have what was needed to make a pilot, and it was his job to make him one.

He could keep a kite straight and level, his turns would do, his take-offs steady enough, but his landings – as was always the case – weren't safe enough. He'd sat through dozens with him, shaken and jarred until his bones ached. But if he didn't let him go alone now he'd never be any good. Now he'd either make it, or break up the kite and perhaps himself.

He began to talk quietly, running over the sequence of the circuit, trying to get the essence of all he had learnt in a thousand hours war flying into a few simple words. 'Relax. Relax completely. Become part of the aircraft, try and feel that the controls are an extension of your own limbs.'

Still talking, he snapped the release of his 'chute harness and slung the heavy pack over one shoulder. The pupil's eyes were bright and he nodded his head as if listening intently; but the instructor knew he was conscious only of the flow of his voice. His thoughts were racing far ahead. Already he was thinking of how he would burst into the barrack block and shout 'I've made it!' Thinking of how the Waaf waitresses in the mess that night would smile appreciatively.

The instructor tried to think of a joke that would help the kid to laugh his way out of his tenseness. His inability to recall anything humorous made him irritable, reviving his resentment at having been posted home to instruct after three years on Stirlings in England. Why should he have to worry about a bunch of kids? he asked himself time and again, thinking how different they were from those of his own training days. They had been an older lot, more world-weary, cynical. Now so many of them came straight from school. Yet he wanted to make the kid feel at ease; the kid's life could depend on how he made him feel.

With a deliberately casual wave of his hand he turned and walked towards the fence, knowing that the pupil was watching him, and never glancing back, trying to give him the feeling that he was so good that he did not need watching. He heard the short bursts of the engine and he knew that the pupil was taxi-ing towards the boundary, and he kept on walking. Then the engine was turning over quietly as the pupil sat cross-wind running through his cockpit drill.

Instantly the instructor thought of things he might have warned him against, but he stifled the impulse to turn around and wave him back. 'Easy now, easy!' he said aloud. He knew that lately he had begun to tense up too much himself. But he felt that the doctor was taking it all too seriously. A spot of leave was all he needed; he'd be as fit as ever. The engine was beginning to rev up as the pupil turned into wind. What if he opens her up too quickly and chokes the engine? He'd get half off the deck and smash back into the trees at the boundary. He looked around. But the roar was rising smoothly, steadily, as the aircraft raced down the field for the take-off. Then the tail was up and the engine wide open.

The aircraft bounced twice and was airborne. 'Too steep! Too steep!' the instructor shouted. The kid hadn't allowed for the loss of his weight. Why the devil doesn't he adjust the trim? Still, if the engine doesn't cut he'll be all right.

If the engine doesn't cut,.if the engine doesn't cut. If he doesn't panic and do something stupid. If he doesn't stall and come back into the deck. He knew how the kid's heart would be racing when he suddenly realized that he was up there all alone. Thoughts would rush through him. He would be intensely aware of the absence of the familiar helmeted head in the front cockpit, and that there was no longer the voice of advice in his earphones. He'd be cursing the day he joined the air force. Cursing all those long days and nights of swot which, seemingly, led up to nothing but the chance to break his own neck. Then he'd look around gradually and he'd think, hell, if the instructor with all his experience thinks I'm okay, I must be.

He heard him throttle back at 500 feet and saw that the angle of climb was less steep. His turn at 700 feet was bad. He was too tense to bank properly, the aircraft slipped inward. Hell, he thought, the kid's too nervous! Why the devil had he sent him up there alone? He suddenly thought of Brent (feeling as if something were pressing on his chest) the night when only four of the squadron's kites came back from the Ruhr – Happy Valley! Brent made it but his crew were dead. Brent didn't have a scratch, but he wasn't much good for anything afterwards. The kid was the same type.

He watched him level out at 1,000 feet and turn surprisingly smoothly. Straight and level on the down-wind leg, the instructor thought, he'll realize for the first time that he's really flying. For a moment he'll eye warily the other aircraft moving around the circuit. Then he'll look beyond their yellow dipping wings to the crumpled foothills and farther back the peaks swimming above the cloud. On the other side he'll watch the crawling line of breakers, the spray sliding back across the withered skin of the sea. He'll relax and become aware of the soft movements as the control surfaces tug the stick in his fingers. He'll glance at his instruments, turn-and-bank indicator, rev counter, altimeter, oil pressure, and he'll begin to feel fine.

But he was going too far. Why doesn't he turn? the instructor thought, becoming impatient. Then he saw the Hudson. It was coming swiftly cross-wind, descending directly into the pupil's line of flight. Obviously the pupil had not seen it. Its operational colours made it difficult to see. The instructor opened his mouth and suddenly he was shouting, 'The fool! The damned young fool!'

There was a sudden roar. In a frozen instant he waited for the sound of rending metal and fabric. But the Hudson was banking steeply, its engines wide open. The skipper had spotted the trainer, which, tossed violently in the slip-stream of the now shrill Wright Cyclones, passed only a few feet beneath.

The instructor saw the pupil regain control and commence to reduce height rapidly on his landing approach. He caught his breath. In his panic to get down the pupil had cut his throttle too soon. Tense again, he skidded his last turn which was dangerously low. Gunning the engine, he just got over the fence. The aircraft ballooned when the wheels hit; it shot up thirty feet and seemed to hang suspended. Rigid, his hands suddenly sweating, the instructor waited for it to stall and dive back into the ground. Then the engine coughed and picked up sharply as the throttle was slammed open. The wings and fuselage shuddered, then the aircraft began slowly to climb.

In a rage the instructor walked up and down at the edge of the field as the pupil began to go around again. By the hangar several pupils, their flying finished for the day, were watching too. On the tarmac the petrol waggon was refuelling each aircraft before it was wheeled into the hangar. Following the trainer as it roared above him, he noted with surprise that the angle of climb was better this time. Throughout the circuit the kid still used too much rudder in his turns, but they had improved. Finally, with the engine throttled back, he was descending steadily. His turn into wind was at just the height and angle. He seemed to have loosened up at last.

Then the landing – most critical of all. He levelled out over the field, but was still too high. He was closing the throttle and easing the stick back, holding off . . . holding off . . . holding off . . . . The instructor clenched his fists, wanting to turn his head away or shut his eyes. The group standing by the hangar was suddenly silent. They knew that if he were to stall now there would be another aircraft wrapped up, and another of their number, at the best, grounded. All heard the throttle opened sharply and then cut back. Then the aircraft was on the ground, a three-pointer.

The instructor picked up his 'chute and walked rapidly towards the hangar, seeing the pupil turn left and taxi around the opposite boundary. He was thinking of Brent again. After all, he had been one of the few in the service who had ever argued or thought seriously about the war, and all that. Perhaps this kid and his kind, younger, less disillusioned, would come out of it all with the energy to make things a bit better. Perhaps –. Half impatient, half ashamed of his philosophizing, he shook off his thoughts. Reaching the tarmac, he strode towards the trainer which had just rolled to a standstill.

A slightly built figure climbed out stiffly. He pulled off his helmet and ran his fingers through his hair, uncertainly. Around his neck he wore a woollen scarf, carelessly tied.

The instructor glared at the trailing ends of the scarf. Christ, how many times did the young fool have to be told? Couldn't he understand the danger of that sort of thing? His cheek was jerking. He was conscious of the pupil pilots behind him, drawing closer together, anxious, watching. His hands shook as he struggled with his anger. Then quickly he stepped forward smiling and gripped the kid's sweating hand.

It was so late

The moment he was left to himself he moved over to the long window overlooking the grounds, still thinking, Why had it to be here, in this house, of all places? Outside there was no wind and the sun slanting against the motionless branches made shadow patterns on the lawns. The native shrubbery stood out darkly against the burnt copper of the oaks. He remembered how the coming evenings would be soft and still, with mist slowly gathering around the trunks. Later there would be rain and the black water of the creek would swell and sweep away spinning clusters of leaves and dead twigs. And after the rain reflectionless pools would lie under the trees and in the hollows of rotting logs.

A man wearing a shapeless hat and carrying a gardening fork stepped out of the trees and walked across the bottom lawn. Jennings! he thought excitedly, almost upsetting the forgotten cup and saucer in his hand. Then he remembered, Jennings had been an old man. He must have died years ago.

A quiet voice interrupted his thoughts, 'Autumn, everything is dying . . . the season of decay.' It was the young man with scanty blonde hair, wearing a clerical collar, whom he had noticed earlier sitting in a corner alone. They stood for a moment without speaking, looking out into the greying light. 'It's always rather sad, don't you think?' the curate continued.

Behind them a faded voice had risen uncertainly above the flickering conversations, '. . . greatest pleasure to welcome these brave boys back into our midst.'

They turned and sat down respectfully. It must be the mayor, he thought, noticing the winged collar and the dark, carefully pressed suit. The voice wavered, then with a confident spurt became louder, '. . . if I may so express myself, these gallant knights of the air, who by their fine record of service with the Royal Air Force, have added lustre to the name of New Zealand. These men to whom we . . . .'

He glanced around at the other uniformed figures. Alan was slumped in his chair, his brow puckered, staring hard at the end of his cigarette. Michael, his face stud' ' expressionless, was fiddling with the strap of his wrist watch. Rex had been trying to attract his attention. He was leaning forward so that he was partly screened from the rest of the room by a high-backed mahogany chair. He was making deprecating gestures and grinning desperately.

Reluctantly, inevitably, his gaze shifted to Mrs Chatterton, the hostess. She was sitting with her head inclined towards the speaker. Her hair that he remembered having glimmers of grey was now white, and harsher lines marked her strong immobile features. Thinking of the first time he had seen that cold implacable face, he felt again the shock and sharp thrust of rising emotion.

He was holding his mother's gloved hand as they walked up a tree-lined drive towards a big house, when they came upon a tall lady walking in the garden.

'Good afternoon,' his mother said.

'Well?' the lady demanded.

'I . . . I answered the advertisement . . . for a maid,' his mother faltered.

'Oh, indeed.' The inescapable eyes held them for several moments. 'Well, if there is anything you wish to know ask Mrs Johnston, the housekeeper.'

'Why so serious?' Mrs Wells said, lowering her wide hips into the chair at his side. He continued to stare at the bone-white knuckles of his still tightly clenched hands. Groping for a reply, he began, 'I was –'

Mrs Wells interrupted, 'I was only saying to Mrs Chatterton– Oh, here she is! So nice of her to have the "welcome home" here when there wasn't a hall available. Hello, my dear! I was just saying to Flight Lieutenant –'

Mrs Chatterton swept past and stood for a moment by the window. Then she turned to Mrs Wells. 'That girl, wherever can she be? Her car isn't in the garage yet!'

'Well, she's young,' Mrs Wells said feelingly. 'When I was her age –'

'I don't know what she does with all her time,' Mrs Chatterton complained.

'Well, she has her Red Cross work, my dear,' Mrs Wells defended.

'You should be thankful, Mrs Chatterton,' Mrs Keeble interposed in a thin, high voice, 'that there are no longer any of these soup kitchens and charity bazaars, or she might spend all her time there, like my Grace and Jeannie did before they were married.'

Mrs Keeble was the wife of Old John Keeble, headmaster of Woodbury. Mrs Chatterton glanced absently at her nervous features, then, dismissing her, continued, 'I do wish Margot would hurry. She might consider me sometimes.'

Margot, he thought, feeling his way back through dim years. Then everything sharpened, came into focus. He saw again a green trellis gate open and a little girl wearing a blue embroidered dress come through. She walked over to where he was sitting at the bottom of the kitchen steps. She was dragging behind her a large wax sleeping doll, and each time its head bumped on the gravel its closed eyes flickered open.

'What is your name?' she demanded.

'Ronny,' he replied. 'What's yours?'

'My name is Margot Chatterton.'

Then she said suddenly, 'See that car. It belongs to my father. Father says next year we will have two. . . . Have you got a car?'

'No.'

'Why doesn't your father buy you one? Where is your father?'

There were rapid footsteps on the drive and a voice called sharply, 'Margot, come here at once!' It was Mrs Chatterton. 'Haven't I told you to keep away from there?'

In the afternoons after school he would sit by the window of the small back room that he shared with his mother, waiting till she could find a moment to slip in and get him something to eat. Sometimes, when there had been visitors, she would smuggle him in something special, such as a cream cake or a chocolate biscuit, which she would take out of a pocket in her black dress under her white apron.

Often he would feel very lonely, waiting, feeling the faint pangs of hunger, listening to the subdued, conflicting noises of the big house. Jennings, the gardener, would stop and talk to him when he was working nearby. Once he had brought him an old cap-gun that he had dug up down by the creek. Sometimes he would see Margot playing on the far lawn. He began to look forward to hearing her bright chatter when she bombarded the gardeners with excited questions, or to watching her movements as she played with her toys. So that later there was always an emptiness when she was not there.

One day she noticed him and ran over to the window. When she smiled he could see how the freckles crinkled round her eyes. 'What school do you go to?' she asked. 'I'm going to school soon. To St Catherine's. Is that where you go?'

'No, I go to Marsh Street.'

'Oh.'

For a moment she seriously traced with the toe of her shoe in the loose soil of the border garden. When she looked up she asked, 'Where is your mother?'

'She's busy.'

'I know something.'

'What?'

'I won't tell, see!'

'What is it, then?'

'The gardener told me.'

'Who, Jennings?'

'Yes.'

A chair grated on the verandah and Mrs Chatterton called, 'Margot.'

Margot turned and ran to where her mother was sitting, shaded from the sun by a rattan blind. 'If I have to tell you again –'

'Mother, mother, I know why the little boy hasn't got a father. It's 'cause he was killed at the war.'

'Margot, go inside at once.'

Mrs Chatterton stamped her foot, her voice broke shrilly.

'Margot! Do as I say, at once! And don't have so much to say for yourself!'

Then it was Saturday, Margot's birthday. Watching Jennings set up the tables for the party, by the fountain in the sunken garden, he remembered how the previous day Jennings had leaned his brown hairy arms over his shovel and said to his mother: 'It's a new country, gal. You don't have to depend upon anyone here, not like at home. You've been out here long enough to know that – plenty of opportunity! I'm old . . . doesn't matter now.'

Mrs Johnston arranged the spread. Watching, he forgot about Jennings; he ceased to wonder why he often told his mother she shouldn't work there any longer. He couldn't look away from the tables. There were plates of feathery cakes bursting with cream, frail white and pink meringues, chocolate cake, a variety of biscuits, some covered in coloured tinsel paper, and finally the birthday cake, encrusted with icing, with five candles on top. Mrs Chatterton came out when the games were finished and watched Mrs Johnston arrange the guests around the tables. The boys wore dark jackets and starched white collars; the girls, white silk dresses, and most had bows in their hair.

He leaned against the window sill, listening to Margot's voice, brighter and quicker, rising above the others. Then he saw that something was wrong. Margot had got down from her place at the top of the table and was shouting, 'I won't. I won't!'

Mrs Chatterton moved towards her, but she turned and ran, stopping with her back to the pond. Her cheeks were flaming as she cried, 'I don't want to sit next to Grace and Maurice! I want Ronny to be here. Ronny . . . .' Mrs Chatterton tried to grasp her daughter's arm but she jumped, evading the outstretched hand, and stumbled against the low stone rim of the pond. For an instant she struggled to hold her balance, then all the children shrieked as she flopped backwards into the water.

When he could bring himself to look again, Jennings had got Margot out of the pond, and Mrs Johnston was trying to get the tittering children back to the tables. Mrs Chatterton half led, half dragged her soaked choking daughter over to the house. As they approached, he moved back from the window into the shadows. His heart was racing and he felt sick, and somehow guilty.

'Well, how does it feel to be back?' asked Old John Keeble, peering shrewdly down his long nose.

'It's rather early to say.'

'I suppose the old country has, well, as they seem to say nowadays, taken a pounding?' Then, scarcely allowing him to reply, Old John went on, 'I must say everyone over there stood up to it wonderfully. Plenty of spirit, eh, Flight Lieutenant? I'd like to go home again some day, just to have a look around. It's surprising how one becomes attached to this little country. I came out here thirty-five years ago, straight from Oxford. Never thought I would stay; there was so much I missed, the finer things. One settles in, though, takes root. . . . It's comfortable here, that's it. . . .'

He was aware of the keen gaze again. 'Now, let me see. . . . What year would you have been in?'

'I beg your – Oh, I see. I . . . I didn't go to college.'

'Oh.'

'Lieutenant, you haven't had a thing to eat!' Mrs Wells interrupted. 'Can I get you something? Another cup of tea, then?'

'No thank you.'

Outside there was the sound of a car being braked sharply, and then the distant boom of a heavy door closing. Mrs Wells was speaking to him, but he could hear only the rhythm of her voice. Out of the corner of his eye he saw Mrs Chatterton leave the room. 'Yes,' he said, 'yes,' struggling to regain the drift of the conversation. Then he heard Mrs Wells say, 'Oh, here's Margot. Now isn't she beautiful? Just like her mother used to be!'

Mrs Chatterton was crossing the room, accompanied by a tall young woman.

'Isn't she beautiful?' Mrs Wells persisted.

'Yes. . . . Yes, she is,' he said, feeling weak.

Then Mrs Chatterton was standing before him. 'Now, what is your name again?' He felt the blood rising in his face, and he couldn't find words. Mrs Wells came to his rescue. 'Brent,' Mrs Chatterton repeated. 'Of course. I simply cannot remember introductions now. Flight Lieutenant Brent.'

He was looking into a pair of clear light eyes, and he felt his lips moving and heard a voice unlike his own acknowledging the introduction. The eyes smiled automatically, then flicked down to the decorations beneath his wings. 'Quite a collection!' Margot said, arching her eyebrows.

'Oh, those,' he said awkwardly. Then in a floundering attempt at humour, 'They gave them away. Must have had too many left over.'

'Will you have a cup of tea, dear?' Mrs Wells asked.

Margot shook her head – 'Thank you.'

'What have you been doing, dear?' Mrs Wells inquired.

'Nothing very interesting, I'm afraid,' Margot smiled sociably.

When Mrs Wells was out of hearing, she turned back to him, saying, 'A cup of tea! Hell, a gin would be more like it. God, what a life. You can't even get anything decent to drink!'

'That's the hell of it,' he said. But she missed the irony of his tone. She was gazing around the room at each of the uniformed figures in turn. Finally she said, 'I suppose you're glad to be back.' Then unexpectedly, 'The roads are just dreadful nowadays. We went for a run out to Newhaven this afternoon and had to crawl all the way. Soon as the needle moved over fifty we got shaken to pieces. It was simply brutal!'

'I see,' he said.

'There was nothing to do when we got there. Sybil wanted to go in for a swim, but it was simply freezing. There's nothing to do anywhere these days, for that matter.'

'How about your Red Cross work?'

'Oh, that. It's only a few hours a week, and it's just about finished now, anyway. Mother wouldn't let me go into a hospital full time. Once I tried to get overseas. I was keen then. You know, Florence Nightingale, and all that. But I never got an answer to my application. I think mother must have had something to do with that, too.'

'Margot,' Mrs Chatterton called.

'Margot.' An echo awoke in the past.

There was a thud, thud of small feet in the passage, changing to a quick slap, slap on the boards, where the rugs ceased in the servants' quarters. Then small fists were beating against the door. His mother put down her darning and opened the door. Margot stood in the passage in her nightgown. Her hair was damp and had just been combed, leaving the ends straight and spiked.

'I want to see Ronny,' she said.   .

'You'd better go back, Margot. Your mother will be angry,' his mother told her.

'Ronny,' Margot called. There were little points of light dancing in her eyes. When he moved up beside his mother, Margot bent down and grasped the hem of her nightgown and pulled it up to her chin. 'See,' she squealed, 'I've just had a bath!' She stood with her feet planted apart and her toes turned in, revealing her body, still flushed from a brisk towelling. The points of light in her eyes were racing. Then she was stamping back along the passage, her excited laughter rising above the sound of her mother's voice.

'Margot,' Mrs Chatterton insisted.

'Yes mother.'

'I want you to meet Flying Officer Grayson. He was at Woodbury with your cousin Roger.'

'A cigarette?' The curate held out a silver case.

'Thanks.'

'I was rather sore at missing out on the show,' the curate said. 'Actually I was in camp for three months, but they turned me out. Apparently the old heart is not what it might be.'

He tried to think of a reply, but his attention kept wandering. 'I don't think you missed much, really,' he said. He could hear Michael Grayson's lisping, 'Ve'y nice . . . . Ve'y fine indeed.' Good old Michael. One of the best, he thought. Margot was answering, her head tipped slightly to one side, a fixed social smile on her lips. Dressed in white, she appeared almost illuminated in the darkening room. His eyes lingered on her costume, shaped by her hips and the full thrust of her breasts. An image from the past returned, and thinking of how Margot had obviously forgotten it all, he smiled. Then he was shaking, struggling against a mounting desire to laugh. He held himself tight, aware that the curate was speaking again.

'It's possible you did more real good being out of it all,' he replied, noticing that Margot had left Michael and was now standing with her mother. Her lips were moving and he tried to separate her voice from the surrounding conversations.

'What I say is, where is all the money coming from?'

'So we had to stooge around until the pathfinders dropped their flares.'

'. . . time they lifted petrol restrictions altogether.'

'Ve'y nice.'

'. . . almost impossible to get servants. And you daren't say a word to them.'

But Margot was talking in a low tone which did not reach him. Her head was slightly bowed, she suddenly seemed to him dispirited, subdued. Still talking, she turned absently in his direction and with a gathering shock he became aware of the change she had undergone. Her face, for the moment unprotected by its cultivated responses, was empty. Her eyes were old and vacant. Their dancing animation that had been so much part of her memory was gone.

The curate's voice brightened. 'You really think so –' He stopped, seeing the officer's changed expression.

He was still looking at the delicate lifeless face, pain and anger mounting in him, spreading, choking. He gazed round the room, his anger giving way to dull wonder. 'I didn't realize . . . I wouldn't have thought that even all this could have . . . .' His voice tailed off.

'I beg your pardon?' The curate was looking at him anxiously.

'I didn't –' He made an effort to dismiss his thoughts. 'I didn't realize that it was so late.'

Mrs Wells turned to Mrs Keeble. 'What a pity the Flight Lieutenant has to leave so soon, he's awfully nice. . . . What dear? Yes, that's him shaking hands with the Mayor.'

He paused at the door and glanced back into the room. Rex was speaking to an attentive group, illustrating his remarks with sweeping movements of his hands. Margot was walking with a studied flowing movement to where Alan was sitting alone. Her face was calm, imperious, bored. Mrs Chatterton was resting her head against the back of her chair, her cheek bones prominent in the sunken flesh. As he watched, the white lids dropped for an instant over her eyes, like the blinking of an old harsh-voiced bird. The curate stood by the window, thoughtfully peering out into the thickening night, which was slowly blacking out the dying trees, the rotting leaves, the silent decay.

He turned and stepped quickly out of the room. Mrs Wells's wide, moist eyes stared after him; but she could see only the light slipping backwards and forwards on the swinging glass of the doors. 'War is dreadful,' she said. But Mrs Keeble had moved away, so she continued, speaking her thoughts aloud. 'He's been through so much. You can see it all in his face.'

MAURICE DUGGAN

Blues for Miss Laverty

Miss Mary May Laverty drank her bitter and solitary drink (gin and angostura and lemonade, pink as a varnished nail) and looked out from the dark room through dark glass to the floor, the strewn floor of lights four storeys down, and out and away to night mountains and the candy stripes of the harbour lights. Mary May Laverty sighed. She screwed at a dull wisp of hair at her temple and pushed it for the millionth time behind her ear where it uncurled and fell listlessly forward again into the waiting twirl of thumb and forefinger. Light, reflected from somewhere, the sky? the stars?, gleamed faint in the burnished piano dark as a coffin, and on the keys. May Laverty played minor chords. She held the glass in her left hand. The wisp of hair curled forward and stayed.

Down at the street entrance Paul Mooney, aged nine years or ten, in his hand a violin aged not less than seventy years rocking in its case, inspected the faded card in the faded light: Miss Mary May Laverty, Violin and Pianoforte. Please ring. He knew it well. He rang long and listened (he could not hear the bell) then stepped back from the doorway into the street and looked up. A window shrilled, a voice called something lost in air, and something metallic hit the pavement, jangling. Paul Mooney took up the keys, picked out the bronze, opened the door, shut it, ascended the four spiralling flights in faded light and sourceless melody:

I hate to see that evenin' sun . . . .

A nameless tenant at the blues.

'Paul Mooney, you're late.'

'Yes, Miss Laverty. Mum said to say sorry but it's the electricity and dinner was late.'

May Laverty sniffed, twisted hair, let the boy advance into the now lighted room and shut the door.

He done left this town . . . .

Very very far now and faint as he sprung his case and began tuning while May Laverty stared down on the lost lights dispersed, destroyed by the room's illumination. She moved backwards until she felt a chair behind her and dropped into it. She was more fatigued than drunk, she was sure. Tired to the middle of the marrow of her bones; the yellow bones of the blue Miss Laverty. She let her head settle back. The dark mohair bristled at her nape. She listened without any particular expression of face to the wailing tuning note and felt inside her something tautening in sympathy. (God send that nothing snaps, that's all.)

'Electricity,' she scoffed, sniffing. 'Last week it was the transport system, and the week before that you didn't come at all. No money, no apology, nothing. Who do you Mooneys think you are, that's what I'd like to know?'

'I don't know, Miss Laverty.'

'I've a good mind, Paul Mooney, to call your mother and see are you playing tricks on me.'

'I'm not, Miss Laverty.'

'That's what you say. How am I to tell? It doesn't matter; but don't think I'm to be won with looks of innocence. I know what they're worth, angelic smiles. Play something, then. I'm not going to give you a full lesson every time you're late. I have to go out.'

'Shall I play the London thing, Miss Laverty?'

'The London thing,' May Laverty said wearily, 'is the Londonderry Air. It has nothing to do with London. Can't you get that clear? No, I'm sick of it. I can't have heard it less than a million times. Play what you like.'

Paul Mooney so clearly gave it thought, without result.

'Then play that thing, what is it, that I keep hearing in my head? It's been badgering me all day.' She hummed it. 'Yes, St Louis Blues. Play that.'

'I think it's what they're playing downstairs. I can't play that, Miss Laverty.'

'No, of course you can't. I was teasing. Give me the fiddle then. And turn off that big light and turn on the piano light. My eyes are burning.'

May Laverty leaned forward, wispy, the angle of her jaw sharpening as if to fury as she strained to hear. She placed the violin and waited with bow poised, inclined to the boy at the angle of an accent acute.

Up through the silent building it rose, tremulous, vague, continuing. May Laverty caught it up in the middle of a bar and thin, melancholy, faintly vibrating, the melody began to fill the room, slow and seeming to expand; seeming to press out to the bare walls and surge back.

'Turn out the light.'

She turned slightly, still playing, and the jewelled floor and beaconed sea glowed from darkness and on the night mountain one light, star or signal, burned and pulsed.

She played a long time, getting the tune sometimes mixed in her mind and straying off into Stormy Weather and coming back, marking her erratic journey with notes as thick as grief. The boy sat still and wondering in the dark, embarrassed by behaviour he found strange. He wished he might go. He too looked down. And when she stopped he could see her, dark against the dark window. And still there rose, oblivious to the violin, oblivious and constant, the sound like fine drawn wire coiling up:

If I'm feeling tomorrow like I feel today . . . .

'Miss Laverty.'

'What is it? You don't like it, is that it?' The figure moved, the light went on. May Laverty had tears on her face, tears black as bruises and black-streaked runnels down either side of her nose. It didn't suggest grief to Paul Mooney.

'Can I go now, Miss Laverty?'

'I'll have to start all over again,' May Laverty said and dabbed at her ruined eyes with toilet tissue. 'Oh damn it; damn everything. I'm sorry. Have you any money for me?'

'Miss Laverty, Mum said there was only a five-pound note and I'm to tell you I'll bring it next time and could you please write it down?'

'Why? I sent the account.'

'I think we lost it.'

May Laverty looked fiercely amused. She threw down the tissue and crossed quickly to the boy. He shrank away slightly as if expecting a blow. 'Only a five-pound note? That's lovely.' She found her purse and took out a card and wrote on the back of it and thrust it into the breast pocket of the boy's shirt. 'It wouldn't occur to your mother, of course, that I have to live too. *Only* a five-pound note – that's rich. Perhaps she fancies I live on air. I have to eat, don't I? Do I look like a canary?'

'No, Miss Laverty.'

'No, and what's more . . . . Oh, what's the use? Run along. It's not fair to be slanging you. Make sure you shut the door after you.'

'You said you were going out, Miss Laverty.' The boy slackened strings and clipped shut the female case.

'You don't miss a thing, do you, Paul Mooney? I was going out to dinner on the money your mother didn't have the decency to send.'

'Won't you have dinner, then?'

May Laverty stared a long moment. 'Don't break your heart over that. I'll have dinner all right. Now run along; and shut that door or we'll have the bailiffs in like a draught.' She lit a cigarette and threw the match towards the empty grate, into a trash of cigarette butts and dead matches. She advanced and ruffled the short brush of the boy's hair. 'You've hair like a doormat,' May Laverty said. 'Like a pelt.'

'What's a bailiff, Miss Laverty?'

'That was a joke, Paul. It doesn't matter. Ask your mother.'

She let him out. Insistent, fine, the slow blues rose faint as a far crying through the quiet building. May Laverty went to the stairwell and bent over the rail and with her hands cupped about her mouth shouted with a surprising, shrill loudness: 'Shut it off, will you? Shut it off.' There was no more response than the echo which quickly ceased. Then the music welled up in volume, a yellow bar of light showed near the bottom of the shaft, and a voice shouted up, ringing: 'Go mind your own business.' May Laverty cocked a thoughtful miming eyebrow. In the silence, faint again, the melody continued.

'It gives me fits,' May Laverty said reasonably. 'To hear a tune being done to death like that, I mean. You'd think once, or even twice, but . . . .'

'Goodbye, Miss Laverty.'

'You've got everything? Down you go then.' She tripped the light and the timing mechanism whirred like a secret beetle in the wall.

Unabashed, persisting, the thread of sound rose to meet the boy as he tiptoed down, fearful of rousing the ire of that rude tenant. May Laverty entered her room and slammed the door behind her: the latch was faulty and she was obliged to slam it a second time before it caught. She made herself another pink gin and turned off the light and sat staring again out and down and away. After a little while she began quietly to hum and then to sing:

I hate to see that evenin' sun . . . .

Her voice was high, a breathy pipe.

'Oh damn,' she said. 'Damn it to hell.' And taking up her purse she made for the door, stumbling in the dark. She found the light and returned to drain the rest of her drink and went out then, plunging the room into darkness again, not waiting to repair the ravage to her smudged, bruised eyes.

On the landing of the first floor she paused. The music, she had to admit, was not loud enough for complaint; it squeezed out as she stood there, squeezed out with a bar of light under the door of Room 3. May Laverty remembered the force and brevity of that rejoinder and went quietly down. The time switch to the stair light was set mean and she was left in darkness with half a flight to go. In spiteful anger she pressed the switch again before she closed the door. The music which had followed her down was finally imprisoned, beyond hearing, behind that shut door where the light burned wastefully.

'Look at this, if you please,' Mrs Mooney said. She dropped May Laverty's card on the newspaper her husband was reading. 'A fine sort of thing.'

Mr Mooney stolidly read: 'Miss Mary May Laverty (lately Music Tutor at Haversham College): Violin and Pianoforte. Tuition for Beginners and Advanced Players. Telephone for appointment'.

'Where's Haversham College?' Mr Mooney asked.

'The other side,' Mrs Mooney said. 'Turn it over: I meant you to look at the other side.'

Mr Mooney turned the card and read: 'No tickee no shirtee. M.M.L.'

'In the matter of impudence,' Mrs Mooney said, 'I've never met anything to match. And from a teacher of music too. You might well ask where Haversham College is: I doubt she's ever been near it. Paul has been there for the last time, I can tell her that.'

'It's direct, certainly,' Mr Mooney said. He glanced at his wife's gaunt and inflamed face. 'I take it we owe her money.'

'After that sort of impudence I doubt that we owe her anything. There's no excuse for that.'

'I'm not suggesting there is. How much do we owe, Ella?'

'How should I know? I don't keep these things in my head. I suppose the account is lying about somewhere. I've had it out with Paul. She didn't even bother to give him a lesson at all tonight. She just sat him in the dark and played him some rubbishy popular song and then pushed him out.'

'In the dark? Is that right, Paul?'

'I think she was angry,' Paul Mooney said. He was distressed by his mother's anger and his sense of being disloyal. 'She said I was late last time, too. And the time before that I didn't go at all.'

'Is she right about that?'

'There were good reasons,' Mrs Mooney said. 'Her card is unforgivable and I don't see any profit in going into it any further. There's no shortage of music teachers.'

Mr Mooney turned the card. 'But she has the phone, Ella. Did someone ring her to say the boy would be late or that he was unable to come?'

'I don't know,' Paul Mooney said.

'That means no, I suppose. We've been rather inconsiderate too, Ella, by the look of it. I mean if we're going to insist on such a standard . . . .'

'We'll see about that,' Mrs Mooney said and snatched the card and went to the telephone. But May Laverty did not reply. It had the effect of short-circuiting Mrs Mooney's anger. For a moment she was nonplussed.

Mr Mooney shook out his paper. 'She has a right to expect payment, Ella. It could be a simple joke, you know.'

'Trust a man to side with a woman,' Mrs Mooney said curtly.

'I think we have to trust to that,' Mr Mooney said, a little amused.

'Just what she's a right to expect, we'll soon decide,' Mrs Mooney said. 'Paul, get your violin, if you please.'

'Now, Ella. You're upsetting yourself unduly. It's a small matter.'

'Robert Mooney, sometimes I just don't understand you. If you think I am going to stand here and be insulted by . . . .'

'All right. Have it your way. Get your violin, son. But tune it up before you bring it in here. I can't stand the sound of those things being wound up.'

The house in grief wailed long and uncertainly for Danny Boy, the violin calling like an aged and faltering tenor.

'Well, that wasn't all that bad,' Mr Mooney said. 'Though I would have preferred some other tune. What was the song this Miss – ah – Laverty played you?'

'I think, Saint Louis Blues.'

'Then what about playing that, now that you're here.'

'Robert Mooney.'

'What's wrong with it, Ella? It's old enough to be respectable, surely? I've always been fond of it.'

'I can't play it,' Paul Mooney said.

'I'm grateful for that, at least,' Mrs Mooney said. 'If you think we're paying out good money for the child to learn that sort of rubbish . . . .'

Mr Mooney was again amused. 'But, Ella, surely that's the whole point: we *aren't* paying out good money. That's what's got under the woman's skin.'

'I've no patience with you,' Mrs Mooney said.

'Then do what you want, between the two of you,' Mr Mooney said. 'The world isn't losing a Paganini, I suppose.' He took up the card and put it in his pocket and bent to his paper, oblivious to his wife's hard, colouring stare.

Of course, you could rely on it to ring when she was in the bath'. Didn't it always? There were times when May Laverty suspected the telephone of being possessed of a malice not usually associated with bits of bakelite and metal or whatever it was. If she had a pound for every time she'd had to get out of the bath to answer the phone . . . . She put on a towelling gown, dried her hands carefully (she had read somewhere that you could get a fatal shock if your hands were wet) and padded out. No hope of just letting it ring: she wasn't quite flush enough for that.

It was Mrs Mooney, mother of Paul Mooney, with a voice as chill as a sliding glacier. (Of course, that stupid card!)

Mrs Mooney clearly and coldly could not be expected to treat the matter as a joke. Her voice crackled to May Laverty down the defective wire. Mrs Mooney hardly thought from her son's report that the account could be treated seriously.

'It's serious all right,' May Laverty said. 'I never joke about money.' She managed to get a cigarette out of the packet and to light it with one hand.

Yes, quite; but didn't Miss Laverty see that it could hardly be thought part of the contract, if you called it that, simply to play the boy a hit-parade tune and send him packing.

'It hasn't been on the hit parade since you were a girl, Mrs Mooney.'

Was that intended as an insult? Mrs Mooney hoped that she herself had more dignity than to behave like a fishwife. She would like Miss Laverty to understand that her son would not be returning for further tuition. And, further, she, Mrs Mooney, would make a deduction from the stated amount and send Miss Laverty a cheque. There was one occasion, and Mrs Mooney regretted the lack of notification, when the boy had been unable to attend; and there was last night.

'Mrs Mooney, I'm sorry. I hadn't understood that you were so hard up. If you're as broke as that we'll just forget the whole thing. I'll make you a gift of the lessons.' May Laverty viciously considered the end of her cigarette.

Miss Laverty was being impudent. The telephone went dead.

May Laverty replaced the receiver with infinite gentleness and went back to the bathroom and lay in the lukewarm water and finished her cigarette. She did not enjoy it. Neither did she enjoy the coffee she made herself when she had dressed. She sat in the high window. There was a fog on the harbour and over the city. May Laverty sat rather glumly above it.

Later she made the four-flight journey down to the mail basket on the street door. The door to Room 3 was shut and the music silenced. There were some things yet that she could be thankful for. And there were two letters in the box. One was a sheet of numbers on pink paper which, searched later for the number of her ticket, showed May Laverty that she had not won the lottery this time either, nor even the most minor prize. The other letter contained a five-pound note from Mr Robert Mooney, pinned to a note asking her to accept this as some reimbursement for the trouble she had been put to over Paul's lateness and non-attendance. Mr Mooney had not yet seen the account, which would be met later. He took the opportunity, in a postscript, of expressing his purely personal preference for the St Louis Blues over and above the Londonderry Air which he referred to as Danny Boy. The letter was on business notepaper: Mooney and Masters, Public Accountants.

'Never say die,' May Laverty said, climbing the gloomy stairs.

In her room she made a note of the telephone number – she had a choice of three – on the scratch pad by the telephone. Mr Mooney must be thanked: the amount was far too much, of course, and May Laverty wondered at it. His tone was, at the least, so different from that of his wife that May Laverty wondered too what this might imply.

May Laverty stood among rings and brooches and wristlet watches in the doorway of the closed jeweller's shop and surveyed the street. There, that was surely him, standing as if on a hot brick on the corner and flushing red and green as the traffic lights changed. He looked as nervous as she felt, though she had only the back and side of him; but on the whole he was more presentable than she had imagined. Yes, all in all he represented something rather better than she had hoped. Didn't this, though, only serve to widen the gap? Hadn't he, she meant, all the more right if he looked like that, to hope on his side for something a little better than herself? Oh Lord: the long panel of mirroring glass too plainly gave the show away, too clearly told the familiar tale and kept too few secrets. Wasn't she all too raddled, all too much the blown and faded rose? She took up her courage and faced her image, prepared to be stern. (Was it what you called an assignation? No, surely that was too antique a suggestion. A blind date might better describe it. On the corner by the jeweller's in Cannon Street I'll be wearing my tweed, my apricot blouse, flowers, my cracked and batty smile; and my expiring perm. Mary May Laverty. Violin and Pianoforte. Please ring.) It had to be faced; no amount of pressing would take the baggy seat out of this skirt, nor the pouched elbows out of this jacket. She felt positively marsupial. Stand though she might, straight as a tent-pole, head alert and shoulders back, she still appeared to be crouched with elbows bent. Damn. True, her legs weren't bad, though you wouldn't venture more than that. And her face? May Laverty wryly contemplated it. Wide eyes, good forehead: take the best things first. But spreading out from the corners of her eyes, from the corners of her mouth, was a system of lines best to be compared with a railway siding or a shunting yard. Perhaps she exaggerated; but the mirror didn't flatter. Her mouth wasn't young; but then what would she be doing wearing the hopeful rosebud of a young girl?

'Miss Laverty?'

He'd made up his mind to approach. May Laverty took him in. A triangle of pocket handkerchief about the size of a postage stamp in his breast pocket; bald and not trying to conceal it; taller than she was with a kind, even an innocently mischievous expression of face; big, well-kept hands. Dark, groomed, good-humoured and rather at a loss, that was her impression. An Irish mug for all the rich trimmings.

'Mr Mooney, I presume.' She advanced her hand and laughed. The gods be thanked, her teeth were her own. 'Tell me immediately, have you an impulse to turn and run? Please say; now's the time.' She thought she sounded like a revivalist coaxing decisions, or just a little too much as though she hoped he *would* turn and run. The gin gave her confidence; but it was ebbing.

'Have *you* that impulse?' He faced her squarely. The street was empty of all but one or two people dawdling past lighted windows.

'Oh me?' May Laverty said. 'No, I've not.'

'No more have I.'

'Then what . . . ?'

'I wondered, well, I wondered whether you'd be interested in a drink? There's a place I know down here; quite ordinary, of course, but not far to go.'

'An excellent idea,' May Laverty said with some relief.

The bar was noisy and rather crowded. He bought her a large pink gin, and gin and water for himself.

'I was sure you would drink whisky.'

'I'm not much of a drinking man, I'm afraid.'

'Look, there's something I want to say right off. I don't know whether *you're* used to this sort of thing. I mean I don't know what you think. Oh, I'm not pretending to be innocent. I just want things to be plain, so that we know where we stand.'

Robert Mooney was puzzled. 'I don't think I see. If you mean am I in the habit of, ah, this sort of thing – no, I'm not. I simply thought . . . .'

'This is rather awful, isn't it? This place, I mean. I can't hear a word you're saying.'

'Perhaps if I got something to take away. Could we find somewhere, some place . . . ?'

'There's my place,' May Laverty said frankly.

'Yes. Would that be in order?'

'I don't see why not.'

She noticed it immediately, before her hand found the light switch. The St Louis Blues was cascading in considerable volume down the dark stairs.

'No,' May Laverty said. 'It wasn't pre-arranged. We mustn't dawdle or we'll find ourselves in the dark.' The switch snapped and the timing mechanism took over, clicking. They passed Room 3, the crest of the wave, and the volume diminished as they climbed. 'You need a stout heart,' May Laverty said. 'I'm convinced, every now and again, that I'm no longer young enough to live at such a height; but the young ones don't seem to care for it either. So there you are.'

'You do need a stout heart,' Robert Mooney said, and his puffing suggested considerable distress.

The light held until they reached the high landing.

The room smelled a little of damp. Except for the piano it was poorly furnished. May Laverty fetched glasses and made drinks. Through their silent constraint ran the thread of music.

I'm gonna pack up and make my getaway . . . .

'It tears at my nerves,' May Laverty said. 'Though I don't mind it at this moment. You find yourself actually holding your breath listening for it; and then you wonder if it hasn't stopped after all and you're imagining you can hear it.'

'No, I can hear it,' Robert Mooney said. He had recovered his breath. 'But I must have misunderstood. I thought Paul said *you* played it to him.'

'Oh that; yes, I did. When it goes on like that it's the first thing and the only thing that comes into your head when you're trying to think of what to play. I've complained; but it won't do any good. It will drive me up the wall if it goes on like that much longer.'

'Who is it?'

'I don't know. It's a man, that's all I know. The others have complained too. But they're scared to do anything because he's drinking in there and they think he might get violent.'

'Have you seen him?'

'No. We had some conversation. I told him to shut up and he told me to mind my own business; if you can call that a conversation. We were shouting up and down the stairs. He's been at it for days: something will have to break soon. Good luck.'

'Good luck,' Robert Mooney looked around. 'You must have a view.'

'Oh, I have,' May Laverty said with excitement. 'I have. It's the whole point. Look.'

She slid the curtains and put out the light and the moment their sight adjusted there, seemingly suspended in dark air, was a liner lighted in tiers and floodlit at funnel and mast, moving slowly across the dark glass, floating as fragile as tinsel above the broadcast yellow jewels of the city lights. Then the harbour lifted from darkness, striped with beacons and navigation lights, red, orange, yellow and green, and the liner or a tug or some incoming ship (who could know?) gave a long forlorn call. A bladder of a moon, partly deflated, hung over the night mountains; and far up were a few faint stars.

'I hardly understand my impulse,' Robert Mooney said in the dark. 'I don't think I was thinking of anything – ah – very much; to be honest.' He sounded embarrassed.

'But why should you? It was me who phoned.'

'Yes, but I suggested we might meet for a chat.'

'And I accepted, I agreed. What are you trying to say? You wish you hadn't is that it? Is that what you want to say?'

'Well, Miss Laverty, I'm a family man, and . . . .'

'Oh look,' May Laverty said. 'The lights are going.'

The lighted liner, suggesting distance, luxury, something mournfully pleasant, sailed slowly out of the darkened pane, into the wall; and where it had been a ruby beacon flashed hard and brief, and after a full minute flashed in darkness again.

'It's all right, Mr Mooney,' May Laverty said. 'You may relax. I'm not after anything, you know; not your money or your life. And I could hardly help knowing you were a family man.'

'Well, I only meant that in a way I've no place to be here.'

'Then why did you come?'

'I don't know, to be truthful. It's pleasant; and you certainly do have a view.'

May Laverty drank and poured. 'You might ask why I let you come.'

'I don't think I . . . .'

'I'll tell you, Mr Mooney. I'm not quite what I seem – picking men off street corners. I'm simply a rather broken-down teacher of music fed up to the teeth on my own company.' She spoke as if the fact were well known and needed no further comment. 'Let me put it another way. I'm not asking for anything more than a little human warmth.'

Robert Mooney stirred. 'Ah, that . . . .'

The light came on full. May Laverty drew the curtains. They both winced at the brightness.

'Why? The other was pleasant,' Robert Mooney said.

'Because I've deceived myself too often, in the dark,' May Laverty said. Two coins of high colour burned in her cheeks. Her expression was one of remoteness, grimness. 'I'm like some bird perched over the city on a dark cliff. And that's not what I want to be at all.' She filled the glasses and went to her handbag and took out his five-pound note. 'Take it, please.'

'Why? I thought you'd agreed to accept. You thanked me for it. I don't want it back.'

'Nevertheless, you'll take it,' May Laverty said. 'I thanked you for it, certainly. I don't think I ever intended to keep it. There's no way I could. Take it, please.'

He took it from her fingers. 'I'm sorry about all this. I thought we might chat a little.'

May Laverty shook her head. 'How could we? You're too afraid.'

'Afraid? Of what?'

'Of me, or what you think I am. You're afraid to be here. You suspect complications, scandals, and I don't know what. You said you've no place to be here; no right, I suppose you mean.'

'I wanted things clear. Anyway, the money has nothing to do with it.'

'But it has. It was a gesture I could appreciate even if I couldn't accept. Oh, this pride over money; it's too sordid.'

'Why did we meet then?'

'Curiosity. I don't know. Curiosity is as good a motive as another. Perhaps gratitude on my part. What does it matter?'

'A little human warmth, was that what you said?' It embarrassed him to repeat it.

'Yes,' May Laverty said. 'You'd think it would be easy, wouldn't you? You'd think it would be simple. Sometimes I wonder if there's anything harder.'

He rose and took up his hat and looked at her directly, for a second. She read relief in the steadiness of his gaze.

'You'll be all right?' he said. 'I mean, a straight out loan, if that would help . . . .'

'There's too little security,' May Laverty said, and laughed with a high skirl of sound. 'No, I'm not grubbing for banknotes,' she said with some contempt. She went to the door and opened it. 'Goodnight,' she said. 'You'll find it's not so hard on the heart, going down. I'll wait and trip the light a second time in case you miss.'

If it weren't for powder and for store-bought hair . . . .

'Goodbye, I'm sorry,' Robert Mooney put on his hat and went down, glancing up to meet her non-committal nod as he turned the first flange of the spiral. He dropped out of sight.

I hate to see that evenin' sun . . . .

She tripped the light a second time. It clicked with a sound that echoed on the landing. When it went out she waited a long time, leaning on the stair rail in the dark, the door of her room swung shut behind her. Clear and full now it rose in the silence like the source and the refrain of all her elderly discontents. Her head was spinning: she felt dizzy. (Nothing. Just a song.)

The record must have ended. There was a break, so brief as hardly to be detected, and it began again.

May Laverty snapped on the light and went down the stairs. She stood at the door of Room 3 and loudly knocked on the painted panelling.

'What do you want?'

She'd expected to confront a violent and unshaven drunk, but if the man in the doorway was drunk he wasn't showing it. He was dressed in sweater and slacks; he was shaved; he was barefooted. The music welled out, beat past him and was magnified in the small walled space of the landing. On a table in the centre of the room May Laverty saw a bottle and a glass and a siphon of soda. An ashtray on the floor spilled cigarette butts. There was no sign of the wild or desperate carousal she had expected: the room was if anything tidier than her own.

'I said, what do you want?'

May Laverty continued to stand in silent indecision.

'Have you come to complain?'

'Would it do any good? To complain, I mean.'

He turned back into the room. The music stopped. He returned holding a record. 'You came at the right moment. Satisfied?'

'No, look,' May Laverty said seriously, frowning. 'I'm not complaining about the music. I admit it isn't even all that loud.'

'Just the one tune, eh?'

'Yes. I'll gladly let you have some records, if you want to go on.'

'No, it's finished. I hope never to hear it again. I've beat it to death.'

'Then what were you doing, punishing yourself or something?' He swayed a little in the bright doorway, looking out at May Laverty. 'Were you wanting something else?'

'Why I . . . no,' May Laverty said. 'But I'm glad it's stopped. It was driving me up the wall.'

'Me too.'

May Laverty greeted it with a surprised and surprising giggle. She was more than a little drunk. Thumb and forefinger found the wayward wisp, twisted, tucked it behind her ear. She peered past him into the room.

'What are you looking for?' He stood there easily, watching May Laverty. He appeared to be amused.

'What was I looking . . . ? I beg your pardon,' May Laverty felt confused.

'It doesn't matter. I wondered what you were looking for, that's all.' He offered the record and she took it. 'Break it in half if you want. It's played to ribbons.'

'A little human warmth,' May Laverty said distinctly.

'What?'

'A little human warmth. I mean, you'd think there'd be nothing simpler, wouldn't you? You wouldn't think it too much to ask, a little human warmth. There was no reason to run; none at all. A little human warmth.'

In the doorway the man straightened. His features, slightly puffed, composed themselves into a frown of wonder. He gently and slowly shook his head and reaching behind him he found the door handle. 'What a hope,' he said. 'Lady, what a hope.'

Then the door shut and May Laverty was on the landing in the dark. She turned and began to climb the three flights to her room, carrying the record, steadying herself with a hand on the banister.

The unfamiliar and persisting sound which filled the stairwell was the sound of May Laverty's laughter: a neighing echo, a falsetto and quavering trumpet. It accompanied her on the steep ascent.

Along Rideout Road that Summer

I'd walked the length of Rideout Road the night before, following the noise of the river in the darkness, tumbling over ruts and stones, my progress, if you'd call it that, challenged by farmers' dogs and observed by the faintly luminous eyes of wandering stock, steers, cows, stud-bulls or milk-white unicorns or, better, a full quartet of apocalyptic horses browsing the marge. In time and darkness I found Puti Hohepa's farmhouse and lugged my fibre suitcase up to the verandah, after nearly breaking my leg in a cattlestop. A journey fruitful of one decision – to flog a torch from somewhere. And of course I didn't. And now my feet hurt; but it was daylight and, from memory, I'd say I was almost happy. Almost. Fortunately I am endowed both by nature and later conditioning with a highly developed sense of the absurd; knowing that you can imagine the pleasure I took in this abrupt translation from shop-counter to tractor seat, from town pavements to back-country farm; with all those miles of river-bottom darkness to mark the transition. In fact, and unfortunately there have to be some facts, even fictional ones, I'd removed myself a mere dozen miles from the parental home. In darkness, as I've said, and with a certain stealth. I didn't consult dad about it, and, needless to say, I didn't tell mum. The moment wasn't propitious; dad was asleep with the *Financial Gazette* threatening to suffocate him and mum was off somewhere moving, as she so often did, that this meeting make public its whole-hearted support for the introduction of flogging and public castration for all sex offenders and hanging, drawing and quartering, for almost everyone else, and as for delinquents (my boy!) . . . . Well, put yourself in my shoes, there's no need to go on. Yes, almost happy, though my feet were so tender I winced every time I tripped the clutch.

Almost happy, shouting Kubla Khan, a bookish lad, from the seat of the clattering old Ferguson tractor, doing a steady five miles an hour in a cloud of seagulls, getting to the bit about the damsel with the dulcimer and looking up to see the reputedly wild Hohepa girl perched on the gate, feet hooked in the bars, ribbons fluttering from her ukulele. A perfect moment of recognition, daring rider, in spite of the belch of carbon monoxide from the tin-can exhaust up front on the bonnet. Don't, however, misunderstand me: I'd not have you think we are here embarked on the trashy clamour of boy meeting girl. No, the problem, you are to understand, was one of connection. How connect the dulcimer with the ukulele, if you follow. For a boy of my bents this problem of how to cope with the shock of the recognition of a certain discrepancy between the real and the written was rather like watching mum with a shoehorn wedging nines into sevens and suffering merry hell. I'm not blaming old STC for everything, of course. After all, some other imports went wild too; and I've spent too long at the handle of a mattock, a critical function, not to know that. The stench of the exhaust, that's to say, held no redolence of that old hophead's pipe. Let us then be clear and don't for a moment, gentlemen, imagine that I venture the gross unfairness, the patent absurdity, the rank injustice (your turn) of blaming him for spoiling the pasture or fouling the native air. It's just that there was this problem in my mind, this profound, cultural problem affecting dramatically the very nature of my inheritance, nines into sevens in this lovely smiling land. His was the genius as his was the expression which the vast educational brouhaha invited me to praise and emulate, tranquillizers ingested in maturity, the voice of the ring-dove, look up though your feet be in the clay. And read on.

Of course I understood immediately that these were not matters I was destined to debate with Fanny Hohepa. Frankly, I could see that she didn't give a damn; it was part of her attraction. She thought I was singing. She smiled and waved, I waved and smiled, turned, ploughed back through gull-white and coffee loam and fell into a train of thought not entirely free of Fanny and her instrument, pausing to wonder, now and then, what might be the symptoms, the early symptoms, of carbon monoxide poisoning. Drowsiness? Check. Dilation of the pupils? Can't check. Extra cutaneous sensation? My feet. Trembling hands? Vibrato. Down and back, down and back, turning again, Dick and his Ferguson, Fanny from her perch seeming to gather about her the background of green paternal acres, fold on fold. I bore down upon her in all the eager erubescence of youth, with my hair slicked back. She trembled, wavered, fragmented and re-formed in the pungent vapour through which I viewed her. (Oh for an open-air job, eh mate?) She plucked, very picture in jeans and summer shirt of youth and suspicion, and seemed to sing. I couldn't of course hear a note. Behind me the dog-leg furrows and the bright ploughshares. Certainly she looked at her ease and, even through the gassed-up atmosphere between us, too deliciously substantial to be creature

down on a visit from Mount Abora. I was glad I'd combed my hair. Back, down
and back. Considering the size of the paddock this could have gone on for a
week. I promptly admitted to myself that her present position, disposition or
posture, involving as it did some provocative tautness of cloth, suited me right
down to the ground. I mean to hell with the idea of having her stand knee-deep
in the thistle thwanging her dulcimer and plaintively chirruping about a
pipedream mountain. In fact she was natively engaged in expressing the most
profound distillations of her local experience, the gleanings of a life lived in
rich contact with a richly understood and native environment: A Slow Boat To
China, if memory serves. While I, racked and shaken, composed words for the
plaque which would one day stand here to commemorate our deep rapport:
*Here played the black lady her dulcimer. Here wept she full miseries. Here rode the knight
Fergus' son to her deliverance. Here put he about her ebon and naked shoulders his courtly
garment of leather, black, full curiously emblazoned – Hell's Angel.*

When she looked as though my looking were about to make her leave I
stopped the machine and pulled out the old tobacco and rolled a smoke,
holding the steering wheel in my teeth, though on a good day I could roll with
one hand, twist and lick, draw, shoot the head off a pin at a mile and a half, spin,
blow down the barrel before you could say:

Gooday. How are yuh?

All right.

I'm Buster O'Leary.

I'm Fanny Hohepa.

Yair, I know.

It's hot.

It's hot right enough.

You can have a swim when you're through.

Mightn't be a bad idea at that.

Over there by the trees.

Yair, I seen it. Like, why don't you join me, eh?

I might.

Go on, you'd love it.

I might.

Goodoh then, see yuh.

A genuine crumpy conversation if ever I heard one, darkly reflective of the
Socratic method, rich with echoes of the Kantian imperative, its universal mate,
summoning sharply to the minds of each the history of the first trystings of all
immortal lovers, the tragic and tangled tale, indeed, of all star-crossed
moonings, mum and dad, mister and missus unotoo and all. Enough? I should
bloody well hope so.

Of course nothing came of it. Romantic love was surely the invention of a
wedded onanist with seven kids. And I don't mean dad. Nothing? Really and
truly nothing? Well, I treasure the under-statement; though why I should take
such pleasure in maligning the ploughing summer white on loam, river flats,
the frivolous ribbons and all the strumming, why I don't know. Xanadu and the
jazzy furrows, the wall-eyed bitch packing the cows through the yardgate, the
smell of river water. . . . Why go on? So few variations to an old, old story. No.
But on the jolting tractor I received that extra jolt I mentioned and am actually
now making rather too much of, gentlemen: relate Fanny Hohepa and her uke
to that mountain thrush singing her black mountain blues.

But of course now, in our decent years, we know such clay questions long
broken open or we wouldn't be here, old and somewhat sour, wading up to our
battered thighs (forgive me, madam) at the confluence of the great waters,
paddling in perfect confidence in the double debouchment of universal river
and regional stream, the shallow fast fan of water spreading over the delta,

Abyssinia come to Egypt in the rain . . . ah, my country! I speak of cultural problems, in riddles and literary puddles, perform this act of divination with my own entrails: Fanny's dark delta; the nubile and Nubian sheila with her portable piano anticipating the transistor-set; all gathered into single demesne, O'Leary's orchard. Even this wooden bowl, plucked from the flood, lost from the hand of some anonymous herdsman as he stopped to cup a drink at the river's source. Ah, Buster. Ah, Buster. Buster. Ah, darling. Darling! Love. You recognize it? Could you strum to that? Suppose you gag a little at the sugar coating, it's the same old fundamental toffee, underneath.

No mere cheap cyn . . . sm intended. She took me down to her darkling avid as any college girl for the fruits and sweets of my flowering talents, taking me as I wasn't but might hope one day to be, honest, simple and broke to the wide. The half-baked verbosity and the conceit she must have ignored, or how else could she have borne me? It pains me, gentlemen, to confess that she was too good for me by far. Far. Anything so spontaneous and natural could be guaranteed to be beyond me: granted, I mean, my impeccable upbringing under the white-hot lash of respectability, take that, security, take that, hypocrisy, take that, cant, take that where, does it seem curious?, mum did all the beating flushed pink in ecstasy and righteousness, and that and that and THAT. Darling! How then could I deem Fanny's conduct proper when I carried such weals and scars, top-marks in the lesson on the wickedness of following the heart. Fortunately such a question would not have occurred to Fanny: she was remarkably free from queries of any kind. She would walk past the Home Furnishing Emporium without a glance.

She is too good for you.

It was said clearly enough, offered without threat and as just comment, while I was bent double stripping old Daisy or Pride of the Plains or Rose of Sharon after the cups came off. I stopped what I was doing, looked sideways until I could see the tops of his gumboots, gazed on *Marathon*, and then turned back, dried off all four tits and let the cow out into the race where, taking the legrope with her, she squittered off wild in the eyes.

She is too good for you.

So I looked at him and he looked back. I lost that game of stare-you-down, too. He walked off. Not a warning, not even a reproach, just something it was as well I should know if I was to have the responsibility of acting in full knowledge – and who the hell wants that? And two stalls down Fanny spanked a cow out through the flaps and looked at me, and giggled. The summer thickened and blazed.

The first response on the part of my parents was silence; which can only be thought of as response in a very general sense. I could say, indeed I will say, stony silence; after all they were my parents. But I knew the silence wouldn't last long. I was an only child (darling, you never guessed?) and that load of woodchopping, lawnmowing, hedgeclipping, dishwashing, carwashing, errandrunning, gardenchoring and the rest of it was going to hit them like a folding mortgage pretty soon. I'd like to have been there, to have seen the lank grass grown beyond window height and the uncut hedges shutting out the sun: perpetual night and perpetual mould on Rose Street West. After a few weeks the notes and letters began. The whole gamut, gentlemen, from sweet and sickly to downright abusive. Mostly in mum's masculine hand. A unique set of documents reeking of blood and tripes. I treasured every word, reading between the lines the record of an undying, all-sacrificing love, weeping tears for the idyllic childhood they could not in grief venture to touch upon, the care lavished, the love squandered upon me. The darlings. Of course I didn't reply.

I didn't even wave when they drove past Fanny and me as we were breasting out of the scrub back on to the main road, dishevelled and, yes, almost happy in the daze of summer and Sunday afternoon. I didn't wave. I grinned as brazenly as I could manage with a jaw full of hard boiled egg and took Fanny's arm, brazen, her shirt only casually resumed, while they went by like burnished doom.

Fanny's reaction to all this? An expression of indifference, a downcurving of that bright and wilful mouth, a flirt of her head. So much fuss over so many fossilized ideas, if I may so translate her expression which was, in fact, gentlemen, somewhat more direct and not in any sense exhibiting what mum would have called a due respect for elders and betters. Pouf! Not contempt, no; not disagreement; simply an impatience with what she, Fanmy, deemed the irrelevance of so many many words for so light and tumbling a matter. And, for the season at least, I shared the mood, her demon lover in glossy brilliantine.

But as the days ran down the showdown came nearer and finally the stage was set. Low-keyed and sombre notes in the sunlight, the four of us variously disposed on the unpainted Hohepa verandah, Hohepa and O'Leary, the male seniors, and Hohepa and O'Leary, junior representatives, male seventeen, female ready to swear, you understand, that she was sixteen, turning.

Upon the statement that Fanny was too good for me my pappy didn't comment. No one asked him to: no one faced him with the opinion. Wise reticence, mere oversight or a sense of the shrieking irrelevance of such a statement, I don't know. Maori girls, Maori farms, Maori housing: you'd only to hear my father put tongue to any or all of that to know where he stood, solid for intolerance, mac, but solid. Of course, gentlemen, it was phrased differently on his lips, gradual absorption, hmm, perhaps, after, say, a phase of disinfecting. A pillar of our decent, law-abiding community, masonic in his methodism, brother, total abstainer, rotarian and non-smoker, addicted to long volleys of handball, I mean pocket billiards cue and all. Mere nervousness, of course, a subconscious habit. Mum would cough and glance down and dad would spring to attention hands behind his back. Such moments of tender rapport are sweet to return to, memories any child might treasure. Then he'd forget again. Straight mate, there were days, especially Sundays, when mum would be hacking away like an advanced case of t.b. Well, you can picture it, there on the verandah. With the finely turned Fanny under his morose eye, you know how it is, hemline hiked and this and that visible from odd angles, he made a straight break of two hundred without one miscue, Daddy! I came in for a couple of remand home stares myself, bread and water and solitary and take that writ on his eyeballs in backhand black while his mouth served out its lying old hohums and there's no reason why matters shouldn't be resolved amicably, etc, black hanging-cap snug over his tonsure and tongue moistening his droopy lip, ready, set, drop. And Puti Hohepa leaving him to it. A dignified dark prince on his ruined acres, old man Hohepa, gravely attending to dad's mumbled slush, winning hands down just by being there and saying nothing, nothing, while Fanny with her fatal incapacity for standing upright unsupported for more than fifteen seconds, we all had a disease of the spine that year, pouted at me as though it were all my fault over the back of the chair (sic). All my fault being just the pater's monologue, the remarkably imprecise grip of his subject with consequent proliferation of the bromides so typical of all his ilk of elk, all the diversely identical representatives of decency, caution and the colour bar. Of course daddy didn't there and then refer to race, colour creed or uno who. Indeed he firmly believed he believed, if I may recapitulate, gentlemen, that this blessed land was free from such taint, a unique social experiment, two races living happily side by side, respecting each other's etc and etc. As a banker he knew the value of discretion, though what was home if not a place to hang up your reticence along with your hat and get stuck into all the hate that was inside you, in the name of justice? Daddy Hohepa said nothing, expressed nothing, may even have been unconscious of the great destinies being played out on his sunlit verandah, or of what fundamental principles of democracy and the freedom of the individual were being here so brilliantly exercised; may have been, in fact, indifferent to daddy's free granting tautologies now, of the need for circumspection in all matters of national moment, all such questions as what shall be done for our dark brothers and sisters, outside the jails? I hope so. After a few minutes Hohepa rangatira trod the boards thoughtfully and with the slowness of a winter bather lowered himself into a pool of sunlight on the wide steps, there to lift his face broad and grave in full dominion of his inheritance and even, perhaps, so little did his expression reveal of his inward reflection, full consciousness of his dispossessions.

What, you may ask, was my daddy saying? Somewhere among the circumlocutions, these habits are catching among the words and sentiments designed to express his grave ponderings on the state of the nation and so elicit from his auditors (not me, I wasn't listening) admission, tacit though it may be, of his tutored opinion, there was centred the suggestion that old man Hohepa and daughter were holding me against my will, ensnaring me with flesh and farm. He had difficulty in getting it out in plain words; some lingering cowardice, perhaps. Which was why daddy Hohepa missed it, perhaps. Or did the view command all his attention?

Rideout Mountain far and purple in the afternoon sun; the jersey cows beginning to move, intermittent and indirect, towards the shed; the dog jangling its chain as it scratched; Fanny falling in slow movement across the end of the old cane lounge chair to lie, an interesting composition of curves and angles, with the air of a junior and rural odalisque. Me? I stood straight, of course, rigid, thumbs along the seams of my jeans, hair at the regulation distance two inches above the right eye, heels together and bare feet at ten to two, or ten past ten, belly flat and chest inflated, chin in, heart out. I mean, can you see me, mac? Dad's grave-suit so richly absorbed the sun that he was forced to retreat into the shadows where his crafty jailer's look was decently camouflaged, blending white with purple blotched with silver wall. Not a bad heart, surely?

As his audience we each displayed differing emotions. Fanny, boredom that visibly bordered on sleep: Puti Hohepa, an inattention expressed in his long examination of the natural scene: Buster O'Leary, a sense of complete bewilderment over what it was the old man thought he could achieve by his harangue and, further, a failure to grasp the relevance of it all for the Hohepas. My reaction, let me say, was mixed with irritation at certain of father's habits. (Described.) With his pockets filled with small change he sounded like the original gypsy orchestra, cymbals and all. I actually tried mum's old trick of the glance and the cough. No luck. And he went on talking, at me now, going so wide of the mark, for example, as to mention some inconceivable, undocumented and undemonstrated condition, some truly monstrous condition, called your-mother's-love. Plain evidence of his distress, I took it to be, this obscenity uttered in mixed company. I turned my head the better to hear, when it came, the squelchy explosion of his heart. And I rolled a smoke and threw Fanny the packet. It landed neatly on her stomach. She sat up and made herself a smoke then crossed to her old man and, perching beside him in the brilliant pool of light, fire of skin and gleam of hair bronze and blue-black, neatly extracted from his pocket his battered flint lighter. She snorted smoke and passed the leaf to her old man.

Some things, gentlemen, still amaze. To my dying day I have treasured that scene and all its rich implications. In a situation so pregnant of difficulties, in the midst of a debate so fraught with undertones, an exchange (quiet there, at the back) so bitterly fulsome on the one hand and so reserved on the other. I ask you to take special note of this observance of the ritual of the makings, remembering, for the fullest savouring of the nuance, my father's abstention. As those brown fingers moved on the white cylinder, or cone, I was moved almost, to tears, almost, by this companionable and wordless recognition of our common human frailty, father and dark child in silent communion and I too, in some manner not to be explained because inexplicable, sharing their hearts. I mean the insanity, pal. Puti Hohepa and his lass in sunlight on the steps, smoking together, untroubled, natural and patient; and me and daddy glaring at each other in the shades like a couple of evangelists at cross pitch. Love, thy silver coatings and castings. And thy neighbours! So I went and sat by Fanny and put an arm through hers.

The sun gathered me up, warmed and consoled; the bitter view assumed deeper purples and darker rose; a long way off a shield flashed, the sun striking silver from a water trough. At that moment I didn't care what mad armies marched in my father's voice nor what the clarion was he was trying so strenuously to sound. I didn't care that the fire in his heart was fed by such rank fuel, skeezing envy, malice, revenge, hate and parental power. I sat and smoked and was warm; and the girl's calm flank was against me, her arm through mine. Nothing was so natural as to turn through the little distance between us and kiss her smoky mouth. Ah yes, I could feel, I confess, through my shoulder blades as it were and the back of my head, the crazed rapacity and outrage of my daddy's Irish stare, the blackness and the cold glitter of knives. (Father!) While Puti Hohepa sat on as though turned to glowing stone by the golden light, faced outward to the violet mystery of the natural hour, monumentally content and still.

You will have seen it, known it, guessed that there was between this wild, loamy daughter and me, sunburnt scion of an ignorant, insensitive, puritan and therefore prurient, Irishman (I can't stop) no more than a summer's dalliance, a season's thoughtless sweetness, a boy and a girl and the makings.

In your wisdom, gentlemen, you will doubtless have sensed that something is lacking in this lullaby, some element missing for the articulation of this ranting tale. Right. The key to daddy's impassioned outburst, no less. Not lost in this verbose review, but so far unstated. Point is he'd come to seek his little son (someone must have been dying because he'd never have come for the opposite reason) and, not being one to baulk at closed doors and drawn shades, wait for it, he'd walked straight in on what he'd always somewhat feverishly imagined and hoped he feared. Fanny took it calmly: I was, naturally, more agitated. Both of us ballocky in the umber light, of course. Still, even though he stayed only long enough to let his eyes adjust and his straining mind take in this historic disposition of flesh, those mantis angles in which for all our horror we must posit our conceivings, it wasn't the greeting he'd expected. It wasn't quite the same, either, between Fanny and me, after he'd backed out, somewhat huffily, on to the verandah. Ah, filthy beasts! He must have been roaring some such expression as that inside his head because his eyeballs were rattling, the very picture of a broken doll, and his face was liver-coloured. I felt sorry for him, for a second, easing backward from the love-starred couch and the moving lovers with his heel hooked through the loop of Fanny's bra, kicking it free like a football hero punting for touch, his dream of reconciliation in ruins.

It wasn't the same. Some rhythms are slow to re-form. And once the old man actually made the sanctuary of the verandah he just had to bawl his loudest for old man Hohepa, Mr Ho-he-pa, Mr Ho-he-pa. It got us into our clothes anyway, Fanny giggling and getting a sneezing fit at the same time, bending forward into the hoof-marked brassiere and blasting off every ten seconds like a burst air hose until I quite lost count on the one-for-sorrow two-for-joy scale and crammed myself sulkily into my jocks.

Meantime dad's labouring to explain certain natural facts and common occurrences to Puti Hohepa, just as though he'd made an original discovery; as perhaps he had considering what he probably thought of as natural. Puti Hohepa listened, I thought that ominous, then silently deprecated, in a single slow movement of his hand, the wholly inappropriate expression of shock and rage, all the sizzle of my daddy's oratory.

Thus the tableau. We did the only possible thing, ignored him and let him run down, get it off his chest, come to his five battered senses, if he had so many, and get his breath. Brother, how he spilled darkness and sin upon that floor, wilting collar and boiling eyes, the sweat running from his face and, Fanny, shameless, languorous and drowsy, provoking him to further flights. She was young, gentlemen: I have not concealed it. She was too young to have had time to accumulate the history he ascribed to her. She was too tender to endure for long the muscular lash of his tongue and the rake of his eyes. She went over to her dad, as heretofore described, and when my sweet sire, orator general to the dying afternoon, had made his pitch about matters observed and inferences drawn, I went to join her. I sat with my back to him. All our backs were to him, including his own. He emptied himself of wrath and for a moment, a wild and wonderful moment, I thought he was going to join us, bathers in the pool of sun. But no.

Silence. Light lovely and fannygold over the pasture; shreds of mist by the river deepening to rose. My father's hard leather soles rattled harshly on the bare boards like rim-shots. The mad figure of him went black as bug out over the lawn, out over the loamy furrows where the tongue of ploughed field invaded the home paddock, all my doing, spurning in his violence anything less than this direct and abrupt charge towards the waiting car. Fanny's hand touched my arm again and for a moment I was caught in a passion of sympathy for him, something as solid as grief and love, an impossible pairing of devotion and despair. The landscape flooded with sadness as I watched the scuttling, black, ignominious figure hurdling the fresh earth, the waving arms, seemingly scattering broadcast the white and shying gulls, his head bobbing on his shoulders, as he narrowed into distance.

I wished, gentlemen, with a fervour foreign to my young life, that it had been in company other than that of Puti Hohepa and his brat that we had made our necessary parting. I wished we had been alone. I did not want to see him diminished, made ridiculous and pathetic among strangers, while I so brashly joined the mockers. (Were they mocking?) Impossible notions; for what was there to offer and how could he receive? Nothing. I stroked Fanny's arm. Old man Hohepa got up and unchained the dog and went off to get the cows in. He didn't speak; maybe the chocolate old bastard was dumb, eh? In a minute I would have to go down and start the engine and put the separator together. I stayed to stare at Fanny, thinking of undone things in a naughty world. She giggled, thinking, for all I know, of the same, or of nothing. Love, thy sunny trystings and nocturnal daggers. For the first time I admitted my irritation at that girlish, hiccoughing, tenor giggle. But we touched, held, got up and with our arms linked went down the long paddock through the infestation of buttercup, our feet bruising stalk and flower. Suddenly all I wanted and at whatever price was to be able, sometime, somewhere, to make it up to my primitive, violent, ignorant and crazy old man. And I knew I never would. Ah, what a bloody fool. And then the next thing I wanted, a thing far more feasible, was to be back in that room with its shade and smell of hay-dust and warm flesh, taking up the classic story just where we'd been so rudely forced to discontinue it. Old man Hohepa was bellowing at the dog; the cows rocked up through the paddock gate and into the yard: the air smelled of night. I stopped; and holding Fanny's arm suggested we might run back. Her eyes went wide: she giggled and broke away and I stood there and watched her flying down the paddock, bare feet and a flouncing skirt, her hair shaken loose.

Next afternoon I finished ploughing the river paddock, the nature of Puti Hohepa's husbandry as much a mystery as ever, and ran the old Ferguson into the lean-to shelter behind the cow shed. It was far too late for ploughing: the upper paddocks were hard and dry. But Puti hoped to get a crop of late lettuce off the river flat; just in time, no doubt, for a glutted market, brown rot, wilt and total failure of the heart. He'd have to harrow it first, too; and on his own. Anyway, none of my worry. I walked into the shed. Fanny and her daddy were deep in conversation. She was leaning against the flank of a cow, a picture of rustic grace, a rural study of charmed solemnity. Christ knows what they were saying to each other. For one thing they were speaking in their own language: for another I couldn't hear anything, even that, above the blather and splatter of the bloody cows and the racket of the single cylinder diesel, brand-name Onan out of Edinburgh so help me. They looked up. I grabbed a stool and got on with it, head down to the bore of it all. I'd have preferred to be up on the tractor, poisoning myself straight out, bellowing this and that and the other looney thing to the cynical gulls. Ah, my mountain princess of the golden chords, something was changing. I stripped on, sullenly: I hoped it was me.

We were silent through dinner: we were always silent, through all meals. It made a change from home where all hell lay between soup and sweet, everyone taking advantage of the twenty minutes of enforced attendance to shoot the bile, bicker and accuse, rant and wrangle through the grey disgusting mutton and the two veg. Fanny never chattered much and less than ever in the presence of her pappy: giggled maybe but never said much. Then out of the blue father Hohepa opened up. Buster, you should make peace with your father. I considered it. I tried to touch Fanny's foot under the table and I considered it. A boy shouldn't hate his father: a boy should respect his father. I thought about that too. Then I asked should fathers hate their sons; but I knew the answer. Puti Hohepa didn't say anything, just sat blowing into his tea, looking at his reputedly wild daughter who might have been a beauty for all I could tell, content to be delivered of the truth and so fulfilled. You should do this: a boy shouldn't do that – tune into that, mac. And me thinking proscription and prescription differently ordered in this farm world of crummy acres. I mean I thought I'd left all that crap behind the night I stumbled along Rideout Road following, maybe, the river Alph. I thought old man Hohepa, having been silent for so long, would know better than to pull, of a sudden, all those generalizations with which for seventeen years I'd been beaten dizzy – but not so dizzy as not to be able to look back of the billboards and see the stack of rotting bibles. Gentlemen, I was, even noticeably, subdued. Puti Hohepa clearly didn't intend to add anything more just then. I was too tired to make him an answer. I think I was too tired even for hate; and what better indication of the extent of my exhaustion than that? It had been a long summer; how long I was only beginning to discover. It was cold in the kitchen. Puti Hohepa got up. From the doorway, huge and merging into the night, he spoke again: You must make up your own mind. He went away, leaving behind him the vibration of a gentle sagacity, tolerance, a sense of duty (mine, as usual) pondered over and pronounced upon. The bastard. You must make up your own mind. And for the first time you did that mum had hysterics and dad popped his gut. About what? Made up my mind about what? My black daddy?

Fanny? Myself? Life? A country career and agricultural hell? Death? Money? Fornication? (I'd always liked that.) What the hell was he trying to say? What doing but abdicating the soiled throne at the first challenge? Did he think fathers shouldn't hate their sons, or could help it, or would if they could? Am I clear? No matter. He didn't have one of the four he'd sired at home so what the hell sort of story was he trying to peddle? Father with the soft centre. You should, you shouldn't, make up your own mind. Mac, my head was going round. But it was brilliant, I conceded, when I'd given it a bit of thought. My livid daddy himself would have applauded the perfect ambiguity. What a bunch: they keep a dog on a chain for years and years and then let it free on some purely personal impulse and when it goes wild and chases its tail round and round, pissing here and sniffing there in an ecstasy of liberty, a freedom for which it has been denied all training, they shoot it down because it won't come running when they hold up the leash and whistle. (I didn't think you'd go that way, son.) Well, my own green liberty didn't look like so much at that moment; for the first time I got an inkling that life was going to be simply a matter of out of one jail and into another. Oh, they had a lot in common, her dad and mine. I sat there, mildly stupefied, drinking my tea. Then I looked up at Fanny; or, rather, down on Fanny. I've never known such a collapsible sheila in my life. She was stretched on the kitchen couch, every vertebra having turned to juice in the last minute and a half. I thought maybe she'd have the answer, some comment to offer on the state of disunion. Hell. I was the very last person to let my brew go cold while I pondered the nuance of thought of the incomprehensible, picked at the dubious unsubtlety of thought of a man thirty years my senior who had never, until then, said more than ten words to me. She is too good for you: only six words after all and soon forgotten. Better, yes, if he'd stayed mum, leaving me to deduce from his silence whatever I could, Abora Mountain and the milk of paradise, consent in things natural and a willingness to let simple matters take their simple course.

I was wrong: Fanny offered no interpretation of her father's thought. Exegesis to his cryptic utterance was the one thing she couldn't supply. She lay with her feet up on the end of the couch, brown thighs charmingly bared, mouth open and eyes closed in balmy sleep, displaying in this posture various things but mainly her large unconcern not only for this tragedy of filial responsibility and the parental role but, too, for the diurnal problem of the numerous kitchen articles, pots, pans, plates, the lot. I gazed on her, frowning on her bloom of sleep, the slow inhalation and exhalation accompanied by a gentle flare of nostril, and considered the strength and weakness of our attachment. Helpmeet she was not, thus to leave her lover to his dark ponderings and the chores.

Puti Hohepa sat on the verandah in the dark, hacking over his bowl of shag. One by one, over my second cup of tea, I assessed my feelings, balanced all my futures in the palm of my hand. I crossed to Fanny, crouched beside her, kissed her. I felt embarrassed and, gentlemen, foolish. Her eyes opened wide; then they shut and she turned over.

The dishes engaged my attention not at all, except to remind me, here we go, of my father in apron and rubber gloves at the sink, pearl-diving while mum was off somewhere at a lynching. Poor bastard. Mum had the natural squeeze for the world; they should have changed places. (It's for your own good! Ah, the joyous peal of that as the razor strop came whistling down like tartar's blade.) I joined daddy Hohepa on the verandah. For a moment we shared the crescent moon and the smell of earth damp under dew, Rideout Mountain massed to the west.

I've finished the river paddock.

Yes.

The tractor's going to need a de-coke before long.
Yes.
I guess that about cuts it out.
Yes.
I may as well shoot through.
Buster, is Fanny pregnant?
I don't know. She hasn't said anything to me so I suppose she can't be.
You are going home?
No. Not home. There's work down south. I'd like to have a look down there.
There's work going here if you want it. But you have made up your mind?
I suppose I may as well shoot through.
Yes.
After milking tomorrow if that's okay with you.
Yes.

He hacked on over his pipe. Yes, yes, yes, yes, yes is Fanny pregnant? What if I'd said yes? I didn't know one way or the other. I only hoped, and left the rest to her. Maybe he'd ask her; and what if she said yes? What then, eh Buster? Maybe I should have said why don't you ask her. A demonstrative, volatile, loquacious old person: a tangible symbol of impartiality, reason unclouded by emotion, his eyes frank in the murk of night and his pipe going bright, dim, bright as he calmly considered the lovely flank of the moon. I was hoping she wasn't, after all. Hoping; it gets to be a habit, a bad habit that does you no good, stunts your growth, sends you insane and makes you, demonstrably, blind. Hope, for Fanny Hohepa.

Later, along the riverbank, Fanny and I groped, gentlemen, for the lost rapport and the parking sign. We were separated by just a little more than an arm's reach. I made note then of the natural scene. Dark water, certainly; dark lush grass underfoot; dark girl, the drifting smell of loam in the night: grant me again as much. Then, by one of those fortuitous accidents not infrequent in our national prosings, our hands met, held, fell away. Darkness. My feet stumbling by the river and my heart going like a tango. Blood pulsed upon blood, undenied and unyoked, as we busied ourselves tenderly at our ancient greetings and farewells. And in the end, beginning my sentence with a happy conjunction, I held her indistinct, dark head. We stayed so for a minute, together and parting as always, with me tumbling down upon her the mute dilemma my mind then pretended to resolve and she offering no restraint, no argument better than the dark oblivion of her face.

Unrecorded the words between us: there can't have been more than six, anyway, it was our fated number. None referred to my departure or to the future or to maculate conceptions. Yet her last touch spoke volumes. (Unsubsidized, gentlemen, without dedication or preamble.) River-damp softened her hair: her skin smelled of soap: Pan pricking forward to drink at the stream, crushing fennel, exquisitely stooping, bending. . . .

And, later again, silent, groping, we ascended in sequence to the paternal porch.
Buster?
Yair?
Goodnight, Buster.
'Night, Fanny. Be seein' yuh.
. . . .
Fourteen minute specks of radioactive phosphorus brightened by weak starlight pricked out the hour: one.

In the end I left old STC in the tractor tool box along with the spanner that wouldn't fit any nut I'd ever tried it on and the grease gun without grease and the last letter from mum, hot as radium. I didn't wait for milking. I was packed and gone at the first trembling of light. It was cold along the river-bottom, cold and still. Eels rose to feed: the water was like pewter; old pewter. I felt sick, abandoned, full of self-pity. Everything washed through me, the light, the cold, a sense of what lay behind me and might not lie before, a feeling of exhaustion when I thought of home, a feeling of despair when I thought of Fanny still curled in sleep. Dark. She hadn't giggled: so what? I changed my fibre suitcase to the other hand and trudged along Rideout Road. The light increased; quail with tufted crests crossed the road: I began to feel better. I sat on the suitcase and rolled a smoke. Then the sun caught a high scarp of Rideout Mountain and began to finger down slow and gold. I was so full of relief, suddenly, that I grabbed my bag and ran. Impetuous. I was lucky not to break my ankle. White gulls, loam flesh, dark water, damsel and dome; where would it take you? Where was there to go, anyway? It just didn't matter; that was the point. I stopped worrying that minute and sat by the cream stand out on the main road. After a while a truck stopped to my thumb and I got in. If I'd waited for the cream truck I'd have had to face old brownstone Hohepa and I wasn't very eager for that. I'd had a fill of piety, of various brands. And I was paid up to date.

I looked back. Rideout Mountain and the peak of ochre red roof, Maori red. That's all it was. I wondered what Fanny and her pappy might be saying at this moment, across the clothes-hanger rumps of cows. The rush of relief went through me again. I looked at the gloomy bastard driving: he had a cigarette stuck to his lip like a growth. I felt almost happy. Almost. I might have hugged him as he drove his hearse through the tail-end of summer.

An Appetite for Flowers

Hilda trod the high and holy street. A Salvation Army group was meagre at the corner. The wind blew grit and papers and beyond the cathedral spire the sky was green. Traffic checked her briefly then she crossed, walking in the black spaces between the stripes, as the words of salvation were blown away. She kept to the inside of the pavement. Men looked quickly into her face, then at her legs, then in quick appraisal. She felt rather than saw this, as she identified objects in shop windows without glancing directly in. There were not many people in the street. She walked with her head down into the gritty wind. Her shopping bag dragged and the coloured paper round the bunch of chrysanthemums – flowers from Mr Rowbotham – crackled and tore. The lion-faced flowers spread their yellow manes.

North of the cathedral the shops thinned out and she turned west and climbed the Jacob's ladder to the terrace street. Here it was darkening and her heels were loud and she held her face gratefully to the clear breeze. She lingered as usual by the camellia branch, blossomless now, and walked on to enter the gate.

She disliked this dense patch of shadow before the door, although she couldn't have said why. Even in summer the entry remained damp and the stones grew mould. And the tree which caused it wasn't worth the keeping; although she could be grateful for greenness. The cat, as usual, she spurned away – a nameless, mangy thing for which she felt no sympathy. She supposed it smelled the meat.

Some nights the stairwell depressed her: tonight she could have sprinted to the highest doorway.

The butcher, a man of forty with at least four children, had asked her to run away with him; as he stood in the meaty sawdust. Hilda had laughed, but not unkindly. Why did he say that, out of the blue, and mean it? But he gave her excellent meat and did not repeat the proposal. She kept clear of thick fingers and palms and watched the blade open marbled flesh.

Now she unlocked her door and entered the wan room, where the last light was dying in a smell of gas and flowers. A letter had been poked under the door. She stooped, keeping a straight back in a movement rather like a deep curtsy, and felt a stocking go. The letter was from Ben, her ex: she put it on the table by the telephone. It could wait; as what couldn't, from him? The stocking was ruined, of course.

What she would like most, she thought, drawing curtains and switching on lamps, would be to sit for a moment in this amber dusk and to drink something cool and delicious, an absolutely foreign drink, exotic. But although there was nothing to prevent at least a pause, or because of that, she took off her jacket and began to unpack the shopping bag, while the kettle boiled and the telephone rang.

'Hilda?'

'Who else?' She raked her fingers through her hair in a practical manner, after the wind. It was his time for phoning, to the minute. A precise man who had been angry at the butcher's proposal, when she told him: a man with children and no runaway thoughts.

'Shall I come round?'

'Now? I'm just about to get my dinner.' They'd quarrelled: she was shaking him off. The silence awaited an invitation she did not extend.

'You're still cross, then?' He seemed to be speaking right into the mouthpiece: there was a hollowness of breathed sounds. A surreptitious phone call, while his wife fed the kids.

'I'm tired,' Hilda said. 'Phone me tomorrow, why don't you?' Or don't phone me at all. Put in a long distance call to your wife, in the next room.

Hilda reached out, full stretch, and could just reach the plug as the kettle rattled and spilled.

'What about later?'

'I told you, Anthony: I'm tired. I want an early night.' Because his days were leisurely he would never believe such a thing.

'Ten minutes, surely?' He was reasonable, and sure of winning. 'I'll phone you back in an hour or so. I must dash.'

Perhaps, thought Hilda, Anthony junior has choked on his raw carrot. It was a familiar story: he must rush. And it could incite her resentment – all the rushing being in one direction. She'd wait if she felt like it. Did she feel like waiting? Better still, she'd be out. Yes, she would be out. Disenchantment was as distinct as indigestion. She would have liked someone to come, simply, with roses and kind hands, to this simple room and her rose simplicities. But it seemed unlikely; and the pan was hot.

On the radio she found fanfares and a long exudation of violin notes to which she paid no attention, wanting only something in the background. She sprinkled salt into the pan and cooked her perfect steak with complete concentration. She ate with it a single slice of fresh white bread, liberally buttered, while she read the evening paper. Ben's unread letter nagged distastefully at the back of her mind; but Mr Rowbotham's chrysanthemums were a consolation on the corner bookcase, an acceptable yellow above the shelves of paper-back detective stories. The sad Mr Rowbotham whose hands would not make fists or talons, whose gentle lusting she did not pity, understanding its inconsequence.

She was Libra: she read: –

A difficult time for your domestic affairs, particularly if you have a Cancer partner. Wisest advice is to take angry scenes with a smile and refuse to be drawn into any arguments. Remember that it takes two to make a quarrel. Take a tip from the stars and do not place any reliance on impractical relationships that may hurt you. Significant shade is tangerine. Best number: one.

To the best of her knowledge she had no Cancer partner, and little in the way of domestic affairs. And tangerine would make her look livid. She hummed to herself over her few dishes, as the coffee jubilantly bubbled. Best number: one.

Perhaps it was what she'd expected of the patch of intense shadow; this man naked and paltry under his spread top-coat, in the tiring wind pathetically exposed. As if suspicion or uneasy imagination bred such things: as if she imagined it. But the man grossly moved and Hilda turned back indoors. She would have had to pass close to gain the street; and refused the indignity of running, in her present shoes. He was a short wraith of a creature: she could have walked up to him and given him a buffet for his silliness.

The pay phone in the hall raised questions: was this an emergency? Hilda doubted it and began to climb. She felt she might as easily have opened the door again and cried 'shoo', flapping her hands.

The sounds were brief and not loud: a scuffling, a thud, a short cry. The door opened and Anthony stood in the porchlight, breathing with a victor's satisfaction. Hilda felt guilty, caught on the stairs, neither ascending nor stepping down, while Anthony rubbed his fist in brute rumination.

'A nice neighbourhood,' Anthony said. 'Was it your butcher friend?'

'I was going for a breath of air. Of course it wasn't. What happened? Poor crazy creature.'

'Pah.'

Anthony picked up the phone and dropped pennies: he was prepared for all emergencies, until they asked him his name. Discretion was a question. They wanted his name, first; it was presumably the immutable order, to start at the beginning and work through the form – name, time, date of call, address of caller. Hilda kept her hip against the banister. Anthony hung up with a bang and pressed button B, just in case.

'I thought I'd just pop round,' Anthony said. 'Good thing I did. Did he accost you?'

Accost? Hilda shook her head and turned and began to climb the stairs. She felt the heaviness in her calf, her buttocks; and two hours earlier she could have run. While Anthony climbed in his own time, adjusting his tie and cuffs. To free herself of this dragging, Hilda leaped the last flight, without daunting him. She hated to be followed on the stairs: the backs of her knees felt naked, her heels strained. Impractical relationships may hurt, she remembered without amusement.

'Ten minutes you said, Anthony. I'm tired.'

'You were going out, nevertheless.'

'A walk before going to bed. You forget, I don't have a great garden.'

'Courting trouble.' He rubbed his knuckles again.

'Nonsense,' Hilda said. 'That sick old man?'

When he had gone, his ten minutes expanded to an hour – the time it took for reconciliation and further recrimination, love of a kind and anger of a kind – Hilda ran herself a bath in the steamy bathroom. She creamed her face and used pink tissues: her hair was tied up in a knot of cloth. Gratefully she descended into the hot, scented water.

This time it was final, and she welcomed it. It was what he had come to say. But took his time, not being one to miss opportunities or leave a body lie about unused. He made his quarrel without her assistance; and his love; and was angry. Remembering her indifference she was pleased, as if she'd won mastery over a habit like smoking or drinking or drugs. She could hardly wait for him to go, to be gone. From on high, even, she heard the roar of his going, the unnecessary fierceness of the engine, the wince of rubber on the road. And she would bruise where he had clenched her arm; but only there. She began to wash, enjoying the generous lather. Anthony, or the poor man in the shadows, or the unopened letter from her ex – she wouldn't embark on comparisons. It was midnight and she yearned for sleep, in the warm water. She definitely needed eight hours, not a minute less. Best number: one.

She might regret it, after all. She'd see.

Roses in season to your love, anywhere in the world. Except the iron curtain, Mr Rowbotham said. Try the pet shop next door, for doves.

But love was always away, if she could believe the messages they wrote on the cards; and the things they said to her, Hilda Preeble (Mrs).

In silver and bronze distinction Mr Anthony Silversteen was buying flowers, for his wife and their fifth.

'You're Hilda Preeble, aren't you? We met once at a Guy Fawkes' party. Years ago, if you remember? I did some business with your husband. Ben, was it? He was in cars. How is he these days?'

'As always, I imagine,' Hilda said. 'Are we to send these for you?' It was obvious from the note.

'If you would.' He peeled money. 'Is this by any chance your own venture?'

Hilda puzzled as she wrapped.

'Your own business, I mean?'

'Heavens no. I work here, that's all.'

'For the gentleman over there?'

'No.' Hilda smiled at the thought. 'That's our Mr Rowbotham. He's a dear. And he has a wonderful way with chrysanthemums.' (Who touched me once, in solemn praise, upon my breast.)

Anthony's wife was named Martha. She was inundated with flowers which Anthony chose but only Hilda might wrap and send. There were some doubt in Hilda's mind as to who was being ransomed, or won, with this profusion. Anthony confessed to being on various boards which precluded frequent visits to the nursing home; and for a moment, remembering a phrase, Hilda took him to be an actor – though it seemed unlikely. She thought a theatrical person would have been less formal, less wealthy. 'Company director' was a disappointment when he took her out to dinner; but he was eager to please, if a little dull. And more eager, driving her home, while she discouraged. After all, as she pointed out, they had so recently met.

If she now remembered beginnings, briefly, running a little extra hot, it was not because she wished to explore the nature of her relationship with Anthony. That was not her way. It was just that it had always pleased her to think of that positive avalanche of blossom, that tornado of flowers in which his wife was whirled, as the prelude to his finally ascending to her flat, where he was eager and dull. He remained that way. For the brief time of their affair he was too unbending a man to command surrender or engender tenderness: his dignity approached pomposity. He was, also, too possessive in his wealth of which she wanted nothing. It was inconceivable to Anthony that Hilda could be happy in the flower shop and content in these small, neat and rather dowdy rooms. He wanted to change her: she wanted him to let her be, in however friendly a way. His plans were too grand for the small future she allowed herself; and he was so married. She simply enjoyed his company, in a limited way, and that was that. He couldn't excite her; there was nothing she could conceivably do for him; and nothing she could permit him to do for her.

Roses in season to your love, anywhere in the world.

Hilda dried herself vigorously on the huge soft towel.

The days were bleak. Mr Rowbotham sat among pale blooms and wrote poetry in a school exercise-book, in exquisite handwriting. He said it was doggerel, really; but the beautiful writing seemed to redeem. He was a sad-looking jowly man, after all, but he had a deeply poetic nature; and he liked to stand close if Hilda would allow. He coughed persistently and his vivid white handkerchiefs smelled of eau-de-Cologne.

He spoke of Persephone, a goddess of whom Hilda had never heard, going now into the earth. It was strange, as she listened to his gentle voice. Mr Rowbotham was known to be a deep reader.

'She will eat poppy seed and sleep in the earth with her dark king, Hades of the black chariot.'

Was this Mr Rowbotham's poetry? Hilda smelled the richness of his breath: he took frequent nips, in private at the back of the shop, hiding the sherry bottle behind empty flower pots.

'Winter, you see,' Mr Rowbotham said. 'I suppose I'm boring you.' His smile was thin and, she thought, rather bitter. He fixed his eyes on her chest. 'An owl cries,' he said, 'and Persephone goes down.'

Hilda was impatient with his sadness, in the warm shop among the flowers. She would not try to understand such an eerie story: she moved away from the timid hands. After all, Mr Rowbotham was not that old and poppy seed or not, or poetry, he was a man like the others – even if his case seemed special.

Now she did not linger before the camellia branch and hurried through the patch of shadow by the door. And no one sent her roses. She kept the kerosene heater burning night and day and her flat was snug; though the nights seemed cold. She had gone past regret of Anthony: she would not have welcomed him; but she was piqued that the telephone did not ring. A stinging finality of tone had been rehearsed.

In the evenings she read detective stories, washed her hair, ironed clothes or cleaned the flat, while the old rooming house slept in gusty age. The butcher sold her eye-steaks and milk-fed veal. Time passed, and she was glad not to be a goddess – in cold earth.

She was late and tired. Friday was late shopping night and after the shop had closed there was still a great deal to be done. Mr Rowbotham was in no condition to assist, at that hour: he was, even, something of a nuisance, flushed and emboldened, and had frequently to be sent home in a taxi. Home to Mrs Rowbotham who had once sung, for Hilda, her one flower song.

> The foxglove bells with lolling tongue
> Will not reveal what peals were rung
> In Faery, in Faery, a thousand ages gone.

Surprisingly, Mrs Rowbotham sang superbly, from a deep globy bosom. She accompanied herself on the piano; and Mr Rowbotham kept time with a waving hand, proud of his wife.

And now Hilda hummed it, as well as she could remember, as she climbed the stairs – to find Adam seated on the floor by her doorway. In the company of a grim suitcase. He was half-asleep, but passed her the note, without speaking. Hilda broke open the envelope and read:

> Hilda old thing I have to be off on urgent business. Plans don't allow for Adam and I thought that seeing you were once mad keen for custody and all that you'd be happy to take him in. I may not be able to get in touch for some time. Your X Ben.

Adam was watching her as she read, in the dim light of the landing. With that curtsy she dropped to him but ventured no embrace. He was wary; and he looked chill, in a thin jacket.

'How long have you been waiting, Adam?'

He exposed an expensive watch. She thought it typical of Ben: the boy would have the best, or at least the ostentatious, while she was dunned for sums of money exactly calculated to distress without bankrupting her outright.

'Since half-past six.'

'You poor dear, you're frozen.' She couldn't touch him: he gave off such waves. She unlocked the door and they entered awkwardly. 'I had absolutely no warning. Why didn't you come to the shop? He could have said. He could have given me time to prepare.'

'There wasn't time. He was in an awful hurry.'

It looked, somehow, wretched – the small room in its neatness and emptiness – as she tried to see it through his eyes. She snatched up under-garments and stockings drying by the heater: the intimacy shocked her, suggesting a sordid abandon, as she stood in her neat dark dress.

'You haven't eaten, I suppose?'

'Yes. It doesn't matter. I'm not hungry, anyway.' He simply stood.

'Bring in your bag, and close the door. It won't take a minute to get you something.'

She could have wept at the vast unfairness. It was what she most wanted to do – collapse in a chair and weep buckets, or floods. But tears had never come easily. So she drew the curtains and turned on the lights – an unvarying routine of quick, precise movements – and unpacked the shopping bag. After all the flat was warm, even if a little fumy.

Adam stood by his suitcase, waiting; waiting for anything or everything. Fourteen this month, she remembered; and over three years since she had seen him. Just an occasional post-card, because her ex had been 'moving about a bit, old thing.'

'Look, love,' Hilda said. 'We'll have to do better. I fancy we're both a bit shy. We'll think of something.'

And then, for the first time in weeks, the telephone rang. She was sure it was Anthony: things never came singly.

'Hilda?'

'Who else?'

'Can we talk?'

'No.'

'Please. Are you alone?'

'No.'

'I see. Anyone I know?' His displeasure was rewarding.

'Adam has come on a visit.' Hilda smiled at her son.

'Adam? Might I ask . . .? No, it doesn't matter.'

Against her first decision, she relented. He may have hurt but hadn't harmed her. He wasn't Ben. 'Adam, my son,' Hilda said.

'Your son? You never mentioned you had a son. I find that strange, Hilda.'

'Do you?' Hilda said. 'I must go.' She smiled again, to involve Adam.

'Shall I phone again?' Anthony's tone was neutral, even official. Hilda wanted the conversation finished: Adam was so embarrassingly unpractised in not seeming to listen.

'Well, we'll see,' Hilda said. It wasn't intended as an answer. 'Goodbye for now.' She wouldn't bolt doors quite tight, in her situation, at her age. She replaced the receiver.

'Am I in the way?' Adam expressed his feeling of being everywhere out of place. Like a fork in the knife drawer, Hilda thought.

'In the way?' She only feigned incomprehension.

'He said not to get under your feet all the time.'

'Your father?'

'Yes.'

Hilda soberly made herself a stiff drink from Anthony's bottle which had lain untouched all this time. She sat down.

'Please sit down, Adam. Over there.' She drank. 'Can I make one thing perfectly plain, Adam? You aren't in the way: you won't be. There's simply no question. Will you take my word for that? You couldn't, you know, be more welcome.' Wondering what else Ben might have said: he was never a reticent man. Meantime the gin assisted.

'If you'll tell me where things are, I'll cook something,' Adam said. 'I'd quite like to.' Wanting perhaps to be out of view.

'You can cook? No, there's no need.' She began to get up from her chair.

'I'm housebroken. He said to tell you that, too.' It was a wry grin of more than fourteen years. He pulled off his jacket and went into the kitchen, where closed cupboards were daunting.

Hilda was decisive: she finished her drink and put away the bottle. 'The best thing you can do, Adam, is to prepare your room. In here.'

She swept aside curtains on the glass balcony. It wasn't promising: the view was of lighted windows and the backs of tall houses. But by day there would be a compensation of green, the slope of a hill, a few dark trees.

'Just throw everything out,' Hilda said. 'Except the bed.' Quite suddenly her good temper returned.

'Out where?'

'Pile it up on the landing. Tomorrow's Saturday: we'll take it down. There's a basement of sorts, and it's only junk, anyway. And open the windows; it may be musty.'

'Where's north?' Adam said, when he had the space cleared.

'Sorry love: I didn't catch?' Hilda had moved to the kitchen: the distance between was not great.

'I wondered where north was.'

It surprised her. 'Well, you get the morning sun so it must be. . . . ' Hilda turned so that the balcony was on her right. 'Why?'

'It's all right.' For the first time he smiled – not a grin, a smile. 'I've worked it out. I don't know why: I just like to know.'

The boyishness reassured her, a little. There was no mystery: but the distance between did not immediately diminish, and the years had not helped. She sensed the intractable, an intransigence: right or wrong, only so far would he go. She hoped she was mistaken; it was Ben's way.

'Fruit-juice?' Hilda said. 'And tea or coffee? Or do you usually have a cooked breakfast? I suppose you should have. It won't take a minute.' Growing boys were said to need a lot, she thought.

'What do you have?'

'Fruit-juice and coffee. Did you sleep?' The balcony looked uninviting.

'Yes. I'd like the same, if I may.'

'Then you use the bathroom first. I'll get things ready.' The constraint had gathered again, in the hours of darkness.

He had made his bed and there was nothing of his lying about. His suitcase was closed. It's probably locked, too, she thought. And when she used the bathroom she found no trace of him except steam, and a towel. She had provided the towel, and it hung neatly folded. She felt intimidated, and nervous of the days ahead. She wondered how long it would be before he emerged, left his mark, let things lie. He was a neat camper and a stranger, for all the blood they shared. And how heavily she had carried him, at the last, braced back to counterbalance the great burden, while Ben disparaged: she remembered that. She remembered too that she had woken half-expecting to find him gone; and determined, now, to take up the challenge and to make things work. He was hers: there was that fact; and she was quite old enough to be his mother.

'Mr Rowbotham, this is my son, Adam. Adam, Mr Rowbotham.'

'A pleasure.' Mr Rowbotham extended a shy hand. 'And a surprise, if I may say. Brother and sister I could conceive, but . . . .'

Hilda laughed: the gallantry wearied her. 'I'm flattered, Mr Rowbotham. Adam has come to stay. We must do some shopping, if you can cope.'

'Monday morning, if you remember, seems not to promote an appetite for flowers. But there are the usual wreaths. Yes, of course I can manage.'

Adam examined the small shop and the figure of Mr Rowbotham.

'Oh, well,' Mr Rowbotham murmured an apology. 'You should see it in the spring. Persephone, as I was explaining to – to your mother – Persephone has left us. Temporarily, of course.'

'Persephone?' Adam looked about, as for a junior assistant.

Mr Rowbotham chuckled, but Adam's puzzlement was brief.

'You mean the goddess, or whatever she was?' Adam was noticeably pleased to have unravelled the clue.

Mr Rowbotham was delighted. 'I congratulate you,' he said to Hilda. 'A well-taught boy. I fancy there aren't many.'

Hilda too was impressed, not least with Adam's awkwardness under the compliment. She would ask him to tell.

That day they bought, second-hand, a chest of drawers, a folding cardtable and a small bookcase. They bought, new, an adjustable desk-lamp, a piece of bright carpet and a bright blanket. Hilda thought she was all right for sheets, in the meantime.

When, in the afternoon, Adam was enrolled at high school, he had to be fitted out in school uniform. He did not wish her to accompany him: he would prefer to manage it alone. He was away a long time but returned, before the shop closed, through the vigorous turbulence of air, all wind blown and ruffled, and handed Hilda the docket and the change. Hilda gasped at how little change there was from so many large notes, but said nothing; and wondered was the boy still growing fast? And Mr Rowbotham, under his fuzz of white hair, spoke of a classical education.

Adam had remained reserved. He had given practical assistance with each purchase, rejecting one chest of drawers as too large and another, to Hilda's relief, as too grand; but apart from that he stood to one side. He appeared to have no curiosity. When Hilda remarked on something he attended, without comment. The city was strange to him but she had very strongly the impression that he would make his own appraisal in his own time, and fix his own landmarks.

She learned very quickly that she was not a woman who could help him, in deeper ways; that help was what he least wanted. He had been removed from her when he was seven; and Ben had taken care that only the bare letter of the agreement should be met. She had seen Adam only briefly over the last seven years, and only rarely alone. He was a stranger, and her son. Yet she could remember summers, faultless vault, unmarked cerulean; but turned from too painful an invasion by the past. To shrug things off; that had always to be her strength. She decided that Adam was naturally shy: she forgot how little choice he had.

She saw that he had found independence of a kind in this shyness, this silence and deep reserve: emotion, she supposed, lay deep. He fitted in with her routine and carefully kept from spilling over into her life – where was no mystery. He seemed impelled to tidy himself away. But, finally, she realized that she could only trust him to deal with his own life, and with a woman he called Hilda; as he searched for his north.

Because these were not things she was good at.

'Don't you go out, or anything?' Adam said.

'I suppose I don't,' Hilda said, struck with it.

It had only been a matter of months: she tried to remember how she had filled her time before he came. She read detective stories. And there had been Anthony; and now there wasn't. And Adam's tastes, or his mountains of homework, did not encourage the former background of the radio.

'Do you mean you'd like to go out? To a film, or something?'

'No. Not particularly. I only wondered. You don't seem to see many people.'

'Oh, all day,' Hilda said. 'That's enough, surely?' And knew it wasn't. 'I'm lazy. I like to sit.'

She'd left her friends in other places; or they'd grown apart. For a while husbands came, just passing through, with a bottle of something for the gay divorcee alone in her convenient flat: for a year or two after the divorce. But she couldn't accommodate so many impingements of another world; and was slow to respond, hinting at strong emotional attachments and hoping the message would go back. To Ben.

'Adam. If you mean you'd like to have friends in.' Why hadn't she thought of it? 'I'd be quite happy to clear the decks.' It was an expression of Ben's: Clear the decks old thing, we've got a mob descending. She hated it. 'I mean, don't think I'd be forced out into the snow.' She hoped he would see the hilarity of that.

'Have you always lived here? Since . . . .'

'Since our divorce? Yes. I like it; and it's handy.' To what she did not ask, but would have supposed she meant her job. 'I suppose it's not ideal, for you.'

'Oh, I like it,' Adam said, and sounded genuine. 'No. I didn't mean I wanted friends in. Not yet, anyway.' He went back to his homework.

Seeing him absorbed again in his books, Hilda was disappointed. She had thought he might be going to open out, to tell her things – even to ask her things. She glanced at him from time to time: she watched him, fearing to find Ben in him and, she abruptly realized, fearing only a little less to find herself. For some time she had thought of her son as this simple amalgam; until she realized that Adam at fourteen already contained his own mystery and was resolved to be himself, seeming even to know what this could be. No urgency of expression revealed it: Hilda had to search for signs. As Adam studied (Why was there so much?) she witnessed a concentration, a slow passionate attention that neither she nor Ben could ever have commanded; and she thought it a blessing that she could not help.

Faultless vault, unmarked cerulean: remembrance of a time when she had been mother, wife and housewife was not a way through to Adam. She could not insist that he share her memory: for him time past seemed to bear no charge. She had tried it, conjuring up one picture that had stayed bright for her.

The bonfires burned like beacons along the spine of hills. Shots rang in the gully: rockets rose to release a slow bright fall of stars: the rose smoke drifted and the air smelled of gunpowder. Small warriors, Adam among them, held out, against the burning night and the encroach of darkness, with a few hoarded shots, a last hushing rocket. While Ben – she would not recall this for Adam – was somewhere in the darkness with her old school friend, Marie Boyd, and Ben's father was sympathetic and touched her elbow and said it was all coming to an end, and one last Catherine wheel blazed. So she agreed, out of revenge, to meet Andrew Mason, Ben's partner, and Ben came into the house hours later and said Marie Boyd was a bloody understanding woman and she had said: 'She must be: you're wearing her lipstick'. And Adam was crying from the smallest burn, and it was over – never having begun.

But how could she make that blaze for Adam? Or feel other than stupid for having tried – the guilty party with uneasy recollections?

Adam arranged a Saturday morning job for himself, for pocket money. He wanted his own and would accept only the minimum from Hilda, giving as reason his supposition that she didn't have so much. He worked from seven in the morning until two in the afternoon at the petrol pumps of a garage in town. And on Saturday evenings, sometimes, they made a small ritual of a bottle of wine, with Hilda's special tender cuts. (Her butcher definitely let her down during the first few weeks of Adam's stay. A standing order of 'enough for two' was not welcome; until Adam was introduced. Then tenderness came back, without a word.)

They were cramped in the small flat. Hilda thought of looking for something larger but rents were against it and convenience favoured the present arrangement. The initial embarrassment faded and was replaced with a formal friendliness. Adam was interested in her day: they laughed together over Mr Rowbotham; and there were always flowers for brightness, while Persephone visited.

Persephone. It caused Hilda to wonder at the magnitude of what she did not know, and at all irrelevance. She simply couldn't conceive of herself swapping fairy stories about goddesses. Mr Rowbotham was definitely weird at times, when she came to think of it. Winter was winter, as if that weren't enough, without any need of dark kings. Really!

Hilda, in fine impatience, flashed the gleaming iron along a seam.

Adam had been with her almost a year when Ben called, without phoning beforehand, on a weekday evening. Hilda had recently taken up knitting again and sat near the heater with a knitting pattern open on her lap. She asked Adam to go to the door.

'Hello, son. Long time no see. You've grown. Hello, Hilda.' He gave Adam a friendly punch.

Dad plays Humphrey Bogart, Hilda thought. She recognized as of old his condition of equipoise between being sober and being drunk – a condition potentially dangerous to the point of violence.

'Going to ask me in?'

Hilda had not yet spoken. Ben came into the room with his hand on

Adam's shoulder and slammed the door carelessly. That too Hilda remembered. Unmindful of the intricacies of her ambitious pattern she continued to knit.

'Must say you're a bit cooped here, aren't you?' His inventory was brief. 'I'd fancied it bigger. Going to offer me hospitality? A reviver after the stairs?'

'There's coffee,' Hilda said. 'That's all, I'm afraid.' She felt her face hardening, the flesh tightening. She remembered all too clearly Adam's expression, that first evening, as she'd poured herself a drink: she'd remembered Ben then, and understood. Adam couldn't draw that sort of distinction; and Hilda wouldn't ask him to. So the occasional bottle of wine they shared represented, as much as anything, her reasoning on the matter, and her reassurance.

Adam was standing about with his thumbs hooked in his side pockets. 'I'll make coffee,' he said.

'Forget it.' Ben took Adam's chair, before the folding table spread with books and papers. 'Your ma help you with this lot?'

'Well . . . .' A hunching of the shoulders expressed difficulties.

'Of course I don't. Hilda was downright. 'As if I could.'

'How's it going, then, Adam? I hear you're doing a stint on the bowsers, Saturday. Helping your ma, is it?'

'It's pocket money,' Adam said. 'I quite like it, really.' He sounded surprised, as if he'd just recognized his enjoyment.

Hilda felt herself being brought into the line of fire, as she steadily knitted rows that would have to be pulled down. It would never be plain, with Ben.

'How's old Anthony, then?' Ben fingered a set square, a triangle, one of whose points he used to scrape a fingernail.

'I haven't seen him in months,' Hilda said.

'I suppose not.' Ben looked from the day bed to Adam's cubby. 'Cramping,' he said.

'You've hardly come for small talk,' Hilda said.

Ben held the perspex triangle against the light and squinted along an edge. 'I've come to get Adam. He can come back now.'

She'd expected it; she'd been expecting it every day for the last month. She registered the evasion, the refusal to look her in the face, the toying with things. She glanced up at Adam, for comparison. Was the boy then like his father? It was urgent that she should know. But she could not tell. Adam's mouth (or did she need to invent it?) had a suggestion of Ben's father. Adam was taller, with his shoulders against the wall: his dark rather closed-in face, his good eyes, gave no hint of what he might be thinking: his expression was a refusal.

'Just like that, Ben?' She hated using his name. 'Out of the blue, with no warning?'

'Ah well, I got through my bit of business earlier than expected. And I've set up in a decent place again, even if it's a bit out of town. You can get the train in to school, Adam. That's no hardship, is it?'

'He's all right here you know, Ben.' How hard would she fight, she wondered? Certainly she would not permit Adam to be, again, rope for this tug-of-war. But what did Adam want? To know that she would have to know what he felt for Ben; and he'd never told her. Would Adam be better off with his father? She couldn't believe it: she simply refused to. She had noticed over the last few months a greater ease in Adam. Oh, no great flowering, no burst of expansiveness and confidence – just a small advance of boundaries he set himself, so that books and an occasional garment lay about.

'I mean he's welcome here,' Hilda said, in the silence. 'He knows that, I hope. And we do manage.' Her neutral tone was not helping; and she was afraid to try more. Adam evaded her smile.

'Sure you're a skinner? Not a drop in the place, I mean?'

Hilda remembered Anthony's gin. 'Look in the cupboard, Adam. I don't know . . . .'

'Holding out on your ex, eh?' Ben greeted the bottle. 'Not that there's much.'

For another it would have been too much: for Ben it would make two drinks, with flat tonic water.

'I took it your note meant you were going away.' Hilda was being cautious.

'For good? No, just a business trip. Adam wouldn't have enjoyed it. And there's the education caper.'

Hilda's knitting ceased to occupy her. 'You do see me, don't you Ben, as someone without rights of any kind? Not even the ordinary politeness applies.'

Ben emptied the bottle. 'You're forgetting the circumstances, old thing.'

'No. I'm not forgetting any circumstances, past or present. Not mine and not yours. Perhaps Adam can decide.'

'You can't have too much gear,' Ben said to Adam. 'I've got a car: there's no need to pack.'

'Ben, that's absurd.' Hilda tried to control her shrillness. 'It's almost ten, and he's got school tomorrow.'

'He can't be doing too well if missing a day makes all that difference.' Ben stared at his manicure. 'Get cracking, old son.'

'I'd rather leave it.' It cost Adam an effort, visibly.

'Weekend suit you better, eh? O.K. I'll go along with that.'

'I mean I'd rather leave it, altogether.'

'Not sure I follow son. Not come at all, you mean?' Ben looked dangerous.

It was a small triumph, whatever it meant; but she knew better than to show it and took little confidence from it. The knitting pattern fell to the floor. Hilda rose and went out to the kitchen and drank a glass of water. The silence was long, while the wind shook a loose latch on the window above the sink. She returned to her chair but let her knitting lie.

'I can come and see you. I'd like that.' Adam looked at his father – an oblique, quick glance.

Ben was thinking, with a tight, grimacing smile. 'You think you might appeal, is that it?' He turned to Hilda.

She met the blue wild stare. A delusive mist of possibilities whirled through her, as Ben downed his drink and waited with cruel patience. Ben had been in trouble; that much she knew. And that she might appeal, yes, she knew that too. She'd taken the trouble to find out where Ben had been: the answer had not been hard to come by.

'No.' Hilda shook her head. 'I've been content to have him here. I'd like Adam to stay, if that were possible. He'd see you: you could help him.'

'With money you mean? I suppose your little flower shop doesn't pay you so much.'

He could always manage contempt, she remembered, for what he called 'the toiling bloody sheep'; and poverty, true poverty, enraged him. His view had nothing to do with injustice.

'I wasn't thinking of money,' Hilda said.

Ben was pensive over his empty glass – a small man with a strained small face. His suit was new. He had married her because she was pregnant; or so she'd believed. Now she thought there might have been other and less obvious reasons. Adam continued to stand, leaning against the wall by the door to the landing.

'Give us five minutes, there's a lad.' Ben ducked his head sideways towards the door.

'There's nothing Adam can't hear,' Hilda said.

But Adam had already let himself out. Ben followed and called down the stairs.

'The blue Chevvy, the new one – look her over why don't you?' He returned to tilt the empty bottle, pulling a pug's face. 'Turned the clucky ma all of a sudden, haven't you? You forget: I'm the one that's brought him up. You don't see him for years and then it's out with the bloody apron strings. There's a great bloody heap he can't hear, it seems to me.'

'How much I saw of Adam was exactly how much you would allow. It's no use pretending otherwise. I begged hard enough. There's no point in going into that. There's nothing against his staying here: you can both see as much of each other as you want.'

'I can come here, do you mean?' He knew this wasn't the suggestion.

'Wherever you have your decent place,' Hilda said. Her smile exhibited no trace of amusement. 'I won't interfere.'

Ben looked his ex-wife up and down. 'Not as young as you were, Hilda. What happened to the boy friend? You get too demanding? A married man with a rich wife and a packet of kids – Christ, do you ever play the long shots. I checked him out.'

'Then we've both been checking.'

'On Anthony?'

'On each other.'

'Ah.' It was not a sigh but a fierce, explosive grunt as though she had winded him.

She thought he would strike her then. His hands made fists and the muscles in his throat went stringy. He stared and trembled.

'So that's it, eh? Now we come to it. That's to be the play.'

Hilda dared to move closer; it cost her an effort. She was not a brave woman; but it forced him to meet her eye.

'No, Ben,' she said. 'There's no play, as you call it. There aren't any threats, any hints. And I don't tell tales: you can be reassured on that point. If you absolutely won't see that Adam counts in this, then I give him up. I'm not going to drag him over all this dead ground between us, with you pulling one way and me another.' Her reasonableness wasn't up to it: she blazed. 'Ben, I'm not.'

'I suppose you're doing it in the backs of cars these days? Now your tidy little prostitute's flat has lost its privacy. Or on the stairs, maybe? You were always hot for it.' He found a tone for his anger – a hiss.

'You've always had a perfectly foul mind, Ben.'

'I suppose you wouldn't consider . . .?'

'If you touch me once more I swear I'll kill you, Ben.' Hilda even looked wildly about and seized a knitting needle; with which she would have been pleased then to inflict a blinding injury.

'Keep your shirt on, old thing.' Ben backed away. 'Let's be reasonable. Sure you haven't got another bottle?'

Hilda returned to her chair, and slumped. 'Reasonable? My God, do you have the faintest idea of what you're saying: do you have any idea of what it means? Have you ever in your whole life done one reasonable thing?' She was closer to exhaustion than to tears.

Had he ever meant to take Adam away – to take him away for more than the time needed to work his vicious little act of revenge? Hilda couldn't know. He had divorced her: he would not, therefore, forget. His memory was as tightly tailored as his clothes: no one could share it.

In the end it was a common 'touch', a piece of petty blackmail which, degrading them both, degraded Hilda more. Business, in fact, had been lousy; it was as much as he would say on that score. He hadn't been what you'd call active. It was his only concession to what she knew and neither would speak of. Hilda was quite right: the boy was better off where he was, in the meantime. The point was that if he, Ben, could just get out, get away, right out of the country altogether – he'd thought Australia where the pickings were better, especially if a man had a bit over and above the fare – well, Hilda was in business: she'd understand the old capitalist argument, *caveat emptor* and that sort of thing.

It was a phrase he had picked up somewhere early in his activities, called by him his career. *Caveat emptor*; it was the pennant at the mast of his pirate craft; and he spelled it various ways. She didn't dwell on it now, nor ask what he might mean by 'the time being'. But the car, she questioned, surely he had some capital in that?

'Not a razoo, old thing. Borrowed.' He grinned, happily. 'Couldn't let Adam think his old man was reduced to walking. Make it out to cash; it's simpler all round. Don't worry, I'll pay you back. That's a promise. Just give us six months and I'll buy up your hat-box of a flower shop – lock, stock and barrel.'

Hilda held out the cheque. 'I wouldn't do that, Ben,' she said. 'You wouldn't like it. All the roses have thorns. That's something you'd never be able to remember.' She thought of Mr Rowbotham.

'Well, of course, old Anthony is loaded anyway, eh?'

'I told you: I don't see him.'

'Pity, old thing. But,' and he impudently walked round her, 'you're still sitting on a gold mine, I'd say. Which is a compliment.'

'I prefer to think of it as an obscenity.' As she moved towards the door.

At this moment she didn't even care that the cheque represented almost exactly the sum of her balance in the bank. She hoped, but was not confident, that it would be the last demand. It had bought what she wanted; and she could think the price a light one, the more so if the transaction were now complete.

'Please go,' she said.

They heard him lingering on the lower landing. Ben leaned over the rail.

'Adam?' he called down, softly.

'Yes.'

'Hold it, son. I'm coming down.'

'If you could make it seem like your decision.' Hilda wondered whose face she was trying to save – Ben's, her own, or Adam's? 'If you could invent some story,' she said. A known talent she had not expected to invoke.

'Goodbye, old thing. It's all right: you're on your own from now. I'll write the lad. Don't give me a bad name with him, if you can avoid it.'

Her silence was all she would offer: victory could borrow too much of the vanquished's sense of defeat. The exchange had soiled them both. He went down, too dapper and wearing an unsuitable tie. The flower he had taken for his buttonhole was incongruous, a seedy flirtation. She turned back into the room and closed the door before he had gone out of sight, while he was looking up to wave.

When Adam returned Hilda was pulling down her knitting. The knitted wool was kinked.

'He said I could stay. He said you'd talked it over.'

'It was a matter of what seemed best,' Hilda said. 'And of what you seemed to want. It needn't be unalterable, you know.'

That motherly tone: because it was involuntary was it therefore natural? She almost looked into her lap for broad stretches of cloth – as though her hips had hugely broadened: she could all but feel her bosom dragging. A single child seemed insufficient reason for turning into a pudding. Tomorrow she would reconsider the butcher's offer, or run off with Mr Rowbotham to grow chrysanths – lion-faced Mr Rowbotham whose long inert hand had lain on her bosom like a pale ornament. She could smile for Mr Rowbotham now, as she picked up stitches: Mrs Rowbotham, in faery, was clearly a more suitable partner, in contralto brown with spanning hands.

Adam had taken the chair before the folding table. He fidgeted there, his silence drumming.

'It's too late,' Hilda said. 'You can't go on with that now.'

'He's in trouble, isn't he? He wanted money.'

'In trouble?' Hilda spread her knitting over her fingers, stretching it to examine the pattern: she was some distance yet from bedrock.

'There was a man down there.'

'A man? Down where?'

'By the door: by the old tree. Waiting.'

Now, thought Hilda, she would phone. It was too much: he'd had his chance. She prepared to leap, in righteousness.

'A policeman,' Adam said. 'I could see his boots, and the trousers without cuffs.'

'What on earth would a policeman be doing, hiding like that?'

'He wasn't really hiding. He was waiting, by the car?'

Her look was startled: she put down her knitting very slowly. So much from one patch of shadow? Absurd.

'It's all right,' Adam said. 'I told him. That's why I came up. I warned him. I didn't go near the car, after all.'

'There aren't any parking restrictions.' Hilda tried for composure, with her heart banging. 'He'd probably forgotten to leave his parking lights on.'

'He went out the back way, through the yard. I could hear him running down the hill.'

Adam put his books into a pile, a neat pyramid with the set-square on top.

Hilda wrapped her knitting in a white cloth and put it away. Ben's empty glass was still on the table. A Cancer partner? When was his birthday, ever? She'd forgotten.

'I expect it was some mistake,' Hilda said, and hoped to dismiss it. 'Will you use the bathroom first, please, Adam? It's late. I have to be at the shop early to make a wreath.' She wished she could show more authority, and ease.

'He is in trouble,' Adam said. 'I knew something was wrong as soon as I opened the door. How much did he want?'

'That sort of tone doesn't suit you, Adam.' It was her first outright rebuke, and a strong one. 'We all get into hot water sometimes, if that's what it is.'

'Can I ask you a question, then?'

'Of course.' She gathered herself tight for it, summoning from remote perimeters her full reserves, wishing for breathing space.

'Do you hate him? Did you? You know.'

It should have been laughably over-dramatic; but she felt only relief at the simplicity. 'Adam, don't be absurd. It's too long ago.'

'He's asked you for money before. I know that.'

She looked at the dark scowl and knew that anything less than her full seriousness, her fullest concentration, would be a danger. 'You forget we were married, Adam. There aren't so many places one can turn to, for help. When you really need it.'

'I don't forget. But he hates you.'

Hilda denied it: she was confident. 'He never really mastered his habits,' she said carefully. 'I'm a sort of habit, and not a very satisfactory one, either. We're too different: he's always wanted to scoop things up, in great handfuls. He can't forgive the pebble-gatherers. It's what he used to call me, a hoarder of pebbles.

He keeps me in view for that – to remind him of how much he hates it. And it cuts another great piece out of his pride every time he comes a cropper, every time he finds he's just got a handful of rubble.'

'You mean every time he asks you for help?' He wanted to be clear. He turned the set-square in his hands; it caught gleams of light, quickly.

'Well, that's perhaps when he does hate me; because it makes him hate himself. But it doesn't last long, Adam, don't you see?'

'He hates you because you help him?'

'That's usual,' Hilda said. 'Only I don't help, not really. He couldn't get by on that. You don't help people like him any more than you help a child. He has all the rights; it's not his fault. I suppose it's the way he's made. Children don't have to say thank you to survive, even to thrive.'

'He's not a child.'

'And neither are you, Adam. Otherwise why would I try to explain, or why would you ask? That's too simple. Oh, just look at the time.' She wailed at the clock and hurried out of her chair, and stood. 'You may know him better, after all: he brought you up. I could be wrong: I'm hardly unbiased.'

Adam waited. It wasn't finished yet; and he looked determined.

'Look, love.' Hilda ploughed into strange waters. 'It's just that there aren't any rules for him, except the ones he feels like using sometimes, the ones he can make use of. Only pebble-gatherers have rules. But you can't hate him for that. He strikes out and it's his own knuckles that are broken.'

'Are there rules for me?'

In the face of these sullen looks she found explanation difficult; but she would try. In the face of this insolence.

'Women are sentimental, Adam. It takes a very strong one not to ruin a man with mothering, or perhaps it takes a weakness that's like strength. I think I wanted to do that, once – to live through Ben, to make him see the rules and to make him keep them. Of course I lost. If he does hate me it's for that, for trying to change him. For most women the man they marry isn't enough: they can't let him be that, for long.'

It surprised her: she would have sworn she had never given it a thought; but it was, after all, the truth as she had seen it – or was as near as she could come.

'We never understood each other,' she said almost fiercely. 'We married and lived together and were divorced, all for the wrong reasons – whatever the right ones might be. I don't think it matters who is to blame. I can't hate him, can I?'

'Why not?'

'Because I have to live too, in my own way. Because pebble-gatherers do have rights. Because there have to be rules, for you.'

She took up the empty glass and the empty bottle and put them through on the bench and stood there, before the sink, hearing running feet and wondering what rights or rules she was thinking of. 'Least of all should you hate him,' she called. 'He did his best, there.'

'I didn't say I hated him.' Adam had moved to the kitchen doorway. 'I don't. I was just trying to understand, that's all.'

Not unthinkingly Hilda chose vagueness and a straightening of cushions. She thought she felt his eyes on her, but when she looked up he had gone and the bathroom door was closed. There was the boomy explosion of the califont and the usual drift of gas. Adam was whistling through his teeth; it didn't amount to a tune. Hilda put away the stack of books. She was cross with herself: that was the trap of words – you didn't say what you wanted to say. Between Ben and herself the dialogue would never be concluded; it was something like that.

This was what you surrendered, finally – the luxuries; the feelings of whatever kind you'd come to depend on. Of course she hated him: of course he hated her. It was the strongest tie. It was what had kept them together those few years; it was what kept him nipping at her heels; it was the reason she scribbled out the requested relief. From the very beginning it had been there, only waiting the extinction of that brief infatuation; and it had loomed full height when she had told him she was pregnant. That was the point at which they both began their long search for revenge, began to nurture the strongest feeling either of them had known – unclouded by affection. It had been the reason for passionless Anthony; and for what else she could not know.

But tonight was an excess; and again she heard running feet. Adam had chosen neither, rejected neither, and she suspected contempt in him for them both; depths, as she hoped it would not be, of a new treachery. Tonight Ben had needed help in a different way; and tonight she too might have benefited from some undefined assistance. And Ben was fleeing down dark streets while she, as urgently and as pointlessly, fluffed out cushions and removed flowers in vases to the kitchen bench. That's what it came to, she thought, listening for steps on the stairs.

Take a tip from the stars.

'It's an illusion.'

Hilda jumped, as if an absolute privacy had been invaded, as if she had been speaking aloud. Adam stood damp and wrapped in the bathroom doorway where steam billowed.

'It's an illusion that people need eight hours of sleep,' Adam said. 'That's twenty-five years in bed out of seventy-five, did you know that?'

'What a luxury,' Hilda cried, in some relief. 'Oh what a luxury. I'd settle for the lot, all in a lump, right now. I'm just the right age for illusions, Adam: I positively need them.'

These were the words; but this was not what they were saying: they both knew that. Hilda felt that her nerves had, finally, gone: strings were breaking, snapping in a darkness she could feel. Adam's smile was a laceration: she wished for spears and locks. She wondered what was happening to her: she remembered that tomorrow was Monday.

'Goodnight, Hilda.'

'Goodnight, Adam.' A pause. 'Adam?'

'Yes?' As he turned back.

'No, it doesn't matter. Goodnight.'

'Goodnight.'

Had there ever been anyone in the shade, the shadows? People, women, were known to invent; and her world, she felt, was an unknown one tonight. Tears and smiles conflicted as she rattled the milk tokens and the cat kept its calculated distance with its flag of tail. Had there been, ever, blossoms on the blossomless camellia? Really?

Pssst!

She took her time, now, dawdling under the mere vault of stars. She set the milk bottle in its rack: she smelled autumn earth. The wind was flurrying in the terrace street, quite strangely, pell-mell from every direction, and chill. Beyond the spire, lights contracted or pulsed. Over there would be north, where lights climbed; and she was sad to think of anyone's running in such a mildness of weather.

Pssst!

Had there? Ever?

As a goddess dragged past with a transistor ear-muff and, Hilda imagined, gooseflesh and blue knees.

Hilda spurned the cat: her anger had gathered in her throat.

They would kill the life in you, she thought; and she could have believed someone spoke, from the shadows. And she thought of tomorrow's wreath. Have you a Cancer partner? It takes two to make a quarrel, remember.

Pssst!

And trod again the high and difficult stairs, hoping Adam was asleep.

And Ben, from running.

And Anthony.

And Mr Rowbotham enfolded in globy places, folded in faery and song – if that was what he wanted, most.

Because tonight it was a long way to climb.

But she was, nevertheless, humming softly beneath it all and grateful to think she was not being followed on the stairs.

Because she hated that.

DAVID BALLANTYNE

Other Gardens

I

My husband was expecting a visitor, so I left him reading the Sunday papers –
he thought it broadening to buy them all; the *News of the World*, he said, was as
instructive in its own way as the *Observer* – and escaped to the common. My
ground-floor tormentors were, as I had hoped, too involved in rest-day rituals
to notice my flight, and although there was a moment in the hall when I seemed
to hear Mrs Fenner calling to one of her daughters to see who was making for
the door, I later reasoned that she had more likely been demanding from her
bed that the kitchen radio be turned up.

I had come to value the common not so much for its own sake – there were
days, particularly in the unexpected heat of the first summer, when I hated it –
but simply as *somewhere to go*. We had gone there together, Bernard and I, in the
slate-grey weeks that followed our arrival in London, and I remember how
awed we were as we walked on a snowy day along the path that encircled the
pond in one corner of the common. The skinny trees were black where they
were not white, and all over the common there was only grey or brown where
there was not black or white. 'It's like a photograph,' Bernard said. I said the
earth was so hushed. 'Like a photograph,' he said, and said again many times in
the several weeks left of winter. Afterwards, when I began going alone to the
common, I was seldom touched by its seasonal aspects, could not tell you when I
noted signs of the miraculous spring I had been warned to watch for, nor which
day it was when the sun I thought I had lost shone from a sky as high and as blue
as any I could remember, nor even when I heard for the very first time (so it
seemed) the sound of leaves falling. I became aware of these things
accidentally; they were small interruptions. If it were sunny, I risked resting in
the wild grass; if it were cold, I stamped my feet and swung my arms as though
exercise were my only reason for being there. Whatever my preoccupation, I
was always aware of the others who used the common. We shared that place.

Anyway, on this particular Sunday afternoon, I was elated about dodging
Mrs Fenner and her spies, and not too sorry either to be away from the room
where Bernard would now feel free to enjoy the scandals that for my benefit he
pretended to disdain. (How gravely he had looked up from his *Observer* to wish
me a pleasant stroll!)

I was half-way across the wider part of the common – it narrowed at the pond
end with the inroads of war-time allotments – before I realized that something
special was in the air. I stopped. It was still too early for the people of this
suburb to be out taking what they could of the pallid winter sun; they seemed to
need the approach of dusk to bring them out. But surely there were more
bicycles than usual? And such strangely naked-looking bicycles. They were
bumping across the common from all directions. Riding them were the sharp
pale youths who had looked so boyish when I first saw them in the High Street,
but so disturbing when I was closer that I had wondered if they had ever been
innocent.

Well, they were innocent today. And they held me for an hour while they
raced their bicycles around a miniature dirt-track close to the railway line on
the far side of the common. They were skid-kids, two teams of them –
Greyhounds and Panthers, according to a blackboard near the starting-point.
They raced four at a time, two from each team, and they jabbed their
iron-tipped leather speedway boots furiously on the pedals, they bucked and

skidded their machines on three furious circuits of the track. But the fury was quiet, so quiet. Tyres scraped in the dust, metal occasionally clinked against metal; yet from neither the riders nor the watchers who had somehow appeared at the low stick fence enclosing the track was there a sound.

I stared at the yellow-shirted Greyhounds and the green-shirted Panthers, and presently I realized that, irrespective of team colours, they formed two classes – the skilled and assured ones who went immediately to the front and remained there, and the straining followers who opened and shut their mouths in wordless desperation as they lunged for illusory openings.

Among the skilled ones was a youth wearing a black-and-white check cap. His face was expressionless, his lips did not part, and although his busy legs won him every other race – every one he competed in – he let no smile temper superiority that to me seemed contemptuous. I watched him closely. I admired him, then I was troubled by him. I tried to be interested in other riders, like the crew-cropped Panther whose silken green scarf lifted briefly in its owner's most strenuous efforts before falling as *his* hopes were doomed to fall. Always, though, I returned to that cap, that blank face.

For some time after I left them I could see those skid-kids going round and round and round. I could feel the intensity of the silence in which they laboured.

II

I had smoked my last cigarette. Even for me, this was fast smoking; I had set out with nearly a full packet.

I smiled at the thought of myself standing entranced by the stick fence, popping cigarette after cigarette into my mouth. No wonder my lips were tender, my throat parched.

Now I must visit my friends at the café, I *must* have cigarettes.

I longed for a cigarette. I wished I had saved one, only one.

The café was twenty minutes away. How could I last that long? Perhaps there was a packet in my other coat? But my other coat was back at the flat, and I did not want to return to the flat yet.

No, there was no alternative. You *will* do these silly things. Oh, you pest!

Perhaps I said this aloud. More likely, Patty Fenner needed no such excuse to stare. I wondered if she had been watching the skid-kids and had seen me; it would be something else for her to pass on to her mother, just as she was now passing on other gossip about me to a youth in drainpipe trousers. Patty was a kittenish-looking girl with a small cheeky body and a tiny white face; she had big brown eyes. I suppose she was pretty. To be honest, there was a time soon after we moved into the flat when I was able to compliment Mrs Fenner on the good looks of her children – and no reservations. I was friendly enough with her then to be told about her jolly times during the war. During the war she had apparently moved in higher social circles than she did now; she was especially tickled by the memory of a party where a fellow-guest had been an actor named (she said) Dean Jaguar. I used to study her old face, her greying blonde hair and her sagging figure, and I used to wonder why she did not talk of the blitz, why she talked only of parties. Her interest in pleasure was so obvious that I believe I felt warm towards her.

But that was ages ago. Before the trouble.

I made the mistake now of watching Patty and her boy friend. I should not have watched them, I should have taken the other path, the one past the pond end of the common. I could have reached the street that way.

Still, my mistake scarcely excused the abuse Patty threw at me.

'Big-head!' she shouted. 'Mind your milk-bottles!'

She shared the joke with her boy friend and off they went, shoulder to shoulder in delight.

Well, at least I knew where I stood with this Patty, this girl in the black duffle coat. She came out into the open. She shouted. She could be recognized.

The others, my other enemies, were so furtive, so teasing. If I were to tell, for instance, how I found myself beside one of them at the local cinema, people would want to know *How? What did he say? Did he touch you?* and so on. They would not think it important that he wore a curious spotted ring; they would not appreciate how subtle these others were.

Patty, at any rate, was not subtle. Childishly she called me Big-Head, added a reminder of the occasion her mother's night visitors kicked and smashed the bottles I had placed on the front steps; she wanted to set me thinking about the nastiness that followed my suggestion to Mrs Fenner that her visitors might at least have picked up the pieces. I had something to grasp when it was Patty's kind of insult.

So I was not too disturbed as I made my way along the path. Patty had taken my mind off the skid-kids, if not off my need for a cigarette.

III

I knew them as Henry and Tess. Why were they my friends? Because I ate often in their little café when Bernard's job took him out of London. Because they were at once affectionate and matter-of-fact in my presence. Because they reminded me in some ways of the people of my childhood. Also, though this affected me hardly at all, Henry had had war-time associations with New Zealanders and would sometimes ask me to repeat my assurances about the happy life awaiting the immigrant in New Zealand. I knew very well he had no deep interest in New Zealand, nor in me. But he was friendly and so was Tess and they committed me to nothing.

'Cigarettes, dear?' said Tess before I had reached the counter.

'I've been watching the Greyhounds and Panthers,' I told her.

'Yes, dear?' she said interestedly.

'One of the Greyhounds was particularly fast, Tess,' I said. 'He wore a check cap. Goodness, he was purposeful.'

'It keeps them out of mischief,' Tess said.

'They were *all* so purposeful,' I said, taking a cigarette from the packet she passed me. 'But the one in the check cap was successful, too. That seemed to make a difference, Tess.'

'Well, it keeps them out of mischief,' Tess said.

'The others would never be as fast as *he* was,' I said. 'But they wouldn't give up. And he knew they wouldn't give up. He knew they would always be there behind him. You know, Tess. *Striving*.'

'Yes, it keeps them out of mischief,' Tess said.

I wondered whether to have a cup of tea. I was the only customer in that shabby café and accordingly felt composed. 'Oh I *will* have one,' I said. 'One of your lovely cups of tea, Tess.'

I watched her put three cubes of sugar on the saucer.

Then Henry, who was carrying a vase of red and purple anemones, came from the kitchen and nodded to me. 'Nice enough day for you?'

'I've been on the common,' I told him.

'She's been watching the skid-kids,' Tess said.

'A nice day for the skid-kids,' Henry said. He put the flowers on a glass case of sandwiches and cakes.

'I thought they were so . . . so purposeful,' I told Henry. I drank some tea.

'It keeps them out of mischief,' Tess said.

'Perhaps so,' said .Henry, his gaze on my cigarette fingers. He had once suggested that a holder would keep my fingers from staining.

I lowered my hand.

A young couple entered the café; I must hurry.

I waited until I fancied Henry and Tess would not notice, then I stepped out into the High Street. Dusk was near enough now and there were more strollers. Noisy youths, men in tweed caps and belted gabardines, gaunt women and self-contented women, grubby barefoot kids and rosier kids with socks to their knees, dark-stockinged girls with amazed eyes and high hair.

I was well aware that if I could be pursued once I could be pursued any number of times. I had been pursued one day by two men in black coats, so I had to be always watchful, even on a Sunday afternoon in the High Street.

My trouble began . . . I suppose it began when I refused to lend Mrs Fenner the sugar she had sent Patty up for. I refused because I was tired of lending her sugar, feeling that if she could entertain as she did most nights she could afford to buy sugar. I was, I thought, reasonable about it; I am always reasonable. I gently warned Patty and her sisters that they must stop pestering me. I was working at the time, and it seemed I was no sooner home of a night than the begging knock sounded on the door. It was this, in fact, that helped to send me to the café when Bernard was out of town.

I am not saying, though, that it was the only cause of the trouble. An involved situation arose, for instance, because another tenant, a Miss Lily, used to come down from the attic to chat with me over a cup of tea. Mrs Fenner did not like Miss Lily and warned me in the early days of the spinster's vicious tongue, as she put it. Anyway, it was from Miss Lily I learned of Mrs Fenner's adventures. I don't believe I ever got them all in sequence, but they had much to do with a soldier-husband returning from the wars, booting out the fellow who had moved in while he was away, then moving out himself. Later there were other men. Oh, it was so sordid and my interest was strictly polite. Indeed, I doubt if Miss Lily would have kept it up if Bernard, who sometimes joined our little tea parties, had not encouraged her. I don't know how often he murmured 'Freudian' as he drew on his pipe and nodded for her to continue. And although 'Freudian' is his favourite irrelevancy whenever people's relationships are being discussed, his use of it has never depressed me as much as it did during Miss Lily's visits. Naïvely, I was pleased when she found herself a room in East Finchley; there would be no more tea parties, no more dirty looks from Mrs Fenner, I would have peace.

I was not to know that Mrs Fenner, the star tenant, had some sort of influence over the landlord, a dentist who came across from Hampstead once a month to collect the rent and the meter coins. How otherwise could she have persuaded him to let the attic to the Liverpool newly-weds? At first they were sociable, so sociable that the girl once told me there was something about her husband, who was short and wore rimless glasses and smirked, that frightened her. She did not elaborate, and when the bumping began on the floor above I supposed it was connected with whatever was frightening the wife. This bumping, which was like furniture being moved or a broom continually whacking bare boards, went on for hours at a time. I said nothing, I did not complain. Yet soon the girl would not look at me if she saw me on the stairs or near the bathroom we shared. So that I became certain Mrs Fenner had been speaking to her about me. The old girl was after me, sure enough.

Well, that was how the trouble began. But this Sunday afternoon, surprisingly, I was not pursued. I say surprisingly because only the other night I had given Mrs Fenner a new grievance. I had overheard a front-steps conversation between Patty and a girl named Elsie, a frequent visitor to the Fenners. It was late and I was sitting smoking a cigarette at the street-side window of our flat; the voices, these voices, meant nothing to me, only that Elsie had evidently been to the local and was quarrelsome. My window was open, I could not *help* hearing what was said. Elsie said something about Patty's mother 'knocking off' some silverware, a remark which instantly had Patty whispering urgently about the need to talk quietly – an extraordinary need for any Fenner to seem aware of, I must say. 'Knocking off' I took to mean thieving, but I did not gasp at the revelation or, I thought, react in any other way. It may be that I moved in my chair; at any rate, Patty was suddenly looking up at the window and yelling 'Old cow! Mind your own business!' I imagine she lost no time in telling her mother about Elsie's indiscretion and my nosiness. For my part, I left the bedroom and went into the living-room, and I looked at Bernard who was absorbed, as he had been for nearly a fortnight, in a book about the French Foreign Legion. But I did not interrupt him. Why should I? 'Your imagination in form, eh?' he would have said.

IV

My husband's visitor this Sunday was a young man in well-cut grey trousers, navy blazer, white shirt, black-and-yellow tie and brown suède shoes. I gave him a happy smile. It was a happy smile because I had been undetected by the Fenners on my way up the stairs.

'Ah, the wanderer returns!' said Bernard.

He was happy, too. He was happy because he had a visitor, somebody with whom he could discuss his career as a window-frame salesman – happy, to be fair, because he liked the company of enterprising people.

The young man's name was Don. The usual things were said – yes, I loved London; yes, it was stimulating to be in a city where there was so much to do, so much to see.

'She's a dinkum Kiwi, our Joan,' smiled Bernard, waving his pipe. 'Don't let her fool you, boy. She'd go back like a shot on the first boat if she could.'

Don looked astonished. 'You *would*?'

How did it go? Like this: 'When I remember the years I wasted back there, when I think how bored I'd be at this moment. . . .' I shook my head.

Don was relieved. 'I see what you mean,' he said.

'Besides, I have Bernard to think of,' I said. 'Bernard has so many chances over here.'

Bernard, of course, put in: 'The perfect wife, Don.'

And that, I reckoned, was as good a cue as I was likely to get. 'Mind if I leave you two alone for a few minutes?' I asked. 'I *must* take off my shoes.'

'Go right ahead, honey,' said Bernard. 'Don and I can cope. Eh, Don?'

I went to the bedroom and I looked from the window. Dusk darkened the sycamore in the garden across the street.

I lit a cigarette and walked from the brown-green-orange rug near the window to the dark-green rug near the door, then back again, and I continued walking from one rug to the other. I knew that while Bernard had his own entertainment primarily in mind when he invited people around, he also hoped they would help to divert me. I should meet nice people, he said. And his visitors were certainly nice. Nice in the way you expect New Zealanders to be in London. Unfortunately, I was fed up with ambitious young men and excited travellers. I recalled the couple, back from a car tour, who were full of an adventure that had occurred in Berlin: the husband had joined a group of tourists staring at a Russian colonel and presently had shouted, 'Up you, Old

Horse!' He had spoken these cheeky words to a Russian and, my God, he had escaped! I recalled the man who had driven to one of the Duke of Edinburgh's polo meetings and had later, during a fuss about parked cars, found himself next to the car in which the Duke sat, and, my God, if the Duke hadn't winked at him! All of which pleased Bernard very much. Wasn't it exhilarating to think of New Zealanders touring Europe, New Zealanders being winked at by Royalty! As for what the visitors made of Bernard: I expect they were satisfied, he generally listened attentively (with clever interjections) before starting his own contribution. Only once had he been disconcerted. Why he should bring a Canadian psychologist to the flat puzzled me then and does now, it really does. Why he should flounder into Couéism when his none-too-searching questions had already disclosed that the psychologist, besides disapproving of generalizations about complexes, was sophisticated enough to take an irreverent view of Freud and, I'm bound to say, of Jung and Adler as well – why Bernard should mention Coué did not puzzle me then and does not now. I felt sorry for him and when the edgy psychologist had gone I soothed him and flattered him until he was back to feeling that every day in every way he was getting better and better. . . .

I lit another cigarette and told myself I should be out there preparing a meal; even now Bernard would be pelting his guest with cheerful references to the inner man, light relief after his grave account of how he intended entering politics when he eventually returned to New Zealand. Oh, perhaps another quarter-hour, I decided.

I stopped by the window. There was nobody beneath the sycamore. Nor could I hear the Fenners. But of course they always saved their best efforts until they knew I was alone; they did not bother Bernard at all – or, if they did, not so much so that he was tempted to examine his belief that this was an excellent flat; so cheap, so handy to the buses, so handy to the High Street, so handy to the common . . . far enough out to give one a feeling of earth rather than stone close by.

I drew the curtains, crossed to the light switch, waited a moment after switching on the light, then forced myself to go to the dressing-table mirror.

V

'The important thing,' Bernard told us over the remains of the meal, 'is to *make* them accept you. What's a compromise here and there? If they like to think I'm an Australian, let them – if it will help me make a sale. If they're happy about spotting my accent they're more likely to save me a lot of time-wasting wheedling.' He raised his eyebrows.

'Not a dinkum Kiwi attitude,' Don joked.

'How's that?' Bernard asked seriously. 'Look at it this way, Don – '

'I was kidding,' Don said.

'Don't you agree it's the tendency for the New Zealander to be sat upon?' asked Bernard. 'You get a lot of New Zealanders bringing over easy-going New Zealand ideas. And they don't suit the place. Correct?'

'Is it a bad thing to be easy-going?' asked Don.

'Now that's the question!' cried Bernard. 'You see, Don, my theory is that people over here reckon New Zealanders are only colonials after all – they can be pushed about. The Aussie, on the other hand, has always made it bloody clear he *won't* be pushed about. That's the Aussie way. The Kiwi way is to say "She's jake" and take what comes. The Kiwi doesn't hit back. The Aussie hits back. Why else do the English, with *their* dreadful accents, think the Aussie accent is so dreadful? It's because the Aussies get under their skins. The Aussies are tough. You *must* be tough over here.'

'I see what you mean,' Don said. 'You mean that's why you don't mind being mistaken for an Australian?'

'It's a compliment,' Bernard laughed. 'But, boy, do they hate me behind my back!' He gazed at Don. 'I didn't get this far by worrying about *that* sort of thing, though. Never did care what people said about me. I was a depression kid, you know. My people didn't have much money, so I left school before I wanted to. But that didn't stop me from getting an education, Don. What if I did have to pick it all up myself? It's the kind of education that sticks, in my opinion.' He pointed his pipe at me. 'Take Joan,' he said. 'She came from a humble country environment – small-town, like myself – but her people had just that little extra in the way of cash, they could afford to send her to High School and University. Now I don't want to boast, Don, but I think if you were to ask Joan whether she thought my course in self-education had been a success – I reckon she'd back me up on that. Eh, Joan?'

It was difficult to be still. I wanted to be away from them. 'Bernard is an enthusiastic reader,' I told Don.

Don noted this pensively.

'I read and I *think* about what I'm reading,' Bernard said. 'A lot of readers skim, you know, Don. I'm not a skimmer. Once I take on an Upton Sinclair, for instance, there's no holding me until I've got that book whacked. Same with anything else I tackle. Even music. Nearest we had to music in *my* childhood home was *Hallelujah I'm a Bum*. These days I can listen to Chopin, say, or Puccini for hours – *and* enjoy them. I'm a great man for opera – '

I happened to be sitting at this moment on the ugly old sofa under the living-room's high windows. Striped cottage-weave curtains fell behind the sofa and one of them was not quite in place and I found myself looking through the crack and, since it was now night and I could see nothing, thinking of the view as it had been on a certain evening in late summer. It was one of the evenings when Bernard was away peddling window-frames; otherwise there should have been nothing special about it. But I remembered, as though it were only yesterday, how I sat in the long dusk and watched from this window. Past the overgrown arbour in the garden of our place – the garden we were not permitted to use because it went with the ground-floor flats, including Mrs Fenner's – was the tall spidery tree that stayed bare longer than any other tree in the neighbourhood. Smoke drifted among the trees in the gardens that stretched away from me towards the higher ground where the red buses went by. There were apples and pears in these gardens, there were lawns and flower-beds, there were television aerials on many of the chimney-pots silhouetted above the red- and grey-brick homes. Indications of cosiness. Had it been envy I felt that night? I could not remember. I remembered wishing I had written to my sisters back home, even to my acquaintances back there. But I had nothing to tell my sisters, they who had frowned about Bernard ('Is he *really* your type, Sis?') and about England ('Isn't it *terribly* distant, Sis?'). Nor did I wish my one-time acquaintances to talk of me; let those who knew us be content with Bernard's breezy bulletins. So it was only a passing weakness that night; the letters remained unwritten. How long, I now asked myself, must exile last? One of Bernard's visitors, a journalist named Plimpton, had said it was two years before he 'got the feel of the place' and another two years before he decided that London was 'the expatriate's only possible home'. But how long for me? Three years? Four? Five?

'I reckon about five years, Don,' said Bernard airily. 'Time enough for a fast worker, eh? Mind you, if I'm an executive at the end of five years, I'm not likely to turn it in. I'm working on another angle too – but keep this under your hat. I might be able to work it so they send me to New Zealand. They're thinking of branching out with factories in the colonies – the Commonwealth. And if they want somebody for New Zealand . . . eh?'

'I see you have it all planned,' smiled Don.

'I'm right on top of things, Don,' said Bernard. 'That's the only way to be, take it from me. Joan will tell you. Joan, you'd agree with that, wouldn't you? I've always been on top of things – especially since we came to England.'

I looked at Don. I said: 'Before then, too.'

'Especially since we came to England,' said Bernard. 'But that's enough of that, Don my lad. A man needs a drink after that lot. I'll take you down to my local. Always introduce the boys to my local.'

Always? Apart from a certain Canadian psychologist, I thought.

Don looked at me.

'That's all right, mate,' said Bernard. 'Joan doesn't want us cluttering up the place. Prefers to be on her own. She doesn't like the noise. Isn't that right, honey? I tell you, Don, she left her job – good job as a typist at the Temple – she left there because it was too noisy. The Temple!' He laughed.

I could see that Don was not convinced. So I said with a smile: 'I wanted a holiday.' That sounded lame, so I added: 'It was so foggy.' Then, briskly: 'I must look for another job.'

'Don't worry, honey,' said Bernard. 'You have a good rest. We'll never be short of cash while I'm in gear. Ready, Don? Want you to sample an ale I regard rather highly. I won't be long, Joan.' He pecked my cheek, said: 'Not too long, anyway.'

'Have a good time,' I told them. 'Mind the traffic.'

'She's kidding,' I heard Bernard telling Don as they went out. 'No traffic in this neck of the wood.'

VI

Perhaps he was right, I thought as I did the dishes. Perhaps I *had* left the Temple job because of the noise. Voices, after all, were noise. Ordinary voices. Somebody speaks to somebody else; the voice is meant to be heard by a third person – by me, for instance. An employer speaks of what *he* believes to be a fact, and in his voice is much more than the wish to correct; there is smugness, contempt, irritation, anger. Seldom compassion. Oh, and don't forget the voices from faces that twist in pity when *you* speak.

I clattered the dishes. 'Dear Bernard,' I said, 'there is noise – and noise.'

Mrs Fenner obviously believed the same. For her radio suddenly surged into a blast of 'Stars Shine in Your Eyes', and I wondered why the radio did not fall apart, I wondered how it was possible for a radio to be so loud and not fall apart.

I put the dishes on the gas-stove rack and drew the curtains around the corner that served as a kitchenette. Bernard would expect a white shirt for the morning; shiny collar, of course. His face would drop if the shirt were not pressed and gleaming when he returned from the local. But what could I do against that blasting below? It would persist too; Bernard's departure had been noted.

I turned on our own radio and selected one of those B.B.C. 'portraits' in which a succession of players, pretending to be contemporaries of the victim (in this case, Dr Johnson), recite breathlessly in voices that are now stern, now chatty, now coy, and so on. I found it frightening and, thankful Bernard was missing it ('The Great Cham once said . . .'), turned off the radio and went to the bedroom.

Without switching on the bedroom light, I lit a cigarette and walked from rug to rug until the cigarette burned down. Then I lit another cigarette and sat on the edge of the bed.

I heard whistling. What sound, if any, did a blackbird make at night? Was this mimicry?

I did not go to the window.

Presently the whistling stopped, and I was left wondering: *Why have Henry and Tess changed?*

I recalled the curiosity with which Henry in particular had eyed me in the café today. His manner, the way he carried the anemones. Like a man who had been told things and was not yet certain how to handle me. Essentially good-natured, he had been reluctant to offend – or to rouse? And Tess, Tess could have been talking of an imbecile when she told Henry how I had been watching the skid-kids. Repeating her comment about keeping the skid-kids out of mischief! There was more to *that* than I had realized at the time. How obvious! She might as well have added 'Get the point?'

Still, I tried not to be bitter. I must be reasonable. Really they were a good and simple pair; it was embarrassing for them to have me in their café. Very well, I would spare them embarrassment; I would stop going to the café.

By the time I returned to the living-room to iron Bernard's shirt it was as though losing one's friends were something that happened every day.

VII

Bernard was, as usual after his pub visits, very solicitous. His solicitude was intended, I knew, to cover up ale-prompted elation.

He thanked me for ironing the shirt.

I asked him if he had enjoyed himself.

'Got trapped into darts,' he said. 'That Don fellow, he's an ass with darts. In other ways too, eh?'

'He seems earnest,' I said.

'I think he's finding the going a bit tough over here,' Bernard said, shaking his head. 'Catching on that London can be heartbreaking.' He thought this over, then remembered the next questions. 'What sort of day did you have, honey? Where did you go this afternoon? How was the walk?'

I shrugged. 'Same old walk. Same people. Same dogs.' He was staring. 'Yes?' I asked.

'Your lipstick,' he said. 'Your lipstick's lopsided, honey. Doesn't cover your lips properly.'

'Have you only just noticed?' I asked. 'Your friend Don noticed.' I laughed. 'It fascinated him.'

Bernard frowned. 'You put it like that on purpose?'

'I *intended* adjusting it,' I said. 'I forgot.'

'Looks odd,' he said. Then he was suspicious. 'Have they been bothering you again?'

'Who?' I asked, wide-eyed.

'Down below,' he said.

'Mother Fenner tortured her radio as soon as you went,' I said. 'And Patty was hostile earlier on – when I was watching the skid-kids.' I spoke calmly.

'Skid-kids?' he asked.

'Greyhounds and Panthers,' I said. 'On the common.'

'You mean you watched those skid-kids all afternoon?'

'I couldn't stop looking,' I told him.

'What about the noise?' he asked.

'There was no noise,' I said.

'Honey, I heard the noise from here,' Bernard said. 'I could hear the crowd. I mentioned it to Don. I said to him there must be something doing on the common.'

'It was the silence that surprised me,' I said. 'Those boys were so quiet – ' I stopped.

'What's the matter?'

'Nothing's the matter.'

'Something *is*,' he said.

'No, nothing,' I said.

I was thinking of myself in a black-and-white check cap, pedalling round and round and round – and of Bernard trying very hard to catch me.

I wished I could weep.

JANET FRAME

Dossy

Only on the shadows, sang out Dossy, and the little girl with straight fair hair sang out answering, only on the shadows, and the two of them went hopping and skipping very carefully for three blocks, and then they got tired, and they forgot, and they stopped to pick marigolds through the crack in the corner fence, but only Dossy could reach them because she was bigger. Pick me a marigold, Dossy, to put in my hair, said the little girl and Dossy picked a big yellow flower and she had to bend down to stick it in the little girl's hair.

– Race you to the convent gate, she said, and together the two of them tore along the footpath and Dossy won, Dossy won easily.

– I'm bigger, she said.

And the little girl looked up at Dossy's bigness and supposed that Dossy must live in a big house to match. Everything matched thought the little girl. Mother and Father. Mother singing and Father singing. Mother washing the dishes and father drying. Mother in her blue dress and Father in his black suit.

And when you were small you did things that small people did, grandma said, and when you were big like Dossy you did things the grown-up way. And the little girl thought that Dossy must live in a big house to match her bigness. A big house at the end of a long long street. With a garden. And a plum-tree. And a piano in the front room. And a piano-stool to go round and round on. And lollies in a blue tin on the mantelpiece for father to reach up to and say have a striped one chicken, they last longer.

The little girl put her hand in Dossy's and said, Can I come to live with you, Dossy. Can I live in your house.

And Dossy looked down at the little girl with her shiny new shoes on and her neat blue dress and her thick hair-ribbon, and then she looked down at her own dirty shoes and turned up dress from her aunties, and she drew away her hand that was dirty and sticky with marigolds and said nothing, but went over to the fence to peep through at the nuns. The little girl followed her and together they looked through at the nuns. They watched them walking up and down with their hands folded in front and their eyes staring straight ahead, and the little girl thought I'll be a nun some day and wear black and white and have a black and white nightie, and I'll pray all day and sit under the plum-tree and perhaps God won't mind if I get hungry and eat two or three plums, and every night I'll comb out my mother's long golden hair with a gold comb and I'll have a black and white bed.

Dossy, said the little girl, will you be a nun with me?

Dossy giggled and giggled. I don't think, she said.

The nuns heard someone laughing and they stopped at the gate to see who it was. They saw a little girl playing ball by herself on the footpath.

It's little Dossy Park, they said. With no mother and living in that poky little house in Hart Street and playing by herself all the time, goodness knows what she'll turn out to be.

The Reservoir

It was said to be four or five miles along the gully, past orchards and farms, paddocks filled with cattle, sheep, wheat, gorse, and the squatters of the land who were the rabbits eating like modern sculpture into the hills, though how could we know anything of modern sculpture, we knew nothing but the Warrior in the main street with his wreaths of poppies on Anzac Day, the gnomes weeping in the Gardens because the seagulls perched on their green caps and showed no respect, and how important it was for birds, animals and people, especially children, to show respect!

And that is why for so long we obeyed the command of the grownups and never walked as far as the forbidden Reservoir, but were content to return 'tired but happy' (as we wrote in our school compositions), answering the question, Where did you walk today? with a suspicion of blackmail, 'Oh, nearly, nearly to the Reservoir!'

The Reservoir was the end of the world; beyond it, you fell; beyond it were paddocks of thorns, strange cattle, strange farms, legendary people whom we would never know or recognize even if they walked among us on a Friday night downtown when we went to follow the boys and listen to the Salvation Army Band and buy a milk shake in the milk bar and then return home to find that everything was all right and safe, that our mother had not run away and caught the night train to the North Island, that our father had not shot himself with worrying over the bills, but had in fact been downtown himself and had bought the usual Friday night treat, a bag of licorice allsorts and a bag of chocolate roughs, from Woolworth's.

The Reservoir haunted our lives. We never knew one until we came to this town; we had used pump water. But here, in our new house, the water ran from the taps as soon as we turned them on, and if we were careless and left them on, our father would shout, as if the affair were his personal concern, 'Do you want the Reservoir to run dry?'

That frightened us. What should we do if the Reservoir ran dry? Would we die of thirst like Burke and Wills in the desert?

'The Reservoir,' our mother said, 'gives pure water, water safe to drink without boiling it.'

The water was in a different class, then, from the creek which flowed through the gully; yet the creek had its source in the Reservoir. Why had it not received the pampering attention of officialdom which strained weed and earth, cockabullies and trout and eels, from our tap water? Surely the Reservoir was not entirely pure?

'Oh no,' they said, when we inquired. We learned that the water from the Reservoir had been 'treated'. We supposed this to mean that during the night men in light-blue uniforms with sacks over their shoulders crept beyond the circle of pine trees which enclosed the Reservoir, and emptied the contents of the sacks into the water, to dissolve dead bodies and prevent the decay of teeth.

Then, at times, there would be news in the paper, discussed by my mother with the neighbours over the back fence. Children had been drowned in the Reservoir.

'No child,' the neighbour would say, 'ought to be allowed near the Reservoir.'

'I tell mine to keep strictly away,' my mother would reply.

And for so long we obeyed our mother's command, on our favourite walks along the gully simply following the untreated cast-off creek which we loved and which flowed day and night in our heads in all its detail – the wild sweet peas, boiled-lolly pink, and the mint growing along the banks; the exact spot in the water where the latest dead sheep could be found, and the stink of its bloated flesh and floating wool, an allowable earthy stink which we accepted with pleasant revulsion and which did not prompt the 'inky-pinky I smell Stinkie' rhyme which referred to offensive human beings only. We knew where the water was shallow and could be paddled in, where forts could be made from the rocks; we knew the frightening deep places where the eels lurked and the weeds were tangled in gruesome shapes; we knew the jumping places, the mossy stones with their dangers, limitations, and advantages; the sparkling places where the sun trickled beside the water, upon the stones; the bogs made by roaming cattle, trapping some of them to death; their gaunt telltale bones; the little valleys with their new growth of lush grass where the creek had 'changed its course', and no longer flowed.

'The creek has changed its course,' our mother would say, in a tone which implied terror and a sense of strangeness, as if a tragedy had been enacted.

We knew the moods of the creek, its levels of low-flow, half-high-flow, high-flow which all seemed to relate to interference at its source – the Reservoir. If one morning the water turned the colour of clay and crowds of bubbles were passengers on every suddenly swift wave hurrying by, we would look at one another and remark with the fatality and reverence which attends a visitation or prophecy,

'The creek's going on high-flow. They must be doing something at the Reservoir.'

By afternoon the creek would be on high-flow, turbulent, muddy, unable to be jumped across or paddled in or fished in, concealing beneath a swelling fluid darkness whatever evil which 'they', the authorities, had decided to purge so swiftly and secretly from the Reservoir.

For so long, then, we obeyed our parents, and never walked as far as the Reservoir. Other things concerned us, other curiosities, fears, challenges. The school year ended. I got a prize, a large yellow book the colour of cat's mess. Inside it were editions of newspapers, *The Worms' Weekly*, supposedly written by worms, snails, spiders. For the first part of the holidays we spent the time sitting in the long grass of our front lawn nibbling the stalks of shamrock and reading insect newspapers and relating their items to the lives of those living on our front lawn down among the summer-dry roots of the couch, tinkertailor, daisy, dandelion, shamrock, clover, and ordinary 'grass'. High summer came. The blowsy old red roses shed their petals to the regretful refrain uttered by our mother year after year at the same time, 'I should have made potpourri, I have a wonderful recipe for potpourri in Dr Chase's Book.'

Our mother never made the potpourri. She merely quarrelled with our father over how to pronounce it.

The days became unbearably long and hot. Our Christmas presents were broken or too boring to care about. Celluloid dolls had loose arms and legs and rifts in their bright pink bodies; the invisible ink had poured itself out in secret messages; diaries frustrating in their smallness (two lines to a day) had been filled in for the whole of the coming year. . . . Days at the beach were tedious, with no room in the bathing sheds so that we were forced to undress in the common room downstairs with its floor patched with wet and trailed with footmarks and sand and its tiny barred window (which made me believe that I was living in the French Revolution).

Rumours circled the burning world. The sea was drying up, soon you could paddle or walk to Australia. Sharks had been seen swimming inside the breakwater; one shark attacked a little boy and bit off his you-know-what.

We swam. We wore bathing togs all day. We gave up cowboys and ranches; and baseball and sledding; and 'those games' where we mimicked grown-up life, loving and divorcing each other, kissing and slapping, taking secret paramours when our husband was working out of town. Everything exhausted us. Cracks appeared in the earth; the grass was bled yellow; the ground was littered with beetle shells and snail shells; flies came in from the unofficial rubbish-dump at the back of the house; the twisting flypapers hung from the ceiling; a frantic buzzing filled the room as the flypapers became crowded. Even the cat put out her tiny tongue, panting in the heat.

We realized, and were glad, that school would soon reopen. What was school like? It seemed so long ago, it seemed as if we had never been to school, surely we had forgotten everything we had learned, how frightening, thrilling and strange it would all seem! Where would we go on the first day, who would teach us, what were the names of the new books?

Who would sit beside us, who would be our best friend?

The earth crackled in early-autumn haze and still the February sun dried the world; even at night the rusty sheet of roofing-iron outside by the cellar stayed warm, but with rows of sweat-marks on it; the days were still long, with night face to face with morning and almost nothing in-between but a snatch of turning sleep with the blankets on the floor and the windows wide open to moths with their bulging lamplit eyes moving through the dark and their grandfather bodies knocking, knocking upon the walls.

Day after day the sun still waited to pounce. We were tired, our skin itched, our sunburn had peeled and peeled again, the skin on our feet was hard, there was dust in our hair, our bodies clung with the salt of sea-bathing and sweat, the towels were harsh with salt.

School soon, we said again, and were glad; for lessons gave shade to rooms and corridors; cloakrooms were cold and sunless. Then, swiftly, suddenly, disease came to the town. Infantile Paralysis. Black headlines in the paper, listing the number of cases, the number of deaths. Children everywhere, out in the country, up north, down south, two streets away.

The schools did not reopen. Our lessons came by post, in smudged print on rough white paper; they seemed makeshift and false, they inspired distrust, they could not compete with the lure of the sun still shining, swelling, the world would go up in cinders, the days were too long, there was nothing to do, there was nothing to do; the lessons were dull; in the front room with the navy-blue blind half down the window and the tiny splits of light showing through, and the lesson papers sometimes covered with unexplained blots of ink as if the machine which had printed them had broken down or rebelled, the lessons were even more dull.

Ancient Egypt and the flooding of the Nile!

The Nile, when we possessed a creek of our own with individual flooding!

'Well let's go along the gully, along by the creek,' we would say, tired with all these.

Then one day when our restlessness was at its height, when the flies buzzed like bees in the flypapers, and the warped wood of the house cracked its knuckles out of boredom, the need for something to do in the heat, we found once again the only solution to our unrest.

Someone said, 'What's the creek on?'

'Half-high flow.'

'Good.'

So we set out, in our bathing suits, and carrying switches of willow.

'Keep your sun hats on!' our mother called.

All right. We knew. Sunstroke when the sun clipped you over the back of the head, striking you flat on the ground. Sunstroke. Lightning. Even tidal waves were threatening us on this southern coast. The world was full of alarm.

'And don't go as far as the Reservoir!'

We dismissed the warning. There was enough to occupy us along the gully without our visiting the Reservoir. First, the couples. We liked to find a courting couple and follow them and when, as we knew they must do because they were tired or for other reasons, they found a place in the grass and lay down together, we liked to make jokes about them, amongst ourselves. 'Just wait for him to kiss her,' we would say. 'Watch. There. A beaut. Smack.'

Often we giggled and lingered even after the couple had observed us. We were waiting for them to do it. Every man and woman did it, we knew that for a fact. We speculated about technical details. Would he wear a frenchie? If he didn't wear a frenchie then she would start having a baby and be forced to get rid of it by drinking gin. Frenchies, by the way, were for sale in Woolworth's. Some said they were fingerstalls, but we knew they were frenchies and sometimes we would go downtown and into Woolworth's just to look at the frenchies for sale. We hung around the counter, sniggering. Sometimes we nearly died laughing, it was so funny.

After we tired of spying on the couples we would shout after them as we went our way.

> Pound, shillings and pence,
> a man fell over the fence,
> he fell on a lady,
> and squashed out a baby,
> pound, shillings and pence!

Sometimes a slight fear struck us – what if a man fell on us like that and squashed out a chain of babies?

Our other pastime along the gully was robbing the orchards, but this summer day the apples were small green hard and hidden by leaves. There were no couples either. We had the gully to ourselves. We followed the creek, whacking our sticks, gossiping and singing, but we stopped, immediately silent, when someone – sister or brother – said, 'Let's go to the Reservoir!'

A feeling of dread seized us. We knew, as surely as we knew our names and our address Thirty-three Stour Street Ohau Otago South Island New Zealand Southern Hemisphere The World, that we would some day visit the Reservoir, but the time seemed almost as far away as leaving school, getting a job, marrying.

And then there was the agony of deciding the right time – how did one decide these things?

'We've been told not to, you know,' one of us said timidly.

That was me. Eating bread and syrup for tea had made my hair red, my skin too, so that I blushed easily, and the grownups guessed if I told a lie.

'It's a long way,' said my little sister.

'Coward!'

But it *was* a long way, and perhaps it would take all day and night, perhaps we would have to sleep there among the pine trees with the owls hooting and the old needle-filled warrens which now reached to the centre of the earth where pools of molten lead bubbled, waiting to seize us if we tripped, and then there was the crying sound made by the trees, a sound of speech at its loneliest level where the meaning is felt but never explained, and it goes on and on in a kind of despair, trying to reach a point of understanding.

We knew that pine trees spoke in this way. We were lonely listening to them because we knew we could never help them to say it, whatever they were trying to say, for if the wind who was so close to them could not help them, how could we?

Oh no, we could not spend the night at the Reservoir among the pine trees.

'Billy Whittaker and his gang have been to the Reservoir, Billy Whittaker and the Green Feather gang, one afternoon.'

'Did he say what it was like?'

'No, he never said.'

'He's been in an iron lung.'

That was true. Only a day or two ago our mother had been reminding us in an ominous voice of the fact which roused our envy just as much as our dread, 'Billy Whittaker was in an iron lung two years ago. Infantile paralysis.'

Some people were lucky. None of us dared to hope that we would ever be surrounded by the glamour of an iron lung; we would have to be content all our lives with paltry flesh lungs.

'Well are we going to the Reservoir or not?'

That was someone trying to sound bossy like our father, – 'Well am I to have salmon sandwiches or not, am I to have lunch at all today or not?'

We struck our sticks in the air. They made a whistling sound. They were supple and young. We had tried to make musical instruments out of them, time after time we hacked at the willow and the elder to make pipes to blow our music, but no sound came but our own voices. And why did two sticks rubbed together not make fire? Why couldn't we ever *make* anything out of the bits of the world lying about us?

An aeroplane passed in the sky. We craned our necks to read the writing on the underwing, for we collected aeroplane numbers.

The plane was gone, in a glint of sun.

'Are we?' someone said.

'If there's an eclipse you can't see at all. The birds stop singing and go to bed.'

'Well are we?'

Certainly we were. We had not quelled all our misgiving, but we set out to follow the creek to the Reservoir.

What is it? I wondered. They said it was a lake. I thought it was a bundle of darkness and great wheels which peeled and sliced you like an apple and drew you toward them with demonic force, in the same way that you were drawn beneath the wheels of a train if you stood too near the edge of the platform. That was the terrible danger when the Limited came rushing in and you had to approach to kiss arriving aunts.

We walked on and on, past wild sweet peas, clumps of cutty grass, horse mushrooms, ragwort, gorse, cabbage trees; and then, at the end of the gully, we came to strange territory, fences we did not know, with the barbed wire tearing at our skin and at our skirts put on over our bathing suits because we felt cold though the sun stayed in the sky.

We passed huge trees that lived with their heads in the sky, with their great arms and joints creaking with age and the burden of being trees, and their mazed and linked roots rubbed bare of earth, like bones with the flesh cleaned from them. There were strange gates to be opened or climbed over, new directions to be argued and plotted, notices which said TRESPASSERS WILL BE PROSECUTED BY ORDER. And there was the remote immovable sun shedding without gentleness its influence of burning upon us and upon the town, looking down from its heavens and considering our infantile-paralysis epidemic, and the children tired of holidays and wanting to go back to school with the new stiff books with their crackling pages, the scrubbed ruler with the sun rising on one side amidst the twelfths, tenths, millimetres, the new pencils to be sharpened with the pencil shavings flying in long pickets and light-brown curls scalloped with red or blue; the brown school, the bare floors, the clump clump in the corridors on wet days!

We came to a strange paddock, a bull-paddock with its occupant planted deep in the long grass, near the gate, a jersey bull polished like a wardrobe, burnished like copper, heavy beams creaking in the wave and flow of the grass.

'Has it got a ring through its nose? Is it a real bull or a steer?'

Its nose was ringed which meant that its savagery was tamed, or so we thought; it could be tethered and led; even so, it had once been savage and it kept its pride, unlike the steers who pranced and huddled together and ran like water through the paddocks, made no impression, quarried no massive shape against the sky.

The bull stood alone.

Had not Mr Bennet been gored by a bull, his own tame bull, and been rushed to Glenham Hospital for thirty-three stitches? Remembering Mr Bennet we crept cautiously close to the paddock fence, ready to escape.

Someone said, 'Look, it's pawing the ground!'

A bull which pawed the ground was preparing for a charge. We escaped quickly through the fence. Then, plucking courage, we skirted the bushes on the far side of the paddock, climbed through the fence, and continued our walk to the Reservoir.

We had lost the creek between deep banks. We saw it now before us, and hailed it with more relief than we felt, for in its hidden course through the bull-paddock it had undergone change, it had adopted the shape, depth, mood of foreign water, foaming in a way we did not recognize as belonging to our special creek, giving no hint of its depth. It seemed to flow close to its concealed bed, not wishing any more to communicate with us. We realized with dismay that we had suddenly lost possession of our creek. Who had taken it? Why did it not belong to us any more? We hit our sticks in the air and forgot our dismay. We grew cheerful.

Till someone said that it was getting late, and we reminded one another that during the day the sun doesn't seem to move, it just remains pinned with a drawing pin against the sky, and then, while you are not looking, it suddenly slides down quick as the chopped-off head of a golden eel, into the sea, making everything in the world go dark.

'That's only in the tropics!'

We were not in the tropics. The divisions of the world in the atlas, the different coloured cubicles of latitude and longitude fascinated us.

'The sand freezes in the desert at night. Ladies wear bits of sand. . . .'

'grains . . .'

'grains or bits of sand as necklaces, and the camels . . .'

'with necks like snails . . .'

'with horns, do they have horns?'

'Minnie Stocks goes with boys. . . .'

'I know who your boy is, I know who your boy is. . . .'

> Waiting by the garden gate,
> Waiting by the garden gate . . .

'We'll never get to the Reservoir!'

'Whose idea was it?'

'I've strained my ankle!'

Someone began to cry. We stopped walking.

'I've strained my ankle!'

There was an argument.

'It's not strained, it's sprained.'

'strained.'

'sprained.'

'All right sprained then. I'll have to wear a bandage, I'll have to walk on crutches. . . .'

'I had crutches once. Look. I've got a scar where I fell off my stilts. It's a white scar, like a centipede. It's on my shins.'

'Shins! Isn't it a funny word? Shins. Have you ever been kicked in the shins?'

'shins, funnybone . . .'
'It's humerus. . . .'
'knuckles . . .'
'a sprained ankle . . .'
'a strained ankle . . .'
'a whitlow, an ingrown toenail the roots of my hair warts spinal meningitis infantile paralysis . . .'
'Infantile paralysis, Infantile paralysis you have to be wheeled in a chair and wear irons on your legs and your knees knock together. . . .'
'Once you're in an iron lung you can't get out, they lock it, like a cage. . . .'
'You go in the amberlance . . .'
'*ambulance* . . .'
'amberlance . . .'
'amberlance to the hostible . . .'
'the *hospital*, an *amberlance to the hospital* . . .'
'Infantile Paralysis . . .'
'Friar's Balsam! Friar's Balsam!'
'Baxter's Lung Preserver, Baxter's Lung Preserver!'
'Syrup of Figs, California Syrup of Figs!'
'The creek's going on high-flow!'
Yes, there were bubbles on the surface, and the water was turning muddy. Our doubts were dispelled. It was the same old creek, and there, suddenly, just ahead, was a plantation of pine trees, and already the sighing sound of it reached our ears and troubled us. We approached it, staying close to the banks of our newly claimed creek, until once again the creek deserted us, flowing its own private course where we could not follow, and we found ourselves among the pine trees, a narrow strip of them, and beyond lay a vast surface of sparkling water, dazzling our eyes, its centre chopped by tiny grey waves. Not a lake, nor a river, nor a sea.
'The Reservoir!'
The damp smell of the pine needles caught in our breath. There were no birds, only the constant sighing of the trees. We could see the water clearly now; it lay, except for the waves beyond the shore, in an almost perfect calm which we knew to be deceptive – else why were people so afraid of the Reservoir? The fringe of young pines on the edge, like toy trees, subjected to the wind, sighed and told us their sad secrets. In the Reservoir there was an appearance of neatness which concealed a disarray too frightening to be acknowledged except, without any defence, in moments of deep sleep and dreaming. The little sparkling innocent waves shone now green, now grey, petticoats, lettuce leaves; the trees sighed, and told us to be quiet, hush-sh, as if something were sleeping and should not be disturbed – perhaps that was what the trees were always telling us, to hush-sh in case we disturbed something which must never· ever be awakened?
What was it? Was it sleeping in the Reservoir? Was that why people were afraid of the Reservoir?
Well we were not afraid of it, oh no, it was only the Reservoir, it was nothing to be afraid of, it was just a flat Reservoir with a fence around it, and trees, and on the far side a little house (with wheels inside?), and nothing to be afraid of.
'The Reservoir, The Reservoir!'
A noticeboard said DANGER, RESERVOIR.
Overcome with sudden glee we climbed through the fence and swung on the lower branches of the trees, shouting at intervals, gazing possessively and delightedly at the sheet of water with its wonderful calm and menace,
'The Reservoir! The Reservoir! The Reservoir!'
We quarrelled again about how to pronounce and spell the word.

Then it seemed to be getting dark – or was it that the trees were stealing the sunlight and keeping it above their heads? One of us began to run. We all ran, suddenly, wildly, not caring about our strained or sprained ankles, through the trees out into the sun where the creek, but it was our creek no longer, waited for us. We wished it were our creek, how we wished it were our creek! We had lost all account of time. Was it nearly night? Would darkness overtake us, would we have to sleep on the banks of the creek that did not belong to us any more, among the wild sweet peas and the tussocks and the dead sheep? And would the eels come up out of the creek, as people said they did, and on their travels through the paddocks would they change into people who would threaten us and bar our way, TRESPASSERS WILL BE PROSECUTED, standing arm in arm in their black glossy coats, swaying, their mouths open, ready to swallow us? Would they ever let us go home, past the orchards, along the gully? Perhaps they would give us Infantile Paralysis, perhaps we would never be able to walk home, and no one would know where we were, to bring us an iron lung with its own special key!

We arrived home, panting and scratched. How strange! The sun was still in the same place in the sky!

The question troubled us, 'Should we tell?'

The answer was decided for us. Our mother greeted us as we went in the door with, 'You haven't been long away, kiddies. Where have you been? I hope you didn't go anywhere near the Reservoir.'

Our father looked up from reading his newspapers.

'Don't let me catch you going near the Reservoir!'

We said nothing. How out-of-date they were! They were actually afraid!

The Bath

On Friday afternoon she bought cut flowers – daffodils, anemones, a few twigs of a red-leaved shrub, wrapped in mauve waxed paper, for Saturday was the seventeenth anniversary of her husband's death and she planned to visit his grave, as she did each year, to weed it and put fresh flowers in the two jam jars standing one on each side of the tombstone. Her visit this year occupied her thoughts more than usual. She had bought the flowers to force herself to make the journey that each year became more hazardous, from the walk to the bus stop, the change of buses at the Octagon, to the bitterness of the winds blowing from the open sea across almost unsheltered rows of tombstones; and the tiredness that overcame her when it was time to return home when she longed to find a place beside the graves, in the soft grass, and fall asleep.

That evening she filled the coal bucket, stoked the fire. Her movements were slow and arduous, her back and shoulder gave her so much pain. She cooked her tea – liver and bacon – set her knife and fork on the teatowel she used as a tablecloth, turned up the volume of the polished red radio to listen to the Weather Report and the News, ate her tea, washed her dishes, then sat drowsing in the rocking chair by the fire, waiting for the water to get hot enough for a bath. Visits to the cemetery, the doctor, and to relatives, to stay, always demanded a bath. When she was sure that the water was hot enough (and her tea had been digested) she ventured from the kitchen through the cold passageway to the colder bathroom. She paused in the doorway to get used to the chill of the air then she walked slowly, feeling with each step the pain in her back, across to the bath, and though she knew that she was gradually losing the power in her hands she managed to wrench on the stiff cold and hot taps and half-fill the bath with warm water. How wasteful, she thought, that with the kitchen fire always burning during the past month of frost, and the water almost always hot, getting in and out of a bath had become such an effort that it was not possible to bath every night nor even every week!

She found a big towel, laid it ready over a chair, arranged the chair so that should difficulty arise as it had last time she bathed she would have some way of rescuing herself; then with her nightclothes warming on a page of newspaper inside the coal oven and her dressing-gown across the chair to be put on the instant she stepped from the bath, she undressed and pausing first to get her breath and clinging tightly to the slippery yellow-stained rim that now seemed more like the edge of a cliff with a deep drop below into the sea, slowly and painfully she climbed into the bath.

– I'll put on my nightie the instant I get out, she thought. The instant she got out indeed! She knew it would be more than a matter of instants yet she tried to think of it calmly, without dread, telling herself that when the time came she would be very careful, taking the process step by step, surprising her bad back and shoulder and her powerless wrists into performing feats they might usually rebel against, but the key to controlling them would be the surprise, the slow stealing up on them. With care, with thought. . . .

Sitting upright, not daring to lean back or lie down, she soaped herself, washing away the dirt of the past fortnight, seeing with satisfaction how it drifted about on the water as a sign that she was clean again. Then when her washing was completed she found herself looking for excuses not to try yet to climb out. Those old woman's finger nails, cracked and dry, where germs could lodge, would need to be scrubbed again; the skin of her heels, too, growing so hard that her feet might have been turning to stone; behind her ears where a thread of dirt lay in the rim; after all, she did not often have the luxury of a bath, did she? How warm it was! She drowsed a moment. If only she could fall asleep then wake to find herself in her nightdress in bed for the night! Slowly she rewashed her body, and when she knew she could no longer deceive herself into thinking she was not clean she reluctantly replaced the soap, brush and flannel in the groove at the side of the bath, feeling as she loosened her grip on them that all strength and support were ebbing from her. Quickly she seized the nail-brush again, but its magic had been used and was gone; it would not adopt the role she tried to urge upon it. The flannel too, and the soap, were frail flotsam to cling to in the hope of being borne to safety.

She was alone now. For a few moments she sat swilling the water against her skin, perhaps as a means of buoying up her courage. Then resolutely she pulled out the plug, sat feeling the tide swirl and scrape at her skin and flesh, trying to draw her down, down into the earth; then the bathwater was gone in a soapy gurge and she was naked and shivering and had not yet made the attempt to get out of the bath.

How slippery the surface had become! In future she would not clean it with kerosene, she would use the paste cleaner that, left on overnight, gave the enamel rough patches that could be gripped with the skin.

She leaned forward, feeling the pain in her back and shoulder. She grasped the rim of the bath but her fingers slithered from it almost at once. She would not panic, she told herself; she would try gradually, carefully, to get out. Again she leaned forward; again her grip loosened as if iron hands had deliberately uncurled her stiffened blue fingers from their trembling hold. Her heart began to beat faster, her breath came more quickly, her mouth was dry. She moistened her lips. If I shout for help, she thought, no-one will hear me. No-one in the world will hear me. No-one will know I'm in the bath and can't get out.

She listened. She could hear only the drip-drip of the cold water tap of the wash-basin, and a corresponding whisper and gurgle of her heart, as if it were beating under water. All else was silent. Where were the people, the traffic? Then she had a strange feeling of being under the earth, of a throbbing in her head like wheels going over the earth above her.

Then she told herself sternly that she must have no nonsense, that she had really not tried to get out of the bath. She had forgotten the strong solid chair and the grip she could get on it. If she made the effort quickly she could first take hold of both sides of the bath, pull herself up, then transfer her hold to the chair and thus pull herself out.

She tried to do this; she just failed to make the final effort. Pale now, gasping for breath, she sank back into the bath. She began to call out but as she had predicted there was no answer. No-one had heard her, no-one in the houses or the street or Dunedin or the world knew that she was imprisoned. Loneliness welled in her. If John were here, she thought, if we were sharing our old age, helping each other, this would never have happened. She made another effort to get out. Again she failed. Faintness overcoming her she closed her eyes, trying to rest, then recovering and trying again and failing, she panicked and began to cry and strike the sides of the bath; it made a hollow sound like a wild drum-beat.

Then she stopped striking with her fists; she struggled again to get out; and for over half an hour she stayed alternately struggling and resting until at last she did succeed in climbing out and making her escape into the kitchen. She thought, I'll never take another bath in this house or anywhere. I never want to see that bath again. This is the end or the beginning of it. In future a district nurse will have to come to attend me. Submitting to that will be the first humiliation. There will be others, and others.

In bed at last she lay exhausted and lonely thinking that perhaps it might be better for her to die at once. The slow progression of difficulties was a kind of torture. There were her shoes that had to be made specially in a special shape or she could not walk. There were the times she had to call in a neighbour to fetch a pot of jam from the top shelf of her cupboard when it had been only a year ago that she herself had made the jam and put it on the shelf. Sometimes a niece came to fill the coal-bucket or mow the lawn. Every week there was the washing to be hung on the line – this required a special technique for she could not raise her arms without at the same time finding some support in the dizziness that overcame her. She remembered with a sense of the world narrowing and growing darker, like a tunnel, the incredulous almost despising look on the face of her niece when in answer to the comment
– How beautiful the clouds are in Dunedin! These big billowing white and grey clouds – don't you think, Auntie?
she had said, her disappointment at the misery of things putting a sharpness in her voice,
– I never look at the clouds!

She wondered how long ago it was since she had been able to look up at the sky without reeling with dizziness. Now she did not dare look up. There was enough to attend to down and around – the cracks and hollows in the footpath, the patches of frost and ice and the potholes in the roads; the approaching cars and motorcycles; and now, after all the outside menaces, the inner menace of her own body. She had to be guardian now over her arms and legs, force them to do as she wanted when how easily and dutifully they had walked, moved and grasped, in the old days! They were the enemy now. It had been her body that showed treachery when she tried to get out of the bath. If she ever wanted to bath again – how strange it seemed! – she would have to ask another human being to help her to guard and control her own body. Was this so fearful? she wondered. Even if it were not, it seemed so.

She thought of the frost slowly hardening outside on the fences, roofs, windows and streets. She thought again of the terror of not being able to escape from the bath. She remembered her dead husband and the flowers she had bought to put on his grave. Then thinking again of the frost, its whiteness, white like a new bath, of the anemones and daffodils and the twigs of the red-leaved shrub, of John dead seventeen years, she fell asleep while outside, within two hours, the frost began to melt with the warmth of a sudden wind blowing from the north, and the night grew warm, like a spring night, and in the morning the light came early, the sky was pale blue, the same warm wind as gentle as a mere breath, was blowing, and a narcissus had burst its bud in the front garden.

In all her years of visiting the cemetery she had never known the wind so mild. On an arm of the peninsula exposed to the winds from two stretches of sea, the cemetery had always been a place to crouch shivering in overcoat and scarf while the flowers were set on the grave and the narrow garden cleared of weeds. Today, everything was different. After all the frosts of the past month there was no trace of chill in the air. The mildness and warmth were scarcely to be believed. The sea lay, violet-coloured, hush-hushing, turning and heaving, not breaking into foamy waves; it was one sinuous ripple from shore to horizon and its sound was the muted sound of distant forests of peace.

Picking up the rusted garden fork that she knew lay always in the grass of the next grave, long neglected, she set to work to clear away the twitch and other weeds, exposing the first bunch of dark blue primroses with yellow centres, a clump of autumn lilies, and the shoots, six inches high, of daffodils. Then removing the green-slimed jam jars from their grooves on each side of the tombstone she walked slowly, stiff from her crouching, to the ever-dripping tap at the end of the lawn path where, filling the jars with pebbles and water she rattled them up and down to try to clean them of slime. Then she ran the sparkling ice-cold water into the jars and balancing them carefully one in each hand she walked back to the grave where she shook the daffodils, anemones, red leaves from their waxed paper and dividing them put half in one jar, half in the other. The dark blue of the anemones swelled with a sea-colour as their heads rested against the red leaves. The daffodils were short-stemmed with big ragged rather than delicate trumpets – the type for blowing; and their scent was strong.

Finally, remembering the winds that raged from the sea she stuffed small pieces of the screwed-up waxed paper into the top of each jar so the flowers would not be carried away by the wind. Then with a feeling of satisfaction – I look after my husband's grave after seventeen years. The tombstone is not cracked or blown over, the garden has not sunk into a pool of clay. I look after my husband's grave – she began to walk away, between the rows of graves, noting which were and were not cared for. Her father and mother had been buried here. She stood now before their grave. It was a roomy grave made in the days when there was space for the dead and for the dead with money, like her parents, extra space should they need it. Their tombstone was elaborate though the writing was now faded; in death they kept the elaborate station of their life. There were no flowers on the grave, only the feathery sea-grass soft to the touch, lit with gold in the sun. There was no sound but the sound of the sea and the one row of fir trees on the brow of the hill. She felt the peace inside her; the nightmare of the evening before seemed far away, seemed not to have happened; the senseless terrifying struggle to get out of a bath!

She sat on the concrete edge of her parents' grave. She did not want to go home. She felt content to sit here quietly with the warm soft wind flowing around her and the sigh of the sea rising to mingle with the sighing of the firs and the whisper of the thin gold grass. She was grateful for the money, the time and the forethought that had made her parents' grave so much bigger than the others near by. Her husband, cremated, had been allowed only a narrow eighteen inches by two feet, room only for the flecked grey tombstone In Memory of My Husband John Edward Harraway died August 6th 1948, and the narrow garden of spring flowers, whereas her parents' grave was so wide, and its concrete wall was a foot high; it was, in death, the equivalent of a quarter-acre section before there were too many people in the world. Why when the world was wider and wider was there no space left?

Or was the world narrower?

She did not know; she could not think; she knew only that she did not want to go home, she wanted to sit here on the edge of the grave, never catching any more buses, crossing streets, walking on icy footpaths, turning mattresses, trying to reach jam from the top shelf of the cupboard, filling coal buckets, getting in and out of the bath. Only to get in somewhere and stay in; to get out and stay out; to stay now, always, in one place.

Ten minutes later she was waiting at the bus stop; anxiously studying the destination of each bus as it passed, clutching her money since concession tickets were not allowed in the weekend, thinking of the cup of tea she would make when she got home, of her evening meal – the remainder of the liver and bacon –, of her nephew in Christchurch who was coming with his wife and children for the school holidays, of her niece in the home expecting her third baby. Cars and buses surged by, horns tooted, a plane droned, near and far, near and far, children cried out, dogs barked; the sea, in competition, made a harsher sound as if its waves were now breaking in foam.

For a moment, confused after the peace of the cemetery, she shut her eyes, trying to recapture the image of her husband's grave, now bright with spring flowers, and her parents' grave, wide, spacious, with room should the dead desire it to turn and sigh and move in dreams as if the two slept together in a big soft grass double-bed.

She waited, trying to capture the image of peace. She saw only her husband's grave, made narrower, the spring garden whittled to a thin strip; then it vanished and she was left with the image of the bathroom, of the narrow confining bath grass-yellow as old baths are, not frost-white, waiting, waiting, for one moment of inattention, weakness, pain, to claim her for ever.

Winter Garden

Mr Paget's wife had been in a coma for two months. Every day he visited her in the hospital, sitting by her bed, not speaking except to say, 'Miriam, it's me, Alec, I'm here with you,' while she lay unresponsive, not moving, her eyes closed, her face pale. Usually Mr Paget stayed half an hour to an hour; then he would kiss his wife, return her hand that he'd withdrawn and held to her side under the bedclothes, pat the clothes into their position, and then, conscious of his own privileged freedom and movement in the afternoon or evening light, he would go home to the corner brick house in the hill suburb, where he would prepare and eat a meal before going outside to work in the garden. Every day in all seasons he found work to do in the garden. His time was divided between visiting the hospital and tending his flowers, lawn and olearia hedge. When the neighbours saw him digging, clipping, or mowing they said, 'Poor Mr Paget. His garden must be a comfort to him.' Later in the evening, when the violet-coloured glare showed through the drawn curtains of the sitting-room as Mr Paget watched television, the neighbours said, 'Poor Mr Paget. The television must be a comfort to him.' Often in the evening he would phone for news of his wife and the answer would be, always, Her condition shows no change. No change, no change. He had learned to accept the words without question. He knew what they meant – that she was no nearer living or dying, that the scarcely perceptible fluctuations he noted in his daily visits were ripples only, this way and that, as the opposing winds blew, but were no indication of the surge of the tide. No change. How intently he watched her face! Sometimes he stroked it; even her eyelids did not blink; they were shut and white like lamp shells.

Mr Paget's garden was admired in the street. His roses were perfect, untouched by blight or greenfly. His lawn shone like fur in the sun. Laid between his lawn and the street his hedge looked like a long smooth plump slice of yellow cake – except that it moved; in the wind it crackled its curly dented leaves with a kindling sound as if small fires were being started; in the morning light it was varnished a glossy green; in the evening it became pale lemon, appearing under the mass of houseshadow as lawns do sometimes, seen beneath dark trees at sundown.

In the corner of the garden overhanging the street a rowan tree grew that was Mr Paget's pride. It was now, in autumn, thick with berries suspended from beneath the protecting leaves of each twig like clusters of glistening beads. Everyone admired the rowan tree, and its berries cheered Mr Paget as he trimmed, mowed, staked, planted. In the early days of his wife's illness, depressed by the funereal association of flowers, he made up his mind not to take them to the hospital; but one day, impulsively, he picked a cluster of rowan berries.

He arrived early, before visiting time. He found on his wife's bedside so many instruments, tubes, needles – all the tools necessary to care for an apparently lifeless body – that at first there did not seem to be room for the berries. Hesitating, he put them on the locker next to a brick-coloured gaping-throated tube. Perhaps his wife, lying in the strange secret garden where those instruments tended her, would notice the berries.

A nurse came into the room. 'Oh, Mr Paget, you're early. I'll remove this tray and put these berries in water. Aren't they from your garden?'

Mr Paget nodded.

The nurse leaned over his wife, tucking in the bedclothes as if to arrange a blanket defence against the living, speaking creature who had invaded her vegetable peace. Then taking her silver tray of tools and the twig of berries she went from the room, and only when she had gone did Mr Paget say, 'Miriam, it's me, Alec,' taking her hand in his. He could feel a faint pulse like a memory gone out of reach, not able to be reclaimed. He stroked the fingers. He was overwhelmed by the familiar hopelessness. What was the use? Would she not be better dead than lying silent, unknowing in a world where he could not reach her?

The nurse came back. She put the berries on the windowsill, where they made a splash of colour. The slim skeleton-shaped leaves soared, like spears, against the glass.

'With winter coming and the leaves turning, there'll soon be only the late berries.'

'Yes,' Mr Paget said.

The nurse looked at him, answering his unspoken question, her face warm with sympathy. 'There's been no change, Mr Paget. But she's not suffering at all.'

'No,' Mr Paget said.

He waited for the nurse to say what everyone was saying to him now, beating the words about his ears until he wanted to cry out for mercy, 'It will be a happy release for her when it comes.'

The nurse did not say it and he was glad. She smiled and left the room, and he sat watching the narrow ribbon of afternoon light that had bound itself across the windowpane and the sill and the berries, surging in their glass like tiny bubbles of blood. Mr Paget shivered. He began to feel afraid. What will it be like, he wondered, when death comes and I am with her?

He looked again at his wife's hand, at the wrinkled soft skin; new skin. He stroked her fingers and his heart quickened and a warmth of joy spread through him as he realized her skin was new; and of course her fingernails had been cut; and if they had been cut they had also been growing; her hair, too. Her hair had been cut. Quickly he leaned to touch her damp mouse-coloured hair. It had grown and been cut. They had cut her hair! Then the wild joy began to ebb as he remembered that even after death the hair and fingernails may grow and need to be cut. Was this growth then more a sign of death than of life?

'Oh no, oh no,' Mr Paget said aloud.

For while his wife lay in a coma, again and again they would need to cut her fingernails and hair, to bathe her, to take from her each day the waste of the food they had given her, and each day was different, had been different all the weeks she had been ill; and he had not dreamed, they had not told him, he thought bitterly. They had said, 'No change, no change,' when each day one speck more or less of dust had to be washed away, one ounce more or less of food was stored, rejected; and one day the wide blade of sunlight pressed burning and sharp upon her face while another day she lay in cool dark shade. She was alive, in the light. In the grave there was no sun, no shadow, touching of hands, washing of body.

When Mr Paget smiled happily as he said goodbye to his wife, the nurse looked startled. Poor Mr Paget, she said to herself.

That evening, Mr Paget took special care in trimming the hedge, stepping back to admire its evenness, putting the clippings into a neat pile. He felt quite frivolous as he ran the old-fashioned mower over the lawn; chatter-chatter it gossiped throatily, spewing out the green minus-marks of grass. Then, before he went inside to phone the hospital and watch television, in a spurt of extravagant joy he picked two clusters of rowan berries, and as he was springing back the branch the neighbour passed on her way home.

She saw Mr Paget. Her face assumed the appropriate expression of sympathy. 'And how is Mrs Paget?'

Mr Paget's accustomed answer flowed from him. 'There's been no change.'

He heard the despair in his voice as he spoke. Then, sympathetically, he asked, 'And how's Mr Bambury?'

The neighbour's husband had been ill. She released her news. 'They're stripping his arteries tomorrow.'

There was a jubilant consciousness of action in Mrs Bambury's voice. Mr Paget groped from a dark void of envy to his new joy: no change, no change indeed!

He smiled at Mrs Bambury. He wanted to comfort her about her husband and his arteries but he knew nothing about the stripping of a person's arteries: the resulting nakedness seemed merciless; he was grateful that his wife lay enclosed in sleep, her arteries secret and unyielding.

'I hope everything will be all right with Mr Bambury,' he said at last.

'Oh, there's a risk but a very strong chance of recovery. I do hope there'll be a change in Mrs Paget's condition.'

'Thank you,' Mr Paget said humbly, playing the game. 'So far there has been no change.'

'No change?'

'No change.'

They said goodbye. On his way to the house he stopped to scan the garden. He looked tenderly at the pile of grass and hedge clippings and the succulent golden hedge with the dark pointed roof-shadow eating into it.

Mrs Paget died in late autumn. It is winter now. The berries are gone from the rowan tree, some eaten by birds, some picked by the wind, others scattered by the small boys switching the overhanging branches up and down as they pass in the street. In a luxury of possession rather than deprivation, Mr Bambury, his arteries successfully stripped, rests in a chair on the front porch of his home, looking across the street at Mr Paget in his garden. Mr Bambury and his wife say to each other, 'Mr Paget is tied to his garden.'

Others notice it, too, for Mr Paget seems now to spend all his waking time in the garden. 'Since his wife's death, he's never out of the garden,' they say. 'Why? Nothing grows now but a few late berries. Nothing grows in the garden in winter.'

They wonder why Mr Paget stands for so long looking at the dead twigs, the leafless shrubs, the vacant flower beds set like dark eyes in the middle of the lawn, why he potters about day after day in the dead world where nothing seems to change. And sometimes they think perhaps he is going mad when they see him kneel down and put his cheek against the skin of the earth.

Insulation

In the summer days when the lizards come out and the old ewes, a rare generation, a gift of the sun, gloat at us from the television screen, and the country, skull in hand, recites To kill or not to kill, and tomatoes and grapes ripen in places unused to such lingering light and warmth, then the people of Stratford, unlike the 'too happy happy tree' of the poem, do remember the 'drear-nighted' winter. They order coal and firewood, they mend leaks in the spouting and roof, they plant winter savoys, swedes, a last row of parsnips.

The country is not as rich as it used to be. The furniture in the furniture store spills out on the footpath and stays unsold. The seven varieties of curtain rail with their seven matching fittings stay on display, useless extras in the new education of discernment and necessity. The dazzling bathroom ware, the chrome and fur and imitation marble are no longer coveted and bought. For some, though, the time is not just a denial of gluttony, of the filling of that worthy space in the heart and the imagination with assorted satisfied cravings. Some have lost their jobs, their life-work, a process described by one factory-manager as 'shedding'.

– Yes, we have been shedding some of our workers.

'Too happy happy tree'?

The leaves fall as if from other places, only they fall here. They are brittle in the sun. Shedding, severing, pruning. God's country, the garden of Eden and the conscientious gardeners.

Some find work again. Some who have never had work advertise in the local newspaper. There was that advertisement which appeared every day for two weeks, full of the hope of youth, sweet and sad with unreal assumptions about the world.

'Sixteen year old girl with one thousand hours training at hairdressing College seeks work.' The *one thousand hours* was in big dark print. It made the reader gasp as if with a sudden visitation of years so numerous they could scarcely be imagined, as if the young girl had undergone, like an operation, a temporal insertion which made her in some way older and more experienced than anyone else. And there was the air of pride with which she flaunted her thousand hours. She was pleading, using her richness of time as her bargain. In another age she might have recorded such time in her Book of Hours.

And then there was the boy, just left school. 'Boy, sixteen, would like to join pop group as vocalist fulltime' – the guileless advertisement of a dream. Did anyone answer either advertisement? Sometimes I imagine they did (I too have unreal assumptions about the world), that the young girl has found a place in the local Salon Paris, next to the Manhattan Takeaway, where she is looked at with admiration and awe (one thousand hours!) and I think that somewhere, maybe, say, in Hamilton (which is to other cities what round numbers are to numbers burdened by decimal points), there's a pop group with a new young vocalist fulltime, appearing, perhaps, on *Opportunity Knocks*, the group playing their instruments, the young man running up and down the stairs, being sexy with his microphone and singing in the agony style.

But my real story is just an incident, a passing glance at insulation and one of those who were pruned, shed, severed, and in the curious mixture of political metaphor, irrationally rationalized, with a sinking lid fitted over his sinking heart. I don't know his name. I only know he lost his job and he couldn't get other work and he was a man used to working with never a thought of finding himself jobless. Like the others he had ambled among the seven varieties of curtain rail and matching fittings, and the fancy suites with showwood arms and turned legs, and the second circular saw. He was into wrought iron, too, and there was a wishing well in his garden and his wife had leaflets about a swimming-pool. And somewhere, at the back of his mind, he had an internal stairway to the basement rumpus. Then one day, suddenly, although there had been rumours, he was pruned from the dollar-flowering tree.

He tried to get other work but there was nothing. Then he thought of spending his remaining money on a franchise to sell insulation. It was a promising district with the winters wet and cold and frosty. The price of electricity had gone up, the government was giving interest-free loans – why, everyone would be insulating. At first, having had a number of leaflets printed, he was content to distribute them in letterboxes, his two school-age children helping. His friends were sympathetic and optimistic. They too said, Everyone will be wanting insulation. And after this drought you can bet on a cold winter. Another thing, there was snow on Egmont at Christmas, and that's a sign.

He sat at home waiting for the orders to come in. None came. He tried random telephoning, still with no success. Finally, he decided to sell from door to door.

– I'm going from door to door, he told his wife.

She was young and able. She had lost her job in the local clothing factory, and was thinking of buying a knitting-machine and taking orders. On TV when they demonstrated knitting-machines the knitter (it was always a she, with the he demonstrating) simply moved her hands to and fro as if casting a magic spell and the machine did the rest. To and fro, to and fro, a fair-isle sweater knitted in five hours, and fair-isle was coming back, people said. Many of her friends had knitting-machines, in the front room, near the window, to catch the light, where, in her mother's day, the piano always stood, and when she walked by her friends' houses she could see them sitting in the light moving their hands magically to and fro, making fair-isle and bulky knit, intently reading the pattern.

– Yes, door to door.

The words horrified her. Not in her family, surely! Not door to door. Her father, a builder, had once said that if a man had to go door to door to advertise his work there was something wrong with it.

– If you're reputable, he said – you don't advertise. People just come to you through word of mouth, through your own work standing up to the test. Well, it wasn't like that now, she knew. Even Smart and Rogers had a full-page advertisement in the latest edition of the local paper. All the same, door to door!

– Oh no, she said plaintively.

– It can't be helped. I have to look for custom.

He put on his work clothes, a red checkered shirt, jeans, and he carried a bundle of leaflets, and even before he had finished both sides of one street he was tired and he had begun to look worried and shabby.

This is how I perceived him when he came to my door. I saw a man in his 30s wearing a work-used shirt and jeans yet himself looking the picture of disuse, that is, severed, shed, rationalized, with a great lid sinking over his life, putting out the flame.

– I thought you might like to insulate your house, he said, thrusting a leaflet into my hand.

I was angry. Interrupted in my work, brought to the door for nothing! Why, the electrician had said my house was well insulated with its double ceilings. Besides, I'd had experience of that stuff they blow into the ceiling and every time there's a wind it all comes out making a snowfall in the garden, drifting over to the neighbours too.

– No, I'm not interested, I said. – I tried that loose-fill stuff once and it snowed everywhere, every time the wind blew.

– There's a government loan, you know.

– I'm really not interested, I said.

– But it's new. New. Improved.

– Can't afford it, anyway.

– Read about it, then, and let me know.

– Sorry, I said.

My voice was brisk and dismissing. He looked as if he were about to plead with me, then he changed his mind. He pointed to the red print stamped on the leaflet. There was pride in his pointing, like that of the girl with the thousand hours.

– That's my name and phone number, if you change your mind.

– Thank you, but I don't think I will.

He walked away and I shut the door quickly. Insulation, I said to myself with no special meaning or tone. How lovely the summer is, how cosy this house is. The people here before me had carpets that will last for ever, the ceiling is double, there are no cracks in the corners, that is, unless the place decides to shift again on its shaky foundations. How well insulated I am! How solid the resistance of this house against the searching penetrating winds of Stratford. The hunted safe from the hunter, the fleeing from the pursuer, the harmed from the harmer.

How well insulated I am!

That night I had a curious ridiculous dream. I dreamed of a land like a vast forest 'in green felicity' where the leaves had started to fall, not by nature, for the forest was evergreen, but under the influence of a season that came to the land from within it and had scarcely been recognized, and certainly not ruled against. Now how could that have been? At first I thought I was trapped in a legend of far away and long ago, for the characters of long ago were there. I could see a beggar walking among the fallen leaves. He was the beggar of other times and other countries, and yet he was not, he was new, and he was ashamed. I saw a cottage in the forest and a young woman at the window combing her hair and – a young man with a – lute? No, a guitar – surely that was the prince? – and with the guitar plugged in to nowhere he began to play and sing and as he sang he sparkled – why, it was Doug Dazzle – and he was singing,

> *One thousand hours of cut and set*
> *my showwood arms will hold you yet*
> *baby baby insulate,*
> *apprentice and certificate,*
> *God of nations at thy feet*
> *in our bonus bonds we meet*
> *lest we forget lest we forget*
> *one thousand hours of cut and set. . . .*

The girl at the window listened and smiled and then she turned to the knitting-machine by the window and began to play it as if from a 90 per cent worsted, 10 per cent acrylic score. I could see the light falling on her hands as they moved to and fro, to and fro in a leisurely saraband of fair-isle. Then the beggar appeared. He was carrying a sack that had torn and was leaking insulation, faster and faster, until it became a blizzard, vermiculite falling like snow, endlessly, burying everything, the trees and their shed leaves, the cottage, the beggar, the prince, and the princess of the thousand hours.

The next morning I found the leaflet and telephoned the number on it.
– I'd like to be insulated, I said.
The man was clearly delighted.
– I'll come at once and measure.
   We both knew we were playing a game, he trying to sell what he didn't possess, and I imagining I could ever install it, to deaden the world. All the same, he measured the house and he put in the loose-fill insulation, and following the Stratford custom, although it was summer, I ordered my firewood against that other 'drear-nighted' winter.

Two Widowers

'I'm making the trip,' he said, 'because my wife died three months ago and they advised me to get away for a change, to go to the Old Country. But I wish I'd never left Australia. As soon as the ship docks at Southampton I'm coming home.'
   He talked to me every morning. He talked about his wife and the leg operation that had killed her.
   'It was successful yet three weeks later she was dead.'
   'King George the Sixth had the same trouble,' I said.
   'Fancy your knowing that! My doctor told me about it. He said, King George the Sixth had the same trouble and not even the best surgeons could save him.

That helped, you know. Having something in common with the King. My doctor knew it would. But she was so well, and then one morning there she was, unconscious.'

'Perhaps,' I murmured, choosing from the array of commonplaces, 'perhaps it's better that she died.'

'Yes. She might have been crippled for life. A blood clot. Only three years ago she had the first illness of her life. *Literally.* A stomach operation.'

Lifting the flap of his shirt and baring his stomach he drew his straightened finger, like a knife, across his skin.

'Twenty-four inches of good stomach cut open.'

His voice became loud, protesting: 'Twenty-four inches of good stomach!'

I could see that his love for his wife had been mixed with practical economy and a hint of animal husbandry.

Then he spoke quietly, confidentially, leaning towards me: 'I'll never marry again. Some do. My friends said: "Marry again." But I'll never marry again. Smoking and drinking is all the women do these days. My wife looked after me. Chose everything. Had taste. Chose this shirt I'm wearing. See?'

He pinched at the sleeve and held it for me to examine.

'Just my colour.'

I agreed.

'Knew what colours to choose.'

He had dispensed with the personal pronoun and was speaking telegraphically. 'Was a businesswoman, too. Had a little dress shop. Knew how to manage money.'

I thought he seemed as if he were making or measuring a new distance which ordinary leisurely sentences could not traverse and which, indeed, would soon be beyond the reach even of telegrams.

'I'm well off, you know. I don't spend my time in the bar drinking and smoking. My home's a nice little flat. I haven't sold up everything like some of these.'

He looked around the empty deck imagining it, I suppose, as it would be later in the morning, crowded with the emigrant families whose torment was known to everyone. They had sold everything. They were returning to Europe. They were restless, apprehensive, the young uprooted from their adopted country and the only language they knew, the old, with no home anywhere apart from a desperate tonguehold in the native language that not even their children understood.

'Yes, "sell out", they said to me. "Go and live away from the memories. Start a new life." My son wanted me to live with him and his family in Brisbane. But why should I? I've got everything at home. Hi-fi, too. And a second TV in the bedroom. If I were home now I'd make my tea – scrambled egg – none of your wine for me, then I'd go to bed and watch a programme. Educational. Great company. My wife had nothing against it. She was getting on so well. They said there was a risk with the operation but until three years ago she'd never had a day's illness. *Literally.*'

Having telegraphed his bereavement to wherever it might be received he had returned briefly to speaking in the third person. My wife. She.

As more people came on deck for the day his emotional focus widened and I could hear him, from time to time, explaining himself to others: 'I'm a widower, you know. My wife has been dead three months. They said it was a good idea to go on a sea-voyage, visit the Old Country.'

He was pale. He had lost weight or acquired an inner formlessness which made his clothes hang loosely on his body and which, for all his professed pride in his appearance, gave him the general untidiness of someone depressed and, for the time being, not quite at home with himself or those around him. Day after day, I, and others, were embarrassed to hear the 'twenty-four inches of good stomach' protest voiced in anger at the wastefulness of good material misused and at the revealed imperfections of his wife and her final unforgivable imperfection of dying. He acted like a man who had been cheated, and I saw him in the coffee shop carefully counting his change and inspecting his coffee for faults.

He behaved also like someone who had been in great danger and must in future exercise caution, so that once he had found himself a routine on board ship he made it his ally, a kind of extra force with a hint of superstition, to control and shape the dishevelled elsewheres of his day.

Everyone knew about his daily goal of a required number of turns of the deck. He was not alone in this. Others for various reasons were trapped in the compulsion, for after all, when the ground has given way to water beneath your feet you have to find some framework. He was determinedly honest in his walking. He never skirted the part by the stairs but walked right up to the bulkhead and even touched it to make sure.

When he'd completed his number of turns he came to talk to me, always beginning with: 'How are you today?' And when I smiled my seasick smile he would give me his advice.

'Get up and walk around the deck. It's the answer, you know.' He was offering me advice, the medicine which others had offered him as being 'the answer' and which he was finding unpalatable.

'Yes, take a walk on deck. There are games you can play, too. I wouldn't go near the bar. They're rotten in there. That was one thing about my wife. She neither smoked nor drank. Yet we enjoyed ourselves. She was always full of surprises. Liked to surprise me. Would have a present tucked away as if it were my birthday. Liked to go away on her own, too. Liked to visit her mother and our son.'

He was sending further telegrams from the supply he had inherited on his wife's death. Some day, I thought, he would find there were no more telegrams and then he would come back into the personally pronouned world.

Now there was another passenger, an elderly man, who appeared to be alone. He too was untidy and as he did not mention a wife (on board ship where almost everyone's tongue behaved like the ocean in constant ebb and flow) it was assumed that he, too, was a widower. The rumour that his wife was ill, confined to their cabin was belied by his apparent aloneness and air of loss.

On his third day at sea he bought two modern marvels – a watch, waterproof, shockproof, antimagnetic, etc.; and one of those transistor radios the size of a small suitcase with all possible wave-bands, a slot for cassettes, a portable microphone, playback at several speeds, impressive dials, indicators, aerials that could be telescoped and twirled. The watch and the radio became the old man's constant companions. He took them everywhere, he showed them to everyone, and one morning when he was leaning over the ship's rail trying to get decent reception on his radio, away from what people called 'the ship's interference', and the Australian was making his required number of rounds of the deck, the two met.

Together they tried to listen to the radio. Together they walked the deck. Later, they sat side by side in their deck chairs drinking their beef tea and talking. Two widowers. The two were so obviously untidy and depressed and bereaved, so much that they embarrassed, with the fraying edges of their lives, many of the oh so neatly hemmed passengers, and there was general relief when the two found each other. Their common ground or wave was their widowerhood.

Some said the old man was a distinguished scholar, that he could speak several languages and he read foreign books from the library. The Australian, they said, was a retired electrician, which fact caused some surprise, for in the sweeping stereotype of international waters, Australians are thought to be 'rangy cattlemen or sheepfarmers'.

For the rest of the journey across the Pacific the two were inseparable. The tale of the twenty-four inches of good stomach was no longer given public recital. The Australian gradually lost his air of dishevelment while the old man no longer slept half the day with his mouth open and his belly poking out between his shirt and shorts and his arm cradling the transistor radio. Both acquired the grooming of friendship, for, make no mistake, when people feel themselves to be within the human race they have a way of grooming one another, invisibly, as birds do visibly, and animals, lions in their pride.

And now when the ship stopped at a way port the two went ashore, tourists together, and returned with their new T-shirts and Panama hats and sandals. They began to take part in the ship's games: quoits, shuffleboard, deck tennis. Soon the new tide of belonging closed over them, submerging, merging them with the other passengers, and their status as 'the two widowers' was seemingly forgotten.

Then one day when the ship was about to dock at Ponta Del Garda I saw the old man standing by the purser's desk checking a number of suitcases. He turned to speak to a tall pale woman whom I'd not seen before. They linked arms.

He saw me and beckoned. 'This is my wife, Ella. She's been ill, confined to the cabin.'

'Oh,' I said. 'I'm sorry. Are you disembarking here?'

'Yes. About time, too,' the old man said. 'We grew very tired of that long journey across the Pacific, didn't we dear?'

I hoped that I wasn't staring too closely at them. He no longer appeared widowed. There was no sign of his cherished watch and radio, still less of his Australian companion. Perhaps his widowed state had been an effect of the voyage, for after all, if the sea can work miracles of cure can it not also work miracles of kill? I wondered.

And then I saw the Australian coming up to the desk. He stopped abruptly, seeing the two. I saw him glance once, then again, and a third time, as if to make sure that it was indeed his friend of so many days, his Pacific friend – the Pacific ocean had driven many of the passengers to a kind of madness – then he looked again at his friend's wife. Surely, I thought, he must have known she existed. I saw the familiar, prim, 'neither smoked nor drank' expression come on his face, transparently over a fleeting hurt and betrayal. He stared again at the two and did not speak. I saw him turn and walk up the stairs, holding fast to the stair-rail.

The next morning when we were once again full steam ahead and the Australian had completed his turns of the deck, he sat down beside me.

'You know,' he said, 'I think I'll make a go of the Old Country after all. An awful waste of money to go straight home again. I've joined this club, I joined it this morning. They take you to your hotel in London, they look after you.

'Might go to the Continent in the Spring. Might even see the Swiss Alps. Be glad to get home though.'

He was sending telegrams to himself now, about himself. Then, having proclaimed the urgency of his own life, he returned to ordinary speech, setting his dead wife at last beyond the reach of the carefully measured distance of dream-telegram.

'My wife would want it this way,' he said. 'My wife would want me to enjoy myself.'

O. E. MIDDLETON

The Will to Win

Although my first contact with the game came when my parents scraped up the money to send me to boarding-school, I did not begin to play chess seriously until I found myself at an Officer's Training School in Egypt during the war.

Despite the meaningful looks of my fellow N.C.O.s, I had grasped the offer of a commission with both hands and was soon posted to the training establishment in Cairo. One of the instructors there, an Intelligence Officer who had seen service in France during the Kaiser's war, was a renowned chess-player, more than once runner-up, it was said, for the British Open Title. The sight of him, blindfold, coolly calling his moves to a fellow instructor as he went from board to board while a dozen junior officers tried vainly to match his skill, gave me my first real taste for the game.

As far as I know, all my forbears were either honest yeomen or, when they forsook the land, men of business of one kind or another. As an importer of tobacco, my father had, it is true, a certain refinement of taste. But I had never observed in my parents any trace of that talent for abstract thought which might have forewarned a more astute merchant of the onset first of depression, then of war and its restrictions.

'Why don't you have a go?' urged one of my fellow cadets as he got up from a round in which the redoubtable major had already routed several of the school's more promising tacticians.

'Haven't played since I was at school,' I faltered, grinning as casually as I could.

But already that voice which had prompted me to leave the ranks when the chance came was urging me to seize this fresh opportunity of showing my mettle. Nor was this simply because the ability to play chess was regarded as a desirable attribute in an officer. Even in those days, I had begun to make plans for the future. A man of business who had some knowledge of abstract tactical principles, who could – like the major – work out everything in his head, would have a decided advantage over his rivals in the post-war world still to come to birth.

Apart from me, only four other players could be found for the next round. The major demolished these without difficulty but to my surprise, took much longer over his game with me. There was never any doubt as to the outcome, but something in the style of my play seemed to disconcert him. At the end of a long game when the mess was almost empty, the ashtrays brimful and the weary orderlies impatient to clear away the coffee trays, he beat me narrowly on an almost empty board.

'Don't believe I've played you before Sansome, have I?' he asked as he slipped off the bandage. (As you might expect, he had an excellent memory.)

'No sir.'

'Your style is, ah, unorthodox but I shouldn't be surprised if you have the makings of a strong player.'

'Thank you sir.'

For some obscure reason, since I was only another war-time volunteer while he was a professional soldier, the major went out of his way to improve my game. The fact that he was from a well-known public school, urbane, civilized, and above all a fine soldier, no doubt influenced me as much as it did my fellow trainees. How else account for that studied conformity of speech and gesture, that charming drawl and diffidence of manner we all acquired as inevitably it seemed as we did the elements of military law and history, the habit of command?

By the time the course had ended, I was as familiar with the finer points of chess as I was with King's Regulations, the feel of my revolver. The major was as much a master of the game as he was a model for officers and gentlemen. I still encounter in unlikely corners of civilian life, pale, ageing copies from that fine mould. Doubtless I owe to him some of the cool-headedness which saw me through the rest of the war. And if I am honest, I must admit that part at least of that ease of bearing, those social graces that so impressed Felicia, were owed to him.

In civilian life, the first tournament successes were an unexpected asset to a young executive whose only other qualification was then commonplace.

'Let Sansome nut that one out,' the senior partner would say. 'He's got the head for it.'

'I see you are among the top players,' clients would greet me over the telephone. Men who had never attempted anything more cerebral than golf or poker seemed to find pleasure in transacting business with a chess-player.

But as competition grew more intense, it became clear that I could not go on spending whole days in tournament play and help run a business at the same time.

'Why not try postal chess?' a veteran player suggested when I told him of my difficulty. 'This would allow you to keep up the game with all the time in the world to make your moves. And don't think it's an easy field, either. The open postal tournament attracts some of the best players in the country, seasoned veterans who put everything into their game and play to win.'

At first, Felicia seemed relieved when I did not go out so much at night. 'If anyone had told me I should become a chess widow, I should have laughed in his face,' she confided one evening as we set out for the theatre. 'But darling, it was almost coming to that!' She was half laughing but there was an undertone in her voice that prompted me to give her a reassuring squeeze. How could she know that at that precise moment I had been going over in my mind the names of the top players in the last open postal tournament? Some of these, it is true, were already known to me through inter-club matches. Others again were strangers, able players in the main who either because of the demands of their daily work or through isolation, rarely had the pleasure of meeting a first-rate opponent face to face.

One of my early games, I remember, was with a lighthouse-keeper on a remote part of the East Coast. Another was against a fire-watcher who spent the summers in a lookout tower surrounded by miles of forest.

In the beginning, Felicia seemed amused by the novelty of my new interest. She would greet me on my return from the office with the news that there was another postcard from Sollars the lighthouse-keeper or Midgeley, the man in the forest. (One of the advantages of postal chess is that one can play several games at once.)

As the post-war boom blossomed, business doubled and quadrupled. It was a relief to get home in the evening and, the board before me, to retrace the manoeuvres of a game against some chess-loving recluse in a remote part of the country. As I pored over the pieces, absorbed in the endless possibilities of my next move, the concerns of commerce seemed as remote as the stars. That *I* might be a kind of recluse quite escaped me then. Even when Felicia began to go off with friends in the evenings to concerts and the theatre, I scarcely spared the time from my game to say goodbye to her.

My first game with Summerfield came only at the end of my second year of postal chess. His cards arrived regularly from a town on the West Coast and to begin with I felt no more curious about him than about the others. He was a strong player and having beaten me in the semi-finals, went on to win that year's national open tournament.

The following year I lasted as far as the finals but was again defeated by Summerfield after a hard-fought game. By now Felicia's temper had begun to show in various ways. She no longer greeted me on my return from the office with the news that a number of postcards awaited me. She had joined an amateur dramatic group and was frequently absent at rehearsals and performances. The news of my second defeat by Summerfield even seemed to give her some pleasure. 'Really darling! Don't you think it's time you gave up? He's probably a retired mathematician with a mind like a computer. What hope has a tired businessman against someone who probably does nothing else but play chess . . .?'

The mere suggestion that I lacked the qualities of which champions are made was enough to arouse in me that determination to succeed which had always stood by me. Instead of being content with the position of runner-up, I made up my mind to become national postal champion, whatever the cost. As my leisure hours at home were already taken up, I bought a small portable chess-set whose pieces fitted into holes in a folding board, so that I could keep my mind well honed even at my office desk. 'Tired businessman', indeed! Were not some of the best, the shrewdest brains taken up with commerce? Only when she began to spend most of her time with her bohemian friends and entered into that defiant association that was to end our marriage did the full force of the taunt strike me. By then, of course, it was already too late. Summerfield had won again, was national champion for the third year running. Not only had I been unable to hold my own with him, I had even had a struggle against an unknown player in the preliminaries. . . .

That princess of ancient India who is supposed to have invented chess to keep her warlike husband at home knew a thing or two. But did she live to grow jealous of a game which though it spared her lord's life, must have kept him from her as effectually as any campaign?

For some months my only thought was to defeat Summerfield. I dug up all the records of his previous matches, replayed the games on the small set I kept in my desk at the office, studied his approach to chess, his style of play. Despite the skill with which he placed his pawns, the power and daring of his knight attack, there was an element of opportunism in his play. He never overlooked an undefended piece, always accepted an exchange when the odds seemed in his favour. His openings, his endgames were orthodox. Only his use of pawns and knights – those footsoldiers and cavalry of chess – showed real brilliance.

Whole days went by without Felicia and I having exchanged more than a few words. How much harder it is, after all, to hold than to win. . . . My colleagues could not fail to mark my preoccupation. Instead of accepting luncheon appointments, I had something brought to my desk and ate alone, at the same time going over on my small board some game of Summerfield's.

The students and bookworms huddled at the tables in the public library must often have wondered at my presence as I pondered some work on chess lore or the thoughts of some Russian master. If the margin between profit and loss were as slight as it often is between devotion and obsession, many a commercial empire might never have been built. . . .

When tournament time came around again, I was so steeped in the game that I eliminated my first opponents without effort. Summerfield drew the new player, Hollinrake, in the semifinals while I was matched against Drury, the master, it was said, of a coastal ship. Drury's moves came on postcards bearing the postmarks of a dozen small ports. Sometimes, too, they carried the prints of a large thumb as though some seaman, or perhaps the captain himself, had pored over them as he stood his watch. But neither Hollinrake nor the captain carried the day and in August I was informed that

Summerfield and I were to play off the final round, the game to be adjudicated if not finished by the end of December.

After those erratic, salt-stained cards of the sea captain, it was a relief to receive again in a small, firm hand, the postcards detailing Summerfield's moves.

Imagination of that feeling sort which fills in the outlines of an unknown face I leave to women or to artists. Calculations based on figures or the close study of rival methods are more in my line. Sometimes, it is true, as I crept out to catch the late post or pondered some particularly subtle move, I suppose I wondered how the fellow spent his time when he was not playing chess: whether he was an ex-schoolmaster or a retired army officer. But once the game was well under way, I gave the *man* no more thought than I do when conducting some complex business deal.

Despite my long preparation and my right to first move, I began badly and allowed Summerfield to get control of the centre of the board.

He gained this advantage by a judicious exchange of pawns and it was with some difficulty that I held my own and began to manoeuvre my pieces. The small board I kept locked in my desk at the office with the ivory pieces firmly pegged into the centres of the black and white squares, became the battleground of my greatest ambition. Although I still pored every evening over the larger set in my study at home, the chilling silences of my wife, her frequent absence, threatened my concentration. Her behaviour had begun to cause me some concern.

One night she stayed out later than usual. I waited up till one o'clock analysing all the implications of Summerfield's latest move and deciding what reply to make, then went to bed. As often happens, the images of the black and white pieces continued to move about their chequered universe long after I had shut my eyes. Like some mechanism which, once wound-up, must run down in its own good time, my mind continued to plan, scheme, manoeuvre. When, because of the noise she made, I awoke to find Felicia preparing for bed, it was plain that she was rather drunk.

Before I set out for the office, I usually refreshed my memory with a glance at the board, if a game were in progress. But that morning the study was in disarray. The pieces had been swept from their places and lay strewn on the floor. The white queen, her head missing, lay under a chair. Rather than wake Felicia, I left the apartment at once, congratulating myself on the greater seclusion of my other realm.

That same night I returned to an empty apartment and a letter from Felicia. She had found someone, she wrote, who understood her, could give her all that I had neglected to give. . . .

Do you know what hurt me more than anything else? She had not stayed to see me take my revenge on Summerfield: it did not matter to her whether I won or lost!

From then on, *all* my energies were directed towards winning. I neglected the business shamelessly. But what great commercial enterprise does not shelter its quota of midweek golfers, barflies, womanizers, or those most flagrant time-wasters, trout fishermen? Each day I spent several hours considering my moves, analysing and anticipating Summerfield's. If I felt the need to be alone, I simply went out for a stroll in the park or buried myself in the reference department of the public library. Now that the apartment held no other distraction, all my leisure there was given to the game.

Summerfield seemed in his usual form. We had each lost a bishop, a knight and two pawns, but there was never any doubt as to who was the stronger player. Almost every move he made was a threat to my peace of mind, seemed to feel out the weak points in my defences. Unless each was encountered in its turn, the game, I knew only too well, might turn into a debacle. The daring gambit of offering my strongest piece for a winning position suggested itself as I brooded over the board in the silent apartment. It would be accepted by my opponent, of course, only if the inevitable outcome remained obscure. The exposure of the queen must come about after a series of moves seemingly initiated by Summerfield himself.

While I awaited the postcard on which would be recorded the fateful move, I wondered if he were pacing up and down, as I often do, while he weighed the consequences in his mind. The opportunist in him proved too strong. 'Knight takes Queen' was printed neatly on his postcard. In seven more moves, the game was over and in December I was presented with the trophy and a certificate and declared National Postal Champion.

Need I say that after all I had put into winning, there was a certain feeling of anticlimax? Perhaps if Felicia had been there things might have been different.

Rather guiltily, I plunged back into the firm's affairs, went out of my way to catch up all I had put off. The chessmen pegged into the small folding board in my desk remained fixed in the positions they had assumed in that memorable game. At first I would look at them from time to time, congratulate myself on my victory; but soon even this pleasure palled. After a while, all battlefields leave one with the same feelings, no matter which side one is on. Besides, for all Summerfield's well-earned reputation as a chess-player, I had not yet met the fellow. When I reflected that he was almost certainly a retired professor with a lifetime of abstract thinking behind him, could I be blamed for wanting to meet my old adversary face to face?

The chance came as it always does when one is determined that it will. A company in the town where Summerfield lived transferred their business to us. When it was decided that one of our principals should go down and meet their executives, it was not difficult to ensure that the assignment fell to me.

Coalport is one of those sprawling mining towns that have seen better days. The moment I got out of the plane and felt that cold wind whipping in from the sea, I regretted having come.

Our new clients' establishment was not only in the main street, but seemed almost the only building in the whole of Coalport not of timber construction and sorely in need of paint. The numbers of recent model cars parked outside, the jaunty, pleasant manners of the office girls reinforced the impression that, business-wise, the trip was well justified. What was left of the morning I spent with their general manager and out of politeness, accepted his invitation to a lunch that even a brash but invigorating bottle of Australian burgundy did not enliven.

Mining towns always depress me. The grime that blears the eyes of the wooden houses has something obscene about it. Every inhabitant is yoked in some way to those who toil like moles far underground. Dalton, the general manager, was a keen fisherman and spent much of the meal boasting of the fine rainbow trout and quinnat salmon to be had in the local streams. I let him talk on, deciding to call on my old opponent unannounced, without any locally garnered foreknowledge, the better to enjoy my triumph and his surprise.

I parted from Dalton late in the afternoon and took a taxi to Summerfield's address on the outskirts of town. The lawn and garden were neatly kept but the house was something of a shock. Clearly, I thought, one could not do *everything*. Besides, superannuation probably did not amount to much, even for an ex-professor. . . .

The door was opened by a woman, attractive and still young, yet with a worn, anxious expression. 'Good afternoon,' I said, 'my name is Sansome. I had to come to this part of the country on business and thought it would be agreeable to look up Mr Summerfield at the same time. As a chess-player, I already know Mr Summerfield very well, but. . . .'

In the instant before she broke in, a shadow flitted across the girl's brow like a bomber over a peaceful street. 'Of course,' she said smiling. 'Mr Sansome of Orkington. I *should* know your name by now.' Was there a trace of irony, almost of bitterness, in her voice?

'Good lord!' I thought, 'surely *she* isn't the celebrated O. T. Summerfield?' Women still assume men's names to write novels, why not to play chess?

Her next words restored my composure: 'Please wait a moment while I tell Mr Summerfield, you are here.' Clearly she was the old man's niece or daughter. Perhaps even his housekeeper.

She left me on the warped, wooden verandah and slipped inside, leaving the door ajar. An ancient basket chair, its covers faded and frayed and darkened by the same film of grime that seemed to smear everything in the town, stood beside the door. I turned from it to survey the drab houses across the street and was still thus engaged some minutes later when the woman reappeared and ushered me in. 'He'll be glad to see you,' she told me politely, but added swiftly in a lower tone: 'I'm sure you'll understand if I ask you not to stay too long.'

We went down a long, dark hallway and into an airy room with a view of paddocks and scrub-covered hills. Sunlight slanted in through west-facing windows, flooding and warming the autumn leaves of the wallpaper, outlining the contours of a man under the covers of a bed. As we entered, his head turned slowly on the low pillow and he looked intently at me.

'Darling, this is Mr Sansome: Mr Sansome, this is my husband,' said the woman, going forward and placing her hand on his shoulder. We smiled at one another, said 'How do you do?' and as soon as I had collected my wits I said, '. . . I wanted to tell you how much I have always enjoyed our games.'

'We have had some tremendous tussles,' he answered in a gentle, musical voice. 'I must say you deserved your win, though. Congratulations!'

Although only his head and neck were visible, it was plain from the outline of his body that he had been a strapping fellow. Despite its resignation, its gentle intellectual quality, his voice still had a resonance that suggested the outdoor man. 'I doubt if I shall manage to beat you next time,' I said and he smiled again.

'I've always put a lot into my chess,' he said simply. 'It's been a wonderful standby – hasn't it Mary?'

'It certainly has,' she answered, adding, 'Would you like a cup of tea, Mr Sansome?'

Naturally I accepted and while she busied herself in the kitchen, Summerfield and I talked chess.

'How long have you been playing?' I enquired at length.

'I started in my student days,' he told me, 'but didn't take it up seriously until after my accident.'

The tea arrived and I told them in a little more detail of the business that had brought me to Coalport. While Mrs Summerfield held the cup and raised her husband's head so that he could drink, I turned and stared through the old double-hung windows at the wind-swept, scrub-covered hills. Not long afterwards I was warned by her expression that time was up so I made ready to go.

'Goodbye,' said Summerfield in his soft, musical voice. 'If you play as well this year as you did last, you'll be hard to beat.' With that same sensation of incompleteness that I had felt at our meeting which showed itself in a twitching of the muscles of my right arm, I hesitated, then went out.

When we reached the verandah, the girl – she was certainly little more – drew the door to and walked with me to the gate. 'It was good of you not to stay,' she said, leaning towards me. 'When I think how strong he was once. . . . He used to be an engineer at the mine, you see . . . . But now the least excitement tires him.'

'I'm so glad I came,' I said. 'I had no idea. . . .'

'You see he's completely paralysed,' she said, her eyes on the houses opposite. 'His chess is everything to him. I set up the men on that little table by the bed. He spends hours working out his moves. When he's ready to move a piece, he calls me and I write it down for him.'

On my return home, I avoided telling my chess-playing friends of my visit to the ex-champion. Some weeks later, my secretary drew my attention to the news of Summerfield's death in a national daily paper. 'Wasn't that the chap you used to play chess with sometimes?' she asked, doubtless remembering things I must have given her to post.

'Yes,' I said, after a pause. 'He was a jolly fine player too.'

'Isn't it sad,' she said, raising her head again from the paper, 'he was only thirty-six. . . . '

For a long time afterwards, I could not bring myself to look at a chess-board, let alone to touch that small set in my desk at the office. My old love of the game had gone forever. Before long, I would, I knew, be expected to defend my title, yet the thought had not the slightest attraction for me.

The idea of writing to Summerfield's widow came to me one evening as I made my way back to the empty apartment. Even after I had composed the letter, however, I could not for some days bring myself to post it. When at last I overcame my scruples, it was somehow reassuring to be able to write that name and address on the envelope.

The day her first reply came, I could not for some moments bring myself to open it. But when, to my great relief, I saw that I had not been imprudent, I set to work to improve and elaborate the dialogue with all the eloquence at my command.

The Loners

As long as he had been working, all had been well. The other men in the timber-yard had been friendly enough once he had got to know them. They had taught him all the gauges, shown him how to tell *rimu* from *matai, totara* from *kauri* and white pine. Once he had grown used to their rough teasing ways, he had come to like working in the timber-yard.

The day the foreman had told him he was to 'finish-up' he had not at first understood.

'Bad luck, Luke!' one of the gang had growled, clapping him on the shoulder. 'There's seven of us been given our walking-tickets today.'

'. . . You too?'

'Yes. Me, my mate Bill here, young Jimmy from the joinery shop and three from one of the other gangs.'

'B-b-but, why?' he had managed to bring out, his eyes searching the man's weathered, unsmiling face.

'Not enough orders. That's why! The country's in a bad way at the moment. The building industry's one of the hardest hit. I've seen it happen before and it'll happen again!' The man had drawn a hand across the grey stubble on his chin, stared past the even stacks of timber at the gleam of sea.

All the next, workless morning, he had sat about, not knowing what to do. There were no labourers' jobs in the paper.

'Why don't you sit on the verandah?' Pine had suggested.

He had gone there meekly enough, glad to be out of the way while the two women made beds and cleaned the house. After a while, though, he had grown uneasy. It seemed to him that the people who strolled past, especially the stiff-faced women with their trundlers and shopping baskets, looked at him disdainfully, as if he had no right to be there. As soon as he had gone back inside, his brother's wife, Rebecca, had begun to scold him.

'Aw, Luke! Can't you give us a chance to get the house straight!'

Ashamed, ill-at-ease, he had gone out again, wandered off alone, not thinking or caring where he went, yet always making for the sea. He had sauntered moodily past the other old wooden houses, all like the one he shared with his brother Matthew, had become aware all at once that this was his first *free* day, his first day to himself since they had got off the ship. From then on, he had wandered through the town, glancing almost furtively into shop-windows. In the window of a fish-shop, something had caught his eye. For some moments he had stared intently, almost affectionately, through the streaming glass at the object; a sizeable squid on a large dish. . . .

He had been on the point of going in to ask the price of the succulent thing, but just in time, realized that he did not know its English name. Besides, he had given Pine all his money the day before, so his pockets were empty.

Moodily, he had turned away. It did not do to go anywhere without money in *this* country. With money in the pocket, there was always something to buy.

At home, he had always gone fishing with friends: either in a boat on the lagoon, or, at night, with torches and spears on the reef. Whatever the catch, there had always been plenty of fun, the warmth of talk and laughter. . . .

Here, everything was different. The people went about singly, many of them with grim, stony faces. Often they passed one another in the street without so much as a greeting.

At last, hardly knowing where he was, he had reached the harbour, walked the length of the old wharf. A solitary fisherman squinting down at a dancing float had glanced at him briefly. In that instant, the two halves of his longing had come together. He would ask Pine for enough to buy a couple of lines and some hooks.

Ever since, he had hardly missed a day. Once he had scanned the job columns, been to see about any work that was offering, his thoughts would turn to the hours stretching ahead. With his gear and a morsel of food in an old basket, he would set out for the wharf.

Though he no longer followed that first, roundabout route, wasted no time gazing into shop-windows, it was still a long way. Sometimes, another man, or even two, were there before him. One day, when he had been to see about a job, he found four of them perched, intent as gulls, at the end of the wharf.

At weekends and late in the afternoons, small boys sometimes drifted down in twos and threes to fish for sprats.

The old man he had seen that first day came down on his bicycle two or three times a week. He used a homemade rod that he carried tied to the bar of his bicycle, rarely stayed beyond midday and usually went home with a fish. He wore spectacles, moved stiffly and sometimes had trouble taking off and putting on the clips he wore around the bottoms of his trousers. He seldom smiled, spoke little, but usually greeted the other regulars with a nod. Once or twice, Luke thought he saw a gleam, like the sudden sparkle of sun on sea, light up the old man's eyes.

Jock, as the others called him, kept all his tackle in a wooden box strapped to the carrier of his bicycle. Nestling in a honeycomb of small cells were hooks and sinkers, swivels, rod-rings, spare coils of fine wire and nylon, spinners and oddments of all kinds. Once, the old fellow had gone to the box, rummaged a while, and handed Luke a sharp new hook to replace one lost on a snag. He had shown him how to tie a stop-knot, how to 'kinch' it tight so that it would never slip. Another time, Jock had tossed him a piece of fresh mullet, signing to him to exchange it for the bait he had been using without success.

Three other men came down to the wharf almost every day. One rode a motor-bike, another drove a battered car, while a third came on foot. All were married men in their late twenties or early thirties. From the few words they exchanged, Luke guessed that all were out of work and came to the wharf as much to get away from their wives, as in the hope of taking something home for the pot. He would have liked to ask them what work they did; to have told them how strange he found everything after the life he had been used to. But the chance never came.

If one of them spoke to him, it was teasingly, as though he were a child. His halting replies usually brought only shakes of the head, pitying smiles. Their eyes would return to their fishing-lines that seemed to transfix the water like fine spears. He guessed that the three had all been born in the town, had grown up there at about the same time. Yet they were not *real* friends. Perhaps they had gone to different schools, belonged to different churches, worked at different jobs? Often, as he sat brooding on these things, Luke's thoughts would return to his wife. He would stare past the breakwater at the great rock thrusting up through the pale sea like a huge, blunt tooth, his heart swelling with love.

It was natural that she should feel anxious, now that she was again with child. At least Matthew still went to his job at the freezing works every morning. When the wind blew from that quarter, the wail of the works siren would come clearly over the intervening sea. Luke would cock his head, stare uneasily across the water.

There had been a hooter at the timber-yard. The first new words he had learned had been *smoko, knock-off, pay-day*: his workmates had seen to that. Each time he heard the siren, it reminded him of the men he had worked with in the timber-yard, the things they had said. The sound seemed to stir some chord in the others too. They would get up, stretch their limbs, swallow mouthfuls of tea from their flasks, light a cigarette or fill a pipe when the smoko hooter went. Whenever the noon whistle blew, old Jock would get up stiffly, begin reeling in. Although the old man lived on a pension and none of the others had regular jobs, the mournful call of the hooter seemed to tug at them all, as the sun and moon affect the tide.

Since they were fond of eating their fish raw, Pine had tried to buy limes at the greengrocer's. But even the shops that sold *taro* had only lemons to offer.

Luke was still out of work in May when the mackerel began to come in. He caught a few of the smaller type known locally as 'English mackerel', found them good bait for larger fish and fine to eat raw when there were enough for a meal.

One day, the other man who also came down on foot hauled in a fine 'horse-mackerel'. 'Don't often get them like that in the daytime,' he said, holding it up to take out the hook. Shy of the light, the fish quivered and fought, its scutes and nacreous sides catching fire. Adroitly, unmoved by its frenzy, the man held the fish, slipped out the hook. He slid the mackerel into a sack where it went on shivering and vibrating.

There were only the two of them on the wharf that morning and it was the first time the man had ever spoken to Luke. The 'horse-mackerel' reminded him of a type of small tuna much prized in the islands for its fine flavour.

'What is the *best* time?' he brought out slowly at last.

'Night-time is best,' the other answered briefly. 'Use a small hook – a treble is best – and no sinker.'

'. . . I used to come down after mackerel a lot at one time,' he went on after a pause. 'It's different now though. My wife doesn't like me coming down here after dark. Says it's too risky for a married man. . . .' He gave a short scornful laugh, spat between his dangling legs into the sea. 'They're beautiful eating, too,' he finished wistfully.

Luke said nothing and the other soon fell silent. Not long afterwards, he rolled up his lines, slung the sugar-bag over his shoulder. 'So long!' he threw out as he set off home.

As he watched him swing away down the wharf, Luke wondered what Pine would say when he told her he wanted to fish at night.

In the paper next morning, there was an advertisement for men to fill and sew sacks of wheat in a grain store. He was one of the early ones, was given three days' work with some other men in a cold, dimly-lit warehouse.

After that, he came down to the wharf at night two or three times a week, took home several fine horse-mackerel. Even after dark, quite a few people came down to the old wharf to fish. They were mostly men in steady jobs with a sprinkling of boys from the High School. The only daytime fisherman Luke recognized among them was the man who drove the battered car. He offered Luke a lift home one night, on the way, told him that he was an out-of-work carpenter.

Late one night, after he had got back from the wharf, a strong wind sprang up. As he cleaned his fish, the old house started to creak and sigh. Matthew's youngest child began to cry and woke the others. By the time Pine had got their own small daughter back to sleep, he was in bed. When at last she slipped in beside him, hugging his back for warmth, they lay awake for a long time, talking in whispers, awed by the strange howling of the wind.

In the morning, the wind still blew from the mountains. Matthew went off to work swathed like an Eskimo in the warm gear he usually wore only in the freezing-chambers. The wind still prowled about the house, fumbling with a loose sheet of iron on the roof, making the branch of an old tree scrape mournfully against the weatherboards. When the children had been wrapped up and sent off to school, Luke went onto the verandah. The sea was an uneven strip of frosty green under scudding clouds. There would be no fishing that day.

Pine pounced on him the moment he went inside again.

'You can do the shopping for us today, man! Too cold for Rebecca and me to go out . . .!' She handed him a kit, a list and her purse, helped him on with the army greatcoat he had bought at the surplus stores.

At the fruiterer's, he saw two women who came from the same village as his wife. They were buying *taro*, weighing the tubers expertly in their hands, searching for blemishes. They gave the customary polite greetings, which he returned. Yet he was glad when they were gone. It seemed to him that there had been something mocking, sly, in the looks they had darted at the kit. When you did not have a job to go to, everyone, even your own countrymen, began to look at you askance. At home, if a man chose to be idle, no one frowned.

At the butcher's and the baker's he felt awkward, out of place. In the grocer's shop, he gave up trying to stumble through the list, handed it to the young assistant.

When he came out at last, the kit was bulging. A bell began to clang from a doorway further down the street over which a banner flapped. People came hurrying, jostling one another to get in. Guessing that it must be some kind of entertainment, he went in too. A man with a face as red as the banner outside and a pencil behind his ear, mounted a platform, began to harangue the crowd in a loud, sing-song voice. Two other men in long aprons hunted among piles of furniture, old radios, crockery, lawnmowers, clothes-wringers, books, peering at labels, turning or holding up the goods for the crowd to see.

Although at first, Luke did not follow all that was said, he soon saw that the things were being sold. How stupid he was! Was not this the very place where Pine and Rebecca had bought most of the things for the house?

The kit was heavy. He put it down, could not help smiling at the antics of the red-faced auctioneer. The man grinned at him, caught his eye; Luke gave an answering nod. Only when a chorus of other bids followed and the auctioneer looked at him again, did he realize that he had very nearly bought a large iron double bedstead with brass knobs. Hastily, he gathered up the basket, hurried out, his face burning. How the women would laugh if they knew!

As he came out onto the footpath, he bumped into someone, almost knocking him over. 'Sorry!' he said, putting out his free hand to steady the man who seemed dazed by the blow.

'So you should be!' the man answered unexpectedly. 'Do you always treat your old mates so rough?'

Luke stared at him, saw with surprise that it was one of the men from the timber-yard – the one who had spoken kindly to him that last day. 'I didn't see you,' he said smiling.

'How are things, Luke? Got a job yet?'

'No,' he said. 'Not yet.'

'Nor me either,' said the man. Their eyes met, held.

The same greying stubble stood out on the man's furrowed cheeks and bony jaws. His breath carried a sweetish reek of alcohol and his pale, blue-grey eyes held a misty, far-off look. 'All on your own?' he asked: then, without waiting for an answer, 'Come and have a drink!'

Luke had been into a pub a couple of times with his brother. Once or twice, he and Matthew had cracked a bottle of beer in the house in the weekend. At home, people had often brewed their own from bananas, oranges, all kinds of things. He had once got very drunk on the stuff when he was still in his teens.

After their third beer, Jack said, 'Oh it's good to have someone to talk to. You get fed-up with your own company and the sight of four walls! . . . I had a missus too, once; and a kiddie. Little girl. I made good wages in those days. Putting up houses for a big builder. . . .' He paused, stared into his glass for a moment before going on. 'Then the Slump came. The builder went broke and for months I was on relief. I started to hit the booze. . . . My wife left me and took the kid. I've never seen them since. I guess the girl will have a family of her own by now.' He raised his glass, tilted his head, closed his eyes as the beer went down.

By the time Luke had swallowed his own drink, much of his shyness had gone and he had forgotten his blunder at the auction. He might have forgotten the shopping too, if Jack had not said to him: 'Now, whatever you do, don't leave that basket behind – or your wife will use you for a chopping-block!'

He wanted to bring Jack home, introduce him to Matthew and their wives, give him a meal. But Jack would not hear of it, kept shaking his head. '. . . I'll have a bite to eat somewhere after,' he said vaguely. 'There's a place I know. . . .'

While he was speaking, he must have made a sign to the barman and before Luke could say anything, two more beers had been bought.

Outside, the wind still blew with the same force, plastering the thick stuff of the greatcoat against him, making him lean forward to keep his feet. Where did the others spend their days? he wondered. Some, he knew, came to the pub. Jack had introduced him to a few of them. He was glad he had met Jack. Another time, when it was too rough to fish, he might look in at the pub. It was good for a man to make friends outside his own countrymen, his own family. Pine would understand.

He was smiling when he reached their gate. Pine, a blanket about her shoulders, looked anxiously out from the verandah. Her face melted into a smile the instant she saw him, but clouded as he stumbled, almost fell, on his way up the steps.

'Luke! Where have you been?'

'Doing your shopping. . . .' Why was she looking so solemn?

'Man, you've been drinking!'

'I – I met a friend. A man I used to work with. I wanted him to come and eat with us. He's out of work too. . . . We went to a pub, had a few beers.'

'Did you do all the shopping?'

'Yes. See, it's here!' He held out the bulging kit, was astonished at the ease with which she took it from him.

'Where's the purse?'

He began to fumble for it in his pants, fished it out at last from one of the deep pockets in the greatcoat.

'Here it is!' he said cheerfully.

Pine opened the purse, counted out what was left. 'Where is the milk-money?' she asked at length.

'What do you mean?'

'There should have been more than a dollar left after you did the shopping. That money was for our next week's milk!'

He stared into her hot, troubled face and the full import of it smote him, left him aghast. 'It's gone,' he mumbled, hanging his head. 'I used it for beer.'

He stood waiting for an outburst from her. It did not come. She simply stood there, looking at him, her eyes wide, the tears close. Then, without a word, she turned, opened the door and went in.

Dumbly, he followed her, his face burning, his limbs beginning to feel numb.

In the morning, while everyone was still asleep, he slipped out of bed, crept onto the verandah. It was still too dark to make out the sea. The wind had shifted but it was still cold.

Silently, he gathered his gear together, shrugged on the greatcoat and went out. A solitary vehicle bumbled about the street. He heard the merry, jingling rattle of bottles in metal crates, hurried his steps as though pursued. Light gleamed from only one or two houses. As though weary from their night-long vigil, even the street lamps seemed to burn with a subdued, worn-out glow.

It was still early when he reached the wharf. The wind was coming straight off the ocean and every so often, breakers boomed against the seaward edge of the breakwater. He baited his small line, turned up the collar of his coat, settled down to wait.

It was the first time he had been out so early. Maybe he should have told Pine? Matthew would not yet be setting out for work. It was a fine place to live, in spite of everything. When you grew used to it, even the cold had something fine about it. Matthew said it helped you work better. The colder water certainly seemed to make the fish taste sweet.

When the sun began to peer over the ridge of hills beyond the town, the air seemed at first to grow colder. He shrugged deeper into his collar, stared out through slitted eyes at the glittering grey-green sea.

Footsteps sounded at the far end of the wharf. He turned to see who it was, could not at first recognize the man because of his parka and woollen head-gear.

'You're early!' the newcomer said. 'Any luck?'

Luke shook his head.

'Cunt of a day, yesterday!' the other remarked when he had set his lines.

'No good for fishing!' Luke agreed.

They fell silent. Under them, the sea sucked and gurgled around the piles. Every so often, a comber smashed itself against the breakwater, sending up a smother of white. All at once, the man in the parka got to his feet, began to haul in one of his lines. Luke could tell from the run of the line, the man's movements, that it was something big. He secured his own lines, went to see if he could help.

'Just as well he grabbed my new line!' the other muttered. As he spoke, the water churned and boiled some way out. A red-gold mass flashed for a moment, then beat back out of sight.

'Big snapper!' grunted the man, paying out line.

Luke said nothing. He slipped off his coat, lowered himself over the end of the wharf, began to climb down. By the time the fish came up again, it was close under him. Its great, humped, red-gold back heaved up, glittered an instant, then was gone. Luke glanced up, met the blue eyes staring uneasily down.

'Don't know how long I can hold him!' the man called, gingerly hauling in again.

As the snapper swam up, Luke bent down, steadying the line with his free hand. With a deft movement, he slipped his fingers into the gills, felt the nails rasp the harsh lining of the gullet. As he inched back over the cross-ties, the kicking and jumping of the heavy fish made his arm ache. At last he felt the rough timber of the combing, a hand gripped his shoulder. With a final heave, he swung the heavy fish onto the decking.

They stood for a long while looking down at the snapper as it flapped and gasped at their feet. 'What a beaut!' crowed the man in the parka for the third time. 'He must be all of twenty pounds!'

Luke smiled, flexing his aching muscles.

The man turned to him. 'You don't often get them like that. He's a moocher. A loner.' His plain, colourless face had come to life. His frosty, blue-grey eyes shone with a pale lustre. 'They say they're the survivors of old shoals. . . .'

Luke nodded, went on smiling, though he understood only part of what the man said. He began to shiver, turned away and put on his coat.

The other man pushed back the hood of his parka. Tufts of fair hair stuck out from under his woollen cap.

Luke felt rapid, sharp bites on his small line. He pulled it up, unhooked a plump little fish spotted brown and yellow.

'Do you want him?' the other man called, his eyes on the small fish.

'No! You take him!' Luke got up, glad to have something to give.

The man in the parka stuck one prong of a treble hook through the body of the little fish just below the dorsal fin, carefully lowered it into the water. Just then, the wail of the starting-whistle at the works came faintly to them during a lull in the wind.

They fished in silence for the best part of an hour. All at once, the other man got up, began to haul in the line baited with the live fish. This time he did not pause, kept bringing in the line hand-over-hand, until an ugly greyish fish with a dark blotch on each side lay gasping on the wharf.

Luke went to look at it. 'What do you call that one?' he asked. He had seen a few of these fish caught, had even watched a man casting a murderous-looking weighted jag at one of the slow-swimming creatures on a still day, but had not liked to ask the name.

'Oh that's a johnny: a john-dory. Best eating fish in the sea! My missus will be pleased! Loves them, she does. . . . Only fish she's keen on.' He began to whistle under his breath, rebaited the line with a dead sprat, lapsed into silence once more. Before long, the men's solitary figures became as still as two bollards. The sun slid over the faces of the rocky islands beyond the breakwater, caught the occasional flash of a diving gannet. The wind never ceased to worry at the grey-green sea, making the white under-fur bristle, plucking at the men's lines until they danced and sang.

The sad, peremptory wail of a hooter came faintly again across the water. The man in the parka lifted his head, looked puzzled. 'It's not smoko yet,' he muttered. He glanced uneasily at the tide, which had begun to drop, got up and began to haul in his lines. As he wound them onto their sticks, his elbows wagged in a comical rhythm and he stared fixedly towards the town.

When he was ready to go, he took the snapper from the sack, put it down beside Luke's basket. 'Better take that home with you,' he said.

Luke glanced up with a smile, made a ritual gesture of refusal.

'Look there's only the two of us. We've got any amount with the johnny. You take the snapper – it's a family-sized feed!' He turned away, his boots thudding dully on the wooden decking, his cowled head turned against the wind.

When the man's footfalls had died away, Luke bent over the fish. The huge tail was dry and stiff where it had stuck out in the wind. But where the sack had covered it, the snapper had kept its moist bloom under the scales, was dappled red-gold, blue-green.

He took out his knife, began to clean the fish. As if by magic, red-legged gulls sprang into the air, began to squall and bicker around him.

Before he set out for home, he slipped a length of cord through the fish's gills, climbed down over the cross-ties once more, rinsed the fish in the sea. All the way back, he had to keep shifting the dead weight from one side to the other, to rest his arm.

As he crossed the railway-tracks near the freezing works, knots of men carrying lunch-cases passed him in twos and threes. One of them chivvied him, asked if the fish were for sale. Grinning, he shook his head, kept on walking.

He felt suddenly hungry, tried to remember what Jack had said about the place where the out-of-work could get bread and hot soup. Anyway, he was almost home. Yesterday, Pine had been angry, but by now she would be glad to see him. Pine was like that. Still, now that he knew that other world, he could always return there when he felt the need. . . .

He climbed the steps to the verandah, opened the front door and went in. For a moment, he thought he had heard Matthew's voice: then Pine ran to him, threw her arms about his neck.

Next moment, he was in the kitchen. They were all there, talking, admiring the fish.

Soon, it was Matthew's turn. Smiling, he spread his knees, cleared his throat, began once more to explain about the strike. They all listened, watching his face. A couple of times, Rebecca asked him to repeat things she had not understood. When he had finished, everyone began to talk at once.

The brothers looked at one another and laughed. 'Might as well make it a *real* holiday,' Matthew said. 'Let's go into the other room.'

As he watched his brother bring in the bottles, take off the caps, pour out the beer, Luke could not help thinking: 'It's all right now. This is only the first day. Wait till the women begin to scold at him. . . .' Matthew was fond of fish but did not have the patience to sit hour after hour, waiting for bites. Since he had come here, he had learned to play snooker, though, and kelly pool. Perhaps he would fill in the time with some of his mates in one of the billiard saloons in the town. As long as he had something in his pocket, Matthew would be happy. If the strike dragged on and he ran out of money, he would soon grow fretful. . . .

But why worry? The beer warmed him, reminded him he had eaten nothing so far that day. Pine came in, offered him some slices of cold *taro*, drank a little from his glass.

'Such a fish will need careful cooking,' she remarked.

'We will have it this evening, when the children are here and we are all together.'

'How long will the strike last?' Luke asked when the women had gone back to the kitchen.

'Maybe a week, maybe a month. Some of the men say it may last even longer.'

From the kitchen came the sounds of running water and of Pine's singing. It was some new song she had heard on the radio, but her voice had all its old warmth, as though she were helping prepare one of the family feasts back home.

Luke remembered the way the snapper had flashed in the early light as it came up out of the sea, its bony gill-plates gleaming. He saw again the look in the frosty blue eyes of the fair-haired man.

'If the wind is not too strong, I will go down again tomorrow,' he decided. 'As long as things are like this, I might as well be the fisherman of the family.'

RENATO AMATO

One of the Titans

He was tired. There was an abandoned slackness in his arms and legs as he stood in front of the concrete-mixer, continuing to wash it even when he did not need to any longer. The bowl was clean. But just now he liked playing with the water; he liked the noise the water made when the solidity of what seemed to be a shaft of glass broke and twirled. It was easy; he did not have to move. He could be still and just flick his wrist one way and the other.

There was concrete, as solid as rock, hardened all round the rim but he would not try to scrape it off. It was not his fault that it had been allowed to settle. He could hardly believe that anybody might be so careless with their equipment, but nobody really cared. Why should he worry? The only thing that mattered was the big money. As big as their mouths could make it. That was all that counted: the big money earned with a constant grudge at being forced to work long hours, and away from the city. But then, to people like him, to all the ditch-diggers and concrete-shovellers and timber-carriers and steel-benders and nail-pushers he knew, money was all they could have. . . .

Once he had seen an old, tall, somehow masculine woman in the bank where he worked before he came away; and now she kept hammering at him, coming back to him, with one sentence that, when he had first heard it, had had no meaning at all.

The woman had been as if iron-bound; she had looked metallic and hard in her antiquated dress – a country woman come to town from the other end of the world – while she stood in front of his teller's window to change her traveller's cheques. She had come from Australia which, then, to him, was only a series of glowing reports from the pages of some propaganda booklet.

He had asked one question of this woman, because he had decided to go somewhere near there, some sort of Paradise on Earth, or Garden of Eden, just like Australia: two islands called New Zealand, another colony of Great Britain. 'What's Australia like?'

Of all the things she might have said, or might have kept to herself, he only remembered a sort of cowed, sorrowful, inward look in her eyes and one short cryptic sentence. 'Yes, the money is good.'

It had not been clear then, but he understood it now. She had said it in Italian, in what she thought was the right way of saying it in Italian, but all she had done was to use Italian words that resembled the English ones but did not render the ideas behind them.

'Si,' she had said. 'La moneta e' buona,' which, to an Italian, meant only 'Yes. The coin is good-hearted.' And that woman, tall, old, faceless, soured by he now knew what, kept saying to him, silently and maddeningly, 'Yes, the money is good; yes, the money is good; yes. . . .'

Of all the tinselled brilliance that this part of the world had been in the pamphlets and statistics and papers he had read before coming, only that remained, that 'Si. La moneta e' buona', which no Italian could understand unless he first understood what 'Yes, the money is good' could mean.

He was tired. Guiliano Martine, the only Eye-tie on the job, the only Eye-tie earning the coin that was good-hearted, was glad that work was over for the day.

It was not that he was physically tired. His tiredness seemed to come from inside, it was all in his mind. It was a sort of numbness that paralysed his brains and for which he had confusedly and conveniently found a name that, in reality, did not apply.

It was more like the continued effect of an unexpected shock. The way that 'La moneta e' buona' had meant to him 'The coin is good-hearted', everything, before he came, seemed to have had a meaning which, here, did not apply. From 'freedom', which now encompassed a peculiar licence to booze-up and brawl and curse to hell everybody and everything within a limited mental reach, to 'Christian love' and 'standards of living' and 'the best in the world'.

He could not say what he might have understood at one time by the words 'building a city' and 'turning the wilderness into a land of milk and honey'. But whatever it might have been, he knew what they meant now – BIG MONEY .

He was helping with the building of a city. The foolish thing had been that nothing had forced him to get a job up country, to go into the middle of nowhere, except perhaps another distorted concept, that of 'man pushing back yet another frontier', or of 'man marching ahead in the name of progress'. Concepts which, as usual, had turned out to be something else.

But . . . 'Oh yes, the money is good.'

There had been nothing when he had first arrived: just a store and the company office and two big huts for the men and a stretch of yellow pumice land where the township was going to be. Now, with the help of God, the houses had been built and the camp with single huts for the men was ready, and he couldn't care less. The way he couldn't care less for the big money that kept growing in his bank account.

Chris, the leading hand in charge of the work on the group of ten houses where they were now working, shouted at him from the door of the toolshed.

'What the hell are you doing? Come on, get moving. Want to sleep here tonight?'

Guiliano started.

'Coming!' he shouted back. He turned the tap off and stored a few tools that were still scattered on the ground. Chris stood aside and watched as Guiliano went into the shed. He made a slight gesture of annoyance at what he thought was the Wop's unwarranted and unnecessary slowness. He liked using 'Wop' better than 'Eye-tie', although 'Wop' was an American term, because it was quicker, sharper. The word in itself was good, he thought, although he wouldn't use it to his face. He could not say why, but Guiliano annoyed him more than all the other Eye-ties he had met or knew of. It was the first time he had actually worked with one, and at times he wished the Wop was working under someone else. He was a funny bird, refusing to tell him what the Italian words were for this, that and the other thing, and never talking of women and never laughing and never singing a song. What the hell had he been lingering for tonight? His annoyance grew.

'Come on,' he said, 'don't forget your gloves. . . .' The Eye-tie with the gloves, the Wop who doesn't want to get his hands dirty. 'Those gloves must cost you a lot of money,' he said again. 'Found the ones you lost?' It was a joke. The boys kept throwing his gloves away, and the Wop kept buying a new pair without saying a word.

'No.'

'What do you wear them for? Nobody else does.'

'I like wearing them,' Guiliano said.

Chris locked the door impatiently and then went towards his car, parked on the road a short distance away.

'No point in giving you a lift,' he said, 'because it'll be quicker for you to walk. You're a fast one, aren't you?' Just a dig that – he hoped Guiliano would know what he meant.

'I'd rather walk myself. Thank you for the thought,' Guiliano said. Just a dig back – he hoped that Chris would know that he meant he didn't want his company. He could have cursed at Chris, following a pattern he knew by heart by now; he could have said, 'Who f—' wants to f—' go in that f—' bomb of yours?' but, somehow, it would have been like putting a mere facade on an empty lot and calling it a complete building. The words would have been there, but the spirit behind them – that sort of automatic conviction that was in the voices of the Johnnies and Chrises and Tommies around him – to give them meaning and a reason to be, would have been missing. 'I'd rather walk myself,' was not what he wanted to say either, but that did not need much spirit behind it.

Chris started his car and drove off, raising clouds of pumice dust along the road. He felt that, in the circumstances, he had done the only possible thing. Confusedly, it seemed unfair to leave a man behind. Still, apart from everything else, if he had asked that joe into his car, the boys might have come to think that he was taking his side. And if they thought that, he would have trouble on the job. What did the Wop think he was doing? he asked himself. Five minutes' travelling time! Only a bloody fool could be so damn stupid.

Guiliano went down to the road and started shuffling slowly towards the camp where his hut was, and the new cookhouse and the shower-block.

He had wanted to be late tonight, to be the last one to leave the job, because he wanted to check again how long it took to walk from the houses on which they were working to the camp where they slept. He knew it took only six minutes, but he just wanted to make sure once again. Then he would go and tell them, then he would show them that they had no reason to make such a fuss about it. Why should he have said a quarter of an hour? It did not take six minutes.

The pumice crunched under his feet. He kept his eyes on the ground. The soil had a dry, gritty quality which did not seem to hold any promise of growth and yield. A ground for digging a hole in and lying down and cursing and crying and shutting your eyes forever. They had had to add cobalt salts to make that artificial forest grow. It was like an ovum in a test-tube, a chick in an incubator. It was like translating a country and its people on to a piece of paper in neat lines of small print. Everything was lies.

Or perhaps it was like translating a country and its people into a theoretical concept in his own imagination. That, too, was lies.

Guiliano kept walking, dragging his feet in the dust, all the time conscious of a dormant desire to run away. Up into those wooded hills on the left – nowhere, that is. Away from nowhere to get nowhere else. Which, he thought, would maybe make him something like the other fellows on the job. They, too, came and went, like shuttlecocks being struck endlessly from here to there, scurrying around like wood-lice when you upturn the stone under which they are hiding. He would then be one of them: not with them, but *like* them. One of the 'builders of a country', an outstanding specimen, drunken and broke, run-down and grumpy, hating everything and fighting everybody.

And then, his loneliness would end.

One of the pioneers, one of the titans, talking and moving and shouting and sweating and swearing, without knowing what or whom he was doing it for. For the country, or himself, or maybe the free world.

Or, maybe, for Archie Mell who ran the taxi business, the cinema, the rental car agency and sold beer and spirits wholesale, or for that fellow Mosom who ran the store and was a J.P. and looked at you with hard pig's eyes as if he thought you were just a bit of dirt, a no-good louse.

Who else could he, and all the others, do it for? Or what else? The legend? Of course, the legend of men who are giants and roam the countryside and master nature; the legend of lands that flow with milk and honey.

And it was good to feel that he himself, by doing that, by swearing and sweating and smelling and going, might just make it and get into the legend.

NOEL HILLIARD

The Girl from Kaeo

Take this one now. Typical. When she was picked up she was wearing a man's shirt and jeans and no shoes, and she had bad teeth and crab-lice and sticking-plaster on a cut in her cheek. Look at her hair and fingernails. Note the tattoos on arms and hands and fingers and knees. There are others you can't see. She's seventeen.

this man he said to me Where you from? and I said Kaeo and he said Thats nice Im from Kaeo too, where abouts in Kaeo? but I said nothing so he said Were you right in Kaeo or round about? and when I still said nothing he said Do you mean Te Huia? and I shook my head so he said Waiare then? Opokorau? Pupuke? Omaunu? and when I said nothing he looked at me in a way to show he thought I was telling a lies about where I come from so I said to him I said All I remember about Kaeo is there was fifteen of us and we all slept on the floor and I never saw my fathers face because I was always looking at his boots

Look into her living conditions. Was she living at home, or boarding, or sleeping around? Would you say her living conditions were very high? high? average? poor? very bad?

If she was not living at home, look into her relationships with her kinsfolk in general and scale them as Very Good/Good/Average/Poor/Very Bad.

What about the people in the house? Are they active criminals? People of dubious reputation? Average types? Very good? Or have you no information?

Now apply the same criteria to her associations and relationships in general and see if the two roughly coincide.

that night I was so late at the cowshed the moon it come up when I was on my way back to the house and Mum she was sitting by herself on the old busted verandah and I sat down beside her in my beret and overcoat and leaky gumboots and Mum she put her arm around my shoulders so warm and she said Did you know the man in the moon is a Maori? and I said No and how do you know that? and Mum she said Is because he got a tattoo face cant you see? just like my great-grand-father and he was OLD when he died

Establish the extent of her possessions, savings, and property from legitimate sources. Estimate the value and classify: over $200; $1–$200; none; in debt $1–$100; in debt over $100.

and my mother she use to have a nice voice one time that was before she lost her teeth, lovely voice to sing my mother and my mother she use to say you cant sing properly without you got your teeth, your mouth is all funny

Examine the extent of her social involvement and community integration. Church or acceptable social-club membership are useful indicators. Find out if she is very active in one or many; moderately active; no interest; resists such activities.

Establish what her attitudes are towards authority in general and particularly towards the police, the probation service, welfare and institution officers. Classify under Very Good/Good/Reasonable/Poor/Antagonistic.

and we use to get our water from the bush, the creek in the bush, but a slip came down and spoilt the place where we use to go and so after we had to get it from the side creek where is all the wiwi and was all right too but not so good the bush water. And my mother she use to say the side creek water was not so good the bush water, that bush water it was beautiful water. Lovely water

and in the city I use to think of my mother and my eyes they would prickle when I thought of the bush water and how my mother said it was beautiful water, lovely water

and how many in the city that all think theyre so smart, how many of thems know about bush water or even there are different kinds of water and it doesnt just only come from out the tap?

and my mother she knew the taste of good water even if she lost her teeth that time my father he came home mad on the dandelion wine he call it his jungle juice even if it come off a paddock

Form an opinion on her manner and ease of communication. Would you say she was very easy to get along with? Would you describe her as moderately open? Is she suspicious and evasive? Does she lie even when she can have no doubt the truth is already known?

Examine her work record before her offence. If you find she had few changes of job, and the jobs were all of the same kind, and she was never dismissed, class her record as Very Good. If you find that her jobs were mostly but not invariably of the same kind, mark Good. If on the other hand you find she had a variety of jobs and stayed in none for long, mark Poor. At the extreme, if you find her indifferent to work, and lax about finding a job, and never attempting to keep one or advance herself in it, mark Bad.

and it was loving and it was always too hard and much too often but always good and warm and loving and it was having a lot of real and touching people close to you and yes Johnny any time Johnny please Johnny too again please yes and how often you want me Johnny how often you like Johnny you so good to me Johnny please too sleepy no not and you must and if you want yes and never stop

and not them Johnny no just only you Johnny please just only us please Johnny just only us this time please Johnny PLEASE

Now look at her other attitudes. First towards her offences. Does she show remorse? Acknowledge guilt? Is she shamed by the exposure? Is she defiant? Is this defiance in your view related or unrelated to feelings of guilt? (Caution needed here.)

Now her attitudes towards incarceration. Is she afraid? apprehensive? indifferent? inured and without fear?

and is it not a fact that to become members of this gang, girls had to submit to intercourse with all male members?

yes

eight and nine and even ten, one after the other?

sometimes more

and did you enjoy it?

the question is irrelevant, mr thing

Im sorry your honour Now is it not a fact that girl members were required to go out and obtain new girl members for the gang?

yes

how did you go about this?

silence

let me put it to you this way then, was force ever used to get other girls to join the gang?

yes

and you yourself used force on other girls to get them to submit to the boys?

yes see there was this boy Johnny see he

thank you And is it not a fact that you ripped a girls pants off and when she resisted further you
  the point is already established, mr thing

Look at her efforts at rehabilitation. Would you say she was trying hard? Making some effort? Making no effort? Determined to keep to crime and anti-social behaviour?
  This leads to an estimate of her criminal future. On the basis of her record and known performance would you describe her as a persistent offender? Do you believe she will be in trouble for some time yet? Is she an occasional offender, depending on associations and circumstances? Could you conclude (this must be approached with caution) that she is unlikely to offend again?

and is it not a fact that when you are angry with yourself you keep hitting your teeth against the windowsill until they bleed?

Look next at her behaviour inside the institution. Has she offended against discipline? How often? More than once a week? Once a month? Is she incorrigible? What is the type of offence? Riot; escape; fighting; theft; writing illegal notes; other (give details); or minor.

Earlier in the year, on a charge of being not under proper control, she had been committed to the charge of the Child Welfare Department. Since then, stated the senior sergeant, she had been 'uncontrollable and a considerable worry' to the welfare and other authorities. She had refused to work, alleging a state of pregnancy contrary to fact.

Does she talk about crime? Is this obsessional, can she talk of nothing else? Does she refer to it only occasionally? Or does she avoid and resist such topics? Can she talk much, or well, on topics unrelated to crime? What is her influence on other inmates? Good, poor, bad, or none? Estimate the extent of her voluntary association with other inmates: more than six; four to six; two; one; solitary.

As the charges were read the accused collapsed, wailing and sobbing bitterly. Police hurried her out of the courtroom. She was still crying softly when the case resumed 20 minutes later and while the senior sergeant continued giving details of her behaviour, tears rolled down her cheeks.

Form an estimate of the interest she shows in her family. Keep a record of the number of outward letters, and after careful perusal give an opinion of their quality. Correlate this with an estimate of the interest her family shows in her, on the basis of letters and visits and inquiries about her progress.

'I cannot criticize any particular section of the police force,' said the magistrate, 'but the force at large is to be censured for keeping any person under the age of 16 in a common jail awaiting trial for seven days.'

Is she able to carry out her work assignment on her own or does she require constant supervision? How good are her relationships with staff? Classify according to Very Good/Good/Neutral/Reserved/Very Distant.

'You are not the only member of the community who is untrustworthy,' the magistrate stated. 'Nor are you the only one who is wayward and dissolute. But from my point of view you are the only one of all the sorry parade I see before me day after day who can only be described as a pest. What is to become of you? You must give some thought to trying to make something of yourself.'

Observe the extent of her involvement in education, hobbies and sparetime interests. Classify according to number and quality, and amount of time spent on them; from more than six down to none.

and this magistrate I seen him before and he got a green fountain pen and white hairs in his ears and pick his nose and he say to me you are nothing but a nuisance, do you know that? in and out of here all the time

Note the amount of care taken of her cell beyond the requirements of normal supervision. Form an estimate of the standard of cleanliness and quality of decoration. Mark her approach to unsupervised personal hygiene as Very Good/Good/Average/Poor/Very Poor.

and we use to meet these boys in Gleeson's and take them up home this place in Lincoln Street in Ponsonby and was all this beer and the old man he use to sell the bottles and was dozens and hundreds so he must get a fair bit off them and the boys they would give him beer too or wine or what he wanted but he got WILD he said to us you not to bring these boys home and we all said we said bugger you we said this is our place what we pay you this is where we LIVE and nobody took no notice and the old man he locked the door and he put boards over the windows in the daytime after a while to stop the boys getting in and the boys come they smashed the boards down yes and broke the glass and put the beer in through the window first and then they come in too yes after the beer yes all these boys gee there was LOT of them and Pauline she was trying to get this boy to give his mate some moneys so he can pay her and they was all yelling and the old man he come in yelling in his pink underpants and he told us he rang for the cops and gee the boys was WILD and gee it was funny with the cops coming in the front door and the boys all diving out the windows and there was these two on the floor and a cop he fell over them gee it was funny and Ruby she was naked and Sandra she only had her skivvy on and the old man in his pink underpants he was just standing there gee he looked funny and the broken glasses on the floor and gee they came in fast and hell they WENT fast too the boys back to the ship and we all went down after and gee was great you know this boy he borrow me his jersey I was COLD and was this old man on the ship and the boys they got him to bring out his pink underpants and one of the boys he put them on and he was making out he was this old man up at Lincoln Street the one that phone for the cops and gee it was funny the way he done it we was all laughing

Corrective Training

After thinking it over for a week Marcia wrote a note:

Dear Henny,
I want to be frends with you. I am so lonely. All the girls in here will not be frends with me. They think I must be someone else frend and they do not want a fight. But I am nobodys I have not been here long enough. And I do not care for that what they do. I have had boyfrends and that is what I like. My boyfrend said he will meet me when I come out. But I need somebody to talk to. Somebody I can trust. I like you Henny you got a kind face. I want to talk about things to you will you let me?

Your frend if you will have me
Marcia

Henny sat in her room. She was a tall good-looking girl of nineteen with large hands. On the first knuckles of her left-hand fingers were the letters E S U K in amateur tattoo and on the right fingers L T F C. She wrote:

Dear Marcia,
I got your illegle note and I have hid it. I liked it when you said you like me. But I did not get that other bit you said about not liking what the girls do. Thats your problem kiddo. You got to sort that one out for yourself. And you never told me how long you are in for. That has a lot to do with it. I have been here on what they call indeteminit sentence but I been a good girl (ha ha) and they letting me out soon. Want to get rid of me I spose. So you dont have long to make up your mind.

Yours in the meantime
Henny
0 4 1 0 E

Dearest Henny,
This is your kiddo again. I have thought over what you said about *that* and if we can meet you can tell me what you want. Or show me. But take it easy because I am new at this. It is raining now and cold and the wind blows leaves on to my window and the rain water makes them stick to the glass. Then a splash of rain hits the window and the leaves wash away. I always feel sad when its raining and I am inside and nowhere to go and nothing to do. And what is worst is, is nobody to talk to. When we meet we will talk and tell each other about ourselves and make frends before we do that. But I will let you. Thats a promise. You are so sweet I like to look at you. Your a bit like my Aunty Sara in Morrinsville.

Your
Marcia
0 4 1 0 E 2

Dear Kiddo,
Your got a cheek to tell me what I can do and I cant do. I dont need you really because I got all the darls I need just now. Your not the only one that wants to be frends with Sweetsie. I will tell you who my darls are and that will make you jelous. They are Cuddles Sister Blanket Noddie Podge Cobra. Hows that now. But I will not tell you who my Special Darl is. That is my secret and I hope you get even more jelous. But I like you and hope you can get some sense into that sweet sixteen head of yours. You got a lot to learn girl.

So long
Sweetsie
(you can call me that so
you are at first base)

PS   Fuck your Aunty Sara.

My dearest Sweetsie Darling,
It was so nice how that happened we never planned it and yet there we were together and nobody else around and at last I had somebody nice and frendly and tender and loving in my arms and nothing else mattered. Nothing else in the world. All the best things seem to happen like that. There was me and this boy once I never even new his name but never mind that. Was worried before but now I no its you I truly love. I am so glad I have met you properly now. This place can never get too bad so long as you are here for me to think about all day long. The sun is shining through the window on to my bed and its nice. It will warm the blankets and that is good this is such a

cold place. After I was with you I felt all sort of loose and good and cheerful. Then I got all tight again and grumpy and all I can think about is you and me and when we can meet again. It cant be soon enough for me. With you close and wanting me I no who I am and I can like myself for a while. Not much but a bit when you want me. I love you Sweetsie and what you said about us that made me feel real good. And that is for the first time since I been in this dump. But it must be all right if a lovely sweet kind darling like you is in here too. I am encloseing some pictures of flowers I tore from a magazine. Thought you might like them for your wall. So this note is a fat one and I hope it gets to you safely.

Your ever loving
Kiddo

XXX   OOO   XXX

Dear Kiddo,
Dont get too smart now. I seen you talking to Porkchop yesterday. She is not one of my darls but you are. I do not like my darls to talk to any girls that are not my darls. You just remember that or your out. But I do not want to be rough on you. Your such a sweet kid. I am sorry I said that just now. I was in a bad mood and I get jelous. If people are going to like me they have to like ME and not anybody else. That is just the way I am. So glad you like me Kiddo darling. When you was talking to Porkchop you never had a coat on. You should of else you might have catch cold. That is no good for my sweet Kiddo. Did I tell you I like your new shoes there nice did your parents send them? I wish I had folks would send me things. I am going to see if I can steal a present for you.

So long for now
Sweetsie

Dearest Sweetsie,
I love you so much I do not want to share you with your other darls. I hate them. Sweetsie my treasure I want to be your Special Darl. I never asked you who your Special is I never want to no else I might kill her. I would too. You no you like me a lot and we have such fun together and I like you telling me all the mad things you done in your life and we laugh together I never laugh with anyone except you Sweetsie my pet. You make me feel good all over and warm and laughing and kind and loving. You have to *ditch* your Special who ever she is and I am going to be your Special Darl from now on. Take me in those cuddly arms of yours and tell me not to worry and that you love me and I am your own Special Darling. I will believe you. I can believe anything you say when you hold me in your warm arms. Gosh you had your hair done nice at chapel today. Real neat and I never took my eyes off you.

Yours for ever
Kiddo
(Special Darling please?)
X X X X X X   O O O O O O

My dearly beloved Kiddo,
I ditched Bonkers but not because you told me to. She was only a fucken shop lifter anyway she got no style and she never had any class. She pisses me off and I will be glad when she gets out of here. But you do not get to be my Special as easy as that. When I see you I will tell you what I mean. I do not want to write it down else someone find this note. I do not want them to know about us. You make me happy Kiddo and I want to make you happy to. But you got to let me. Next time I see you I will give you some lollies I pinched

from Charmaine's room. She is a dead loss any way just like her fucken mate Bonkers.

Love
Sweetsie

PS I thought yesterday you was looking a bit thin are you sure your eating properly? Its not much what they give us here but you should eat it.

My closest darling lovely Sweetsie,
I just had a letter from Mummy and my Aunty Sara died. Yes she died in our old house where we use to live before and my uncle Bob (that is Saras husband) he moved there family in there after. I feel so sad and lonely and awful. I got a brooch my Aunty Sara gave me I use to wear it on my hat when I wore a hat. She was the one to make pikelets. We use to pick lemons from our tree and cut them in four long ways and sqweeze them on her pikelets. Gee they were nice. I thought I would hate it in here and I did at the start but now I dont because it brought us together you and me Sweetsie and I feel safe with you and I would stay in here for ever if it meant being with you. Now without my Aunty Sara nothing is settled for me up there. Sweetsie my darling we will try the other one tonight. I promise. That one you told me about for me to be your Special. The one I would not do. I want to now. But only for you. So please come. I will do it but only with you. Come tonight. I cant stand to be alone. Your been here much longer and will no how to work it. Or see if you can meet. Please Sweetsie. My empty arms are longing to hold you.

from your Kiddo
who tonight becomes your
SPECIAL DARL (please)
come here for X and O and?

Dear Kiddo,
No I do not show your notes to any one else. I might do that with my darls but not with my Special Darl. Thats what special means and you have ernt it. You dont want to get so suspishus. Or jelous because I am nice to all my darls not just you. I am alowd to make other girls happy arnt I? They think a lot of me to you know. And when I was talking with Blanket no we were not talking about you so there. Anyone who hurts any of my darls hurts me to so just you remember that. Or is against them. You better watch out I don't see you talking to girls who are not my darls. Other girls want to be my darls now and other darls want to be my Special. I will not tell you there names. I trust you but dont get smart. You say when I talk to my other darls I hurt you. Sweetheart I know what it is to be hurt. That is why I never go all one way. That is how to get real bad hurt. You trust me and stick to me and I will look after you and protect you. I told you I love you and when I say that I mean it. Of course I am not forgetting you. So stop your fucken moaning. There I go getting wild again. I get these moods. What it is sweetest is that I am scared you might stop loving me. Just a bit. That would be awful. I need your love so much. There is nothing else in here just only our love for each other. That is the most precious thing in all the world. I feel good now I have told you that because I know you will believe me. We should make up a special tattoo for you and me and put it on ourselves where nobody can see it only us when we are going to be special. But it might be to sore. I have been worried about you since I heard you coughing in the bathroom you sure your all right? Think of a night together just us. Wonder what we would be like in the morning a sight I bet. Put your hand down there and swear you will always be true to me. I am doing that now to you and its good it always is with you and that is why you are

my Special Darling. Must lie down and think about you. Do the same for me when you get this.

> Must rush
> Sweetsie

PS Later – I have not sent this yet because I lost my best messenger today she is gone outside where we all want to be.

> I FLY

My dearest darling Sweetsie pet,
Your going today and I will give this note to Miriam to give you at the door. I feel like killing myself and it is only your promise that is stopping me. You said you will write and that is what will keep me going. The thought of a letter from you. Am deeply hurt to no we are to part. I saw the new girls today that has just come in and I was wishing it was you and me. That is a mad thing to say I no but if it was us we could start all over again. I do not no what I am going to do without you. Sweetsie my Special and Only Darling your the only one who talks to me and tells me jokes and makes me laugh and loves me for *real*. I owe every thing to you. The only nice things that happened to me in this dump was when I was with you. After I seen you I always lie awake in bed and think over all the things we said to each other. The ways you have of loving me they make me feel real close to you. I can not have any secrets from you after we been doing that. Only just a while. Now your going away from me. Have nothing left but dreams. I will be a good girl (true) and try to get out soon with remishun and you will be waiting for me. I will be true to you and you no I will because I never liked any these other girls here much you no that. Never like I love you. So I will not fall for any one else and will do any thing you want when I am out there with you. Promise. Sweetsie my darling that Special Darl one you got me to do to you the one on my knees it took some getting use to. I have been thinking we might try that one together you and me. But not any one standing or kneeling you figer it out. And take our time. I will keep out of trouble and if they want me at home after all this I will go but you must come too. You told me you had no where. I can easy be faithful when I think of our times together. And the times that are to be. I never seen any one in the new girls as nice as you. Now I am lonely again and now I am crying. Gosh it is hard and cruel them letting you out and not me and yet it is what we all long for and in a way I am glad for you. I have your photo for my treasure. The half with Bonkers in it I tore that half off and put it down the toilet. Good job. You must promise me you will not start going with Bonkers again now you are going out and she is out too. She must think she is smart. She is out there and me in here. I wish you the best of luck and love you more than ever. I am still crying and I cried before when I went past and saw your things gone and new you was in the office and soon you would be gone for ever. And another girl in your room and to sleep in your bed and put her things where all your dear things use to be on the dressing table and the shelf and put up new pictures. It will hurt me every time I look there to no you have gone. God I am feeling awful. Wish I could stop being me and be some body else for a while. That is until this goes away. But I do not think it will ever go away so long as I am in here and you gone. My heart is yours and my body and soul and I can not see the paper any more. I hope you will be very happy. Keep your promise.

> For ever and ever YOURS
> Marcia (Kiddo S D No. 1)
> X X X X X X O O O O O O
> x x x x (for you no where)
> WAIT FOR ME

Marcia got off the train in Wellington. She walked up the platform and stood in the concourse, her suitcase in her hand, looking for Henny. The masses of people were bewildering. She looked at the women's clothes and particularly the girls'. She put the suitcase at her feet.

Henny came out of the women's rest room. She wore a shirt and jeans and no shoes. They smiled, and put their arms about each other, and kissed. Henny was a head taller. She nearly lifted Marcia off her feet. They kissed again. People at the bookstall turned to look at them.

They went to a seat. Henny put an arm around Marcia's shoulders and Marcia put one around Henny's waist and they gripped hands on their knees. They kissed again.

'Kiddo.'

'Sweetsie.'

Henny gripped Marcia's hand and placed it on her thigh.

'You cold?'

'Not now.'

'You should of borrowed a coat though. You look cold.'

'Not any more.'

'Glad to be here?'

'Glad to be away. Out. At last. With you.'

'Counting the days.'

'Only till I see you again.'

They kissed. Henny licked Marcia's lips.

'I've missed you Kiddo.'

'Me too. You.'

Henny pressed her hand harder. 'You know what I like about you Kiddo? You're so affectionate.'

'I feel frightened here. All these people.'

'You're with Sweetsie now Kiddo.'

'Where we stay tonight?'

'I don't know.'

'Where you last night?'

'Never mind. Dead loss anyway.'

'Where's your things.'

'Got none.'

Henny went to the bookstall and bought the evening paper.

'Let's see what's all it say here.'

They searched the classified advertisements for the accommodation section. 'You read it,' Henny said.

'I can't read too good. You.'

Henny squinted at the page.

'Nothing here,' she said. 'Nothing here for *us*.'

'You sure?'

Henny screwed up the paper and pushed it under the seat.

'How about Tawa then?' Marcia asked.

'You know anyone in Tawa?'

'One or two.'

'But it's a cold dump, Tawa. Cold and wet and too long to get to.'

'What about Newtown?'

'It's changed a lot. You wouldn't know it now. It's not cheap up there any more. Same at Aro Street.'

'Where we go then?'

'I don't know.'

'So long as it's just you and me Sweetsie.'

'It will be.'

'Promise?'
'Course.'
'Even if it's just only tonight. Please?'
'Sure.'
'Promise?'
'I said so, Kiddo.'
'Where we go then?'
'We'll find somewhere.'
'Anywhere. Just you and me.'
'That's all there'll be. Nobody else. Promise.'
'Come on then.'
Hand in hand, Henny carrying Marcia's suitcase, they walked out into the street.

The Tree

1

This had once been a collection of raupo huts but now it was a village of neat houses with gaily coloured tile roofs and tar-sealed streets. The meeting-house stood, still, and the marae was clear of thistle, but the old matai occupied the site needed for the new community centre and it would have to go; its root system was stopping the installation of sewerage pipes for a new block of houses. The Government had taken the land under the Public Works Act and the tree's removal had been decided on and nothing could be done, now, to save it.

Work parties arrived on Friday morning with chain-saws and later a bulldozer. Stripped to their singlets the men sawed at the tree well into the morning but made little mark on its hard flanks and became more and more exasperated. The elders, Wi, Pare, and Tu, sat on a seat outside the meeting-house, smoking and muttering and shaking their heads. When at last the bulldozer clanked towards the tree at top speed and hit it with a loud *chunk* and the driver pitched forward over the levers, winded, the elders leaned back and chuckled. 'E koe!' said Wi. 'E nga!' said Tu.

After school the children of the village came to watch. They enjoyed the whirring rip of the chain-saws and they liked to see the bulldozer jolting over the grass, straining on its cable. They all hoped to be watching when the great tree tipped over and hit the ground with a thump. Some went to their grandfathers, the elders sitting on the seats, to ask for money to buy ice-creams; it was always good to have something sweet in your mouth while watching an exciting piece of action, like at the pictures or in the sitting-room at home lying in front of the TV.

One of the workers, he looked part-Maori but he wasn't from around here, stood beside the elders rolling a smoke.

'E tama!' said Pare. 'Kei te raweke koe i to tipuna, i a Tane!' ('Hey son! You are fooling with your ancestor Tane!')

The young worker, not wishing to say he did not understand, shook his head.

'You are cutting Tane's throat!' Wi said. He was a little deaf and thought he had missed the reply. 'Have a care!' he said. 'Watch your step!'

'She's a tough one all right,' the worker said.

'Ae.' The three nodded.

'Like we say up in Te Whaiti, that's the tree Te Kooti tied his horse to.'

The three sat silent a moment.

'Te Kooti was never down this way,' Tu said.

The worker lit his smoke and walked away. A minute later there was a yell and a flash of blood; shouts; running. A chain-saw had slipped and bucked and the young worker had been cut. His mates gave him first-aid and in a while the ambulance came whining up to take him off to hospital. Nobody did much work after that, and the tree stood quiet and still.

Wi leaned towards Pare and Tu and they spoke together.

Word spread quickly and by the time the Ministry of Works men had packed their gear and left for the weekend, everyone in the village knew there was to be a korero tonight.

2

The people gathered in the meeting-house after tea. Wi was the first to speak.

'Respect,' he said, 'respect has to be paid to parents. Always. It is traditional and also scriptural. If we do not honour our origins, how can there be respect between those who now are, and those who were, and those who are to come? So it is with Tane and his works. This tree is the child of Tane, as we all are, and we must recognize and respect this parenthood. I am a Christian, at least I try to be. But there is nothing in the Christian faith to say I may not honour the feelings and beliefs of my forefathers. Not when it means showing respect for life.'

'Ae,' the people murmured. 'Kia ora, Wi.'

'We have come to live too close to the pakeha, we are too eager to adopt his ways. We have been too ready to take on his beliefs without examining them. Too ready to put our own thoughts aside. Yet we Maori had such a richness of belief, in the old days, it would be impossible for the pakeha to understand. And for many of us Maori too because we have forgotten. We were then the children of the sky and the earth. What are we now? What have we allowed the pakeha to make of us? In those days we never knew what it was to be alone or unwanted. To us all things were the children of the Sky Father and the Earth Mother as we ourselves are. The trees and plants, the birds and fish, even the rocks and the sand and the wind, all possessed a spirit as we do, they too were touched by the wairua, and this we knew and respected. The mauri ora, the great life principle in all things.

'What of now? This tree that resists so strongly, what is the secret of her strength? To me the answer is simple. She is the child of Tane the Great Fertilizer, as we are. She fights for her life as we do when attacked. Fights for her dignity as we do when insulted. She has wounded one of her foes as a warning. This tree is protected and knows her strength. She grew up to feel she was among kinsfolk here, friends, people who would love her and care for her when she grew old. Instead we cuff her and kick her and make her feel friendless among strangers and enemies; alone. We should be ashamed.

'Let me remind you that we are of the younger branch of Tane. When we wish to slay a member of the elder branch, we must be careful to go about it the right way. We are meddling with the work of our great common ancestor and we must be sure we know what we are doing.'

'Ae,' the people murmured. 'Kia ora, Wi. Ka pai!'

Pare stood up. 'E hika e! Let us think for a moment of what this tree means in our lives. She is the only survivor of an earlier time. Of all our great ancestors she is the only one who still lives, who still has her being among us. She saw us all as children playing about her roots, she saw our fathers too, and our grandfathers. All the great men of our hapu have sat in her shade and eaten and joked and talked of courage and honour, and we heard them and believed.

We must love her in her own way, this tree. As Wi has said, we respect age. How much more respect is due to this old-timer? Scarred and deformed, perhaps; long past her best; a nuisance in some ways, a menace in others. Yet let us remember that many of us were conceived within the sound of her clashing branches. We are as close to this tree as the birds are, and the wind.'

'Kia ora, Pare.'

'Life– life is what this tree of ours has still. What upstarts they are, who decided to condemn this tree to death! She has no voice to plead for her life. No voice that the pakeha can hear. But she speaks to us. If we will listen. She spoke to us today in the way that the God of all things speaks only to the Maori. We did not listen. And already with their chain-saws and their bulldozer they have made her existence a burden and her survival unlikely. But it is not too late for us to make up for our failure.'

'Ae, ae.' The people nodded their heads.

'This is a strong tree still, untouched by the decay that comes to even the mighty. It is not time which brings death to our tree, but change. It is we who have changed, and the world about us. Not our tree. From the time when an insect could shake her little stem she has grown to such a size that even a hurricane cannot bend her. She might have become a canoe, this tree. She might have been made into houses for our parents, been cut into rafters to rib them in. But the axe never touched her and she has served us in a different way. With her great body she has been cover to us in storms and shade from the sun and shelter from the wind and rain. How grateful our people must have been to her in past days. Now she must give up the fight she has fought all her life to stay with us and help us. She must bow. At last. To us. But she will not do this without a struggle. I agree with Wi, we must go about this the right way.'

'Kia ora, Pare.'

Tu stood up. 'I too feel we must respect this tree. Think of all the great labours she has accomplished. Staying alive! Once she was small enough to be hidden in the hand of a baby. When she took root and grew her first two leaves, the grass could cover her and a kick or a blow or a rolling over when fighting or loving would have destroyed her. How fortunate we are that nobody broke her off to wave in the hand when greeting visitors to our marae in times long past, or set her in their hair to show grief for a lost one. They might have used her to make a decoration in the meeting-house. All this hugeness and strength could then have been held within the arms of a girl. But the rain soaked to her roots, the wind was kind, the sun caused the damp to rise, and the child grew into a beautiful woman. Nourished and made virile by the juices of the earth. Mother of many. And with age came wisdom. How many true things this old tree knows. If only she could speak! How much she could tell us about our parents, our grandparents, and the people before them; she knew them all when they were young. The stories that have come down to us, first this version, then that: how we have wondered what the truth is. Yet the truth is here, in this old tree. We are so used to her, she is so much a part of our lives, we have forgotten what she is to us. This tree is the living record of all our days and nights together in this place, back longer than any person now living on the earth.'

'Kia ora, Tu.'

The people decided they would take care of the matai themselves. When the Ministry of Works men arrived on Monday they would find the job done. Wi would take charge.

3

Before dawn on Saturday morning Wi left his bed and instead of putting on his trousers and shirt he went to the wardrobe and took down his piupiu from the hook. He slipped a box of matches into the waistband, and took from the drawer the stone axe, an heirloom left to him by his father. Barefooted, he went out to the verandah and waited for Pare and Tu. He looked at the moon: fortunately it was at the right phase. But it was cold; he shivered.

Tu and Pare arrived, also in piupius. Wi took up a tawa stick he had whittled the night before, and without a word the three elders walked to the church. Inside the fence grew a tall and spreading puriri tree. Wi picked the largest leaf he could reach, and fitted it carefully into a cleft at the end of the tawa stick; it was now a long-handled axe with the leaf as the head.

The three walked slowly to the old matai, approaching it along the shadow it cast in the moonlight. Chips and sawdust lay scattered about from the Ministry's efforts in the afternoon, and the ground was churned.

They stood with heads bowed. Wi said quietly:

'Kai te hiahia	A desiring
Kai te koronga	A wishing
Kai a Tane.'	For Tane.

He then stepped to the tree, raised the tawa stick and tapped the trunk gently with the puriri-leaf at the spot where the felling scarf would be made.

'He ao pukapuka
He ao mahamaha
He toki henahena
He toki ta wahie
Ka pa ki tua, ka pa ki waho, ka pa ki a Tane.'

As he spoke the last line of the invocation he passed the stick to Pare and on the words *ka pa ki a Tane* he hit the bark of the tree twice with his stone axe. A chip flew out, a small one; he searched for it and picked it up and, passing the axe to Tu, he walked away from the tree, passing into the moon-shadow. Tu continued cutting into the trunk and collecting the chips.

Wi kept walking into the darkness until he could no longer hear the sound of Tu chopping the tree. He found himself near the school. He went into the playground, gathered dry sticks and leaves together in a heap, took the box of matches from the band of his piupiu and lit a small fire. While searching for sticks he trod on a snail and felt sorry; but he had not meant it, he reflected. When the fire was blazing he squatted beside it and placed the chip, the first chip from the matai, in the heart of the flames. He chanted quietly:

'Hika ra taku ahi
E tumutumu whenua
E aneane whenua
E raro timu, e raro take, e Hawaiki
Ka hika ki te ihi o Tane
Ka hika ki te mana o Tane
Noho mai i tua na
E tapu ana Tane
E maota ki te rangi o Hawaiki . . . e!'

When the chip had burnt he waited for the sacred fire to die down. The embers ashed over grey and faded to black. Except for the matches, all the essentials of *tumutumu whenua* had been met: the chip of the tree marked for death had been claimed by the gods.

He returned to Pare and Tu at the base of the matai. They had put together the chips, and Wi made another fire and placed them in it. Tu took three small potatoes from his piupiu-band and put them in the embers. The three gathered chips and sawdust and some of the bluish-black bark of the tree ripped off by the Ministry men during the afternoon, and put these on the fire. As the flames grew higher and the potatoes steamed and began to blacken on the outside, Wi chanted and each line was repeated by Pare and Tu.

'Hika ra taku ahi, e Tane!   Generate my fire, O Tane!
Hika ra taku ahi, e Tane!
He ahi purakau, e Tane!   A ceremonial fire, O Tane!
Ka hika i te ihi o Tane
Ka hika i te mana o Tane
Ka hika i te marutuna o Tane
Ka hika i te maruwehi o Tane
Ka hika i te pukapuka a Tane
Ka hika i te mahamaha o Tane
Ka kai koe, e Tane!   You will eat, O Tane!
Ka kai hoki au, e Tane!   I also will eat, O Tane!
Ka mama nga pukenga   Thus will the adepts be
                                        freed,
Ka mama nga wananga   Thus will the wise ones be
                                        cleansed,
Ka mama hoki ahau,   As I too, this disciple,
   tenei tauira.'   will be freed.

The chips and sawdust were dry and burnt quickly and cleanly. Wi felt sure the tapu had now been taken off the tree and that Tane was satisfied with the sincerity of their devotions. No further harm would come to those who intended death to one of his children; there would be no more accidents, no blood would flow, they would be safe and they would work well.

With the tawa stick he cleared the embers and took out the three potatoes, charred on the outside. He waited while they cooled, then broke one open and recited:

'Tenei te pou ka eke
Te pou kai a koe
Ko te pou o tenei mahi
Tiaho i roto, wananga i roto, korero i roto
Tena te umu, te umu ka eke
Ko te umu o tenei whaihanga
Ka ma taku hau tu
Ka ma taku hau mahi
Ka ma moe tu, ka ma moe rere
Ka ma moe te whakaarahia
Whakaarahia i te ata hapara
Ka mau tatua mau wawe i te ata hapara
Ka ma nga pukenga
Ka ma nga wananga
Ka ma hoki matau, enei tauira.'

He ate the potato, and Pare and Tu broke theirs open and ate too. Sunrise was coming, and they felt cold; the warm potato lay like a burning ember in the stomach.

The sun came from behind the hills and its rays slanted through the level layers of smoky cloud; mist rose from the grass. The elders walked to their homes for breakfast and changed into working clothes for the day.

4

The matai was sixty feet high and the trunk three feet in diameter. The main attack began after breakfast. Wi and Tu, now wearing denims and checked shirts, brought their stone axes to the tree and eight men, working in pairs, took turns to deepen the scarf into the trunk. The first man cut the top and bottom of the scarf, and the second pecked with his axe at the wood between. Making an opening into the tree in this way, with such tools, was hard slow work.

Pare, in a faded khaki boiler-suit, built a fire of tawa branches and when the gap in the trunk was wide enough he placed burning tawa logs in it crosswise. The fire failed to take until the men sprinkled on dry grass and fern and small twigs. When the fire had burnt into the trunk a little way the logs were pulled out, the glowing embers doused with water brought in buckets from the creek, and the axemen went to work again, first chipping away the charred wood and then deepening the scarf ready for the next burn.

'When I saw how this tree stopped that charging bulldozer yesterday, I had an idea,' said Tu. 'I believe this tree had a charm said over it long ago koi tukitukia e Tawhiri-matea – in case it might be destroyed by the wind spirit. This has made it especially strong against any pushing or pulling.' So crews were sent off in trucks to the swamp to cut and bring in flax, and on trestle-tables outside the meeting-house Tu's wife supervised the women as they plaited three thick ropes each a hundred feet long.

The men worked hard and sweated a lot and wanted to drink beer but Wi would allow them only water; beer they could have when the job was finished and not before, he said. The fires burnt and the chipping went on into the afternoon. Some of the younger men despaired of the blunt and cumbrous stone axes; they asked Wi to let them use saws and sharp metal axes.

'This is a stupid old Maori idea this,' one of the young men said. 'Why can't we use a saw or a decent axe? Something with a blade to it? We'll be here for hours.'

Wi glared at him 'And this tree has been here for centuries,' he said. 'It's not just a matter of cutting down a tree.'

They were reminded of what the elders had said in the meeting-house the night before.

'It took *men* to use these axes,' Wi said. 'Today you like the tool to do the work. Before, it was the man. He liked to feel he was giving something of himself. So try to be worthy of the ones who went before. Just today. And be patient.'

As the afternoon wore on they overcame their exasperation. Forces had been released which they did not understand but which they could feel working inside them. They became more accustomed to the stone axes, to their weight and balance, and began to compete with each other in seeing who could make the deepest bite into the tree in the shortest time. The past was coming to them again, and working through them; and far from being resentful, they welcomed it.

In the meeting-house the women cooked the tree-fellers' food separately from the food for the other workers, and they ate before anyone else was allowed in. After they had eaten and gone back to work, the floor was carefully swept to remove any chips or dust that had fallen from their clothes, and the sweepings were taken out and thrown into the fire beside the tree.

While the cutting and burning and chipping went on, the elders took turns to chant:

> 'Haruru te toki, ngahoa te toki, haramai te toki
> Ngau atu te toki ki te uma o te rakau
> Tenei te toki ka haruru, tenei te toki ka ngatoro
> Ko toki na wai? Ko toki na Whiro te tipua
> Oi whiti ka ao.'

The workers toiled in rhythm to the words, and when they had learnt them by heart they chanted them without the elders having to lead.

'I was just thinking,' Wi said. 'We are shifting this tree to make room for our community centre. But we have always had one. Our own community centre. Right here. Under this tree.'

'No shops though,' said one of the young workers. 'No pool room. No hot and cold water.'

'No lights,' said another. 'No bowls, no table tennis. No housie, no cards, no darts. No orchestra. No band.'

'Plenty of room to dance though,' said Wi. 'The light of the moon and the stars. And all the air to fill with singing. But you are right. The times change.'

'And what will we do with this matai when we get her down?'

'We will mill her and use the boards in the community centre. Very good for weatherboards and floors. Strong, and lasts well. And she will still be with us.'

'I hope she hears you,' called Pare. Wi did not hear so he called again.

'I'm sure she does,' Wi said, nodding his head.

When the cut was deep enough, Wi called a halt. The plaited ropes were brought from the tables and laid out on the ground. A man stood at the treetrunk, another climbed on his shoulders, and Tu, the spryest of the elders, with the ends of the flax tied to his belt, climbed up the other two men into the lowest branches of the tree. He tied one rope to the trunk, and the other two to branches on either side. Many willing hands took the strain below. Tu climbed down.

Wi put his ear to the scarf.

'I can't hear too well,' he called. 'Please be quiet. Turituri at the front.'

He kept his ear to the tree for a long time while the people waited in silence.

'The tree is speaking to us,' he said at last. 'Quick now, we must lose no time. We have all been part of her life and we must all be part of her death; we must share! Bring all the whanau, quickly.'

They came from the meeting-house, the women still with their aprons on and the visitors in their best clothes; and from all over the village the children came running. Tu walked up and down, carefully measuring the fall and placing the people beyond the reach of the topmost branches. Women took places on the ropes, and children, and the visitors and the aged; even a few pakehas who had come to watch.

They grasped the flax and pulled. The tree stood firm. Wi began to chant, and as they pulled on the ropes the people repeated each line of the chant after him:

> 'Tena te ara, te ara ka iri
> Ko te ara o Tane
> Tane i te pu,
> Tane i te aka,
> Tane i te tamore
> I tupu ai te whanaunga ariki
> E Tane whiwhi make ngutaha ki te ra
> Tena te ara, te ara ka iri
> Ko te ara o Tane.'

A crack rang out and echoed and re-echoed in the hills, a sound like the breaking of a rock in a fire. The timber at the scarf in the matai began to moan like an old woman in pain. The people leaned forward, pulling hard, and suddenly the ropes became slack. They turned to watch. The tree seemed to fold her branches about her like a shawl for warmth and comfort, and the leaves grew strangely still, and with a snapping crackle at the scarf she leaned with the breeze and bowed slowly and with great dignity to the earth; and the birds rose from her branches and sang in shrilling chorus as they circled like gulls above the wake of a vanished ship. It was as if a curtain had been torn open and the light poured through, and the watchers marvelled at the sudden vast and terrible emptiness in the sky.

'E! kua hinga a Tane!' cried Wi; and his face was wet with tears.

YVONNE DU FRESNE

The Morning Talk

The weeks marched up to Midwinter Day. It never stopped raining. Brown rain, brown paddocks.

'Daneweather!' exulted the Bedstemoder, squinting out of the streaming windows like a Vikingwife. 'But of course, not the *ice*!'

Astrid had to admit the beauty of the Lillebaelt, the pink ice in the sunset, after hearing so much about it.

'Lit candles we pushed into the snowbanks in the garden,' intoned the Bedstemoder. 'The flames and the black birch-trunks. . . .'

Astrid could see that picture, but she was concentrating on the creek. Each day it rose a little higher and threatened Mr Semple's beautiful new road. Soon it would be covered, they would be cut off from school. Out of the ground-fog on an impossible morning she would see with eyes that gleamed with welcome the first Daneship steal over the flood. A neat Daneship, accommodated to small-sized floods, it would be manned by her six-foot cousins standing motionless and golden-haired, broad-swords at the salute, ready to take their cousin Astrid on board and show their flag, the Dannebrog, to the Wainui District Primary School.

It was dark in the mornings and dark in the late afternoons. Gleams of watery sun at midday glanced over the sodden grass in the muddy playground at school.

'Aak! Aak!' screamed the children, like ravens, swooping over the mud, under the brown sky. Doing her solitary reconnaissance before school, Astrid roamed the school hall, spying on the British Empire, looking at the English heroes in the pictures on the walls. They were all dying very gently, held up in comrades' arms on bloodied ships' decks, or on trampled battle-fields. Two were active dying heroes, waving swords and leaping elegantly toward distant clumps of the enemy, who wore striped turbans too low for fashion over their brows, and drooping pantaloons. Everywhere, *Ragnarok*, the world's last battle, was being fought, but nobody was laughing.

Inside the classroom, the Englanders struggled with overflowing inkwells and light upstrokes and dark down-strokes. And Morning Talks. The dark classroom ceiling beams were pointed like an ark, the rain drummed on the roof, and the Headmaster gave his regular morning commentary on the war-news. Astrid felt keenly the empty space at her waist that should have held the comforting shape of her Danegirl's knife, freshly whetted that morning. Just a little flash of blade in weak sun would have sufficed as a warning in Harald Bluetooth's time, but like Prince Amleth, this was a game of wits. No weapons but one's brain. In the bleak reality of the present, the Second World War, Denmark had fallen in a matter of hours. A fight had raged around the King's Palace for six hours, waged by the traffic police, among others. Rumour had it that the King had waved a handkerchief as a sign of surrender. Holger the Dane, fast at his marble table at Kronborg, had failed to rise up and bring lightning down from the skies on Denmark's foes. The situation needed Astrid's smiling, golden cousins, sitting at the tip-up desks in a solid circle around her to maintain a show of solidity and calm. But they were twenty miles away, no doubt fighting their battles of wits in their own schools. She remained, the sole representative of the over-confident, treacherous, fallen European nations in the district, and accepted the responsibility proudly.

'Over-excitable, over-emotional, unreliable, unprepared. . . .' The well-trodden words rolled over Astrid's head as she sat wearing a new neutral smile to avert a little of the flood-tide. She dwelt on the pictures in her mind that became richer day by day, of the long-ships bearing down on the English coast, and fires starting here and there.

She apologized inwardly for her over-blonde hair and wolf's eyes. The Headmaster seemed confused in his knowledge of the ethnic groupings of Northern Europe. She suspected that he lumped the Danes in with the Northern Germanic tribes, which had also muddled the Romans in their reluctant forays into her homelands. And if *they* had been confused, what chance had he to clear his mind?

'Foreigners,' he stated on this morning of the flood, 'have the gift of the gab. Can you give us a little talk tomorrow? A *brief* talk, if that is at all remotely possible, Westingad.'

'Westergaard!' snapped an irritable voice in Astrid's mind. She must check her temper; Prince Amleth would have stumbled in his contest if he had been led astray by rage. She was a master of the English Public School language, knowing *Tom Brown's Schooldays* nearly off by heart.

'I can only try, Sir!' she essayed. Right on the nail.

'Try Denmark then. Entertain us. *Dazzle* us!' A wintry smile. 'If there's anything left there to talk about.'

A neutral chuckle. Incautious. Nobody laughed in this class.

Astrid sat stolidly on. In her mind, more long-ships beached. The Golden Warriors leapt into the surf. The Headmaster and his family made a clumsy attempt to run up a hill, but were losing ground. . . .

After school, at the gate the car waited. Fader leaned out.

'The flood's come. Hurry!' he shouted, and laughed. The rain fell like Thor's hammers. The Golden Warriors raced up the crown of the main road, beating the quivering line of speeding water rising on each side.

'Alley-oop!' roared Fader, hitting the side of the car with clenched fist. Spray flew in their bow-wave. They landed. On the verandah the women shouted exultantly. Brown water stretched over the land, up to the house.

'You are *home*!' they called. Bedstemoder waved a dressmaking ruler.

'Three feet!' she screamed, a Warrior Queen, 'and still rising!'

'Ah!' gasped Fader, and swooped her over the flood to safety.

The wind blew, the rain fell and the flood hissed past the house. Inside the fire blazed, the soup bubbled in its pot on the stove, and the talk swung between floods defeated and the Morning Talk.

'A little talk about our Denmark. An honour!'

Astrid dug into her good soup, working out chillier tactics. It would have to be, she decided, a war of wits, she being weaponless and but ten years old. Wits— and magic. She prayed for Prince Amleth's cunning.

After dinner they went out on to the verandah. In the night before Midwinter's Day the flood roared over the paddocks, a boiling current ran past the verandah steps, but the wall Fader had cleverly built by the creek was slowing it down. The house rode the waters like a Viking ship. *Ragnarok* was at hand, when the warriors rode the sky, the battle-maidens sang and the arrows fell hissing in the hail.

'Not through the floorboards yet!' said Fader and went restlessly inside to put the *Karelia* on the gramophone to give them heart to design the Morning Talk. Astrid chanted to his prompting –

'Reaching out into the sea in the north of Europe lies the small, but brave Kingdom of Denmark. . . .' Butterfat yields, the draining of the marshes, the Silver Kings buried in the peat at their house door in Jutland, universal education, agrarian reform. . . .

'You tell them – *everything*!' instructed Fader, stabbing his pen at Astrid's chest. 'And our families fighting in the Underground. You tell them that!'

The women took up the needle work and by the bright eye of the fire showed Astrid how to make a running stitch trace a magic bird, a marsh flower, a ship and a crown. They beamed at her while Fader's pen drove over the paper and the rain thundered on the roof.

'Tell them the stories, Astrid!' commanded the Bedstemoder, cheeks red with excitement. Then she paused and looked keenly at her, taking in the situation with her fingertips, as usual.

'Storytellers,' she said softly, 'hold all men. Stories win all hearts. The voice, well used, ends wars.'

Astrid looked up sharply.

'Tell them the stories, Astrid,' said Bedstemoder, 'of love and death and brave men. *Lille Fortaeller* Astrid.'

Astrid went to sleep muttering statistics of butterfat returns and the Silver Kings in the marshes. In the dawn she cried out in her sleep, and woke herself. By the edge of her bed, where she had rolled in her dream of ice and war, lay two little signs, put there by the Norne, the reader of signs, Bedstemoder. A little Dannebrog, its cross of white on scarlet bright in the dim light, and a picture of her example, the fourteenth-century Queen Margrethe, with the motto 'God's Help, the People's Love, Denmark's Strength' printed underneath.

Next morning, even though the flood crouched and drew in breath for a fresh onslaught that day, Fader got the car through for the honour of the Morning Talk. She sat perched on the hard draughty seat beside him and held the Dannebrog furled in both hands. As the true warriors of old had gone into battle chanting the sacred runes, she chanted the Talk inside her head, and the words, 'God's Help, the People's Love, Denmark's Strength', for the sake of Dronning Margrethe.

She still held it as she reluctantly climbed on to the bar of the black-board easel to try and find Denmark in a welter of black names on the old yellow varnished school map of Europe. The Headmaster watched in mocking silence as she regrettably stabbed the Dannebrog on to Holland.

'Lost at sea?' he inquired.

'*Nej!*' she answered curtly, searching for the maddeningly small patch that said 'Jutland'.

'Here lies Jutland!' she cried, unmanned with delight, giving it the full glottal stop. The class lifted heads in alarm.

'Reaching out into the sea in the north of Europe lies the small, but brave Kingdom of Denmark – ' she began, and rolled on through the butterfat returns, the agrarian reforms and so on. Squinting sideways at the Headmaster, she saw him lean against the fireplace and yawn.

'Vikings,' she said abruptly, 'had their training camps at the back of our farm at Trelleborg.' The class lifted its drowsy head.

'From the marshes the Golden Warriors have been raised and we have seen their faces,' she announced. The silence she had heard people speak of when the *skalds* struck their first silver chord was in the class-room. She obeyed it. She climbed carefully off the wobbly easel and advanced towards the class, pointing the Dannebrog at them.

'I will tell you the old story,' she said. 'Today is Midwinter's Day. Today Jarnvid strikes his harp. The wolf-children of Fenris break forth to hunt the sun and moon, and Garn, the hound of Hel, leaps over the earth.'

The Headmaster straightened his tie as if summoned to a meeting of Inspectors. Astrid, the mouthpiece, recited the Fortaelling of her people.

'Nidhaggr gnaws through the last root of Yggdrasil, and Jormungan, the serpent that circles the world, turns itself so that a wave sweeps over the earth.

Sleipner bears Odin to his last battle. The sky is split by a flaming sword. *Ragnarok* is upon us. The Gods die. Darkness falls over the earth. *Ragnarok* is upon us now.'

The class looked apprehensively at the rain outside and back again. 'But I will tell you of the end,' said Astrid. 'For thousands of years there is darkness, and then a small star, no bigger than a little spark, appears. Thousands of years pass, and it slowly grows. Until at last the first faint dawn appears. First we will have the flaming sword rending the sky in two, and then our dawn. But the darkness will be always on the edge of the world, because of that sword in the sky.'

The pattern of that old Fortaelling had been changed when she had been its mouthpiece. The Gods are here, she thought humbly.

'The years,' she said clumsily, 'we can read as meaning "days". Then Denmark rises again. And England!' she added hastily, careful not to offend.

'Kind of you,' said the Headmaster. But the silence still held. Astrid folded up the Dannebrog and started the drained-out tramp back to her desk. The Gods departed in a breath. The class rustled and several people turned and looked at her. *Skalds* had awkward lives – to *foretael* one moment and do the spelling tests the next.

'Well,' said the Headmaster, 'if we survive *Ragnarok* you could give us another sample next Monday, Westingad.'

'Westergaard,' said Astrid. '*Astrid* Westergaard.'

'Astrid,' repeated the Headmaster with a shocking accent. 'Any other bits you have straight from the horse's mouth would be welcome. It quite takes one's mind off the rain.'

'I'll do my best, Sir!' answered Astrid. Denmark's Strength, in vintage Tom Brown language.

BARRY MITCALFE

Black Cat

I have eliminated six men, or should I say, four men, a woman and a child. There may have been others that I don't know about but those I do know because, for once in our lousy lives, we had time to stop and count.

A body is just a thing, not very nice to look at.

The first was perhaps the worst, because I didn't know what to expect and it had no hardware, but then who's to say it's not Charlie? In the bush they're all Charlie, otherwise they wouldn't be there.

Turning it over and finding just that small hole in the forehead – unlike the back which was pretty messy – I got quite a bad feeling to see it was just a young boy, perhaps twelve, though I couldn't tell their ages too well. Not then.

That one was not too good, because I kept wondering, was he, wasn't he? Trouble was Charlie could be anybody.

So what if I'd made a mistake? It was V.C. country, wasn't it? He'd been told to get out and he hadn't gone.

He had a sort of soft look about him, for Charlie. But that didn't mean a thing, their women would skin and tan a living man, no trouble. Some of the pictures we saw in Orientation would turn your guts over. But this one didn't even have the old Charlie Chang look that most of the dead ones got, he was just a skinny kid, much the same dead as alive, apart from the mess where the back of his head had been.

He reminded me of another mistake – or was it a mistake – back at Matamau, which is south of Norsewood, which is in the North Island of New Zealand, which is and was my home. Got me placed now?

That was the time I killed the kitten. I'd been after the mother cat for months, she was a wild one, black with a white patch. Bloody townies, haven't got enough guts to get rid of their own cats, put them out to live or die. She'd lived, because she was smart and there was – or had been when she first started – a hell of a lot of birds.

Funny thing, though I was only fourteen or fifteen at the time and hadn't heard of 'Nam, I'd called that little kitty 'Charlie' and I was out to catch him because soon he'd be getting too wild.

So I was going to bowl the mother and tame old Charlie. I could have sneaked the gun and skittled the mother, no sweat, but trouble was the old black cat would only show up when I was bringing the cows in for morning milking and I didn't want to send our daily bread and butter stampeding back into the bush or half way through the boundary fence. Dad'd have me guts for garters. Anyway, it seemed more of a sporting proposition to 'have a go' with the quarry rocks off the race. I was a pretty deadly shot. Too deadly. Zang, zowie and I got the wrong one, little kitty jumping and kicking and going no place, with a piece of his head hanging over one ear and the blood thick as gravy on his fur. I stomped him with my boots, stuffed him down an old rabbit hole and crumbled the bank over the top so that he was out of sight, but not out of mind. Poor old Charlie.

I can still see him, he would have been a mighty cat, much better than the two kittens I'd already more or less tamed. Only thing was, he'd been left with his mother a bit too long and his face and shoulders were all patchy with ringworms. Like that kid. Couldn't help noticing down his arms and legs, the scabs and scars of what we used to call 'Maori sores'.

Both cases I went to the nearest water to wash. With the kitten it was a long way, with the kid it was a well, just beyond the row of huts. I was leaning over beginning to haul up the bucket when bhwam! if you've ever heard a gun fired in a well you'd know how loud it was. We'd been warned never to drink the stuff but hell, nobody said anything about snipers in it! I'd gone back a few paces, just enough to drop him a pineapple, which I did. The whole well rose up and fell in on itself. Instant grave, much tidier that way, sergeant said. Hell of a sense of humour, that fellow. I felt a lot better about what had happened to that kid and somehow forgot all about any handwashing. Lucky to have hands.

It was a funny war, that one. There weren't too many of us from the S.A.S., but I know us and the R.T. (artillery that is) were getting stuck in. Don't ask me what the Yanks were doing, the place was lousy with Air-Cav and Cal-tex and Tam-pacs, bloody useless and bloody everywhere, noisy as a fart in a nunnery. It was almost a relief to be given bivvies next to the R.O.K.s at Quang Ngai. Well named, those bloody Koreans weren't nothing but head hunters – those babies didn't care whose so long as it wasn't theirs. Bit like some Aucklanders I know. So apart from a few of the Aussies, there was only ourselves we could really trust – especially after our R.T. plastered an Aussie platoon. It weren't our fault, the R.T.'d been given the wrong co-ordinates, could just as easy been us on the end of the bread-run.

But we did our job and it was just a job, what we'd been trained to do, only this was for real.

Like the 'Christmas pudding', that's what the Maoris called it – boy, they've got a sense of humour, I'd sooner serve with Maoris than with white men, but God help the man who rubbed them the wrong way – Christmas in 'Nam is just a little more and less than usual, a little less of this and more of that, but Tet is Charlie's big time, not Christmas, they never heard of it, though why we should observe their Tet and they should ignore our Christmas never seemed right to me. Anyway, this Christmas finds us a damn long way from home, air-dropped into Hill 840 which is just a bare, bloody piece of dirt with a bunch of Montagnards, real head hunters who'd even put the bloody R.O.K.s to shame, and a black American sergeant who claimed Charlie squeezed 'em so tight last night he woke up to find one in bed with him. Anyway, that was Christmas, calling in air-strikes all round, watching the scrub go up in smoke and flame, 'palm and phosphorous, some of it so thick we had to wear gas masks on the clean-up. That was Christmas, easing the squeeze on Hill 840.

Like I said, call came on the radio, that Christmas morning, 'Gotta little Christmas surprise for you Kiwis, just keep your heads down, we're coming right over.'

And it surely was the most god-awful Christmas present anybody ever had, they'd developed these screamers that would go deep into the earth, then blow, whoomp! which was the only way to dig Charlie out. After them came the usual incendiary stuff – they had this new napalm that really stuck, you could jump under a creek and it would still sizzle the skin off your bones. Well, they did that whole goddam ridge until the gravy ran out of the clay. It was a good few hours before it was cool enough for us to go out and mop up. That was when we saw their 'Christmas pudding'. Must've been a good twenty or thirty of them, all joined together, burnt and blackened, so at first a man didn't know what his eyes were seeing. That was the only time I was sick, I mean, really spewing, a lot of us were, otherwise I'd've never heard the last of it.

Reminded me of the time before. There was this hillside up the back where the wild cats used to give me the slip every time, it was all gorse and manuka. Having bowled little Charlie, I reckon I'll have his ma, one way or another. So I ask my Dad about a burn-off, and we take the kerosene and matches and set the whole hillside alight. I waited up the top end, well armed with rocks, while Dad worked below, stopping the fire from burning back into the grass. But no sign of that cat, only a few half-cooked hedgehogs and that was that. All we did was give that bloody black cat the kind of cover she needed in amongst the black stumps, so that she was able to get stuck into the birds that came into feed on the grubs and beetles.

Hill 840 was the same. Charlie came in unseen, dusk not dawn, which was unusual, so much so that we took half our casualties of the whole bloody war, right there.

So it was back to base for the unit, the nearest to R&R we ever got. Not like the Yanks, it was all laid on for them, every six months out to HK or Tokyo, but we had our compensations. You might think it funny after what happened at the Hill, but there were these two laundry boys, we called them Rin and Tin Tin, that the unit sort of adopted. We tried to take them with us when we were ordered out on stand-by outside Duc Tho, where there were the usual so-called 'disturbances'. All we saw was smoke by day and a little more small arms fire than usual each night, otherwise nothing. After a week of it we were ordered back to Qui Nhon, back to Rin but not to Tin Tin. 'Where's Tin Tin?' It took a lot of pressure to make Rin tell what had happened – the A.R.V.N. had used the Tet disturbances as an excuse to clamp down hard on the shanty towns, the huts of cardboard and tin on the sand flats between the airbase and the sea. They'd found all sorts of military gear we'd given Tin Tin and that was that.

We went to see the A.R.V.N. District Commander and he called in an interpreter, and in the end we got the story – or rather their story. Tin Tin had tried to make a run for it, they'd fired, 'only to wound, you understand,' but one shot had gone too high. I don't think even they knew what had really happened and they certainly couldn't understand why we should carry on like this all for the sake of one lousy little kid. But they'd been thoughtful enough to call out what looked like a whole regiment of A.R.V.N. – we found them waiting as we came out, so we didn't wreck the joint, which had been our original intention.

Again, the cat, or rather its kittens came to mind. The two kittens I'd caught early on – before I'd bowled poor old Charlie – were getting pretty tame and cheeky, in fact too cheeky, because one came up to old Tip's meat. One snap and it was flipping and somersaulting all over the lawn. Old Tip had broken its back. It was really my fault. I shouldn't have given Tip his meat with the kitten around, I mean, Tip is naturally a gentle dog, but a bit bad tempered where food is concerned – what dog isn't? But at the time I blamed Tip. Two down and one to go, the runt of the litter, a scrawny, frightened female that never tamed down enough to come except when food was laid down.

Well, I came home. And what do I see, rubbing round Dad's slippers? that same kitten, black with a little patch of white, just like its mother, but purring fit to burst. 'Hi, kitten.'

'Kitten,' said Dad, 'that mangey thing died of rickets a month or two after you left. This one's the mother.'

I couldn't get over it. How the hell had he done it. After all the time I'd spent trying to get it tame, hunting it over hill and bloody dale, feeling bad about it, saying to myself it was the best thing, couldn't afford any more wild cats cleaning out the quail.

'The mother! What did you do?'

'Do? Nothing. Started comin' in for feeds. Now she's in for keeps.'

Now, every time some smart ass comes up to me and says Vietnam this and Vietnam that, as if he's got all the answers, I tell him about my little old black cat. Only I never get time to finish me tale before they're off somewhere else on their own track.

But I dunno. Guess everyone's gotta find out for themselves. The hard way.

PHILIP MINCHER

The Mace

On the first day of barracks an instructor had made a fool of him over a bren. He had been listening to the band practising on the other side of the field, and this young army chap had shown him up for inattention.

'What's the effective range of this weapon, cadet?'

Fainy had felt his face reddening. He had not actually known until then that he was a cadet, and he was not sure whether or not the soldier could make trouble for him. He had stood dumb with his throat thick and his eyes beginning to sting, and let the soldier bawl him out while everybody snickered.

That had been the first jarring note of his grammar school career: something beyond the initiation things, and the hard, frightening knot of the preliminary exams. What they referred to at the school as the first week's barracks had not turned out so nicely for the new boy. It was a school, he reasoned, like any other school. He wanted to do his best and stay out of trouble.

So that when a Mr Lewis came upon the scene seeking new prospects for the trumpet band, Fainy remembered the nasty glint in the young army instructor's eyes, and put up his hand.

Mr Lewis was a nervous, untidy little man with long dry hair and insipid features. Fainy could tell at once that he would not be one of the popular masters. He was in charge of the trumpet band because he knew something about music, but he never took any drill or made a great deal of noise about anything. He had few volunteers: most were drawn more towards gunnery than to music. He eyed Fainy hopefully:

'Which interests you, the trumpet or the drum?'

'The trumpet, sir.'

'Can you play?'

'No, sir.'

'But you have the general idea?'

Fainy felt that Mr Lewis wanted him to have the general idea, wanted it to be all right.

'I think so, sir.' He wanted very badly to be able to play the trumpet.

'Report to the drum major after lunch,' Mr Lewis said.

'Yes, sir. Thank you, sir.' Fainy thought now that he might have got himself into something. He remembered the eyes of the army instructor, and shivered.

The drum major was a stocky, muscular sixth-former named McCall. He was kind to Fainy without really appearing to see him, and passed him on to the trumpet sergeant, a tall, pouting youth named Clift who put a trumpet into Fainy's hands and forgot about him, looking over his head until he went away.

Fainy stood self-consciously among the grouped bandsmen, waiting to fall in. He held the trumpet awkwardly. It was the worse for wear, dented in the bell, with its braid shredded.

McCall gave the order to fall in. Fainy just found himself in the ranks, quickly placing the trumpet beneath his arm the way the others were holding theirs. The bass drummer hooked on his great bass drum, and they dressed behind the side drummers spacing with their sticks crossed to either side.

McCall held his mace braided with the school colours. He walked seriously down the ranks. Fainy stood stiffly to attention among the motionless bandsmen. The drum major came abreast of him and stopped.

'Can you play that thing?' he asked.

He looked a good-natured young man and his eyes were smiling. But in spite of himself Fainy saw in his mind the cutting eyes of the army instructor, and he heard himself blurting out like a fool, 'No, sir.'

McCall smiled, and a ripple of mirth ran through the ranks. Fainy knew he had done it again. He wanted to die.

The drum major passed on, then returned to face the band. It wasn't his fault, Fainy thought, his face red, his eyes stinging once more. He envied McCall his poise and his self-assurance. He kept his eyes on the drum major. He had to go through with it now, whatever happened.

The drum major took up his place at the head of the band. Fainy tried to lose himself in what was happening, to be a part of the band and nothing more. Then McCall gave his order and it worked.

'Band – double flam, school tune, by the centre, quick . . . march!'

The drums began to beat and they were marching, and he was in fact a part of the band, feeling at last he was where he wanted to be. He felt himself caught up in the drum music, and he marched as he might well have marched a thousand times before.

The drum major marched with the mace in front of his band. They swung out of the school gates and Fainy could feel everybody watching. McCall signalled with the mace and blew his whistle, and as the bass drummer gave his double flam and the side drums rolled in introduction Fainy knew that the trumpets were going to play. Trumpet sergeant Clift barked out the name of the tune.

They marched up the road away from the school, and Fainy felt himself inside the music, the drums rolling and the trumpets blaring, the whole band one single piece giving out its grand noise to the world. He saw without staring the people on the street stopping to watch. He carried the trumpet proudly beneath his arm, and he knew that he was going to learn to play it, and that he was always going to be a part of this magnificent noise.

It was a grand march. They marched around the block and into one of the back playing fields. Then they drilled for an hour. Towards the end of it Mr Lewis wandered across the field from the main school, a solitary figure crossing the green. They watched him come, and cruel remarks were passed. Fainy was not surprised: they hated him for his meekness.

After some preamble, Mr Lewis and the trumpet sergeant took Fainy aside for an introduction to the instrument. He was nervous, but he put his heart into it. He knew the others were listening, ready to make fun of him, but he could overcome that now. He tried with everything he could muster, as if his life depended on it. Clift played the notes with a casual perfection, then stood by with his constant, disarming pout while Fainy struggled to follow him. Mr Lewis stood willing him to play. Fainy felt that well enough. Mr Lewis wanted him to learn, perhaps he could sense how much it had come to mean to him.

He put his soul into the test, and at last they decided he had the necessary potential. He marched from the field in the centre of the grand noise they made, not yet playing, but a part of it.

That was the start of it. The problems that followed were made to be overcome: the matter of somewhere to practise, for instance.

He had to be far enough away from the house not to activate his mother's migraines, yet a respectable distance from the nearest neighbour. As it was, his best possible site, the woodshed, was well within earshot of the man next door, a retired pork butcher named Sigley, who always managed an ungracious, easily-audible comment at the first blast.

But that could be overcome, too. Mr Sigley had never marched inside the great brass wonder of a trumpet band, or he would have given up before he started.

Surprisingly, it was Mr Sigley's nasty comments that helped to bring Fainy closer to his brother, Tom. One evening Fainy sat down to practise, and with the first note came Mr Sigley's sour remark, and as he closed his mind and redoubled his concentration, there was Tom's voice cutting into the old butcher's with a well-worded counter-blast. Fainy was startled. Tom's sentence was long and furious, and a hair's breadth from libel. There was silence, and then Tom came into the shed:

'You play as long and loud as you want to, mate.'

He was ten years older than Fainy, and a working man. He had never been much of a one for school, and at Fainy's age had been working out his own destiny in the engineering trade.

'That old pork chop doesn't worry me,' Fainy said, holding the instrument awkwardly.

'Yes he does,' Tom said with authority. 'I've got a better place.'

Fainy followed him in wonder, across the yard to the other building, and into the secret world of the young man, his brother. Tom unlocked the door and switched on the light. The three stripped motorcycles gleamed before them.

Tom cleared pieces of machinery from a chair, and set it clumsily before the boy.

'You'll be able to concentrate better here,' he said.

'Gee, thanks, Tom.'

'I'll give you a key,' Tom said awkwardly. 'You just come in any time you want to get clear of old Porky. . . . And watch out you don't touch anything, or I'll knock your bloody head off.'

'Gee, Tom. . . .'

Tom began to make his exit on the gruff note intended, then paused:

'Is it hard to play?'

'Not really. D'you want a try?'

'No,' Tom said flatly. Then, 'What's it feel like in the band – I mean, when everything's playing?'

'It's the best feeling in the world,' Fainy said truthfully. He felt the colour coming to his cheeks, because he had spoken from the heart, but there was no sneer from Tom.

'Well, you do it, then,' Tom said. 'Don't let anybody stop you.' He hesitated again. 'Your braid's pretty well shot.'

Fainy looked, knowing it was so.

'I could make you a new one,' Tom said.

'Boy, could you?'

'Sure. I can do braiding, all right. That's one of the things Grandad taught me when I was younger than you.'

'And you still remember how to do it?'

'I remember, all right. Your grandad had a sail ticket; what he had to say was worth remembering. He taught me every knot in the book, and I could show you them all now.'

'He gave me *The Sea Wolf*,' Fainy said. 'He must have remembered those days. He must have been a young man when Jack London was alive.'

'I read *The Sea Wolf*,' Tom said.

'I've got some Joseph Conrad books,' Fainy said.

'I don't get any time for reading now,' Tom said, and went out.

But after that things were different between them. Fainy felt closer to Tom than he had ever been before. He felt how Tom was tolerating him now, respecting him where previously he had been prone to scorn.

He felt himself maturing. The term developed, and he settled into his studies, and there was no fear any more of being caught out of line, or making a fool of himself. And all the while his love was the trumpet, and his secret was the grand, incredible thing that came about when the band played.

And although the other boys were keen enough, he felt that they didn't see it in the same way as he saw it himself. For Fainy it was as though something was brought to life when they played, something martial and magnificent that had come down to him through a thousand years, a spirit evoking the names of Waterloo and Balaclava and a million shows of splendour, and feats of sword and lance he had never even heard of. This was the thing that was there in his head when they played.

And always in front of the band marched McCall, the drum major, with the school mace.

The mace was a magnificent thing of polished wood and chrome, with the school crest moulded into the head of it, and richly braided with the school colours. When you looked closely you knew that it had seen better days, but it was well balanced, and in use it was the focal point for band and spectators alike.

One day Mr Lewis released the news that the band was to appear in a parade. There was going to be a show in a month or so for a famous American general, and the band had been given the job of leading a unit of Waafs on to the field. Everybody was excited, and they began to drill in earnest. The drum major, too, began to brush up on his mace work. For the first time Fainy saw him throw the mace in the air. They were marching across the field, playing their heads off, with McCall giving the mace everything he had, and then up it went, at the very peak of the music, up and up and over and down, and Fainy nearly died with apprehension as it came down and was taken mechanically, and spun again in the drum major's hand.

After that McCall threw the mace at least once every time they trained, and they knew that he was going to throw it in the parade. In front of thousands, Fainy thought. Thousands!

Then one morning, drilling in the quadrangle, McCall threw the mace and missed. It hit the asphalt with a crash they could all hear right through the music, and everybody stopped without the whistle and stood anxiously watching. It had fallen heavy end first, and the moulding about the head had been shattered.

It was a blow to the whole band. The mace was its essence, the kernel of its concord. There was no mending it, although the tragedy might be disguised. But you couldn't throw an imperfect thing like that, not in front of thousands and an American general to boot. The whole act was going to go sour without that big toss of the mace.

Mr Lewis was most concerned, but offered no immediate hope. A new one would have to be imported, he said. They didn't make them here. That was when an idea began to form itself in Fainy's head. Why couldn't they make them here?

That evening as usual he practised in the private sanctuary. He had finished a tune, and was draining the instrument of spittle, when Tom came in with yet more pieces of machinery.

'Carry on, mate,' he said.

Fainy kept on with his draining.

'Needs a vacuum cleaner,' he said.

'Why not?' Tom said, appearing to consider it. He got busy at his workbench. 'You must be getting pretty good at it by now.'

'I hope so,' Fainy said. 'We've got a big parade next month.'

'Big deal,' Tom said.

'McCall busted the mace today.'

'Oh, how?'

'He threw it up and missed, and busted it on the asphalt.'

'He's the one who should have practised,' Tom said.

'They can't get it fixed,' Fainy said. 'They say they don't make them here.'

'Tell them they don't know what they're talking about,' Tom said. 'And bring it home with you.'

His words rang in Fainy's ears like music.

So next day he was bold enough to approach McCall and tell him that the mace could be saved. It was a proud moment. McCall must well understand and feel the band thing as he himself felt it.

McCall pricked up his ears at the news.

'Does your brother do that kind of thing?'

'He's an engineer,' Fainy said proudly. 'If he can't do it, nobody can.'

'All right,' McCall said. 'Take the mace home tonight then, Burridge.'

Fainy's heart swelled with pride. He took the mace reverently. It was all there, locked in the wood and the braid and the damaged metal head of it.

He carried it proudly and delicately home to Tom, who received it with a different kind of interest. Fainy watched with fascination as he tapped it over. Tom measured, weighed and otherwise tested the mace, with all the care and gravity of a surgeon projecting a brain operation. He made a couple of realistic sketches and gave the mace back.

'Give me a week,' he said, and seemed to forget all about it.

'Is that all?' Fainy asked uncertainly. 'Shall I take it back?'

'Oh, yes,' Tom answered indifferently. Fainy felt it might be part of an act. Staking so much on his brother, he carried the mace back to McCall.

'He says about a week,' he passed the message on.

'Can he fix it?'

'Oh, sure as eggs.'

He left McCall, feeling like a man on a tight-rope. It was going to be a long week.

Every day, he could feel all eyes in the band upon him. At home, Tom went on with his 'I have spoken' act. Fainy thought seriously about prayer.

Then one evening Tom came into the sanctuary with a long object wrapped in old newspapers.

'See how this hits you,' he said, and got busy at his bench.

With trembling fingers Fainy stripped away the wrapping. It was a new mace, complete save the braiding, resplendent in its polished wood and gleaming, chrome-plated head and ferrule. Fainy wanted to shout. It all caught in his throat.

'Gee, Tom . . . .'

'What d'you think?' Tom was going through with the act.

'Gee . . . but the whole thing!'

'Thought it was the best way,' Tom said. 'I'll braid it for you after tea.'

'But how'd you do it, the wood and all . . . and the crest and the lions?'

'It was nothing,' Tom indulged himself a little. 'Mate of mine turned the wood. I know a dame at art school and she modelled the lions and stuff and I got them cast. That's a furniture ferrule on the end; I made the dome piece out of a toilet float, screwed the castings on and got it all chrome-plated. You feel the balance, mate. If he drops this one, he doesn't know what he's doing.'

'Gee, Tom. I . . . .'

'Is it okay?' Tom nearly gave himself away.

'Is it ever!' Fainy couldn't find the words. He was lost in the presence of the mace.

After tea Tom was true to his word and got busy with the braiding. He braided the mace with the school colours, naming with authority the various knots, passes and tassels as they appeared. Fainy's head reeled with a myriad of terms such as coach-whipping, Nelson braid, shroud knots and six-pass turk's heads. As the mace grew in beauty there were things in his head as great and as profound as the deep impenetrable thing he had about playing in the band. There were things now about his grandfather, who had sailed in ships as had Jack London and Joseph Conrad, and had lived as they had lived, and whose every word that he could remember would now be as precious as gold to him. And there were things too about his brother Tom, who had known their grandfather better, and had kept his words as sacred things, and was sure of his hands, and was a great craftsman, and had made the school mace for love.

When it was finished, the words wouldn't come; he was silent before its beauty. But he knew that Tom understood.

He all but burst with pride when he took the mace to McCall. He knocked on the band-room door before morning school, and someone from the select hierarchy opened it. When they saw the parcel, they let him in.

He thrust it into McCall's hands and waited as they all gathered around. The paper fell away and there it was.

'My God,' somebody said. Somebody else whistled. McCall held it up to catch the light, and they all gaped. Fainy felt their eyes as one by one they remembered he was there and turned to him.

He drank deep of their praises and fled. Most of all he would remember McCall's grateful acknowledgement, and friendly hand on his shoulder:

'This parade's going to be one out of the box, now, Burridge.'

All that week he was somebody in the band. Mr Lewis thanked him, and asked that his compliments be passed on to Tom for such a fine job. The older boys seemed suddenly to be aware that he existed, and even trumpet sergeant Clift appeared not to look over his head so much when he spoke to him. McCall, who had always been kind, was exceptionally warm about the whole thing.

That was during the first week. Then it began to die off, and Fainy became himself once more – the third-former Burridge, with the oldest, brightest trumpet, and the newest, cleanest braid. All interest focused once more on the mace alone.

It never struck Fainy that it had really been the mace alone that they had seen in the first place. It never occurred to him that the boys had no particular respect for Tom as an artisan, or that, except in this one case, they wouldn't have given twopence for his craftsmanship. When the affair settled down, the mace assumed its rightful proportions, and they trained for the big event as before. But for Fainy there was so much more that came out of the music when they played.

Finally, the big day arrived.

It was a Saturday afternoon. Fainy was ready before time, and sat needlessly polishing the gleaming trumpet. He felt there was something he wanted to say to Tom, but he was not sure about it. Finally, he wandered uncertainly into the sanctuary.

Tom was busy at his work bench, ringing a motorcycle piston.

'All ready then, Tiger?' he said.

'I'm a bit early,' Fainy said.

'Better early than keep the general waiting,' Tom offered.

Fainy answered yes, and started to say what he wanted to tell Tom, how he felt about the mace and what Tom had done for him, and it wouldn't come. He stammered, and stood there like a fool.

Tom bent over his work.

'Never mind about that,' he said, without looking up. 'You just go in there and blow their eyes out.'

'All right,' Fainy said. 'All right, Tom.'

He went out quickly, knowing he was going to blow their eyes out all right.

He arrived early, the first bandsman at the rendezvous. They were to meet and fall in at a small playing field a couple of blocks from the main park, then lead the Waafs down the street and into their place in the show. Fainy stood anxiously waiting for the others.

They came at last, all excited but trying to play it cool. Finally, they were all there except Barrett, one of the senior trumpeters. McCall was there with the mace, discussing the programme with the Waaf officers.

Barrett arrived at last. He had no trumpet. He spoke earnestly with sergeant Clift. It seemed somebody had brought his trumpet into town for him, and there had been a mix-up, and it had been left in a car some place.

There was a hasty council of war. Fainy knew before they spoke to him what they were going to do.

He felt himself handing over his trumpet, hearing Clift's soft, brutal logic: 'Well, it *is* for the good of the band, Burridge. . . .'

'That's all right,' Fainy heard himself saying. 'I don't mind.' He was afraid that his voice might crack, his eyes water and give him away.

Barrett accepted the trumpet apologetically: 'Sorry about that Burridge. . . .'

'That's all right,' Fainy said. He let go the trumpet, wondering how anybody could care so little. Just because he can play so well, he thought: to think that it ends there! He stood in a vacuum of shock, holding on to himself, coaxing himself to be brave.

It was time. McCall brought his band together and they fell in like professionals, dressing with precision behind the drummers with their crossed sticks. Fainy stood without his trumpet, well in the middle of the middle-most rank. Something came to him, and he tried to drive the idea from his head, but it persisted. He felt that they would have stood him down entirely except for the space to be filled. He remembered Clift's cruel, pouting logic: 'It *is* for the good of the band, Burridge. . . .' Nobody need know, of course. He wondered if he would be able to describe the show to Tom afterwards without actually lying.

They were ready. The Waafs were ready and waiting. As McCall gave his order, the mace shone in his hand.

'Band – double flam, school tune, by the centre, quick . . . march!'

They marched out of the little playing field and on to the road. The drums played the school tune and Fainy, truly in the centre of the band, thought of how the Waafs were marching behind him. He saw without moving his head the people lining the streets. Then McCall gave the signal for the trumpet tune, and the bass drummer gave his double flam and the side drums rolled, and as the trumpets began to play he felt himself encased in their music, so close to being a part of the thing they made it didn't really matter that he wasn't playing. He marched proud and erect, his eyes on the mace.

They marched up the road and through the main gates into the park. The field was a vast arena surrounded by a bubbling, vibrant crowd. The distances appeared very great, and the troops already assembled seemed so far away. They marched out on to the field and the people began to applaud.

Fainy was a part of the music. It didn't matter any more about the trumpet. A million visions burst in his brain as they marched, splendid deeds and splendid names like Blenheim and Waterloo and Balaclava, and the march became the ultimate tune of glory, the epitome of a million battle hymns raised to the heavens.

They marched on before the cheering crowd. Then right in front of the grandstand McCall threw the mace.

Fainy saw it from the heart of the music. The mace soared – up and over, and up and over and down – and he heard the roar of the crowd while it was still in the air, as the metal gleamed in the sun and the tassels with the school colours flared, and his ears rang and his eyes stung and the back of his neck tingled with it, and the splendour of it stayed on as the mace returned correctly to McCall's hand, and he saw it still, on and on as they marched, etched into his soul for as long as he might live.

He was fourteen years old, and life was long, and the world was very wide. And the flashing splendour of the mace, flung high with all the joy and flaunted pride of youth, soaring into the afternoon sun while all the world cheered, was the splendour of an instant that would never fade.

MAURICE GEE

The Losers

I

Dinner was over at the Commercial Hotel and the racing people were busy discussing prospects for the final day. The first day's racing had been interesting; some long shots had come home, and a few among the crowd in the lounge were conscious as they talked of fatter, heavier wallets hanging in their inside pockets. Of these the happiest was probably Lewis Betham who had, that day, been given several tips by trainers. The tips had been good ones, but it would not have mattered if they had been bad. The great thing was that trainers had come up and called him by his first name and told him what to back. He thought he had never been so happy, and he told his wife again how the best of these great moments had come about.

'He said to me, "Lew, that horse of mine, Torrid, should run a good one, might be worth a small bet." He's a cunning little rooster, but he's straight as they come, so I just said to him, "Thanks, Arnold" – I call him Arnold – and I gave him a wink. He knew the information wouldn't go any further. See? I didn't have to tell him. And then Jack O'Neill came up and said, "Do you know anything, Arnold?" and he said, "No, this is a tough one, Jack. They all seem to have a show." He's cunning all right. But he is straight, straight as a die. He'd never put you wrong. So I banged a fiver on its nose. Eleven pound it paid, eleven pound.'

Mrs Betham said, 'Yes, dear. Eleven pounds eleven and six.' She sipped her coffee and watched the people in the lounge. She was bored. Lew hadn't introduced her to anyone and she wished she could go out to the pictures, anywhere to get away from the ceaseless jabber of horse names. None of them meant anything to her. She realized how far apart she and Lew had grown. If someone came up and murmured Torrid in her ear she would just stare at him in amazement. But this whispering of names was the only meaning Lew seemed to demand from life these days. He had always dreamed of owning a horse and she had not opposed him. She had discovered too late he was entering a world with values of its own, a world with aristocracy and commoners, brahmans and untouchables. He, new brahman, was determined to observe all its proprieties. And of course he would receive its rewards.

Lew's horse, Bronze Idol, a two-year-old, was having its third start in the Juvenile Handicap tomorrow. It would be one of the favourites after running a fifth and a third. Lew was sure the horse would win and his trainer had told him to have a solid bet. He was tasting his triumph already. He excused himself and went into the house-bar to talk to Arnold. He wanted now to give a tip in return for the one he had received. Arnold would know the horse was going to win, but that was beside the point.

Mrs Betham watched him go, then looked round the lounge. This place, she thought, was the same as the other racing hotels she'd been in. There were the same pursy people saying the same things. There were the same faint smells of lino and hops, vinegar and disinfectant. And Phar Lap, glossy and immaculate, was on the wall between lesser Carbine and Kindergarten. The Queen, richly framed, watched them from another wall, with that faint unbending smile the poor girl had to wear. How her lips must ache.

Duties, thought Mrs Betham, we all have duties.

Hers, as wife, was to accompany Lew on these trips. To wear the furs he bought her and be sweet and receptive and unexceptional. Surprising what a hard job that was at times. She yawned and looked for the clock, and found it at length behind her, over the camouflaged fireplace, over the polished leaves of the palm in the green-painted barrel. With straight dutiful hands it gave the time as ten past eight. She yawned again. Too late for the pictures, too early to go to bed. She prepared her mind for another hour of boredom.

There were a dozen or so men in the house-bar but only two women. Lew recognized one of these immediately: Mrs Benjamin, the owner, widow of a hotel man. She was sitting at a small table sipping a drink that appeared to be gin. The hand holding the glass sparkled with rings. Between sips she talked in a loud voice to her brother, Charlie Becket, who trained her horses. Arnold, wiry, tanned, and deferential, was also at the table.

Arnold saw Lew and jerked his head. Lew went over, noticing Mrs Benjamin's lips form his name to Charlie Becket as he approached. When he had been introduced he sat down.

Mrs Benjamin said, 'You're the Betham who owns that little colt, aren't you? What's the name of that horse, Charlie?'

'Bronze Idol,' said Charlie Becket. 'Should go well tomorrow.'

Lew nodded and narrowed his eyes. 'We've got a starter's chance,' he said.

Arnold said, 'Well-bred colt. You've got the filly in the same race, Mrs Benjamin.'

'Ah, my hobby,' cried Mrs Benjamin. 'I bred that filly myself. If I can make something of her I'm never going to take advice from anyone again.'

'She should go a good race,' said Arnold.

As they talked Lew watched Mrs Benjamin. She was over-powdered, absurdly blue-rinsed; her nose was flat, with square boxy nostrils, and her eyelids glistened as though coated with vaseline. He'd seen all this before, and refused to see it. This was not what he wanted. He wanted the legend. He remembered the stories he'd heard about her. It was said she had a cocktail bar built into the back of her car, and the mark of entry to her select group was to be invited for a drink.

Perhaps, thought Lew, perhaps tomorrow. He found himself wanting to mention the bar.

It was said she carried a wad of notes in her purse for charitable purposes connected with racing. Nobody had ever seen the wad, nobody had seen her pay out, but there were stories of failed trainers mysteriously re-entering business, always after being noticed in conversation with Mrs Benjamin. Lew did not believe these stories, but he felt it was more important for them to exist than for them to be true.

Mrs Benjamin said, 'And Bronze Idol is your first venture, Mr Betham?'

Lew told her of his lifelong ambition to own a horse. He kept his voice casual and tried to suggest that he was one of those who would do well at racing without having to do well. He was trying to make it a paying sport.

Charlie Becket twisted his mouth. He spoke about Bronze Idol and said the horse was promising. Lew said it was still a bit green; tomorrow's race was in the nature of an 'educational gallop'. He saw Charlie Becket didn't believe him, and was flattered.

Mrs Benjamin interrupted the conversation to ask Charlie if he would like another drink. Lew understood that the question was a request. Her own glass was empty while Charlie's was still half full. He was about to say, 'Let me, Mrs Benjamin,' and take her glass, when he realized it might be wiser to pretend he hadn't understood. He must not appear over-anxious. And his knowledge of women told him Mrs Benjamin was not the type that liked to be easily read. Perhaps when she brought her request a little more into the open. . . .

But Charlie gulped his drink and stood up. He had a broad face, a broad white nose, and squinting eyes that looked everything over with cold appraisal –

an expression, Lew thought, that should have been saved for the horses. Lew wondered if it was true that at training gallops Charlie always carried two stop-watches, one for other people, showing whatever time he wanted them to see, and one he looked at later on, all by himself. Of course, he thought, watching the eyes, of course it's true. I wish he was training my horse.

Charlie said, 'Don't feel like drinking right now. Come on, I'll take you for that drive.'

Mrs Benjamin barely had time to open her mouth to protest when he added shortly, 'It was your idea, you know.'

She said, 'Oh Charlie, why have you got such a good memory?' but she stood up, smiled at Lew and Arnold and said, 'Excuse us.' Charlie nodded and the pair left the bar. The eyes in the steam-rollered fox head on Mrs Benjamin's shoulders glittered back almost sardonically.

Arnold sucked his lips into a tight smile and nodded in a way that showed he was pleased.

'Charlie must be mad about something. He doesn't often turn on a performance like that in public.'

'So Charlie's the boss,' said Lew softly.

'Always has been. It just suits him to let her play up to things the way she does. All the horses she's got, they might just as well belong to him. Even this filly of hers – that'll only win when he wants it to.'

Lew nodded and tried to look as if he understood. It was a shock to have Mrs Benjamin, the legendary figure, cut down to this size. But he experienced also a thrill of pleasure that he was one of the few who knew how things really were. It meant he was accepted. He was one of those Charlie Becket didn't pretend to.

'Good thing too,' Arnold was saying. 'Most of these women get too big for their boots if they start doing well. And hard. My God, that one, she's sweet as pie on the surface but you scratch that and see what you find. She's got one idea, and that's money – grab hold of it, stack it away, that's how her mind works. Don't you believe these yarns about her giving any of it away. If there's one thing you can be sure of it's nothing gets out of that little black purse of hers once she's got it in.'

Lew nodded and said, 'I knew they were just yarns, of course.'

'There's been some fine women in the racing game,' said Arnold. 'But most of 'em go wrong somehow. Look' – he jerked his head – 'you take Connie Reynolds over there.'

Lew looked to a corner of the room where a young blonde woman with a heavy figure was arguing with a group of men.

'You've heard about Connie?'

Lew shook his head reluctantly.

'Christ man, she's been banged by every jock from North Cape to the Bluff. And now, believe it or not, she's got herself engaged to Stanley John Edward Philpott. You've heard of him?'

'I've heard the name,' lied Lew.

'Stanley John Edward Philpott,' Arnold said, and he swept a hand, palm down, between them. For a moment Lew wondered what racing sign this was, then understood it was a personal one of Arnold's, meaning the man was no good.

'I could tell you a few stories about him. Could tell you some about Connie too.' Arnold smiled, and the smile deepened, and Lew leaned forward, breathing softly, waiting for the stories, feeling fulfilled and very, very happy.

At half past eight Connie Reynolds left the men in the house-bar corner and went into the lounge. She left abruptly after one of them had made an insinuating remark about her engagement. He said it wasn't fair to the rest of them to take herself out of circulation. As she went towards the door she felt she was behaving as she'd always wanted to behave. She was simply walking out on them. She glanced at the ring on her finger: pride and anger were two of the luxuries she could now afford. And the freedom of not having to please made her for a moment see Stan in the role of champion and liberator, riding to slay the dragon and unchain the maiden. But this image, the unreal figures springing on her from the white delicately haunted innocence she had left long ago, forced her into a hurried retreat, and 'Maiden?' she said, shrugging and giggling, 'that's a laugh.' And Stan as a knight on a white charger, poor battered old Stanley, who had strength only to assert now and then that one day he'd get his own back on all the bloody poohbahs, just you wait and see if he didn't? No, nothing had really changed, except that she was walking out on them, that and the fact that she didn't care if she had drunk too much whisky. She didn't have to care any more.

Mrs Betham saw Connie come through the door and say something to herself and giggle.

The poor girl's drunk, she thought, and she looked round for the dark tubby little man who'd been with her at dinner. There weren't many people in the lounge. Most had gone out or into the bar. She remembered that the man had gone upstairs with friends some time ago and she half rose and beckoned the girl.

'If you're looking for your husband,' said Mrs Betham, 'he's gone upstairs.'

Connie stopped in front of her. 'He isn't my husband,' she said, 'he's my boyfriend.'

'Fiancé,' she corrected. She sat down in a chair facing Mrs Betham. She saw the woman smiling at her and thought she looked kind.

'Do you believe in love?' asked Connie.

Mrs Betham could not decide whether the girl was serious. She was a little drunk, obviously, but drunk people often talked of things they managed to keep hidden at other times – the things that really troubled them.

'You know, a man and a woman, to have an' to hold – all that stuff?'

'Yes, I do,' said Mrs Betham.

'Well, I was hoping you'd say no, 'cause I don't. And I don't think it's passed me by 'cause I've had my eyes wide open all the time an' I haven't seen anything that looks the least bit like it.'

Mrs Betham thought of several clever things to say, but she didn't say any of them. 'Would you like me to try and find him for you?' she asked.

Connie said, 'No, he'll keep. And you can bet your life he's not worrying about what's happened to me. Still, I'm used to looking after myself. I shouldn't kid myself Stan's going to take over just because I got a ring on my finger.'

'You know, dear,' said Mrs Betham, 'these aren't the sort of things you should be saying to a stranger.'

'You aren't a stranger. You're the wife of the man who owns Bronze Idol. Stan told me. Stan's got a horse in the same race. Royal Return. You heard of Royal Return?'

Mrs Betham shook her head.

'Well, don't ask me if it's got a chance because it isn't forward enough. That's what I been told to say.'

Mrs Betham laughed. 'And my instructions are to say that I don't know anything at all. Haven't we been well trained?'

Connie said, 'Yeah, but not as well as the horses. My God, I'd love to be groomed, just stroked an' patted an' brushed that way. Any man who treated me like that would have me for life. But I haven't got a chance. I'm just an old work horse, the sort that gets knocked around. The day'll come I'll be sold for lion's meat.'

'My dear, you sound very bitter.'

'You know why I'm getting married?' Connie put her hand on Mrs Betham's knee. 'I'm getting married because I'm tired and I want a rest. Is that a good enough reason?'

'I'll find your fiancé,' said Mrs Betham. But she couldn't get up while the hand was on her knee.

'Is it a good enough reason?'

Mrs Betham closed her eyes. She had involved herself – the old mistake.

'Yes, dear,' she said, 'I think that's a very good reason.'

Connie thought for a moment, eyes gazing at the Queen on the wall.

'And what's the way to be happy, then?' she asked.

'Why . . . to be happy,' said Mrs Betham, but she could find no answer. 'I suppose each one's got to put the other first,' she said lamely.

'No,' said Connie, her eyes bright and questioning, 'I don't mean him, I mean me, the way for me to be happy?'

Mrs Betham knew she should say, My dear, I think you'd better not get married at all, but instead she said, with sharpness, 'You've got to make sure he needs you more than you need him. That's the only way I know.'

She forgot Connie and thought of herself and Lew. After twenty-five years the roles were reversed. Now she didn't need him any more and so she couldn't be hurt. But over the years he had grown to need her, she was the faithful wife, part of his sense of rightness. Without her his world would crumble. So I'm still a prisoner, she thought, just the way I always was. But now it doesn't hurt, and it doesn't mean anything either. It's just one of the things that is.

She turned back to Connie. The girl was almost in tears.

'Well then,' said Connie, 'it's all wrong. It isn't Stan who needs me it's me who needs him – because I'm tired and I've got to stop, just stop you see and be still and let things go past me for a while. And Stan had to have some money to buy the horse, so I gave it to him and he's got to marry me.'

Mrs Betham tried to speak, but the girl said fiercely, 'It doesn't matter if he needs me. That isn't important at all.'

'No, of course, dear,' said Mrs Betham, trying to soothe her. 'As long as you both put each other first. That's the main thing.'

But Connie jumped up and ran from the room. Mrs Betham wondered if she should follow, then decided against it. She couldn't think of any advice to give if she did catch the girl. She could only tell the truth again, as she knew it. She wasn't the sweet fairy-godmother type to heal with a sunny smile.

After a while she took a magazine from the rack under the coffee-table and opened it at random. *Plump Correspondent Puts In Cheery Word For The Not So Slim*, she read.

She smiled wrily.

Not So Slim. Why couldn't that be the most serious affliction? A world made happy by dieting and menthoids.

She put the magazine aside and looked round the room. The glossy horses posed, the slim Queen smiled down, and over the fireplace the clock said that at last it was late enough to go to bed.

She yawned and went up the stairs, thinking about Connie, and the impossibility of ever helping anybody.

Stan Philpott was playing poker in the room of Jeff Milden, an ex-bookie and small-business man who had failed to survive tax investigations and a heavy fine. He now worked on the wharves, where several sly gambling ventures had shown disappointingly small returns, a fact he put down to working-class prejudice against an ex-employer. The truth was that nobody he had ever known had liked him. He was aware of this in a dim uncomprehending way, and tonight he was directing most of his energy to finding other reasons for his guests' preoccupation. He supposed Joe Elliot the trainer was worried about money or his horses, whereas Joe was really worried about having a stable boy who blushed and giggled whenever he was spoken to and cried when threatened with being sent home. He supposed Stan Philpott was worried about money and Royal Return. In this he was right. The tremendous complex of preparation, bravado, fear, assessment of skill and luck, that had driven Stan frantic for weeks past had reduced itself on the eve of the event to an urgent knowledge of necessity: Royal Return must win tomorrow or he was finished. It was as simple as that. He, Stanley John Edward Philpott, was finished.

Fingering his cards he told himself that if the horse didn't win there was only one way left to get some money, and that was a way he could never take. He tried to read in the hand he held a sign that he should never even have to consider it. The hand was poor; he threw it aside and watched the others bet.

'Can't seem to get one tonight,' he muttered, and Jeff Milden, pulling in winnings with one hand, pushed the cards towards him with the other, saying, 'Come on, Stan. Stop worrying about that donkey of yours. Deal yourself a good one.'

Stan treated this as an invitation to talk. As he shuffled the cards he said, 'You know, it's that bloody thing of Becket's I'm scared of.' So that he might talk about Royal Return he had told the others to back the horse tomorrow, but had suggested enough uncertainty about winning to make sure they wouldn't.

Joe Elliot shook his head and said with an air of sad wisdom, 'Don't hope for too much, Stan.'

'If there's one bastard who could beat me it's Becket. He's got it in for me.' Stan continued to shuffle, though Jeff Milden was showing impatience.

'I'm one up on Becket and I don't reckon he's going to rest till he gets it back on me.'

'Christ, Stan, that happened years ago,' said Jeff. He snapped his fingers for the cards. But Joe Elliot was tired of playing. He asked to hear the story.

Stan smiled, recalling his victory. 'Was when I was riding over the sticks. Becket was just beginning then. He had a pretty good hurdler called Traveller's Joy. I used to ride it in all its starts so I knew when it was right. We waited, see, we got everything just like we wanted it, an' I said to Becket, right, this is it. So he pulls me aside in that sneaky way he's got an' he says, I've got twenty on for you. So then it's up to me, and sure enough I kick that thing home. And then do you think I can find Becket. I chased him all over the bloody course. After a while I give up, and I take a tumble to what's happening. I'm getting the bum's rush. And sure enough the next time this horse starts there's another jock up. So I get cunning, see. I think out a little scheme to put Mr Becket where he belongs. I know he thinks the horse is going to win again, an' I think so too, so I decide to do something about it. Becket's got some kid up, and that's a mistake he wouldn't make now, so just before the race I go round and make myself known to this kid, an' I say, Listen kid, I've ridden this horse lots of times an' I know how he likes to be rode, an' I tell this kid he's got to be held in at the jumps. Take him in tight, I say, he's got to be steady, an' the kid thinks I'm being decent an' he says, Gee, thanks, Mr Philpott, or words to that effect. Well, this horse Traveller's Joy is a real jumper, he likes to stretch right out, so at the first fence the kid takes him in on a tight rein and gets jerked clean over the bloody horse's head, an' I look round an' see Becket standing there with his face all red an' I spit on the ground an' say, That's for you, bastard, an' he looks at me, an' I reckon he'll be asking that kid some pretty pertinent questions when he gets hold of him.'

'When the kid gets out of hospital,' said Jeff. 'Come on, deal 'em round.'

Joe Elliot said nothing. Stan hadn't enjoyed the story either. Surprisingly, he had lost heart for it as he went along and the climax hadn't been convincing. He said in a puzzled voice, 'That bloody Becket.'

The telling of the story hadn't changed Becket; he'd stood through it hard and aloof, clothed in success; and Stan saw that the stories a hundred Philpotts could tell wouldn't change a thing about him, wouldn't draw them up or him down in any way that mattered. There was no way to attack him.

Stan thought, It's only the poor bastards who don't like themselves much that you can get at. A man's only piddling in his own boot if he tries with Becket and the rest of them poohbahs.

He was so shaken by this that he wanted to get off alone somewhere so that he could cry out or swear or beat the wall, break something to prove himself real. He stood up and left the room. There even Joe Elliot's silence, the familiarity of a has-been like Milden, were working for Charlie Becket.

He slammed the door behind him and went along the passage. He was angry that his feet made no sound on the carpet, and when he came to his room he slammed that door too.

'Stan?' said a voice from the bed. It was wet and husky, ending with a little ridge of panic. For a second he didn't recognize it.

'Connie?' He turned on the light.

She was lying on the bed fully clothed except for her shoes. One shoe was on the floor, the other balanced on the edge of the coverlet. This was so typical of her, of what he called her sloppiness, the way she let her money, her time, even her feelings dribble away, the way she dressed and undressed, and spoke and ate, that he broke into a rage. Becket, grey-suited and binoculared, seemed to stand beside him reproaching him with this blowzy fifth-hand woman. He entered a grey dizzying whirl made up of all he had never won and never achieved, a past of loss and failure, of small grimy winnings, a past of cheap beds and dirty sheets and bad food, of cards, smoky rooms, overflowing ashtrays, of women you could only want when you were drunk, of scabby horses, pulled horses, falls, broken bones, stewards' committees and lies, a past of borrowing and forgetting to pay back, of bludging and cheating and doping, a past of asserting your worth and greeting your winnings with a bull's roar so that you could believe in them, a past of noise and dirt and slipping lower and lower until a frayed collar and a three-day growth and a fifth-hand woman were part of you you weren't even conscious of. All these ran out in words he had never known he could use and broke against the hard withdrawn figure of Becket and made the woman on the bed curl and shrink and turn sobbing into the blankets until she was just tangled yellow hair and a shaking back. And these, the hair and back, were all Stan saw as he freed himself at length from the grey clinging fragments of his past.

He went slowly to the bed.

'Connie?'

He sat down and put a hand on her shoulder.

'Connie. I'm sorry. I didn't mean it.'

He sat stroking her shoulder. In a few moments she was quiet. He turned out the light and lay down with her. His feet knocked her balancing shoe to the floor. She gave a small start that brought her body more firmly against his. After a while she said, 'Stan?'

'Yes, Connie?'

She turned suddenly and they lay close together, holding each other.

'Tell me it's going to be all right.'

'It'll be all right. Don't worry about it.'

'Can we get married soon, Stan?'

'Don't worry. We'll get married. Stanley's got it all figured out.'

It was the first time, he realized, that he'd ever been with her and talked quietly, held her like this and not wanted her. He felt her going to sleep, and soon he heard her gentle snoring; and this sound, that she always refused to believe she made, brought him even closer to her, made him realize how helpless she was.

Yes, he thought, it'll be all right. As long as the horse wins. He stroked her hair as she slept, then carefully drew away and found his coat and laid it over her softly so that she wouldn't wake.

II

Charlie Becket walked from the saddling paddock to the jockeys' room. By the time he was there he had the instructions clear in his mind. The filly looked good, but she wasn't quite ready – and there was too much money on her. A poor race, a run home in the ruck, would lengthen her price for the next start. He'd get good money off her, but not today.

He beckoned the jockey and spoke to him in the corridor. The little man nodded thoughtfully then went back to the room to smoke. The instructions were simple. He'd ridden work on the horse and knew her well. She always went wide at the turn. He wasn't to check her: let her dive out, pretend to fight her, make her look green. It was a simple job – if you were a good jockey, a top jockey. He smiled and drew deeply on the cigarette and thought about how much he'd tell Becket to get on the big race for him. There was a sure win there.

Charlie went back to the stand and smiled as he climbed the steps. Betty was looking at him anxiously, like a grandmother fox in her furs. She was waiting to be told how much to bet. She must bet on her dear little filly. Twenty quid he'd tell her. It would teach her a lesson to lose.

He took the money and went to the tote. Bronze Idol was surprisingly long. A tenner each way would net him sixty. And a little bit on Philpott's horse. There was sly work going on there. He placed the bets and went to stand beside the judge's box. He liked to be alone. A quarter hour without Betty twitching at his sleeve was something to be valued.

At the saddling paddock Stan had Royal Return ready. The horse seemed jaded and was slightly shin-sore. He shouldn't even be in work with the tracks so hard, but Stan told himself not to worry. He aimed his habitual punch of affection at the horse's ribs and murmured, 'It's over to you, you goori.' Royal Return responded by ambling in a circle. Stan placed his mouth beside its ear and pretended to whisper. The almond smell of the dope-pill had gone. He grinned as though at his clowning and led the horse past Connie on the fence and into the birdcage. Everything was as right as he could make it. It was over to Lady Luck now. And as he walked Royal Return round and round and saw the white silks of the jockeys moving in the corridor he began to sweat. This formal part of the business had always made him nervous. He felt shabby on the green lawn, and was made to realize how much he had lost, how much he had to win back, and he tried not to think of the things he still had to lose. It was over to Lady Luck – she owed him for a lifetime of losses.

Connie had come to the birdcage fence and was watching the horses circle. Presently the first jockeys came out and mounted, and she wondered how they managed to look so serious. Perhaps just getting into those colours and looking neat and clean made the difference. One of the first things she'd learnt about men was that they were horribly vain. But knowing things like that didn't seem to help women – or rather, not her sort of woman. She'd read stories about the siren type who could charm men to them and play them like harps, and she'd tried to be the siren type herself but it hadn't worked. It had failed so badly that now it was all she could do to hold even Stan who, as far as she knew, had never been wanted by another woman anyway. He looked rather grimy out there among the glossy horses and bright little jockeys. He didn't compare very well with all those stewards and owners and trainers under the members' stand verandah, with Mr Betham for instance. Betham was short and red-faced, but very handsome in his suit and Stetson and fancy shoes, very prosperous and distinguished looking. She'd tried to catch men like that and once or twice had thought she'd succeeded. But she couldn't hold them and soon she discovered that they'd caught her. They'd tossed her back like an eel from a slimy creek.

She wondered what it was that made the difference, and she looked from Betham to Stan. Clothes, money – or not having to worry about so much? Perhaps all three put together. But Stan at least was real, you knew where the real part of him began and where it ended. That was something you'd probably never find out about Betham.

She watched as Stan talked to his jockey and helped him mount. Then Stan went off somewhere and the horse was on its own. Everything was naked and simple now. The future was that horse out there and a Maori jockey in red and white silk. This was somehow a point, an end, the top of a hill or something like that, but she couldn't see how she'd reached it. She couldn't even see how she'd started on the way. Perhaps, she thought, it had begun back there at school. She liked some things and didn't like others. Did a hundred thousand little things and didn't do the hundred thousand others she might have done. Then some time later had understood that really she'd been making a great big simple choice. What was her choice? Slut, race-course bag. Once she'd thought she might be a model. But all the little things she'd done had made her a slut. She'd wanted so much to enjoy herself.

There should be some way of letting people know what they were doing. It was all so serious. Every little thing was so serious.

A voice beside her said, 'They're really rather beautiful, aren't they?'

She turned and saw Mrs Betham there. Mrs Betham nodded admiringly at the horses.

'Yes,' said Connie.

Watching the horses in the birdcage was the only thing Mrs Betham enjoyed at the races. They were so clean and so polished looking, so sleek and yet so powerful. They seemed to dominate the men, and she wondered how the jockeys found courage to climb up on their backs. Most of the jockeys were only boys. Yet they sat there so unconcernedly – some of them even chewed gum. There was a Maori boy on number eleven who looked like a trained chimpanzee, but the jockey on her husband's horse was quite old and looked rather tired. She felt sorry for him and wondered how on earth he'd survive if the horse fell over. He looked consumptive; the purple and orange colours didn't suit him at all.

'Which one is yours, dear?' she asked Connie.

Connie pointed to the one with the Maori on and Mrs Betham said, 'He looks rather nice.' But the horse that had really taken her fancy was a little black one. It moved daintily, prancing sideways, then going backwards with tiny mincing steps. She was annoyed that the effect was spoiled by the dull moon-faced jockey sitting hunched on its back. The horse was definitely superior. She would have liked to turn it loose in the hills and see it gallop away along the skyline.

Odalisque, she read. *bl. f. Owner Mrs E. Benjamin. Trainer C. F. Becket.* She was pleased it was a filly (smiled that she hadn't noticed) and that a woman owned it, and she made a mental note to look up odalisque in the dictionary when she got home.

The first horses went out for their preliminaries and a bell began to ring over at the totalizator. The horses came back down the track, some galloping, others just cantering. Mrs Betham thought again there was something really graceful and exciting about it all. The worms in the apple were the people. There were queues of them still stretched out at the totalizator scrabbling away at their money.

Connie said she was going round to the hill and Mrs Betham asked if she could come too. Lew would want to be with the trainer for this race. They went round the back of the stand, past the refreshment tents and the smelly bar where men were gulping down their last drinks. Mrs Betham saw the man who was Connie's fiancé come out and hurry into the crowd, wiping his mouth. Before she could point him out he had disappeared in front of taller people. She realized then how short he was; and he seemed some shades darker too, but perhaps that was because of his old-fashioned navy-blue suit.

The stream of people moved on and they moved with it until they found a place halfway down the hill. The horses were at the five furlong start when they arrived. The race would soon begin.

'I hope one of us wins,' said Mrs Betham. She was finding it embarrassing to be with Connie. She couldn't get the girl to talk. She decided that if there were things on her mind it would be kinder to keep quiet. She tried to concentrate on the horses, but couldn't pick any of them out, and she knew she'd have to listen to the course announcer to find out what happened. And she'd have to listen carefully. It was one of those short races that was over almost as soon as it started.

'Don't you wish you had binoculars?' she remarked wistfully, thinking of Lew's expensive pair. There was no reply, and she turned, rather annoyed now, and saw that Connie was staring away down an alley in the crowd. At the end of it was the man in the navy-blue suit, her fiancé. Mrs Betham could see that their eyes were meeting.

'Your fiancé,' she said. 'Why doesn't he come up?'

The man seemed to be trying to say something, though he was too far away for them to hear. He smiled, with a small twist of his mouth, and lifted his fingers in a V sign, Churchill's way, rather pathetically she thought. Then he moved to one side so they couldn't see him any more.

'He should have come up,' said Mrs Betham.

Connie began to stare at the horses again. Her face seemed thinner and more bony. 'Get them started,' she said. She moved a few steps away.

Mrs Betham shrugged and told herself not to be angry. Connie was perhaps not so ungracious as she seemed – the race must mean a lot to her. For that reason she hoped Royal Return would win, if Lew's horse didn't.

No, she thought, no, I hope it beats Lew's horse. They probably need the money more than we do.

The announcer's voice blared into her thoughts. 'The field is lining up for the start of the Juvenile Handicap.' He mentioned the horses that were giving trouble. One of them was Royal Return. But soon they were all in line and she saw the heave of brown and heard the crowd rumble as they started. She still couldn't pick out any of the horses.

'Bronze Idol has made a good beginning and so has Odalisque.' Then there was a list of names with Royal Return in the middle. She wondered how the announcer picked them out. She couldn't see any horse clearly. They were all melted together and their legs flickering under the rail made them look like a centipede.

'As they come round past the three furlong peg it's Bronze Idol a length clear of Samba with Odalisque next on the rails on the inside of Conformist. A length back to Song and Dance getting a trail, a length to Sir Bonny.'

The next time he went through them she counted and found that Royal Return was eighth. Bronze Idol was still a length clear of the field. Lew would be getting excited.

At the turn it was the same except that she was pleased to hear Royal Return had ranged up on the outside of Conformist. Then the horses came into the straight and they seemed to explode. They spread out right across it. She thought this was normal, but the announcer was excited and said Odalisque had run wide and had carried out two or three others and Bronze Idol was holding on a length clear of Samba. She didn't hear Royal Return's name. But she was excited herself now. She could see Bronze Idol looking really beautiful, heaving along with his head out straight and his tail flowing and his body slippery with sunlight as the muscles moved; the little consumptive jockey was crouched very low on his back, not using his whip. They were past too quickly for her. She would have loved to see them going on like that for ever.

Above the roar of the crowd the announcer said Bronze Idol was winning as he liked. She was pleased for Lew's sake, and, she admitted, a little bit for her own too. It had been very exciting.

Then she remembered Royal Return. It hadn't been mentioned after the corner. The girl would be disappointed.

She looked round to find her. But Connie hadn't waited for the finish. She had seen Royal Return go out at the straight entrance, and had turned and gone back through the crowd. She had broken past the red paralysed faces of people staring stupidly away at something they didn't know was already over.

III

Mrs Benjamin wanted to stay the night at the Commercial Hotel but Charlie Becket insisted on going home. Finally, after he had threatened to leave her behind, she agreed, and a few minutes before nine o'clock they left town and set off along the Auckland highway. It was a fine night, mild and cloudless. The stars were very bright.

They drove for some time in silence, then Mrs Benjamin began to complain about the meeting. There hadn't been anyone interesting there. All her friends were dying or losing interest.

'Common thing with old people,' said Charlie, hoping to quiet her.

But she seized on the statement and began to worry it with persistent whining energy and he knew she was working to the complaint that nobody cared about her any more. He broke abruptly into her talk, saying, 'That filly isn't right yet. You've been making me push her too fast.' She grasped this subject eagerly. 'Oh Charlie, I know she'll be good. I've never seen a horse I liked better.'

'She over-reaches,' said Charlie. 'Cut herself one day, you see.'

'But I can't afford to lose twenty pounds on her,' she continued. 'Why did you tell me she was going to win?'

'Because I thought she was,' said Charlie. 'It's not my fault if the jockey can't ride her. I'll get someone different next time.' He smiled, remembering how perfectly Armstrong had let her go on the corner. Not even a question from the stewards. A good jockey, a good man to have, even if he was expensive.

Mrs Benjamin sighed.

'She looked as if she was going to go down, pushing those big horses right out. She's so tiny.'

Charlie said, 'Yeah, funny thing happened about that too.'

He told her how after the race, when he was talking to Betham, Philpott had come up and accused him of sabotaging Royal Return.

'I told him I'd hardly do that when I had a few quid on it myself, and that seemed to make him worse. I've never seen anyone sweat so much or look so mad. He'd have stuck a knife in me if he'd had one. He's got a kink I reckon. He'll end up in the nut-house.'

'What happened?' said Mrs Benjamin.

'He followed me all over the course until I had to tell him to clear out or I'd call a cop.'

'What did he do?'

'He cleared out. They're all the same these broken-down jocks. Yellow. No guts. That's why they don't last.'

'But he was a good jockey once.'

'Plenty of good jockeys. They're a dime a dozen. Plenty of good horses too. What I'm interested in is good prices.'

'Sometimes you're just too hard, Charlie.'

Charlie said, 'We're not here to make friends.' It was his favourite saying and it never failed to please him. He drove on smiling, and Mrs Benjamin lay back stiffly in her corner and tried to sleep.

After a time she said wearily, 'It was a boring meeting. I didn't meet anyone I liked.'

Charlie grunted.

A little later she said, 'That Betham man is rather nice.'

'Got a good horse,' said Charlie.

'It's a pity his wife's such a mousy thing.'

'Anyway,' she said, 'I took him out for a drink.'

'You drink too much,' said Charlie.

They wound down a long hill. The lights ran off down gullies and over creeks and paddocks. Charlie fought the car, making it squeal in a way that pleased him.

They came to a level section of road. It ran for a mile without a curve and then went sharply left. Just round the corner the headlamps picked out two cars and a group of people standing at the back of a horse-float. The tail of the float was down and men were clustered in its mouth, white and yellow in a glare of light.

Charlie drove past slowly.

'Horse is probably down.'

Then, as Mrs Benjamin said, 'Let's stop, Charlie,' he saw the float was coupled to a big pre-war Oldsmobile.

'Philpott,' he said. He increased speed.

'But Charlie, I want to see what's happened.'

Charlie didn't answer. He changed into top gear. Soon the speedometer reached sixty again.

'There's plenty of people there. Joe Elliot was there. He'll know what to do.'

'Charlie, why can't you do what I want to, just for once?'

But again Charlie didn't answer. A hundred yards ahead the lights had picked up the figure of a woman walking at the side of the road. She was going their way but she didn't look round as they approached or make any signal. The car sped past.

'It's Connie. Connie Reynolds. Stop, Charlie.' Mrs Benjamin was peering back.

'Charlie, *stop*.'

'I don't feel like it,' he said. The speedometer kept level at sixty.

For a while Mrs Benjamin sulked in her corner. She didn't see why she couldn't know what was happening. Then she grew morbid. She was old – she wondered how many more pleasures she was to be allowed. Perhaps she couldn't afford to lose this one.

Charlie said, 'For God's sake don't start the waterworks.'

Mrs Benjamin had not been going to cry but she allowed herself two or three tears and held her handkerchief to her eyes. Then she rearranged herself fussily in her seat, grumbled about its hardness, and watched the road in an effort to stay awake. Her frequent desire to sleep had worried her lately. But this time she found reason for it in the motion of the car. She closed her eyes and let her mouth loosen comfortably. Her body sagged a little and she felt a settling lurch in her bowels. Her hands turned in her lap until the palms faced upwards.

She slept, as heavily as a child, and soon Charlie Becket put out his hand and tipped her against the door. He did not want her falling over him as he drove.

Connie had not found Stan until two races after the Juvenile Handicap. She knew at once he'd been drinking, but believed him when he said he wouldn't drink any more. He was determined to win back everything and he asked for money. She gave him the few pounds she had, keeping only enough for petrol to get home on. The hotel bills could be paid by cheque and though the cheque would bounce that was a worry for another day. Now the only thing that mattered was to keep Stan from doing anything crazy. He went off and she sat down shakily on a bench. She had never seen him looking so ill. His face was always blue-bristled by mid-afternoon, but now the skin under the bristles seemed more yellow than white, and his eyes were blood-shot, the lids scraped looking and salty. She wanted desperately to help him; and she wondered what was wrong with her, as a woman, that the only way she could help was by giving him money.

After the sixth race he came to her again. He had won a little, enough to bet more solidly with. But after the seventh he did not come. That would mean he had lost. She went to sit in the car. From there she heard the course announcer describe the last race. A horse called Manalive won. She had never heard Stan speak of it, and it paid only a few pounds.

Most of the traffic had gone by the time he came. He told her he'd won twenty pounds on a place bet in the eighth. They drove out of the course without picking up the float. He said there was a card game he wanted to get to. His voice was rough and urgent, and impersonal, not directed at her.

'But Stan,' cried Connie, 'you can't win enough in a card game.' She didn't know what she meant by enough but the word frightened her, it seemed so full of things that might happen, it uncovered years that might go any way at all.

'I can win something,' said Stan savagely. 'I can win enough so I won't have to. . . .' He could not finish, and she became frightened. It was almost as if she had to open a door knowing there might be something terrible behind it. She wanted to put everything further off.

'Stan, don't let's talk about it. Just drive.'

The card game was in a shabby house down by the harbour. She could see the sad battered hulk of a scow sunk lower than the wharf it was moored to, and over beyond a spit of land three sleek launches in front of a white-sand beach. It seemed they were only lazing, it seemed they could fly away out of the harbour at any moment they chose.

She waited two hours without any tea. The launches slowly faded into the dusk. Then Stan came.

He had lost.

He made her go to a restaurant and went to get the horse. He was gone for a long time. When he came back she tried to buy him some food but he said he wasn't hungry. He wanted to get on the road.

They were some miles out of town when she remembered their bags at the hotel. He said quickly, 'We can't go back for them now.'

She argued. They were hardly out of town. It would only take a minute.

'We can't go back,' he shouted. Behind the anger in his voice was a drawn-out sound of despair so that she knew he had done something that was frightening him.

'Stan, you haven't . . .?' But he began again before she could finish.

'What are you talking about? What do you mean, haven't? I just say we're too far out of town and you start thinking all sorts of things.'

She knew then that he had done something back there. For a moment she even wondered if anyone was chasing them, and she looked at the petrol gauge. But the tank was almost full. Shocked, she said under her breath, Stan what's happened? Stan never bought petrol. It was one of the things he always had to be reminded of.

Now as they drove on she grew more aware of the float, and she thought, That's the trouble, that's what causes all the trouble, we're tied to these horses and we can't get away. We're like servants or slaves.

Why couldn't Stan get another job? Why did he have to do things they had to run away from? Why couldn't he go out to work every day, to an ordinary job, like other men? Everything was so complicated. Why couldn't it be simple, as clean and white as that beach and those launches?

The float dragged heavily, lifting the front of the car in a way that gave her almost a feeling of lightheadedness. In this slight dizziness she knew she must speak of the marriage. She must have that chance, the chance for something different even if she couldn't make it just the resting place she wanted.

She said, hesitating, 'Stan, do you – remember last night?'

He broke out again.

'I said I'd marry you, didn't I? What more do you want me to say? I won't break my promise. That's one of the things I don't do.'

'Stan, why can't you – I mean, you could sell the horse and then get a job.'

'Sell the horse,' he said, and now he spoke softly, as though not thinking of what he was saying.

'He ran a good race today. He was going well until the turn and that wasn't his fault. Somebody would buy him.'

'He's a mongrel,' said Stan. 'He was so full of dope he could hardly breathe. Without it he wouldn't have got to the barrier.'

His hands were light on the wheel so he could feel it move and jump. The float was swaying as they wound down a long hill.

Connie began to speak again, but stopped when she saw he wasn't taking any notice. He seemed to be listening. And then, from the way he was driving, she saw he was aware of the float.

'Is something wrong, Stan?'

He turned on her irritably.

'What do you mean, wrong?'

'Back there, in the float?'

'What could be wrong? God damn it you say some stupid things.'

The car sagged heavily into the road at the foot of the hill and she heard a faint whinnying scream from the horse, and then a scraping sound that lasted only a second. She looked at Stan quickly.

'Excitable – excitable horse. Doesn't like bumps,' Stan jerked out. He tried to smile at her.

They came to a straight level stretch of road and he began to drive faster. His hands were white on the wheel. He was sweating, and the float was rattling louder than it ever had before.

'Stan, have you done something to the horse? Is he down?'

Then Stan seemed to go crazy. He began to swerve the car over the road. The float lurched and dragged, and the horse screamed again.

'Mongrel, bloody mongrel,' he groaned. He ran the car halfway over the broken shoulder of the road. It bucked and jolted along; stones rattled against the mudguards and thumped on the chassis.

'Mongrel,' he shouted.

Connie was screaming at him and jerking his arms, almost running the car off the road. She turned and opened her door. Grass and bracken whipped on the metal. She looked back but could see only the yellow half-lit face of the float, so close it seemed to overhang and threaten.

'Stan, for God's sake stop.'

There was no sound from the horse.

'Stan,' she screamed. She tugged at his arm again and the car jumped to the middle of the road. The door beat once, like a broken wing.

'Stan.' She fell against him. She was crying, beating his shoulder softly with her fist.

At last they came to a corner and he slowed the car down. His first words came on the rush of a long-held breath. 'All right, we'll stop, but nothing's wrong. Excitable, that's all. Just might have got himself down.'

She had time only to half realize the weakness of his pretence before the car stopped and she was out and back at the float. He followed slowly.

The horse was moaning.

'Christ,' said Stan, but his voice was flat. He pulled her away from the locks and lowered the ramp.

Royal Return was down. At first she could not make out how he was lying. Then she saw that his chest was on the floor and his body was twisted left and right from it, the hind quarters turned one way and raised so she could see a leg that dug spasmodically at the straw (like a chicken's, she thought, and the unnatural likeness struck a sort of terror into her), head and neck turned the other and forced erect by the wall so that a great pit was dug in the horse's shoulders. One eye was turned towards her, held in a blind and desperate steadiness just above agony.

'Get the torch,' said Stan.

'Oh God.' Connie moved away from him. 'Stan. You *did* it.'

'Get the torch,' he repeated dully.

She stopped at the roadside grass. 'You *did* it.'

'Connie, I. . . .'

'You *did*, Stan.'

'Connie, it was for you. Don't you see?'

She turned at that and stumbled down the road.

'Connie, don't go away.'

She made no answer.

'Connie.'

Soon she was out of sight.

After a while Stan walked to the car himself and got the torch. He went down on his knees and looked underneath the float; and stood up immediately, leaving the torch on the ground. He moved to the roadside and sat down in grass with his feet in a gutter. Soon he began to retch. He didn't notice that another car had stopped and other people were climbing into the float, but he heard the horse scream, and he felt himself travelling back with terrible urgency to times and places where there had not been even the smallest beginning of things like this. He was riding back to salute the judge after his first win, a tiny apprentice in gold and green on a chestnut colt with a white blaze. It was a sunny day and people were clapping.

But then Joe Elliot and another man pulled him to his feet and started asking questions. All he could answer, with his face in his hands, was, 'I'm sick, I'm sick.'

They threw him back into the grass.

The Bethams left the hotel shortly after Mrs Benjamin and Charlie Becket. Mrs Betham wondered if Lew had taken so long over his last drink in order to drive back to Auckland behind them. His pleasures, it seemed, were becoming increasingly simple; but they seemed to satisfy him as nothing had done before – as she herself had never done: he spoke of Bronze Idol with an enthusiasm he had never displayed for her. In thinking this she was frightened. She did not want her memories attacked, she did not want them involved in this business at all. The present must not be allowed to war on the past. She wondered then what the past really was. Just a few short years after all – the slump years, when they had lived on porridge and rice and turnips in a tin shed that filled with smoke from a fire that couldn't warm it. How could those be the happy years? Yet she thought of them as a sort of Golden Age. Lew and she had been together in a way that could never be broken. The outside world didn't touch them. Or was it, she wondered, just that memory had run the good things together, creating a closeness that had never really existed? It had all happened so long ago. But in spite of her doubts those years would continue to live.

It was a sort of Golden Age, she thought, and now's the depression when we've got everything we want.

She began to study Lew. He was concentrating on his driving, trying to catch Charlie Becket.

Perhaps the immortals are equipped with faster cars, she thought. Or perhaps their cars have wings and can fly while ours remain earthbound. Her amusement was brief. She seemed suddenly to be driving with someone she knew only slightly. The face was familiar, but the intentness was created by an ambition she could never understand.

Lew seemed to sense her mood. 'What are you so quiet about?'

She could tell by his voice he expected her to complain.

I should, she thought, but it wouldn't do any good.

'Nothing.'

'Haven't you enjoyed yourself?'

'Yes,' she said.

'Well, what is it then? You don't seem very excited. Don't you realize some people own dozens of horses before they get a winner?'

'Yes, dear. And you've done it first time. That's very clever of you.'

Sarcasm had come in spite of her. She had now to listen to a lecture on her lack of wifely enthusiasm, her inability to enjoy herself as other women did.

'I don't understand you,' he finished. 'I do everything I can to make you happy.'

She had many answers to that but he had heard them all and not been impressed. So she sat watching the dark bush, trying to see into it, imagining some primitive settlement deep in there, a place where life was simple and people had time to know and like each other. But the headlamps never rested on anything for long. Her mind couldn't settle. Lew was driving too fast. There was a car going down the hill ahead of them, disappearing round a new corner every time they caught sight of it. He was trying to get closer to see if it was Charlie Becket's.

On the flat at the foot of the hill they saw it wasn't and Lew seemed to lose heart. He drove more slowly.

'I think I'll stop and have a whisky.'

Just then they went round a corner and saw what looked to be an accident. Two cars were pulled up behind a horse-float and a third was in front of it. There were some men at the mouth of the float and two inside. They couldn't see the horse.

Lew went past slowly and pulled in at the front of the line. He told Mrs Betham to wait where she was and went back to the float. He was gone for perhaps five minutes.

Mrs Betham would have liked to see what was happening, but she thought if the horse was sick or hurt she'd only be in the way. Besides, she hated to seem curious. But she did notice two rather strange things: this was horse business and Charlie Becket hadn't stopped, and back beside the float a man was sitting in the grass. At first she thought he was a small tree or a clump of bracken. Then the shape became clearer. He was bent forward with his arms across his knees. Nobody was taking any notice of him although the way he was sitting made him appear lonely and in need of comfort. She felt she should go along and see if there was anything she could do.

When Lew came back she said, 'Who's that man sitting in the grass?'

'Philpott.' It was not so much an answer to her question as something he was saying to himself. Then he swore, using a word he'd never used in front of her before.

'What's happened, Lew?' she asked nervously.

Lew was pouring himself a whisky. When he'd drunk it he looked at her and said, 'He's just butchered his horse.'

'Butchered? You mean he's killed it?'

He shook his head and she saw his eyes fill with tears. 'It's not dead yet. They've gone to get a gun to shoot it.'

She couldn't understand, but she listened as Lew told her what had happened. Philpott had loosened the boards at the front of the float so the horse's legs had broken through when the car hit a bump.

'They must have been trailing along the road for miles. They're almost torn off. Just hanging in tatters. You can see bits of bone.'

Lew poured himself another drink. His hands were shaking and whisky slopped on his trousers.

Mrs Betham was saying to herself, But that's awful, how could he, how could a person do a thing like that? – but she couldn't say it aloud. Nothing was adequate as she pictured the tattered legs and pieces of bone.

'But, Lew. . . .'

'He did it for the insurance,' said Lew. 'You knew horses were insured didn't you?'

'There are people who could do a thing like that for money?'

'For money.' Lew threw the whisky bottle into the glove-box. 'I hope he gets ten years. If I was the judge I'd order a flogging.'

'What about the girl?' said Mrs Betham. 'Was she in it?'

'His girl? Connie Reynolds? She wasn't there. How do you know her?'

'I saw her on the racecourse today,' said Mrs Betham.

Lew grunted. His mind was still on the horse. Mrs Betham too, though relieved about Connie, could not keep her mind from turning back to the horrible picture he had painted. She looked again at the figure in the grass. It was motionless, in a hunched cowering attitude.

It's too late for him to be sorry, she thought. Her loathing increased. But strangely it changed so that it was not so much for him as for what had been done. He seemed now to exist outside the act. The act was unimaginable, but he was there, part of the horror he had brought into existence, the only part she could really see.

She knew that soon she would feel sorry for him, and she told herself it wasn't right to have so much pity. It was dangerous to forgive too much. There must be things that could never be forgiven, and surely this. . . .

The tattered legs and pieces of bone. . . .

Lew had started the car and they were moving again. He drove without talking, and she was glad, though she expected him to break out at any minute. Her mind was calmer now, and she was trying to convince herself a person couldn't do a thing like that for money. There must be other reasons.

No, she thought, it's not just money. That's too simple. It's everything money means. You can't blame a person for failing to survive that. And yet you can't forgive. Here I am trying to forgive.

But as she thought of the horse with its legs torn off, and the man sitting in the grass, both seemed equally terrible mutilations, the one as pitiable as the other.

'There's his girl now,' said Lew. He didn't slow down and they flashed by almost before Mrs Betham saw her.

'Stop, Lew. We'll pick her up.'

'After what happened back there?' said Lew.

But she argued with him and made him stop and back up to the girl. He was angry and showed his disapproval by not looking round or speaking as Connie got into the back seat.

Then, as he drove on and heard his wife explaining that they knew what had happened and heard the girl break into long scratching sobs, he was seized by an almost physical revulsion. He felt he wanted to be sick. The girl and the crying, and Philpott and the horse, were a sort of disease; he felt unclean having her in the car. There must be ways of avoiding things like this, ways of getting about so that you never saw them.

God, why can't things be perfect, he thought.

He heard the girl say, 'I don't know what to do. I don't know.'

'Then wait,' said his wife. 'Just don't do anything. You'll find out what's right.'

A little later Connie said, 'I want to go back, but I *can't*.'

'Just wait,' said his wife. 'Don't think of anything.'

He recognized her 'soothing' voice. It made him jealous when she used it for anyone but him, and he stabbed savagely with his foot to dip for an oncoming car.

The girl said, still crying, 'This is the first time he's ever really needed me – and I can't go.'

'Shh,' said Mrs Betham.

But Connie had not been talking to her, and hadn't listened. In a few moments she stopped crying.

'He said he did it for me,' she whispered. She gave a little moan.

'Shh. Don't think,' said Mrs Betham.

'So really – really. . . .' She stopped and seemed to talk to herself, and almost cry again.

'So really – it's as much my fault as his.'

'No. Don't even begin to think that,' said Mrs Betham. She tried to take Connie's hand but the back of the seat made it awkward for her and Connie made no move to help. So she rested her arm along the seat-back with her fingers brushing the sleeve of Lew's coat, and smiled kindly at the girl, wishing there were something she could give her, something she could do: the dead paws of the fur, dangling over her arm, were no more useless than she was.

Later, when they thought she was sleeping, Connie leaned forward and said, 'Stop please. I want to get out.'

Lew stopped quickly. His wife leaned back and put a hand on Connie's arm. 'What are you going to do?'

'I don't know,' said Connie.

She opened the door, got out clumsily, and came to Mrs Betham's window to say something. Lew couldn't hear for the noise of the engine, and didn't want to hear. He thought her face was yellow and ugly; he wanted to get away.

The car began to move again; Mrs Betham said nothing. She watched until the girl was lost in the darkness. Then she leaned against her door with her cheek against the cold window.

Lew let a little time pass. He said, 'You want to save the Good Samaritan act for somebody worth while. I could tell you stories about that girl.'

'I don't want to hear,' said Mrs Betham.

He shrugged and drove on. He was happy now that Connie had gone.

Soon he saw a tail-light shining in the darkness ahead, and he increased speed, wondering if at last he had caught up with Charlie Becket.

MAURICE SHADBOLT

Figures in Light

for Pat Hanly

I do not see my sister often. Strange, for we were intimate as children. Or perhaps not so strange, perhaps that is the reason. We didn't grow apart; we fell apart. I had little use for her friends, when we were students, and she had little use for mine. I started university only a year behind her, but the gap was sufficient: she was already established among friends of her own temperament and inclination, and the gap soon widened. Since then, I've seen less and less of her.

Once I marvelled that children of the same parents could be so different. Nowadays, of course, we live in cities some four hundred miles apart. It is true that there is seldom a year in which we do not see each other, but in this case 'see' is the critical word. I cannot honestly say that we converse. She asks after my children, I ask after her life: there is no real exchange. I no longer, for example, ask why she has no husband, no children. No more than I would pose such a question to a total stranger. On the other hand, I am not suggesting that my sister is a total stranger to me. I think I understand her rather better than she will ever allow. Perhaps I deceive myself, but I do not think so. That tall, sullen, untidy woman is not really so remote from the elder sister I worshipped, to put it mildly, through childhood into adolescence.

The failure, then, is not one of understanding, at least not on my side. Yet when I try to define some other point of failure, I know beforehand that I cannot do it. And if I cannot define failure in myself, I can scarcely impute it to her; it surely cannot all be hers. And if we do not share the failure, where then must we look? Where? Questions like that ring in my head on sleepless nights; I slide soundless from beneath the bedcovers, careful not to disturb my sleeping wife, and brew black coffee in the kitchen until the multiplying questions, at first churning wildly, collapse exhausted in my brain. Unhappiness is not uppermost of my emotions when I return to bed beside my wife, or when I wake heavily in the morning. It is more perplexity – if one can call perplexity an emotion, as I certainly do. For I am sure that my sister is unhappy, but why? And I know that I should help her, or should be able to help her, but how?

If I feel baffled and helpless, it is at least in part because I have gone through the usual motions. We once, my wife and I, invited Ruth – my sister – to stay with us. I imagine my idea was to help Ruth feel part of a family again; aside from our father, who has since died, I have been her only close relative. But her visit was not a success. My wife, Helen, usually so understanding in so many things, was troubled by Ruth's presence in the house. That was clear from the beginning; and, since I could exact nothing by way of confession from Helen, and perhaps offer some explanation to clear the air, there was very little I could do about it.

There was no real unpleasantness. It was all a matter of discomfort. Ruth was uncomfortable in our house; Helen was uncomfortable with Ruth. Caught between, I was uncomfortable for them both; uncomfortable, and for a while unreasonably though quietly angered. For our house, of all houses, warm and carpeted and cushioned, and sheltered by a remnant of native bush high above the city, seemed designed to contain every possible situation with some degree of comfort; my actual physical security seemed threatened, along with my peace of mind, as if the solid scenic windows in the living room had split, allowing frosty winds off the mountains entrance to our lives. The mountains are literal; on clear days it is possible to see them from our windows, across the rough water of the Cook Strait. In the steeply descending foreground there are treeferns which toss their fronds in the wind against the tall trunks of spiky cabbage trees; in the middle distance, the oval harbour busy with shipping and the city of Wellington tight-packed beneath bleak hills and eroded gullies which freak with shadow in the late sunlight; beyond are the peaks of the South Island, blue and remote in summer, often white and close in winter.

Ruth spent a great deal of her time flopped in a basket chair before the wide windows. As quiet and sleepy as a cat, her eyes dreamy with distance, her long loose body apparently empty of all tension, she seems in my memory of her visit to have spent all her time there. Her half-brushed hair fell untidily over the hand which propped her head; she seldom changed out of her check woollen shirt and jeans during her stay, and rarely left the house at all, though the fact that she had business in Wellington, some plan for a future exhibition in the city, was part of my excuse for inviting her to stay. Apparently it was all quickly settled, in a single afternoon, and the city as such had no further attraction for her.

I imagined that she missed some excitement or vivid interest which was part of her daily life in the north; though I had never known that life well, this appeared a reasonable supposition. On the other hand she seemed content – or as content as she could be – with our remarkable view. Common sense tells me, though, that she couldn't have been all the time in that chair with the city and harbour, hills and mountains for company. For the one small success of her visit was the pleasure she took in the children. I was about to say surprising pleasure, but in retrospect I see there was nothing surprising about it at all. With our children Ruth established a satisfying relationship, one which was impossible with the adults of the family, Helen and myself. She told them stories; she walked them up the patchily pine-clad hill behind the house on fine days, and romped with them on the needles among the trees. There was no doubt of Aunt Ruth's popularity. The children asked about her for a long time afterwards. I saw clearly that Helen did not like it. It was as if Ruth had left infection in the house, as in a way she had.

Certainly things took time to settle after she left, and comfort was slow to return. Nothing was said. Helen has never once raised the subject of Ruth with me and, though I've tried fitfully, I've never yet persuaded her to talk about my sister, so I have been unable to get to the bottom of her dislike or distaste, whatever it is.

'Your sister,' she once said, 'is an exceptional girl.'

Which is the nearest she has ever come to passing judgement. Well, perhaps not quite. Judgement of a kind was passed a month or two after Ruth's visit. I came home from the office one evening to find a decisive change in the living room. The paintings were rearranged, and one had vanished altogether, to find a new place on the wall of the small spare bedroom (Ruth's, when she stayed) which I use, when the children are at large in the house, as a study; with the idea of escaping my job in market research for something more stable in the university or civil service I am taking a second, part-time degree, which means I need a certain minimum of peace and quiet at home.

Anyway the painting was the one Ruth had given us when we married. Surprised, for things like this seldom happen in our house without prolonged consultation, I made some comment.

'You need to change paintings round now and again,' was all Helen said. 'Otherwise you stop seeing them. Everyone knows that.'

This was, of course, perfectly true. The subject was dropped. The infection Ruth had left behind her was still at work. As I took my glass of sherry behind the evening paper I wondered what it was that so much troubled Helen.

Perhaps there had been some argument with Ruth, when I was out of the house, and about which I was still ignorant? Hardly likely. There would have been some echo. No: the whole thing seemed impossible, beyond explanation. The two did not get along, and that was that. It was odd, even so, because I should have thought them extremely compatible. Helen herself was by no means a conventional girl and that, I admit, was part – a large part – of her appeal at the time I married her. If Ruth had been with me at the time I was first involved with Helen, I am sure she would have approved. Even to the extent of nudging me and urging, 'Yes, her. Don't hesitate, you idiot. She's the one for you.' Now that I have said this it seems to me, quite uncannily, that Ruth *was* at my side at the time, and did nudge me and say those words. But it is absurd. Ruth was never near me in those days, no more than she has been since; she came to the wedding, a rather sullen stranger among Helen's friends and mine, and departed in the middle of the wedding breakfast – without a word, and while I was on my feet fumbling with a speech. My words crumbled, my voice faltered; there was one prolonged, horribly blank moment– or minute– while I stood there foolishly, my mouth open, staring at the empty seat at the long, festive table. I seemed to be struggling up out of some slippery pit to find myself, and my voice, again. Which, after a time, I did. Was that Helen's grievance, then, that incident at the wedding breakfast? We never talked of that, either; as I recall the incident was lost, forgotten, in all the change and commotion of the time. Could it be, though, that Helen had never forgotten or forgiven that ungraceful and unexplained departure? We should have talked of it, we should have talked freely of Ruth from the beginning. The fault is mine. I see that now. I should never have allowed Ruth, or some notion of Ruth, to become an irritation in our lives.

I think it is safe to say that ours is a comfortable marriage. With Helen I have felt a degree of security which I once thought impossible in my life; it pleases me to think that my children will live and breathe this security in the house as they grow. Perhaps Helen saw, from the beginning, exactly what I needed; if so, she was more perceptive than I would have thought at the time I married her. She was lively, flighty, scatty. I plodded in her wake. From coffee bar to rehearsal (she did a good deal of acting before we married) to parties, rather rowdy and jammed with people of whom I scarcely approved; I didn't conceal this from Helen, any more than I had ever concealed my disapproval of Ruth's erratic friends – for they were much the same, at least similarly casual to the point of being downright destructive in their personal lives. (I may be too harsh; my attitude may be too coloured by first impressions. Nowadays I can recognize that they, as the first real friends Ruth ever made, signalled the possibility of change in both our lives; perhaps I would have resented them whoever they were.) In this sense it is true that Helen's circumstances, before we married, were not so unlike Ruth's. But it is not fair to myself, or to Helen, to make too much of similarities. Or to Ruth, either. Where Helen was always slightly diffident, Ruth was impertinent and thrusting. After all, Ruth is herself and has always been. The woman is not so different from the girl, or from the child. Perhaps – and this is the terrible, frightening thing – she will never change.

So that evening, months after Ruth's departure, I stood puzzled before the painting which now hung in my study. Helen, of course, was right. Paintings obviously did need to be changed around regularly, seen in a new context. For I had stopped seeing this one a long time before. That night I looked at it, really looked at it, for the first time in years. The children murmured sleepily in their bedroom, Helen clattered about in the kitchen, and I stood frowning before a painting I seemed never really to have seen before.

It was not a painting I had ever liked particularly, for like so much of Ruth's work it seemed to have very little to it; it lacked depth, in every sense of that word. There was a flatness, a lack of any perspective, in the scene – a fragment of seacoast, rocks and water and lumpy hills vaguely crowded and barely separable, a red dinghy drawn up on pale sand; it could have been, and possibly was, a memory of one of the many places where we spent our childhood. What I saw for the first time, though, was not detail – familiar enough – but the strange, almost unearthly light which filled the frame: I could have sworn that it had not been there before; that it was something which had sprung magically from oil and canvas as it aged. Vivid, timeless and dancing, it was impossible to place, and difficult to connect with any sunrise, sunset or noon that I had ever known. On the other hand, and this was perplexing, the flawless light seemed not at all unfamiliar to me; there was a tinkle of response, coming and going faintly, in some distant delta of my mind. I listened, but heard no more. What I saw clearly was that I had somehow missed the point of the painting before; the light *was* the point. And the detail, into which I had earlier peered without success, seeing no depth or perspective, was in fact there only to give the light depth and perspective; or at least to indicate that the light was of this time, this place. Yet the light itself, its source, still escaped explanation. I stood there puzzling until the children quietened, and Helen called me to dinner. Looking at my small blonde wife across the table, observing her tired and rather harassed face, I resisted an impulse to thank her for having shifted Ruth's painting: she might have sensed irony, which I certainly did not intend. For a while we ate in uncustomary silence. Then, as if each stirred by guilt, we spoke simultaneously – I of the office, she of her family. The family won, naturally; or perhaps I should say unnaturally. Never having known normal family life until I married, the intrigues of Helen's family, even the most trivial, still fascinate me; with some wealth and little common sense, it has more intrigues than most. Helen had just had, that day, a telephone clash with her mother and another, for good measure, with an unmarried sister who was running wild with a bass-player in a jazz band.

'Be tolerant,' I advised.

'Tolerant?' she cried. 'That's just the wishy-washy sort of thing I'd expect you to say. That bitch thinks she can get away with anything.'

'Perhaps she can,' I suggested. 'Anyway let her find out. You can't affect the issue.'

'God,' she said, 'sometimes you're hopeless. You just don't want to see.'

'She'll settle down,' I predicted with confidence. 'Just give her time. After all, you had your fling. Why shouldn't she have hers?'

'It's different,' she said. 'That's why: Besides, she's been carrying on like this for years. If she's not careful she'll finish up like – ' She hesitated.

'Yes?'

'Well, if you must know – like that sister of yours.'

'Like Ruth? But Ruth's different.'

'Of course. She has to be, doesn't she?'

But, as usual, Helen was content to leave it at that: she had no wish to make a frontal attack. The main thing was that she reduced me to silence. Perhaps that is the only way I can defend Ruth, by way of silence. It was unusual for Ruth to lurch into our domestic conversation, and interesting to observe the fact that she had that night in particular; it confirmed all I felt about the shifting of the painting.

When Helen called me in my office early next morning to say there was a message, a telegram, from Ruth, I was not as surprised as I should have been; my sister seemed once again central in my life. Yet this was one of the few communications I'd had from her in my married life, certainly the first urgent one.

'Yes?' I said.

'It arrived a few minutes ago,' Helen said irrelevantly. 'I would have redirected it, but I thought you might be out of your office. So I took it down over the phone.'

She sounded strained and nervous.

'All right,' I said, impatient. 'So what is it, what does it say?'

'It's your father,' Helen said.

It seemed my father was dead. *Our* father, Ruth's and mine. After I replaced the receiver I sat in my office a few minutes longer, trying to feel things I did not feel. I could summon up regret but no grief; it obstinately refused to rise to the occasion. I suppose I am still a stranger to real grief: my mother died when I was young, too young to know or remember, and I have had no other close bereavement. It was, I thought, useless to pretend that my father had been anything but remote to me, to either of us. It wasn't that he denied us affection, in his way. It was just that patience and sympathy for the young, and any real love, were missing; we were a sad encumbrance, constantly reminding him of the love of which he had been robbed, and which he no longer wished to remember. He appears to have turned in upon himself, to have become remote from the world entirely, after our mother's death. It might have been easier for all three of us if he had put down roots there and then; but he was apparently unable to do this, and in any case it was partly in the nature of his work – he was an engineer, a man licensed to tug the earth apart – to travel from place to place, job to job. Even so, there was something frantic in his wandering; I imagine that often he must have walked off projects half-finished. It was as if he were determined to bury all memory beneath the tumbling soil and rock of landscape after landscape. There was never any question of his marrying again, and he had few friends. At some stage in my childhood I overheard a conversation with one of the few who remained.

'You can't mourn her for ever,' this friend said. 'It's not right. You've got to snap out of it. You owe it to yourself.'

'I owe nothing to myself,' my father said. 'Nothing.'

'Well, to your kids, then.'

'Am I in debt to them?' he demanded. 'I do my best.'

That was undeniable. He did his best. When he had seen us both through school and packed us off to university, his relief was perceptible. And when we were independent in every sense, he turned from engineering to work menial and manual. Eventually he became the odd-job man of the tiny seaside community into which he retired. There is something awe-inspiring and humbling about a grief which can persist across the years and blight a lifetime. Love, like happiness, is something which can best be defined in its absence; I should be grateful to my father, then, for having in his life taught me the meaning of both, even if his death could teach me nothing of grief.

So our childhood, at least in appearance, was an unsettled one, with its spasmodic shifts from place to place. In this I suppose we were only a little more extreme than most New Zealanders, an itinerant people always pulling themselves up to see how deep their roots have grown; the shallowness of growth can't entirely be explained by the fact that our seed falls in hardened ruts rather than on virgin ground.

When I was young, Ruth was the only constant and settling factor in my life: housekeepers, tired and bulky middle-aged women, flicker faintly across my memory; towns, valleys, rivers, bush and beaches; and my father's haunted face looms now and again. I seldom have the impression that he was even with us physically, though in truth he was never far away. But this doesn't mean our childhood was miserable. It was never that; it was always exciting and full of promise. Perhaps because no adult, and almost no other children, intruded upon our shared imagination. As children we were seldom in one place long enough to make real friends. Our imagination was our world: each move, each new scene, was grist to the mill and fuel to the fire. There was never loss of continuity. Ridiculously, some people called us lonely children. We were never that; we had each other. It rarely struck us that this might end, any more than it struck us that childhood would end. 'Always' and 'for ever' were favourite words in Ruth's vocabulary, and thus in mine too.

'Do you think this summer will go on for always?' I remember asking – perhaps one day when we lay naked and browning in deep dry grass by a riverside, tall trees and taller hills around us, and cicadas singing thick in the afternoon heat. 'I mean, do you think it would if we wished hard enough?'

'If we really want it to,' she said, 'it will go on for ever. In our minds, I mean. That way we can stay warm in winter. Just remembering.'

She was perhaps sixteen then, large and long-limbed, and her answers just a step ahead of my questions in sophistication. But she wasn't impatient with me; that didn't come till later. Possibly that was the last year we were really ourselves. Like summer, childhood had an end, even if we might later warm ourselves with the memory.

Something of all this raced through my mind while I sat at my desk looking at the telephone. I picked it up again, booked a seat on an afternoon flight to Auckland, and then went home to pack. It was May, with Wellington's winds already wintry; my work wasn't pressing, and since it was the middle of university vacation I should miss no lectures. There was nothing to stop me staying away as long as was needed. 'All the same,' I explained to Helen, 'I shouldn't be away too long. There can't be much to tidy up. I imagine his affairs are pretty simple and straightforward. But obviously I can't leave it all to Ruth. She just wouldn't be interested. After the funeral I'll stay till everything's tidy. It'll save another trip later.'

There was concern in Helen's face. 'Are you sure – ' she began.

'I'm sure it'll be all right,' I told her. 'There's no need for you to come along too. After all, there will probably only be Ruth and myself at the funeral. And you hardly knew him anyway.'

Though I made my coolness plain, Helen insisted on treating me as if I were shrunken with grief. While waiting for my flight number to be called at the airport she gave me a comforting hug and an earnest kiss, then placed the palm of her hand gently against my cheek and said, 'Look after yourself, darling. And don't – '

She hesitated.

'Don't what?' I asked.

'Well, don't stay away too long. Remember we want you back.'

'But of course I'll be back. What on earth are you worried about?'

Her smile trembled. 'Nothing,' she said finally. 'I'm just being silly. You know me.'

For a moment I wondered if I did.

Our actual farewell, when the call came from my plane, was more sedate: a quick passionless peck and I walked across the tarmac. I might have been off on a business trip.

I'd sent a telegram ahead to Ruth, and she was waiting for me when I arrived after the flight at the airways terminal in Auckland. In her habitual jeans and sweater, with a duffel-bag slung over her shoulder, she was conspicuous, at some distance, among sleekly clad citizens of that city. She looked subdued, and was silent as she placed a welcoming hand on my arm. We walked together to the baggage counter.

'What are you planning to do?' she asked.

'There's only one thing we can do. Rent a car and get up there as soon as we can to make arrangements for the funeral.'

My father had lived some seventy or eighty miles north of Auckland all his retirement; a rough road in the later stages meant we had more than a two-hour journey ahead.

'Someone up there is making arrangements. A friend, the one that rang me up. A Mr Slegel.'

'Well, that's something. It hadn't even struck me that there might be a friend to do all that. Knowing Dad.'

'It was all sudden. No sickness, nothing. He died in his sleep.'

I felt guilty: I realized I should have asked about that in the first place. The fact that he was dead had been sufficient for me.

'I see,' I said. 'Well, I'm glad it was easy.'

Ruth was quiet.

'Come on,' I said. 'Let's see about that car. We'd better get moving if we want to be there tonight.'

The car was quickly procured.

'We've still a couple of hours of daylight,' Ruth observed. 'Let's run home to my place. You can straighten yourself up with some coffee while I fetch out some clothes for the funeral. That's going to be a job. To find something to wear, I mean.'

I made no comment, and concentrated on getting through Auckland's dense and noisy traffic. Ruth lives just outside the central city area, in a flat off Parnell Rise. It is part of a decrepit house among ugly warehouses, but overlooking the city and sea and sidelong to the sun. The front part of the house swarms with two large families of Samoans. The back part is Ruth's. It doesn't seem to me an ideal situation for her. But she insists that she likes the noise, the life around. Her flat consists of a small and cluttered kitchen-living room and a combined workroom and bedroom.

'Brother mine,' she instructed, 'park yourself in a seat while I get you coffee.'

'Don't worry about that. Hurry up and find those clothes you're talking about.'

'It was only ten days ago I went up to see him,' she said.

'Him?'

'Dad. A friend ran me up there in his car for the weekend.'

'I didn't think you saw him often.'

'I didn't. Not until recently, at least. But I seem to have got up there to see him every two or three weeks lately.'

'Since your trip to Wellington, you mean?'

'I'm vague about dates. I suppose it is since then. I saw a lot more of him than usual, anyway.'

I sat puzzled. I supposed I had seen my father, on average, once every year or two; Ruth, who lived so much nearer him, hadn't seen him much more often. Why the change?

'Did he have very much to say?' I asked.

'No more than usual.'

'Then why the sudden interest in the old man?'

'I don't know,' she said, clicking switches and planting the coffee percolator on the stove. 'Perhaps I had a premonition. I just felt like seeing a little more of him, that's all.'

'Did you have something you felt you wanted to talk to him about? Was that it, then?'

'Not really,' she said, and disappeared into the bedroom to look for clothes. More puzzled than ever, I sat at the bare board table in her kitchen, looking out of a dusty window at the haze on the Waitemata harbour and the neat blue crater of Rangitoto rising beyond. I thought briefly of the bleak landscapes visible from our window above Wellington, and Ruth's obvious enjoyment of them. There man still perched precariously on an island's spiny edge; here where everything was so much gentler, so much milder, man overwhelmed. Even the hills were shaped by ancient Maori settlement, and now pale houses were scattered in clumps of green around; native trees, tropical palms, and Norfolk Island pines planted back in missionary times. One could still feel warmth in a May sun; summer was never too far away. It never seemed far away in childhood either, for this was more my part of the country. For the sake of a career, for the sake of my family, I'd gone among colder hills.

No matter how I tried, though, I couldn't get it out of my mind that Ruth's belated interest in her father had something to do with the failure of her visit to Wellington. And more, with some failure of my own. But how had I failed her, and why should she have turned to him?

The percolator began working. Ruth appeared, still in jeans and sweater, swinging her duffel-bag. 'I thought you were getting dressed,' I said.

'No point in that. Not till the funeral tomorrow. And there's the car trip ahead. I always feel sticky after a car trip, don't you? Nothing seems clean. I've got all I want here.' She slapped the duffel-bag. 'Clothes for tomorrow, toothbrush for tonight. How's the coffee?'

She poured from the percolator into two chipped cups. 'Brother mine – ' she began.

'Why do you keep saying that?'

'Saying what?'

'Brother mine. It's something you haven't said for years. It sounds quite odd now.'

'I didn't realize. Sorry. If it upsets you, I mean.'

'It doesn't upset me. I said it sounds odd. After all this time.'

'Does it? Well, now. Fancy that.'

'It would sound just as strange if I began calling you "sister mine" again.'

'Would it? I hadn't realized.' She passed me the coffee. 'Stir with the spoon in the sugar bowl.'

'You're not offended?' I asked. 'I mean, I was just pointing the fact out.'

'Why should I be offended?'

There was a silence between us as we sipped the coffee. I was still trying to adjust to the ground again, after the flight, and after being torn so abruptly from my life in Wellington.

'I must say,' I said after a while, 'that we don't look a particularly grief-stricken pair. But it's no use pretending, is it? We hardly knew him, really.'

'I think I was getting to know him,' she said slowly, as if measuring each word for weight. 'I feel I was, anyway. I think it was a question of approaching him on his own terms. And not expecting him to be other than what he was. Which we always did. We wanted a father like other fathers. Wouldn't you agree?'

'But even then – ' I began, and faltered. I remembered my own visits, on holidays, with Helen and the children. I had hoped grandchildren, the idea of grandchildren, might produce some response from him. He was kindly enough, true; he picked them fruit from his garden, patted them on the head, walked with them down to the beach near his cottage. But there was something missing all the same. I felt that, as far as he was concerned, they could have been any children. Just as Helen, say, could have been any woman; not a daughter-in-law. 'I think you're simplifying,' I went on. 'I think there was a little more to it than that. After all, fathers don't come in a special mould. They're not all alike, I mean. Speaking as one myself.'

'Well,' she sighed. 'Perhaps I'm wrong about that. But I feel I was getting to know him, all the same.'

'In what way?'

'I told you. In his way.'

I was perplexed and unreasonably irritated, as if I had just found her cheating me of something.

'We must talk some more about this,' I said, and rose. 'It's time we were moving.'

We used the last of the daylight on the journey and travelled the last twenty or thirty miles with the headlights flashing over fern, gorse and rutted road; inland places had the chill of coming frost, but the air was warmer as we neared the sea. Ruth smoked steadily and had little to say.

'Where to?' I asked, as we drove into the settlement. Drawn-up boats and ramshackle cottages, deserted by their summer residents, rose pale in the headlights. Few windows were lit up anywhere.

'His place, I suppose,' Ruth said. 'I mean we'll have to spend the night somewhere.'

'I was thinking in terms of a motel,' I said. 'Something like that.'

'Why pay money? His place is there. And it's ours now, anyway.'

'That hadn't struck me, I admit. I mean, it doesn't seem right that his place should be ours. But what about – ' I hesitated.

'The body, you mean? An undertaker's looking after it all. That's what Mr Slegel said. The man who rang me up. He found the body early this morning and he told me everything was being taken care of. He must have told me that at least four times. It seems he expected to spend the morning fishing with Dad.'

More boats, more darkened cottages. Above the engine noise we could hear the sea, the beat of surf, off to our right. A couple of shops floated through the headlights, then pale sandhills and marram grass.

'You sure we'll be able to get into the place?' The more I thought of it, the less I liked the idea of spending the night in my father's house.

'Mr Slegel said everything would be taken care of.'

Lights were even fewer at the north end of the beach. I slowed the car and changed into low gear as the road deteriorated. The last few yards were very bumpy. When we reached the beginning of my father's drive I was startled to see lights burning beyond his sub-tropical jungle of banana trees, passion fruit and paw-paw.

'Someone in occupation,' I said.

'Probably Mr Slegel. Waiting for us.'

'Who is he, anyway? Never heard of him.'

'A friend. I told you. Probably Dad's only friend. A German Jewish refugee, retired now. He got out of Germany with his wife just before the war. But his wife insisted on going back to fetch some relative. He never saw her again. She died in Auschwitz, Belsen, one of those places. He was interned himself as an enemy alien for a while. He bought himself a place here with compensation from the West German government. Dad told me the whole story.'

'I'm surprised he could get so interested in someone else. I really am.'

'You're bitter, brother. Too bitter. Don't let it rankle. Not now.'

'All right,' I said. 'Any further instructions?' On that note I stopped the car. We climbed out and made our way along the winding, rising path to the house. The place was at the extremity of the beach, against a hillside and above rocks washed by surf. In this sheltered place, on volcanic soil, his plants had flourished. We ducked beneath banana leaves heavy with dew on our way up to the house. The surf was very loud now.

A waiting figure filled the doorway and, when we approached, a hand was thrust roughly into mine. 'Slegel,' a thick voice said. 'I thought you would be here tonight.' He guided us through the door.

The inside of the house was warm. Logs blazed in the fireplace. 'You have eaten this night?' Mr Slegel said with concern.

'We had a bite on the way, thanks.' We hadn't really eaten, apart from a toasted sandwich with coffee at a roadside stop, but I didn't want to put him to any more trouble. It was obvious he'd slaved to get the place ready for us. Everything was prepared, neat and comfortable. Miraculously he seemed even to have tidied away the idea of death. The only thing missing, really, was my father himself. I half expected him to walk out of the bedroom to greet us, and then to sit with us before the log fire.

'So long as you are all right,' Mr Slegel said. 'That is the main thing. Anyway, if you want more, your sister knows where to find food in this house. There is a fish in the refrigerator which your father caught yesterday, a twelve-pound snapper of which he was proud. His last. I weighed it for him.'

He hesitated, a heavy and rather clumsy man who apparently found even the shortest speech an effort. It was then I realized, having just grown used to the light, that his eyes were red and puffy and still faintly damp. He'd wept as he waited for us. Perhaps wept all day. I cringed from this grief of a stranger, and perhaps Ruth did too, as we stood there fresh-eyed from the city.

'Your father was good friend to me, so good I can never tell. Life is not worth so much to me today. Perhaps tomorrow we will talk more. For is not the time, this night. Main thing now is that you are comfortable. In the morning we will speak again.'

Before I could reply, thank him for everything, he ducked out of the door.

'Well,' I said, and Ruth and I were left looking at each other. Ruth moved slowly towards the fire and warmed her hands.

'I think he was rather like Dad,' she observed finally. 'I mean they were much of a muchness, lonely here, and they got along together. They kept to themselves. I don't think they even talked much between themselves. They just liked to be with each other.'

'I see.'

She looked into the fire for a while. 'He'll miss Dad,' she added.

'Obviously.'

'Hungry?'

'I suppose I am. It's been a long day. Everything's starting to catch up with me. I mean, a lot has happened in the last twelve hours or so. I think I must have eaten, at some stage, but it's hard to remember.'

'I'll get something,' she said, and turned from the fire.

I looked at her. My voice seemed to strain across the stillness and quiet of the house. 'I suppose this is an event,' I said. 'Back in my father's house, and my sister cooking for me again. How long has it been?'

Ruth sighed as she went through to the kitchen. 'Let's not count the years,' she called over her shoulder. 'Just for once.'

I took her place before the fire and tossed a couple of fresh logs into the grate. Mr Slegel had left us plenty of wood. Then I relaxed in a chair. I felt my father's presence more strongly than ever: our old familiar furniture; his books; the photograph of the fragile stranger who was my mother, on the mantelpiece. Though I had never actually lived in this house, it could have been any one of a dozen places I had known in childhood. Ruth was right: there was no point in counting the years. For it was as if the years had been banished. My father could have been out on a job, late, while Ruth and I fended for ourselves, as we often did, in the absence of regular housekeepers.

The fire crackled; I was lost in the thought.

Ruth appeared from the kitchen. I looked at her, she looked at me. For a moment she said nothing. Then she asked, 'Why are you looking at me like that?'

'Like what?'

'So strangely.'

'Things are strange all of a sudden. I can't help it.' It was as if Helen had never existed, nor my children; as if I didn't have a warm house, warmth of any kind, waiting five hundred miles away. All my adult life seemed to crumble and vanish. 'Don't you feel it too?'

'In the sense that Dad is gone,' she said, 'yes.'

'No,' I began. 'I mean – ' But I faltered and finished, 'It's too difficult to explain. Just now, anyway. What were you going to say?'

'I came to ask whether you'd like meat, or that fish Dad left.'

'What do you think?'

'I think I'd prefer to leave the fish. If you would. Perhaps Mr Slegel might like it. Not that there's anything wrong with it. It's just that – '

'I know,' I said.

Ruth went back to prepare the meal, humming softly to herself. My insecurity ebbed slowly; I felt the return of older warmth, older certainties. As a child I had often been utterly dependent on Ruth, on her judgement. She had stood between me and the world. Her presence at the funeral would make it all so much easier. Perhaps she would even know what to say to Mr Slegel.

'How about a drink?' Ruth called. 'I couldn't rely on Dad having anything, so I put a bottle of sherry in my duffel-bag. You might get it out of the car.'

I went out into the chilly evening. The surf was noisy, the stars bright. A light wind rattled the damp foliage in the garden. I paused beside the car and looked back to the lighted house. It seemed to me now that the place strangely enclosed all the half-forgotten perplexities and mysteries of my life: if I was still alien, it was because I felt alien to myself. I fetched our bags from the boot of the car and carried them inside.

I uncorked the bottle and poured the wine. Ruth came to sit beside the fire while the food cooked. We raised our glasses.

'I'm not sure what we can toast,' I said, 'except Dad's memory.'

'To us, then,' Ruth said decisively. 'To our futures. That's simpler.'

The sherry was cheap and faintly metallic. It soothed, though, and warmed. Ruth kicked off her shoes and placed her bare feet close to the fire.

'So Dad's brought us under the same roof again,' I observed.

'I was under your roof a few months ago,' she said.

'That doesn't count somehow.'

'All right, so that doesn't count. What does count?'

I shrugged.

'My dear sweet brother,' she said, 'I don't expect some gnomic utterance. Just a simple answer. What does count with you?'

'Doing my best, I suppose. Doing my best, in every sense.'

'You think you've done it?'

'How would I know?'

'Don't be so coy. Really, you're very pleased with yourself, aren't you? And proud of your good safe job, your pleasantly tamed wife, your happy family? Isn't that so?'

'Well, I suppose I've reason to be. Proud, I mean. I refuse to be ashamed, anyway.'

'Good Lord,' she said. 'Who's asking you to be ashamed?'

She padded barefoot back to the kitchen and began serving the food. I set the table for the meal: that had always been my job. Then I fetched and refilled my glass and leaned in the kitchen doorway, watching Ruth set out the food on plates. I realized I was still a little afraid of her. My elder sister had always seemed to know best.

'What do you want me to do?' I challenged.

'To be yourself for a change. To be a little less stuffy.' She looked at me sharply; her hair drifted lightly over her vivid eyes. 'To be a little less bloody pompous.'

'Fair enough,' I said. 'So what am I supposed to do now? Run round in jeans? Be a thirty-two-year-old beatnik?'

An oblique attack seemed to me the best form of defence. But she didn't bite.

'Anything,' she said, 'anything but the way you are now. You were such a bright-eyed kid. Sorry, but I can't help remembering.'

'And I can't help feeling you're unfair,' I said. 'There should be room for all kinds in this world. And if there's not room for your kind, and my kind, then it's a poor look-out. That's all I can say.'

'You enjoyed life,' she went on. 'You really did.'

'How do you know I don't still enjoy it?'

'How could you?' She shrugged. 'That house of yours, it's a living death. Really. No honest emotion could survive there five minutes. It's the kids I feel sorry for most of all, though. They just haven't a chance.'

She couldn't have surprised me more if she had struck me across the face.

'What do you want them to have? A childhood like ours? Is that it?'

'They could do worse. A lot worse. All things considered.' She gave me another sharp glance, then took up the two steaming plates of food and carried them through to the living-room table. As we sat down, she added, 'We didn't do badly. We were pretty lucky, in fact. Not many have a childhood as rich as ours, and you ought to know that by now.'

'I've thought about it,' I confessed.

'We ought to be grateful to Dad.'

'For ignoring us?'

'For leaving us alone.'

'What's the difference?'

'The difference between oversight and insight. I've only come to understand some things lately. As I've come to understand Dad himself. It's true that he was stunned when our mother died. And it's true that he didn't seem to know we were around for a while. But when he tried to acknowledge our existence again, he found that we didn't acknowledge his any more. We didn't need him. We'd grown self-sufficient in the meantime. And he seemed to think we were better for it. So he withdrew, and left us alone. Deliberately. It might have cost him a lot, for all we know.'

We began to eat in silence. The surf seemed to move closer to the house.

'That may be so,' I said reasonably, trying to sum up, 'but I still think there's a certain failure of imagination on your part if you think my kids are unhappy. You think everyone should be like we were.'

She didn't acknowledge the point. 'Then there's your wife,' she said.

'Helen? She's happy enough.'

'That shows a considerably greater failure of imagination on your part. A more insecure girl I've never seen.'

This time Ruth had gone too far.

'That's bloody ridiculous,' I said, 'and you know it. A sense of security is the one thing that Helen has got. She has precious few worries – with the house, or with the kids. I've seen to that. I've worked for it.'

'I'm not talking about that kind of security.'

'Then pray tell me what you are talking about.'

'She's not secure in herself, in her own mind. Don't ask me why. It's an impertinence to explain someone else's discontent. I felt it as soon as I walked into your house. In fact I was on the receiving end. She took it out on me. For a while, there, I was a kind of whipping-boy. I don't suppose you noticed that Helen and I didn't get along.'

That assumption irritated me even more. 'I'm not altogether blind,' I said.

'Well, then,' she went on, 'if you saw she wasn't easy in mind, you might have wondered why. After all, she is your wife; the subject must have some interest for you.'

'I did wonder why. I've tried to talk to her. Without much success, I admit. But I have tried.'

'Great. So you've tried. And, having failed, did you draw the only possible conclusion?'

'I concluded that she didn't like you much.'

'That's a fact, not a conclusion. You didn't go very far, did you? Or were you afraid to go too far? The only possible conclusion, it seemed to me, was that she was jealous.'

'Jealous?' The word, usually so hard and angular, suddenly became rubbery and meaningless; it seemed to slither away from me. 'What in God's name has Helen got to be jealous about? Why should she be jealous of you?'

Ruth shrugged. 'I suppose I could list any number of reasons – none of them good ones, mind you. But then people are seldom jealous for good reasons, are they?'

'Go on, then.'

'Well, one could simply be that I'm your sister and in this situation a kind of mother-in-law. That I belong to part of your life, a good part of it, which is still much of a mystery to her and which she resents not possessing too. But that's only half a reason, isn't it? It doesn't explain anything really. The real question is why she, or any human being, should crave total possession of another, when it's so impossible.'

'Perhaps life's like that. Perhaps love's like that. And perhaps you wouldn't know.'

She took that coolly.

'We can always fall back on love, can't we?' she observed with a faint smile. 'The best whipping-boy of all.'

'All right,' I said. 'Anything else?'

'Another thing could be that she feels she's missing something. Something she imagines I've got, because I haven't married, and she lacks because she has. She may resent being tied to house and children, and may resent even more a woman who is not tied down. Can't you see?'

'No,' I said stubbornly. 'It's no use bringing the children into it. Helen's perfectly happy with the children.'

'But you admit she wasn't easy in mind – '

'That may just be you. You're an upsetting influence.'

'All right. Please yourself.'

The meal moved to its end in prickly silence. I found myself remembering the incident of Ruth's painting: the way it had vanished, after so long a time, from the wall of the living room. I decided to say nothing about it. I would interpret the incident for myself; I wasn't going to supply Ruth with ammunition.

Afterwards we sat for a while in front of the fire. Towards the end of the evening, since Ruth was taking my father's room and bed, she made up a bed for me on the couch in the living room. By that time the long day had caught up with me, and I was hazy with exhaustion. Ruth made herself a last cup of coffee and stood sipping it before the diminished fire. I lay flopped in a chair. She lit herself a cigarette, and flipped the packet into my lap.

'Thanks,' I said. 'I've stopped, but I still like one now and again, when the occasion demands. It certainly does demand today.'

The cigarette, though, only complemented my sense of strangeness; I felt a little giddy. I looked at Ruth, half silhouetted against the firelight, and realized what a lean and handsome woman she had become. It had always been difficult for me to see Ruth other than as a sister. But men must surely have found her disconcertingly attractive. In figure and manner there was an animal economy, a natural elegance of movement at odds with the erratic life she led. They must have been drawn to her. Suddenly, with a faint twinge, I was sure they had. There must have been many men, many, who had sought purchase on those firm breasts and thighs. But what had happened to them? Had there never been one who meant more than others?

'Ruth,' I said suddenly, startling myself, 'why haven't you settled down?'

'I'm perfectly settled, thanks.'

'But your life, it's so untidy.'

'As far as I'm concerned, it's perfectly tidy. Everything in its proper place.'

'It's never seemed that way to me.'

'That's because you're not living my life.'

I supposed that a stupid question had, after all, deserved a stupid answer. I blamed my own reluctance to be direct.

'Well, marriage, then,' I said. 'Marriage and children. Hasn't that ever appealed to you? Tempted you?'

'Once it might have.' She shook her head. 'I really don't know now. I really don't know at all.'

I felt close to her again, for the first time that evening; her answer was disturbingly honest. As if scrub and undergrowth had parted to reveal a tall, clean-limbed tree.

'You mean you put temptation behind you?'

'It put itself behind me. Suddenly it wasn't there any more. It just wasn't an issue.'

'I see,' I said, and brooded.

'Well,' she said, 'I suppose we've another big day tomorrow.' She washed the coffee cups, said goodnight, and went off to her bedroom.

Though I was probably even more tired, I remained some time longer in the chair before the fire, still puzzling. Eventually I rose.

'Ruth,' I called. 'Just one more thing. Something I've always meant to ask you, but never have.'

The bedroom door was open. I went to stand beside it. In an undergarment luminously pale against her very brown skin, Ruth was in the act of climbing into bed.

'Yes?' she said.

'Why did you walk out on my wedding breakfast? You remember?'

'Of course I remember. I walked out because I just couldn't stand it.'

'Couldn't stand what?'

'If you must know, I couldn't stand watching my brother make a clumsy clown of himself, before a lot of drunken idiots. I don't care if they were your wife's relatives, I don't care if it was expected of you. I just couldn't stand it, that's all.'

'You were disappointed in me, then?'

'Since you've said it, yes.'

'Well,' I said, 'I suppose I've always known that, in a way.' I hesitated, and realized there was nothing more I could say. 'Goodnight, then. See you in the morning.'

'Goodnight, brother mine.'

I shut her door, and began the long night. Though I was tired and the couch comfortable, my body twisted painfully in search of sleep; after an hour of restless turning I was as far from it as ever. I blamed the strangeness of everything. The strangeness of our arrival, the lights burning eerily beyond the trees in a dead man's house, the weeping stranger at the door; the strangeness of being in my father's house again, beneath the same roof as my sister, alone with Ruth for the first time in years.

And there was the unfamiliar thud of surf outside.

I realized I should have rung Helen. Her voice would have reassured me and I mightn't have felt so vulnerable. And I might have had some sense of continuity instead of a sense of a widening crack down the middle of my life. I felt gusts of doubt, and doors creaked open on strange places in my mind. My father's face danced dimly before my closed eyes, then Ruth's; finally the puffy-eyed Mr Slegel's. All seemed, in some way, accusing. It was absurd.

Then Ruth again, but younger and different. She was slight and lean in a swimming costume and running ahead of me down to the sea. The water was silver, the early sunlight vivid on sand-dunes and stumps of bleached driftwood. Ruth plunged down from the dunes, skidding, laughing. She looked back at me and cried, 'Come on, slow-coach.' Breathless, I followed. We skimmed like gulls together over the sand.

There was a savage and piercing pain in my foot. I cried out and tumbled forward. Ruth was suddenly beside me, tender with concern.

'Why don't they leave us alone?' she said angrily. She was biting her lip and weeping. 'Why don't they?'

My foot was sliced open, and my blood bright on the sand. When Ruth lifted my head I saw for the first time the ugly half-buried glass of a broken beer-bottle.

She bandaged my foot with a torn strip of towel and, leaning on her shoulder, I hobbled home.

Restless on that couch the night after my father's death, twenty years later, I could still feel the shredding glass in my flesh. I could still twitch with the agony of it, yet feel at peace with Ruth's gentle hands and tender voice.

It was no use. Sleep was hours away.

I rose, switched on the light, and heaped some fresh wood on the fire. Then I heated the coffee and helped myself to another of Ruth's cigarettes.

Remembering how we had bickered so fretfully all evening, seeking to wound in tender places, I wanted to cry to her shut bedroom door, 'Look what they've done to us, sister mine. Just look what they've done to us.'

But I didn't. Instead, wide awake and tense, I hunted along my father's bookshelves for something to read, something to pass the night. But it was hard to find anything appealing. It wasn't really the time to begin an exploration of my father's collected classics, or to examine the works of Karl Marx, Daniel De Leon or Edward Bellamy; socialism had flowed strongly in my father's thought and speech when he was younger, when he could still see all mankind's problems as moral and economic. After my mother's death, an event which may have given his views some cosmic qualification, his interest and involvement in the affairs of men became more academic: Trotsky's *Revolution Betrayed* stood alongside Winwood Reade's *Martyrdom of Man*; Koestler and Deutscher beside William Morris and Thomas Paine. Certainly he didn't argue or attend meetings any longer. His views became so much his own they were vague even to his children. And now – as I passed over a two-volume work on ancient Egypt, Gibbon's *Decline and Fall* – his books served still to conceal rather than reveal the man. I could not associate them with the father I knew.

Was that my fault? Should I, like Ruth, perhaps like Mr Slegel, have made some effort? My frustration at not finding something ephemeral to read merged into something larger. Even at this late stage, it seemed, I would never be able to see him clear. I would never be able to assign him a place in my mind and say: Yes, that is, that was, my father. He would always perplex me.

And there wasn't even a magazine. In the cold night foliage from warmer climates rubbed and rustled against the house, as if craving the heat within. I sat by the fire, drank coffee, listened to the surf, and smoked more of Ruth's cigarettes. It was clearly too late to search out my father, set him straight in my mind. But what had he made of us, Ruth and myself? In one way, at least, we must have disappointed him, for neither of us had taken more than a mild interest in things political; we were like passengers insulated in a ship, trapped placidly, listening now and then to faint and distant storm surges. Yet in our different ways we were children of a world he and men like him had made as surely as we were children of a country he had made: he had seen society tugged apart as well as landscape; in his lifetime the socialist idea may have faltered here and failed there, may have been stalemated by its own successes, may in desperation have assumed grotesque and fearful shapes, but nothing had been left unchanged by it, no country and no person. Had there been satisfaction in this for him? It was unlikely. I could see that, easily enough, but what I could still not see was how Ruth and I, in our separate lives, must have appeared to him. Had he been amazed that we should remain indifferent to his late urgencies, or had he been able to make some imaginative and compassionate leap into our world? For actually we weren't so much indifferent as perplexed and powerless, seekers of refuge. Had that been at all plain to him?

I would, of course, never know. An hour or two later I put out the light and tried sleeping again.

I must have slept – for a time, at least – before I became aware once more of the surf's din. The darkness was perhaps less dense beyond the windows, but dawn still some way off. Then I became aware of what had woken me: the light was on in the kitchen, and I heard Ruth moving round there. I could smell cigarette-smoke, as if she'd just been standing beside my couch.

'You're up early,' I called.

'I couldn't sleep.'

'You too.'

'Coffee?'

'Thanks.'

A minute or two later she came to sit beside me on the couch. We sipped our coffee in silence. 'I suppose I must have slept for a couple of hours,' she said blearily, pulling up the lapels of my father's dressing-gown against the morning chill. 'Then something woke me – a tree scratching on the window – and I couldn't go back off again. I seem to have been awake, thinking, for hours. I'm sorry if I was unpleasant to you last night.'

'You weren't unpleasant. Just blunt.'

She seemed pained, uncertain of herself. She fidgeted a new cigarette out of a flattened packet, lit it, and then ran a vague hand through the hair which streamed over her eyes.

'I seem to remember being unpleasant, all the same. It wasn't a particularly nice way to behave on the night after Dad died. I'm sorry if I hurt your feelings. I didn't mean it. All that stuff about the wedding breakfast – '

'It was true enough, wasn't it?'

'Half true. Let me put it that way.'

'What's the other half, then?'

'You're being difficult.'

'Come on. Otherwise I will be hurt, after all.'

'Let's face it, then. We were pretty close as children.'

'That's no news.'

'No, when I say pretty close, I mean pretty close. I mean pretty incestuous, in fact. If I have to spell it out.'

'Well, I wouldn't go so far as to say that.'

'I would.'

I shrugged. 'Please yourself. Perhaps I'd better have one of those cigarettes too.'

'I think it's best to be honest with ourselves. I mean, it's easier that way. My trouble is, I've never been able to make up my mind just where incestuous regard ends and sisterly concern begins. You see?'

'No. Not really.'

'Naturally you could object that you've not seen sisterly concern much in evidence lately, anyway. Fair enough. Blame that on my suspicion of the first. My suspicion of myself.'

'Ruth, you're taking yourself much too seriously.'

'I have to, you see. So when I look back on something like your wedding breakfast I wonder if I haven't just been concealing the whole truth from myself. About why I walked out, I mean.' She paused. 'I suppose Helen is so right to be suspicious. I don't blame her.'

'Now you're trying to dramatize everything.'

'Trying? I didn't think I had to try.' She laughed bitterly. 'We're adults now, for God's sake.'

The windows were brightening to pale grey. Ruth sighed, rose, and carried our empty cups back to the kitchen.

'Ruth,' I called after her, 'there was nothing wrong with our childhood, with us. Nothing unnatural.'

'No. That's just it, I suppose. That's just it.' She ran a tap, washed the cups, and then walked past my couch on the way back to the bedroom. 'Feel like a walk? I'm going to have a look at the sea while I've still got a chance today.'

I swung my feet gingerly to the floor and dressed quickly. Ruth didn't take long either. Then we let ourselves out of the cottage into the keen morning. Dew dripped slowly from frond and leaf; the sea in the east was pale and bright. The air was perfectly still. Below us, the land sloped sharply to rocks patchily black with mussels and tangled with shiny kelp: the tide was out. The beach began with a wide curve into the land and then swept away in a straight line until it was lost in spray-haze and distance. Banked up behind the beach were silky white dunes. Islands floated upon the first light of day. The sky was clear.

'A pleasant enough day for a funeral,' I observed. 'Even if I can think of better uses for it.'

Ruth walked slowly and silently ahead of me. It required some effort to walk slowly down that slope to the sea. A yellow scarf trailed about her neck and her hands were thrust deep in the slit-pockets of her windbreaker. She held herself very erect, as if deliberately pacing out the correct distance to the beach. For myself, it was all I could do to keep from breaking into a jog-trot and hurtling past her on the way to the sand. Once we would have careered down this slope in an instant, skimmed over the beach, thrown ourselves into even this wintry sea. We had never walked together so sedately before.

We reached the sand by way of the rocks at the end of the beach. It was a slight scramble, and the surf kicked spray over us. The razor-ridged rocks were slippery, and once Ruth lost her poise and teetered dangerously above a deep crevice filled with foam. I grabbed her hand and helped her the rest of the way.

'Thanks, brother mine,' she said, when we reached the actual beach safely.

We separated again, and trod the sand carefully, almost tenderly, a yard or two apart, as if there were glass underfoot; as if our feet were unshod.

The sea was green and uninviting, the spray fresh on our faces. The sand squeaked underfoot as we walked in silence. Once more Ruth seemed to be pacing out the distance between one point and another. At length she paused beside an amputated tree-trunk which some spring tide had flung into the dunes with such force that it had actually pierced the hirsute cover of marram grass, between bulging flanks of sand.

'Let's just sit here,' she said. 'And watch the sunrise.'

We hadn't long to wait. The cold silver of sea and sky vanished; there was spurt after spurt of colour above a reddened sea. Before long the light, diluted to pale yellow, was touching our faces with a faint promise of warmth. Lean gulls swayed above the rising tide.

'It's nice to know it's still there,' Ruth observed. 'The sun, I mean. It's about the only thing you can rely on.'

But she shivered, all the same.

'The only bloody thing,' she went on, 'and even then only sometimes.'

She hunched forward, hair falling over her face, and with a stick began drawing in the sand. Once she looked back up at our father's house, perched at the end of the beach.

'It'd be nice to stay here, though,' she said. 'Everything unimportant stripped away. Why don't we?'

'You're not serious.'

'I couldn't be, could I?' She paused. 'Just the same,' she added dreamily.

'Ruth, please – '

'Oh, of course I'm not bloody serious. Don't panic.' She stood up. 'Let's go back. We've had our free time for today, children. Now back to the business of life. Or isn't it death?'

She gave me her hand, and pulled me to my feet. We faced each other for a moment. Her eyes searched mine.

'You forgive me, don't you?'

'For what?'

'Everything.'

'In that case,' I said, 'there's nothing to forgive.'

She laid her head silently on my shoulder, then lifted it again. We walked back to the house. On our way we gathered enough mussels for breakfast.

The funeral was straightforward and almost painless. A retired clergyman, for whom my father had done odd jobs, conducted the service. He made brief reference to my father's professed agnosticism, dismissing this as altogether irrelevant. With the exception of Mr Slegel, all the faces at the graveside were strange; there were about twenty people present, all from the village. Only Mr Slegel wept. Ruth all but wept, I suppose; as the coffin dipped into the earth she shivered, and I slid an arm about her waist. When the service ended, I helped her along a muddy track to the car. Then I went to thank the clergyman, and shake hands with all the pleasant strangers who had attended my father's funeral. It wasn't as difficult as I expected to say the right things, since they had very little to say themselves: none of them had really known my father well. But when I looked for Mr Slegel, he had gone. I went back to the car and sat in silence beside Ruth. She lit a cigarette, and placed it between my fingers.

'So that's the end of it,' I said at last.

'The end of what?' she asked softly.

'Of something. Of him, of us, of whatever we were to each other and whatever we weren't.' I paused. 'Listen, Ruth,' I added, 'I've been thinking about things this morning. It would save a whole lot of trouble if you took over Dad's place.'

'You're not serious.'

'I am. Perfectly serious. Otherwise we'd only have the problem of selling it and dividing the proceeds between us. It's hardly worth it. I doubt if Dad's got any other asset to speak of. Another thing, I'm quite settled. I've got a house, all the security I want. You haven't. With a place like that, even if you use it only as a weekend cottage, a holiday place or a workplace, and let it to other people when you don't need it, you'll have some stability.'

'And you won't need to worry about me?' she said shrewdly.

'If you put it like that, yes. I'd worry less about you, anyway.'

'All right,' she said. 'I'll think about it. And just what is Helen going to think about your brotherly generosity?'

'She can think what she likes. It's my business. In any case she should be able to see that it will solve a lot of problems. About what to do with all Dad's possessions – his library, for example. I can put the whole thing in the hands of an Auckland lawyer and fly straight home to Wellington.'

'Ah,' Ruth said, 'I see. The truth, at last. You want to fly straight home.'

In the distance a solitary gravedigger was heaping the last clay on my father's coffin. It was just noon and there was warmth in the day: the wintry sun was gentle on the small cemetery, the straw-coloured grass, the headstones gripped by convolvulus. Beyond a line of peeling bluegums the sea was very blue.

'Why not? There's no point in spending more time away in the north than I need to.'

'Are you tired, brother? Are you tired, depressed, miserable, uneasy, in fact bloody awful? Try Wife, then. Try Wife, the friendly all-purpose remedy. Back again in standard sizes or in our special flip-top box. Watch for the trademark and beware of substitutes. Obtainable today from – '

'For God's sake,' I said.

'Superior to all other brand names,' she went on. 'Get with it, be in the swim. Tests show that nine out of every ten men prefer Wife. And the others are probably homosexuals anyway.'

'Shut up.'

But she was weeping; she had her face buried in her arms. I put the car into gear and drove back through the village to the house. Ruth went quickly inside, through to the bathroom, to wash her face and brush her hair. I fell heavily into a chair and looked beyond green growth to the sea. After a while she reappeared.

'Sorry about all that,' she said calmly. 'I didn't mean it.'

'I know. You never do.'

'True enough,' she agreed. 'I never do.'

She went into the bedroom to change. Then we packed, tidied, and ate a quick lunch. Ruth defrosted the refrigerator and removed the fish for Mr Slegel. As we moved to the door, I paused and said, 'Well, there you are. It's all here, all yours, if you want it.'

'Yes,' she said. 'All right.'

'All right?'

'I'll take the place over. And if you and Helen and the kids ever want a holiday here, I'll move out – if I'm in residence, which probably I won't be, often. It might give us some sense of continuity after all. If there's something to be salvaged, I suppose that's it – some sense of the importance and relevance of the past. We may need that more and more. I don't mean just us. I mean people in general. If your children are ever going to have a sense of continuity, a sense of family, we might as well start here as anywhere, if we're going to start at all.'

'And your children?' I said.

Ruth shrugged, and we went out of the door together.

I am in my home. It is evening. The lights of Wellington glitter far below my study window. In another room the television has just been silenced and now Helen is reading to the children. I am familiar with the story she is reading them. It is about a comical, clumsy, well-meaning elephant. Whatever he touches, he seems to damage. When he tries to play with other animals, he inadvertently hurts them. But – since this is a story for children – he manages to do the right thing in the end; it all ends happily. I can see myself briefly in the story, at least my clumsiness. Have I done the right thing in the end? The fact is,

I've tried to buy off my sister; tried to buy her off my conscience. I may actually have done the right thing by Ruth. As for myself, I cannot tell. I just wish I felt happier in mind.

Before we left the village we sought out Mr Slegel, thanked him for everything, and presented him with that fish we hadn't been able to bring ourselves to eat. He was delighted to know that Ruth would be returning to the house regularly, and promised to look after the place for her, and tend the garden.

'Your father,' he told us, 'was a good man, good and gentle. And I can see, for it is easy to see, that he had two fine children of which he was proud. I know that always he dreamed of only the best things for his children.'

Was that the truth? Or was he just saying that for something to say? I couldn't be sure. It left me uneasy.

'I think,' he went on with a sad smile, 'that he would have liked the house kept. It would have done him good to know that he had not made a home there for nothing – not just for himself, but for his children too.'

I was glad to say goodbye to Mr Slegel, for he disturbed me – I felt drawn to him; I suppose that was the simple truth of the matter. I felt drawn to him as I had never been to my father. And I was sure at last that it was my fault, not my father's.

It was too late in the day to see a lawyer and catch a plane home when we got to Auckland. I spent the night with Ruth – again an improvised bed on a couch, this time in her untidy kitchen. She had greater assurance on home ground again. We talked of her work, which sells moderately well in Auckland galleries, and I looked over some of her newer paintings. I was interested to see again, in painting after painting, that curious light which had perplexed me. I was about to remark on it when there was a noise, then knocking, at her door.

'Oh God,' she said. 'Visitors. I was afraid I'd have them tonight. I just had a feeling.'

Four friends, three men and a girl, swamped us. They planted a dozen bottles of beer on the floor and arrayed themselves around Ruth's bedroom-studio. With glasses supplied by Ruth, they quickly set about emptying the bottles. They all seemed to know Ruth well: I had the impression that they might be as close to her as anyone she knew. They examined me without great curiosity when I was introduced, and went on talking to Ruth. She didn't explain my presence, or mention the death in the family, until the beer was gone and the gossip exhausted.

'It's midnight,' she said wearily. 'And my brother and I have had a funeral today.'

Even that didn't particularly shake them. It simply caused a new outbreak of talk, and they didn't leave for another hour or more. Since I had little to say for myself, I had more than enough time, that evening, to sort them out as individuals; it helped keep me awake. A lean young man with thin bristly moustache, apparently some kind of writer or journalist, certainly an art critic, treated Ruth with particular deference: I guessed he was having, or had had, an affair with my sister; Ruth seemed edgily polite when she spoke to him, so I imagined the affair was a thing of the past. The other two men were bearded, and wore tight jeans; they were difficult to separate until I learned that one with dark hair was a sculptor, one with brown an artist. The girl, who in some ways might have been Ruth ten or twelve years younger, remained totally in the background and anonymous. Small and fair and frail, she curled into a corner where she smiled mysteriously to herself now and again. She gave me the impression she had heard most of the conversation before. Perhaps she had. Aside from gossip and character dissection, it mostly concerned the founding of an art magazine.

'Money,' the lean young critic said. 'Lots of lovely money. That's all we need. With a wealthy backer we could go ahead tomorrow.' He swung round on me abruptly. 'You know anyone in Wellington?'

'Me?' I shook my head.

'It's no use looking south, anyway,' the sculptor intervened. 'The further south you go, the more barbarous this country gets. God help us, they're still assimilating French impressionism down there.'

'It's not quite as black as you suppose,' I said. 'There are islands of enlightenment in the capital.'

'It's not enlightenment we're looking for,' observed the artist. 'But cash. And plenty of it.'

'Mind you,' said the critic, 'I feel sure we could pull in enough money to cover expenses on prestige advertising. Once we got started. It's just a question of getting started. There's money around all right. If only we could get our hands on it.'

'You would receive a regular salary as editor, of course,' Ruth said.

'Naturally. The thing should be done professionally, or not at all.'

'Wait till we're all rich, then,' Ruth said, 'and we'll all put money up for your magazine.'

'No,' said the critic. 'The point is that it's got to be done now. To create the climate, can't you see? To give you people a place in the sun. Damn it, I want to make you rich.'

Wherever the conversation travelled, it always seemed to circle back to the same point: money, or the lack of it. Even some new exhibition was discussed in terms of inflated prices which had or hadn't been paid; I didn't quite get the drift of what was said, because by that time I was too depressed to listen – but quite unreasonably depressed, it seemed to me. After all, there was no good reason why artists shouldn't worry about money as much as other people. In fact I – a philistine in their eyes, I supposed – should have been relieved and impressed to know they were much the same as other people. That they weren't so unworldly as one might expect. Had I needed to imagine, for my own peace of mind, that Ruth existed on a different plane from the rest of us? Well, there it was: prices, patrons, dealers, prestige advertisers; my life in the actual world of commerce began to seem positively academic and monastic. Had I needed to imagine also that Ruth lived in an interesting world, with exciting friends? Well, there it was, or there they were: the critic, artist and sculptor, and muse for good measure. As people they didn't exactly dazzle me.

When Ruth finally revealed that it was our father we had just buried that day, appropriate things were said and apologies made. Someone launched into an account of a strange funeral *he* had recently attended while Ruth, in despair, made black coffee to hasten the evening to its end. In my melancholy I felt the bleakness of Ruth's flat as a grey oppression; in my tiredness the electric bulb above our heads seemed to become dimmer and dimmer, and the figures around me more and more shadowy and remote. Voices rose and merged into one long monotonous and meaningless sound.

The next thing, Ruth's hand was on my cheek. The room was empty. The visitors had vanished.

'Hello there,' she was saying gently.

'Sorry,' I said. 'I've disgraced you. Falling asleep like that.'

'Don't be silly. It was all I could do to stay awake myself. Besides, it worked wonderfully well. I mean as soon as they saw you were asleep they all cleared out.'

'These people,' I said, 'they're really friends of yours?'

'Yes,' she said. 'Why not?'

'No reason. I just wondered. I mean I couldn't really make up my mind whether they were good friends or not. Though I supposed they must be.'

'They're good friends, all right. As good as I'll ever have, I suppose. And they're very loyal.'

'I see. Well, time for bed, I guess.'

'Something worrying you, brother?'

'Not especially.'

'Come on. Tell me.'

'It's nothing I can tell.'

'But something's worrying you. What is it?'

'I suppose I'm worried about dying. That's all.'

'Dying? What on earth – ' She knelt beside my chair, took my hand affectionately, and looked into my eyes with concern. 'Is something the matter? Really?'

'No. I just had a sudden vision of myself dead. You too. That's all. No reason. Except the funeral – and that's not it really. I'm just tired. Perhaps that's why. I need–' I shook my head helplessly. Then I knew what I needed. I needed to get home, the sooner the better. 'I need sleep badly.'

'That's no problem. I've just made your bed up on the couch.'

'Sorry. Rather a morbid way to end an evening.'

'But natural enough, considering. The shock about Dad is just filtering through to you, that's all. It's just starting to register.'

'No,' I said. 'It's something different, something more. I can't explain it.' I stood up, as if to shift the weight of my depression. 'Ruth,' I went on, 'you will look after yourself, won't you?'

'What do you say that for?'

'In case I forget to say it when I rush off in the morning. You will, won't you?'

'Of course. But why?'

'You mean a lot to me, that's all I'm trying to say. Without you, I wouldn't have any past, and I mightn't even be able to weigh my future. Without you I wouldn't be myself. That's probably what I mean. I'm not saying it very well. I'm too tired. Sorry.'

'Brother mine,' she said, and smiled. 'I think you've said it very well.' She reached up and ran a hand through my hair. Then she kissed me lightly on the cheek. 'Sleep well tonight.'

She started to turn away, but I didn't allow her to escape. Without considering why I pulled her head clumsily against my chest and held it there. Her body, her shoulders, breasts and thighs, rested inert and almost weightless against me. Yet she lived, and breathed, and possessed warmth; it seemed I needed to know that, to be reassured. Then, as if to confirm it even more, something like a sigh or a shudder shook her body. It seemed she needed reassurance too. I lifted her head and covered her lips with mine. I was sure I could still taste salt on her lips and smell sea in her hair, something of the lost day and lost summers, and I had a sense of wintry space around us.

Again her body shook. Abruptly she pushed herself away, and held me at arm's length.

'If that,' she said, 'was all I wanted, don't you think I could have got it long ago?'

Her eyes were strange, her smile thin.

'You would have been easy,' she went on. 'Dead easy. After all, I've slept with enough men. A brother here or there wouldn't make a great deal of difference.'

Astonished, I realized at last that she was trying to be brutal. It was just that for once she wasn't very good at it.

'No,' I said. 'I suppose not.'

She relented. Her hand gripped my arm tightly.

'Now turn around,' she said, 'and don't look back. Sleep well tonight and hurry home to your wife and children tomorrow. But don't look back. Don't ever look back, ever again.'

'That's your privilege?' I said.

'Mine,' she agreed. 'Goodnight, brother mine.'

The couch in the kitchen wasn't particularly comfortable. I sat on it for a while, before I tried sleeping, and smoked a cigarette in the dark and looked out Ruth's window at the lights trembling on the harbour; the fact was that I was wide awake again, at least in thought. My mind and body were fighting in separate directions. I remembered the cold beach that morning, Ruth walking silently on the sand; then the coffin descending into a dry clay hole, and Mr Slegel's stricken face.

I put my head down on the pillow but it was no use. My mind continued to race in a fever; it unreeled image after image of its own accord, as if it was searching for something. Then, as its progress steadied, as the images became less frightening, I began to understand that it was really travelling in the same direction as my exhausted body. It was collaborating, after all. Now I was wandering with Ruth, along a rocky creek, beneath huge fern; now pulling at the oars of a dinghy, while Ruth trailed a line from the stern; now lowering my rifle and bending to lift a shot rabbit from the tussock while Ruth hid her eyes; now swimming beside her in sunlit water, and the wild spray danced silvery from our bodies. Then I came, as I knew I would, to that beach: Ruth leapt ahead of me over the sand dunes, skidding and laughing and calling back. I plunged after her, down on to the beach. I prepared myself for the impact of that half-buried glass; I could not avoid it. Tensed, I knew exactly the pain to expect; exactly the moment to call out to Ruth. The colours of the world swam gently in the hazy early light. Then, miraculously, I was still running. Running on, after Ruth, over unblemished sand, and diving with her into cool water.

Light was in my eyes, and it was morning; Ruth was in the kitchen, cooking an omelette over a primus. 'I can't let you go home to Wellington half-fed,' she announced. Half an hour later, dressed and shaved, I set out to find my life again.

The house is quiet now. The clumsy elephant has made his peace with the world, the children are asleep; and Helen, whom I can hear now and then as she moves quietly about the kitchen, is preparing dinner. She has just, without saying a word, set a glass of sherry on the desk beside me. Ruth is in another city, four hundred miles away; but she might as well be in another country. I find it hard to imagine what she might be doing at this moment; possibly eating, or preparing to go out, or waiting for friends to call. For she could. I suppose, be anticipating an evening with friends like the one I remember enduring. That is her way; fair enough. She finds my way a living death, I find hers intolerably bleak. We do not share much in our lives, except the past; but that, when fanned in memory, can still glow so as to make the present seem lustreless and the future drably predictable. Of course I understand that the logic of that past dictates that she should be as she is, and that I should be as I am; we really have had no chance for escape. It is not a matter for regret, nor even for speculation. For Ruth was, of course, wrong when she said we were self-sufficient as children: she was speaking only for herself. Without Ruth I was always incomplete; as incomplete, say, as I am without Helen now. Perhaps that is something Ruth cannot understand. And yet . . . .

Love; she tried to make that an explanation. It wasn't good enough, really. For it explained everything and nothing. This is the paradox I still contemplate on sleepless nights when I rise disturbed from my marriage bed and sit solitary, with black coffee in the kitchen.

Again I wonder what she is doing at this moment. At last I find a satisfying picture. She is at home, in my father's house, at the beginning of a lonely evening. She is settling down to work she has neglected, painting her way slowly and thoughtfully into a new scene. Of course; that must be it. To imagine her at work reassures me. My eyes flick up to the painting above my desk – the red dinghy on pale sand, and that strange haunting light. The light no longer baffles me. It is perfectly obvious, perfectly familiar. That serene light flows in and out of our childhood, leaving no shadows: could there ever be glass beneath that sand? All things melt beneath it – even the dinghy is insubstantial, a brittle stick to fuel the incandescence, as it speaks of this time and this place; every time and every place. Unreal? Of course. As unreal as her belated explanation of love, her romantic's rationalisation. She is in love not with me, but with what we were and can never be again. More than that, she is in love with what we never were. But who am I to say? That light speaks eloquently where she and I cannot.

I do not see my sister often. But I recall that once, confused travellers at a junction, we met, or almost met, before we fell back into our separate journeys towards –

Well, where else? Towards the extinction of light.

C. K. STEAD

A Fitting Tribute

I don't ask you to believe me when I say I knew Julian Harp, but I ask you to give me a hearing because in every detail the story I'm going to tell is gospel true. I've tried to tell it before. After Julian's flight I even got a reporter along to the house and he wrote me up as 'just another hysterical young woman claiming to have known the National Hero'. That was a year or more ago and I haven't mentioned Julian Harp since.

What reason can a person have for telling a story that she knows won't be believed? I have two: a cross-grained magistrate and a statue. You might have heard about the case in Auckland in which a woman, a shopkeeper in court for trading without a licence, happened to say in evidence that Julian Harp had once come into her shop and bought one of those periscopes short people use for seeing over the heads of a crowd. The magistrate asked her to please keep calm and stick to the truth. Then he called for a psychiatrist's report because he said she was obviously a born liar. Next day, which happened to be the anniversary of Julian's flight, he sentenced her to a month in jail and the *Herald* published an editorial saying No one knew Julian Harp. Julian Harp knew no one. A privileged few watched his moment of glory; but he died as he had lived, a Man Alone. . . .

Of course if the woman hadn't mentioned Julian Harp she might have got away with a fine. But she insisted she remembered his name because he asked her to keep the periscope aside until he had money to pay for it. And she said he wore his hair down around his shoulders. That was unthinkable!

When I read about that case I knew what no one else could know, that the woman was telling the truth. But it was the statue that really persuaded me it was time I tried to write down the facts. I was walking in the Domain pushing my baby Christopher in his pram. Some workmen were digging on the slope among those trees between the main gates and the pavilion and what pulled me up was that they were working right on the spot where Julian first got the idea for his wings. Then a truck arrived with a winch and a great slab of polished granite and in no time all the workmen were round it swearing at one another and pulling and pushing at the chains until the stone was lowered into the hole. I thought why do they want a great ugly slab of graveyard stone there of all places? I didn't know I had asked it aloud, but one of the workmen turned and said it was for the new statue. The statue was to go on top of it. What new statue? The statue of Julian Harp of course. The one donated by the Bank of New Zealand. *The statue of Julian Harp*! You can imagine how I felt. I sat down on a bench and took Christopher out of his pram and rocked him backwards and forwards and thought how extraordinary! Miraculous! That after all the arguments in the newspapers about a site, not to mention the wrangling about whether the statue should be modern or old fashioned, they had at last landed it by accident plonk on the spot where Julian thought of his solution to the problem of engineless flight.

I sat there rocking my baby while he held on to my nose with one hand and hit me around the head with the other, and all the time I was thinking, I might even have been saying it aloud, what have I got to lose? I must tell someone. If they laugh at me, too bad. At least I will have tried. And besides, I owe it to Christopher to let everyone know the solemn truth that he is the son of Julian Harp. By the time I had wheeled the pram back through the Domain I was ready to start by telling Vega but when I saw her there in the kitchen cutting up beans for dinner and looking all straggly and cross I knew I oughtn't to tell anyone until I had the whole story sorted out in my head and perhaps written down.

I should explain before I go any further that Vega is a sort of awful necessity in my life. Before Christopher was born I had to give up work and I didn't know how I was going to pay the rent. I wanted to stay on in the house I lived in with Julian, because although everyone says he is dead no one knows for certain that he is. I wasn't planning to sit around expecting him, but I had to keep in mind that if he did come back the house would be the only place he would know to look for me. The house and Gomeo's coffee bar. So when someone advertised in the *Auckland Star* that she was a respectable middle-aged female clerk wanting board, I took her in; and now there are the three of us, Christopher and Vega and me, sharing the little two-storeyed wooden house with three rooms upstairs and two down that sits a yard from the footpath in Kendall Road on the eastern edge of the Domain. Vega isn't a great companion or anything. She hasn't much to say – except in her sleep; and then although she goes on for hours at a time it isn't in English or any other language. But when I was ready to start work again at Gomeo's I discovered I had been lucky to find her. I needed someone in the house at night to watch over Christopher, and when I mentioned it to Vega she said in her flat voice I could stop worrying about it because hadn't I noticed she never went out at night. She was afraid of the dark! Then she told me she was named after a star we don't often see in the Southern Hemisphere; and she made a noise that sounded like a laugh and said had I ever heard of a star going out at night.

All the time I was feeding Christopher that evening after seeing the workmen in the Domain I kept thinking about the statue and how wrong it would be if no one ever knew that Julian had a son. So when Christopher was asleep and I was helping Vega serve the dinner I asked her whether she thought Julian Harp might have had a family. She said no. I asked her what she thought would happen if someone claimed to be the mother of Julian's child. She said she didn't know, but she did know there was a good deal too much money being spent on a statue that made him look like nothing she'd ever seen and that kind of sculpture was a pretty disgusting way to honour a man who had given his life. I said but leaving aside the statue what would she think if a girl in Auckland claimed to be the mother of his child? Vega said she thought some of the little minxes had claimed that already, out for all they could get, but she didn't think Julian Harp would have been the marrying kind. She said she imagined him like Lawrence of Arabia, married to an idea. When I said I hadn't mentioned marriage but only paternity she said there was no need to be obscene.

I gave up at that and I didn't have time to think about Julian for the rest of the evening until it was quite late and something happened at the coffee bar that made me remember my first meeting with him. I was bending over one of the tables when Gomeo came out of the kitchen and put his hand on my buttocks and said in a sort of stage whisper you could hear all over the shop that tonight he'd gotta have me or that's the end. The sack. Finish. I said nothing and went to wipe down another table but he followed me and said in the same whisper well was it yes or no. So I swung round and said no, no, no – and each time I said it I pushed the wet cloth in his face until he had backed all the way into the kitchen. By now the people in the shop were waiting to hear me get the sack but Gomeo only said one day I would really make him mad and my God that would be the finish of us both.

You might wonder why that should remind me of Julian. It's because Gomeo threatens to sack me and for the same reason nearly every time there's a full moon and it was after one of his more spectacular performances I first talked to Julian. Julian was in the shop and like everyone else he took it all seriously and thought I had lost my job. So when I had finished pushing Gomeo back into the kitchen where he belongs Julian asked could he help me find a new job and he said he would even be willing to hit Gomeo for me if I thought it would help. I had to explain that Gomeo isn't quite one hundred per cent and he doesn't mean what he says. But you have to pretend he means it and fight him off. If you just laughed at him, or if you said yes you'd like to go to bed with him, you would be out on the pavement in five minutes, because Gomeo only wants the big drama, nothing real. I explained all this to Julian and he looked relieved but then he said he was sorry because now there wasn't any excuse to invite me to his bed-sitter after I finished work. When I looked at his face I could see he meant just what he said so I asked him did he have to have an excuse.

And thinking of Julian's face reminds me I ought to say something about his appearance because reading about him in the papers will have given you a wrong picture of him. It's well known there's only one photograph of Julian, the one taken by a schoolgirl with a box camera just before he took off. His face is slightly obscured by the crash helmet he's just going to put on and the camera hasn't been properly focused. So all the local Annigonis have got to work and done what they call impressions of him and I can tell you quite honestly the more praise the picture gets the less it looks like Julian. They all dress him up in tidy clothes and cut his hair short and some of them have even put him in a suit and tie and stuck his hair down with Brylcreem. Well if it's important to you that your local hero should look like a young army officer I'm sorry but the fact is when I first knew Julian he was one of the most disreputable looking men I had seen. His clothes never seemed to fit or match and he never went near a barber. Every now and then he would reach round to the back and sides of his head and snip off bits of hair with a pair of scissors but that was all. I think he had given up shaving altogether at the time but he didn't have the kind of growth to make a beard so he was what you might call half way between cleanshaven and bearded. He wore a rather tattered raincoat done right up to the neck, and at midnight when I finished work and he took me to a teen club under the street where you could twist and stomp he kept it on and buttoned up until I began to wonder whether he had a shirt underneath.

I hadn't turned eighteen then but I was older than most of the others in the teen club and Julian was probably twenty-two or three so I felt embarrassed especially because Julian looked such a clown. When we arrived we sat at a table and didn't dance until one of the kids called out Hey Jesus can't you dance? and several others laughed and jeered. Julian laughed too and clapped in a spastic kind of way and looked all round like a maniac as if he couldn't see who they were jeering at and then he got up without me and drifted backwards into the middle of the dancers and began to jerk and twist and stamp and roll in time to the music. Julian could certainly dance and in no time they had all stopped and made a circle round him clapping and shouting and urging him on until the sweat was pouring off him. He had to break out of the circle and make his way back to our table waving one hand behind him while they all shouted for more.

After that we drank coffee and danced and talked but you couldn't have much of a conversation above the noise of electric guitars and when we came out at 2 a.m. I felt wide awake and not very keen to go back to my bed-sitter. Julian said I should come to his and I went. We walked up Grey's Avenue under the trees and then between two buildings and through an alley that came out at the back of the house where Julian had a room. I followed him up a narrow outside stairway right to the top of the building and through French doors off a creaky verandah. He threw up a sash window and we sat getting our breath back looking out over a cluster of old wooden houses like the one we were in and the new modern buildings beyond and the harbour and the bridge. Julian said the nice thing about coming back to Auckland after being away was the old wooden houses. I had thought that was what people coming back complained about, a town where nothing looked solid, but Julian said it was as if people lived in lanterns. He liked the harbour too and the bridge and everything he looked at and I found that unusual because the people who came into Gomeo's were forever arguing about which buildings in Auckland were any good and which were not and nobody was ever enthusiastic about anything, least of all those like Julian who had been away overseas.

Julian said he liked living right in the busy part of the city and he liked to be up high. He had worked as a window cleaner on the A.M.P. building in Sydney and as a waiter in the Penn Top of the Statler Hilton in New York. And before coming back to Auckland he had driven a glass elevator that ran up and down the face of a hotel at the top of Nob Hill in San Francisco looking out over the harbour and the Golden Gate Bridge and the Bay. He said that was the best job he had ever had and he was willing to make a career of it but they made the elevator automatic to save the expense of an operator. Julian offered to run it for nothing and live off whatever tips he could get from sightseers, and when the hotel managers refused he still spent hours of every day going up and down as a member of the public until it was decided he was making a nuisance of himself and he was told not to come into the building again. A week or so later when he tried to slip in wearing dark glasses someone called the police and Julian decided it was time to leave San Francisco.

We sat without any light drinking and talking or rather Julian talking and me listening and I remember being surprised when I noticed the wine bottle was half empty and I could see the colour of the heavy velvet cloth it stood on was not black but dark red. It had got light and still I didn't feel tired. Julian said he would make us some breakfast and while he cut bread and toasted it I had a chance to look around at his things, and especially at a big old desk that had taken my eye. It was half way down the room facing one wall and it was covered with a strange collection of letters, newspaper clippings, stationery, bottles of ink of all different colours and makes, every kind of pen from a quill to a Parker, and three typewriters. Pinned to the wall above the desk there was a huge chart, but before I could begin to read it Julian saw me looking at it and called me over to help him make the breakfast.

I got to know that chart well later on because it was the nerve centre of what Julian called his Subvert the Press Campaign. On it were the names and addresses of all the people Julian had invented to write letters to the editor, then a series of numbers which showed the colour of ink each one used, the type of notepaper, and the kind of pen – or t^1, t^2, or t^3 if one of the typewriters was used; then examples of their scripts and signatures and details about their opinions and prejudices. Each name had stars beside it to show the number of letters published, and the letters themselves hung in bulldog clips at the end of each horizontal section. It had come to Julian that a newspaper really prefers letters signed with pseudonyms because it can pick and choose among them and print the opinions it likes but within reason it has to print all the signed letters that come in. So the idea of his Subvert the Press Campaign was very very gradually to introduce a whole new group of letter writers who all signed their names. They had to be all different types and live in different parts of town so the paper wouldn't suspect what was going on; but as Julian explained to me later, once he had established his group he could concentrate them suddenly on one issue and create a controversy. He called them his Secret Weapon because he said only a small group of people reads the editorials but everyone reads the correspondence columns.

But when it was put to the test and Julian decided to bring the Government down (I think it was over the cancellation of the Lyttelton scaffolding factory and the issue of extra import licences) the Secret Weapon misfired. He sent letter after letter, not only to the *Herald* and the *Star* but all over the country and soon there was a raging controversy. But he wrote his letters in a sort of daze, almost as if voices were telling him what to write, and what each letter said seemed to depend on the person supposed to be writing it instead of depending on what Julian himself really wanted to say. In the end his letter writers said as many different things as it was possible to say about the cancellation of the contract and when Parliament assembled for the special debate not only the Opposition members but the Government ones as well were armed with clippings of letters Julian had written. That was a great disappointment for Julian. He lost faith in his Secret Weapon and when I tried to get him going again he said what was the use of secretly taking over the correspondence column of a newspaper if when you succeeded it looked exactly the same as it looked before.

But it wasn't until I knew Julian well that he let me into the secret about his letters. That first morning he called me away to help with the breakfast before I had got more than a quick glance over the desk and when I thought about the chart afterwards all I could guess was that he might be the ringleader of a secret society of anarchists, or even a criminal.

We sat at the big sash window eating breakfast and watching the sun hitting off the water on to the white weatherboards and listening to pop songs and the ads on 1ZB. Julian sang some of the hits and we did some twisting and while the ads were on we finished off the wine. Julian told me the Seraphs were his favourite pop singers and that was weeks before anyone else was talking about them or voting them on to the Top Twenty. I often thought about that when Julian got to be famous and the Seraphs were at the top of the Hit Parade with 'Harp's in Heaven Now'. And when the N.Z.B.C. banned the song because they said it wasn't a fitting tribute to the national hero I felt like writing some letters to the editor myself.

It must have been eleven o'clock before I left to go home that morning and I left in a bad temper partly because I hadn't had any sleep I suppose but partly because Julian had stretched out on his divan and gone to sleep and left me to find my own way out. He hadn't said goodbye or anything about seeing me again and when I thought about it I didn't even know his second name and he didn't know mine.

I slept all that afternoon and had a ravioli at Gomeo's before starting work and I spent a miserable evening watching out for Julian to come in. It wasn't that I had any romantic feelings about him, the sort I might have had in those days about one of those good looking boys in elastic sided boots and tapered trousers. But I had a picture fixed in my head of Julian with his straggly hair and mottled blue eyes going up and up in that glass elevator like a saint on a cloud, and I kept looking for him to come into Gomeo's as if it would be almost a relief to see just the ordinary Julian instead of the Julian in my head.

He didn't come of course because he was busy writing his letters to the newspapers, but I wasn't to know that. The next day was Sunday and I spent the afternoon wandering around the lower slopes of the Domain among the trees — in fact it must have been somewhere near where they've built the Interdenominational Harp Memorial Chapel. I was feeling angry with Julian and I started to think I might get back at him by ringing the police and telling them he was a dangerous communist. I probably would have done it too but I didn't know his address exactly and I only knew his Christian name.

I still go for walks down there, with Christopher in the pram, and sometimes I sit inside the chapel and look out at the trees through all that tinted glass. People who come into Gomeo's say it's bad architecture but I like it whatever kind of architecture it is and sometimes I think I can get some idea in there of how Julian felt in the glass elevator. I've had a special interest in the chapel right from the start because Vega belongs to the Open Pentecostal Baptists and her church contributed a lot of money to the building. She told me about all the fighting that went on at first and how the Anglicans tried to get the Catholics in because of the Ecumenical thing. She said they nearly succeeded but then a Catholic priest testified to having seen Julian cross himself shortly before he put on his wings and the Catholics decided to put up a memorial of their own. Vega said it was nonsense, Julian Harp couldn't have been a Catholic, and I agreed with her because I know he wasn't anything except that he used to call himself a High Church Agnostic and an occasional Zen Buddy. Of course Vega was really pleased to have the Catholics out of the scheme and so were a lot of other people even though it meant raising a lot more money. Vega said it was better raising extra money than having the Catholics smelling out the place with incense.

It must have been nearly a week went by before Julian came into Gomeo's again and when I saw what a scraggy looking thing he was I wondered why I had given him a second thought. I ignored him quite successfully for half an hour but when he asked me to come to his bed-sitter after I finished work I went and the next night he came to mine and before long it seemed uneconomical paying two rents. We more or less agreed we would take a flat together but weeks passed and Julian did nothing about it. By now he had told me about his Subvert the Press Campaign and I knew how busy he was so I decided to find us a flat myself and surprise him with it. I answered probably twenty ads before I got one at Herne Bay at a good rent with a fridge and the bathroom shared with only one other couple. I paid a week's rent in advance and when Julian came into Gomeo's and asked for a spaghetti I brought him a clean plate with the key on it wrapped in a note giving the address of the flat and saying if Mr Julian Harp would go to the above address he would find his new home and in the fridge a special shrimp salad all for him. I watched him from behind the espresso machine. Instead of looking pleased he frowned and screwed up the note and called me over and said he wanted a spaghetti. I didn't know what to do so I brought him what he asked for and he ate it and went out. When I finished work I went to his bed-sitter to explain about the flat. He wouldn't even go with me to look at it because he said anywhere you had to take a bus to get to was the suburbs and he wasn't going to live in the suburbs.

I decided I wouldn't have anything more to do with him. I knew he was friendly with a Rarotongan girl who was a stripper in a place in Karangahape Road and I thought he was possibly just amusing himself with me while she did a three-month sentence she had got for obscene exposure. A few days later when he came into Gomeo's and said he had found a flat in Grafton for us I brought him a plate of spaghetti he hadn't asked for and when I finished work I went out by the back door of the shop and left him waiting for me at the front. The next evening and the next I refused even to talk to him. I was quite determined. But then he stopped coming to Gomeo's and began to send me letters, not letters from him but from his people who wrote to the newspapers. Every letter looked different from the one before and told me something different. Some told me Julian Harp ought to be hanged or flogged and I was right to have nothing to do with him. Others said he was basically good but he needed my help if he was going to be reformed. One said there was nothing wrong with him, it was only his mind that was disordered. One told me in strictest confidence that J. Harp was too good for this world and would shortly depart for another. They were really quite funny in a way that made it silly to stay angry about the flat, so when he had run through his whole list of letter writers I went round to his place and knocked and when he came to the door I said I had come to sing the Candy Roll Blues with him. It wasn't long after that we took the little two-storeyed house in Kendall Road, the one I'm in now with Christopher and Vega.

The first few months we spent there Julian wasn't easy to live with. He liked the house well enough and especially the look of it from the outside. He used to cross the street sometimes early in the morning and sit on a little canvas stool and stare at the house. He said if you looked long enough you would see all the dead people who had once lived there going about doing the things they had always done. But I soon discovered he was missing the view he had from his bed-sitter of the city and the harbour, and if I woke and he wasn't down in the street he was most likely getting the view from the steps in front of the museum. I used to walk up there often to call him for breakfast or lunch and I would find him standing on the steps above the cenotaph staring down at the ships and the cranes or more often straight out across the water beyond the North Shore and the Gulf and Rangitoto.

We had lots of arguments during those first couple of months. I used to lose my temper and walk up and down the kitchen shouting every mean thing I could think of until I ran out of breath and if I was still angry I would throw things at him. Julian couldn't talk nearly as fast but he didn't waste words like I did, every one was barbed, so we came out pretty nearly even. But Julian caused most of the fights and I used to make him admit that. It was because he didn't have anything better to do. His Subvert the Press Campaign had ended in a way he hadn't meant it should and now there didn't seem to be anything especially needing to be done. He took a job for a while as an orderly in the hospital because the money he had brought back from America was beginning to run out but when they put him on duty in the morgue he left because he said he didn't like seeing the soles of people's feet.

It was Anzac Day the year before his flight that Julian first thought of making himself a set of wings. In the morning there were the usual parades, and the servicemen and bands marched up Kendall Road on their way to the cenotaph. Julian wasn't patriotic. He couldn't remember any more about the war than I can. But he liked crowds and noise so he tied our tablecloth to the broom handle and waved it out of the upstairs window over the marchers until a man with shiny black shoes and a lot of medals on a square suit stopped and shouted what did he think he was up to waving a red flag over the Anzac parade. Julian said it wasn't a red flag it was a tablecloth and that made the man angrier. He shouted and shook his fist and a crowd gathered. When the Governor-General's car arrived on its way to the cenotaph it was held up at the corner. By this time Julian was making a speech from the window. He was leaning out so far I could only see the bottom half of him and I couldn't hear much of what he was saying but I did hear him shout:

Shoot if you must this old grey head
But spare my tablecloth she said.

Then the police arrived and began clearing a path for the Governor-General's Rolls and I persuaded Julian to come in and close the window.

By now he was in a mood for Anzac celebrations and we followed the crowd up to the cenotaph and listened to the speeches and sang the hymns. After the service we wandered about in the Domain. Julian kept chanting Gallipoli, El Alamein, Minqar Qaim, Tobruk, Cassino and all the other places the Governor-General had talked about in his speech until I got sick of hearing them and I turned up my transistor to drown him out. He wandered away from me across the football fields and kept frightening a flock of seagulls into the air every time they came down. When he came back to where I was sitting he was quiet and rather solemn. We walked on and it was then we came to the place where the workmen are putting in the statue and right on that spot Julian stopped and stared in front of him and began slowly waving one arm up and down at his side. I asked him what was the matter and he said quick come and have a look at this and he ran down the slope and lay flat on his stomach on one of those park benches that have no backs and began flapping his arms. When I got down to the bench he asked me did his arms look anything like a bird's wings. I said no but when he asked me why I couldn't think of the answer. Then he turned over on his back and began flapping his arms again and asked me did they look anything like a bird's wings now. At first I said no but when I looked properly I had to admit they did. His forearms were moving up and down almost parallel with his body and the part of his arms from the shoulders to the elbows stayed out at right angles from him. So I said yes they did look more like a bird's wings now because a bird's wings bent forward to the elbows and then back along the body and that was why his arms hadn't looked like wings when he lay on his stomach. As soon as I said that he jumped up and kissed me on both cheeks and said I was a bright girl, I had seen the point, he would have to fly upside down.

It wasn't long before I began to notice sketches of wings lying about the house and soon there were little models in balsa wood and paper. One of the things that annoy me every time I read about Julian's flight is that it's not treated as a proper scientific achievement. People talk as if he flew by magic or just willed himself to stay in the air. They seem to think if no one in human history, not even Leonardo da Vinci, could make wings that would carry a man, Julian Harp can't have been human or his flight must have been a miracle. And now Vega tells me there's a new sect called the Harpists and they believe Julian wasn't a man but an angel sent down as a sign that God has chosen New Zealand for the Second Coming. I've even wondered whether Vega doesn't half believe what the Harpists say and it won't surprise me at all if she leaves the Open Pentecostals and joins them.

Gradually I learned a lot about the wings because designing them and building the six or seven sets he did before he got what he wanted spread over all that winter and most of the following summer, and once Julian had admitted what he was doing he was willing to explain all the stages to me. I don't suppose I understood properly very much of what he told me because I haven't a scientific sort of brain but I do remember the number 1.17 which had something to do with the amount of extra energy you needed to get a heavier weight into the air. And also .75 which I think proved that animals as big as man could fly if they used their energy properly but animals that weighed more than 350 pounds, like cows and horses, couldn't, not even in theory. But the main thing I remember, because Julian said it so often, was that everyone who had tried to fly, including Leonardo da Vinci, had made problems instead of solving them by adding unnecessarily to the weight they had to get into the air. The solution to the problem Julian used to say was not to build yourself a machine. It was simply to make yourself wings and use them like a bird. But you could only do that by making your arm approximate to the structure of a bird's wing – that was what he said – and that meant flying upside down. Once you imagined yourself flying upside down it became obvious your legs were no longer legs but the bird's tail, and that meant the gap between the legs had to be filled in by a triangle of fabric. In theory your legs ought then to grow out of the middle of your back, about where your kidneys are, and that of course was one of Julian's biggest problems – how he was to take off lying flat on his back.

But his first problem and it was the one that nearly made him give up the whole project was finding the right materials for the framework. He must have experimented with twenty different kinds of wood and I was for ever cleaning up shavings off the floor, but they were all either too brittle or too heavy or too inflexible. Then I think he got interested in a composition that was used to make frames for people's glasses but you would have needed to be a millionaire to pay for it in large amounts. It was the same with half a dozen other materials, they were light enough and strong enough but too expensive.

By the middle of that winter Julian was ready to give up and go to work. It was certainly difficult the two of us living off what I earned at Gomeo's and paying the rent but Julian was so happy working on his wings even when he was in despair about them I said he must keep going at least until he had given his theory a proper trial. It was about this time he decided nothing but the most expensive materials would do and he wasted weeks thinking up schemes to make money instead of thinking how to make his wings.

It must have been June or early July he hit on a solution. He had gone to Sir Robert Kerridge's office, the millionaire who has a big new building in Queen Street, and offered to take off from the building as a publicity stunt if K.O. would put up the money for making the wings, but he hadn't got very far because the typists and clerks mistook him for a student and he was shown out of the building without seeing Sir Robert. It had begun to rain heavily and Julian had no coat and no bus fare and he walked all the way back to Kendall Road that day with nothing to keep him dry but a battered old umbrella with a broken catch and a match stick wedged in it to keep it open. When he got home he couldn't get the match out and he had to leave the umbrella outside in our little concrete yard. He was standing at the kitchen window staring out and I didn't ask him about his idea of taking off from the Kerridge building because I could see it hadn't been a success when suddenly the match must have come out and the umbrella sprang shut so fast it took off and landed on the other side of our six-foot paling fence. I could see Julian was very angry by now because he walked slowly into the neighbour's yard and back with the umbrella and slowly into the shed and out again with the axe and quite deliberately with the rain pouring down on his back he chopped the umbrella to pieces. I went into the other room to give him time to cool off and when I came back ten minutes or so later he was sitting quite still on one of our kitchen chairs with the water running off him into pools on the floor and held up in front of him between the thumb and the forefinger of his right hand was a single steel strut from the framework of the umbrella. He seemed to be smiling at it and talking to it and even I could see what a perfect answer it was, light, thin, strong, flexible, with even an extra strut hinged to the main one.

Julian was impatient now to get on but he needed a lot of umbrellas because his wings were to be large and working by trial and error a lot of struts would be wasted. We couldn't afford to buy umbrellas and in two days searching around rubbish tips he found only three, all of them damaged by rust. The next morning he was gone when I woke and when I walked up to the museum steps where he was standing staring out across the harbour he said we would have to steal every umbrella we could lay our hands on. So that afternoon and every afternoon it rained during the next few weeks I left Julian at home working and I went to some place like the post office or the museum or the art gallery and came away with somebody's umbrella. It was easy enough when Julian wanted women's umbrellas but when he wanted the heavier struts I always felt nervous walking away with a man's. Occasionally there were umbrellas left at Gomeo's in the evenings and I took these home as well. Soon the spare room upstairs, the one Vega sleeps in now, was crammed with all kinds and I got expert at following a person carrying the particular make Julian needed and waiting until a chance came to steal it. I still have a special feeling about umbrellas and sometimes even now I steal one just because it reminds me of how exciting it was when Julian was getting near to finishing his final set of wings. I even stole one at the town hall on the night of the National Orchestra concert when that poet read the ode the Government commissioned him to write about Julian and the Orchestra played a piece called 'Tone Poem: J. . . H. . .' by a local composer.

I should mention that all the time this was going on Julian was in strict training for his flight. I used to tell him he was overdoing it and that he didn't need to train so hard, because to be honest I always felt embarrassed in the afternoons sitting on the bank watching him panting around the Domain track in sandshoes and baggy white shorts while Halberg and Snell and all those other Auckland Olympic champions went flying past him. But Julian insisted that success didn't only depend on making a set of wings that would work. It depended on having enough stamina left to keep using them after the first big effort of getting into the air. The flight he said would be like running a mile straight after a 220 yard sprint and that was what he used to do during his track training. He had put himself on a modified Lydiard schedule and apart from the sharpening-up work on the track he kept up a steady fifty miles jogging a week. There were also special arm exercises for strength and co-ordination and he spent at least ten minutes morning and evening lying flat on his back on the ironing board flapping his arms and holding a ten-ounce sinker in each hand. Julian was no athlete but he was determined and after six months in training he began to get the scrawny haggard look Lydiard world champions get when they reach a peak. It wasn't any surprise to me when he timed himself over the half mile and found he was running within a second of the New Zealand women's record.

By now the framework for the final set of wings was built and ready to be covered with fabric and there were only a few struts still to be welded in to the back and leg supports. Julian had bought a periscope too and attached it to the crash helmet so he could hold his position steady, flat on his back, and still see ahead in the direction of his flight. Everything seemed to be accounted for except there was still no answer to the problem of how he was to take off lying on his back. He needed a run to get started but he could hardly run backwards and jump into the air. He considered jumping off something but that seemed unnecessarily dangerous and besides he thought it would be important to hold his horizontal position right from the start and that meant a smooth take-off not a wild jump.

I suppose I won't be believed when I say this but if it hadn't been for an idea that came to me one morning while I was watching Julian lying on his back flapping on the ironing board he would probably have had to risk jumping off a building. It came to me right out of the blue that if the ironing board had wheels and Julian was wearing his wings he would shoot along the ground faster and faster until he took off and left the ironing board behind. I don't think I realized what a good idea it was until I said it aloud and Julian stopped flapping and stared at me for I don't know how many seconds with his arms out wide still holding the ten-ounce sinkers and then he said very loudly my God why didn't I think of that. The next moment he was gone, clattering up the stairs, and then he was down again kissing me and saying I was the brightest little bugger this side of Bethlehem and for the rest of the day he got nothing done or nothing that had anything to do with his flight. Of course Julian dropped the idea of actually putting wheels on the ironing board, and the take-off vehicle he did use is the only publicly owned relic of his flight. I find it strange when I go to the museum sometimes and see a group of people standing behind a velvet cord staring at it and reading a notice saying this tubular-steel chromium-plated folding vehicle on six-inch wheels was constructed by the late Julian Harp and used during the commencement of his historic flight. It puzzles me why no one ever says good heavens that's one of those things undertakers use to wheel coffins on, because that's what it is. Julian had seen undertakers using them – church trucks they call them – when he was working in the hospital morgue, and when I suggested putting wheels on the ironing board he immediately thought how much better a church truck would be. I don't know where he got the one he used but I think he must have raided the morgue or an undertaker's chapel at night because one morning I came down to breakfast and there it was gleaming in the middle of the kitchen like a Christmas present.

If I'm going to tell the whole story of the flight and tell it truthfully I might as well come straight out with it and say Julian didn't get any help or encouragement from the organizers of that day's gymkhana. It makes me very angry the way it's always written about as if the whole programme was built around Julian's flight, and the way everyone who was there, Vega for example, talks as if she went only to see that part of the programme and even tells you she had a feeling Julian Harp would succeed. Up in the museum under glass that's supposed to be protected by the most efficient burglar alarm system in the Southern Hemisphere they show you the form Julian had to fill in when he asked the gymkhana organizers to put him on the programme. They don't tell you he had to call on them six or seven times before he got them to agree. Even then I don't think he would have succeeded if he hadn't revived two of his letter writers and had them send letters to the *Herald*, one saying he had seen an albatross flying in the Domain and another, a woman, saying she didn't think it was an albatross, it looked remarkably like a man.

Then you find there's a lot of fuss made by some people about the fact the Governor-General was there and how wonderful it is that the Queen's representative went in person to see Julian Harp try his wings. The truth is the Governor-General was there because the gymkhana was sponsored jointly by the fund-raising committees of the Blind Institute and the Crippled Children's Society and he agreed as their patron to present the prizes for the main event of the day. And in case like everyone else I talk to you have forgotten what the main event was and allowed yourself to think it was Julian Harp's flight, let me just add that it was an attempt on the unofficial world record for the one thousand yards on grass. In fact Julian had to sit round while the mayor made his speech, a pole-sitting contest was officially started, twelve teams of marching girls representing all the grades competed, the brass and Highland bands held their march past, and the police motor cycle division put on a display of trick riding. And when he did try to begin his event at the time given on the programme he was stopped because the long jump was in progress.

Of course now it's different. It's different partly because Julian succeeded, partly because he's supposed to be dead and everyone likes a dead hero better than a live one, but mostly because he made us famous overseas, and when all those reporters came pouring into the country panting to know about the man who had succeeded where men throughout history had failed – that was what they said – everyone began to pretend New Zealand had been behind him on the day. People started to talk about him in the same breath as Snell and Hillary and Don Clark, and then in no time he was up with Lord Rutherford and Katherine Mansfield and now he seems to be ahead of them and there's a sort of religious feeling starts up every time his name is mentioned.

There's nothing to get heated about, I know, but when I hear the Prime Minister (Our Beloved Leader, Julian used to call him) on the radio urging the youth of the nation to aim high like Harp I can't help remembering Julian so nervous that morning about appearing in public he even cleaned his shoes and with me just as nervous the only person there to give him any help or encouragement. And then when we got to the Domain Julian was told he couldn't have an assistant with him because the field was already too cluttered with officials and sportsmen, so there he was crouching down in front of the pavilion with his shiny coffin carrier and his scarlet wings for hour after hour waiting his turn while I sat on the far bank knowing there wasn't a thing more I could do for him. We were nervous partly because he hadn't given the wings a full test and partly because he had tested them enough to know they would carry him. They couldn't be tested in broad daylight and remain a secret, so Julian had to be satisfied with a trial late one night. I remember it almost as clearly as the day of the flight, Julian's church truck speeding across the grass getting faster and faster until I could just see the wings, black they looked in the dark, lift him clear of it. Each time he was airborne he let himself drop back on to the truck because he didn't trust his vision through the periscope at night and he was afraid of colliding with overhead wires. But there was enough for us both to know what he could do and to put me in a terrible state of nerves that afternoon watching the marching girls and the bands and waiting for Julian to get his chance.

Everyone knows what happened when that chance came. I don't think many people saw him climb on to his truck and lie down and the few around me who were watching were saying look at this madman, he thinks he's Yuri Gagarin. But by the time the little truck and the scarlet wings were shooting full speed across the grass everyone was looking, and when somebody shouted over the loud speakers look at the wheels and the whole crowd saw the truck was rolling free there was a tremendous cheer. There was a gasp when he cleared the trees at the far end of the ground and then as he veered away towards the museum with those scarlet wings beating and beating perfectly evenly something got into the crowd and it forgot all about the athletic events and surged over the track and up the slope through the grove of trees by the cricket scoreboard, then down into the hollow of the playing fields and up again towards the museum. I would have followed Julian of course but I didn't have to make up my mind to follow. I was one of the crowd now and I was swept along with it running and tripping with my eyes all the time on Julian like a vision of a heavenly angel rising on those wings made out of hundreds of stolen bits and pieces. He rose a little higher with each stoke of his wings and even when he seemed to try for a moment to come down and almost went into a spin I didn't understand what was happening. I didn't think about whether he intended to go on climbing like that I was so completely absorbed in the look of it, the wings opening and the sunlight striking through the fabric showing the pattern of the struts, and then closing and lifting the tiny figure of Julian another wing-beat up and out and away from us. I had stopped with the crowd on the slopes in front of the museum and Julian must have crossed the harbour and crossed the North Shore between Mt Victoria and North Head and got well out over the Hauraki Gulf towards Rangitoto before it came to me and it came quite calmly as if someone outside me was explaining to me that I was seeing the last of him. I don't know any more than anyone else whether it was a fault in the wings or whether flying put Julian into some kind of trance he couldn't break or whether he just had somewhere to go, but it seemed as you watched him that once he began to climb there was no way to go but higher and further until his energy was used up. I stood there with everyone else watching him get smaller and smaller until we were only catching flashes of colour and losing them again and finally there was nothing to see and we all went on standing there for I don't know how long, until tea time anyway.

After that I was ill and I lay in a bed in hospital for ten days without saying a word seeing Julian's wings opening and closing above me until I was sick of the sight of them and all through the day hearing people talking about him and reading bits out of the newspapers about him. By the time I began to feel better he was famous and I remember when a doctor came to see me and explained I was pregnant and asked who the father was I said Julian Harp and I heard him say to the sister she needs rest and quiet. Soon I learned to say nothing about Julian. He belongs to the public and the public makes what it likes of him. But if you ever came out of a building and found your umbrella missing you might like to believe my story because it may mean you contributed a strut to the wings that carried him aloft.

KATHLEEN CRAYFORD

Duncan

1

Whenever she heard the sound of banging coming from the vicinity of the back door, my mother would raise her head slowly and say in sepulchral tones,
'I hear a knocking at the South Entry.'
If the noise continued she would turn, throw her arms wide, and cry out in a wild, grief-stricken howl,
'Wake Duncan with thy knocking! I would thou couldst.'
In fact our back door was fitted with perfectly adequate bellchimes whose ringing could be heard all over the house. The banging my mother heard usually came from one of the neighbouring sections where somebody was busy mending a fence or chopping wood. When we did have visitors, which was not often, my mother would open the door, all bright-and-smiling like any other housewife. The perceptive visitor might have wondered at her immaculate make-up, thought the eye-shadow a little overdone, the nail varnish not entirely appropriate. The flourish with which she opened the door into her shining kitchen, her expansive gestures, and the theatrical emphasis with which she would proffer a cup of tea, might have seemed out of place in the state house and its child-loud suburban setting. But our visitors were infrequent and could rarely have been described as perceptive. My mother's make-up, like the gleaming crockery displayed on the dresser, was there for her own satisfaction. Admiration, if it came at all, came as a bonus. She lived within her own fantasy, with my brother Tahu and I serving both as audience and supporting cast. The house was her stage, and she was forever her own leading lady.

As a small child I used to wonder who Duncan was. Pondering about this, picking up bits and pieces of information not meant for my ears and supplementing these meagre scraps from my own imagination, I came to the conclusion that Duncan must have been the name of the baby brother who choked to death the night I was conceived. My mother had had a lover, a man she had first known at Drama School in London, years ago. He'd looked her up when he was here on tour, and his stay had coincided with her husband's night-shift. On this particular night, with Tahu sleeping his sound, two-year-old sleep, she had tucked up the new baby with his bottle to keep him quiet while she had entertained her exciting red-headed lover. Next morning she had found the baby dead in a pool of vomit. Her lover took the next plane out, and was never seen again. Her Maori husband stayed until I was born, and I was registered as his child. And so I grew up with an English mother, a Maori surname, and a flaming halo of red hair. There was no way the neighbours could have overlooked the incongruity. As it was, they didn't even try.

I never knew if it was the local people who ostracized my mother, or whether it was she who cut herself off. She never spoke to them, nor they to her. We neither visited nor received visits from our neighbours. Quoting Macbeth was the nearest she ever came to acknowledging their existence. But there was never any doubt about their awareness of us. Conversation stopped when we entered a shop or passed a crowded bus-stop, and resumed with redoubled vigour as soon as we were out of earshot. Unruffled she glided by, oblivious both to their gossip and to my discomfiture. For along with his red hair, I had inherited from my father his thin, sensitive skin, skin which my mother assiduously protected from sunburn, but whose susceptibility to public opinion she apparently failed to notice. And so I would blush, and my mother seemed to be the only person in the entire neighbourhood who did not comment upon it.

As well as quoting Shakespeare, my mother used to enjoy reciting poetry and reading fairy stories. As pre-schoolers Tahu and I would listen spellbound and horrified to her rendering of the more gruesome stories of the Brothers Grimm. As we moved out of our pre-school years through the lower and middle standards, she added Greek myths and Maori legends to her repertoire, with the odd bit of Edgar Allan Poe thrown in.

Of poetry, she loved the long narrative poems of Keats, the *Pot of Basil* being her especial favourite. How she lingered over the scene where the maiden cut off the head of her dead lover and concealed it beneath the soil of a flower-pot. We even had a Pre-Raphaelite picture of the lady draped over her pot plant, mourning her dead love.

In the summertime on our immaculate lawn, or in the winter in the lounge which was furnished and lit like the set for a Noel Coward play, she would arrange us and herself in suitable theatrical positions and enmesh us in webs of horror. With her hands, her eyes, the slightest inflexion of her voice she would transport us out of our clean suburban world into lands of dungeons and giants, where men could be changed into animals, witches could cast spells, and nothing was what it seemed. With a word, a sigh, a wave of her hand, she could transform a gentle summer's day into a howling blizzard where helpless children were set impossible tasks by implacable ogres. In our bright lounge we would hear about children killing their parents, and parents devouring their children, and when at last we were released even the carpets we walked on held menace untold as we made our way to our nightmare beds.

Sometimes, for light relief, she would recite to us passages from Lewis Carroll's *Jabberwocky*:

> "Twas brillig, and the slithy toves
> Did gyre and gimble in the wabe,'

she would intone, and we could practically see them, invested with terror unspeakable by the croak she'put into her voice and the widening of her eyes. There were no dark corners in our house, so how did she manage to fill it with so much anxiety?

But of all the shuddering words she came out with, it was one apparently innocuous line which had the power to hold me rigid and trembling, longing to run away and yet too terrified to move.

> 'And hast thou slain the Jabberwock?
> Come to my arms my beamish boy.'

Not even the worst excesses of Edgar Allan Poe could inspire in me the terror conjured up by that dreadful invitation.

Once I tried to find out how my brother felt about her stories.

'Do you like it when Mum reads to us?' I asked him.

'I never listen,' he said.

This reply absolutely astonished me.

'But she makes us listen,' I said.

'Well I got fed up with her carrying on. So one day I pretended I was playing football. Now I do it every time. Pretend I'm playing games, or do sums in my head. That's the best way I've found for getting away from her. Doing sums or saying tables.'

And so I lost the only comfort I ever had. Sometimes when she paused for breath I would look at my brother's face and long for eyes to meet mine and break the spell. But they never did. As he got older I lost even the reassurance of his physical presence, for my mother could not always compel him to stay home, and he took to going out more and more with his friends. He'd come in at mealtimes and then be off out again immediately. He treated her as though she didn't exist, and she didn't even notice. Except as an audience he had no meaning for her. It was a long time before I realized that the same truth applied to me.

The conversation with my brother was not, however, entirely without effect, for it drew my attention to the rewards that could be gained from school. Although I never really mastered his trick of being able to cut himself off from the present situation, I did begin to realize that school, and especially maths, could add another dimension to life. I began to appreciate the beautiful orderliness and predictability of figures. Because most of the other children fumbled and struggled through basic principles which were as clear as daylight to me, I was allowed to work my way through the maths book alone. When I surfaced between exercises it was to hear with irritation the teacher going over ground which I had left behind weeks ago. I was so desperately shy in the classroom that she had given up trying to make me read aloud. I answered questions only under duress, and then in never more than a whisper, but once I discovered mathematics the classroom held no fears for me. I was kept supplied with the appropriate books and left alone. Sometimes the teacher would look at me in a puzzled sort of way, but so long as I had my maths to do I was largely unaware of what else went on in the classroom. Nobody bothered me, and I was comfortable enough.

I suppose most children take it for granted that the way their family behaves is the way every family behaves. Our family pattern did not seem abnormal to me. It did not seem strange that apart from the readings and recitings, my mother seldom spoke. She never addressed me directly, nor called me by my name. Instructions came by way of proverbs and clichés. She had one for every occasion. 'Cleanliness is next to Godliness,' she would say, handing me a clean towel and propelling me towards the bathroom. 'A little water clears us of this deed.' I took it for granted that this was the normal means of intercourse between parent and child. I had never known anything different.

The first indication I had that all was not well was when the headmaster requested an interview with my mother following a mid-year survey in which the teacher had used words like 'withdrawn', 'self-absorbed', and 'unsociable'.

My mother made a good impression at the school. She enjoyed the role of concerned, bewildered parent. She smiled bravely as she told how her husband had left her years ago. She managed to indicate how gallantly she strove to bring us up decently, how determined she was that we should not suffer by being members of a one-parent family. Apparently the school was unaware of those facts about my origin which were common knowledge among our more immediate neighbours.

Gratifying as this interview must have been for my mother, it would have had little effect upon me had she not made a point of stressing how much time she spent reading to me and telling me stories. We had no television, which she held to be a corrupting influence, but she was quite sure, so she told the headmaster, that I had a far wider knowledge of poetry and literature than any other child of my age. I loved being read to.

In their eagerness to build a bridge between home and school, the staff assembled a collection of fairy stories which my mother had said were my absolute favourites. These were given to my teacher for classroom story-time, and she called them her Special Collection. The first time the haven of school was invaded by one of my mother's stories I think I must have fainted, though one of the other children said I'd had some sort of a fit. Whatever it was, it happened every time the teacher began to read from her Special Collection.

'Put your maths book away now Jeannie,' she would say. 'We are going to have a story.' I became so nervous that soon it was happening every time she opened a book of any kind. The slithy toves would come gimbling out from the corners of the room, I'd close my eyes and hold my breath to stop myself from screaming, and then suddenly I'd find myself flat on my back on a couch in the medical room, with one of the Teacher's Aides sitting worriedly beside me.

Later that year I was seen by the school medical officer. After examining me, he referred me to the hospital to have my hearing tested, and when it was found to be normal, my mother was asked to take me to yet another department. There, long loops of wire were stuck on to various parts of my head. The woman who did this explained to me that it wouldn't hurt, that it was simply a device to measure the electrical activity of my brain, to see if they could find out why I was having these fainting fits. But I already knew why I was having them. It was because of the slithy toves. Of course, I couldn't tell anyone that. They would have thought I was mad.

2

In contrast to the drama and alarm of being hooked up to the hospital's measuring devices, the School Psychologist entered my life quietly. He was a small man with thinning hair and bright blue eyes. When I first saw him he was talking to my teacher. She was showing him her special collection of fairy tales and folk stories. I hurried away in case she should open one of the books and let the slithy toves come out. I thought she might lend them to him, but when he turned to speak to me, he had nothing in his hands but a small folder of printed papers. He said his name was Mr Rogers and he asked me if I would go to the staffroom with him to do some written work instead of listening to a story with the other children. He made it sound as though I would be doing him a favour. In the staffroom he opened the folder and showed me the papers. He explained what he wanted me to do, and once I had got started he quietly left the room, saying he'd be back in about half-an-hour.

There were a number of maths questions on the papers, so I did them first. Then I went over the paper again to look at the other questions. They were about words, and the meaning of words. I became confused and frightened. So I checked the maths again, and having gained what comfort I could from them, I pushed the papers away and sat and waited.

Mr Rogers came back. He had more papers with him, only this time he said he'd fill in the answers if I told him what I thought they were. Then he said half a sentence and asked me to finish it, but I couldn't. He asked me to draw him a picture, but I couldn't do that either. Then he showed me some pictures on a card and asked me to tell him a story about them, and I started to feel frightened again. He piled all the cards up, gathered the papers together, glancing at the ones I had been able to tackle.

'You enjoy mathematics,' he said.

I nodded. He was quiet for a while, just sitting there looking at the papers. Then he said,

'You don't enjoy stories much, do you?'

I was so surprised that I looked quickly up at his face and whispered, 'No.'

I had been too shy to look straight at his face before, but when I did I found there what I had looked for and failed to find in my brother's. I dropped my head, and suddenly, without knowing it was going to happen, I began to cry. I went on and on, until I thought I was never going to be able to stop. He pushed a box of tissues across the table to me and said, 'It's all right. Don't worry about it,' and then he just sat and waited. No words. No fuss. Just quietly waited.

It was a funny feeling when I blew my nose, as if I'd been all cleaned up inside. I used up two or three tissues, and when I had thrown them into the rubbish bin, I glanced at him quickly again. He didn't seem to have changed. There was a feeling of rightness about him. I don't know how else to put it.

'Jeannie,' he said, as though he had come to a decision about something, 'I have to write a report for your teacher, and I want you to read it. Do you understand?'

I nodded.

'All right,' he said, 'we'll make a start right now.'

He pulled a sheet of paper towards him and wrote across it in big scrawly writing.

I looked at the note. It said, 'No more fairy stories please!' For a moment I thought I was going to cry again. Then an extraordinary thing happened. The corners of my mouth began to twitch, and a smile came on, a great big smile, and I couldn't turn it off, no matter how hard I tried.

I picked up the paper and left the room. I thought my troubles were over, which only goes to show how little I had understood my mother, and how much I had underestimated the cruelty of the other children.

It was almost home-time when I got back to the classroom. I had handed over the note, and as I returned to my place one of the boys said, 'Been to see the shrink, have you?'

I didn't know what he meant, but I felt myself blushing. There was a ripple of suppressed giggles, and I heard the word 'shrink' whispered around the room. After school they started again.

'Been to the headshrinker today, have you?'

My hands flew to my head, but it was still the same size. They laughed, and someone said they always knew I needed my brains tested.

I ran home.

At Mr Roger's suggestion the Visiting Teacher came to see my mother next day. She brought with her a small pile of books which she told me Mr Rogers had recommended as being more suitable than fairy stories. She addressed me directly. She said, 'He asked me to tell you that you may find them a little young, but he's been thinking it over, and he thinks that as you've never had this kind of book before, you may enjoy them. You can go on to something more sophisticated when you get tired of these.'

She spoke to me as though I were a proper person. I felt very surprised.

My mother enjoyed having the Visiting Teacher call. She showed her over the house, discussing the books and pictures, and telling animated little stories about the various ornaments and mementos in the lounge. I had never realized that every one of her things had a history of its own. They were treasures that had had an existence long before I was born, in a time and place when she had been young and beautiful. I found the thought very strange.

At first, my mother seemed to enjoy reading to me from the books Mr Rogers had recommended. Certainly she gained great satisfaction from the knowledge that the school staff were interested in what she was doing. As for me, I found the stories enchanting. Some were about a little girl called Milly-molly-mandy who lived with a family of loving relatives in a farm cottage in the country. She had a friend called Susan, and another called Billy Blunt. They rode bikes, built tree houses, and went for picnics. Once they made a miniature garden in a big pie-dish and entered it for a competition where it won first prize. It was a gentle, interesting world, full of small adventures of childhood, and I loved it.

Until that time the worlds of home and school had been completely separate, so that upon entering one, the other had ceased to exist. But since my mother's visit, each began to impinge increasingly upon the other. To and from school I ran an uneasy gauntlet through the nudges and giggles of the other children. They would have forgotten it soon enough had that first interview with Mr Rogers been the only one. But regular appointments were made for me, and once a week I was sent over to the staffroom for what the teacher euphemistically referred to as Individual Tuition. The term fooled no-one. My sessions with Mr Rogers were just frequent enough to maintain the children's interest. They had noticed that they could make me blush by referring to him. It almost seemed as if home and school had reversed their roles in my life. The jabberwocky nightmares receded, and I stopped having fits, but school was no longer the haven it had been. Home now became a refuge from the attentions of the other children, where I entered into the safe, consistent world of Milly-molly-mandy and her friends. It was the walk to school, and the playground, and the classroom, that became the nightmare then. Those, and the days when Mr Rogers came.

It was not Mr Rogers himself who made such an ordeal of our relationship, it was the other children's distorted evaluation of it. Any pleasure I might have gained from the anticipation of seeing him was ruined by the teasing I had to cope with before and after every interview. And there was pleasure in seeing him. When I had stumbled and blushed my way out of the classroom and into the quiet corridor, I would stand a moment, taking deep, slow breaths, and wait for my burning skin to become cool again. In the time I spent with him, I experienced myself increasingly as a real person. He accepted my nods and whispered monosyllables as valid communication, and his friendliness and courtesy were unfailing. But the price of person-hood was high. The other children's blood-lust seemed to be insatiable.

And then my mother began to tire of reading children's books. I think I must have contributed to this by my growing impatience at being read to. For the first time in my life, I wanted to read the books myself. Obviously I could read, or I'd have never coped with maths, but I had never voluntarily read a story-book: in any case, children's stories gave little scope for my mother's histrionic talents, and she decided I was ready to move on, as the Visiting Teacher had said, 'to something more sophisticated'.

And so we moved rapidly through teen-age romances to Barbara Cartland, and thence to the kind of intellectual porn that is such a feature of the drug-and-sex orientated seventies. At first I tried to cut myself off, but my own biochemistry dictated otherwise. I found things happening to my body as I listened to my mother's throaty renditions of some of the most explicit seduction scenes in the English language. How I longed for Tahu's ability to imagine himself away into a game of football. But Tahu was seldom home, and within days I was caught up in my mother's dream-world of rape and seduction, incest and adultery. The books she selected were the best of their kind, describing anatomical and physiological details I had not known existed. Sometimes it was hard to believe that they meant what they seemed to mean, and then I never knew whether it was depravity coming from within myself that held me fascinated and repelled, or whether the writer and my mother were really as depraved as they seemed to be. For now I had difficulty in distinguishing the story from the story-teller.

And once again the poison crept from home to school. The blushes that had previously spread from my face and neck, now became focused in that part of my body which had always been private and inviolable. They would start in unseen places and spread outwards like a consuming fire, throbbing and burning till I was beside myself. It seemed as if the slithy toves that had once haunted the classroom had somehow got inside me, and now there was no escape.

If the teasing I had had to put up with had been painful before, now it became intolerable. And suddenly, I didn't want to see Mr Rogers any more.

On the occasion of his next visit I was called out of the classroom as usual. I heard the familiar giggles and whispers, saw the nudges and grins, and felt the blushing fire pouring and burning out from between my legs. And then suddenly everything stopped. Ice is the antithesis of fire, and as though someone had thrown a switch my body solidified and turned to ice. There behind my desk, half sitting, half standing, the power was turned off and I was immobilized. Somewhere, like a third eye outside myself I watched my vision glaze over, heard my hearing die, and saw my body bent and rigid behind the desk that was my fortress no longer.

3

Someone must have brought me to the hospital. I have no memory of how I got there. But when I came to myself I was aware that some change had taken place in me. There was a peaceful lassitude that was unfamiliar, and I kept drifting in and out of some kind of a reverie, waking to be washed or fed, or to swallow pills, and then drifting off again. I experienced everything as though I were one step removed from myself, detached and uninvolved. I had watched myself in the classroom as I lost consciousness, and I was watching myself now as I regained it. I felt almost like two separate persons. One of me was lying on a bed, drifting. The other was becoming increasingly alert, appraising, remembering, trying to make connections.

As the days went by, the alert part of myself became irked by the ministrations of the hospital staff. I had thinking to do, and I wanted to get on with it.

Soon the nurses began to encourage me to get out of bed. They took me for walks around the hospital gardens, and into rooms where people were working or playing or talking. All I really wanted was to be left alone to think. I needed solitude, and it was the only thing they denied me.

The strange feeling of detachment continued. I saw and heard everything that was said and done as though it had no relevance to myself. I became a puppet, and yet at the same time I was an observer at the show, watching how the strings were being pulled, wanting to take charge, and yet powerless to move of my own volition. Once, a fat doctor brought a group of people to have a look at me. He told them that the acute phase had passed and I was now undergoing a period of intensive socialization training. Some of them asked questions, and he told them that the aim was always towards adjustment and discharge. I was progressing satisfactorily, he said, and would be coming up for assessment before very long.

And that brought me eventually to the Case Conference. The nurse who looked after me told me about it. This nurse had been around most of the time since I had recovered consciousness, and was said to be Specialling me. I hadn't taken much notice of her at first, because they all looked alike in their uniforms, but after a while I had noticed her voice. She talked to me and explained what she was doing. Sometimes I felt that I was her doll, and she enjoyed playing with me, brushing my hair and helping me dress, and holding conversations in which she replied to her own questions and comments with words which no doubt she thought I would have used, had I been able to speak. But I didn't always feel like her doll. Once when she took me into a room where people were busy making things, and asked me to join in, and took me away again after a little while, she put her hand under my chin and lifted my face up and said, 'Oh Jeannie, please get better.' But I didn't know how to.

Anyway, on the day of the Case Conference she was clearly excited. Excited and nervous. She helped me shower and wash my hair, which she dried with a hand-held dryer. She brushed it, playing the dryer over it as she did so, totally absorbed. Then she gave me a mirror.

'See how nice you look,' she said.

I studied the reflection in front of me. I saw a girl with clear delicate skin, wide hazel eyes and a cloud of shining red-gold hair. I had always thought I was ugly, but I could see now that I was not. I remembered the time I had cried in the staffroom at school, and I began to wish the nurse would stop being so kind to me.

We took a lift up to the Conference Room. She was carrying a folder with some notes in it. Just before we got out of the lift she said, 'This is my first Case Conference. You are my first Special. I hope everything will be all right.'

I lifted my head and glanced at her quickly. She was a girl not much older than me. She caught my glance and tried to hold it, but I dropped my head. The lift came to a halt, the doors opened and we stepped out.

I find it hard to describe my first impression of the Conference Room. The difficulty arises from my strange double awareness of every situation. I stood outside myself and watched as the nurse and I entered the room. It was full of strangers and cigarette smoke. It seemed that they had just had a coffee-break, for there were used cups on the low table, and even on the floor. White-coated men and women were standing or sitting around chatting. The fat doctor was there. We stood inside the door like two intruders. I tried to detach myself, but I was too aware of the nurse, whose hands were trembling. The fat doctor saw us and told us to come in, indicating two chairs by the window. The chatter ceased as he seated himself behind a desk and began leafing through some papers. As we sat down I risked a quick glance round the room, and I saw something that made the two parts of myself snap violently into focus. Mr Rogers was there!

Inside my head, several things seemed to happen at once. I became alert and aware of every nuance of feeling in that room. My memory for past events came back. I remembered the blushing at the same time as I became aware that it had ceased. The feeling of powerlessness had gone. The puppet-strings had been cut and I ceased to experience myself as the object of other people's manipulations.

Another glance around the room and I caught Mr Rogers' eye. He smiled, but I remained impassive. I had never seen him in other people's company before. He was the only one not wearing a white coat, and he looked out of place.

The doctor put aside his papers and began to speak. He spoke of the tragedy of schizophrenia, especially its effect on young people. He explained that its cause was still largely a mystery. Within the last fifteen years attempts had been made to trace its origin to faulty relationships between parent and child. In his opinion this was a grave mistake, as the case before us showed. This child's mother was an intelligent, cultured woman who had coped without help for years, and wanted nothing more than to have her child restored to her, cured or not. 'It is our responsibility now, to decide whether it is fair to burden the mother with this grossly disturbed child. It may be that she should remain in hospital until she is completely stabilized on the appropriate medication. Her mother is asking for her back. The question is, should we let her go?' He said this not without a touch of drama. I couldn't help wondering why he said, 'We have to decide,' since it was clear that it was he who was the puppet-master.

He turned towards the nurse sitting beside me. I could feel her trembling.

'Now nurse,' he said. 'I understand you have been Specialling this patient for the past three weeks. What can you tell us about her?' The nurse opened her folder and began to read from her notes. The tremor transferred itself to her voice. She told them I was a good patient, quiet, showing no signs of violence. She had wondered if I might be either deaf or retarded, as I was so slow to respond when spoken to. I was totally lacking in initiative and showed no interest in other people. Here she paused and looked up from her notes, troubled.

'Well,' said the doctor. 'Was there something else?'

She replied diffidently. 'It's hard to know. It's just that when I was brushing her hair . . . I gave her a mirror to show her how nice she looked. She seemed . . . interested, sort of. . . .'

The doctor smiled kindly.

'Even schizophrenics are not entirely devoid of vanity, nurse. Was that all?' She hesitated.

'It was just something I felt,' she said, 'in the lift coming up here. I spoke to her, and I felt. . . . It was the first time ever . . . I felt as though she'd heard me. I felt as though she wanted to reply.'

The words came tumbling out in a breathless rush, and as they did, something extraordinary happened to me. I felt myself caring about what somebody else was feeling. It was hard for her to speak as she did. She was saying something that was not in the script.

'Nurse,' the doctor said gently, 'We all have to protect ourselves against emotional involvement with our patients. I guess this girl has become pretty important to you over the past few weeks. It's natural that you should want her to respond to you. But you can hardly expect us to take seriously something you felt, fleetingly, coming up in the lift to your first Case Conference, now can you?'

'No doctor,' she said, and subsided into silence.

'However, the suggestion of retardation is an interesting one. We have among us today a guest from the Department of Education. Mr Rogers. You are a teacher I believe. You knew this girl at school.'

'I'm not a teacher. I'm an Educational Psychologist,' said Mr Rogers, 'and yes, I did know Jeannie at school.'

'A psychologist. Yes, of course. You have a B.A. in the subject I believe.'

I glanced at Mr Rogers and saw him flush slightly.

'An M.A. actually,' he said.

'Quite. But no medical training I take it? Well what can you tell us about this girl?'

The tremor I heard in Mr Rogers' voice was not that of fear, as the nurse's had been, but of suppressed anger.

'Dr Cardew,' he said, 'at your request I have provided a detailed assessment of Jeannie's potentialities. That report has been with you for several weeks, and I think you know that there is no question of retardation. I have found her above average in intelligence, distinctly gifted in mathematics, but extremely shy. I should also like to point out that she is well aware of what is going on in this room and that she probably understands every word that is being said.'

The doctor ignored the last remark and took up the question of shyness.

'You are aware, no doubt, that what you call shyness is one of the earliest symptoms of schizophrenic withdrawal?'

'Yes, I am aware of that.'

'Then why did you not refer the girl for treatment sooner?'

'Because I didn't want her labelled. I knew she was disturbed, but she was beginning to respond and I felt sure that given time, she'd come right.'

'Well you were mistaken, weren't you, Mr Rogers?'

Mr Rogers looked at him and then looked at me long and earnestly. 'No,' he said. 'I don't think I was. Something else happened. Some other factor intervened. I don't know what it was, but she was responding, and she did begin to improve. I think if you look at the test papers she did for me. . . .'

Dr Cardew looked around the room and addressed himself to the listening staff.

'I think we have here yet another example of the dangers of emotional involvement. This child is exceptionally attractive, and no-one wants to believe she is mad.'

I saw Mr Rogers wince. The Doctor went on talking.

'But unless and until we accept the fact of this disease we will get nowhere in treating it. We have to decide whether, appropriately medicated, this child can survive in the outside world, and how soon we can return her to her mother. . . .'

During this exchange my eyes had returned repeatedly to Mr Rogers' face. As with the nurse, so with him, I began to find myself inexplicably concerned about somebody else's feelings. Something was going dreadfully, frighteningly wrong in that room, but it was not I who was being threatened. It was Mr Rogers. Never in my life before had I realized that I was not the only person in the world who could be frightened. But I realized it now, as I watched that small man with his thinning hair and his tired eyes, standing up to ridicule and disparagement for my sake.

Unexpectedly, he stood up and walked firmly across the room to where I was sitting. He knelt down in front of me and took both my hands in his.

'Jeannie,' he said. 'Jeannie, can you tell me what's troubling you. Can you tell me now, before it's too late?'

I felt the words inside me. I felt his longing to reach me. I felt what it had cost him to cross the room in front of all those people. The nurse beside me held her breath. There was silence as they all watched and waited, a silence only distantly broken by the voices of the other patients at their recreation outside. Someone was bouncing a ball, thump, thump, thump, and someone else was crying out, 'Here, here, over here.'

I disengaged my hands and stood up. Raising my head slowly, I opened my mouth and let the words come out.

'I hear a knocking at the South Entry!'

The tension broke. Someone giggled nervously, and the doctor smiled. 'Well Mr Rogers, you have provided us with yet another example . . . a classic example . . . of a well-known symptom. A random utterance, totally unrelated to anything. Frequently one finds such random utterances to be the only speech schizophrenics are capable of. I'm sorry Mr Rogers. It was a nice try.'

Mr Rogers looked desperate.

'How can you call it a random utterance? This is the first piece of coherent speech she has produced for over a year. You saw what the effort cost her. It cannot be without significance.'

He turned to me. The nurse too was on her feet.

'Please, Jeannie,' he said.

Once more I felt words inside me. I lifted my eyes to his face, and though it cost me my soul I was determined to tell him exactly where the trouble lay. And so I said, in a loud voice whose urgency nobody could mistake,

'Wake Duncan with thy knocking. I would thou couldst.'

And then I think I fainted, for the next thing I was aware of was that I was back on my bed, drifting, separated into two parts again, one self watching the other, waiting to see what would happen next.

4

In fact, very little happened. The hospital resumed its inexorable routine. I had a different nurse looking after me, and after a period of rest she started trying to get me to join in games and discussion with the other patients, but I was not interested. Two things remained with me from the Case Conference. One was the memory of the fat doctor saying I was exceptionally attractive and no-one wanted to believe I was mad. The other was that, given the strength, the puppet-master could be resisted. I had seen the nurse do it, and I had seen Mr Rogers do it. I began to see that my lack of interest in the hospital's games was my own way of refusing to be bound by the script.

My mother visited sometimes, but she was more interested in impressing the staff than in paying attention to me. She brought me clothes and sweets, which latter she took away almost at once and began sharing around the ward with the other patients. So I didn't take very much notice of her. I didn't care whether she came or not.

At least, I didn't until the day she came looking very different from her usual self. The make-up was missing. Her nails were their natural colour. And instead of sweeping into the ward with a flourish and greeting staff and patients alike as though she were some kind of Lady Bountiful, she walked in quietly and came straight over to where I was sitting.

'Hello Jeannie,' she said. It was the first time she had called me by my name. She sat down beside me. There was a long silence, and then she said awkwardly, 'Would you like me to read to you?'

I said nothing. She pulled a book out of her bag and held it out to me.

'It's one of the Milly-molly-mandy books. Would you like to choose a story?'

This was something new. Never before had she offered me a choice of what stories I would listen to. That had always been her decision. I took the book and opened it at random. She read the story. I don't remember what it was, I remember only that her voice had changed. She was no longer acting. She was trying to communicate.

When the story was finished she said, 'Would you like to sit in the sun for a while?' and stood up. I followed her out into the garden and we sat down on a bench. There was another silence. My mind took off and became absorbed watching the antics of a bumble-bee on a nearby flower-bed, and I forgot she was there. She cleared her throat and I felt her preparing to speak.

'Mr Rogers rang me up,' she said.

My mind scrambled back into my body so fast that I almost laughed out loud, but I said nothing. I continued watching the bumble-bee, and I waited.

'He asked me to go into his office and see him. He said you'd said something.' She stopped, and then went on again with an effort. 'He told me you'd said something about . . . about Duncan. He asked me if I knew what it meant.'

She stopped again. I began to feel frightened, brittle and precariously balanced, as though the least movement would knock me over and shatter me into a million pieces.

'I told him. I told him about how the baby died, and all about . . . everything.'

She leaned forward and put her elbows on her knees, clasping her hands in front of her and looking at the ground.

'He asked me if you knew. He said I should tell you. He said I should talk to you about. . . .' Her voice dropped and became husky.

'About Duncan.'

We sat there a long time, saying nothing. Slowly the brittle feeling went away. At last she stood up.

'I can't talk about it now. He says I have to be honest with you, and tell you about real things. He says it's important for both of us. Perhaps next time. Will you walk with me to the gate?'

My mind did not leave my body again. That night I refused to take my medication. There was no fuss about it. I just lifted my head and said, 'No!' and pushed it away. A doctor came to see me, a young man I had not noticed before.

'You don't want to take your medication?' he said.

Again I lifted my head and said, 'No!'

He turned to the nurse.

'It's the first time she's shown any initiative since she's been here. There must be a reason. Scrub it for tonight and just keep an eye on her. She may be coming right.'

I continued steadfastly to refuse to take any more tablets or pills. By the time my mother came back again, the feeling of detachment had almost gone. I slept badly, but that gave me time to think.

The nurse who had accompanied me to the Case Conference came back on the ward, and when I saw her the edges of my mouth began to twitch, and a tiny little smile came on. She saw it, and came rushing over to me absolutely beaming, but before she reached me she stopped dead and looked upset, remembering no doubt, about the dangers of emotional involvement. Then she came on more slowly, composing her face.

'I'm so glad you are feeling better,' she said primly.

I had heard about people's eyes twinkling, though I had never understood what it meant. But if eyes can really twinkle, I'm sure that mine did then. The smile stretched my mouth a bit more. It felt most strange. We stood grinning at each other like a couple of idiots, and then she turned abruptly and left the room. Later, I heard her singing.

Although I no longer needed to be Specialled by any particular nurse, this nurse became very special to me. She was unable to conceal her pleasure in my continuing recovery, and it was for her sake that I finally agreed to join the group of patients who went to the Occupational Therapy workshop every afternoon.

My mother came to see me twice a week. She brought books to read, and soon a pattern began to develop. It almost seemed as if she could not get her voice going unless she read to me first. Then she'd put the book away and start to talk. On the first few occasions she prefaced her conversation by some reference to Mr Rogers.

'I was telling Mr Rogers,' she'd say, 'about the time when . . . .'

But after a while it came more easily to her. She told me about her life in London, and about the drama school where she had first met my father. She told me about the places they went to and the things they did; about the London river-buses, and Kew Gardens, and Buckingham Palace where they had seen The Queen come out onto the balcony. It wasn't anything like the awful magical spell-weaving she used to do. She was just a lonely woman, talking about times when she had been happy.

And so the weeks went by. In the hospital garden, the dayroom or the corridor, or anywhere that was quiet and private, she picked up the pieces of her life and began to put them together again. I used to go down to the gate to meet her, and we'd walk up the drive together, and she'd talk to me. The possibility of my going home came up. I could see she was nervous about it, because she started referring to Mr Rogers again. It was, 'Mr Rogers says . . .', or 'Mr Rogers thinks . . . .' One day she said it and I looked at her and grinned. She laughed. 'Oh well. *I* think . . .' she said, and went on to say what she had to say. And that was the last reference she made to him.

And then one day, slowly and painfully, with many pauses and long silences, she began to talk about the occasion of my conception. As though it had happened only the day before, she went through the whole awful agony again. I had picked up a good deal from around the neighbourhood when I had been too young to understand it, and I had woven my own fantasies around the event. But no fantasy of mine could have been as bad as what she went through, both at the time, and in the telling. There had been an inquest on the baby, and the coroner had had some hard things to say. It had been in all the newspapers. Everybody knew.

And yet, when she had told all this, she was still not at an end. There was something else that, strangely, had never got into the newspapers, nor come to the neighbours' ears. Or rather, the accident which killed my father had been to them no more than a distant event in the history of aviation. A plane had crashed upon landing at Singapore Airport. There had been no survivors. There was no reason for the neighbours to connect that news with the departure of my mother's lover. Nor was there any reason why the airport authorities should know that one of those mangled bodies they managed to identify held any interest for one obscure family in a State Housing area in New Zealand.

Telling the story with tears, with pain, but with infinite relief, my mother produced an old press-cutting about the crash. Although she had kept no memento of the baby who had died, no newspaper reports of the event which had haunted my childhood, she had kept this tattered account of an aviation disaster that seemed to have no bearing on my life. And yet she showed it to me, complete with a list of the casualties, and a blurred photograph of an actor with a touring company, an actor who, the newspaper reported, would never have been on that flight had he not been called to return home urgently, because of a family crisis.

And that was how I learned what perhaps I should have guessed right from the start. I had been mistaken about the name of the baby who died. I had been mistaken about the origin of my mother's continuing grief. And more than anything, I had been mistaken about its relationship to myself. The baby had not been called Duncan.

Duncan was my father's name.

RUSSELL HALEY

Fog

Simon Fesk's mother had a sense of humour. There was no denying that. She was seventy-five years old and still wrote to him when she believed the occasion significant. These times were not always personal though they often were. Once she wrote to him on Armistice Day: 'Imagine all the silent people,' she said. Another time he received a telegram on *her* birthday which simply read: 'But for me.'

Today was his birthday. He thought of it as half-way to ninety. His mother, though, felt differently. The home-made card stood on the side-table.

That is less than an exact description. The card could not stand by itself. It was not made from paper stiff enough to support an upright position. It leaned idly against a milk bottle, insolently concave – a spiv of cards with its trilby hat tipped over its eyes working out a paper deal. A breeze could set it flapping around the rented room.

Nor was the table an ideal surface. He had bought the thing, knocked-down in both senses, at an auction in Karangahape Road. The legs were shaped like the side frames of a lyre and they slotted into grooves on the underside of the top. A smaller shelf fitted near the feet and prevented the legs from splaying or collapsing inwards. The surface of the top was carved with jungle blossoms of an unknown species and of such high bas-relief and low intaglio that even the milk bottle was unstable.

Fesk bought it because he liked the colour – dark honey. He also needed a table. Simon had a streak of practicality.

Such was the form of the card. Its contents were no less pliable.

'Think only of the future,' his mother wrote. 'You have your whole young life ahead of you.' The card was quarto size, folded once across the centre. These words were written in pencil on the front. His mother's hand was still firm. Inside, however, were two printed charts.

A physical impatience welled inside Fesk. He was sitting in his old brown uncut moquette armchair. The chair was also from an auction. It rattled and chimed mysteriously whenever it was moved. No doubt it contained treasures of small change, lost pens, shopping lists. Fesk did not feel this impatience in his head. It stemmed from his legs. He raised his feet in turn from the carpet as though he were walking in a crouch and then he squeezed his thigh muscles. He wore Donegal tweed trousers. Fesk bought them in a Mission shop.

They were not charts. Inside the cards were two tables. If he had been in a better mood he might have laughed. A thin card containing two printed tables slumped on his decisively carved table.

He did smile. His eyes lit up. Simon forgot his legs. His impatience ceased to exist. Like the tree in the forest which falls unseen and unheard. So large in this country that you could make a whole house from one of them. But people would have to come in and out of doors and switch on radios.

Table One described the various classes of fog signals in use on the 1st of January, 1910, in certain countries. Fesk's own adopted country was not mentioned. As far as fog was concerned this country might not have existed in 1910. Hundreds of years of Polynesian voyaging had been made in the clear sunlight of the Pacific. New Zealand was not tabulated. Fog was infrequent in Auckland though it existed in the thermal areas. Perhaps too in the Marlborough Sounds. Fesk's meteorology was sketchy. So too his geography. He had sailed here on a ship which took many weeks to arrive. Since then he had not moved. His memories of Suez and Aden were dim and blurred. He could not remember whether he saw the Bitter Lakes first or the Red Sea. There was an image of the heat-hazed coastline of North Africa.

But in this table England, Scotland, Ireland, France, the United States, and British North America were fully examined in terms of fog and signals: sirens, diaphones, horns, trumpets, whistles, explosive devices, guns, bells, gongs and submarine bells.

To lie there underwater and listen to bells – undersea Sunday – aqua-Christmas!

1910 must have been a festive year if foggy. His mother would have been six years old. He thought of her as a small girl called Lydia clutching a penny. Her maiden name was Martello. But she was born in Ravensthorpe far away from these detailed sea signals. Almost as far away from the sea as you could get in England. Unlike here where he could look out to the islands and the Gulf if he opened his curtains.

But the local blanket mill did fire a cannon at ten o'clock every evening fog or no fog. It was called the ten o'clock gun. You could set your watch or close a pub by it. And hooters signalled lunch.

Perhaps she married his father because of the gun – future nostalgia. He was a sailor – shipped out of Hull for Rotterdam and Antwerp. Maybe this card came from prodigious papers. With senility he had lost the ability to control them. Instead, he grew massive sunflowers in the narrow garden of the new bungalow.

Last Christmas his mother sent him a clipping from the local newspaper. His father, lined beyond comprehension, pouring the dregs of his tea on the earth at the foot of the sunflowers. She wrote a different message then: 'Keep us always in mind.'

Fesk kept them in his head. Where else? They were his prototypes for the future. Though he would have no children to send clippings and obscurities.

His birthday came in cold weather in this country. If he'd remained in Ravensthorpe it would occur in summer. Impossible to blow out the breath like this and make a small cloud of mist. Bigger there then at eleven and a half, winter, a plume from your lips. Adding minutely to the fog-bank which obscured the poplars on the boundary of the football field. Thicker and closer than that suggested. Run three paces and lose yourself. Or your friends. Screaming in wet wool.

'Nobody can get me!' Lighting a tab with his last match. Woodbine smoke and breath pouring from both nostrils. Perfect freedom.

His cat jumped up on the arm of his chair. It ripped at the upholstery and then forced its head against his hand. There were beads of moisture on its whiskers. Titus turned his head as though it were articulated on a ball-joint. The underside of his chin was white. Ten. Close to senility.

'Grow flowers,' Fesk said. He prodded the cat and it jumped to the floor. Titus landed awkwardly.

Half-way to ninety. Two-thirds of the way to nothing. The last fog. Lying there in your cold sheets with the room dissolving.

There was an unclear patch already. In the top corner of the living-room where last winter's rain soaked through obscuring the pattern of the wallpaper. It looked like a small cloud. Miniature gun, diaphone, or bell? Some tiny warning signal: bang – hraarnm – ting!

But perfect freedom. The field like iron. They did that game with breathing. Deep. Deep – sucking in the fog. Then hold it with Wally squeezing his chest. Fooo! Falling forwards on hands and knees with the world crashing. Rehearsals.

It was bigger, that blurred patch. A slide of mucus in his eye. It moved when his gaze altered.

Fesk got up and bathed his eyes in warm water at the sink. He put the kettle on for tea then went to the table to re-read the card.

According to Sir Boverton Redwood (1904), duplex burners which gave a flame of 28 candle-power have an average oil consumption of 50 grains per candle per hour.

Grains of oil! Solidified fog. You could reverse anything with words. His mother implanting him in the past. The cat sailing up from the floor, its startled look turning to placidity. The head turning. The white chin. Striations in the moquette fading.

Steam issued from the spout of the kettle. Simon knew less about physics than the little he retained of geography. But he remembered that certain bits of water were agitated and changed their form. Slow them down and they turn to ice. Tea does not taste the same at the top of Mount Everest. Water boils quicker and colder. So the tea fails to mash, to draw.

He drank his cup in his chair. A knowing smile passed over his face.

She was a cunning old bugger. Fog itself was the warning. Not the signals. She was telling him about change, mutability: fog was the future. Everything gone out of shape. A low ceiling.

He had once caught a bus in thick fog. So dense that the conductor walked ahead, showing the driver the way. And the passengers trudged behind. Walking to keep warm and following the bus so that they did not lose their way. He'd paid full fare. Sixpence to walk!

Whatever light Sir Boverton tried to cast we were walking into darkness. Follow the bus.

It was late now but Simon did not turn on his light. A cruise ship hooted three times as it left the harbour. He had seen flying fish, an albatross, dolphins. The stern and a white trail blazed across the sea. You have been there. You leave your own wake.

After he left home he moved to London. In those days fog was green and frequent. He lived in Archway. Could walk to Hampstead Heath. The fogs drove him wild with desire. He was young. The possibility was held out of meeting a fellow-soul in the fog. Lighted windows took on a special diffuse quality. You could draw close. Who curtained against that blanket?

The city changed shape and decayed under that floor of fog. Lagan to be retrieved in discrete fragments of treasure. A girl dressed in mist – her hair like dark water.

Meetings were an astonishment – looming, distorted, and immediate. And people talked excitedly, their breath catching.

'Are you there? Are you there?'

'Where am I?'

'Haa! I thought I was nearly home.'

'Is this the kerb?'

'I've passed that corner three times.'

And were there really smudge-pots burning in the roads? One could walk naked and undetected.

There were more deaths. The old and frail gave up when their boundaries dissolved. They simply merged with whatever was to come. Their bits vibrating in a different mode. Passing out into something else. Steam or ice.

The young survived. They kept their shape because their memories were sharper. Matter is solidified memory of form. In fog a key which had been too long a key could slip its form and run as a bright trickle of amnesia down the thigh. So the old flew out from there. Officials called it pneumonia or influenza.

Fesk knew now that he loved it, fog, as some men loved danger. He should not have washed his eyes although the room was comfortingly dark now. It was a poor simulation but it would have to serve. He should be colder than he was, his skin transparent to the air.

Simon removed everything he had on and sat in his armchair, nude.

Rather than take those sounds as warnings, one could orchestrate them into a hymn in praise of fog:

Boom crack wheep bong ding blah hoooo
dong fooo crash ting boom wheee!

Repeat and vary. A fifty-grain candle burning as an offering.

Finally Simon knew what he was celebrating. He would leave this meridian of sun where fog, at the very best, came three times a year. He would seek out some industrial valley in a northern clime where factory chimneys poured out their libations to invisibility. Perhaps Ravensthorpe if it had not been ruined by the Clean Air Act.

Certainly not that bright little suburb on the outskirts of York where sunflowers grew in profusion. It would have to be a mucky place where dark bricks absorbed acid from the air. Where the skin was an osmotic device and not a dry barrier tanned and leathered by the sun.

She had made him homesick after all these years.

He would find desire again. One evening. Some dark girl in a mackintosh. Walking huddled streets glazed with rain, inundated with mist.

Fesk sang, the old song, before he retired:

> Oh I am a bachelor and I live all alone
> And I work at the weaver's trade
> And the only only thing I ever did wrong
> Was to woo a fair young maid
> I wooed her in the winter time
> And in the summer too
> And the only only thing I ever did wrong
> Was to save her from the foggy foggy dew.

He straightened the card against the milk bottle. It bent again. A meniscus of hope.

Before Simon went to bed he emptied the tea-pot outside the back door. He flung the soggy leaves against the agapanthus growing there.

Somewhere or other his father smiled a blank bright unimpassioned smile. His mother prepared a congratulatory sheet.

Fog descended immediately on all points.

WARREN DIBBLE

A Way of Love

Dust kicked up by the ewes settled all along the margin of the road, on grass, blackberry, manuka.

Dust and sweat smeared the face of the spectacled farmer.

It was a listless, burning afternoon, with a pulsating drone of cicadas in the air. The sheep were tired and hot. Paddocks away could be heard the distant throb of a baler.

The farmer walked his horse behind the mob.

Once he stopped to break himself a switch from an osier willow and a green and gold ladybird glinted up into the sun and alighted on his singlet. He flicked it off.

He had two dogs with him. One was a pup in training, the other a big black thing that seemed to be always grinning.

A car, an old model Morris, rolling huge clouds of pumice dust behind it turned a bend and slowed down as it came upon the sheep. Some of them scrambled wildly against each other and tried climbing up the bank. The pup went leaping and barking excitedly after them.

In low gear the car began to nose very slowly through the sheep. The older dog trotted after it, sprung up and onto the running board and carefully began to work himself, slithering and scratching, in between the headlamp and mudguard. The manoeuvre successful he stretched himself comfortably and began barking at the sheep, clearing a way for the car through the mob. His tail thumped madly against the body of the car and despite his barking he seemed to be grinning more than ever.

As soon as the car had got through he wriggled forward and floundering a little, sprang down to the road some three yards ahead of it and then trotted back through the sheep.

The car drove on a short distance and pulled up. A middle-aged couple got out and waited till the farmer came up to them.

'I guess he'll have to take us through again now. But I've never seen a dog do that before. My wife wants to take a photo of it.'

'Where did he learn to do that trick?' smiled the woman.

'Eh?'

'He's a great dog,' she said to the farmer.

'Buck? He's o.k.'

'Here boy!' called the man. 'Here boy!'

The dog made no response. It haunched down for a moment, panting; and snapped half heartedly at a fly.

'Here boy!' called the woman.

The farmer took out a tin of tobacco from his khaki shorts.

'He don't answer no one but me. He's trained for it.'

He rolled a cigarette, lit it, and then called: 'Buck.'

The dog crossed to them.

'Sit.'

'You lovely old fellow,' said the woman stooping down and patting his sides with both hands. 'You nice old boy.'

As she straightened, the dog jumped up with his forepaws against her dress.

'Down boy!' she said, laughing.

'Buck!' called the farmer sharply. 'I said sit! Sit!'

The dog squatted again.

The farmer removed his spectacles and wiped them against his singlet. Then he stepped forward a couple of paces to the dog, drew back his boot and slammed it hard and savagely into the dog's stomach.

The dog screamed and backed painfully.

While her husband watched amazed the woman gave a little cry and ran towards the dog.

'Poor boy! Poor fellow! Poor old chap!'

She bent down to pat him but the dog uttered a low snarl and snapped at her hand. She pulled it away hastily.

'He won't hurt you,' drawled the farmer. 'He don't hurt anyone.'

The woman and the farmer stared into each other's eyes.

In It

'Put one up the spout and shoot the bastard!'

He hung up. His wife asked:

'Who was that?'

'Mick. That big black dog of Wilson's been hanging round the ewes again.'

'You'd better go. You're late.'

He grunted.

'Is your uncle going to stay with us?'

'Don't know.'

'I expect he'll want to.'

'He can please himself.'

'When's he go into hospital?'

'Tomorrow I think.'

She took his gumboots outside to the porch, saying:

'Why's he coming all the way down here to the reception? If he goes into hospital tomorrow?'

'Reception my ass. He's come down to put the bite on me for a few thousand.'

'Do you think so?'

'He sent me thirty typed pages on his affairs. He's been diddling the tax men for years.'

'Are you going to give it to him?'

'Don't know.'

He drove fast, nonchalantly, to the pub. His uncle, a farmer from up north, had not yet arrived. He joined a few farmers in the private bar.

He was young, of big build, especially powerful in the legs, and worth a couple of hundred thousand. Nobody's fool. He ran three farms, two dairy and one sheep. He didn't put on airs but had nevertheless a natural authority. At boarding school he had been head prefect. Up to a few years ago he'd represented the province as a rugby lock. Older farmers listening to one of his forthright, contrary pronouncements might say dubiously, 'Well, I don't know . . .' but in discussing him critically among themselves one of them was sure to add, 'Mind you, he's got brains. Once he's made up his mind he won't mess around.' There were one or two rumours about other women but no one knew anything definite. All the same it was certain that women found his curt, take-it-or-leave-it style and his faint aloofness intriguing.

He had fairish brown hair that sometimes needed cutting on the neck. Well over six foot, he slouched rather than slumped. When not in working gear he dressed casually. At the moment he was wearing a white open shirt, expensive herringbone sportscoat, crumpled grey flannels and sneakers.

One of the farmers greeted him.
'Gooday Jess. What are you having?'
'Gin.'
'Right.'
'Been to the saleyard?'
'Yes. Very iffy market.'
It was twenty minutes or so before his uncle showed up; a bulky man with high colouring, grizzled tufts of eyebrows and a nose that ballooned out like a spinnaker. He was dressed in an ageing but well cut suit of some cinnamon coloured material, with matching waist-coat.
'How are you?' his nephew asked, stretching himself from the barstool and shaking hands.
'Not bad, Jess, not bad.' He had a deep, almost fruity voice.
'First time I've seen you wearing a hat.'
'It's a new one, too,' said the uncle.
'Well you must be doing well. Dough in the wool, eh?'
'Hah!'
'Yes, well: what are you going to have? I'd better introduce you. Henry. Bill. Mac.' He indicated his uncle. 'This is Jim Burton. My uncle. Silly old bugger, really.'
'Your face is familiar,' said one of the men.
'Yes,' said the nephew, 'I think you've met the old boy before. I try to keep him away – but you know – !'
'Last year, wasn't it?'
'That's right.'
'Whisky, uncle?'
'Yes. And lots of water.'
'Right.'
The uncle placed a pound on the bar. His nephew shoved it back at him.
'Put it away. I'll shout.'
'Hah! Nothing like having a wealthy nephew.'
'Nothing like having a destitute uncle.'
The uncle made a grimace and asked seriously:
'You got the typed packet I sent you?'
'Yeah.'
'Yes, well then, you've got my finances at your fingertips.'
'And I don't think much of them. That enough water?'
'Good.'
'Cheers.'
'Cheers.'
The uncle said doubtfully:
'I suppose I'd better book in.'
But his nephew instead of extending the expected invitation merely replied:
'It's not a bad pub. Good table, they tell me.'
The uncle swallowed his whisky and said, with a troubled expression:
'Well, I don't know what's going to happen to me tomorrow.'
'Why?'
'They may have to amputate my leg.'
'That bad, eh?'
His uncle launched into a long and detailed account of X-rays and the opinions of his specialist. 'Still, no use worrying,' he concluded.
'If they cut it off,' commented his nephew, 'you'll really have one foot in the grave then, eh?'
The young man turned and drew the others into conversation and the talk became general.

His nephew's bantering tone threw the uncle off balance a little. Understandably he was worried. He needed several thousand to clear his tax arrears and of late had found himself unable to make decisions. He didn't know whether to sell up his farm or not. If he did, where would he go? All his friends and associations were in the district. City life had few attractions. He was hoping that Jess would lend him some ten thousand. In fact, if he didn't. . . . But it was a delicate subject to broach. The boy seemed almost flippant about things. And he knew he'd have to put it delicately to his nephew, mention at least ten per cent, because if Jess once made up his mind to pass the deal, nothing would change it. But whenever I try to get him on the subject, he thought, he dances away from it; surely he's aware that I need to know before I go into hospital?

He felt dispirited and began to brood. His nephew, a little boisterous with gin, jabbed him on the arm.

'Come on you silly old bankrupt bastard. You'd better have a few more drinks before they amputate you. You won't be playing much golf after tomorrow, either.'

'By the way, Jess. I didn't tell you. I had a hole in one. It was on – '

'Oh shut up. No one believes you.'

'No, truly. I did. Cost me a packet, too.'

'Drink up. You talk like a bloody politician.'

A little while later the uncle thought: I feel drunk, and I've got to get in a serious talk with Jess, damn it.

But his nephew had swung away into a kind of larky, facetious mood. The uncle looked around for the Gents.

'Where are you off to now?'

'For a long spit.'

'Well don't stand there all day looking at it.'

But the truth was, he wanted to be alone for a moment. He was rather dazed by all this downrightness from his nephew. It was so far from his own mood. When he returned, Jess, who was smoking a cigarette and chewing his empty pipe at the same time, had just begun a description of some calves he'd sold.

'. . . to Harrop. I said I'd deliver 'em, so I drove them to the Patai bridge, half way, where this bloke met me. Do you think I could get 'em across that bridge? I'll be damned if I could. We tried everything. Forcing them, leading them. We even put hay on the bridge.'

'Were they weaners?'

'Yeah. In the end we had to get some milk from a cocky down the road. That brought 'em. Well, we just about had them all across when two of the buggers broke. Those two cows! Do you think we could get them to come back? In the end I had to bring the whole bloody herd back to them. Then they all came across like lambs.' He said suddenly to his uncle:

'That's not your gin. That's yours on the ledge.'

'Oh yes. I didn't notice.'

'You wouldn't notice if I had a horse with me.'

'I shouldn't be into the top shelf, you know.'

'If you conk out I'll put you to bed.'

'No you won't. I don't need to be picked up and nursed.'

'Don't you, you old bugger. I should pick you up and bounce you on your head to give your brain a shakeup.'

Desperately, the uncle said:

'I'm worried, Jess.'

'So you ought to be.'

'Can't we have a talk?'

'What do you want to talk about?'

'I thought you might be able to give me – some advice. I mean I may have to lose the farm. Sell up to pay the tax people.'

His nephew frowned slightly.

'And you know. It's a good farm, Jess.'

'Then what the hell are you going round buying new hats for?'

'Christ, it's not funny.'

'Sell out then.'

'But I've got that farm up to peak production. It's showing good returns.'

'You don't want a lot of money, you'll only spend the stuff. But if you're going to spend it, spend it.'

'But I don't want to give up the farm.'

'Look, you're going to die soon. Sell out and spend it. If they slice your leg off you won't be able to work, anyway.'

'I suppose I could sell half, or lease it. But it's the tax I'm worried about.'

'Get on the right side of your bank.'

'I'm on the wrong side of my overdraft already.'

'You'll just have to push on regardless.'

'Yes, but it's critical Jess. I've just had another letter from the tax people. A nasty one.' He took a deep breath and said slowly:

'I'm liable for nine thousand.'

There was a pause.

'W-e-ll, I'll tell you what,' said the nephew in his slurred, nasal and not unattractive voice. He gave his empty pipe a suck. 'I think you're in the shit.'

And from the settled, almost malevolent tone in which it was said, the uncle knew that he was.

JOY COWLEY

The Silk

When Mr Blackie took bad again that autumn both he and Mrs Blackie knew that it was for the last time. For many weeks neither spoke of it; but the understanding was in their eyes as they watched each other through the days and nights. It was a look, not of sadness or despair, but of quiet resignation tempered with something else, an unnamed expression that is seen only in the old and the very young.

Their acceptance was apparent in other ways, too. Mrs Blackie no longer complained to the neighbours that the old lazy-bones was running her off her feet. Instead she waited on him tirelessly, stretching their pension over chicken and out-of-season fruits to tempt his appetite; and she guarded him so possessively that she even resented the twice-weekly visits from the District Nurse. Mr Blackie, on the other hand, settled into bed as gently as dust. He had never been a man to dwell in the past, but now he spoke a great deal of their earlier days and surprised Mrs Blackie by recalling things which she, who claimed the better memory, had forgotten. Seldom did he talk of the present, and never in these weeks did he mention the future.

Then, on the morning of the first frost of winter, while Mrs Blackie was filling his hot water bottle, he sat up in bed, unaided, to see out the window. The inside of the glass was streaked with tears of condensation. Outside, the frost had made an oval frame of crystals through which he could see a row of houses and lawns laid out in front of them, like white carpets.

'The ground will be hard,' he said at last. 'Hard as nails.'

Mrs Blackie looked up quickly. 'Not yet,' she said.

'Pretty soon, I think.' His smile was apologetic.

She slapped the hot water bottle into its cover and tested it against her cheek. 'Lie down or you'll get a chill,' she said.

Obediently, he dropped back against the pillow, but as she moved about him, putting the hot water bottle at his feet, straightening the quilt, he stared at the frozen patch of window.

'Amy, you'll get a double plot, won't you?' he said. 'I wouldn't rest easy thinking you were going to sleep by someone else.'

'What a thing to say!' The corner of her mouth twitched. 'As if I would.'

'It was your idea to buy single beds,' he said accusingly.

'Oh Herb –' She looked at the window, away again. 'We'll have a double plot,' she said. For a second or two she hesitated by his bed, then she sat beside his feet, her hands placed one on top of the other in her lap, in a pose that she always adopted when she had something important to say. She cleared her throat.

'You know, I've been thinking on and off about the silk.'

'The silk?' He turned his head towards her.

'I want to use it for your laying out pyjamas.'

'No Amy,' he said. 'Not the silk. That was your wedding present, the only thing I brought back with me.'

'What would I do with it now?' she said. When he didn't answer, she got up, opened the wardrobe door and took the camphorwood box from the shelf where she kept her hats. 'All these years and us not daring to take a scissors to it. We should use it sometime.'

'Not on me,' he said.

'I've been thinking about your pyjamas.' She fitted a key into the brass box. 'It'd be just right.'

'A right waste, you mean,' he said. But there was no protest in his voice. In fact, it had lifted with a childish eagerness. He watched her hands as she opened the box and folded back layers of white tissue paper. Beneath them lay the blue of the silk. There was a reverent silence as she took it out and spread it under the light.

'Makes the whole room look different, doesn't it?' he said. 'I nearly forgot it looked like this.' His hands struggled free of the sheet and moved across the quilt. Gently, she picked up the blue material and poured it over his fingers.

'Aah,' he breathed, bringing it closer to his eyes. 'All the way from China.' He smiled. 'Not once did I let it out of me sight. You know that, Amy? There were those on board as would have pinched it quick as that. I kept it pinned round me middle.'

'You told me,' she said.

He rubbed the silk against the stubble of his chin. 'It's the birds that take your eye,' he said.

'At first,' said Mrs Blackie. She ran her finger over one of the peacocks that strutted in the foreground of a continuous landscape. They were proud birds, irridescent blue, with silver threads in their tails. 'I used to like them best, but after a while you see much more, just as fine only smaller.' She pushed her glasses on to the bridge of her nose and leaned over the silk, her finger guiding her eyes over islands where waterfalls hung, eternally suspended, between pagodas and dark blue conifers, over flat lakes and tiny fishing boats, over mountains where the mists never lifted, and back again to a haughty peacock caught with one foot suspended over a rock. 'It's a work of art like you never see in this country,' she said.

Mr Blackie inhaled the scent of camphorwood. 'Don't cut it, Amy. It's too good for an old blighter like me.' He was begging her to contradict him.

'I'll get the pattern tomorrow,' she said.

The next day, while the District Nurse was giving him his injection, she went down to the store and looked through a pile of pattern books. Appropriately, she chose a mandarin style with a high collar and piped cuffs and pockets. But Mr Blackie, who had all his life worn striped flannel in the conventional design, looked with suspicion at the pyjama pattern and the young man who posed so easily and shamelessly on the front of the packet.

'It's the sort them teddy bear boys have,' he said.

'Nonsense,' said Mrs Blackie.

'That's exactly what they are,' he growled. 'You're not laying me out in a lot of new-fangled nonsense.'

Mrs Blackie put her hands on her hips. 'You'll not have any say in the matter,' she said.

'Won't I just? I'll get up and fight – see if I don't.'

The muscles at the corner of her mouth twitched uncontrollably. 'All right, Herb, if you're so set against it – '

But now, having won the argument, he was happy. 'Get away with you, Amy. I'll get used to the idea.' He threw his lips back against his gums. 'Matter of fact, I like them fine. It's that nurse that done it. Blunt needle again.' He looked at the pattern. 'When d'you start?'

'Well – '

'This afternoon?'

'I suppose I could pin the pattern out after lunch.'

'Do it in here,' he said. 'Bring in your machine and pins and things and set them up so I can watch.'

She stood taller and tucked in her chin. 'I'm not using the machine,' she said with pride. 'Every stitch is going to be done by hand. My eyes mightn't be as good as they were once, mark you, but there's not a person on this earth can say I've lost my touch with a needle.'

His eyes closed in thought. 'How long?'

'Eh?'

'Till it's finished.'

She turned the pattern over in her hands. 'Oh – about three or four weeks. That is – if I keep it.'

'No,' he said. 'Too long.'

'Oh Herb, you'd want a good job done, wouldn't you?' she pleaded.

'Amy – ' Almost imperceptibly, he shook his head on the pillow.

'I can do the main seams on the machine,' she said, lowering her voice.

'How long?'

'A week,' she whispered.

When she took down the silk that afternoon, he insisted on an extra pillow in spite of the warning he'd had from the doctor about lying flat with his legs propped higher than his head and shoulders.

She plumped up the pillow from her own bed and put it behind his neck; then she unrolled her tape measure along his body, legs, arms, around his chest.

'I'll have to take them in a bit,' she said, making inch-high black figures on a piece of cardboard. She took the tissue-paper pattern into the kitchen to iron it flat. When she came back, he was waiting, wide-eyed with anticipation and brighter, she thought, than he'd been for many weeks.

As she laid the silk out on her bed and started pinning down the first of the pattern pieces, he described, with painstaking attempts at accuracy, the boat trip home, the stop at Hong Kong, and the merchant who had sold him the silk. 'Most of his stuff was rubbish,' he said. 'You wouldn't look twice at it. This was the only decent thing he had and even then he done me. You got to argue with these devils. Beat him down, they told me. But there was others as wanted that silk and if I hadn't made up me mind there and then I'd have lost it.' He squinted at her hands. 'What are you doing now? You just put that bit down.'

'It wasn't right,' she said, through lips closed on pins. 'I have to match it – like wallpaper.'

She lifted the pattern pieces many times before she was satisfied. Then it was evening and he was so tired that his breathing had become laboured. He no longer talked. His eyes were watering from hours of concentration; the drops spilled over his red lids and soaked into the pillow.

'Go to sleep,' she said. 'Enough's enough for one day.'

'I'll see you cut it out first,' he said.

'Let's leave it till the morning,' she said, and they both sensed her reluctance to put the scissors to the silk.

'Tonight,' he said.

'I'll make the tea first.'

'After,' he said.

She took the scissors from her sewing drawer and wiped them on her apron. Together they felt the pain as the blades met cleanly, almost without resistance, in that first cut. The silk would never again be the same. They were changing it, rearranging the pattern of fifty-odd years to form something new and unfamiliar. When she had cut out the first piece, she held it up, still pinned to the paper, and said, 'The back of the top.' Then she laid it on the dressing table and went on as quickly as she dared, for she knew that he would not rest until she had finished.

One by one the garment pieces left the body of silk. With each touch of the blades, threads sprang apart; mountains were divided, peacocks split from head to tail; waterfalls fell on either side of fraying edges. Eventually, there was nothing on the bed but a few shining snippets. Mrs Blackie picked them up and put them back in the camphorwood box, and covered the pyjama pieces on the dressing table with a cloth. Then she removed the extra pillow from Mr Blackie's bed and laid his head back in a comfortable position before she went into the kitchen to make the tea.

He was very tired the next morning but refused to sleep while she was working with the silk. She invented a number of excuses for putting it aside and leaving the room. He would sleep then, but never for long. No more than half an hour would pass and he would be calling her. She would find him lying awake and impatient for her to resume sewing.

In that day and the next, she did all the machine work. It was a tedious task, for first she tacked each seam by hand, matching the patterns in the weave so that the join was barely noticeable. Mr Blackie silently supervised every stitch. At times she would see him studying the silk with an expression that she still held in her memory. It was the look he'd given her in their courting days. She felt a prick of jealousy, not because she thought that he cared more for the silk than he did for her, but because he saw something in it that she didn't share. She never asked him what it was. At her age a body did not question these things or demand explanations. She would bend her head lower and concentrate her energy and attention into the narrow seam beneath the needle.

On the Friday afternoon, four days after she'd started the pyjamas, she finished the buttonholes and sewed on the buttons. She'd deliberately hurried the last of the hand sewing. In the four days, Mr Blackie had become weaker, and she knew that the sooner the pyjamas were completed and put back in the camphorwood box out of sight, the sooner he would take an interest in food and have the rest he needed.

She snipped the last thread and put the needle in its case.

'That's it, Herb,' she said, showing him her work.

He tried to raise his head. 'Bring them over here,' he said.

'Well – what do you think?' As she brought the pyjamas closer, his eyes relaxed and he smiled.

'Try them on?' he said.

She shook her head. 'I got the measurements,' she said. 'They'll be the right fit.'

'Better make sure,' he said.

She hesitated but could find no reason for her reluctance. 'All right,' she said, switching on both bars of the electric heater and drawing it closer to his bed. 'Just to make sure I've got the buttons right.'

She peeled back the bedclothes, took off his thick pyjamas and put on the silk. She stepped back to look at him.

'Well, even if I do say so myself, there's no one could have done a better job. I could move the top button over a fraction, but apart from that they're a perfect fit.'

He grinned. 'Light, aren't they?' He looked down the length of his body and wriggled his toes. 'All the way from China. Never let it out of me sight. Know that, Amy?'

'Do you like them?' she said.

He sucked his lips in over his gums to hide his pleasure. 'All right. A bit on the tight side.'

'They are not, and you know it,' Mrs Blackie snapped. 'Never give a body a bit of credit, would you? Here, put your hands down and I'll change you before you get a chill.'

He tightened his arms across his chest. 'You made a right good job, Amy. Think I'll keep them on a bit.'

'No.' She picked up his thick pyjamas.

'Why not?'

'Because you can't,' she said. 'It – it's disrespectful. And the nurse will be here soon.'

'Oh, get away with you, Amy.' He was too weak to resist further but as she changed him, he still possessed the silk with his eyes. 'Wonder who made it?'

Although she shrugged his question away, it brought to her a definite picture of a Chinese woman seated in front of a loom surrounded by blue and silver silkworms. The woman was dressed from a page in a geographic magazine, and except for the Oriental line of her eyelids, she looked like Mrs Blackie.

'D'you suppose there's places like that?' Mr Blackie asked.

She snatched up the pyjamas and put them in the box. 'You're the one that's been there,' she said briskly. 'Now settle down and rest or you'll be bad when the nurse arrives.'

The District Nurse did not come that afternoon. Nor in the evening. It was at half-past three the following morning that her footsteps, echoed by the doctor's sounded along the gravel path.

Mrs Blackie was in the kitchen, waiting. She sat straight-backed and dry-eyed, her hands placed one on top of the other in the lap of her dressing gown.

'Mrs Blackie. I'm sorry – '

She ignored the nurse and turned to the doctor. 'He didn't say goodbye,' she said with an accusing look. 'Just before I phoned. His hand was over the side of the bed. I touched it. It was cold.'

The doctor nodded.

'No sound of any kind,' she said. 'He was good as gold last night.'

Again, the doctor nodded. He put his hand, briefly, on her shoulder, then went into the bedroom. Within a minute he returned, fastening his leather bag and murmuring sympathy.

Mrs Blackie sat still, catching isolated words. Expected. Peacefully. Brave. They dropped upon her – neat, geometrical shapes that had no meaning.

'He didn't say goodbye.' She shook her head. 'Not a word.'

'But look, Mrs Blackie,' soothed the nurse. 'It was inevitable. You knew that. He couldn't have gone on – '

'I know, I know.' She turned away, irritated by their lack of understanding. 'He just might have said goodbye. That's all.'

The doctor took a white tablet from a phial and tried to persuade her to swallow it. She pushed it away; refused, too, the cup of tea that the District Nurse poured and set in front of her. When they picked up their bags and went towards the bedroom, she followed them.

'In a few minutes,' the doctor said. 'If you'll leave us – '

'I'm getting his pyjamas,' she said. 'There's a button needs changing. I can do it now.'

As soon as she entered the room, she glanced at Mr Blackie's bed and noted that the doctor had pulled up the sheet. Quickly, she lifted the camphorwood box, took a needle, cotton, scissors, her spectacle case, and went back to the kitchen. Through the half-closed door she heard the nurse's voice, 'Poor old thing,' and she knew, instinctively, that they were not talking about her.

She sat down at the table to thread the needle. Her eyes were clear but her hands were so numb that for a long time they refused to work together. At last, the thread knotted, she opened the camphorwood box. The beauty of the silk was always unexpected. As she spread the pyjamas out on the table, it warmed her, caught her up and comforted her with the first positive feeling she'd had that morning. The silk was real. It was brought to life by the electric light above the table, so that every fold of the woven landscape moved. Trees swayed towards rippling water and peacocks danced with white fire in their tails. Even the tiny bridges –

Mrs Blackie took off her glasses, wiped them, put them on again. She leaned forward and traced her thumbnail over one bridge, then another. And another. She turned over the pyjama coat and closely examined the back. It was there, on every bridge; something she hadn't noticed before. She got up, and from the drawer where she kept her tablecloths, she took out a magnifying glass.

As the bridge in the pattern of the silk grew, the figure which had been no larger than an ant, became a man.

Mrs Blackie forgot about the button and the murmur of voices in the bedroom. She brought the magnifying glass nearer her eyes.

It was a man and he was standing with one arm outstretched, on the highest span between two islands. Mrs Blackie studied him for a long time, then she straightened up and smiled. Yes, he was waving. Or perhaps, she thought, he was beckoning to her.

Apple Wine

Ellen was looking for three perfect roses to go on the table. 'The storm has done almost no damage at all,' she said as she leaned over the bushes, her secateurs probing like the pincers of a large beetle. 'Which do you prefer, Hetty? White or pink?'

But her sister was in the hall talking on the telephone to Muriel. 'I said the garden, dear.' Her voice came out the front door and rolled across the verandah, every word clear and the shape of a bell. 'We decided to have the reading out-of-doors today. Yes dear. Oh indeed, yes. Quite superb. Ellen's put the seagrass chairs under the walnut tree and there's plenty of shade, but I suggest you bring your panama. No dear, your hat. Do bring your hat.'

Ellen pulled a pink rose towards the secateurs and waited. Her sister often said things were quite superb. It was a figure of speech which described Hetty's vitality more than anything else, but today the expression was so rightly fitting it had taken on a new sound, magnificent, like a phrase from the Hallelujah chorus. To Ellen's mind there was no better way of describing the transformation wrought by an overnight change in the weather. It was quite superb.

The lawn was still very damp, of course, but it had risen from the earth as thick as living fur, glistening, patched at the edges with the shadows of trees. And the roses, yesterday half-drowned, had inhaled the sun and expanded until they were almost bursting with colour and perfume.

Ellen touched the face of the pink rose and thought, angel skin, it was like blushing angel skin, then, hearing Hetty on the verandah, she called out, 'Do you remember what Daddy used to say about the rain? How it was the angels weeping for their sins?'

'Did he, dear?' said Hetty, shaking the white cloth over the table. 'No Ellen, those are too pale for the tea set. That red one, dear, growing by the thingamy— yes, yes, that's it.'

'I wonder if it was original,' said Ellen. 'Knowing Daddy, it probably was.'

Hetty didn't comment. She had changed the focus of her spectacles by lifting them away from her nose and was watching Ellen select the flowers. 'Muriel thinks it's time we had a chat to Olive,' she said.

Ellen carefully trimmed a stem. It was an old rose with single petals round yellow stamens and a heavy perfume unrefined by breeding. Too rich for the tea table, she thought.

'Did you hear me, dear? I believe at times you're as deaf as Muriel. I was talking about Olive. Muriel feels we've let it go far too long and the sooner we say something, the better for Olive's sake. Wouldn't you agree? Ellen? Ellen, are you listening?'

She closed the secateurs and brought the flowers over to Hetty. 'They're a nice colour,' she said. 'But I fear everything will smell of roses.'

'Muriel saw Stella last night. Stella says she can't come back to the reading group while Olive's in it.' Hetty flattened the creases in the cloth. 'We should do it today,' she said.

Ellen took the cut crystal vase from the tea trolley and set it at the centre of the table with the three red roses leaning out from its rim. The light through the walnut tree lay in shivering shapes on the table, striking the vase so that its reflection on the cloth held splashes of white fire extending into rainbows and two red spots like wine stains.

She turned. 'Hetty, let's have a bottle of the apple wine.'

Her sister stopped mid-sentence as though someone had put in her mouth something to be tasted. She smiled. 'What a superb idea. Yes, indeed yes, a bottle of the good batch and we'll serve tea after the reading. Oh Ellen, you are a clever thing with flowers. It's so pretty – ' She softly clapped her hands. 'We'll use the decanter,' she said.

It seemed rather frivolous to get out Daddy's decanter for their home-made apple wine and Ellen was surprised that Hetty had suggested it. As she opened the cabinet door she felt her father's disapproval in the stiffness of the hinges and she called to Hetty in the kitchen, 'We'll use the good glasses too, won't we?'

'Of course, dear!' Hetty shouted back and in a voice so reckless that Ellen laughed over the dark teak shelves.

Muriel came before they had finished setting the table, deliberately early so that she could talk about Olive. She was wearing a white and navy dress with a green silk scarf to hide the cord of her hearing machine, and a hat of yellowing straw. In a paper bag under her arm she carried the large-print edition of *Lorna Doone*. For some small time she stood by the verandah to fully admire the garden and comment on the lavender, geraniums, roses, stocks, the table under the tree. 'Gosh Hetty, your apple wine. We are in for a treat.' Then she sat heavily in one of the seagrass chairs and pulled off her gloves finger by finger. 'I came in a taxi cab. Olive offered to bring me, which was jolly decent of her.' She looked at Hetty. 'She's been more than generous with her motor, I don't deny it.'

'We always pay for the benzine, dear,' said Hetty.

'The spirit of generosity,' said Muriel. 'We'll find it difficult to accept the loss of our little excursions, especially the concerts. We'll miss the concert season. I say, Hetty, there must be someone in the village. Are you sure you haven't overlooked a possibility? What about that friend of yours related to the Scott-Turners – Mrs Calder – doesn't she drive a motor-car?'

'She had a stroke,' shouted Hetty.

'Pam Calder? Oh Hetty, what a shame. I am sorry to hear that. Perhaps Ellen has a suggestion. Ellen, do you know anyone with a motor?'

'I'm afraid I don't,' said Ellen.

'Pardon, dear?' said Muriel.

Hetty leaned over Muriel's chair. 'Ellen doesn't want to talk about it. She thinks we're being unfair. Unfair. To Olive. She thinks we're trying to put poor Olive out in the snow. Muriel, do switch on your deaf aid.'

'Unfair?' Muriel fumbled with the pocket on her bodice and her hearing machine whistled like an untuned wireless. 'Does she?' The noise stopped. 'Is that what you really think, Ellen?'

But Ellen didn't know what she thought, only that she believed no one had the right to turn a beautiful day to unpleasant purpose, so she nodded affirmation and sat in the opposite chair, leaning back until Muriel's head was barely visible above the table.

Muriel laughed. 'Olive, I imagine, will be vastly relieved. Of course she will, Ellen. Poor soul gets so fearfully bored with our fuddy-duddy ways her only refuge lies in sleep or photos of her grandchildren. She'd have drifted away months ago if she didn't have our only means of private conveyance. Loyalty, Ellen. Loyal and generous to a fault, that's our Olive. Years ago Winkie had a batman cast in the same mould. The salt of the earth, was the way he described him, the salt of the very earth.'

Ellen said nothing. The table rose between them like an altar with the white linen cloth, the decanter and glasses, the crimson roses already open to the stage of dropping. There was no sediment in the wine. It glowed in the decanter a pale gold colour but with a look of age to it, as though they had fermented pre-war sunshine in a vintage year. The long-stemmed glasses which had been covered with the fine dust of a locked cupboard, were now so clean they looked as frail as soap bubbles.

And, as Ellen had predicted, everything smelled of roses.

'Our poor little group,' Hetty was saying. 'We've been disappearing like the ten little nigger boys. Do you remember, Muriel, the meeting at Cynthia's and how she used to read from that very odd lectern with the carved monkeys on it? Cynthia's gone. It was quite sad, dear, so far away. A nursing home in Auckland, I believe.'

A stillness came into the garden and a quiet which they held not so much for the passing of Cynthia who had, God bless her, been a little difficult at times, but for the resurrection of her drawing-room and the afternoons they'd spent in it.

After a while Muriel sighed and said, 'I know, Hetty. You told me several times.'

'Did I, dear?' said Hetty. 'I don't remember.'

Olive came late and in a hurry. They were about to pour the wine when they heard the little motor-car crying out with the suddenness of its halt outside their hedge, and they put the stopper back in the decanter. A car door slammed, then immediately, another. Hetty and Muriel looked at Ellen who shook her head and stood up, stretching on her toes to peer through the trees. She sat down again quickly. 'I think she has brought a gentleman friend,' she said.

'A what?' whispered Muriel, but it was clear from her expression that she had heard and understood.

'Oh dear,' said Hetty, turning her chair away from the gate.

None of them got up to greet Olive. She came up the path, large in pink and lavender, with a young man following several paces behind.

Very young, observed Ellen, very tall and so fair his hair caught the sun like thistledown.

He saw them first and said something to Olive who turned at the point of knocking on the front door, and gave a cry of surprise. She came across the lawn with small, quick steps, calling, 'Oh now! Oh my, I mean to say, isn't that just lovely? Isn't it beautiful? Like a scene from the movies, you know, with the garden in the background – oh, I never in all my born days saw such a picture. You girls, you look just like royalty, don't they, Gareth?' She turned back to the young man. 'Girls, this is Gareth Miller, my eldest grandson.' Then, taking him by the arm, she introduced him to each in turn.

He was only a boy, Ellen decided, tall and well-grown but with a freshness to his complexion which indicated that a shaving brush was still new to him. He had blue eyes and straight fair hair which fell over his eyes when he leaned forward. His trousers were of a coarse cream fabric with buttoned pockets on the legs and he wore a pink and white striped shirt open at the throat. Round his neck hung a gold chain with some kind of coin or medal attached.

He was exceedingly polite for a young man of the day and seemed well enough at ease in their company. 'Nan's always talking about her reading group,' he said. 'I was glad for the opportunity to meet you at last.'

'Gareth's not staying,' said Olive, taking the empty chair. 'He's just dropped me off so he can borrow the car for the afternoon, haven't you, love?' She smiled up at him. 'He's coming for me again, later.'

He might have gone then, but Hetty, perhaps touched by his charming manner or her own initial coldness, held on to the arms of her chair and almost stood. 'Before you go, Mr Miller, will you please join us in a glass of apple wine?'

'Sure,' he said. 'Thanks very much. I'd like to.'

'We have extra glasses,' said Hetty, 'and Ellen will get you a chair.'

But he insisted he'd rather sit on the ground. No, it wasn't damp, he said, and no, no, he wouldn't get grass stains. See? He unfolded his handkerchief and spread it by the base of the walnut tree. Then he came back to the table and offered to pour. 'It's my job,' he said. 'I'm a wine waiter.'

'Just listen to him,' laughed Olive. 'Of course he isn't a waiter. He's at university – going to be a lawyer. Don't let him kid you, girls, he's an awful tease.' She smiled at him as though he were made of precious metal.

'It is my job,' he said. 'Two nights a week I pour wine and I'm very good at it. Allow me – ' He took the stopper from the decanter and held it under his nose. 'Seventy-seven,' he said. 'A very good year for *Granny Smiths*.'

'Just listen!' cried Olive. 'The cheek!'

Even Muriel laughed immoderately. 'Granny Smith, indeed. Could you not have thought *Splendour* or *Rome Beauty* or even *Delicious*? Couldn't you have allowed our vanity that much?'

'He's right,' said Hetty. 'They were *Granny Smiths*.'

Olive eased off her shoes and stretched her feet in the grass. 'I do love a drop of cider now and then. Only a glass or two. It's got a kick like a mule if you over-indulge yourself any.'

'This isn't cider, dear,' said Hetty, 'It's apple wine.'

'Oh?'

'They're very different,' said Hetty.

'Well go on, you could have fooled me,' said Olive.

The young man poured the pale wine into a glass, neatly twisting his wrist so that not a drop spilled on the tablecloth. His hands were yet at the bony stage, long fingers, large knuckles. 'What's the difference?' he asked.

'One can make cider of any apple,' said Hetty. 'Any type, any quality. If one leaves the apples to fall off the tree and rot in the grass of their own accord, they will make cider.'

'And wine?' he said.

'Predominantly cooking apples with a few dessert and a few crab apples, only the best quality, and refined sugar. The process is the same for any wine, Mr Miller, but there is much to go wrong – yeastiness, haze, rope, thinness, acidity. We find that only one year in four produces excellence.' Hetty nodded towards the glasses. 'This is one of our better rackings.'

'It looks like a sylvaner riesling,' he said.

Muriel snorted. 'Nothing so innocuous. Hetty's wine is ambrosia. You'll need the stamina of the gods if you're going to drink it like your riesling.'

'It is – ' admitted Hetty, ' – a substantial wine.'

He brought the glasses to them with the small niceties of formal presentation, heels together, a flourish from the waist that turned a stoop into a bow, then he took his own glass and sat with his back against the tree trunk. 'Your very good health,' he said.

'Cheers,' said Olive.

'Good health,' said Muriel.

The wine had only the faintest taste of apples, Ellen thought. Mostly it was flavoured with the season of the picking, the light chill of mist, the crispness of a little frost and over it all, the warmth of the sun. She leaned back against the cushions to savour better the total effect of the beautifully balanced glass and its straw-coloured liquid.

'It's a marvellous wine,' the young man was saying. 'So smooth on the palate, so – so rounded.'

'Yes,' said Hetty. 'It is quite superb, isn't it?'

'Just goes to show you're never too old to learn something new,' said Olive.

'I assume you're on holiday,' said Hetty. 'From where, may I ask?'

'Christchurch,' he said. 'A week off to visit kith and kin before I go back to work.'

'I've got two daughters in Christchurch,' said Olive, opening her handbag on the arm of Muriel's chair. 'Here's a snap of Edna, my eldest, Gareth's mother, and here's the one I showed you the other day, all five of them outside their new home. That's Gareth by his Dad.'

Ellen sipped in silence. The green shade was spotted and barred with sunlight which moved every time a breeze disturbed the tree so that they seemed to be in the flickering current at the bottom of some woodland pool, like a group of trout or grayling. She watched the shadows move across the young man's face and saw his hair float over his forehead as he nodded, listening.

I'm so glad I've got Hetty, she thought suddenly. The warmth of the wine had made her feel sad for Muriel living on her own, no one to care for. Poor Muriel, her only daughter had married a dark gentleman from the Islands who had taken her away to live with his family, and Muriel had not seen her in twenty-seven years.

I don't know what I'd do without Hetty, Ellen thought. I've so much to be grateful for.

Muriel had taken the photographs from Olive and was holding them at arm's length towards the young man. 'I say, Hetty, he looks awfully like a young John Ridd.'

Hetty slowly nodded.

'He does most certainly,' said Muriel, deliberately teasing. 'Such a coincidence. We have a visitation from the hero of this very novel.' She patted the package in her lap. 'Look, Ellen. Wouldn't you say he was none other than John Ridd in person?'

'No,' said Ellen. 'John Ridd was of much broader stature and he had a beard.'

'I'm sure he didn't always have a beard, dear,' said Hetty, and their laughter surrounded the boy who blushed and put his head down, his composure gone.

Olive said, 'You know John Ridd, don't you, love? A big fellow, built like an ox but a real kewpie doll underneath, kind, everybody's heart-throb.'

The boy's face was pink and his eyes were drowning. He tried to dismiss the conversation with a few hand movements.

Muriel was still laughing and patting her chest as though to regulate her breathing. 'He gets – John Ridd gets – most awfully intimidated by compliments.'

Hetty said, 'Have you read *Lorna Doone*, Mr Miller?'

He shook his head.

'What a pity,' she said. 'It's a book best read in one's early years. Ellen selected it for the reading group because it was a favourite of her girlhood, but I think it's a mistake to revisit the places of one's youth. Wouldn't you agree? Everything seems so small and ordinary when one goes back. With *Lorna Doone* one feels that all the best pages have been removed.'

'I don't,' said Ellen. 'I find the story as touching as ever. As for the descriptions of the English countryside, they're beautifully written and quite wasted on a child. I'm sure I didn't appreciate Mr Blackmore's penmanship nearly as much when I was young.'

'Oh yes, indeed, yes,' said Hetty. 'He paints delightful little landscapes. But what about the romance, Ellen, that splendid passion between Lorna Doone and John Ridd – how improbable to the adult reader. At no time in the history of men and women since Adam, could friendship have existed on such stilted utterances. My dear, it's so childish.'

Ellen smiled. Hetty, she thought, was getting a little tiddly.

Muriel had taken their large-print edition from its bag and was turning the pages. 'We missed an extraordinary thing, Hetty. Going back, I discovered an unaccountable change in the character of Mrs Betty Muxworthy. Most extraordinary.' She looked at the boy. 'Betty Muxworthy is a domestic servant in the Ridd household.'

'An unpleasant woman,' said Hetty.

'Embittered by fortune,' said Muriel. 'Here it is. On page forty-nine when she first appears, she has an Irish brogue. Listen to this: "Men is desaving," she says, "and so is galanies; but the most desaving of all is books, with their heads and tails, and the speckots in 'em, lik a peg as have taken the maisles. Some folks purtends to laugh and cry over them. God forgive them for liars!" But look here, a few pages further on and for the rest of the book, she has a broad Devon accent: "Zailor, ees fai! ay and zarve un raight!" There. What do you make of that?'

'Nothing,' said Hetty, waving her glass.

'But he changed her speech pattern totally.'

'He made a mistake, dear,' said Hetty.

'Do you think so?'

'Of course. Mr Blackmore was not the most gifted in portrayal of character but at least he was a kindly man. John Ridd assures us of that.'

'Assures us what?' said Muriel, whose hearing machine was whistling again.

'That he was kind,' shouted Hetty.

Quite tipsy, thought Ellen, and in a fine mood. By evening she would have one of her heads.

'I see,' said Muriel, looking puzzled.

Ellen said, 'Hetty, how do you know John Ridd was an autobiographical portrait?'

'He was,' said Hetty. 'Indeed he was, my dear. When only one character in the book is real, one can be sure he's the author.' She held out her glass. 'Perhaps our John Ridd will be good enough to fill our wineglasses.'

Ellen didn't see what happened next. In standing to take Hetty's glass, the boy somehow knocked over his own. The noise of breaking crystal was loud and discordant as though someone had upset a harpsichord. Ellen heard it in every part of her body.

The boy sucked in his breath and stood with his back to Ellen, looking at the fragments.

'Jolly bad luck,' said Muriel.

'It's not important,' said Hetty. 'Don't concern yourself.'

'It must have hit the root of the tree,' he said. 'I'm sorry, I didn't see it. I must have kicked – Jees, I'm sorry.'

Daddy's wineglass, mourned Ellen, rocking with pain. Oh how awful. Daddy's beautiful glass.

'Don't give it a thought,' said Hetty.

Olive got out of her chair. 'Gareth, Gareth!' With her hands on her knees and her arms set like wings, she bent over, looking for fragments in the grass by the tree. 'You're such a clumsy boy. That was antique, you know. You can never replace it for love or money.'

'Olive, don't make a fuss,' said Hetty. 'There are five of us and we still have five glasses. Olive. Please. You'll cut your fingers.'

'I'm sorry,' said the boy. 'I know they're rare. I feel terrible.'

'All his life he's had two left feet,' said Olive.

'It just happened,' he said.

'No, no,' said Muriel. 'Not in your kerchief, that could be nasty. She handed him the brown paper bag which had held the book. 'In there and do be careful of the splinters. Oh I say, cheer up, it's not the end of the silly old world. Did you know? John Ridd also had two left feet.'

'All of you leave the wretched thing,' said Hetty. 'Mr Miller, put that down and we'll attend to it later. Come over here. Now. You may pour us all some more wine, my dear.'

He stood up slowly and brushed his hair away from his forehead. 'Do you trust me?'

Hetty laughed. 'Of course I trust you. When a woman gets to my age, she can trust any man.'

'It was a stupid thing,' he said. 'I should have – '

'Enough!' said Hetty, clapping her hands twice. 'We will have a complete change of subject. Ellen, you've been very quiet, hardly a word, dear. You can introduce the next topic of conversation.'

Ellen looked away from their eyes. She could think of nothing new, nothing at all. She let the boy take the empty glass from her hand. 'I don't know,' she said. 'Unless you want to talk about the English countryside.'

'Not of general interest, dear,' said Hetty.

'Gareth's been to England,' said Olive.

'Have you?' Hetty turned to him. 'Have you really?'

'Only three weeks,' he said. 'The tourist view of London and a quick skid round Buckinghamshire and Oxford. I don't know it the way you do.'

'I absolutely adore the Cotswolds,' said Muriel. 'Tell me, did you get down to Aldershot?'

But he was looking at Ellen.

'No,' she said. 'I've never been to England.'

'Haven't you?' He seemed surprised, and that pleased her.

'Mother and Daddy were both English, of course,' she said. 'But Hetty and I have never been outside of New Zealand.'

'We were considering a sea voyage a few years ago,' said Hetty. 'People advised us against it. They warned us we'd find the old country changed so much, we'd be disappointed.'

'Terribly,' said Muriel.

'Did you find it changed, Mr Miller?' said Hetty.

'I don't know what you mean by changed,' he said. 'That would depend on your expectation.'

'Believe you me, Hetty,' said Muriel, 'London is unrecognizable.'

'But the countryside,' said Ellen, 'is it as green as they say it is?'

'It was a drought year,' he said. 'The paddocks were burned to a crisp, more like the colour of Spain or Greece.'

Oh no, thought Ellen. Not paddocks. Fields. Fields and meadows, woods and copses, spinneys and hedgerows and thickets.

'These days,' said Muriel, 'you can go from the Bayswater Road to Regent Street and not see a Londoner.'

'Yes,' said the boy, passing their filled glasses. 'I reckon it'd just about be possible.'

'You haven't poured one for yourself,' said Hetty.

'No,' he said. 'I'd like to, but if you don't mind, it's time I excused myself.'

'So soon?' said Hetty.

'I wish I was able to stay – '

'He's taking the car into town,' said Olive.

'Oh yes,' said Hetty. 'You have an appointment.'

He stepped backwards. 'Thank you for the wine. It was really fantastic. And thank you for being so nice about the you-know-what. No, stay there. Please don't bother to get up.'

'Don't be any later than five on the dot,' said Olive.

He had moved beyond the trees but even in full sunlight he looked cool, as though he were made of shade itself. 'See you later,' he called. His right hand was palm out towards them, instructing them to remain seated, but when he reached the path, he moved it in a sweeping circle and called, '*Ciao*'.

After he'd gone they sat quietly for a while, sipping wine and listening to the sounds of bees in the garden. The air was hot and still and beyond the shadow of their tree the lawn shimmered at an uncertain level as though it were in the process of being dissolved. On the table one of the red roses made a small noise like a sigh and dropped its petals all at once on to the white cloth.

'You must be proud of him, dear,' Hetty said to Olive.

'I am,' said Olive. 'But I mean to say, I would be, wouldn't I? There's always something special about the first grandchild.'

'He's charming,' said Muriel.

'He didn't want to come in,' said Olive. 'I had to force him and then I thought we'd never get rid of him. He looked – ha ha. Rid of him. Ridd. Oh, he lapped that up a real treat, did you see? See him blush?'

Ellen put her glass back on the table. She felt exhausted, unreasonably tired, and yet at the same time wide awake as though she had narrowly missed some frightful danger. She rested her head back on the cushion and listened to the birds and insects. Somewhere in the garden a grey warbler had started up. It trilled in the upper register like a drunken flautist, a beautiful extravagant sound.

'Are you ready?' said Muriel.

'Yes please,' said Olive.

Muriel read in clear and careful tones, 'You may suppose that my heart beat high, when the King and Queen appeared, and entered, followed by the Duke of Norfolk, bearing the sword of state, and by several other noblemen and people of repute. . . .'

Ellen shut her eyes.

It could almost have been a nightingale.

VINCENT O'SULLIVAN

Palms and Minarets

'You're the one who will have to decide. You're the one who knows whether you're run down or not.'

My wife sat under the lampshade made from a sheet of old monk's music we had brought back from Spain.

'I'll decide,' I told her. 'I'll decide before next weekend.'

Her needles clicked while she knitted. The shiny pages of a pattern book lay open on the sofa beside her, and even as she spoke her eyes moved from the needles to the instructions in the book, then back to her work. I looked past her to the red lines drawn on the curved stiffness of the parchment, at the heavy black squares to tell a monk's voice where exactly to go, where in the huge cool greyness of a church his voice was to rise or fall, the light from a high window over the shaved heads of the monks. Because I saw that once in Spain. My wife was looking for a shop that sold filigree work, the kind she had seen in Toledo and decided not to buy, and had then thought about and spoken about for the next three days. We were in a town whose name I forget, where we had not meant to be. She lay down in the afternoon and I walked through streets which were high white walls and stiff shadows. Then late in the afternoon she had decided to go after her filigree and I walked into a church, into the rise and fall of the voices behind the heavy leather curtain at the door, the black squares on the red lines behind my wife's head.

'If you don't decide to take a rest now who knows where we'll finish up?'

There had been a smell in the greyness like concrete, like water sprinkled on concrete. There was a young monk with a beard who looked like a movie star.

'I told you I'd go next week.'

'You know very well with a specialist you need to make an appointment well ahead.'

'I'm sure I'll last that long,' I said. My wife's needles clashed, they were steel and clashed softly but she may also have been cross that I kept putting things off. Her hair which once I had thought so lovely was drawn close against her head. It was red in the light from the monk's singing, from the music which had no tune to follow, no notes I could read although I had learned the piano for several years. My mother had said *He'll never be a concert pianist mind you but he sticks to a thing.* She had said it to my aunt while she stood at the kitchen sink. She wore pink rubber gloves which almost made me feel ill if they touched my skin. *You can play that piece you did for the examinations* she told me, *the piece you played last night for your father.* But it was for *him*, I thought, I am not playing it for anyone else.

I'll play it when she comes round next week I told her. I watched her pink gloves shine each time she raised them from the water and their pale dry insides when she peeled them off. *Next week, auntie. I'll be better at it by then.*

Only a few times, once or twice in the Army and another time in a church group, have I been with men who talked about their fathers. I do not mean the way one reminisces with friends, because it is likely they would have known him or heard about him anyway. I mean the times when men try to tell others what their fathers were like. That doesn't happen very often, and I think that when it does, most men will tell lies.

My own father was short, his features as sharply fine as if clipped from paper. In these past months I have thought of him a great deal. I believe I remember the first time he walked down the street with me. He held my hand as I stepped across the dappled footpath through circles and patches of brightness and moving shadow, when I was still too young to know that the pavement wasn't shifting but the flickering was from the trees that grew right along the street. We would come to a puddle of light and when I paused he would take both my hands in his and say 'Over we go, digger.'

I am the only person I know whose father was a dandy, a man who failed at almost everything except keeping his shoes polished to perfection, and at a kind of kidding all the time that he was more melancholy than anyone understood. He loved standing on the back porch with his jacket off but his white sleeves rolled down, the cuffs held with slender jade cufflinks, his waistcoat buttoned and his watch-chain shining across his lean stomach. He would stand with a book open and resting on one palm and in the sunlight (it is never winter when I remember him), from the distance, he was lithe and solitary, a kind of figure from a western who held a book instead of a gun. But he would take books up and lay them down as though there were something in them which roughness would spill.

My father's single hobby was pool. Several nights a week he went out after we had eaten our dinner. My mother would say it was all very well having an interest but it would be nice if it was something that put food on the table. One of the delights of my childhood was to be taken to the saloon which was across the road from the library. Children were not meant to enter the bluish darkness with the great pyramids of light from the lamps above the tables, but my father nodded his head to the man at the doorway and said he's keeping an eye on me. He looked down at me and said *Don't you break the place up, do you hear me?* The tables were so brilliant and green that my hope for weeks was simply to touch one. It was my fourth or fifth visit before I asked if I might, and my father surprised me, he gave a quiet laugh and pressed my shoulder and said 'You just go ahead and touch it if that's all you want.' He spoke as though it was nothing at all that I had keyed myself up to ask, and I ran my hand along the side of the table on the smooth varnished wood, then on the table itself, backwards and forwards on the pliant crushed firmness of the felt.

My partner is the one who really makes the money. He brings ideas to me for new lines and especially for new promotion methods and at the board meetings he always begins 'We've decided' or 'We came to the conclusion' and the board believes that when he says 'we' he naturally means the two of us. He is loyal because ten years ago I brought him in against opposition. He had no official qualifications and he is as ugly a man, I suppose, as you are going to get. At the staff barbecues (it is there, I mean, one most notices it) he wears a short sleeved shirt and his guts sag over his belt. His arms are fat and pale and hairless, his hair has receded from a forehead which shines always in a slight glaze of sweat. One looks at him because one must. There is no way of working with a man, of sharing with him the responsibilities of a company, and avoiding his physical insistence. Nor would one ever call his wife attractive, but at least she is not gross, she does not make you want to reach out your hand to remove plate or glass, to spirit away both food and drink because one knows how it will sag and weigh against the strained belt, puff those disagreeable arms. She is a smallish woman and when he stands beside her she seems less than half his size. The lines of her clothes hang parallel from her shoulders to below her knees. It is of no consequence of course what she looks like, whether she were all rotundities or a breathing pencil, but I notice because she is so incongruous beside her husband. They are each a kind of distorting mirror to the other. She lays her thin fingers on the cushion of his forearm, he sometimes rests his arm across her shoulders, his hand hanging loosely in front of her slight breast as though to protect it. Perhaps because her skin is so sallow, so much the colour of a kind of tawny soap, I am reminded of an Eastern woman, perhaps an Indian I may have seen in *National Geographic*, with a plump snake relaxed about her neck. Yet I admit one has so little right to be fastidious with the lives or the choices of others.

Sometimes I see his eyes slightly puckered as against a drift of smoke, and he is taking in my wife and myself. I wonder why he is so meticulous to present me favourably to the board, to share with me what he has a right to keep for himself. Or why when he speaks to the staff in his joking way does he pretend it is my way as well? There is nothing more he can get from the company, he is my full partner although I took him in when the board said quite openly did I know what I was doing? Even then he was fat and smiled. When he covered his eyes with one pale hand at the very first meeting, had opened his fingers and looked at them like a child to see if he was going to be attacked before he explained his figures, they had laughed and they had loved him. Several times over the years they have said they have me to thank for him. And over and over when he begins in those meetings 'We decided' or 'We think it best', he is saying over and over too that he has *me* to thank for them.

I sat on the bench in the hospital corridor, leaning my head on the wall behind me. I wore one of those shapeless blue-towelling hospital gowns and sat cross-legged, while nurses pushed at the noisy swinging doors of the X-ray rooms. An old man sat a few yards from me in a wheelchair. His eyes were receded and his hands constantly smoothed the blanket across his knees. I feel uncomfortable among the sickly, but I continued to watch him. I was wasting the better part of an afternoon to satisfy a doctor I had visited because of occasional digestive pains in my chest. ('We don't know however that it's nothing until we see these,' he told me a few weeks later. He slipped a large negative from its brown envelope and held it against the window so we both could inspect the overlapping of shadow and outline, an aerial photograph it might as well be of a city I did not know, taken through cloud and gathering darkness.) I looked down at the incongruous shoes and socks which the attendant had told me I could keep on, and across to a young man opposite me who sat with bare feet, in a gown identical to my own. Again I glanced at my watch, I suppose with some impatience. A woman beside me said 'Would you like this to look at? It might pass the time.' She held towards me an *Australian Post* which had become dog-eared with handling by the bored and the ill. 'No, thank you,' I told her. I saw her own hands joined together on her lap, the band of a wedding ring on one of her fingers. Beneath the sleeves of her gown the bones of her wrists stood up like little domes. I went back to looking at the old man, at the gleaming lino along the long corridor, hearing the squeak of rubber soles as the nurses came and went. The woman beside me was Eva, and for as long as I was to know her that was her way of sitting, knees together and the fingers of her hands interlacing as they rested across her skirt or her paisley house coat at home, or her naked legs during the summer.

We would joke that we met in a hospital corridor, in our ill-fitting gowns among the clattering of metal trays and the constant swinging of the doors. Later when she went for other X-rays or for tests, I would wait in the larger room at the end of the corridor. It became so much easier to take time away from my office than ever I had thought. I would leave at ten or at twelve or at three, whenever I wished, and I felt the freedom of a boy deciding simply to walk away from school. We would drive to Cornwall Park to the grey constantly stirring olives which Eva loved or to the kiosk in the Domain and once, on a flawless day in early September, we crossed the harbour bridge and walked on sloping paths between the dark green of native trees, above the glitter of the sea. Or more often, and what I preferred, we sat at Eva's home, a small state unit on the other side of the city to where I lived. In our one winter we would sit on a settee in front of an open fire, burning thick lengths of pine which her brother had sent down to her from his farm. The logs hissed and gave out a clean delicate scent. In the part of our one summer we lay in deckchairs at the back of the house, on the small square of grass, protected from neighbours and from wind by a screen of corrugated plastic sheets I had erected for her.

When I think of us it is seldom of one particular time, hardly at all of what we spoke about. I think of that simplest of things, the closeness neither of us needed to work at. It is as though when we were together we moved always under a canopy of content, like some ikon in a procession (which again I saw in Spain). And always Eva's physical stillness is in my mind, her voice which was almost harsh, which knew and carried more of life than any other I have heard. Yet she had not even been to the South Island, where her husband had settled with another family.

For the past eight years, since she came to the city from a small town in the north, she had worked at a warehouse I drove past every day. From the window behind her desk she could see our factory, with my name along the side.

I have said to my wife that I do not want to go out in the next few weeks, not to dinners nor parties nor to the Old Boys' Ball she has mentioned several times. 'You go by all means,' I tell her. 'We have gone with the same group for ten years, you will know everyone there.'

'I wouldn't dream of it,' she says. She smiles to let me know that her disappointment will never show. My partner has said to me several times 'She's a brick, that woman,' so I do not fuss when she is heroic. I say simply 'You may change your mind. You may want to go when the time comes.' She smiles again and shakes her head and there is the faintest of metallic sounds from the movement of her ear-rings.

My wife is the kind of woman everyone says has charm. The last time we were out together, the week before last at another company's social, the woman I was dancing with said 'Your wife's got him eating out of her hand.' She meant one of the directors who wore a hairpiece and who slid his spread hand over my wife's buttock when they turned into the shadow at the further end of the hall. She took the hand and raised it back to her waist. I danced with this younger female because I was obliged to. She was the wife of one of our up and coming men, a boyish petulant man who sat drinking in one of the booths at the side of the floor, his leg out stiffly in front of him in the swathed bandages of an ankle sprained while skiing. When his wife spoke she smiled at me and shook back her hair and I presume I was meant to be a little taken with her charm too. 'Oh,' I said to her, 'has she?' And the young woman I held and turned with and was bored to death by said 'There, every man with a lovely wife likes to play it down.' She gave her gay young executive wife's laugh, and it was like a stick being run across a child's xylophone. I thought as I glanced at the young throat and the breasts raised up by her dress and the folded lace handkerchief affair tucked like some small animal between them that Eva, without looks or charm, was all that mattered in my life after even fourteen months.

As on that night, dancing with the young wives of my staff, or at any other time I think of, alone with my family or going through the hoops with my equally well-trained guests, it is all much the same. I look at the faces in front of me as though at cardboard and plastic; I think of a woman who is nothing and nowhere, and she is more real to me than my own hand. Always as I think of her I am tapping my thick square nails (which Eva liked to play with, to snick her own nails against or press the bands of quick towards their base) on whatever happens to be near me. The vile marble thing on my desk at work or on an ashtray at home, until my wife says 'I don't like to nag but would you mind stopping that? It gets on my nerves.'

'So would breathing if you could hear it,' I answer her. Or once when she asked me if I did it simply to pass the time I said No, it was more than that, it was hearing time pass as well, and she and her daughter looked across at each other 'significantly', as I suppose they would think it. Their look is to say observe how husband and father is over-strained, is in advanced depression, when in fact I am bored, bored. Recently I dreamed of myself fishing a lake. I was sort of trawling with several lines from the back of the boat as we moved along. There was no water in the lake and the hooks dragged at the bottom like the teeth of a plough. As far back as I could see were the neat parallel lines of the dragging hooks. But while I tap my nails against ashtray or table or the wooden arm of a chair, my wife turns her head and raises her hands when she speaks, and her rings and ear-rings sparkle and her voice 'tinkles', as she likes to be told. She sheers like late-afternoon water, I see her standing in life and splashing as a child in the shallows of a river. That is where she speaks from, and I answer from the dry floor of my lake.

My father stopped with me one afternoon at a house much finer than our own. I had been with him at the library for the whole morning. At two o'clock he slipped his jacket over his long white sleeves with the jade links, and the dark waistcoat he did not take off when he worked. I liked to be with him in the room where he did his tasks, and breathe in the odours of glue and ageing paper and the shiny leather chair. His job was to sort out all the papers which came to the library, and put them in the wooden frames that held them together in bunches. There were brass hooks in the frames and the frames hung in rows, and between the rows was like being in a tunnel of papers.

He took his hat from a high shelf and turned it as he always did against his sleeve, while he held the edge of his sleeve in his hand. Sometimes on Saturdays we would go to the snooker saloon where I watched him play, or sometimes to the afternoon pictures. What I remember are stories about the desert and sheiks in long flowing robes and headpieces which flapped behind them as they galloped their horses in a smear of flying sand. There were often clumps of palms where they spoke to women inside silken tents, or cities with wonderfully white walls and high thin towers. After the pictures I would hold his hand when we came onto the street, and everything was so grey and ordinary and dull after what we had seen. But this day he said 'Nice afternoon to stretch the old legs, wouldn't you say?' Often I did not quite know what he meant. Yes, I would say to everything. He took up a parcel of books from the table where a stack of folded newspapers were still in their brown paper wrappings. We walked up the long street to the bridge and then across the tops of the trees. I looked down on the gully through the flicker of the gaps in the concrete fence. Towards the end of the bridge he lifted me right up and I held the small squares of wire and pressed my face close against them. I could look down to the rounded crowns of the trees, and in the bright summer light some of the leaves were shining like glass.

We walked until we came to a house with a verandah around three sides. A lady opened the door and when we stepped inside it was like going into a deep cool cave. My father placed the books on a small table in the hallway where there was a leaning white tower she said was carved out of one tusk of ivory. My father and the lady sat in a large room with heavy curtains folded like in a picture theatre. They sat in there and drank tea from cups which had little flecks in them that you could see through when they were held against the light. The lady took out to the verandah a little tray with a glass of lemonade, and cake I did not like with seeds in every mouthful. I walked round and round the verandah and put my hands through the spaces between the railings, and pulled over a stool from where wire baskets of trailing ferns and creepers were hanging from the roof. I knelt on the stool and leaned against the railing as though I were on a ship. I could look over the gully we had walked across, see the whole span under the bridge like part of a huge hoop. And far down was the harbour, so brightly blue I am sure I remember it as more brilliant than it was.

After our visit to the lady we walked back across the bridge and it was back to what was ordinary. We would just say we had been for a walk when we got home, my father said, this would be our secret. We waited on the safety zone for the tram to take us home. Usually my father let me sit on the thick curved end of the platform while I held on to his arm, but I remember that day we only stood. When we were walking down the small hill towards our own house my father said, as we came near the gate which always snagged for a second because part of the catch had come away, 'Mecca, eh, old man?'

'Yes,' I said to him. I knew that was a kind of secret too, long before I knew whatever else it was.

There is a marble inkstand on my desk, a present my wife brought me back from Mexico two or three years ago. I find that I tap my nails against it most of the time I am sitting at my desk. The lump of marble is off-white and yellowish on different sides, the veins merely darker unattractive streaks. It is like snow when it begins to thaw, that seeping and trickling and discoloration you see in diminishing banks stacked against the side of a road, when it is eaten at the edges and irregular and stained. This is what Zelma's present has reminded me of since the moment she placed it on my lap at home and said 'This is yours, señor,' while the children pranced about in their broad brimmed and sequinned hats. She had loved Acapulco even more than she had thought she would, miles more than Spain on our trip before we had the children, when we had pretended to ourselves that we would return there to live.

'More than Honolulu?' my son asked.

'You don't have to compare things, silly.' She tipped the boy's hat forward so that the brim rested against his shirt front. The shirt was a present too, blue linen with eagles embroidered on the shoulders.

'I almost bought you a shirt, you know,' she said to me.

'Almost?'

'Would you have worn it?'

I looked at the bright embroidered wings and lied, I said 'You just never know.'

'Of course he wouldn't,' my daughter said. 'He'd die if he wore anything with colour in it.'

'You can see him with this hat on too, can't you?' The children held their arms stiffly and strutted as we used to for marching as wooden soldiers, but they were being their father. The boy put his head a little to one side as I suppose I do and gave the curtest of nods several times, his father acknowledging the neighbours. He and the girl and their mother became quite hysterical, 'The idea of him in that gear!' My wife had to sit back and flap herself with both hands until she said 'Now that will do, you've all had your joke.' I put my folded hands beneath my chin and watched them, the eagles moving when the boy's arms moved and the hats flashing as they turned.

'Did you see a bullfight?' I asked her.

'Do you think I'm sick or something?' she said. 'He says did your mother go and watch those barbarians torture a bull to death?' she exclaimed to the children. She closed her eyes at the thought of it and the girl said 'I'd certainly hate to see one, I know that.'

'What about you?' I said to the boy. 'Reckon you could face a bullfight?'

The boy was turning the hat in his hands now, his thumbs edging the brim round and round. He shrugged his shoulders when I asked him what he thought about it. 'Not interested enough to even know?' I said, and my wife and my daughter looked at each other and each raised her eyebrows at the same time. 'We'll leave it there shall we?' my wife said. 'Before we're fighting again.'

I have noticed time and again that they are so close they do not have to speak. I have seen them at parties, they circle and move about like two animals you think are unaware of each other, and yet once they get home each knows exactly what the other has done, to whom the other spoke and when. As they sit together and talk of something again they are feline, precise. They sit above whatever they speak of and nose it, as it were, prod it about with swift careful taps.

One night very recently they were discussing bridal patterns when I came into the lounge before dinner. They were speaking rapidly together, unaware that their husband and father had come into the room until they heard me at the bottles, and I asked them why there was no ice. 'There's ice all right,' my wife said. She moved to stub her half-smoked cigarette.

'Don't you go,' my daughter said to her. 'I'll get it for him.' While she banged at the refrigerator, inserting her arm behind the frozen vegetables and the television dinners to where the one small tray of ice was stuck fast against the back wall, my wife placed her hands palm downwards on the arms of the leather chair, and closed her eyes. She was like an Egyptian statue, something at the door of a monument.

'You'll have to get it for yourself,' my daughter called out. 'It's stuck too hard for me to move.'

'It must have been back there a long enough time,' I said.

'Hard to see how that could happen, the way you go through ice.'

'Well?' I asked her. 'Is that leading up to something?'

'The carving knife's there if you need it,' she said. I chipped between the wall and the metal tray while the girl went back to her mother. As I tugged at the tray to edge it free my hand slipped and my fingers caught against one of the sharp fittings inside the ice-box. Suddenly on the white encrusted ice I saw the small blooms of my own blood, splashes that opened like minute flowers. I looked at the drops for a moment, at the close sequence of stains across the ice, and felt my stomach lift with a kind of disgust. I must have stood for quite some time, fascinated at those vivid splashes that were myself. The others picked up the silence after my chipping with the knife and my daughter called out 'Managed, have you?'

'I've cut my hand,' I said.

'On the knife?'

'On the fridge.' I waited because I thought one of them might move. I pressed my finger in my handkerchief but there was no depth to the cut. Yet I still expected one of them to come across to say is it all right, even to take the tray out for me and put the cubes into my glass. When I turned towards them I saw that both of them were looking at me.

'There's plaster in that drawer,' my wife told me. 'That one right beside you.' I opened the drawer and moved my other hand through the jumble of papers and stamps and rubber bands and tins.

'Manage?' she called again.

'It'll be all right,' I told her. I had found the spool but when I took it from the drawer it was not plaster but masking tape. I left my finger wrapped in my handkerchief and attended again to my drink. I ran the hot tap on the frozen tray, the ice cracking under the stream of steaming water. Neither of the women – for she is that, too, I suppose, my daughter – asked me how it was when I went back into the lounge, my hand concealed in my pocket. I sipped at my gin, the ice-cubes nudging and clicking against one of the thin Danish glasses which my partner had given us last year for a Christmas present. 'Not that I believe in Christmas,' he had said as he gave the box with its gay seasonal wrapping to my wife, 'but I believe in presents.' That was the first night – last Christmas Eve – when I knew how clearly I was watching something on a screen. I have thought of that comparison many times, each time I feel more strongly that what I watch does not really have much to do with me. I now watched the two women and turned my glass slowly to hear the ice. They spoke of whether my daughter's hair would need to be cut if that style were to suit. I watch them as if there is an audience between us, like a man who wonders when he sits in a cinema what those actors must be like once the cameras stop filming, is there any small movement, any inflexion in their voices, which tells him what they are really like? There is no one I know who is not behind make-up, not across a deep pit. I try to think of people who are not on a screen, and I think only of two, of my father and of Eva.

I have said that my partner's strength is that he can get on with people, whether he knows them or not. He tells me that is what selling is about. It is a way of putting your arm around someone's shoulder, talking to him so that he knows you're his friend. I have heard him explain this several times, to the staff or to the board. His hands open and close while he speaks. His face eases into its broad smile or he looks at whoever he is talking to quite solemnly, sincerely. When he opens his hands and shows his palms he has let out the dove of confidence and intimacy. It hovers over the heads of his audience and they feel its presence too, they look back quite as solemnly. Then when his palms meet and close and his thick fingers interlock or rub over each other in a kind of love-making with themselves, the bird has returned, it has disappeared into the magical hands, and those who have listened smile back, or laugh at his own laughing. It is like a man performing in front of a mirror, and his mirror is people.

Once my partner said to me 'I know you think my methods are brash but they are also twenty-six per cent better than those anyone else in this outfit would think of using. That's not a bad return on brashness.' He sat opposite me while I tapped my nails against the marble inkstand. His hands were folded across the rise of his guts, as they usually were when we spoke together. He is far from being a fool and I believe he knew very early on that I did not believe in the dove. He had just delivered his latest advertising thoughts on to the broad unstained blotter of my desk. What he had placed there was a coloured photograph of a foetus, the tiniest veins in the creature's disproportionate head quite visible through its surrounding transparent sac. There were words typed beneath it. *Nobody packages more carefully than we do.*

'I can't claim it's my own idea altogether,' he admitted. 'I've seen it in an American magazine, but no one here's to know that.'

I looked again at the glossy photograph and the words on a narrow strip of paper gummed beneath it. The hands in the picture were like small fins.

'It's a logical extension, though,' he went on. 'Remember that one we used last year of a girl sealed in cellophane for the new Airtex Lunchwrap? Remember that?'

Yes, I told him. There was still a lifesize enlargement of it on the wall of the staff cafeteria.

'We're all a lot more ecologically aware now than we were even twelve months ago,' he said. 'That free advertising we did for the Beech Forest buffs on our food cartons for example. People associate our name with caring about such things.'

'The public?' I asked him.

'People,' he repeated. 'That's why we can't go wrong with this one.' He leaned forward on his thick thighs and a length of pale pink cuff was exposed as his hand spread above the foetus. 'You don't use a photograph like this lightly,' he told me. 'It's something pretty important, after all, pretty delicate. People would know we were serious because we're serious about what we market. Serious the way nature is when it wraps this up, if you like.' The features on the oval face were obscured by the square jut of his index finger. 'We want them to know we take packaging as seriously as that.'

I continued to look down at the photograph when he removed his hand and settled back in his chair. His legs were crossed and one foot jerked slightly as he waited for me to speak. I was amazed at the clarity of what I looked at, the fine detail of the utterly vulnerable and trusting curve of the incompleted body. I had read once how an embryo goes through the whole of evolution, through various stages of fish and other life before it reaches the fully human. I remembered how appalled I had been twenty years ago when the doctor had called me into my wife's room and shown me my newly delivered daughter. The nurse was washing her with a wad of dampened cotton wool, and there were streaks of blood and foam over the tiny chest and legs. The doctor had said *Well aren't you pleased with her?* and I watched the wad move under the mottled arm, the look of discomfort or even pain on the tight screaming face.

'We'll go ahead then?' my partner asked.

'You'll go ahead anyway,' I told him. 'Everyone else will think it's splendid whether you kidnapped it from an American magazine or conceived it yourself.'

He laughed broadly and said 'But you think it's shit?'

'You know what I think of it,' I said.

'Like a bet sales are up fifteen per cent at a minimum on this line within three months?'

'I'd rather bet we'll be into glass coffins before the year's out,' I told him. 'Your concern for the living and the unborn can be carried further than this.'

He stood with one hand on the handle of my door and his other rubbed the back of his neck while he clucked and shook his head. 'Don't know what we're going to do with you, pardner,' he said in a drawling voice.

Before he shut the door I called to him 'Don't you need the photo?'

'I've had half a dozen run off for Friday's meeting,' he said. 'You're welcome to it.'

I slanted the photograph towards the light to examine it more closely. There were even little fingernails on the hands, branched veins in the sac which enveloped the body. I wondered at the minute and intricate being which in time would become one of my partner's people, one of our tenfold profit increase for total additional production costs of maybe five per cent. And then a curious feeling stirred in my stomach as I realized that of course the thing was dead. There could not be a photograph like that unless the child had been removed from its mother. The idea disturbed me, and yet I was amused at my partner's self-congratulation that our care for the people was a huddle of human meat perhaps an hour or two from the first workings of decomposition.

As I said, I watch them. And now they are watching back, even addressing me, which people on a screen or stage should never do. And I remember once I had said to Eva when we were in Wellington together, standing at the window of a hotel from which we could look across the clutter of streets beneath us, would she like to go to a play? I had seen one advertised in the *Dominion* we read together in the taxi from the airport. The paper was spread out over our knees like a sheet, and her hand had rested on mine while she leaned close to the page to read it, because she would not wear glasses. I had kept the play for a surprise.

Through the afternoon, between two meetings, I found my way to the theatre and bought the tickets. We could never go out together like that in Auckland and so now I said, as though I might have asked it any night, did she fancy the theatre? *Love* she said *let's not waste our time together.* I said nothing about the tickets and instead we simply walked about the city. She held my arm and we strolled along the finely curved road beneath the hotel. Every few minutes she would press my arm, bring us to a halt as she pointed or remarked on something which held her eye. When it was dark the lights twinkled up and down the hills. Right above where we stood, as though supporting itself, was the large cross illuminated on the wall of a monastery. I began to say something about religion. Eva said nothing and we were walking on, her hair lifting and blowing across her face and touching my own cheek. She raised her hand to draw back and smooth her hair, and her skin seemed so pale against the darkness. A little further on she said *Do you mind if we rest a while?* She sat on the wall which ran along the seafront, and now we were drenched in the orange glare from the lights along the Parade.

'Tired?' I asked her. And she said to me *Never, I just want to soak it up.* The harbour was streaked with the broad flowing band of a moon which had risen above the hill across the city. It seemed almost exaggerated, like an enormous backdrop. I sat beside Eva on the wall and I said we would never be more contented than this, which of course was true, but at the time Eva said, teasing me, it was because like so many rich people I am sentimental.

'Not that rich,' I said to her. The sea slapped against the wall a few feet beneath us and Eva sat with her head rested against my shoulder. A little later I said that it was turning cool, and although she said she did not notice it, when we stood she asked *could we take a taxi back, love? was that all right?* At the hotel she lay on the bed and told me to switch on the television, it was the night of a programme she knew I usually watched. She lay there with her hair spread across the pillows. *You'll wake me if I nod off?* she demanded. *I don't want to miss a minute of this.*

Eva's brother was a tall man about my own age, his face lined and weathered, with the same grey eyes as his sister. He waited on the top step leading up to the foyer and reception desk, and he moved down the steps as I came towards him. It was eight o'clock in the morning, March the twenty third. There was a cool wind coming in from the mudflats which lifted the soft corners of the man's checked collar. The girl at the reception desk was standing and looked down on us. She must have pointed me out to him as I left my car in the carpark on the other side of the road.

'I'm Eva's brother,' he said. 'I don't want to spend any more time with you than I need.' He looked at me with the hard stare that some men who work the land seem to take on, a hardness that dismisses all divergence as weakness, other ways of life as directly hostile to its own. I have seen his face a hundred times at football matches and on the streets of country towns. Eva had told me, when she first spoke of going to stay with him for a few weeks, that he belonged to some small religious sect. His wife was his only help on the farm, they worked difficult land with the singleness of prophets. She had felt the rest and the country air would help her pick up some of the weight she had lost in the last few months. I said I would drive her north but she had demurred at that, she said her brother wouldn't approve of us, it was better if he didn't know. 'I've come to see you because I could not avoid it, because Eva is dead.' I saw the blue-checked collar rising with the wind and lean back against his jaw. I saw the girl still looking down at us from behind the shine of the plate glass, and Eva's brother cleared his throat. 'The service and the rest of it is over,' he said. 'She wanted to make sure I saw you.'

'She knew?' I said. The words were like dry flakes in my mouth, they were colourless sounds.

'She knew she was pretty sick,' her brother said. 'I'd have thought you'd have known that much. I thought there was more between you than sin.'

'She didn't say that?' I asked. His tongue moved quickly along his lips, he turned from me to look over towards the sea. 'She said nothing very much,' he told me.

There was nothing now I wanted to say to her brother, nothing more for him to say to me. I walked up the steps and through the doors with their gentle hushed closing and into my office. I sat among the routine noises of the morning, looking out between the various factories and across the open patches of land to the slight caps of foam on the shallow inlet, the mud-brown shoreline. I watched the odd movements of wind from inside the stillness of a closed room, watched the rocking of an empty drum in the yard behind the factory. There was the stretched emptiness of the sky above the buildings and the low slope of the hills. 'Eva,' I said. *He would scoop the coloured balls into their wooden triangle and then lean at the end of the table for only the slightest moment, because he seemed always to know what to do, while the other men waited and took practice shots and stooped until their chins were tucked back and quite disappeared, and their eyes were level with the table. His cue was back resting upright in his hand before I had seen it move, the packed balls were scattered and brilliant and flowing across the cloth. Then he would pick them off one by one,* tock *and* tock, *then the soft catching noise as the first fell into the pockets, and the different kind of click as one after another bulged out the nets in the corners or in the centre of the table.* As I said Eva's name I had stood for a second in the intensity of what never comes back, in the curling bluish drifts of smoke and under the bright pyramid of light which I had not thought of for years. And yet now I seem to think always of two things at once, or of one person who immediately brings to mind the other. They are not ghosts, they are what everything else is seen by, is paled against, until what I look at in front of me is not even a film. It is a negative hung at a window, I see by the light from the other side.

They have come to look at me and so to sympathize, to take my elbow on one side with the wifely hands of concern and duty, my elbow on the other with the feeling and the intimacy of having spoken with me daily for a dozen years. I am part of their rights, I am what they have worked at and are entitled to. I am their guarantee that *they* are sane. I let them take me across the yellow earth to where my daughter's fiancé holds open the door of the car.

My daughter with tears in her eyes and my wife who does not wear make-up because her paleness is the marking of her grief, now sit one on either side of me in the back seat. My fat partner accelerates and the white line in the middle of the road disappears beneath the long shining bonnet of his car, an endless ribbon he devours. I sit quite calmly and consider how I am branded because I have stood for longer than usual in one place among the machines and graders of the extended motorway, looked down into a hole where a beautiful house once stood. There was a verandah on the house, and leaning on its rail, my knees supported by a stool, was like leaning over the rail of a ship. I stand on the wet clay and remember my father, and a woman I loved, who are also gone into smaller but identical holes. To think of that seems to me the very best of reasons to stand so still, to wonder what there can be to make moving a matter of any consequence. I have looked things in the face because they are not there.

Yet my wife and my daughter, my partner and my daughter's boyfriend, for all their love of things, their touching and their endless talk and their hating to be alone, do not believe in what they see. All *that* – the bodies, the cars, the Mexican ashtrays – is for them no more than a sketch of what is real, of what might be. They believe that reality is something they shall make from all these things, not these things themselves. They now look at me from either side, in discreet glances in the rear-vision mirror. I am smiling slightly which confirms all that they suspect. I am smiling because I am with four people who think that our travelling at forty miles an hour along Great North Road, in the silence of tact and apprehension, will make some difference to anything at all. They are like those mad saints of centuries ago, men who would not believe that the world is what it is, but a distortion from its true shape that love and charity and worship could somehow wrench it back to.

We are now travelling past the used-car marts with their bright strings of flapping plastic flags, with words spelled out in little metal discs which shimmer endlessly against the light and wind. We are coming towards the turn where a church sits high on one's left, a tall grey finger of stone against the sky. I consider for a moment with some amusement that we are a procession from that old time I was thinking of. My partner who is like St Francis opens his thick hands and the doves of fifteen per cent hover at his shoulder, move with their strutting walk along his extended arms. My own wife with her eyes cast down, my daughter like a novice, my devoted son-in-law of two months' time, beside and behind that franciscan flesh as he leads me to where I shall be questioned, dressed in a special robe, touched and tampered with by men who will work towards that miracle, to turn my world to theirs. They shall give me the cool pastures of a private room, the quiet waters of their choice. And on the green slats of their garden seats I shall be silent as a boy who walks from a picture theatre holding his father's hand, who looks at the bald streets with eyes fresh from palms and minarets.

The Professional

I decided pretty early on that if the only way you can survive this tangle we call 'life' is by telling lies, then you can't be too careful about the lies you're going to tell. Before I was ten it occurred to me that the kids who were great liars, who were caught and thrashed and stood in corners were the lesser brotherhood, they were *bad* liars. They were fabulists, fantasists, they in fact wanted a different world to the one they existed in. They wanted a lie to be like a cowboy film that they suddenly lived in, as if their doctoring truth would set them on the dappled horse, make the pearl-handled guns blaze in their hands. They are the ones who never knew what the true point of lying was – that its gift is balance. It is carrying across a room a glass with the water not only to the brim, but a little above the brim, while everyone expects it to spill. A lie is that meniscus. It's the arc where you control the appearance of things.

Let me start with a story.

Zeta Adams was a girl in my class at primary school. She was at least a foot taller than any other girl, and her face was nearly flat. I mean her chin was level, exactly, with her forehead, and her broad nose rose only slightly from the plane of her face. Freckles crowded on its bridge then spread out more sparsely across her cheeks. She had a younger brother called Leo in another classroom. He used to foul himself occasionally, and his sister would be sent for. It was a kind of sport for the rest of us, when the crisis arose, to line up along the windows of the standard four classroom, above the school hall, and look down on the pair of them. Tall Zeta, her legs shapeless and dead white beneath the gymfrock which she wore without the plaited gold girdle that the girls were supposed to wear; and beside her, holding her hand, her young brother walking awkwardly, comically, towards the school lavatories, where one supposed the crisis somehow would be attended to. When she came back to class she would grin at the calls that went up. If she was provoked too far, she would pick up a book, an inkwell, a pencil case, and heave it towards whatever angered her.

Of course, Zeta was several other things besides her brother's keeper, and as tall as a grown up. She was also dumb, and fairly dirty, and the skin on her neck tended to flake. Anyone who sat next to her moved over towards the wall and called out 'Snow storm. Watch it!' She was always worth provoking because her temper could run to teachers quite as much as to her fellow-pupils. Once she threatened to jump out of the window, to leap twenty-five feet to the asphalt playground beneath, if the bitch of a teacher, as she called out, took another step towards her. And so she was sat finally by me.

I was the smallest, and the cleverest, and perhaps the best-behaved in the class. I think the teacher thought I was the last chance of shaming her into some kind of couthness. Zeta took her books, and a ruler with the figures almost totally hidden beneath layers of red ink, and shifted in next to me. I made a point of helping her, which no one else would do, and I believe that marginally her pages of grubby confused schoolwork improved. I told her what the simple words were that she baulked at, and once when the message came through from the other block of classrooms that Leo needed his sister, I offered to go with her. The teacher insisted it wasn't necessary, there was no reason at all, she said, why other people should be roped into a family concern. So Zeta once again walked from the classroom, her broad face silly and flushed with the attention. A few minutes later we looked down on the pair of them, Leo bow-legged, clutching his sister's hand. But she had heard my offer to go with her, and from then she was as attentive to me as a pet dog. She would have torn anyone apart had I sooled her onto them. And knowing she was at heel like that pleased me, I suppose, more than actually using her. The less she could do for me, the more she wanted to do. A few times she picked up imaginary slights, and jumped to defend me. She would stand between me and the supposed enemy, a wall of defensive and stupid flesh. 'Leave them, Zeta,' I would order her. And as the minister who used to talk to us about religion recently had gone over Easter week with us, and explained that strange part of the story where Peter cut off the soldier's ear, and Christ joined it on again, even though that soldier may have been the very one who scourged him a few hours later, I felt a sense of virtue when I restrained her.

There's nothing more interesting to say about Zeta Adams once those few facts are told. The point of her story is that about six weeks after she became devoted to me, I stole a green propelling pencil from Irene Duffy. It was a present from her aunt who had travelled round the world, the kind of souvenir that could be bought for a dollar, but was a thing of exotic beauty to the whole class. There were tiny holes near the top, and when you held these close to your eye, and turned towards the light, you saw St Mark's Square in one, and the Houses of Parliament in another, and in the third an avenue in Paris, stretching on and on, trees in leaf along its sides, a great stone arch in the distance. I had never coveted a thing so much. I thought of it when I was at home, and walking to school, and years later when I first saw those places for myself, there was an excitement that went back to Irene Duffy's pencil, held up against the light. After a week, when its glamour was wearing thin for everyone else, I saw it lying on her desk while the class was at the windows, watching a truck dumping earth for the new playground. In the same second I saw it, and knew no one else was looking, I took it in my hand and slipped it under my desk. I then joined the press of children at the window, watching the earth on the raised back of the truck begin to slip, slowly, then gather force, then rush in a brown rapid arc from the tray. The teacher said 'Go back to your desks now,' and a second later the cry went up that Irene's pencil had disappeared. We all had to change rows and search each other's desks, and the pencil was found between Zeta's books and mine. There was confusion for the next few minutes, the class turning and pointing and accusing, the teacher calling for silence, demanding that Irene stop bawling, for goodness sake, the thing had been found, hadn't it? We were told to go back to our places, whoever was responsible would be properly punished. This long after, I don't remember what that was. What survives is the feeling I had while I stood and faced the teacher and said nothing for Zeta, nor against her. It was a feeling of great clarity, as I saw what power there was in saying nothing: a feeling that control and indifference are perhaps the same thing, as the plane of Zeta's face turned towards me and I saw the afternoon light fall across her paleness, her eyes a little distended like an animal's in panic, her new and sudden confusion because she did not know whether I lied or not, whether I should be defended or not.

I could tell you three, four stories like that. One would be about my husband, a tall, gentle man who forty years ago had to hold onto the rail of a verandah to cover the trembling of his hands when I said to him 'No, Desmond. I am sure about it. I know it was from that weekend.' I was twenty-six, he was a year younger, we were on his uncle's farm and I didn't look up when I told him but wound a thread of clematis stalk, I remember, around my finger. 'Who else?' I asked him. 'Who else could it be?'

That would be one story, say.

Another could be about Desmond's friend, the partner in his firm, and the man he sailed with half the summer. He was a widower, and my lover. And Desmond asked me once if it was true, and I said 'Ah, poor Tom. Why did he have to spread stories like that about us? Because our life is something he doesn't have?' There are one or two others. If I want an image for them it would be something like a boat running before a breeze on a splendid day. You move the tiller really to make your course a little finer, you don't do it to overturn. You do it for the excitement of control.

The children come to visit me, my dark son, my fair daughter, my grandchildren who prop *their* children on the foot of my bed, and I pass the young ones the grapes they have really come to see me for. There is a girl like Desmond in early photos of him, who looks down and doesn't know what to say when I ask her does she like me best, or me and my big bowl of fruit together? And a boy, a little younger, who is my favourite, who tells me 'Oh, you don't have to say you like one thing more just because you like something else as well, do you Gran?'

The staff here tend to fuss me because I'm a 'good' patient. That means I'm not senile nor dirty nor complaining. I know there's not a thing, in the long run, that can alter things by a jot, so why perform about them? I've never been one to ask for that dappled horse, for that blazing pistol, so to speak. But there's a young man who used to call once a week, who now pops in every day because, as he says, he just happens to be passing. He puts his bible on his knee and smiles at me, he hardly mentions his wares. I expect he works on the principle that a bald man couldn't sit with a wig salesman every single day and not *hint* at the little bag of samples, could he?

So I tell him 'Yes, do come again,' and 'It's very good of you to drop in.' And when he says a short prayer just before he goes, I close my eyes until it is over. One of these days we may catch each other in the right light, the way one had to turn Irene Duffy's pencil. If I'm that impressed again, if the trees look as leafy and green and the lagoon shines still just as brightly as it used to, then I may well want this little window to peer through too. I may want the young man to talk on about what he's waiting, of course, to tell me. Hold my hand, I may ask him, help me to cross the room without spilling a drop.

PATRICIA GRACE

A Way of Talking

Rose came back yesterday; we went down to the bus to meet her. She's just the same as ever Rose. Talks all the time flat out and makes us laugh with her way of talking. On the way home we kept saying, 'E Rohe, you're just the same as ever.' It's good having my sister back and knowing she hasn't changed. Rose is the hard-case one in the family, the kamakama one, and the one with the brains.

Last night we stayed up talking till all hours, even Dad and Nanny who usually go to bed after tea. Rose made us laugh telling about the people she knows, and taking off professor this and professor that from varsity. Nanny, Mum, and I had tears running down from laughing; e ta Rose we laughed all night.

At last Nanny got out of her chair and said, 'Time for sleeping. The mouths steal the time of the eyes.' That's the lovely way she has of talking, Nanny, when she speaks in English. So we went to bed and Rose and I kept our mouths going for another hour or so before falling asleep.

This morning I said to Rose that we'd better go and get her measured for the dress up at Mrs Frazer's. Rose wanted to wait a day or two but I reminded her the wedding was only two weeks away and that Mrs Frazer had three frocks to finish.

'Who's Mrs Frazer anyway,' she asked. Then I remembered Rose hadn't met these neighbours though they'd been in the district a few years. Rose had been away at school.

'She's a dressmaker,' I looked for words. 'She's nice.'

'What sort of nice?' asked Rose.

'Rose, don't you say anything funny when we go up there,' I said. I know Rose, she's smart. 'Don't you get smart.' I'm older than Rose but she's the one that speaks out when something doesn't please her. Mum used to say, Rohe you've got the brains but you look to your sister for the sense. I started to feel funny about taking Rose up to Jane Frazer's because Jane often says the wrong thing without knowing.

We got our work done, had a bath and changed, and when Dad came back from the shed we took the station-wagon to drive over to Jane's. Before we left we called out to Mum, 'Don't forget to make us a Maori bread for when we get back.'

'What's wrong with your own hands,' Mum said, but she was only joking. Always when one of us comes home one of the first things she does is make a big Maori bread.

Rose made a good impression with her kamakama ways, and Jane's two nuisance kids took a liking to her straight away. They kept jumping up and down on the sofa to get Rose's attention and I kept thinking what a waste of a good sofa it was, what a waste of a good house for those two nuisance things. I hope when I have kids they won't be so hoha.

I was pleased about Jane and Rose. Jane was asking Rose all sorts of questions about her life in Auckland. About varsity and did Rose join in the marches and demonstrations. Then they went on to talking about fashions and social life in the city, and Jane seemed deeply interested. Almost as though she was jealous of Rose and the way she lived, as though she felt Rose had something better than a lovely house and clothes and everything she needed to make life good for her. I was pleased to see that Jane liked my sister so much, and proud of my sister and her entertaining and friendly ways.

Jane made a cup of coffee when she'd finished measuring Rose for the frock, then packed the two kids outside with a piece of chocolate cake each. We were sitting having coffee when we heard a truck turn in at the bottom of Frazers' drive.

Jane said, 'That's Alan. He's been down the road getting the Maoris for scrub cutting.'

I felt my face get hot. I was angry. At the same time I was hoping Rose would let the remark pass. I tried hard to think of something to say to cover Jane's words though I'd hardly said a thing all morning. But my tongue seemed to thicken and all I could think of was Rohe don't.

Rose was calm. Not all red and flustered like me. She took a big pull on the cigarette she had lit, squinted her eyes up and blew the smoke out gently. I knew something was coming.

'Don't they have names?'

'What. Who?' Jane was surprised and her face was getting pink.

'The people from down the road whom your husband is employing to cut scrub.' Rose the stink thing, she was talking all Pakehafied.

'I don't know any of their names.'

I was glaring at Rose because I wanted her to stop but she was avoiding my looks and pretending to concentrate on her cigarette.

'Do they know yours?'

'Mine?'

'Your name.'

'Well . . . yes.'

'Yet you have never bothered to find out their names or to wonder whether or not they have any.'

The silence seemed to bang around in my head for ages and ages. Then I think Jane muttered something about difficulty, but that touchy sister of mine stood up and said, 'Come on Hera.' And I with my red face and shut mouth followed her out to the station-wagon without a goodbye or anything.

I was so wild with Rose. I was wild. I was determined to blow her up about what she had done, I was determined. But now that we were alone together I couldn't think what to say. Instead I felt an awful big sulk coming on. It has always been my trouble, sulking. Whenever I don't feel sure about something I go into a big fat sulk. We had a teacher at school who used to say to some of us girls, 'Speak, don't sulk.' She'd say, 'You only sulk because you haven't learned how and when to say your minds.'

She was right that teacher, yet here I am a young woman about to be married and haven't learned yet how to get the words out. Dad used to say to me, 'Look out girlie, you'll stand on your lip.'

At last I said, 'Rose, you're a stink thing.' Tears were on the way. 'Gee Rohe, you made me embarrassed.' Then Rose said, 'Don't worry Honey she's got a thick hide.'

These words of Rose's took me by surprise and I realized something about Rose then. What she said made all my anger go away and I felt very sad because it's not our way of talking to each other. Usually we'd say, 'Never mind Sis,' if we wanted something to be forgotten. But when Rose said, 'Don't worry Honey she's got a thick hide,' it made her seem a lot older than me, and tougher, and as though she knew much more than me about the world. It made me realize too that underneath her jolly and forthright ways Rose is very hurt. I remembered back to when we were both little and Rose used to play up at school if she didn't like the teacher. She'd get smart and I used to be ashamed and tell Mum on her when we got home, because although she had the brains I was always the well behaved one.

Rose was speaking to me in a new way now. It made me feel sorry for her and for myself. All my life I had been sitting back and letting her do the objecting. Not only me, but Mum and Dad and the rest of the family too. All of us too scared to make known when we had been hurt or slighted. And how can the likes of Jane know when we go round pretending all is well. How can Jane know us?

But then I tried to put another thought into words. I said to Rose, 'We do it too. We say, "the Pakeha doctor", or "the Pakeha at the post office", and sometimes we mean it in a bad way.'

'Except that we talk like this to each other only. It's not so much what is said, but when and where and in whose presence. Besides, you and I don't speak in this way now, not since we were little. It's the older ones: Mum, Dad, Nanny who have this habit.'

Then Rose said something else. 'Jane Frazer will still want to be your friend and mine in spite of my embarrassing her today; we're in the fashion.'

'What do you mean?'

'It's fashionable for a Pakeha to have a Maori for a friend.' Suddenly Rose grinned. Then I heard Jane's voice coming out of that Rohe's mouth and felt a grin of my own coming. 'I have friends who are Maoris. They're lovely people. The eldest girl was married recently and I did the frocks. The other girl is at varsity. They're all so *friendly* and so *natural* and their house is absolutely *spotless*.'

I stopped the wagon in the drive and when we'd got out Rose started strutting up the path. I saw Jane's way of walking and felt a giggle coming on. Rose walked up Mum's scrubbed steps, 'Absolutely spotless'. She left her shoes in the porch and bounced into the kitchen. 'What did I tell you? Absolutely spotless. And a friendly natural woman taking new bread from the oven.'

Mum looked at Rose then at me. 'What have you two been up to? Rohe I hope you behaved yourself at that Pakeha place?' But Rose was setting the table. At the sight of Mum's bread she'd forgotten all about Jane and the events of the morning.

When Dad, Heke, and Matiu came in for lunch, Rose, Mum, Nanny and I were already into the bread and the big bowl of hot corn.

'E ta,' Dad said. 'Let your hardworking father and your two hardworking brothers starve. Eat up.'

'The bread's terrible. You men better go down to the shop and get you a shop bread,' said Rose.

'Be the day,' said Heke.

'Come on my fat Rohe. Move over and make room for your Daddy. Come on my baby shift over.'

Dad squeezed himself round behind the table next to Rose. He picked up the bread Rose had buttered for herself and started eating. 'The bread's terrible all right,' he said. Then Mat and Heke started going on about how awful the corn was and who cooked it and who grew it, who watered it all summer and who pulled out the weeds.

So I joined in the carryings on and forgot about Rose and Jane for the meantime. But I'm not leaving it at that. I'll find some way of letting Rose know I understand and I know it will be difficult for me because I'm not clever the way she is. I can't say things the same and I've never learnt to stick up for myself.

But my sister won't have to be alone again. I'll let her know that.

Valley

Summer

The sun-filled sky wraps the morning in warmth. Already the asphalt has begun to shimmer with light and heat, and the children are arriving.

They spill out of the first bus with sandwiches and cordial, in twos and threes, heads together, strangely quiet. Uncertain they stand with bare feet warming on asphalt, clutching belongings, wondering. They are wondering what I will be like.

It is half past eight. I am watching from my kitchen window and see them glance this way, wondering. In a minute or two I will be ready to go over for them to look at me, but now they are moving away slowly, slapping feet on the warmed playground.

They are wondering what he will be like too. He is in his classroom already, sorting out names, chalking up reminders, and cleaning dead starlings from the grate of the chipheater in the corner. They stand back from the glass doors and stare, and he comes out with the dead birds on a shovel and gives them to a big boy to take away and bury. They all stare, and the younger ones wonder if he killed the birds, but the older ones know that starlings get trapped in the chimneys every summer and have to be cleaned out always on the first day of school.

I pick up the baby and my bag and walk across. Their eyes are on me.

'Hullo,' I say, but no one speaks, and they hurry away to the middle room, which is Tahi's, because they know her. Some of them call her Mrs Kaa because they have been told to; others call her Auntie because she is their aunt; and others call her Hey Tahi because they are little and don't know so much.

At nine he rings the bell and makes a come-here sign with his arm. They see, and know what he wants, and walk slowly to stand on the square of concrete by the staffroom steps. They stand close together, touching, and he tells them his name and mine. Then he reads their names from a list and Tahi tells each where to stand. Soon we have three groups: one for the little room which is mine, one for the middle room which is hers, and one for the big room which is his.

We find a place for the sandwiches and cordial and then they sit looking at me and not speaking, wondering what I am like.

I put the baby on a rug with his toys. I put my bag by the table, then write my name on the board to show them how it looks. And I read it for them so they will know its sound. I write baby's name as well and read it too, but they remain silent.

And when I say good morning they look at one another and at the floor, so I tell them what to say. But, although some open their mouths and show a certain willingness, no sound comes out. Some of them are new and haven't been to school before and all of them are shy.

The silence frightens me, beating strongly into the room like sun through glass.

But suddenly one of them speaks.

He jumps up and points excitedly. Necks swivel.

'Hey! You fullas' little brother, he done a mimi. Na!'

And there is little Eru with a puddle at his feet. And there we are, they and I, with a sentence hanging in the sun-filled room waiting for another to dovetail its ending.

I thank him and ask his name but his mouth is shut again. The little girl in shirt and rompers says, 'He's Samuel.'

'Mop?' Samuel asks, and means shall I get the wet mop from the broom cupboard and clean up the puddle. Which is friendly of him.

'Yes please,' I say, but again he stands confused.

Shirt and rompers shoves him towards the door. 'Go,' she says.

He mops up the water and washes the mop at the outside tap. Then he stands on the soggy mop-strings with his warmed feet, and the water squeezes out and runs in little rivers, then steams dry. Samuel wears large serge shorts belted with a man's necktie and there is one button on his shirt. His large dark eyes bulge from a wide flat face like two spuds. His head is flat too, and his hair has been clipped round in a straight line above his ears. The hair that is left sticks straight up as though he is wearing a kina.

Shirt and rompers tells me all the names and I write them on the board. Her name is Margaret.

> Samuel
> Margaret
> Kopu, Hiriwa
> Cowboy
> Lillian, Roimata
> Glen
> Wiki, Steven
> Marama, Evelyn
> Michael, Edie
> Hippy
> Stan.

We have made a poem. The last two are twins; I don't know how I'll ever tell them apart.

We find a place for everyone at the tables and a locker for each one's belongings, but although they talk in whispers and nudge one another they do not offer me any words. And when I speak to them they nod or shake their heads. Their eyes take the floor.

The play bell rings and I let them go. They eat briefly, swig at the cordial or go to the drinking taps. Then they pad across the hot asphalt to the big field where the grass is long and dry. Then they begin to run and shout through the long grass as though suddenly they have been given legs and arms, as though the voices have at that moment been put into them.

Ahead of them the grasshoppers flick up and out into the ever-heating day.

Hiriwa sits every morning at the clay table modelling clay. He is a small boy with a thin face and the fingers that press into the clay are long, and careful about what they do.

This morning he makes a cricket – female by the pointed egg-laying mechanism on its tail. He has managed the correct angles of the sets of legs, and shows the fine rasps on the hind set by lifting little specks of clay with his pencil. Soon he will tell me a story so I can write for him; then later he will show the children what he has made and read the story for them.

We collected the crickets yesterday because we are learning about insects and small animals in summer. The crickets are housed in a large jar containing damp earth and stones and a wine biscuit. The book tells me that this is the way to keep crickets, and they seem content enough to live like this as they begin their ringing in the warmth of mid-morning.

Two weeks ago we walked down past the incinerator to where nasturtiums flood a hollow of ground at the edge of bush, covering long grass and fern beginnings with round dollar leaves and orange and gold honey flowers blowing trumpets at the sky.

The first thing was to sit among the leaves and suck nectar from the flowers, which wasn't why we had come but had to be done first. And it gave us a poem for the poem book too. Roimata, who finds a secret language inside herself, gave us the poem:

> I squeeze the tail off the nasturtium flower
> And suck the honey,
> The honey runs all round inside me,
> Making me sweet
> Like sugar,
> And treacle,
> And lollies,
> And chocolate fish.
> And all the children lick my skin
> And say, 'Sweet, sweet,
> Roimata is a sweet, sweet girl.'

The next thing was to turn each flat nasturtium leaf carefully and look on the soft green underside for the pinprick sized butterfly eggs. We found them there, little ovals of yellow, like tiny turned-on light bulbs, and found the mint-green caterpillars too, chewing holes in their umbrellas.

The next thing was to put down the leaves they had picked and to begin rolling down the bank in the long grass, laughing and shouting, which wasn't why we had come but had to be done as well:

> I rolled busting down the bank
> On cold seagrass,
> And I thought I was a wave of the sea,
> But I am only a skinny girl
> With sticking out eyes,
> And two pigtails
> That my Nanny plaits every morning
> With spider fingers.

Now all the eggs have hatched, and every afternoon they pick fresh leaves for the caterpillars. Every morning we find the leaves eaten to the stems, and the table and floor littered with black droppings like scattered crumbs of burnt toast.

The caterpillars are at several stages of growth. Some are little threads of green cotton, and difficult to see, camouflaged by the leaf and its markings. Others are half grown and working at the business of growing by eating steadily all day and night. The largest ones are becoming sluggish with growth, and have gone away from food and attached themselves to the back of the room to pupate:

> The caterpillar,
> Up on the classroom wall,
> Spins a magic house around itself
> To hide from all the boys and girls.

Then yesterday on coming in from lunch we found the first of the butterflies, wing-beating the sun-filled room in convoy. We kept them for the afternoon, then let them out the window and watched them fly away:

Butterfly out in the sun,
Flying high by the roof,
'Look up there,' Kopu said.
'Butterfly. Na.
The best butterfly.
I want to be a butterfly flying.'

I said that he would tell me a story to write about his cricket. And that later he would show the children what he had made and read the story for them. But I turned and saw his arm raised and his fist clenched. His thin arm, with the small fingers curled, like a daisy stem with its flower closed after sundown. The fist came down three times on the carefully modelled insect. Head, thorax, abdomen. He looked at what he'd done and walked away.

'Why?' I asked but he had no words for me.

'That's why, he don't like it,' Samuel told me.

'That's why, his cricket is too dumb,' Kopu said.

Those two have made a bird's nest out of clay and are filling it with little round eggs, heaping the eggs up as high as they will go.

'I made a nest.'

'I made some eggs.'

I made a cricket as best I could with my careful fingers. Then my flower hand thumped three times down on the cricket. Abdomen, thorax, head. And my cricket is nothing but clay.

Autumn

Autumn bends the lights of summer and spreads evening skies with reds and golds. These colours are taken up by falling leaves which jiggle at the fingertips of small-handed winds.

Trees give off crowds of starlings which shoot the valley with scarcely a wing beat, flocking together to replace warmth stolen by diminishing sun.

Feet that were soft and supple in summer are hardening now and, although it is warm yet, cardigans and jerseys are turning up in the lost-property box. And John, our neighbour, looks into his vat one morning and sees a single sheet of milk lining the bottom. He puts his herd out and goes on holiday.

Each day we have been visiting the trees – the silver poplar, the liquid amber, and the plum, peach, and apple. And, on looking up through the branches, each day a greater patch of sky is visible. Yet, despite this preoccupation with leaves and colours and change, the greater part of what we see has not changed at all. The gum tree as ever leaves its shed bark, shed twigs, shed branches untidily on its floor, and the pohutukawa remains dull and lifeless after its December spree and has nothing new for this season.

About us are the same green paddocks where cows undulate, rosetting the grass with soft pancake plops; and further on in the valley the variegated greens of the bush begin, then give way to the black-green of distant hills.

They have all gone home. I tidy my table, which is really a dumping ground for insects in matchboxes, leftover lunches and lost property. Then I go out to look for Eru. The boys are pushing him round in the wood cart and he is grinning at the sky with his four teeth, two top and two bottom, biting against each other in ecstasy.

Tahi is in the staffroom peeling an apple. She points the knife into the dimple of apple where the stem is and works the knife carefully in a circle. A thin wisp of skin curls out from the blade. She peels slowly round and down the apple, keeping the skin paper-thin so that there is neither a speck of skin on the apple nor a speck of apple flesh left on the skin. Nor is there a ridge or a bump on the fruit when she has finished peeling. A perfect apple. Skinless. As though it has grown that way on the tree.

Then she stands the apple on a plate and slashes it down the middle with a knife as though it is nothing special and gives me half.

'Gala Day in five days' time,' she says.

'Yes,' I say. 'They'll want to practise for the races.'

'We always have a three-legged and a sack.'

Then Ed comes in and picks up the phone.

'I've got to order a whole lot of stuff for the gala. Gala in five days' time.'

We wake this morning to the scented burning of manuka and, looking out, see the bell-shaped figure of Turei Mathews outlined by the fire's light against the half-lit morning. He stands with his feet apart and his hands bunched on his spread waist, so that his elbows jut. With his small head and his short legs, he looks like a pear man in a fruit advertisement, except that he has a woman's sunhat pulled down over his ears.

Beside him Ron and Skippy Anderson are tossing branches into the flames and turning the burning sticks with shovels. We hear the snap, snap of burning tea tree and see the flames spread and diminish, spread, diminish – watch the ash-flakes spill upwards and outwards into lighting day.

Yesterday afternoon Turei, Ron, and Skippy brought the truckload of wood and the hangi stones and collected the two wire baskets from the hall. They spat on their hands, took up the shovels, and dug the hole, then threw their tools on the back of the truck and went.

Yesterday Ed and the boys put up the tents, moved tables and chairs, and set up trestles. The girls tidied the grounds, covered tables with newspaper, and wrote numbers in books for raffles.

We were worried by clouds yesterday. But now on waking we watch the day lighting clear; we pack our cakes and pickles into a carton and are ready to leave.

By eight o'clock the cars and trucks are arriving and heaving out of their doors bags of corn, kumara, potatoes, pumpkin, and hunks of meat. Women establish themselves under the gum tree with buckets of water, peelers, and vegetable knives. Turei and his helpers begin zipping their knives up and down steel in preparation for slicing into the pork. Tahi is organizing the cakes and pickles and other goods for sale. Eru is riding in the wood cart, and Ed is giving out tins for raffle money. I take up my peeler and go towards the gum tree.

Roimata's grandmother is there.

'It's a good day,' she says.

'Yes,' I say. 'We are lucky.'

'I open these eyes this morning and I say to my mokopuna, "The day it is good." She flies all around tidying her room, making her bed, no trouble. Every smile she has is on her face. I look at her and I say, "We got the sun outside in the sky, and we got the sun inside dancing around." I try to do her hair for her. "Hurry, Nanny, hurry," she says. "Anyhow will do." "Anyhow? Anyhow?" I say. "Be patient, Roimata, or they all think it's Turei's dog coming to the gala." '

Opposite me Taupeke smokes a skinny fag, and every now and again takes time off from peeling for a session of coughing. Her face is as old as the hills, but her eyes are young and birdlike and watchful. Her coughing has all the sounds of a stone quarry in full swing, and almost sends her toppling from the small primer chair on which she sits.

'Too much this,' she explains to me, pointing to her tobacco tin. 'Too much cigarette, too much cough.'

And Connie next to her says, 'Yes, Auntie. You take off into space one of these days with your cough.'

She nods. 'Old Taupeke be a sputnik then. Never mind. I take my old tin with me. No trouble.'

Hiriwa's mother is there too. She is pale and serious-looking and very young. Every now and again Hiriwa comes and stands beside her and watches her working; his small hands rest lightly on her arm, his wrist bones protrude like two white marbles. I notice a white scar curving from her temple to her chin.

Tahi comes over and says, 'Right give us a spud,' then spreads her bulk on a primer chair and begins her reverent peeling. A tissue-thin paring spirals downward from her knife.

'How are you Auntie? How are you Connie? How are you Rita? Gee Elsie you want to put your peel in the hangi and throw your kumara away.'

'Never mind,' says Elsie. 'That's the quick way. Leave plenty on for the pigs.'

'Hullo Auntie, hullo ladies. How are all these potato and kumara getting on?' asks Turei. He takes off his sunhat and wipes the sweat from his neck and head.

'Never mind our potato and kumara,' Tahi says. 'What about your stones? Have you cooks got the stones hot? We don't want our pork jumping off our plates and taking off for the hills.'

'No trouble,' Turei says. 'The meal will be superb. Extra delicious.'

'Wii! Listen to him talk.'

'You got a mouthful there Turei!'

'Plenty of kai in the head, that's why,' he says.

'And plenty in the puku too. Na. Plenty of hinu there Turei.'

'Ah well. I'm going. You women slinging off at my figure I better go.'

He puts his hat on and pats his paunch. 'Hurry up with those vegies. Not too much of the yakkety-yak.' He ambles away followed by a bunch of kids and a large scruffy dog.

The sacks are empty. We have peeled the kumara and potatoes, stripped and washed the corn, and cut and skinned the pumpkin. The prepared vegetables are in buckets of water and we stand to go and wash our hands.

But suddenly we are showered with water. We are ankle deep in water and potatoes, kumara, pumpkin, and corn. Connie, who hasn't yet stood, has a red bucket upside down on her lap and she is decorated with peelings. Turei's dog is running round and round and looks as though he has been caught in a storm.

'Turei, look what your mutt did,' Tahi yells, and Turei hurries over to look, while the rest of us stand speechless. Taupeke's cigarette is hanging down her chin like an anaemic worm.

'That mutt of mine, he can't wait for hangi. He has to come and get it now. Hey you kids. Come and pick up all this. Come on you kids.'

The kids like Turei and they hang around. They enjoy watching him get the hangi ready and listening to him talk.

'They're the best stones,' he tells them. 'These old ones that have been used before. From the river these stones.'

The boys take their shirts off because Turei wears only a singlet over his big drum chest.

'How's that, Turei?' they ask, showing off their arm muscles.

'What's that?' he says.

'What you think?'

'I seen pipis in the sand bigger than that.'

'You got too much muscles, Turei.'

'Show us, Turei.'

'Better not. Might be you'll get your eyes sore.'

'Go on,' they shout.

So he puts the shovel down, and they all watch the big fist shut and the thick forearm pull up while the great pumpkin swells and shivers at the top of his arm.

'Wii na Turei! Some more, Turei.'
'You kids don't want any kai? You want full eyes and empty pukus?'
'Some more, Turei. Some more.'
But Turei is shovelling the white-hot stones into the hangi hole. 'You kids better move. Might be I'll get you on the end of this shovel and stick you all in the hole.'
He makes towards them and they scatter.
The prepared food is covered with cloths and the baskets are lowered over the stones. Steam rises as the men turn on the hose. They begin shovelling earth on to the covered food.
'Ready by twelve,' one of them says.
'Better be sweet.'
'Superb. Extra delicious.'
'Na. Listen to the cook talk.'

Over at the chopping arena the men finish setting up the blocks and get ready to stand to. The crowd moves there to watch as the names and handicaps are called. Hiriwa stands opposite his father's block watching.
Different, the father. Unsmiling. Heavy in build and mood. Blunt fingered hands gripping the slim handled axe.
Hiriwa watches for a while, then walks away.
The choppers stand to and the starter calls 'Go' and begins the count. The lowest handicapped hit into their blocks and as the count rises the other axemen join in. The morning is filled with sound as voices rise, as axes strike and wood splits. White chips fly.

By three o'clock the stalls have done their selling. The last bottle of drink has been sold, many of the smaller children are asleep in the cars and trucks, and the older ones have gone down to the big field to play. Some of the tents are down already and the remains of the hangi have been cleared away. At the chopping arena the men are wrenching off the bottom halves of the blocks from the final chop and throwing split wood and chips on to the trucks.
Turei's dog is asleep under a tree. Finally the raffles are drawn.
Joe Blow wins a bag of kumara which he gives to Ed. Ed wins a carton of cigarettes which he gives to Taupeke. And Tahi wins a live sheep, which she tries to put into the boot of her car but which finds its feet and runs out the gate and down the road, chased by all the kids and Turei's dog.
The kids come back and later the dog, but the sheep is never seen again.

> I said to Nanny,
> 'Do my hair anyhow,
> Anyhow,
> Anyhow,
> Today the gala is on.'
> But she said, 'Be patient, Roimata,
> They'll think it's Turei's dog.'

Winter

> It rains,
> The skies weep.
> As do we.

Earth stands open to receive her and beside the opened earth we stand to give her our farewell.

'Our Auntie, she fell down.' They stood by the glass doors touching each other, eyes filling. Afraid.

'Our Auntie, she fell.'

And I went with them to the next room and found her lying on the floor, Ed bending over her, and the other children standing, frightened. Not knowing.

'Mrs Kaa, she has fallen on the floor.'

Rain.

It has rained for a fortnight, the water topped the river banks then flowed over. The flats are flooded. Water stirred itself into soil and formed a dark oozing mud causing bare feet to become chapped and sore and hard.

> 'Like sky people crying,
> Because the sun is too lazy
> And won't get up,
> And won't shine,
> He is too lazy.
> I shout and shout,
> "Get up, get up you lazy,
> You make the sky people cry,"
> But the sun is fast asleep.'

The trees we have visited daily are bare now, clawing grey fingered at cold winds. Birds have left the trees and gone elsewhere to find shelter, and the insects that in other seasons walk the trunks and branches and hurry about root formations, have tucked themselves into split bark and wood-holes to winter over.

Birds have come closer to the buildings, crowding under ledges and spoutings. We have erected a bird table and every morning put out crumbs of bread, wheat, bacon rind, honey, apple cores, and lumps of fat. And every day the birds come in their winter feathers, pecking at crumbs, haggling over fruit, fat, and honey. Moving from table to ground to rooftop, then back to table.

On John's paddock the pied stilts have arrived, also in search of food, standing on frail red legs, their long thin beaks like straws, dipping into the swampy ground.

'Our Auntie she has fallen.'

I took them out on to the verandah where they stood back out of the rain, looking at the ground, not speaking. I went to the phone. Disbelief as I went to the phone.

An emptiness and an unbelieving.

Because they had all been singing an hour before, and she had been strumming the guitar. And now there was a half sentence printed on the board with a long chalk mark trailing, and a smashed stick of chalk on the floor beside her.

Because at morning break she'd made the tea and he'd said, 'Where's the chocolate cake?' Joking.

'I'll run one up tonight,' she'd said. 'But you'll have to chase the hens around and get me a couple of eggs. My old chooks have gone off the lay.'

'Never mind the eggs,' he'd said. 'Substitute something, like water.'

'Water?' It had put a grin on her face.

'Water?' It had brought a laugh from deep inside her and soon she'd had the little room rocking with sound, which is a way of hers.

Or was. But she lay silent on the schoolroom floor and he came out and spoke to them.

'Mrs Kaa is very sick. Soon the bus will come to take you home. Don't be frightened.' And there was nothing else he could say.

'Our Auntie, she fell down.'

Standing by the glass doors, the pot bellied heater in the corner rumbling with burning pine and the room steaming. She had laughed about my washing too, that morning. My classroom with the naps strung across it steaming in the fire's heat.

'I'm coming in for a sauna this afternoon. And a feed. I'm coming in for a feed too.'

Each morning the children have been finding a feast in the split logs that the big boys bring in for the fire. Kopu and Samuel busy themselves with safety pins, digging into the holes in the wood and finding the dormant white larvae of the huhu beetle.

'Us, we like these.'

And they hook the fat concertina grubs out on the pins and put them on the chip heater to cook.

Soon there is a bacon and roasted peanut smell in the room and the others leave what they are doing and go to look. And wait, hoping there will be enough to go round.

Like two figures in the mist they stood by the doors behind the veil of steam, rain beating behind them. Large drops hitting the asphalt, splintering and running together again.

Eyes filling.

'Mrs Kaa, she fell down.'

Gently they lower her into earth's darkness, into the deep earth. Into earth salved by the touch of sky, the benediction of tears. And sad the cries come from those dearest to her. Welling up, filling the void between earth and sky and filling the beings of those who watch and weep.

'Look what your mutt did Turei.'

'We always have a three-legged and a sack.'

'Water?' the room rocking with sound, the bright apple skinless on a plate, smashed chalk beside her on the floor.

'A sauna and a feed.'

'Our Auntie.'

'Mrs Kaa. . . .'

It is right that it should rain today, that earth and sky should meet and touch, mingle. That the soil pouring into the opened ground should be newly blessed by sky, and that our tears should mingle with those of sky and then with earth that receives her.

And it is right too that threading through our final song we should hear the sound of children's voices, laughter, a bright guitar strumming.

Spring

The children know about spring.

Grass grows.

Flowers come up.

Lambs drop out.

Cows have big bags swinging.

And fat tits.

And new calves.

Trees have blossoms.

And boy calves go away to the works on the trucks and get their heads chopped off.

The remainder of the pine has been taken back to the shed, and the chips and wood scraps and ash have been cleaned away from the corner. The big boys make bonfires by the incinerator, heaping on them the winter's debris. Old leaves and sticks and strips of bark from under the pohutukawa and gum, dry brown heads of hydrangea, dead wood from plum, peach, and apple.

Pipiwharauroa has arrived.

'Time for planting,' he calls from places high in the trees.

'Take up spade and hoe, turn the soil, it's planting time.'

So we all go out and plant a memorial garden. A garden that when it matures will be full of colour and fragrance.

Children spend many of their out of school hours training and tending pets which they will parade at the pet show on auction day. They rise early each morning to feed their lambs and calves, and after school brush the animals, walk them, and feed them again.

Hippy and Stan have adopted Michael, who hangs between them like an odd looking triplet. The twins have four large eyes the colour of coal, four sets of false eye lashes and no front teeth. They are a noisy pair. Both like to talk at once and shout at each other, neither likes to listen. They send their words at each other across the top of Michael's head and land punches on one another that way too.

Bang!

'Na Hippy.'

Bang!

'Na Stan.'

Bang!

'Serve yourself right Hippy.'

Bang!

'Serve yourself right Stan.'

Bang!

'Sweet ay?'

Bang!

'Sweet ay?'

Until they both cry.

Michael is the opposite in appearance, having two surprised blue eyes high on his face, and no room to put a pin head between one freckle and the next. His long skinny limbs are the colour of boiled snapper and his hair is bright pink. Without his shirt he looks as though the skin on his chest and the skin on his back is being kept apart by mini tent poles. His neck swings from side to side as Hippy punches Stan, and Stan punches Hippy. And Michael joins in the chorus. 'Na Hippy! Sweet? Sweet Stan ay? Serve yourself right.' And when they both cry he joins in that as well.

New books have come, vivid with new ink and sweet with the smell of print and glue and stiff bright paper.

We find a table on which to display the books, and where they can sit and turn the pages and read. Or where I can sit and read for them and talk about all the newly discovered ideas.

'Hundreds of cats, thousands of cats, millions and billions and trillions of cats.'

'Who goes trip trap, trip trap, trip trap over my bridge?'

'Our brother is lost and I am lost too.'

'Run, run, as fast as you can, you can't catch me I'm the gingerbread man!'

Hiriwa makes a gingerbread man with clay, and Kopu and Samuel make one too.

Out of the ovens jump the gingerbread men, outrunning the old woman, the old man, the cat, the bear. 'That's why, the gingerbread man is too fast.' Then is gone in three snaps of the fox's jaws. Snip, Snap, Snap. Which is sad they think.

'Wii, the fox.'

'Us, we don't like the fox.'
'That's why, the fox is too tough.'
'Cunning that fox.'
Then again the closed hand comes down on clay. Snip. Snap. Snap.

He writes in his diary, 'The gingerbread man is lost and I am lost too.' One side of his face is heavy with bruising.

On the day of the pet show and auction his mother says to me, 'We are going away, Hiriwa and I. We need to go, there is nothing left for us to do. By tomorrow we will be gone.' I go into the classroom to get his things together.

The cars and trucks are here again. The children give the pets a drink of water and a last brush. Then they lead the animals in the ring for the judges to look over, discuss, award prizes to. Some of the pets are well behaved and some are not. Patsy's calf has dug its toes in and refuses to budge, and Patsy looks as though she is almost ready to take Kopu's advice. Kopu is standing on the sideline yelling, 'Boot it in the puku Patsy. Boot it in the puku.' And when the judges tell him to go away he looks put out for a moment. But then he sees Samuel and they run off together, hanging on to each other's shirts calling, 'Boot it in the puku. Boot it in the puku,' until they see somebody's goat standing on the bonnet of a truck, and begin rescue operations.

Inside the building, women from W.D.F.F. are judging cakes and sweets and arrangements of flowers. I go and help Connie and the others prepare lunch.

'Pity we can't have another hangi,' Connie says.

'Too bad, no kumara and corn this time of the year,' Elsie says. 'After Christmas, no trouble.'

Joe Blow stands on a box with all the goods about him. He is a tall man with a broad face. He has a mouth like a letter box containing a few stained stumps of teeth which grow out of his gums at several angles. His large nose is round and pitted like a golf ball, and his little eyes are set deep under thick grey eyebrows which are knotted and tangled like escape proof barbed wire. Above his eyebrows is a ribbon width of corrugated brow, and his hair sits close on top of his head like a small, tight-fitting, stocking stitch beanie. His ears are hand sized and bright red.

'What am I bid ladies, gentlemen, for this lovely chocolate cake? Who'll open the bidding?
Made it myself this morning, all the best ingredients.
What do I get, do I hear twenty-five?
Twenty I've got. Thirty I've got.
Forty cents.
Forty-five.
Forty-five. Forty-five. Gone at forty-five to my old pal Charlie, stingy bugger. You'll have to do better than that mates. Put your hands in your pockets now and what do I get for the coffee cake? Made it and iced it myself this morning. Walnuts on top. Thirty.
I have thirty. Thirty-five here.
Forty-five. Advance on forty-five come on all you cockies, take it home for afternoon tea.
Fifty I have, keep it up friends.
Fifty-five. Sixty, now you're talking.
Sixty-five, sixty-five, seventy.
Seventy again. Seventy for the third time. Sold at seventy and an extra bob for the walnuts, Skippy my boy.
Now this kit of potatoes. What am I bid?'
'Do we keep the kit?' someone calls.
'Did I hear fifty? Fifty? Fifty I've got. Any advance on fifty?'

'Do we keep the kit too?'

'Seventy-five I've got. Come on now grew them myself this morning. Make it a dollar. A dollar I've got.'

'What about the kit?'

'One dollar fifty I've got. One seventy-five. Make it two. Two we've got. Two once, two twice, two sold. Sorry about the kit darling we need it for the next lot.' He tips the potatoes into her lap and gives the kit to one of his helpers to refill.

'Two geranium plants·for the garden. Two good plants. What do I get? Come on Billy Boy, take them home for the wife. Make her sweet.'

'I already got something for that.'

'That's had it man, say it with flowers.'

'I got much better.'

'Skiting bugger, twenty-five I've got. Thirty I've got. Advance on thirty? Forty. Forty. Forty again. Forty, sold!'

'Now here's one especially for Turei. Filled sponge decorated with peaches and cream. Come on cook, I'll start you off at forty.

Forty cents ladies, gents, and Charlie, from our friend Turei at the back. And forty-five at the front here, come on Turei. Sixty?

Sixty. And seventy up front.

Eighty. Ninety.

One dollar from the district's most outstanding hangi maker and a dollar twenty from the opposition.

One dollar fifty. Two? Two up front. Two fifty from the back.

Two fifty, two fifty . . . three.

Three we have, come on friend.

Three fifty. What do you say Turei?

Five. Five from the back there.

Five once, five twice, five sold. One cream sponge to Turei the best cook in the district. Thank you boys.

Time's getting on friends. What do you say to a leg a mutton, a bunch a silver beet, a jar a pickle, a bag a-spuds, there's your dinner. A dollar? Two? Two ten, twenty, fifty, seventy. Two seventy, two seventy, two seventy, no mucking around, sold.

Another kit of potatoes. I'll take them myself for fifty. Will you let me take them home for fifty? Seventy. Seventy to you, eighty to me. Ninety to you, a dollar to me. Dollar twenty, OK, one fifty. Let me have them for one fifty? One fifty to me, ladies and gents and Charlie. One seventy-five? OK, one ninety. Two?

Two we have once, two we have twice, two for the third time, sold. All yours boy, I've got two acres of my own at home.

Here we are friends, another of these lovely home made sponges. What do you say Turei . . .?'

But Turei is away under the gum tree sharing his cake with a lot of children and his dog.

And back again to summer, with all the children talking about Christmas and holidays, their pockets bulging with ripe plums.

The branches of the pohutukawa are flagged in brilliant red, and three pairs of tuis have arrived with their odd incongruous talking, 'See-saw, Crack, Burr, Ding. See-saw, See-saw, Ding.' By the time they have been there a week they are almost too heavy to fly, their wings beat desperately in flight in order to keep their heavy bodies airborne.

On the last day of school we wait under the pohutukawa for the bus to arrive, and a light wind sends down a shower of nectar which dries on our arms and legs and faces in small white spots.

They scramble into the bus talking and pushing, licking their skins. They heave their belongings under the seats and turn to the windows to wave. Kopu and Samuel who are last in line stand on the bus step and turn.

'Goodbye,' Kopu says, and cracks Sam in the ribs with his elbow.

'Goodbye,' Samuel says and slams his hands down on top of his kina and blushes.

As the bus pulls away we hear singing. Waving hands protrude from the windows on either side. Hippy, Michael, and Stan have their heads together at the back window, and Roimata is there too, waving, chewing a pigtail –

> 'I am a tui bird,
> Up in the pohutukawa tree,
> And a teacher and some children came out
> And stood under my tree,
> And honey rained all over them,
> But I am a tui bird,
> And when I fly
> It sounds like ripping rags.'

Between Earth and Sky

I walked out of the house this morning and stretched my arms out wide. Look, I said to myself. Because I was alone except for you. I don't think you heard me.

Look at the sky, I said.

Look at the green earth.

How could it be that I felt so good? So free? So full of the sort of day it was? How?

And at that moment, when I stepped from my house, there was no sound. No sound at all. No bird call, or tractor grind. No fire crackle or twig snap. As though the moment had been held quiet, for me only, as I stepped out into the morning. Why the good feeling, with a lightness in me causing my arms to stretch out and out? How blue, how green, I said into the quiet of the moment. But why, with the sharp nick of bone deep in my back and the band of flesh tightening across my belly?

All alone. Julie and Tamati behind me in the house, asleep, and the others over at the swamp catching eels. Riki two paddocks away cutting up a tree he'd felled last autumn.

I started over the paddocks towards him then, slowly, on these heavy knotted legs. Hugely across the paddocks I went almost singing. Not singing because of needing every breath, but with the feeling of singing. Why, with the deep twist and pull far down in my back and cramping between the legs? Why the feeling of singing?

How strong and well he looked. How alive and strong, stooping over the trunk steadying the saw. I'd hated him for days, and now suddenly I loved him again but didn't know why. The saw cracked through the tree setting little splinters of warm wood hopping. Balls of mauve smoke lifted into the air. When he looked up I put my hands to my back and saw him understand me over the skirl of the saw. He switched off, the sound fluttered away.

I'll get them, he said.

We could see them from there, leaning into the swamp, feeling for eel holes.

Three long whistles and they looked up and started towards us, wondering why, walking reluctantly.

Mummy's going, he said.

We nearly got one, Turei said. Ay Jimmy, ay Patsy, ay Reuben?

Yes, they said.

Where? said Danny.

I began to tell him again, but he skipped away after the others. It was good to watch them running and shouting through the grass. Yesterday their activity and noise had angered me, but today I was happy to see them leaping and shouting through the long grass with the swamp mud drying and caking on their legs and arms.

Let Dad get it out, Reuben turned, was calling. He can get the lambs out. Bang! Ay Mum, ay?

Julie and Tamati had woken. They were coming to meet us, dragging a rug.

Not you again, they said taking my bag from his hand.

Not you two again, I said. Rawhiti and Jones.

Don't you have it at two o'clock.

We go off at two.

Your boyfriends can wait.

Our sleep can't.

I put my cheek to his and felt his arm about my shoulders.

Look after my wife, he was grinning at them.

Course, what else.

Go on. Get home and milk your cows, next time you see her she'll be in two pieces.

I kissed all the faces poking from the car windows then stood back on the step waving. Waving till they'd gone. Then turning felt the rush of water.

Quick, I said. The water.

Water my foot; that's piddle.

What you want to piddle in our neat corridor for? Sit down. Have a ride.

Helped into a wheelchair and away, careering over the brown lino.

Stop. I'll be good. Stop I'll tell Sister.

Sister's busy.

No wonder you two are getting smart. Stop. . . .

That's it missus, you'll be back in your bikini by summer. Dr McIndoe.

And we'll go water-skiing together. Me.

Right you are. Well, see you both in the morning.

The doors bump and swing.

Sister follows.

Finish off girls. Maitland'll be over soon.

All right Sister.

Yes Sister. Reverently.

The doors bump and swing.

You are at the end of the table, wet and grey. Blood stains your pulsing head. Your arms flail in these new dimensions and your mouth is a circle that opens and closes as you scream for air. All head and shoulders and wide mouth screaming. They have clamped the few inches of cord which is all that is left of your old life now. They draw mucous and bathe your head.

Leave it alone and give it here, I say.

What for? Haven't you got enough kids already?

Course. Doesn't mean you can boss that one around.

We should let you clean your own kid up?

Think she'd be pleased after that neat ride we gave her. Look at the little hoha. God he can scream.

They wrap you in linen and put you here with me.

Well anyway, here you are. He's all fixed, you're all done. We'll blow. And we'll get them to bring you a cuppa. Be good.

The doors swing open.

She's ready for a cuppa Freeman.

The doors bump shut.

Now. You and I. I'll tell you. I went out this morning. Look, I said, but didn't know why. Why the good feeling. Why, with the nick and press of bone deep inside. But now I know. Now I'll tell you and I don't think you'll mind. It wasn't the thought of knowing you, and having you here close to me that gave me this glad feeling, that made me look upwards and all about as I stepped out this morning. The gladness was because at last I was to be free. Free from that great hump that was you, free from the aching limbs and swelling that was you. That was why this morning each stretching of flesh made me glad.

And freedom from the envy I'd felt, watching him these past days, stepping over the paddocks whole and strong. Unable to match his step. Envying his bright striding. But I could love him again this morning.

These were the reasons each gnarling of flesh made me glad as I came out into that cradled moment. Look at the sky, look at the earth, I said. See how blue, how green. But I gave no thought to you.

And now. You sleep. How quickly you have learned this quiet and rhythmic breathing. Soon they'll come and put a cup in my hand and take you away.

You sleep, and I too am tired, after our work. We worked hard you and I and now we'll sleep. Be close. We'll sleep a little while ay, you and I.

MARGARET SUTHERLAND

Codling-Moth

We talk about it a lot. It is as unattainable, as desirable as beauty. In secret we crave it; cynics, we talk about it as we sit together under the gum trees at lunchtime, eating peanut butter sandwiches.

'It's ridiculous, the way they go on about it all the time,' says Mel, tossing her crusts to the predatory gulls. We aren't supposed to feed them but we do. 'I mean, it's one thing in the pictures and books and poetry and that stuff, but take real life. Take my parents. Or yours. They love each other but you don't see them slopping all over each other and going on as though that's all there is to think about. Do you?'

'No, you don't,' I say. When my father comes home he kisses my mother, or rather he kisses the air by my mother's cheek, and if he's late, as he often is when shift work or his mates at the pub delay him, my mother, rattling plates, says 'Your dinner's in the oven and if you don't hurry up and eat it it'll be dried up to nothing.' I suppose they love each other.

'Of course they have been married a long time,' Mel says, thinking. You know when she is thinking. Her eyes go away from you, like a blind person who, in following the direction of your voice, misses and looks past your shoulder. 'It's probably different when you're married. Romeo and Juliet never got married did they.'

I think of Romeo coming in late from work and Juliet rattling plates and saying 'Your dinner's in the oven.' It makes me feel sad. Mel and I saw the film. I cried at the end. Mel's more sensible than I am. She doesn't believe in crying, as a rule, but she didn't want to look at me when we came out.

'It's different, being married,' I say, to bring her back to sitting under the trees and feeding the seagulls. 'It must be. I've never seen any married people who love each other so they'd rather die than stay alive if the other one died.'

Mel bites into an apple – glossy, red, perfect. 'Ughff, look at that,' she says, spitting out the words and the apple together, and showing me the core. A dull greyish powder spreads from where the worm has tunnelled.

'Codling-moth,' I say. Mel has a quick look round and shies the apple at the bossiest gull, which lumbers into the air, settles a few feet away, and regards us with the icy outrage of our headmistress objecting to complaints of behaviour on the buses with the boys from St Pat's.

A thought has just occurred to me. 'Maybe they make it up,' I suggest. 'I bet there's no such thing as love. That kind anyway. Maybe people know there isn't and wish there was, so they make it up and write books and compose songs and all the time it isn't true.'

That makes us silent. I wish I hadn't had that thought. I hope I'm wrong.

'I think you're right,' Mel says suddenly. When she's finished thinking, she's back with you, snap; quite startling if you've gone away into your own thoughts while you've been waiting for her. 'There's no such thing. Jolly good thing too. Who wants to go all sloppy and slushy about some idiot with sweaty hands and pimples. It's absolutely disgusting when you think about it. It makes you sick.'

'But they're not all like that,' I say quickly, trying to unthink my thought. 'What about Jolyon Townsend?'

'You certainly see a lot like him,' says Mel, who can be sarcastic. 'At the school ball the floor was littered with boys like him, wasn't it. You tripped over them at every step. Or they tripped over you more likely.'

'Well . . .' I say.

'Well?' she says. Mel likes to be sure she's won the point.

'Well,' I say, 'they can't help it. They might look better when they're older.'

'Like twenty years older.'

'Anyway what about us?' I've remembered the photo of Mel and me, in flocked nylon dance frocks and long mittens, standing in front of the artificial gladioli. 'What about that photo of us?' There is nothing to say.

I try again. 'How about Mr Krassmann then?' I ask in a very insinuating way. I think Mel has a crush on Mr Krassmann, who tutors her privately on Saturday mornings in German. When she came round to my place after her lesson last week her face was quite pink, and *Heute und Abend* isn't the sort of thing to put roses in anybody's cheeks. Mel is giving nothing away.

'Mr Krassmann?' she says, drawing it out as though I've suggested old Harry, the school caretaker, who is about seventy and smells of tobacco. He spits too. 'You must be joking.'

In *The Importance of Being Earnest*, our play for English Lit. this term, Mel has the part of Lady Bracknell. I concede. 'Okay,' I say. 'Love's an illusion.' I've heard that somewhere. To agree with Mel is the best way to call her bluff, sometimes. She looks at me. It's her other look, the opposite of her far-away one. She has unusual eyes – flecked, the iris blue and green and grey and gold and each colour distinct; the white part is very white. Mel's eyes are her best feature. But when she looks at you this way you stop noticing her eyes, as though you can see past them to a small secret place where the real Mel lives. She doesn't let you in very often, which is only natural.

'Gabriel? You don't really think that's true, do you?'

'I hope it isn't true,' I tell her honestly.

'I hope it isn't too,' she says. The game is over. We're in agreement, which we usually are though we like to pretend. We go down to the pool for a swim.

The pool is new. For two years we've had raffles and class fund-raising contests and limp fudge cake from the school tuck-shop, sixpence the piece. And now we have a swimming pool. Mel and I stand beside the steps that lead down to the water, eau-de-nil water that reminds me of polar seas, lapping on smooth tiles white as ice floes. My bathing-suit is regulation black and my skin is very pale.

I tried to tan last year when Mel and I went camping with her cousins. The tan stayed for two days and peeled away, like dirt. All that stayed in my skin was the smell of sunshine when I breathed on my arm. We kept to ourselves in our ten-by-ten canvas world and waited for sunburnt boys to pay court. We wore eyeshadow, and four changes of beachwear every day. The boys went by our tent and we noticed that the girls beside them looked like Ann, who never wore eyeshadow, and said 'somethink'. We were not grateful to Ann for taking us camping, in the same way that we were not grateful to our parents for conceiving us in their middle age. We did not think about it. Mel and I did not talk about the boys. We bought chocolate-dipped ice-creams, and walked along the beach with our heads close together to hear over the wind and surf.

The light went quickly one evening when we were still on the beach. The two boys came silently out of the sandhills so that at first we were startled. We walked, the four of us, towards the rocks at the end of the beach, together at first, later in pairs, Mel and her boy ahead. His walk was almost a shamble; his arms, before he put one round her shoulders, swung loosely. Smugly, I felt sorry for Mel. The boy beside me was tall and his hand felt firm and warm. It grew dark, and I could have walked on to the rocks for ever.

Mel and her boy drew further ahead as we turned back and went towards the dunes. I wished that Mel was following to notice that my boy didn't shamble and was tall. The juice of the succulent plants, closed now against night, ran out between my toes as he turned me to him and kissed me. His lips, like his palms, were dry and warm. But then his tongue was terrible, slithering wet, strong, a dark eel belonging under stones in the river. He held me tightly but I pulled away and ran back, on and on, to the camp, to the tent. My chest hurt with fright and running. I waited for Mel and was angry because she hadn't stayed with me.

She came back soon. I was curious to know if she had been kissed by her boy but she didn't say and I didn't like to ask. Nor did I tell her about the kiss that had made me afraid. I knew I had not behaved with sophistication, although my eyeshadow was silver and glistened under light. We went to bed soon, on the double mattress that Ann had brought on the trailer for us. Mel's warmth, her solidity, the faint spicy smell of her hair near my face comforted me and I fell asleep against her.

Holidays end; school brings back the pleasures of challenge, approval, Mel's company. We vie in class. While other girls form friendly circles at lunchtime, Mel and I sit apart. In wet weather the shelter sheds smell of sour milk and sandshoes, and wasps hang around the overflowing rubbish tins. When it's fine we sit under the gum trees, and sometimes after lunch we go for a swim.

I look at the pale water, and think that I'm not a good swimmer, that I don't like cold water, that I don't want to go in. Mel, beside me, reaches out and touches a finger behind my shoulders. 'You have such a smooth back,' she says, sounding surprised as though she's just noticed something. Compliments are unusual: from adults who are watchful of praise, from Mel, who tries as I do to be adult. Her words sink like smooth pebbles to the bottom of my thoughts; later I will take them out, turn them over, fondle them. I am flattered. I am happy. I leap suddenly into the water and without a single rest I swim a full width of the pool.

After school we catch the bus to town. It is Friday afternoon, the first Friday of the month. Mel and I are making the Nine First Fridays, in honour of the Sacred Heart. When we have finished we shall be certain of going to heaven; as promised to St Margaret-Mary by the Lord Himself we shall be allowed the grace of final repentance on our deathbeds. Death seems beyond us, as impossible as the committing of horrible, mortal sin, but then one never knows. The Nine Fridays may save us in the final count. Mass and Communion for nine consecutive First Fridays of the month is a little price to pay for heaven. Besides, before Mass at seven o'clock, there's afternoon tea and a five o'clock session of the pictures. We never see the end of the film because we can't be late for Mass. It doesn't matter a lot. We make up our own endings.

Mel's watch is fast. We are early for Mass. Men and women tread quietly past the confessional boxes into the great cave of the church. Confessional doors open and close; voices too muted to understand exchange private words as Mel and I, kneeling together, examine our consciences. HailHolyQueen. HailOur LifeOurSweetnessAndHope.   ToTheeDoWeCome.   BeforeTheeWeStand. SinfulAndSorrowful. Sinful. Even the just man falls seven times daily. Why so hard to put together a respectable list for Father who waits gravely in there, in the small cave smelling so strongly of old planed wood? His profile beneath the dim bulb appears as the window slides back. Latin phrases of absolution switch suddenly, like light, to the patient, 'Yes, my child?' My child? Can he see me? How does he know this is not an old woman, a murderer, a sinner come to repentance after thirty years? Oh, to have the choice of thirty years' wickedness from which to pick sins like cans from a supermarket shelf; oh, how disappointing a display of sin. Disobeyed Mother. Several times. Told lies twice. No. Not harmful to anyone. Not calumny. One about the music practice. One about the chocolates. Mother knew anyway. 'And anything else?' Anything else, anything else. . . . Surely, surely, *something*? Answered back, but she deserved that. I answered back, Father. Impure thoughts? Had an impure thought. 'Yes,

my child. I see. And anything else now?' Anything else anything else Father I'm
almost wetting my pants because it's so dark and there's nothing else so please
give me my penance – a thought only, unspoken. Would that be a sin, to do that
in Confession? Surely not, not even there. Has anyone ever? . . . dear child,
pray for help, Our Blessed Mother, temptation is no sin, remember that the
Devil tempted Christ Himself in the desert. . . . Yes Father. Pray my child. Yes
Father. You do remember your prayers always? Mostly Father. 'I see, my child.
And nothing else?'

When I was small I used to clutch when I felt I couldn't wait and Mother
would say don't, Gabriel, don't do that. Nice little girls don't do that. I do it now,
praying that Father can't see, praying there won't be a little trail of wetness left
behind on the brown linoleum when I emerge, absolved, into the light.

For your penance three Hail Marys, and now a good Act of Contrition.
OhMyGodIAmVerySorryThatIHaveSinnedAgainstThee.   BecauseThouArt
SoGood. AndIWillNotSinAgain. Amen. *Te absolvo*. Thank you, Father. The
window closes.

I open the door, go back to the church and the faces looking up from their
conscience-stricken hunting. Have I been a long time? Too long? Fall
gratefully, blushing, into any pew. Disappear. A light-headed feeling of
freedom like the last day of term. Sin all gone. Sorrowful? Happy. Bury eyes
down on to clasped hands. Three Hail Marys, one, two, three. A soul now,
round and white as a peppermint, the smuts of sin rubbed out. Gabriel shriven.

Most people leave as soon as Mass is over. Mel and I stay behind, kneeling side
by side. The church is a great high cave where we are together, lost, alone. The
candles sparkling on the side altar remind me of glowworms high up on the
caves at Waitomo, cold caves, dark, with lapping black water sensed more than
seen. 'My, now *this* is *something!*' the American woman says, impressed again. I
think of black sky, no moon, the death of a star, and I am glad to climb the
rickety wooden steps up to the light again. Caves are sinister places, running
back to no-exits of darkness and dripping water. Mel isn't afraid of caves. She is
practical. She will be saying the fourth decade of the rosary and planning her
weekend essay. Her beads move, tapping lightly the polished pew cut with the
initials J.B., rayed round with lines like a child's sun.

The church smells warmly of flowers and incense. I ease my weight to one
knee, to the other, and rest my face against my bent arms. It's no good. I give in
and sit down, tracing through the lisle stockings the deep indentations that
mark each knee. Mel's back rises straight and rigid as the brown-robed St
Joseph who gazes past us from his niche. His head does not wear a beret, but
clustered curls and a plaster beard, set stiffly on his chin like old spaghetti.
Looking at Mel I am ashamed. I kneel down again, notice the blunt renewed
ache in my knees and the warmth of Mel beside me. Her blazer filters a musky
smell like faded incense. HailHolyQueenMotherOfMercy. HailOurLifeOur
SweetnessAndOurHope. ToTheeDoWeCome. BeforeTheeWeStand. Sinful
AndSorrowful.

Grateful when Mel's nudge comes, I stand up stiffly, like the old women who
wear headscarves and chew on their prayers without caring who listens in to
their conversations with the Lord. How sad, I think, how impossible to ever be
old like that. I follow Mel down the side aisle, my legs forgetting their stiffness,
my callous soul ignoring the sad dimmed oil paintings of the Way of the Cross.
Dip, splash, the holy water font an ivory shell. Catholic Truth Society
pamphlets, red, blue, purple, on the rack in the church porch. *Have you a
vocation? Sacramental Grace. Youth and Problems of Purity.* I cannot go and take
that title out of the rack, not with Mel or somebody to see me and wonder why
I'm buying that one; but it sounds more interesting than *Fallacies of Jansenism*.

We pass the pamphlets and go outside. It is March and by eight o'clock night has settled down cosily. I was sleepy in the warm church. Now, feeling the thin cold air trickle through my nose, I am suddenly wide awake, and pleased with myself.

'Well, that's eight,' I say.

'Eight what? Oh, you mean Fridays.'

'Only one to go. Did you think we'd really do it, Mel?'

'We haven't yet. There's one more, remember.'

Sometimes I find Mel's precision annoying, but I don't mind tonight. What does it matter? Mel is coming to stay the night and I am happy.

We have never been less tired than we are now, at bedtime.

'Straight off to sleep now,' Mother says firmly, hopefully. In the darkness I sense Mel in the other bed. We talk in whispers, muffling giggles in our pillows.

'Mel? You know when we were up at the beach last summer, and you went down to the rocks with that boy?'

'The one with the acne? The friendly monster from outer space?'

'He wasn't *that* bad.'

'He was. You were jolly pleased the other one picked you.'

'I was not.'

'Yes, you were. He was a crumb.'

'Yes, but did he . . . did you . . .?'

'What?'

'Oh *you* know.'

'For heaven's sake!'

'Did you, well, kiss him?'

'*He* did. I didn't.'

'Didn't you like it?'

'No. I don't think so. It was wet.'

'Was it? So was mine. All sloppy. He just about stuck his tongue down my throat.'

'Mine didn't do that. He kind of chewed, like those old men who don't wear their teeth.'

'Ugh.'

'Yuck.'

Exquisitely funny. We scream silently into our pillows.

'Licking ice cream.'

'Slurping soup.'

'Gob-stoppers in your mouth. *Two*.'

Excruciating. We roll on our stomachs, hysterical. We have forgotten that Mother, in the next room, is tired and is trying to have an early night. Bang on the wall. Bangbang. Stop that noise, girls. Off to sleep. At once.

Silence.

'Gabriel?'

'Ssshh! She'll hear. Come over here.'

Mel in blue pyjamas brings her incense smell into my bed. We arrange ourselves together, bump to hollow, hollow to bump. 'Gabriel? What do you think about it? You know what I mean. Did your mother tell you or what?'

'She told me. Did your mother?'

'She gave me a book. Last year.'

A whole book! My information had been received in the five minutes between rosary and night prayers.

'What was it like?'

'Awful drawings.'

'Like biology class?'

'Worse. There wasn't much about it. The actual part. It had a lot about getting pregnant and how not to and diseases and that.'

Disappointing. I thought there might be something Mother had forgotten about. What she had told me had seemed really rather pointless.

'Mel? Didn't you think it sounded silly? I mean, don't you wonder why people *do* it?'

'It sounds mad, I think. Don't ask me. You'd think they'd have a better system, wouldn't you? An incubator plant or something.'

'Yes. I think it sounds awful.'

'Well I'm not going to do it anyway. Ever.'

'Neither am I.'

Is it incense, powder, faint sun-on-skin perspiration, this special warm smell that is Mel? The winceyette cloth of her pyjama coat has rubbed into tiny balls under my fingers. I am alive, I quicken with awareness like the vibration of a single hair when we sit, heads not quite touching, in the pictures. I will change my mind and be embarrassed, so I say it quickly before I have time to think. 'Mel,' I say, 'I do like you.'

She turns her head back as though she hasn't heard me. The toothpaste on her breath reminds me of the pink smokers we buy in cellophane packets as she answers.

'Well I like you,' she says. I am happy. I find her lowest rib and tickle. We have forgotten again. Bang. Bangbangbang.

'Get to SLEEP!'

Silence.

'Mel?'

'What?'

'I thought you were asleep.'

'No.'

'Oh.'

At the back of her neck, in the hollow, the hair is fine, like a baby's. I feel it for an instant, lighter than a touch on my lips, and wonder if I imagine its softness.

'G'night, Mel.'

'Mmhmm. G'night.'

Then it is morning and Mother is standing by the bed, wearing her least-pleased expression. We stumble up from sleep and go in dressing-gowns to the kitchen for breakfast. The air is thick with Mother's bad mood and fumes from the kerosene heater. Our plates are whisked away, dealt ferociously into the sink. The silence trembles with crashes. I ask with guilt if I can dry.

'Don't bother yourself,' Mother says, passing the tea-towel to me. 'You go and enjoy yourself with your friend. Don't think of your mother.'

'Didn't you have a good night?' I ask foolishly. Mother snatches her trump.

'Good night? Good *night*? The pair of you talking and giggling half the night. . . . My word, wait till you're my age. Young people are selfish today. Very selfish.' I dry in silence.

'Is it all right if Mel and I do some homework now?'

'Do as you like. Don't bother to ask me what you can do or can't do. You'll do what you please. You're just like your father.'

I go back to the bedroom. Mel is dressed. 'What's the matter with your mother. Isn't she feeling well?'

'Oh,' I say vaguely, 'she gets like that. She didn't have a very good night or something.' It does not seem reasonable that Mother's sleep is dependent on my own. A heavy burden.

Homework is done. Mother is ironing.

'Mel wants me to go over to her place. Can I?' I ask.

'You and that girl are always in each other's pocket,' Mother says with resentment. 'If it's not her coming to our place it's you wanting to go there. I don't know what her mother thinks, I'm sure.' It hasn't occurred to me that Mel's mother thinks at all. She is a doing person, never still, always washing, ironing, busy in the kitchen. She uses the weekends to catch up on the week when she's away at work.

'We have to finish this project on pollution by Monday, and Mel's got a book about it.' (BlessMeFather, I told one lie.)

'Go if you must,' says Mother, branding Father's shirt with a vicious stab. 'Please yourself. If her mother can put up with your nonsense and carrying on, go. It makes no difference to me. What I'd like to know is, where are all those nice little friends you used to have to your birthdays, that nice little what's-her-name, Rosemary, Mary Rose, what's happened to her?'

I am patient. 'Mother, that was years ago. Absolute ages. She's gone all stupid now. All she talks about is boys.'

'There's worse than boys,' says my mother, thumping the iron fast. 'A lot worse. You want to think about that, my girl.'

'What d'you mean?' I ask. The damping-bottle flies, sprinkling me with drops, like holy water from the Benediction procession.

'I'll tell you what I'm talking about; you see far too much of that girl, that's what I'm talking about. In case you don't know it there are some funny people about, very funny men, and funny women too, and no girl of mine is growing up into one of them. That's what I'm talking about.'

'I don't know what you mean,' I say. 'I don't understand you.'

'I hope you don't,' she says, and says no more, for she has looked at me and seen my face and I think she is sorry that she let her tiredness and her oldness make her say that, that way. But I think also that she is glad it has been said. At least that is what I decide, later on. As I turn and run away out of the kitchen, into the bathroom, lock the door, sit on the edge of the bath, let the hot hot tears run down, I understand nothing, and everything, and I feel sick to my heart. A grey web of guilt is spinning itself about me. For the first time in my life I learn what it is to be quite alone.

Mel and I go to town. We have afternoon tea. We go to the pictures. We go to church, and kneel side by side. The doors of the confessionals open, close; inaudible words murmur a thread of melody. Mel leaves me and closes the door behind her.

Bless me, Father, for I have sinned. Anything else, my child? Anything else? Sin unspoken makes a worse sin, the sin of deceit, for the priest is the ear of God. Have I sinned? I remember the softness of old winceyette, the fineness of young hair at the back of the neck, in the hollow.

Mel comes out, composed as always. 'I'm not going,' I say. And I turn my back on her surprised face and walk up the church away from the confessionals.

The Ninth Friday. Nine consecutive First Fridays and nine communions and heaven is a promise. This is My Body. And This is My Blood. Mel goes up to receive communion. I do not go. I stay in my seat, kneeling very straight, and I try to concentrate on the pain in my knees and not think of the other pain. I have not made the Nine Fridays and I am trying not to cry.

OWEN MARSHALL

Mr Van Gogh

When he went into hospital our newspaper said that Mr Van Gogh's name was Frank Reprieve Wilcox, and that was the first time I'd ever heard the name. But I knew Mr Van Gogh well enough. He came around the town sometimes on Sunday afternoons, and he would excuse himself for disturbing you and ask if there were any coloured bottles to carry on the work of Mr Vincent Van Gogh. Whether you gave him bottles or not, it was better never to enquire about his art; for he would stand by any back door on a Sunday afternoon and talk of Van Gogh until the tears ran down his face, and his gaberdine coat flapped in agitation.

Only those who wanted to mock him, encouraged him to talk. Like Mr Souness next door who had some relatives from Auckland staying when Mr Van Gogh came, and got him going as a local turn to entertain the visitors. 'Was he any good though, this Van Gogh bugger?' Mr Souness said, nudging a relative, and, 'But he was barmy wasn't he? Admit it. He was another mad artist.' Mr Van Gogh never realized that there was no interest, only cruelty, behind such questions. He talked of the religious insight of Van Gogh's painting at Arles, and his genius in colour symbolism. He laughed and cried as he explained to Mr Souness's relations the loyalty of brother Theo, and the prescience of the critic Aurier. They were sufficiently impressed to ask Mr Van Gogh whether they could see his ears for a moment. Mr Souness and his relations stood around Mr Van Gogh, and laughed so loud when it was said, that I went away from the fence without watching any more. Mr Van Gogh was standing before the laughter with his arms outstretched like a cross, and talking all the more urgently. Something about cypresses and the hills of Provence.

Mr Van Gogh had a war pension, and lived in a wooden bungalow right beside the bridge. The original colours of the house had given up their differences, and weathered stoically to an integration of rust and exposed wood. The iron on the roof was stained with rust, and looked much the same as the corrugated weatherboards. The garden was full of docks and fennel. It had two crab apple trees which we didn't bother to rob.

Mr Van Gogh didn't appear to have anything worth stealing. He used to paint in oils my father said, but it was expensive and nothing ever sold, so he began to work in glass. No-one saw any of his art work, but sometimes when he came round on Sundays, he'd have a set of drinking glasses made out of wine bottles, or an ash tray to sell made out of a vinegar flagon. My father was surprised that they were no better than any other do it yourself product.

Although he had no proper job, Mr Van Gogh worked as though the day of judgement was upon him. He used his attached wash-house as a studio, and on fine days he'd sit in the doorway to get the sun. There he'd cut and grind and polish away at the glass. He would even eat in the doorway of the wash-house as he worked. He must have taken in a deal of glass dust with his sandwiches. Often I could see him as I went down to the river. If I called out to him, he'd say, 'Good on you,' still working on the glass; grinding, cutting, polishing. If I was by myself I'd watch a while sometimes before going down to the river. One piece after another; none of them bigger than a thumb nail. A sheet of glass sheds the light he said. They had to be small to concentrate the light. Some of the bits were thick and faceted, others so delicate he would hold them to the sun to check. Mr Van Gogh liked to talk of individual paintings as he worked – the poet's garden, street in Auvers, or starry night. He stored the different colours and shapes in cardboard boxes that said Hard Jubes on the sides. Yellow was difficult, the colour of personal expression, Mr Van Gogh said, but so difficult to get right in glass. He bought yellow glass from Austria, but he'd never matched Van Gogh's yellow. He never thought so much of his yellow glass he said, even from Austria.

Mr Van Gogh wasn't all that odd looking. Sure he had old-fashioned clothes – goloshes in winter and his gaberdine coat with concealed button holes, and in summer his policemen and firemen braces over grey work shirts. But he was clean, and clean shaven. His hair was long though, and grey like his shirts. He combed it back from his face with his fingers, so that it settled in tresses, giving him the look of a careworn lion.

Because my father was a parson it was thought he should be responsible for Mr Van Gogh and other weird people. Mr Souness said that it was just as well that my father had something to occupy his time for the other six days of the week. Ministers get some odd people to deal with I'd say. Reggie Kane was a peeping tom who had fits whether he saw anything or not, and Miss O'Conner was convinced that someone was trying to burn down her house at night, and she used to work in the vegetable garden in her nightdress. Our family knew Mr Van Gogh wasn't like the others, though most people treated him the same. My father said that Mr Van Gogh's only problem was that he'd made a commitment to something which other people couldn't understand. My father had a good deal of fellow-feeling for Mr Van Gogh in some ways. Mr Van Gogh would've been all right if his obsession had been with politics or horse-racing. He wouldn't have been a crack-pot then.

Two or three times Mr Van Gogh came to our house to use the phone. He'd stand quietly at the door, and make his apologies for coming to use the phone. He was ordering more yellow glass from Austria perhaps, or checking on his pension. Mr Van Gogh's humility was complete on anything but art. He was submissive even to the least deserving. On art though he would have argued with Lucifer, for it was his necessity and power. It was what he was. His head would rise with his voice. He would rake back his grey hair, and for a moment the backward pressure would rejuvenate his face before the lines could appear again; the plumes of hair begin a faint cascade upon his forehead. He could be derisive and curt, fervent and eloquent; but people didn't understand. A naked intensity of belief is an obscene exposure in ordinary conversation. It was better not to start him off, my mother said.

When the Council decided to make the bridge a two lane one, Mr Van Gogh's house had to come down. The engineers said that the approaches to the new bridge would have to be at least twice the width of the bridge itself, and Mr Van Gogh's house was right next to the old bridge. Even the house next to Mr Van Gogh's would probably have to go, the consultant thought. Mr Van Gogh took it badly. He stuck up the backs of the letters the Council wrote, and sent them back. He wouldn't let anyone inside to value the house; he wouldn't talk about compensation. The Council asked my father to get Mr Van Gogh to see reason. My father said he was willing to try and explain the business, but he didn't know if he could justify it. The Council didn't seem to recognize the distinction.

As far as I know Mr Van Gogh never let anyone into his house. Even my father had to stand on the doorstep, and Mr Van Gogh stood just inside the door, and there was a blanket hanging across the hall behind him; to block off the sight of anything to a visitor at the door. My mother said she could imagine the squalor of it behind the blanket. An old man living alone like that she said.

My father did his best. So did the council and Ministry of Works I suppose. They selected two other houses to show Mr Van Gogh, and a retirement villa in the grounds of the combined Churches' eventide home, but he wouldn't go to see them. He became furtive and worried. He'd hardly leave his house lest the people come and demolish it while he was away. The Council gave Mr Van

Gogh until the end of March to move out of his home. Progress couldn't be obstructed indefinitely they said. Mr Souness looked forward to some final confrontation. 'The old bugger is holding up the democratic wishes of the town,' he said. He thought everyone had been far too soft on Mr Van Gogh.

In the end it worked out pretty well for the Council people. Mrs Witham rang our house at tea time to say she'd seen Mr Van Gogh crawling from the wash-house into his front door, and that he must be drunk. My father and I went down to the bridge, and found Mr Van Gogh lying on his back in the hallway, puffing and blowing as he tried to breathe. 'It's all right now,' said my father to Mr Van Gogh. What a place he was in though. For through that worn, chapped doorway, and past the blanket, was the art and homage of Mr Van Gogh. Except for the floor, all the surfaces of the passage and lounge were the glass inlays of a Van Gogh vision. Some glass was set in like nuggets, winking as jewelled eyes from a pit. Other pieces were lenses set behind or before similarly delicate sections of different colours to give complexity of toning. The glass interior of Mr Van Gogh's home was an inter-play of light and colour that flamed in green, and yellow, and prussian blue, in the evening sun across the river bank. Some of the great paintings were there: Red Vineyard, Little Pear Tree, View of Arles with Irises, each reproduced in tireless, faithful hues one way or another.

Mr Van Gogh lay like clay in the passage, almost at the lounge door. I thought that I was looking at a dying man. I blamed all that glass dust that he'd been taking in for years, but my father said it was something more sudden. He pulled down the blanket from the hall, and put it over Mr Van Gogh to keep him warm, then went down the path to ring the ambulance. The blanket hid Mr Van Gogh's workshirt and firemen's braces, but he didn't look much warmer. His face was the colour of a plucked chicken, with just a few small veins high on his cheeks. Very small, twisted veins, that looked as if they didn't lead anywhere. I stood there beside him, and looked at his work on the walls. The yellow sun seemed to shine particularly on the long wall of the lounge where Mr Van Gogh had his own tribute to the man we knew him as. In green glass cubes was built up the lettering of one of the master's beliefs – Just as we take the train to Tarascon or Rouen, we take death to reach a star – and above that Mr Van Gogh's train to Tarascon and a star rose up the entire wall. The cab was blue; and sparks of pure vermilion flew away. It all bore no more relation to the dross of glasses and ash trays that Mr Van Gogh brought round on Sundays, than the husk of the chrysalis to the risen butterfly.

My father came back and waited with me in the summer evening. 'It has taken years to do, years to do,' he said. 'So many pieces of glass.' The fire and life upon the walls and ceiling defied Mr Van Gogh's drained face. He'd spent all those years doing it, and it didn't help him. It rose like phoenix in its own flame, and he wasn't part of it anymore; but lay on his back and tried to breathe. All the colour, and purpose, and vision of Mr Van Gogh had gone out of himself and was there on the walls about us.

Both the St John's men were fat. I thought at the time how unusual it was. You don't get many fat St John's men. They put an oxygen mask on Mr Van Gogh, and we all lifted him onto the stretcher. Even they stood for a few seconds; amazed by the stained glass. 'Christ Almighty,' said one of them. They took Mr Van Gogh away on a trolley stretcher very close to the ground.

'What do you think?' asked my father.

'He won't necessarily die,' said the St John's man. He sounded defensive. 'He's breathing okay now.'

Mr Van Gogh went into intensive care. The hospital said that he was holding his own; but Mr Souness said he wouldn't come out. He said that it was his ticker; that his ticker was about to give up on him. Anyway there was nothing to stop the Council and the Ministry of Works from going ahead. People came from all over the town to see Mr Van Gogh's house before they pulled it down. There was talk of keeping one or two of the pictures, and the mayor had his photograph in the paper, standing beside the train to Tarascon and a star. But the novelty soon passed, and the glass was all stuck directly to the walls with tile glue. The Town Clerk said there were no funds available to preserve any of it, and it was only glass anyway, he said. Someone left the door unlocked, and Rainbow Johnston and his friends got in and smashed a lot of the pictures. Mr Van Gogh's nephew came from Feilding, and took away the power tools.

My father and I went down to the river to see the house demolished. With Mr Van Gogh's neighbours, Mr Souness, and the linesmen who had disconnected the power, we waited for it to come down. There were quite a few children too. The contractor had loosened it structurally, and then the dozer was put through it. The dozer driver's mate wore a football jersey and sandshoes. He kept us back on the road. Mr Van Gogh's place collapsed stubbornly, and without any dramatic noise, as if it were made of fabric rather than timber. The old walls stretched and tore. Only once did my father and I get a glimpse of Mr Van Gogh's work beneath the weathered hide of the house. Part of the passage rose sheer from the wreckage for a moment; like a face card from a worn deck. All the glass in all its patterns spangled and glistened in yellow, red and green. Just that one projection that's all, like the vivid, hot intestines of the old house, and then the stringy walls encompassed the panel again; and stretched and tore. The house collapsed like an old elephant in the drought, surrounded by so many enemies.

'Down she comes,' cried the driver's mate, and the driver raised his thumb and winked. There was a lot of dust, and people backed away. Mr Souness kept laughing, and rubbed his knuckles into his left eye because of the dust.

'All the time Mr Van Gogh spent,' I said to my father. 'All that colour; all that glass.'

'There'll always be a Mr Van Gogh somewhere,' my father said.

The Master of Big Jingles

I know what it's called now, it's called fennel. Knowing the name doesn't make it what it was however. I see it rarely now. It peers occasionally from the neglected and passing sections, like the face of a small man over the shoulders of others in a crowd. Its fronds are the pale green of hollow glass, and it has a look of pinched resignation, as if it can foresee the evolutionary course before it.

When Creamy Myers and I were young, it was in its prime. There were forests of it pressing in on the town, and it reared up confidently in waxy profusion. The rough strip below the bridge was its heartland, and there Creamy and I had our hut. We could reach it by tunnel tracks from the river bank, and the fence. We built it in the summer which ended our standard four year, and in the summer after that we renewed it in our friendship. The year we finished primary school we restored it again. We cut out the tunnel tracks as usual; so narrow that the top foliage showed no tell-tale gap, and even Rainbow Johnston wouldn't find them. We evicted the hedgehog and its loosely balled nest from the hut, and spread new sacks to mark our occupation. In a biscuit tin we kept the important things, wax-heads, shanghais, tobacco, fishing lines and the tin of cows' teat ointment I found on the bridge.

Fennel is the great home of snails: it is their paradise, nirvana and happy hunting ground. The matchless abundance of the snails was a fascination to us, and a symbol of the place itself. The snails were the scarabs of our own hieroglyphic society, and the snail hunt was the most satisfying of our rituals. From the length, breadth and depth of the river terrace we took them. From time to time one of us would return, and lift his shirt from his trousers, to tumble the catch into the biscuit tin. When we had a massed heap of them, perhaps 150 or more, we would sit in the hut and anoint them. We used the cows' teat vaseline; rubbing it on the shells to darken the pattern and make them shine. We would lie the snails in handfuls amongst the fennel, just off the sacks, and in the penumbral green light. As we watched the snails would begin their ceremonial dispersal: large and small, sly and bold, all with the patterns of their shells waxed and gleaming. Scores of snails, each with its own set angle of direction. The gradual, myriad intersection of the planes of their escape through the fennel was like an abacus of three dimensions.

The friendship of Creamy and myself was the smallest and strongest of several circles. We often played with Arty and Lloyd, and there were other faces that we expected at other times. If we went swimming at the town baths for instance, we joined up with the Rosenberg twins. They didn't seem to do much else but swim. But sometimes when Creamy and I were sick of what the others were doing, or after school when we'd rather be alone, then we'd make our signal, just a movement of the head, that meant we'd meet later at the hut. The hut was something apart from the rest of the world. In its life were only Creamy and me. As long as we agreed, our word was law, and no conventions but our own were followed.

I remember just when Creamy told me about going to Technical. We'd had a snail hunt, and were sitting by the river to wash. Creamy had his shirt off, and the snail tracks glistened on his chest. The linear droppings, inoffensively small, clung there too. 'Dad told me I'm not going to Boys' High after all,' he said. 'He's sending me to Tech.' Creamy's voice was doubtful, as if he wasn't sure if it marked an important decision or not.

'But I thought we were all going to High?'

Creamy leant into the shingle of the river. He supported himself on his arms, and lifted first one hand then the other to wash his chest. 'Dad said if I'm going into the garage with him, I need the Tech courses. He doesn't go much on languages and stuff.' Creamy had a broad, almost oriental face, and his upper lip was unusually full. It sat slightly over the bottom lip, and gave his face an expression of thoughtful drollery.

'I suppose after school we'll be able to do things together just the same. Maybe it's just like being in different classes at the same school.' I had a premonition though that Creamy's father had done something which would harm us.

'I did try to get Dad to change his mind,' said Creamy. He said it almost as if he wanted it recorded; lest some time in the future he might be blamed for not putting up more of a fight. Creamy flexed his arms, and recoiled with easy grace out of the water. He pulled the back of his trousers down, and showed the marks of a hiding. 'I did try,' said Creamy, and his upper lip quirked a little at the understatement.

'I don't see why it should make that much difference.' I could say that because it was weeks away in any case. When you are thirteen, nothing that is weeks away can be taken seriously. Creamy and I controlled time in those days; we could spin out one summer's day for an eternity of experience.

'Maybe I'll play against you in football,' said Creamy speculatively.

'I'll cut you down if you do.' We smiled, and Creamy skipped stones across the surface of the river with a flick of his wrist. The sun dried the water from us, and snapped the broom pods like an ambush on the other side of the river.

Already I was surprised at my innocence in thinking that all my friends must go like myself to the High School.

Time made no headway against us that summer; not while we were together. But then my family went on holiday to the Queen Charlotte Sounds, and I returned to find the world moved on. The new term was before us, and Creamy was indeed going to the Tech, and I to the High.

I didn't see Creamy after school during the first week, and on Saturday when we went after lizards on the slopes behind the reservoir, we didn't wear uniform. But the next Tuesday we met at the hut, and the nature of our division was apparent. Although I should have expected it, Creamy's Tech uniform was a blow. His grey trousers to my navy blue; his banded socks and cap, distinct in a separate allegiance. Creamy was never deceived by outward appearance. A smile spread out under his full upper lip, and creased his tanned face. 'I see you've lost your knob, too,' he said, and lightly touched the top of his cap.

'The fourth formers tore them off. Initiation,' I said.

'Same with us.' It was typical of Creamy that he should notice first about our uniforms a subtlety we had in common; whereas I couldn't help seeing us from the outside. Even my friendship with Creamy hadn't given me a totally personal view. Creamy didn't mention the uniforms again. We left our caps with our shoes and socks in the hut, and waded in the river to catch crayfish. As long as we maintained the old life separate from the new, then both could exist. It was like those studies I did at High School, about the primitive societies existing for hundreds of years, and then collapsing when the white man came. Creamy and I couldn't change much in the old way, because our ideas came from different sources that year. Sooner or later the white man would come; the white man comes one way or another to all the pagan societies of our youth.

I never sat down to think it out, but if I had, it must have seemed that as Creamy and I had held our friendship through the end of that summer, and the first term at our new schools, then there was no reason why we shouldn't go on. That wasn't the way of it however. In the winter months I didn't see much of Creamy. The days were short, and the rugby practices we went to almost always came on different nights. I made new friends too; like big Mathew and Ken Marsden. When I was with Creamy, I sometimes found myself assuming that he knew all about High, and then half-way through some story I'd realize that it must have been meaningless to him. Creamy never showed any impatience. Creamy had a natural and attractive courtesy. He would sit there smiling, his expanding lip faintly frog-like, and say, 'He sounds a real hard case,' or, 'I wish I'd seen that.' Unless I asked him, he never said much about Tech. The odd thing perhaps about sport, or the time he saw Rainbow Johnston smash the windows in the gym. Rainbow was the baron of all our childhood fiefdoms. He had a job at the piecart in the evenings, and made more money by stealing milk coupons. Birds stopped singing when Rainbow came past. He knew how to twist an arm till the tears came, did Rainbow, and it was said he made little kids put their hands in his trousers.

In the third term, when it became summer again, we began going back to the river. Not just Creamy and me anymore though, for I'd grown accustomed to spending my time with Mathew and Ken. The first time I took them to the hut, Arty was with us too. Arty knew Creamy from primary school, but Mathew and Ken didn't. I could see them measuring themselves against Creamy, as the afternoon went on. Creamy didn't seem to mind; Creamy liked a challenge in his own unassuming way. Creamy could stand measurement beside anyone I knew.

The mentality of youth is able to unhook its jaws like a snake, and swallow up whole antelopes of experience. Youth is a time for excess; for breaking through the ice to swim, for heaping up a mountain of anointed snails from the fennel, for sledging until your hands are bleeding from the ropes, and sunstroke smites you down. Youth is a time for crazes; hula-hoops and under-water goggles, bubble gum and three-D cardboard viewers.

But that year it was knuckle bones. The year when Creamy and my new High School friends met, it was knuckle bones. Knuckle bones had risen obscurely, like an Asian plague, and swept as an epidemic through our world – brief and spectacular. Creamy excelled at knuckle bones of course: Creamy was insolently good at knuckle bones. Like chickens about a hen, the knuckle bones grouped and disbanded, came and went around Creamy's hand. Creamy had begun with plastic knuckle bones. The soft-drink colours of the pieces would rise and fall, collect and separate, at Creamy's behest. He won an aluminium set in the Bible class competition. The aluminium ones were heavier and didn't ricochet. Creamy was even better with the aluminium ones. Cutting cabbages, camels, swatting flies, clicks, little jingles, through the arch, goliath, horses in the stable; Creamy mastered them all.

Creamy's expression didn't change when Ken challenged him to knuckle bones. He seemed interested in my new friends. His fair hair hung over his forehead, and his complex face was squinting in the sun. Ken was good at knuckle bones; as good as me, but he wouldn't beat Creamy I knew. Creamy was a golden boy, and it's useless to envy those the gods have blessed. Ken and he went right through knuckle bones twice without any faults. 'What do you think is the hardest of all?' said Creamy. Ken considered. He pushed the knuckle bones about the ground with his finger as he thought.

'I reckon big jingles,' he said.

'Ten big jingles on the go,' said Creamy,. 'I challenge you to ten big jingles without a fault.,

'You go first then,' said Arty. 'You go first and if you make a mistake then Ken wins.'

'All right,' said Creamy. The injustice of it didn't seem to worry him. He started out as smoothly as ever, allowing no time for tension to gather. His rhythm didn't vary, and his broad face was relaxed.

'That's good going,' said Mathew when Creamy had finished, and Ken had failed to match him.

'They're small though, these aluminium ones.' Arty seemed jealous of the praise. 'Smaller than real or plastic knuckle bones. It's a big advantage to have them smaller in big jingles.'

'Stiff', said Creamy.

Later in the afternoon we found ourselves fooling about by the bridge. Along the underside of the bridge was a pipe which Creamy and I sometimes crossed to prove we could do it. 'Creamy and I often climb across that,' I told the others. They looked at it in silence.

'Shall we do it now,' said Mathew at last. He thought he was strong enough to try anything.

There's no dichotomy of body and spirit when you're young. Adults see the body as an enemy, or a vehicle to be apprehensively maintained. There's just you, when you're young; flesh and spirit are indivisible. For Creamy and I then, for all of us in youth, any failure in body was a failure of the spirit too. Creamy went first. As always when he was concentrating, his lunar upper lip seemed more obvious, the humorous expression of his face more pronounced, as though he were awaiting the punch line of some unfolding joke. He leant out, and took hold of the pipe. He moved his grip about, as a gymnast does to let his hands know the nature of the task, then he swung under the pipe, and began hand over hand to work his way to the central bridge support. He used his legs as a pendulum, so that the weight of his body was transferred easily from one hand to the other as he moved. When he reached the centre support, Creamy rested in the crook of its timbers, and looked down to the river. Then he carried on, hanging and swaying below the pipe, becoming smaller in silhouette against the far bank as he went.

'Seems easy enough,' said Arty.

'You go next then', said Ken. Arty measured the drop between Creamy's swaying figure and the river beneath.

'I would,' he said. 'I would, but I've got this chest congestion. I see the doctor about it.'

'Sure.'

Mathew could only think about one thing at a time, and as he was busy watching Creamy he found himself next in line for the pipe. The rest of us by slight manoeuvrings had got behind him. 'It's me then,' said Mathew. He took a grip and his body flopped down beneath the pipe, and stopped with a jerk. His up-stretched arms were pulled well clear of his jersey, and his hands were clamped onto the pipe. The crossing was an exercise in sheer strength for Mathew; he pulled himself along clumsily, and his legs hung down like fence posts below his thick body. I went next. I didn't want Arty in front of me in case he froze, and I couldn't get past. The few feet just before the central support were the worst, for if I looked down there I could see the concrete base of the timber supports on which I'd fall, instead of into the water. I used to count the number of swings I made just there; one, two, three, four, until I was able to put my feet on the wooden supports. The second half wasn't so bad, because at the end if you were tired, you could drop off onto the grassy bank which rose up towards the underside of the bridge.

Arty and Ken didn't go over at all. Arty pretended he'd seen a big trout in the hold beneath the bridge, and he and Ken went down and poked under the bank with a stick. When we came back over the bridge, we couldn't see any big trout in the hole. 'Want to go over the pipe again?' said Creamy mildly.

'That's hard work, that.' Mathew was always honest.

'Good though,' said Creamy.

As we scuffed about in the shingle at the end of the bridge, a horse and rider came past. The horse paused, and with flaunting tail deposited vast rolls of waste. Mathew watched the horse with awe. 'I bet horses are the biggest shitters around,' he said.

'No, in proportion guinea pigs are far greater shitters,' said Creamy.

'Guinea pigs?'

'Yea, in proportion they are.'

'Rabbits are good shitters,' said Arty.

'I don't see how anything could beat horses and elephants', said Ken. As an ally he weakened Mathew's argument. The rest of us recognized the subtlety of Creamy's reasoning.

'Guineas are by far the best shitters in proportion.' Creamy knew he was right. 'Imagine a guinea pig as big as a horse. Now there would be a shitter.'

'Yea,' said Mathew in wonder, and capitulation.

We had a swim, and threw fennel spears at each other during the rest of the afternoon. We forgot about the time, and Ken's sister came looking for him. She left her bike by the road, and came down to the fence, calling out for Ken. 'You've got to come home,' she said. Her breasts caused furrows across the material of her blouse.

'Have you been eating too much or something,' said Arty. We had a good laugh at that witticism. 'Turning into a moo-vie star,' continued Arty, pleased with his reception. He tucked his thumbs into his shirt, and paraded before her and us.

'Oh, get lost,' she said. She began to go back up the bank towards the road. 'You'd better come Ken. You know what'll happen,' she said.

'Hubba hubba, ding ding, look at the tits on that thing,' we sang.

'Watch out for Rainbow Johnston,' I called out.

'Hey, Rainbow, here she is.'

'Quick Rainbow.'

For the first time Ken's sister seemed flustered. She looked back along the river bank, and then hurried on to her bike. I don't know why I called out about Rainbow. Perhaps in looking at her smooth legs and breasts, I found some part of Rainbow in myself; some desire to reach out and pinch her, or twist her arm, or worse.

Ken stayed a little longer, trying to show he wasn't afraid of being late, but we soon all began straggling back down the road. Creamy and I walked the last part together. 'I'm looking forward to the full summer,' I said. Creamy agreed. He played with his knuckle bones, and whistled as he walked, his upper lip funnelling out and creating a very clear, penetrating whistle. His shoes, worn by water and grass during the afternoon, were almost white at the toes. Creamy stopped whistling, and asked me if Ken and Mathew were the two I liked best at High School. I told him I quite liked them.

'I'm getting sick of Arty,' said Creamy thoughtfully. 'You know that. I'm finding Arty pretty much of a pill.'

'So am I', I said. Creamy tossed his aluminium knuckle bones up and down again in the palm of his hand. We were nearly at the street where Creamy turned off. 'You didn't mind Ken and Mathew being there?' I asked him. Creamy didn't give any glib answer. He walked on for a while.

'I suppose it's selfish to just have one or two friends,' he said. 'I suppose as you get older, you meet more and more people and make friends with them. Only I don't seem to find as many as you. There's an awful lot like Arty.'

As Creamy went off home, I thought about that; for the first time I realized that despite being good at everything, Creamy didn't have that many friends. Being good at everything was in itself a disadvantage even. That's what was the matter with Arty; he resented Creamy's ability. Somewhere, sometime, he'd like to see Creamy take a fall.

The next Saturday I went again. Ken couldn't come, but Mathew and Arty did. I hadn't seen Creamy, but I thought he'd be there. He had another Tech boy with him. None of us knew him. He had eyebrows that grew right across the top of his nose. I'd never seen anyone with one long eyebrow like that before. His name was Warwick Masters. When he thought something was funny, he let his head fall forward, bouncing on his chest, and gave a snuffling laugh on the indrawn breath.

Creamy and I hadn't had any snail hunts that summer. No decision was made not to, we just didn't do it. As third formers we were growing out of snail hunts, and onto more fitting things like knuckle bones, and calling hubba hubba, ding ding, at Ken's sister. Yet the way Warwick treated the snails made me so angry, I could feel my throat becoming tight. 'Christ almighty,' said Warwick, 'look at these snails.' He reached into the fennel walls of the hut, and plucked out the snails. 'Just look at these snails will you.' He let his head bounce on his chest, and gave his idiotic, sucking laugh. He arranged a line of them by the wall, then smashed each one with his fist. The shells cracked like biscuits, and what was left of the snails seemed to swell up in visceral agony after Warwick's fist was lifted. Creamy made no attempt to stop him; he hardly seemed to notice what he was doing.

'Don't do that,' I said to Warwick.

'Bloody snails.'

'It only makes a mess in the hut.'

'Stiff,' said Warwick. 'That's really stiff.'

'Just leave them alone.'

'Yea?'

'Yea.'

'Yea?'

'Yea.' The verbal sparring quickened into a semblance of humour, and Warwick bounced his head and laughed.

'Anyway,' said Arty, 'I don't think you Tech guys should come to the hut.'

'It's always been my hut too,' said Creamy seriously. Three summers are an accepted eternity when one is young.

'It's got to be either Tech or High ground,' said Mathew. He like things simple for his own peace of mind. 'All the places got to be either Tech or High.' Mathew's simplicity had found the truth. All the places that mattered in our town were either High or Tech ground. The territories were marked, and only the adults in their naivety were unaware. My father never understood why I wouldn't take the short cut through the timber yard on my way to school.

'This side of the bridge is ours,' said Arty.

'But it's closest to the Tech swimming hole.'

'Stiff.'

Warwick picked up some of the squashed snails and quickly wiped them down Arty's face, then crashed away through the fennel a few paces, and stood bouncing his head and snorting. Creamy's subtle and unique face creased with delight, but he made no movement. Arty flung the remaining mess of snails at him, and urged Mathew to grab him. 'Grab him Mathew, grab him.' Creamy dodged Mathew's first clumsy attempt; he seemed as if he were about to say something, but Arty got in first. 'High onto Tech,' he shouted.

'Yea,' I heard myself say, but without reason. It seemed to come from a surface part of me, and not deeper where I thought things out. Creamy slipped from the hut, and stood with Warwick.

'For today you mean,' he said, smiling. Creamy loved a battle.

'For always,' said Arty. Arty was pleased that at last he had something over Creamy. Creamy was Tech, and the rest of us were High. Creamy was quicker, stronger, better at knuckle bones and swinging under the bridge, a true friend, but he was Tech. Arty, like most weak people, enjoyed advantages he couldn't himself create. 'For always. No more Tech farts on the bank. Fight you for it.'

It was three onto two, but that didn't worry Creamy. He had a sense of occasion though, did Creamy. If it had to be Tech against High after all, then it should be done on a fitting scale. 'Thursday night then,' said Creamy. His full upper lip expanded as he thought about it, and his eyes took on the visionary look with which he regarded his schemes. A look that hinted at the appreciation of more colours than existed in the spectrums of the rest of us. 'On Thursday after school we'll have the full fight between Tech and High for the bank. You get all you can, and we'll meet you. All out war.'

'I don't know,' said Arty. 'Maybe we should set rules and numbers.' Arty's brief moment of initiative was over; Creamy had as always taken control.

'All out war,' he repeated, and Warwick's head bounced and his laugh sounded through the fennel.

'Is it really all out war?' I said. I could see Creamy's face not many paces away, but he didn't answer. 'All out?' I said. Creamy's face was relaxed and droll; so difficult to read.

'Full scale,' cried Warwick. 'Tech against High.' And still Creamy didn't answer.

'We'll win easily,' said Mathew. 'We can round up a dozen or more easily.'

'Look out for Rainbow Johnston, that's all,' called Warwick. He went off laughing, to follow Creamy, who had turned away and begun walking towards the fence below the bridge.

I watched Creamy climb up to the road with Warwick, and I knew it had happened. I knew that him going to Tech and me going to High had ruined our friendship after all. I looked at Arty and Mathew standing by the hut, and I knew that neither of them was half the friend that Creamy had been. 'Do you think they'll really get Rainbow?' said Arty hollowly.

'I've heard things about Rainbow. I think we need plenty of guys.' Mathew's slow logic was depressing.

'Can we get enough though?' said Arty.

'Jesus, Arty,' I said, 'will you stop moaning.'

That week at school we started getting as many allies as we could. Arty wrote the names down at the back of his pad. He had two lists – one headed possibles and one headed probables, like trial teams. There were some names in the possibles that I hardly knew. Not even all the probables were at the gate after school on Thursday though. Arty himself didn't show up until we were just about to go. We told him he was trying to get out of it. 'No I'm not. I'm coming; of course I'm coming. I just had to put off other things, that's all. What do you think of this stick?' Arty had a short piece of sawn timber. He hit it against the five courts, and then tried not to show that he'd jarred his hand. 'I reckon I'm ready,' he said.

We began walking towards the river but a car drew up over the road, and the man driving it called out to Arty. It was Arty's father. Arty went over and talked with him, then came partly back. 'Wouldn't you know it,' he said. 'I've got to go up to the hospital for my tests. It has to be tonight.' With Arty's father watching from the car, it wasn't any use saying much. 'Maybe the Tech will be there again tomorrow night. I'll be right for tomorrow.'

'Sure,' said Ken. Arty walked over the road quickly. As he got into the car he let his stick slip onto the roadway.

'He rang his dad,' said Lloyd. 'That's what he did.' Arty couldn't meet our eyes as the car pulled away.

'What a dunney brush he turned out to be,' said Mathew, and we laughed. I was on the point of telling them what Creamy had said about Arty, Creamy had him picked all right, then I remembered that Creamy had become the enemy.

That left seven of us. Mathew, Ken, Lloyd, Buzz Swanson and the Rosenbergs. And me of course. As we got closer to the bridge I had a strange feeling that our group was becoming smaller, although the number remained the same. Ken was walking beside me, and I saw how frail he was. His legs were so thin they seemed swollen at the knees to accommodate the joints. He had little, white teeth that looked as if they were his first set. Even as Ken smiled at me, I thought to myself that he was going to be useless. I didn't want to be by Ken when we were fighting. I'd keep by Mathew. Mathew's dirty knees were comfortingly large, and he plodded on resolutely. 'Perhaps we should scout around first, and find out how many of them there are,' I said to Mathew.

'I've got to be home by half-past five,' said Ken. I bet you do Ken, I bet you do, I thought. I resolved that not only would I stick with Mathew when it started, I'd make sure Ken wasn't protecting my back. I had some idea it was going to be like the musketeers of Dumas; us back to back against the odds of the Tech boys.

We stood on the raised road leading up to the bridge, and looked over the bank from the fence, across the frothing fennel to the greywacke shingle of the river bed, where the larger stones crouched like rabbits in the afternoon sun. Creamy stepped out from the cover of the willows two hundred yards away. He raised one arm slowly, and lowered it again. It caught the significance of our presence, as a hawk becomes the sky. It had nothing to do with friendship or compromise: it was a sign of recognition. It was a sign of deeper cognizance too, in that we were there. Unlike Arty and the others on the list, we had come. So Creamy acknowledged our equality of hostility.

Life was drama when we were young. The power of it made Lloyd's voice shake when he reminded us to keep together as we broke our way through the fennel. Creamy watched us coming for a bit, then disappeared behind the willows. 'Where are they?' said Ken. They were below the bank, where the terrace met the river bed. As if to answer Ken's question, they began throwing stones which snicked through the fennel.

'Let's head for the willows,' I said. The Tech harried us as we went. I could hear Warwick's indrawn laugh, and I had a desultory stick fight with a boy who used to be in cubs with me. The Rosenberg twins were the best fighters on our side. They probably had the least notion as to why we were there in the first place, but they were the best fighters all right. They seemed to fight intuitively as one person; four arms and four feet. They rolled one Tech kid over the bank, and winded him on the shingle below. Mathew seemed unable to catch anyone to fight in this sort of guerrilla warfare. Nobody took him on, but he was too slow to take on anybody himself. He kept moving towards the willows, and we skirmished about him.

I think the whole thing might have petered out, if Rainbow hadn't come. Even in an all out fight there were rules: you knew that no-one would deliberately poke anything in your eye, or hold your head under water longer than you could hold your breath. Rainbow was different. He liked to hurt people did Rainbow. He stepped up onto the bank by the willows, and halted our forward progress. He had a thick stick. 'So it's Tech against High,' said Rainbow. His features were gathered closely on his round head, like sprout marks on a coconut. He held the stick in front of Ken, and Ken stopped. The rest of us did nothing. We did nothing not just because Rainbow Johnston was a fifth former, but because he was Rainbow Johnston. And deep down we were glad he'd picked on Ken, and not on us.

'I'm pax,' said Ken. It was the best he could think of, and its incongruity set the Tech guys laughing.

'Pax!' said Rainbow bitterly. 'We don't have any pax between Tech and High.' He drew back his stick, and speared it out at Ken, catching him on the side of the chest. Ken fell on his back, and as his head hit the soft grass his hair flopped away from his face, making him seem even younger.

'Ah Jesus,' said Ken, and he got up and felt his side where he'd been struck. He laughed shakily, and picked up his own stick in a show of defiance. Then he dropped his stick again, and began to cry. He slumped down on his knees and held his side. He arched his back and squeezed his eyes closed with the pain.

'We've won,' said Creamy, before anyone else could think of a reaction to what had happened. Rainbow motioned with his stick towards the rest of us. 'We've won,' repeated Creamy quietly. 'You can stay and play in the hut, Rainbow.' Creamy had found the right note as ever. With the fight declared over, Rainbow felt a bit ashamed to be with third formers. He vaulted over the sagging willow trunk onto the river bed, and slouched off upstream. 'See you, Rainbow,' said Creamy.

'Yea,' said Rainbow.

Ken was still crying. There was some blood showing through his shirt from the graze, and Mathew and I helped him up. We began to go back to the bridge through the fennel. 'They can't come here again, Creamy, can they?' called out Warwick. 'It's Tech now.'

'They can't come here again,' said Creamy. His face was the same; relaxed, and with the upper lip creating the impression of incipient humour. He didn't speak with any special triumph.

We broke down the fennel in our retreat, paying no attention to the tunnels Creamy and I had made. I was glad Tech had won. I joined in the talk about the injustice of Rainbow being there, but I was glad they'd won. It gave a more general explanation for the end of our friendship– Creamy's and mine. There couldn't be any personal betrayal when it was a matter of Tech and High; a commitment to a cause. Ken was still crying, but with greater artifice as his sense of heroism grew. He leant to one side, and he held his shirt out so it wouldn't stick to his graze. The fennel fronds were like miniature conifers, smaller and smaller, each in the join of the other as marsupial embryos in a pouch. The oddly coastal smell of the crushed fennel was all about us. 'I don't know that we lost, not really fair and square,' said Mathew. 'If Rainbow hadn't been there I mean.' They could say what they liked, but for myself I knew I'd lost all right. And it was worse that as I climbed from the fennel, up onto the road, I could understand what it was I'd lost, and why.

MICHAEL HENDERSON

Freedom's Ramparts

January 1, 1954 This is the First day I have had a diary to enlist in. This diary was given me by the kindness of Granpa, Dr Ernest Happenstance. It is a special doctor's diary, so each day has a medicine. Now for my recordings. Nice day at beach. Had 3 swims. Dad accompnied us in one. Had big bonfire last night to celebrate New Year. Water was phosferescent.

CALCIUM-S: *Allergic states*

Once bronze fists called Victoria – *long to reign over us!* – annexed the toilet fixture tight at the level of his upcrouched eyes, the virginal scroll ever giving cause to sing with heart and voice *God Save the Queen!* And he, holding fast to the high cold throne while parental steps patrolled the linoleum court, learned too soon the joys of monarchy; he was an infant despot wielding a septic sceptre, leaning victorious on the ancient plunge flush in that inaugural dike and disposing the common law of his people's principality. No such thing as a wet bed, plague and death, no fowls to be fed, aeroplanes could not find him. He launched his dream raft and turned all his woes to mirth.

January 15, 1954. 11.20 a.m. Amazing sight rendered us from the heavens. In the midst of reading, excited cackling from the ducks roused me and upon looking out the window I saw large vapour trails headed by some object, beyond explanation, at an amazing speed. Three objects were seen. Newspaper report: 'Royal Air Force Vampires flying at 400 m.p.h. at 35,000 feet.' MESANTOIN: *Psychomotor seizures. January 16. Went to Nelson to see Queen. After a very interesting procession of floats we had lunch with my Granpa, Dr Ernest Happenstance. Shortly after 2 o'clock the Queen drove past allowing a quick glimpse.* CALCIBRONAT: *Rhume des foins. Notes. We must remember the 16th was the day of the Queen's visit to Nelson. It was a typical Nelson day, on the 16th, hot sunny and cloudless. On the way to Nelson all cars were held behind an endless stream of cars. I did not get a medal because I did not go with my old school class (Std. 4). All the school got a medal a flag and a QE2 ice block.*

Neither at school could they get him there. Not the masters smelling of chalk, strange blunted men with their pencils in their pockets. Not Jerp nor Straight nor Piles nor Sack. Not one of those blackboard dusters. Nor Scrooge nor Greasy nor Hori nor Fungus. No not one of those dry-cleaned gaffers could enter his dike *built by Nature for herself* and say Now Look Here Young Man When I Was Your Age I Read The Dictionary. Reassuring us on our spiteful behinds. *Vivant professores!* Vivant Scobie, Shag and Moon! Let sense be dumb, let flesh retire – he who would valiant be 'gainst all disaster, let him incontinently wallow the master!

Nor the boys smelling of morning milk, blobs who clotted together. They could not get him there though they might knee-see his feet and lob water overtop. There he sat divining the patterns in the concrete, praying he was in The Team for Saturday. *February 27. In morning play cricket for C team. Go in last man score 0 not out. Did not bowl. Clubs in morning as usual.* PURSENNID: *Atonic constipation.* There after lights out he chocolate-chippie read unconfiscated books. *Notes. Books read during April Man Alone worth 4/5 Down in the Drink 3/5 Merchant of Venice (School) 4/5. Notes. Every night pranks in dorm are numberless: Pillow fighting, throwing slippers, stripping beds, fighting, arguing, throwing property outside etc.* While there on his dike – *Sanctify our every pleasure!* – he read The Perfumed Garden and waterlogged his dream raft, O balsa balsam, balm of Mecca, Hercules' inceptive labour, flowering *Impatiens Balsamina!* – for when golden youth is wed, and in marriage our joys are dead, *nos habebit humus, nos habebit humus.*

Pavilioned in splendour, he let the name calling assembly rant on. Father Son and Holy Ghost. Pilate's voice called your name and Dangle Smith's and Smoothie Gascoyne's and Hangman Harper's and Corkscrew Coney's and Dropsy Duncan's and Glorious God's. These People Report. Do Shall Did Not. Own Up. Stand Up. Hands Up. Line Up. Speak Up. Shut Up. Socks Up. *Ad Alta.* Fear Not The Heights. With Three Times Three Shout Lustily. World Without Amen. Follow Up. On Your Balls! *Adeste Fideles.* Sing Up. *Alleluia.* Once More Boys. On Our Balls! On Our Balls! We'll Shout As We Roll On Our Balls! Send Forth A Proud Rajah! Never The Battle Raged Hottest But In It! Lest We Forget Uprightness. Lest We Forget *Probitas.* Lest We Forget. They turned the calendar of his teens with dippoldic digits until the days stuck; with paraphiliac prohibition inspissated tongues saccharined the moth of youth until he sang twinkle twinkle little star while they sang god defend new zealand *in the nations' Butcher van selling beef and* Truth *to man*, until on his dike he– O still the small voice of alarm – sang *Set down my name, Sir. Sitfast. I'll fear not what men say. They do but themselves. My strength the more is.*

February 18. Every morning we have a cold shower and then practise clubs, which you have to swing like a bag-pipes dumb major. METHERGIN: *Post-partum period.* Dumb-bells, clubs, hakas, military parade, church parade, fagging, fatigues, hard labour, fives, showers, prep, first bell, cross country, second bell, boxing, prayers, preparing young men, roll call, preparing young men to be Old Boys, bend over, face the wall, bending young men to be Upright old boys. *March 20. Schedled to play for C's against Old Boys, who did not arrive, so had pick up game between ourselves.* DIGILANID: *Paroxysmal tachycardia.* Reading under the blankets with a Woolworth's torch; talking after lights out. *February 16. Caned in pyjamas by Mr Algernon, commonly known as 'Fungus Face' or 'Fungus Bum'.* OPTALIDON: *Antalgique non stupéfiant.* Talking in prep, talking in assembly, talking in church, talking in English. Gated. *March 23. We, the new boys, are suffering countless amounts of shoes, cricket boots, shirts, socks, jockstraps, football jerseys, etc. to clean for* Great Seniors! *Ha! Ha! They send us to shops for whitebait hooks and left-handed pocket knifes. By end of this month we have to know by heart College Song, Board of Governors, Cowdeamus, School motto, God Defends NZ, 1st XI, House XI, and what is on the sundial. If you do not know, the old boys cane you. They make you put your head in a tuck locker. Or go in the Drying Room or boiler room. If you stay on the dike you can not be tested.* PLEXONAL: *Terreur nocturne.* Report in, report out. *March 22. School parades in cadet companies to see film on Royal Coming at Majestic Theatre. Am in F Company.* HYDERGINE: *Arteriosclerosis obliterans.* No crew-cuts, no Yul Brynners. *Notes. Every morning now we have clubs in squads. Clubs—at which hopeless. March 2. Clubs. Usual school work. Cadets. Practise clubs murderously during day. Have been at College 4 weeks today.* BELLADENAL: *Peptic ulcer. March 4. Fine day with shifty breeze. Clubs. Ordinary school day. Caned by Algernon. Practise for C's in nets. Violin practise. Bible-class.* CALCIUM-S OINTMENT: *Dermatitis. March 31. Clubs. School. Military parade. Violin Practise. Caned twice by Mr Sawney-Beane for playing with ruler and not saying sir.* BELLERGAL: *Acrodynie infantile.* Squads. Quad. Physical reject. Shooting. Life saving. Debating. *April 3. Sports Day. Dad comes in morn. In afternoon I run in 100yds under 12. Governor General presents prices. After dinner Dad leaves for home. I cryed profusely. Caned by Buttons for not cleaning his sports gear enough.* HYDERGINE: *Dead fingers.* One man had one talent, another had two. Pull your talons out. *April 25. Holiday, but we have to parade in Anzac Day parade. Headmaster saluted as College Band played God defends NZ. Buttons and other seniors attacked demonstrators.* CALCIUM-S: *États allergiques. Notes. The Headmaster said this fight for the War Memorial was in our War Record. He made Buttons R.S.M.* At the mowing down of our sons and in the mourning we shall remember Buttons.

May 6. Home for Holidays: – Hooray!!!! Catch 8.45 Newmans bus, arrive home safely. Been away 93 days in all. Bevan sick in bed with German meals. Beaut to be home. ALLISATIN: *Infectious intestinal catarrh.* Report in. Roll call. First bell. Second bell. Second term. Lights out. *May 25. Back at College. Military parade for resumtion. Two new boys arrived from Chch. Moved to dorm 6 so as 2 new boys can stay together.* HYDERGINE: *Intermittent claudication. June 2. First Dancing glass for me (Alright).* STROPHOSID: *Paroxysmal nocturnal dyspnoea. June 3. Gym: – hurt wrist, pissed off. There is now alot of mumps going round, & we think that if theres a few more we might be able to go home! Mr Algernon confiscated my book.* HYDANTAL-S: *Jacksonian seizures.* Boaters, waistcoats, collar and studs to church: do not buy Sports Post and do not go by Crouse. *June 6. 1st XV play Wellington Old Boys. (Am Ballboy). Buttons gave me all his gear to wash after the game. School sees 'D-day, sixth of June'. We have to know School haka, house haka, 1st XV, house XV, forty years on and all the prefects by heart. The only way not to be reached is to stay in the dike. Three chaps in San. in our dorm. Kerr, Jack, Pahar. Who will be next? Quite alot of sickness. Join Drama Club, hope it will be worthwhile. Campbell's Kingdom 4/5.* BELLERGAL: *Anxiété.* Dumb-bells. Hakas. Preparing young men to be old boys. *Tempus fugit. Pietas probitas et sapientia. July 3. Brown I was 4 wrong in Pick the All Blacks: – Bowers Elsom Hill Pryor diffed out. Mr Norman McKenzie says 5 fundamentalls of Rugby are: – 1. Tackle balls and all. 2. Kick balls with both feet. 3. Dribble. 4. Fall on balls. 5. Catch all types and pass. (Buttons says to learn well all these).* CALCIBRONAT: *Post-concussional disorders.* Clean shoes clean mind. Sixpence in the church plate. *August 9. Junior Speaking, have quite a crap. After school have kicks with football. Dancing. Go up rifle range in drill period for 1st time. Don't do to bad, get 52/100. (Experience will tell.) Do Hard labour for Algernon, shovelling coke and grubbing gorse on Grampians.* Bible-class. HYDERGINE: *Troubles circulatoires cérébraux. August 15, Sunday. Church. Drama Club rehearsal. Go off alright. First time I've had make up on.* CALCIUM-S: *Exudative conditions.* Dotheboys' Balls. *September 20. Royal Air Force Vampire came over at about 1.40 p.m. School stayed out to watch. Had super views of it as it came over us three times. Supposed to be very powerful plane. Headmaster saluted under school flag. Military parade instead of cross-country run, to celebrate. Afterwards play Brown I and King II in fives. Then bible-class.* HYDERGINE: *Insuffisance coronarienne.* Dining-room maids out of bounds. Fifteen minutes after the dance. Fifteen inches between partners. *Vivant omnes virgines!* Hands off. Hands up. Bend over. Uprightness. *Vivat Alma Mater! September 25. Cold showers in morning supervised by Mr Algernon. Buttons caught me walking on seniors path. Massed choir practise after tea. New headmaster announced. A Mr Bercich. He will move in next Feb. All we know is he has a good war record and was a colonel and is in Territorialls. Mr Marfell fainted during tea. At lights out Jerp told us Mr Marfell had been a batchelor to long.* PARTERGINE: *Induction de l'accouchement. Note. Jerp is our housemaster. He said we do not now how the Nelson mother's sceme for their daughters. Only Prefects may walk past Crouse. Note. Crouse is the Girls' College.* The Power of The Badge. Respect all badges: Prefect R.S.A. Boy Scout Rotary Rosicrucians Round Table M.R.A. Lions Royal Overseas League Y.M.C.A. Salvation Army Royal NZ Vampire Force Navy League L.M.V.D. P.P.T.A. *October 9, Saturday. Muck around all day. Had book confiscated. That night 'Cantate Domino' in concert with National Orchestra in Assembly Hall. Have pretty bad cold, my nose bled alot.* FERRONICUM: *Essential hypochromic anaemia. October 15. During morning, rehearsal for tomorrow nights' Music Festival. Have still got pretty bad cold, can't seem to get rid of it.* CEDILANID: *Auricular fibrillation. October 16, Saturday. Fine to wet. That night Music Festival (Was in 4 items.) (Of the prefects – Blundle is pissing me off now.)* CALCIBRONAT: *Sédatif et neuro-équilibrant. October 20. Finals of boxing: Brown I did well out of our house. After tea, house music competitions. We sang 'Rule Britannia' and we were second.* MESANTOINE: *Epilepsie – Grand mal. October 30, Saturday. Wet day. The weather has pissed me off lately – . In morning wash clothes. Meet Brown II's father,*

General Brown, who is Chief of N.Z. scouts. In afternoon (too wet for cricket) others go to pictures but I Do preparation of form magazine. A bit off a piss off of a day. CALCIUM-S: *Piqûres et morsures d'insectes. November 20, Saturday. Only 27 days to end of first year! Buttons caned me for not knowing clubs. MEM: – Write to Gran, home. SWOT. (Write to: – Secretary French Consul French legation, Wellington, for Facts on france.* OPTALIDON: *Céphalées. November 22. School certificate begins for fifth formers. Just think, in four years I'll have to sit. . . ! What a crap! Jerp tore up book I was reading. Past-Present cricket match. The whole house has been gated on General Principle. Hard labour for me: wash quad with scrubbing brush.* BELLAFOLINE: *Spastic constipation. November 28, Sunday. Bloody piss off of a day. Nobody in the House is aloud out after College Service. Just muck around. Today Brown II learnt he didn't have a father and through a wobbly. Brown I isn't really his brother either. He wasn't meant to learn but he saw one of Jerp's papers.* PARTERGINE: *Uterine inertia. December 6. Annual Physical measurements – which are, unfortunately, a bit of an embarrassment to me. I seem to be a naturally light and thin boy – but I am becoming increasingly unheeding and unworrying over physical appearance: anything anyone says etc. I got 5/- from the Quiz Kids for having a question selected – it was answered. Then I was sent some french material and had a letter from Uncle Thrumbull. MEM – Write letter one prep night to Uncle Thrumbull telling all news.* MESANTOIN: *Electro-shock therapy. December 10. Caned for being out of bounds, also for not wearing cap, by Algernon. Find out I have won a prize for drawing. I was very pleased and surprised.* SCILLAREN: *Portal cirrhosis with ascites.* One man had five, another ten, another one. To every man according to his.

All This Free To The Age Of Nineteen!

June 6, 1956 Buttons caned me for not knowing God defends New Zealand. Am considering writing book. HYDERGINE: *Labile hypertension.*

CHRIS ELSE

Big Jim Cook and the Wheel of God

Big Jim Cook woke up. It was Saturday morning. The sunlight oozed through the slats of the venetians and trickled down like the lemon icing on one of the Old Sheila's sponges. Big Jim imagined it flowing slowly over the house, worming out of the sky from the nozzle of a cosmic icing bag softly squeezed. From out there, in the bright space of day, the world was just a fancy cake decorated with liquorice roads and sugar houses in bright pastel colours. Big Jim would have seen it clearly if he had closed his eyes, but he was awake and troubled, as furtive as one of the curled-up ants beneath the gnawed-out surfaces.

Behind him, in the soft Sleepyhead sprung foam warmth, the Old Sheila turned over and began to snore. Big Jim listened without anger or interest. Time was when he had thought her the best-looking little snorer in town but feelings had hardened into habit over the years. It wasn't her fault, just as it didn't seem to be his. They were both getting on, sagging a bit with the wrinkles coming, and somewhere between hired labour and the bar of the Whitby RSA Big Jim had bought himself a round white gut bristling with hairs like a side of raw pork. The Old Sheila had a right to snore. She did most of the work in the business these days, keeping the books and answering the phone while Big Jim stood around being the boss and watching other people sweat. Worked himself into a corner.

The sunlight trickled through the blind and over the window sill but it still hadn't dripped onto the La-z-boy, lay-back, padded chair beneath where his trousers and his checked shirt lay wrestling in a shadowy heap. The trousers had a head-lock on an arm or maybe the shirt was working a half nelson on the left leg, it was hard to tell. Neither had much advantage as far as Big Jim could see and both were waiting for him to stop looking so they could get down to it again. He stared and kept on staring. After a while, he had been staring so long he thought he might be dead.

The sound of a motor mower ripped through the wall from outside. Eight-thirty. The joker next door was shaving his lawn again. The Old Sheila snorted and twisted awake.

'Oh, Lord,' she said, 'does he have to do that at this hour?'

'Looks like it.' His voice sounded too loud, booming like a coffin lid.

She grabbed the alarm clock and stared at it, heaved back with a yawn.

'What's wrong with you, then?' she demanded. 'You're usually up by this hour.'

'Don't feel like it.' And what did he feel like?

'Suit yourself.'

At breakfast, fresh as an ice cream in her pink housecoat, she served bacon and eggs and tea and toast. Big Jim watched Kevin stuffing his eighteen-year-old face and reflected on the mystery of having grown-up children. It seemed another reason for doing nothing. Viciously, he stabbed his bacon and eggs through the left eye.

'I reckon we ought to get one of those new wall-to-wall deep freezers,' the Old Sheila said, working over the plastic tomato with the sauce in it. Was that what she said?

'What for?' he asked.

'It'd be a lot more economical. Eat better for less.'

'We eat good enough now.'

'You are in a mood. I hope you're not going to spend the whole day moping.'

'I'll fix the bathroom tap and then go down the Raza.'

'Boozing,' Kevin said, his mouth full.

'And what'll you be up to?'

'Dunno. I might drag the bike round to Lenny's.'

'Bikes!' Big Jim echoed his son's tone deliberately. 'An idiot's game!'

'A bloody sight better for you than sitting round the Raza with a bunch of old twits what forgot to die in the war.'

'Don't you speak to your father like that!' the Old Sheila said, waving her knife.

'Well, it's true. He never even saw any fighting anyway. All he did was count socks in Malaya for a year.'

'That's no excuse!' the Old Sheila said.

Big Jim looked from one to the other. What were they arguing about? 'The kid's right,' he said. 'Everybody's right. That's the trouble.'

'He's not going down the RSA anyway,' the Old Sheila told Kevin as if Big Jim was somewhere else. 'Not first thing, he's not.'

'What is he doing, then?' Big Jim asked.

'Taking me to the Show.'

'What you want to go there for?' Kevin demanded.

'Why not?'

'It's full of fuddies looking at stuff they're never going to buy.'

'That's right. Like me and your father. I want to see them freezers.'

At the entrance, the turnstiles clicked like a pair of turbine pumps sucking in the air to keep the exhibition hall blown up to full pressure. Bits of the population were being dragged along in the draught. The Old Sheila in blue and beads was happy on her stack heels. Big Jim paid the money. Between the iron webbed roof and the concrete floor, partition walls rose up dividing the space into booths and stands. A model bathroom in pink and chrome presided over by a man in a neat striped suit. A cooking demonstrator red-faced, chef's hat, stainless steel voice whining soft instructions.

'What about these blinds?' the Old Sheila asked, pointing.

'We got blinds.'

'But those are the new ones, double-action, reverse pull nylon cords. I've seen them on telly.'

The young woman's smile fixed bright as they approached. Not long ago, yesterday even, Big Jim would have enjoyed looking at her and thinking about her body trapped in the tailored trouser-suit. Now it didn't seem to matter. Blinds with icing dripping through them squeezed by the cosmic cook in the chef's hat, soft instructions. Blind like a fried egg, split and bleeding yolk and tomato sauce. Kevin was right. A couple of fuddies, just looking.

The Old Sheila slipped the pamphlets into her bag. 'That freezer stand must be down here some place.' Down through the strings of people. Music blared from the amusement arcade. Across the aisle, above their heads, hung a great banner: 'Twelve o'Clock Today. THE GREAT GOD GIVING LOVE SHOW. Live on Stage.' To the right, a thin man with a bald head was trying out a La-z-boy lay-back armchair while his wife looked on. Something to die in, maybe.

'Here we are,' the Old Sheila said, stepping up onto the stand amid the white enamel.

'Yes, madam, can I help you?'

'We want to look at the big one.'

'Ah, the new Freezemaster. Here we are. Eighteen cubic feet. Special section compound lid. Racks for easy handling.'

'That's nice.'

'And along this end we have the super quick freeze drop well.'
'For the gumboots,' Big Jim said.
'I beg your pardon, sir?'
'For the gumboots. I wear a lot of gumboots in my work.'
The young man's face tightened into a nervous smile beneath his black moustache. 'In the freezer, sir?'
'I don't wear 'em in the freezer. I keep 'em there.'
'Don't be a fool, Jim,' the Old Sheila said, nudging him.
The demonstrator laughed at the joke. His moustache quivered as if it was trying to polish his teeth.
'Frozen gumboots are the best thing in the world for tinea,' Big Jim said. 'You know what tinea is?'
'Er, no.' The smile came back.
'Athlete's foot. Big problem with gumboots.'
'Look,' the Old Sheila said, 'if you can't be serious, why don't you go throw coconuts or something. I want to talk to this man.'
'See you later.'
'Certainly, sir.'

Big Jim stood on a plywood corner and rolled himself a smoke. The coconuts didn't appeal but it was good to be shot of the responsibility of spending money. He couldn't cope with decisions, not today, not with the strange feeling of unreality which had scattered his waking thoughts even before he had got them together. Where was the man who had built a business out of nothing, working nine hours a day in clay trenches with a shovel until he could afford machines to do the job? He ought to be thinking of expanding instead of standing around on street corners. He ought to take an interest. In what? The question shrugged at him. He eased his belt around the only expansion he had done for a year and pulled morosely on his smoke. There must be something in the world a joker could do with himself. A child, its face buried in pink candy floss, stopped to stare at him until its mother dragged it away. I'm turning green, Big Jim thought, running his fingers round his unshaven jaw.
Down the corridor, between the blue spark of the welding demonstration and the insulation stand, there was a blare of music and a coloured roll of light. A knot of people was gathering. Big Jim sauntered towards them assailed by mute appeals for interest on both sides. Get your chain saws here, ladies and gentlemen! Every one a virgin, guaranteed! See the strongest lavatory bowl in the world! The tattooed bathmat! Daring bareback dishwashers perform death-defying feats! The crowd, thickening gently, moved on, ignoring such phrenetic claims, drawn to the dark squared doorway where the lights moved, blue, green, yellow, red, across the bodies packing in.
Big Jim peered round the lintel into the darkened hall. Dim figures moved together, jostling expectantly. Beams of colour flicked over their faces, momentarily distorting features with unfamiliar shadows. The lights came from a slow-moving wheel fitted with lamps which swung back and forth as they circled the dark centre, floating their random selection over the audience in a slow, hypnotic rhythm. Beside the wheel, illuminated by a single, white spot, stood a man in a dark suit and a bow tie. He held a book in one hand and he was leaning forward over the knob of a microphone.
'Jesus saves,' he crooned, in a healthy bass. 'Jesus saves and so do you.'
'What's it all about?' a voice whispered at Big Jim's side.
Another voice answered. 'Quiet. They'll start in a minute.'
'A load of rubbish, if you ask me.'
The man at the microphone tensed suddenly. He spread his arms and leaned back: 'And the Lord said "Let there be light"!' A triumphant shout of joy and

suddenly the stage was filled with brightness. The people gasped. There before them was a vast display of manufactured wealth: lawn mowers, refrigerators, stereograms, lounge suites, vacuum cleaners, washing machines, outboard motors, colour tv sets, all arrayed as if conjured forth by the compere's dramatic gesture. The great wheel, with its coloured beams, turned slowly, smearing the walls and the bodies below with dabs of soft pastel. Above it hung a huge banner which proclaimed in bold, black letters: 'THE GREAT GOD GIVING LOVE SHOW starring JUMPING JOHN THE BAPTIST by courtesy of GOLDEN WONDER CHICKEN, Tennessee, U.S.A.'

'Hi!' the man at the microphone breathed, sweeping the audience with his loving eye. 'A big, wide welcome to the Showgrounds here today. A big, wide welcome to all those who have the Faith, brothers and sisters. And if you don't have the Faith, then don't go away. We're going to show you the Power of God, here today. Oh, yes indeedy, the POWER OF GOD. For the Lord will lay his hand upon the Righteous and raise him up, but the Sinner will be cast down, even to the DEPTHS OF HELL.'

Big Jim, who had never had too much time for the Lord one way or the other, was not very impressed by this speech. He turned to go but, as he did so, his eye caught a face on the other side of the hall, a face briefly lit by a shaft of red light. It was Kevin, surely. Denim jacket and long dark hair, attention fixed on the slowly revolving wheel as if he was hypnotized. Big Jim changed his mind and began to edge his way through the crowd.

'This is the Lord's game,' Jumping John was saying, 'and the rules are simple. One easy question and if you get it right you can come before the altar and pray. One easy question and the light falls on you. Here we go now. The first question is . . . Who was the first president of the United States? Wait for the Light of God, brothers and sisters, wait for the light. Who was the first president of the United States?'

Big Jim squeezed through the press, apologizing for the toes he crushed. Nobody seemed to notice him. Everyone's gaze was fixed on the lights which played their mesmeric rhythm over the waiting faces. Suddenly, the movement stopped.

'The red light, brothers and sisters. It's the red light. You there lady, with the glasses. That's right, ma'am. Who was the first president of the United States?'

'George Washington?'

'That is correct! Come up before the altar, sister. Come up, come up. And while she comes, folks, we'll have another question.'

Kevin and his mate Lenny were standing close to the stage, their upturned faces stilled by tension. The lights stopped again. Another question was answered correctly. A collective sigh of satisfaction and envy swept up from the audience. Kevin shifted nervously and whispered something to Lenny. Big Jim touched his sleeve.

'Dad?' A startled look as if he'd been caught at the whisky bottle.

'Full of old fuddies, eh?'

'This is different, Dad. That trail bike, see?' He pointed to the gleam of chrome and paint on the stage. 'We're after that.'

'How do you reckon you're going to get it?'

'Answer the question and pray. If the lights pick you.'

'Pray?'

'That's what you have to do.'

And why not? Big Jim wondered. It made as much sense in his mind praying for a trail bike as for a clear conscience. You were just as unlikely to get the one as the other. He looked at his son's earnest face and remembered himself at eighteen, signing up for the regular army because he didn't know what else to do. A trail bike was an easy answer to a lot of problems and he could have wished he had a desire of his own to match it, something to lay his hand on and say 'Right, I'm a happy man,' something to make sense of the sunlight through the blinds.

The air had gone strange, green as peppermint, soft like a bedspread. Big Jim was hardly aware of the change until Kevin nudged him.

A voice spoke: 'Where did Davy Crockett die, brother? That's all you've got to tell me. Where did Davy Crockett die?'

Big Jim turned his head and gazed into the green light which shone full in his face. The glare spread outwards from a cold, white-green centre. There was nothing else to see.

'Come now, brother,' the voice told him, beckoning him forward into the bright mystery. 'Where did Davy Crockett die?'

'Go on, Dad. The Alamo. The Alamo.' Kevin's excited voice was whispering at his shoulder.

'The Alamo,' Big Jim said like a megaphone.

'And you are right, brother! Come up, before the altar.'

The green light swung away, drifting once more in its endless probing. Big Jim stood bemused, wondering exactly what had happened.

'Go up on the stage,' Kevin said.

'What?'

'Get on the stage.'

'I'm not going up there.'

'Oh, come on, Dad. Think of that trail bike.'

'You can't sell out on us now, Mr Cook.' Lenny, pale and eager, appealed to him. And a man had to do something with his life.

Big Jim was the third in line after the woman with glasses and a small, bald man whose hands were shaking. There were people behind him too but he didn't know how many because the light at the side of the stage was dim. What time was it? It must be afternoon still but in the gloom of the hall he felt as if night had already fallen, as if he had jolted awake out of a dream he could not now remember, and was standing on the floor beside the bed wondering where the bathroom was. Except that there was no bed, only a gleaming line of appliances and gadgets in a flood of white light and the man in the dark suit holding the microphone. The lights had stopped scanning the audience now. The coloured beams cut straight down the hall through the darkness onto a screen at the far end where they turned slowly to the rotation of the wheel.

'Brothers and Sisters! Here are the sinners!' Jumping John the Baptist pointed to the line of waiting people. 'They have eaten of the tree of knowledge, folks. They have come before the altar seeking grace and forgiveness and God's Gifts. How will the Lord God receive them? You don't know, brothers and sisters, and I don't know. Only the Lord God can see into their hearts and tell if they are truly repentant.' He turned and beckoned to the woman with glasses. 'Come up, sister. Come up and pray.' The woman stepped forward.

'What's your name, sister?'

'Doris.'

'Well, Doris, and what do you do then?'

'I'm a housewife.'

'Aha. And what do you want to pray for? Which of God's gifts have you got your eye on, eh?'

'I'd like the washing machine.'

'The Mighty Tub Double Action Fully Automatic Condor? That's number nine. Okay, Doris, we'll see how pure your heart is.' He pointed down the hall to the turning circle of lights. 'There's the wheel of God, sister. Pray your prayer for number nine and we'll see if the Lord will answer.'

The woman stood staring down the hall. The Wheel of God turned. Slowly, a number defined within the circle. It was seventeen.

'Oh, ho, ho,' Jumping John crowed, hovering over the woman, his face twisted in a satanic grin of triumph. 'Your sins have found you out, sister. God gives a no-no. You're unclean, sister. Your soul is a mass of weeping sores, ulcerated with sin. How dare you come before the Lord in a state like that?' The woman began to cry, still staring at the far wall. 'Tears won't help you either. You're bound for hell, sister. Unless you go back and repent for another time.' He turned to the audience. 'Where's she going, folks? She's going to Hell. Where there are no Mighty Tub Double Action Fully Automatic Condors and you have to wash your clothes in stinking mud. Begone, sinner.'

The woman turned away and walked back to where the waiting contestants were standing. Her face was folded in a grimace of pain, puzzlement, and disbelief. The man with the shaking hands looked up at Big Jim.

'I'm not going on there,' he said.

'Why not? You got something to be ashamed of?'

'Plenty. Haven't you?'

'I never thought about it,' Big Jim told him.

'You're next, then. You can have my turn if you're so sure of yourself.'

Sure of himself? Big Jim was never sure of anything.

'Come up, come up and pray, brother,' Jumping John was saying. There seemed no reason not to.

'What's your name, brother?'

'Jim Cook.'

'Uhuh. And what do you do, Jim?'

'Drainage contractor.'

'Make a good living, do you?'

'Fair enough.'

'To him that hath shall be given!' Jumping John announced. 'You've picked out a blessing, of course.'

'Yer. I'm after that trail bike. My boy wants it.'

'Number forty-seven for you, brother Jim. Number forty-seven for your boy.'

The lights turned, red, yellow, green, blue, slowly at first and then faster and faster until they blurred into a brown-grey-white glowing ring. Big Jim stared. His mind was as blank as a dawn breakfast. He did not feel the audience below him or the grinning compere by his side. He could no more think of God than he could of the trail bike or the number he had been given. Somewhere in the depths of memory was the vague image of an eighteen-year-old on his first parade, wondering what the hell he had got himself into. He could picture the Old Sheila pursing her lips like a cash bag full of good sense because he was making a fool of himself again. Forty-seven came up in the middle of the circle.

'Hallelujah, brother!' Jumping John shouted and there was a burst of cheering and clapping from the audience. 'Hallelujah for a sinner saved! Your prayers are answered, brother Jim, and because the Lord finds favour you can try again. Three prayers for the Faithful, Jim boy. Three prayers. What's it to be this time?'

'My wife has her eye on that freezer over there.'

'Selfless again! Your number is now five. Five, brothers and sisters. Five for the sinner who came back to the fold. Pray with him, folks. Bow your heads before the power of Almighty God.'

The wheel turned. What did it matter if he made a fool of himself? He had been doing that ever since he had outgrown his ambition. In the days when he had shovelled clay for a living he had had some sense of purpose. Now he was fit only to stand on a stage and raffle his desires in public. Number five came up in the centre of the wheel. The crowd cheered and hooted. Jumping John the Baptist leapt high into the air and screamed delight. An angel stepped out of the darkness behind him. Her wings were silver, sparkling with rainbow sheen. Her long gold dress rippled softly as she walked and she smiled with all the mystical assurance of a photograph. Smiling, with perfect painted lips, she took Big Jim's hand.

'Your Guardian Angel,' Jumping John said. 'She's here to help you with the Star Prize. Pray for the Star, brother Jim. Pray this one for the Holy Ghost.'

Big Jim stared at the long white fingers which had gripped his own. The nails were delicate and painted red. He wondered what he was supposed to do with them. The angel had blue eyes and blonde hair. Her face held a slightly peeved expression as if she wished she was back in Heaven. She didn't seem too interested in a drainage contractor who was pushing middle age and forty round the waist. She didn't seem delighted when a star came up in the Wheel of God.

There was a burst of organ music and a choir began to sing the Hallelujah Chorus. A spotlit, golden throne descended from the roof in a blaze of glory. Jumping John the Baptist could hardly make himself heard.

'Paradise, brothers and sisters! Paradise by courtesy of Air New Zealand and the Tourist Hotel Corporation. A year's holiday in every part of the country with free travel and accommodation and fifty dollars a day spending money. Thus is the Lord's Anointed raised in benediction for the Glory of God and the Wonder of Mankind.'

The angel led him to the throne. They sat together side by side. As the choir sang and the audience cheered, they rose into the heavens. The angel's wing got caught in the pulley but Big Jim untangled it. He looked down as the world receded below him.

MICHAEL MORRISSEY

After the Flood

If things are unique, when they go, it's a loss. But you can always look at it the other way: endlessly you can begin again.

No solace for how she feels afterwards when it's mid-July and outside there's a dog on heat. No doubt the cabbages are drowning. Dangerous to walk along the verandah: too many holes larger than a human foot. Between the angel and the telephone the rain leaks . . . what kind of a world to bring someone into. But there's never a time, says another voice, when you're entitled to dismiss everything. Outside the world is asking a huge relentless question and upstairs his fingers on the guitar were asking. . . .

Maybe he wasn't good enough to record but he was damn good just the same. And the concentration: he looked as though he cared. Sometimes after a smoke he'd be amused at what his fingers did, they were apart from him. Like me, she thought.

The life she had, most of it, was here in this half intended room where the curtains weren't properly hung, and the scrim exposed. It was neither small nor large, but she could tuck the bed away in the alcove or place it near the sealed fireplace where it would jut out, an intrusion. There was a room inside her too with an extra burrowed bit at the end, as though an animal had gnawed its way into the centre. She'd signed the paper, of course, her signature said she understood, but they never told her how cold everything would feel. Those long metal instruments made it like going to the dentist; an enormous rotting tooth whose base had to be cleaned out. They'd cranked her open like one of those truck carcasses in the yard, cranked her open and scraped out the rust. Deep reds and blacks savagely pulled out – but despite their raw look she thought of the beautiful windows, the blazing two dimensional church, the stylised hills and the plain glass pathway incandescing in the morning sun.

She hadn't seen it happen for two weeks; it had been raining for several hundred hours, the sides of the house were running, flaking like an old man's skin. The house would never float, it rested on stone, its great weight pushing down like an argument, but it might become an island. Would they still burn fires she wondered, knocking down the dividing walls until they lived in a barn . . . or was life out there on the lawn, swimming with jellyfish. . . .

Oh you're back, he said, his voice sealing things over. It took what had happened as past. Too much presumption in it, she thought.

Can I get you a drink, he said.

It was raspberry leaf tea, nice and hot. He had remembered. They walked up the wide cold stairway, plunk, plunk like a strummed note, the drips between the dirty angel and the telephone. A friendly sound once, she hated it now.

He lit a fire, two candles; her silhouette danced hugely on the wall looking no different, though inwardly not the same. He often undressed her by the fire, the heat striking across her groin like a pain. One time he'd tucked a roll of money down her front, said he'd like to see her hitch her skirt up and stick it under her suspender belt, like they did in French movies, or was it American movies? Then he'd pick up his guitar and make a sound in his throat. . . .

Outside faces would appear at a neighbouring window. Nine small squares, all of them blacked out except the centre one. Someone was painting out all the lighted windows of the world. Those faces could see she'd lost something. I'm like a spider, she thought, making new lives without understanding the one I've got.

The house, rambling, eight, nine, ten bedrooms – colossal 'dream' house, colonial mansion, orphanage, boarding house, had finally dispersed the struggle to master it, assumed power over its occupants. Once she had liked the great hallway, the solid stairwell, now she felt herself shrinking back. In the bedrooms couples might be making love but she wouldn't hear the sound of human lovemaking tonight, only the vast wet whispering chord and the dog on heat.

She touched the wall. It was moist, sweating, her own body also had a damp heat as though it was about to boil. I'm ninety per cent water she thought, nothing but a thin tissue between me and that other great bag of water beating on the roof. Outside the guttering was rusted for several feet, and rinsing streams sluiced through onto the windows. What menacing opacity water, colourless water, could assume. It should purify, not reflect; it had no business being a mirror.

Long before she had seen this house she had imagined it, dreamt him by a fire playing, and here he was, the loved instrument in his hands, fingering out a memory. Nothing else ought to matter now, not even the dog howling outside; it ought to have been enough, this moment, but the state of peace had not yet been coaxed forth. She still felt a deep gulf between them, worse, far worse than that bitch ceaselessly barking for an answer.

Of course if life wasn't unique, if it was a spider laying eggs, there was no loss. Life would grab a purchase in some damp corner. If you howled long enough you'd get an answer, even over the annihilating voice of rain; no loss, no loss barked the dog.

She had lain down on the couch to look into the warming flicker. He put down his guitar tenderly as though it was a body and came over to her. His face, rashed, looked redder than ever in the firelight. She saw his hands reach out and take her head, face, scanning, examining her.

Looking in the mirror, she thought. She was afraid to look too closely into his eyes, but she could not turn away, for he would demand to know why she was avoiding his glance. She caught his gaze quickly, letting her eyes wander slowly over his face.

No, don't say it.

Don't say what.

What's wrong with my face.

No, I wasn't she said opening herself out to him. He believed, accepted, everything was all right now, the moment was coming, their arms slid together, their faces no longer confronting. She dared to think there was peace, nothing could be heard in the house: there were only empty rooms where love was being made, unheard over the whisper of rain. There was the sound of water in the fire, the hissing made by the damp wood as it caught slowly; the room was pushed out to its limits by the shadows. Far over the dreaming earth other fires burnt while their fire talked on insistently like a storyteller in love with its own voice, every so often pulling them up with a splutter of exclamation as though it was repeating something which they had failed to hear.

There was something in the fire. One of those things with a hundred legs, she couldn't get the name. It was twisting at the end of a log, deciding. She pushed it off into the blaze where it quickly curled, died. *If things are unique . . . if not, no loss.* Too easy, and nothing solved. He hadn't noticed – or said nothing. He could be that removed, especially now, head down, fingers eating at the strings.

He got up and put another log on the fire. She remembered the grate had been broken until he wrapped chicken wire around it. The fire wouldn't fall apart again. She lay back and listened to the house, and to the fingering out of their existence on the guitar. This moment is unique, she thought; it will be lost, but I will remember it.

In the morning the worms were out, the sun high, burning. The bathtub outside, weedy but topped with water, shimmered with light; webs were spun across the hedges. Down in the hall he was pulling out old nails and ripping up the frayed lino.

Two days later she hung the curtains, re-arranged her room and dyed her hair, began again.

WITI IHIMAERA

A Game of Cards

The train pulled into the station. For a moment there was confusion: a voice blaring over the loudspeaker system, people getting off the train, the bustling and shoving of the crowd on the platform.

And there was Dad, waiting for me. We hugged each other. We hadn't seen each other for a long time. Then we kissed. But I could tell something was wrong.

– Your Nanny Miro, he said. She's very sick.

Nanny Miro . . . among all my nannies, she was the one I loved most. Everybody used to say I was her favourite mokopuna, and that she loved me more than her own children who'd grown up and had kids of their own.

She lived down the road from us, right next to the meeting house in the big old homestead which everybody in the village called 'The Museum' because it housed the prized possessions of the whanau, the village family. Because she was rich and had a lot of land, we all used to wonder why Nanny Miro didn't buy a newer, more modern house. But Nanny didn't want to move. She liked her own house just as it was.

– Anyway, she used to say, what with all my haddit kids and their haddit kids and all this haddit whanau being broke all the time and coming to ask me for some money, how can I afford to buy a new house?

Nanny didn't really care about money though. Who needs it? she used to say. What you think I had all these kids for, ay? To look after me, I'm not dumb!

Then she would cackle to herself. But it wasn't true really, because her family would send all their kids to her place when they were broke and she looked after them! She liked her mokopunas, but not for too long. She'd ring up their parents and say:

– Hey! When you coming to pick up your hoha kids! They're wrecking the place!

Yet, always, when they left, she would have a little weep, and give them some money. . . .

I used to like going to Nanny's place. For me it was a big treasure house, glistening with sports trophies and photographs, pieces of carvings and greenstone, and feather cloaks hanging from the walls.

Most times, a lot of women would be there playing cards with Nanny. Nanny loved all card games – five hundred, poker, canasta, pontoon, whist, euchre – you name it, she could play it.

The sitting room would be crowded with the kuias, all puffing clouds of smoke, dressed in their old clothes, laughing and cackling and gossiping about who was pregnant – and relishing all the juicy bits too!

I liked sitting and watching them. Mrs Heta would always be there, and when it came to cards she was both Nanny's best friend and worst enemy. And the two of them were the biggest cheats I ever saw.

Mrs Heta would cough and reach for a hanky while slyly slipping a card from beneath her dress. And she was always reneging in five hundred! But her greatest asset was her eyes, which were big and googly. One eye would look straight ahead, while the other swivelled around, having a look at the cards in the hands of the women sitting next to her.

– Eeee! You cheat! Nanny would say. You just keep your eyes to yourself, Maka tiko bum!

Mrs Heta would look at Nanny as if she were offended. Then she would sniff and say:

– You cheat yourself, Miro Mananui. I saw you sneaking that ace from the bottom of the pack.

– How do you know I got an ace Maka? Nanny would say. I know you! You dealt this hand, and you stuck that ace down there for yourself, you cheat! Well, ana! I got it now! So take that!

And she would slap down her hand.

– Sweet, ay? she would laugh. Good? Kapai lalelale? And she would sometimes wiggle her hips, making her victory sweeter.

– Eeee! Miro! Mrs Heta would say. Well, I got a good hand too!

And she would slap her hand down and bellow with laughter.

– Take that!

And always, they would squabble. I often wondered how they ever remained friends. The names they called each other!

Sometimes, I would go and see Nanny and she would be all alone, playing patience. If there was nobody to play with her, she'd always play patience. And still she cheated! I'd see her hands fumbling across the cards, turning up a jack or queen she needed, and then she'd laugh and say:

– I'm too good for this game!

She used to try to teach me some of the games, but I wasn't very interested, and I didn't yell and shout at her like the women did. She liked the bickering.

– Aue . . . she would sigh. Then she'd look at me and begin dealing out the cards in the only game I ever knew how to play.

And we would yell snap! all the afternoon. . . .

Now, Nanny was sick.

I went to see her that afternoon after I'd dropped my suitcases at home. Nanny Tama, her husband, opened the door. We embraced and he began to weep on my shoulder.

– Your Nanny Miro, he whispered, She's . . . she's. . . .

He couldn't say the words. He motioned me to her bedroom.

Nanny Miro was lying in bed. And she was so old looking. Her face was very grey, and she looked like a tiny wrinkled doll in that big bed. She was so thin now, and seemed all bones.

I walked into the room. She was asleep. I sat down on the bed beside her, and looked at her lovingly.

Even when I was a child, she must have been old. But I'd never realized it. She must have been over seventy now. Why do people you love grow old so suddenly?

The room had a strange, antiseptic smell. Underneath the bed was a big chamber pot, yellow with urine. . . . And the pillow was flecked with small spots of blood where she had been coughing.

I shook her gently.

– Nanny . . . Nanny, wake up.

She moaned. A long, hoarse sigh grew on her lips. Her eyelids fluttered, and she looked at me with blank eyes . . . and then tears began to roll down her cheeks.

– Don't cry, Nanny, I said. Don't cry. I'm here.

But she wouldn't stop.

So I sat beside her on the bed and she lifted her hands to me.

– Haere mai, mokopuna. Haere mai. Mmm. Mmm.

And I bent within her arms and we pressed noses.

After a while, she calmed down. She seemed to be her own self.

– What a haddit mokopuna you are, she wept. It's only when I'm just about in my grave that you come to see me.

– I couldn't see you last time I was home, I explained. I was too busy.

– Yes, I know you fullas, she grumbled. It's only when I'm almost dead that you come for some money.

– I don't want your money, Nanny.

– What's wrong with my money! she said. Nothing's wrong with it! Don't you want any?

– Of course I do, I laughed. But I know you! I bet you lost it all on poker! She giggled. Then she was my Nanny again. The Nanny I knew.

We talked for a long time. I told her about what I was doing in Wellington and all the neat girls who were after me.

'– You teka! she giggled. Who'd want to have you!

And she showed me all her injection needles and pills and told me how she wanted to come home from the hospital, so they'd let her.

– You know why I wanted to come home? she asked. I didn't like all those strange nurses looking at my bum when they gave me those injections. I was so sick, mokopuna, I couldn't even go to the lav, and I'd rather wet my own bed not their neat bed. That's why I come home.

Afterwards, I played the piano for Nanny. She used to like *Me He Manurere* so I played it for her, and I could hear her quavering voice singing in her room.

Me he manurere aue. . . .

When I finally left Nanny I told her I would come back in the morning.

But that night, Nanny Tama rang up.

– Your Nanny Miro, she's dying.

We all rushed to Nanny's house. It was already crowded. All the old women were there. Nanny was lying very still. Then she looked up and whispered to Mrs Heta:

– Maka . . . Maka tiko bum . . . I want a game of cards. . . .

A pack of cards was found. The old ladies sat around the bed, playing. Everybody else decided to play cards too, to keep Nanny company. The men played poker in the kitchen and sitting room. The kids played snap in the other bedrooms. The house overflowed with card players, even onto the lawn outside Nanny's window, where she could see. . . .

The women laid the cards out on the bed. They dealt the first hand. They cackled and joked with Nanny, trying not to cry. And Mrs Heta kept saying to Nanny:

– Eee! You cheat Miro. You cheat! And she made her googly eye reach far over to see Nanny's cards.

– You think you can see, ay, Maka tiko bum? Nanny coughed. You think you're going to win this hand, ay? Well, take that!

She slammed down a full house.

The other women goggled at the cards. Mrs Heta looked at her own cards. Then she smiled through her tears and yelled:

– Eee! You cheat Miro! I got two aces in my hand already! Only four in the pack. So how come you got three aces in your hand?

Everybody laughed. Nanny and Mrs Heta started squabbling as they always did, pointing at each other and saying: You the cheat, not me! And Nanny Miro said: I saw you, Maka tiko bum, I saw you sneaking that card from under the blanket.

She began to laugh. Quietly. Her eyes streaming with tears.

And while she was laughing, she died.

Everybody was silent. Then Mrs Heta took the cards from Nanny's hands and kissed her.

– You the cheat, Miro, she whispered. You the cheat yourself. . . .

We buried Nanny on the hill with the rest of her family. During her tangi, Mrs Heta played patience with Nanny, spreading the cards across the casket.

Later in the year, Mrs Heta, she died too. She was buried right next to Nanny, so that they could keep on playing cards. . . .
And I bet you they're still squabbling up there. . . .
– Eee! You cheat Miro. . . .
– You the cheat, Maka tiko bum. You, you the cheat. . . .

Big Brother, Little Sister

He burst out of the house and was halfway down the street when he heard Janey yelling after him, her cry shrill with panic. He turned and saw her on the opposite pavement, appearing out of the night. As she passed under a street light her shadow reached out like a bird's wing to ripple along the fence palings toward him.
– Go back, Janey, he called.
She cried out his name again, and pursued her shadow across the street. A car screamed at her heels and slashed her with light as she fluttered into her brother's arms.
– I'm coming with you.
She wore a jersey and jeans over her pyjamas. In her hands she was carrying her sandals. She bent down and began strapping them on.
– You'll be a nuisance, Hema grunted. Go home.
He pushed her away.
– No.
She wrapped her arms and legs round him. He wrestled her off and she fell on the pavement.
– Hema, no.
He began running, down that long dark street of shadowed houses towards Newtown. Behind, he could hear Janey chasing after him again.
– Don't leave me, Hema.
He turned. His face was desperate.
– You're too small to come with me, he yelled. Go home, Janey.
In desperation, he picked up a stone and pretended to throw it at her. She kept on running. He picked up another stone.
– Go back, he raged.
– No. No.
She gritted her teeth, closed her eyes with determination and launched herself at him. Hema felt her trembling in his arms. She seemed to shake his rage apart.
– You'll just be a nuisance, he growled.
– Where you go, I go, she said.
Then she looked trustfully at him.

Hema had been asleep when Janey began to peck at his dreams. He had turned on his side away from her. She began to shake him.
– Hema.
The two kids slept in the same bed in one of two bedrooms in the flat.
– Hema, wake up.
There was the sound of a crash. Hema sat up. He saw a crack of light under the closed door. Mum and Dad were back from the party. They were quarrelling again.
– Don't be scared, Hema said to his sister.

He went to the door and pushed it open. How long Mum and Dad had been fighting he didn't know. He'd never heard them as violent as this and he had to close his mind against the pain. He went back to the bed and sat on it. Janey crawled into his arms. They watched the light stabbing past the edge of the door and listened as their parents fought.

– Don't you talk to me like that, Wiki, Dad was threatening Mum.

– I'll talk to you any way I like, you rotten bastard.

– And don't you answer me back, Wiki.

– You don't own me, Mum screamed. You and your black bitch, you and her were made for each other. And keep your hands off me. They stink of her. Get away. Get out.

Hema could hear his mother panting and struggling in the bedroom. There was a ripping sound, a helpless woman-cry and a sudden crack of an open hand against her face.

– You bastard, she cried.

She spat into Dad's face. He slapped her again and threw her against the wall. Janey gripped Hema with fright.

– Damn bitch, Dad swore.

Hema saw Dad's shadow cut through the lighted crack of the door. He heard his father walk down the passage to the front door. And he heard his mother's voice, filled with fear.

– No, John, don't leave me. Don't.

Dad laughed. Their mother cried out, ran to the bedroom and began to pull open drawers and throw clothes at Dad, her breath exploding with grief.

– Here then. And here. And here. See if I care.

Dad began to turn the handle to leave. Their mother looked up at him, pleading. Her body became limp.

– You bastard. Well, two can play your game.

She picked up the telephone in the passage. She began to dial a number.

– Taxis?

– Can't wait to get rid of me, ay! Dad was laughing.

Then Mum dialled another number.

– Hullo? Is that you Pera?

Dad's laughter stopped. There was the sound of scuffling in the passage and shapes flicked across the crack in the doorway.

– You been playing around, ay Wiki?

– You're hurting me.

– You and Pera? Ay? Ay?

Hema ran to the door and opened it. Dad had forced Mum against the wall and his hands were squeezing her throat.

– Dad. Mum. Don't.

Dad yelled at him and pushed him back into the bedroom.

– Get back to bed, you damn kid.

The door cracked shut against the faces of his father and of his mother – her face wide with agony and blood streaming from her mouth.

– Leave them alone you bastard, she screamed.

On the other side of the door, Hema and Janey heard her clawing at their father. Then they heard her fall heavily to the floor.

Hema opened the door again. Dad was standing there, his fists clenched, kicking at Mum. Hema tried to shield his mother and lay over her. For a while, his father kept on kicking. Kicking. Until he was exhausted.

Mum leant against the wall. Her face was bruised and covered with sweat and tears. She beckoned Janey. She cradled Janey and Hema close to her.

– You bastard, she whispered to Dad. Don't think we'll miss you. Get out. Get out.

Dad looked at them. His face was grim. He was silent for a while. Then he lurched out of the flat.

Uncle Pera had come to stay.

Janey tugged at Hema's hand. He looked down at her. She was squirming and fidgeting and holding her other hand across the front of her jeans.

– I knew you'd be a nuisance, Hema growled.

– I can't help it, Janey answered lowering her head.

They were just passing Wellington Hospital. A taxi swerved into the kerb in front of them. Hema could see a man inside with a smashed face. As the taxi driver and a woman took the man into the main entrance he began screaming through a red hole where his mouth used to be. Hema pulled Janey away through the crowd of fear-filled bystanders.

– There was a lav a few streets back, he said to Janey. Why didn't you tell me then?

– Because you were in a hurry. And I didn't want to have a mimi till *now*.

– Well you'll just have to wait, Janey.

Newtown was busy. Cars had double-parked all along the main shopping centre impeding the stream of traffic. A trolley bus had snapped its poles, and the showering blue sparks made it appear like a giant red beetle writhing in pain. Along the crowded pavement echoed the voices of people talking in strange languages. The shops spilled their crates of fruit, bolts of cloth and other wares almost to the street. Two small children sold evening newspapers. A Salvation Army band exhorted the passers-by to come to God. A man in a fish shop swung his cleaver and cut off the gaping head of a large grey fish. Crayfish seethed in a tray near him.

A woman haggled over the price of an old cabinet stacked with other junk outside a second-hand mart. Her face was wan and desperate.

– Hema, Janey wailed.

– Hold on just a bit longer, he said.

He pulled her after him through the littered pavement towards the lights at the corner of John Street. He glanced back at the hospital clock. It was still early. Not half past seven yet. Mum and Uncle Pera would be in the pub till ten and afterwards they would go to a party. So there was still plenty of time to get away – even if Janey might slow him up. Not that Mum would miss them. She'd probably be glad they'd gone.

The traffic punched to a stop as the lights turned red.

Come on, Hema said to his sister.

Car motors revved and roared at them and unblinking headlights watched them cross. Then the lights turned green and the traffic leapt through the intersection into the crush of Newtown's main street.

For a moment, Hema stood undecided on the opposite pavement. No, better not keep to the main road for that would take them past the Tramway Hotel, and Mum and Uncle Pera might be there. Be safer to go up John Street.

– Hema, Janey cried again.

– All right, he answered. Look, there's some trees over there. You better have your mimi there.

Janey rushed into the shadows. Hema kept a look-out. Across the road, fading billboards announced an industrial fair of a month before. Emerald lights were strung across the dead facade of the Winter Show Building.

– Hema, you still there?

– Just hurry up, Janey. Quick, before some people come and catch you.

She hurried out of the trees, hitching up her pants. Hema brushed her down and tucked her clothes in. There were stains on her jeans.

– Eeee! he smiled.

– Well, you told me to hurry, she said.

Quickly they walked along the road. Cars slewed past in a steady stream. A few yards ahead people were arguing on the pavement. They began to fight and a beer bottle smashed on the asphalt. Hema and Janey skirted them, their sandals crunching on broken glass. They hurried on. All along the street the lights from the houses shone down on them.

– Where we going, Hema? Janey asked.

– You'll see.

His mind was working fast. He'd previously planned to make for the railway station and get a ticket for Gisborne. That was where his Nanny George lived. Now that Janey was with him he knew the money he'd saved wouldn't stretch to two tickets. Perhaps he could put just her on the train. Somehow, he would follow after her.

He made up his mind. Yes, that's what he'd do. He couldn't think of anything else to do or anywhere else to go. He told her they were going to the railway station. Her eyes widened.

– Are we going to walk all the way? she asked.

He nodded.

– You said you wouldn't get tired, he said.

Her face set with determination.

– No, I won't get tired, she answered.

Hema grinned at her and she grinned back. They walked on, past the lighted windows, the row of singing windows, toward the city.

When Uncle Pera had come to stay Mum began pushing Hema and Janey away from her. It happened slowly and with only small things at first – Hema, dress Janey for me, ay? Janey, go out and play for a while? You kids do the dishes for Mum? Go away now, kids, because Pera and I want to be by ourselves. Go away. Away. Go.

Janey would be hurt and puzzled. For a time she asked Mum when Dad was coming back. She was confused about the strange man who'd come to live with them. As time went by, she stopped asking her mother about Dad. He was never coming back. Mum had Uncle Pera now.

Actually he was quite nice at first, was Uncle Pera. He seemed to like the kids or be amused by them anyway, as if they were a novelty in his life. But he wasn't interested in them really; only in Mum. Sometimes, when he was fondling her, he would dart them a look of irritation and whisper in Mum's ear.

– Go away, kids, Mum would say. Uncle Pera and I want to be alone now.

Her anxieties about pleasing Uncle Pera began to affect Hema and Janey. They became careful when he was around, treating him with as much caution as their mother did. Trying to please him. Trying to please Mum. Because she seemed happy with this man and wanted him to stay with her.

But he was much younger than Mum. His lips were moist for pleasure and his eyes reckless for fun. Hema felt that one day this man would leave Mum too. Watching her lying in his arms, he would feel sad. Sad enough to hate Uncle Pera. For Hema could see from Mum's eyes and the little nervous things she did that even she knew that one day this man might walk away from her; and Uncle Pera, knowing her fear, would play on it and twist their mother round his finger whenever he wanted to. As the weeks went by he began to twist her tight like a rope. He became bored with the children.

He frowned one night when Janey clambered into Mum's arms. Mum pushed her away. From then on, Janey only went to her mother when Uncle Pera was not around.

– Do these kids have to eat with us? he asked at dinner.

The kids began to have dinner before he came home. Afterwards, watching television in the sitting room, Hema would be aware of his mother's anxious glances at her children. He would take Janey by the hand and lead her to bed.

The happiest times for the children were during the mornings after Uncle Pera had gone to work when Mum was getting them ready for school. In the mornings their mother always kissed them.

– Look after your sister, she would tell Hema.

Once, in a moment of truth, she said to him:

– I'm sorry, son. Your mother was always lousy at picking her men.

She was strong-willed, but not strong enough with Uncle Pera. She was passionate; she needed a man. Perhaps she was frightened of being left alone with her kids. Whatever the case she began doing whatever her man wanted her to do.

– Let's go to the pub, he would say. Let's go to a party. Let's go to the pictures. Let's just go somewhere.

– All right, she would answer.

The long nights of being left at home began for the kids again. They weren't any different from those nights when Mum and Dad would go out except that now, every time Mum walked out the door, the kids felt as if she was leaving them. Mum had Uncle Pera now. They only had each other and could depend only on each other.

Sometimes, while Janey was asleep, Hema would creep to the window-sill and look out. Across the road, he would see people sitting behind lighted windows. He would glance at Janey where she fluttered in her dreams. No. For them there were no lighted windows.

The night cracked open. Through the gap the bikies rode like helmeted harpies with high silver-chromed wings. Their bodies were carapaced with leather and studded with silver and as they shrieked through the dark they trailed black scarves from their necks like clotted blood.

– My feet are sore, Hema.

Hema watched the bikies as they passed. He and Janey had come down Taranaki Street and were at Pigeon Park.

– We'll go and sit over there, he said.

They ran across the busy road. The bikies rumbled into the concrete canyons of the city. Janey sat on a bench and began unstrapping her sandals.

– Let me have a look, Hema said.

He found a small sharp stone in one of the sandals. It had bruised his sister's heel. He rubbed it.

– No wonder your feet are sore, he told her. Never mind. All better now. Why didn't you tell me before?

– I've already been a nuisance.

– Well, we'll have a little rest, Hema said. I'm feeling tired too.

They sat there, watching laughing people walk past and the traffic glittering in the streets. Further along, on another bench, an old man sat with his head hunched between his legs. The ground was stained with his vomit. A group of girls walked past the old man and giggled at him. They giggled again when they passed Hema and Janey.

– I like your maxi coat, one of the girls laughed through her thin painted lips.

Hema flushed, but he didn't really care. The park seemed littered with people like him and he had a strange sense of being part of them.

Then he saw a policeman coming, jabbing at others in the park, hustling them on.

– We'll go now, he said to Janey.

As they hurried away, Hema saw the policeman shake the old man on the nearby bench. The old man fell to the ground. The children passed beneath trees where pigeons cramped themselves tight against one another.

Janey pointed to a bus standing at the corner of Cuba Street.

– We haven't got enough money, Hema said.

– I've got some, Janey answered.

She reached into the pocket of her jeans and showed her brother some coins. Hema smiled at her. Her money would never get them on a bus.

– Better keep it for later, he said to her. Just in case we need it for something else. Okay?

– Okay, she answered.

She grinned proudly and put the coins back in her pocket. At the corner, while waiting for the lights, Hema saw a man thumbing through green notes and stuffing them carelessly into his wallet.

– Now hold on tight, he said to Janey as they crossed the street. I don't want you to get lost. If you lose my hand you stop right where you are and don't move. I'll find you.

Ahead, the pavement was crowded with people. Thrusting through them was like struggling through a land of giants, of people who did not look down or see the boy and his sister.

– Are you holding on tight? Hema asked.

His sister nodded back, scared. Her fingernails dug into his arm. Heavy bodies slammed into Janey as her brother dragged her after him, and loud voices boomed about her.

Along Manners Street the children went. Into Willis Street. From a movie billboard a grim-faced man pointed a gun at them. In a television set in a shop a woman was being stabbed to death. A gaunt youth staggered into them out of a hotel, shouting loudly.

– Hema? Janey cried.

Couldn't people see her down here?

– Just keep holding tight, he said.

They came to another intersection. A thick crowd was waiting to cross. For a brief moment Hema's eye was caught by a beautiful shop display – a family table laid with silverware.

Then the lights changed and the crowd began to move. From the four corners of the crossing they came to merge in the middle and jostle, shove and push their way across the road. Hema felt Janey's hand wrench away from his.

– Hema, she yelled.

He looked back and glimpsed her fluttering in the crowd. He tried to get back to her but the rush of people pushed him along to the pavement. Stragglers were dashing across the street. The lights were changing. The cars were beginning to move. Janey was still standing there, turning round and round looking for him, alone, in the middle of the street. Round and round. As if she was a bird in a cage. Looking.

– Janey.

She heard him calling and saw him. Her eyes lost their frightened look and filled with trust. He rushed out from the pavement and put his arms tightly round her. The traffic roared on both sides of them and drivers were shouting and horns were booming but he didn't care. Then a car braked in front of them. The traffic came to a stop.

– Get your sister off the road, boy, a voice called.

He picked Janey up in his arms and carried her to the pavement. He heard a bystander mutter something about mothers who let their children roam the streets at night. He felt eyes piercing him like sharp needles

– You told me to stay right where I was if I lost your hand, Janey said.

Hema looked down at her. He nodded.

– Come on, he said. Not far to go now.

They hurried down Lambton Quay. Department store windows gleamed with rich brilliance. Behind the glass-paned window of a coffee bar a man jabbed at a blood-red steak with a fork.

It happened slowly at first, their mother pushing them away from her, but it increased as Mum's life twisted more and more around Uncle Pera. Her kids were her own – she owned them – but she did not own her man. Some need for security made her attempt to possess him and, in the attempt, she pushed her children further into the background of her life. They became as unsure of her as they were of Uncle Pera, trying to read the signs that flickered across her face. Once they thought they'd known everything they needed to know about Mum. The signs became strange, clouded and opaque. It wasn't that she didn't love them anymore; it was just that possessed as she was with Uncle Pera she became more and more like him. Her moods were inconsistent. Sometimes she would laugh and play with her kids; at other times she would growl them or appear not to notice them. At one moment she would kiss them; the next moment she would lash out at them with a harsh word or hand. They could never tell with their mother now.

Once, Hema had returned home late from school. He'd asked his mother where Janey was. She said that Janey was probably sulking somewhere. Mum had given her a thrashing.

Hema had known instantly where Janey would be. He'd gone into the bedroom and looked under the bed.

– Come out, Janey, he had said. No use crying.

– Mum hit me.

– She didn't mean to.

– Yes she did. She hit me.

He'd crawled under the bed and put his arms round her. Although Hema consoled her, he'd felt Janey was comforting him too. He had thought of his mother and realized he and Janey were secure only in each other.

– Look after your sister, Mum would say.

Always those words even when Mum and Uncle Pera were home.

– We're having a party tonight, Hema. *Look after your sister.* Uncle Pera and I want to watch television. *Look after your sister.* We want to be by ourselves. *Look after your sister.*

His mother had always been careless about keeping the flat clean. After Uncle Pera came she was more careless. Hema had begun making the breakfast for himself and Janey, washing their clothes, doing the dishes and sweeping the floor. Sometimes his mother noticed, sometimes she didn't. Not that it mattered. It had to be done. Mum was too busy enjoying herself. As long as she was happy, Hema was happy too.

Yet he could not help wondering whether or not she was really happy. He wondered constantly what his mother really meant to Uncle Pera. Whenever parties were held at the flat Uncle Pera would often flirt with other women – kissing them, fondling them – and treat Mum with amusement. Mum would drink more, sit on other men's laps and her eyes would glitter with despair. Hema would watch her sometimes through a crack in the bedroom door. She was very pretty and gay. Yet when she danced by herself while everyone else clapped and told her to dance faster she looked so desperate and haggard – her hair swinging free, sweat dripping down the neck of her dress, thighs grinding and face given to the passion of the dance – that he would feel ashamed of her. He would look at the others in the room and wish they would go away and leave Mum alone. That Uncle Pera would go away and leave her alone too.

The morning after, the children would clear up the debris of the party. They would sweep the floor, wash the glasses, stack all the flagons downstairs in the hall, set the chairs in their places and open the windows to get rid of the smell of stale cigarettes and spilt beer. More and more often they would find their mother flaked out wherever she'd fallen – on a chair, on the floor or across the sofa. Uncle Pera, he always made it between the blankets.

– Come to bed, Mum, Hema would whisper. Come on.

He would shake her gently. Her eyelids would flicker and then shut again.

Sometimes Hema and Janey would be able to pull her to bed. Other times she'd be too drunk to move, so they would get some blankets and tuck them in round her. If she'd been sick, Hema would wipe the stains from her lips with a towel.

– Poor Mum, he would say.

Once, she had heard him and looked at him and her face had screwed up with sorrow.

– You're good kids, she'd whispered. Too good for a rotten thing like me. I'm sorry.

She wasn't rotten; she should never feel sorry for the way she was. She was Mum. Her children loved her. If anyone was rotten it was her man. He did not love her the way they did.

Fists thudded in a sudden fight outside the main entrance of the railway station. Two men argued over ownership of a taxi at the rank. Within the pillared shadows thin faces gleamed.

– At last, Janey said.

The station was crowded. It was half past eight. Late night shoppers rushed to catch their units to the Hutt or Porirua. Above the clamour, the loudspeaker announced departure times, platform numbers, welcomes and farewells to passengers. Everyone seemed to have a place to go, a destination.

– You wait here, Hema told Janey.

He sat her on a bench next to a middle-aged Maori woman. The woman looked at them with eyes shattered by tiredness.

– What are you going to do? Janey asked.

He told her. Her eyes glistened.

– I'm not going on the train without you, she said.

– We've only got money enough for one ticket, he answered.

– I don't care, she said stubbornly. I won't go without you.

He pulled her out of the railway station. He shook her and tried to explain to her why she had to go on the train by herself. Then he took her back to where the Maori woman was sitting. Janey put an arm around his neck.

– You got to do what I say, he said.

He walked towards the ticket office and joined one of the queues. Every now and then he looked back at Janey. Would she be all right travelling by herself? Would she? What if. . . .

– Yes?

The voice boomed at Hema from behind thick glass. A bored face looked down at him.

– Please, can I have a ticket for Gisborne, please.

– For where? the face asked.

– Please, Gisborne.

– When for?

– Tonight, please.

– No trains go to Gisborne tonight.

The concourse shuddered beneath his feet. A unit roared into the station. An old man tripped and fell. Two youths swore at a woman who had bumped them.

Hema looked back at the man behind the thick glass. The man's face was curious.

– Where you sitting, sonny?

– Over there.

The face looked towards Janey and the woman sitting next to her. It became thin.

– Why didn't your mother come to get the ticket herself? I've better things to do than muck around with kids.

He waved Hema away.

– No trains tonight, he told Janey.

She tried not to smile too much.

– What do we do now? she asked.

– I'll think of something, he answered. Are you hungry?

Janey gave him a guarded look.

– Have we got enough money? she asked.

– Enough.

– Are *you* hungry?

– A bit.

– Well, I'm a bit hungry too then, Janey said.

They went into the station cafeteria. Hema bought a pie to take away. They went outside the main entrance steps. People ebbed and flowed around them. Then they returned to the seat they had left and sat down.

Hema closed his eyes. Nowhere to go. Nowhere.

– I wouldn't have gone without you, Janey whispered. You could have hit me but I wouldn't have gone. Where you go, I go.

Hema grinned at her.

– I knew you'd be a nuisance, he said.

He saw a couple dragging a stubborn child towards the train. The man muttered to the boy and then raised his hand and hit him.

And Hema felt as if Uncle Pera was hitting him again and put his hands across his body to protect himself from the blows.

Last night. Hema, Janey and Mum, sitting in the kitchen having tea. Mum's face was tight and her hands kept smoothing down her dress, moving down her thighs and up again, brushing the room with tension.

– Mum . . . Hema had begun.

– Just eat your kai, she answered.

The night before, she and Uncle Pera had argued. He was tired of her, he said. He was pissing off.

Yet he'd rung up that day to say he was coming back. Tonight. He'd just wanted to teach Mum a lesson, he'd said. Just to let her know he was boss. Did she want to see him? Oh yes, she'd crooned. Yes. Yes.

Now, they were waiting for him. Hema was feeling sick at his mother's weakness for this man.

The door opened downstairs. Mum gave a cry and ran down the steps to her man. He was drunk. She didn't care. He saw Hema and Janey sitting in the kitchen.

– Go to bed now, Mum said. Look after your sister, Hema.

Her voice was deep-throated with happiness.

– Didn't you hear your mother? Uncle Pera growled.

The kids hadn't finished their dinner. Hema began clearing the table. Behind him, he could hear Mum kissing this man, and when he turned he saw Uncle Pera's hand squeezing her buttocks. Tears spilled in his eyes.

– Why didn't you just stay away, he yelled. You don't love my mother. You'll never look after her.

– Get to bed, Mum hissed. Take Janey with you.

He turned on her.

– Why don't you look after Janey yourself, Mum. And me, too. Tell him to go, Mum. Tell him.

His mother recoiled from his words.

– We don't want you, Hema yelled at Uncle Pera. Janey. Mum. Me. We can look after ourselves.

But Mum had not understood. She had not seen Hema or Janey. Her eyes were filled only with the man standing next to her.

– Get out, she'd screamed at Hema.

– No.

– Do as your mother says.

– You're not my father. I don't take orders from you.

Uncle Pera had pulled him along the passage. Mum was saying to him:

– The kid doesn't mean it, Pera. He doesn't mean it.

Janey ran to Mum and hid her face in Mum's dress.

– Pera, no, Mum pleaded.

– He needs a lesson, Uncle Pera answered. He needs to know who's boss around here.

Uncle Pera had taken off his belt. Just before he began to thrash Hema with it, he kicked the door closed.

– Mum, Hema had called.

The door was closing on her face. She did not come to stop this man. She did not come to her son. She did not. . . .

The *pain*. He held his body tight against the blows. All he could think of was his mother, standing there, not helping him. Only two hours afterwards had she come, from the bedroom she shared with her man.

– Don't interfere, she said. You only get hurt if you interfere.

She'd reached out to caress him.

– Don't touch me.

– Try to understand, Hema.

– Don't touch me.

They'd gone out later, Mum and Uncle Pera. Janey had crawled into Hema's arms. Hema had cradled her softly.

– Mum doesn't need us any more, he'd said. She doesn't need me. She let that man give me a hiding. She let him.

They had sat there, watching train after train pull out of the station, carriage after carriage of lighted windows flowing past like dream after dream. Now, a newspaper scraped across the concourse floor. The station was becoming a derelict place strewn with cigarette butts, spilled food, lolly wrappers, ripped magazines – all the rubbish discarded by people during their passage through the station. The stalls in the concourse had closed for the night. Only a few people remained – an old man, three youths, and a young girl with her boyfriend in the darkness of a railway platform. A late night porter whistled his way across the concourse. He cast a curious look at Hema and Janey.

– We can't stay here, Hema said.

– I'm cold, she answered.

Mum had just stood there. She'd let that man give him a thrashing. She'd let him.

– Do you think Mum will be home yet? Janey asked.

– Too early, Hema answered.

And when she got home and saw they weren't there she would cry out their names and run from room to room and down into the street looking for them, looking, looking. . . .

– Where shall we go, Hema?

She got off the bench and began rubbing her legs.

There was no place to go. There was no use running away.

– We can't stay here, ay Hema?

He began to think of his mother. Love for her overwhelmed him. Their mother was a weak woman. She needed people. One day, when all others had left her, she might need Hema and Janey again.

– We'll go back, Hema said.

– Home?

Home. Yes, life with Mum was home. He and Janey would have to make the best of it. Home was here, in this place, now.

He took his sister's hand. They walked out of the railway station. Janey shivered. The city was not yet dark but it was so quiet – a waste land punctured with street lights. Just outside the station was a police car.

Janey clutched Hema tightly. She was like a little bird seeking his shelter.

– You'll never leave me, ay Hema?

– No, he answered. Not now. Not ever.

They hurried through the night. A patrol car screamed along the street. A star burst across the sky. The lights of the city tightened round them.

Yellow Brick Road

Follow the yellow brick road,
Follow, follow, follow, follow,
Follow the yellow brick road. . . .

We're almost there! Almost at Wellington, the Emerald City! Me and Dad and Mum and Roha, we been travelling for two days now in our car which Dad bought from Mr Wallace last week. No dents and honk honk goes the horn. Dad, he said I could have a drive of it myself when we left Waituhi but then it conked out on the Whareratas and that made him change his mind.

– I told you we wouldn't get to Wellington in *this*, Mum said to him while he was fixing it up.

– We'll get there.

– But I want to get there in one piece! Mum answered.

– Throw some of your junk out then, Dad told her.

Our car sure is loaded down all right. Mum's stuff is in the boot, some belongings are tied under the canvas on the roof and there's even some squeezed in here with us. Boy.

But you won't conk out now, ay car? There's just one hill to go and we'll be there. So up we go, up the hill, slowly but surely. And who cares if cars bank up behind us! They can beep all they like. We got as much right to be on this road as they got.

Road, road, yellow brick road, yellow with the headlights sweeping across it. Just like in that book Miss Wright, my teacher, gave me before we left Waituhi. A neat book. About the straw man, the tin man, the cowardly lion and the Emerald City and . . . we're almost there!

I bounce up and down on the seat. I can't wait to see all the sparkling green towers glittering in the dark ahead of us.

– Matiu, you just sit still! Mum growls. What's gotten into you, ay?

– Sorry, Mum.

Poor Mum. She's very tired and still unhappy about leaving Waituhi, our whanau, our family. Her eyes are still red with the crying when all the people had waved goodbye to us like little flags fluttering far away. At least she hasn't cried as often as Roha has for Hone though! Roha and Hone, they went round together and once I saw them having a pash. Eeee!

I grin at my big sister. Never mind, Roha. Plenty other boys down in Wellington and you can pash up large with them when we get there, ay.

– What you grinning for, Smarty? Roha snaps.

– I'm allowed to grin if I want to, aren't I? I ask, suddenly hurt.

– All right, all right, you don't have to scream.

I make a funny face at her. It would teach her a good lesson if even the pakehas didn't want to pash with her! Lots of pakehas in Wellington. Not like in Waituhi. Makes me scared to think about it.

I turn to Dad.

– Dad, will the pakehas like us in Wellington? Dad?

He doesn't answer me because he is driving carefully. He has to lean forward to see the road in front of him. It has started to rain.

Wish I was older and knew how to drive better. Then I could give him a rest at the wheel.

I press against him and he puts an arm round me. His face looks tired, just like it looked when we were walking to a garage yesterday after our car ran out of petrol. There we were, miles from anywhere, walking along the road while car after car sped past us without stopping. Some of them blared loudly at us. Others made a lot of dust come over us. And always as they passed the faces would be looking back and staring at us. I felt puzzled.

– Why don't they stop, Dad?

He had shrugged his shoulders.

– We're in a different country now, son.

I began to hate those faces. I wanted to throw stones at them all.

But things will be different when we get to Wellington, won't they? And we will be happy, won't we?

Course we will. You just wait and see, Dad. We'll make lots of money and be rich as anything because Wellington is where the money is. And you have to go where the money is, ay Dad. No use staying in Waituhi and being poor all the time, ay.

I lean back in the seat and burrow under the blanket. It is getting cold and there is a draught coming through a hole in our car. I feel my bag of lollies in my pocket.

– You want one, Mum? You want one, Dad? Roha?

I pass the bag to Roha and she takes two, the greedy thing. I put one in my mouth and count what's left. Seven.

Boy, these are the dearest lollies I ever bought. When we stopped at that shop yesterday I gave the man thirty cents and he didn't give me any change. When I asked him for it, he told me thirty cents was how much these lollies cost. But he was lying. He was a thief and he stole my money. How would he like it if someone rooked him? What's more, these lollies are stink, just like him.

I watch the road as it twists ahead through the dark. Every now and then, there is a loud whoosh of a fast car passing us. Those fast cars don't like us. We're too slow for them.

Suddenly, I see two lights ahead like eyes glaring at us. The eyes open wider, grow larger, looking like the eyes of a . . .

– Dad! I yell, afraid.

A big truck descends on us with its headlights blazing full. I seem to see taloned fingers reaching out to claw me.

– Bloody hell, Dad mutters.

He swerves. The car kicks gravel. The truck thunders past, screaming in the wind.

I look at Mum. Her face is shaken.

– I better keep both my hands on the wheel, Dad says.

He lifts his arm from me and I feel suddenly alone. I begin to think of Waituhi, our whanau, and that makes me sad. All our family was there and Emere was our cow. Haere ra, Emere. And haere ra to you, e Hemi. You'll always be my best mate.

I start humming to myself. Quietly.

– *Follow the yellow brick road,*
Follow, follow, follow, follow . . .

Miss Wright, she taught us that song at school. A neat song. We made a long line, joined by our hands, and danced crazy patterns over the playground and . . .

There is a snapping sound and the flapping of canvas.

– What's that, Dad?

He pulls the car over to the side of the road and steps out. Mum winds down her window.

– What's wrong?

– Rope's snapped, he yells back.

– You better get out and help your father, Mum says to me.

I jump out into the rain. Boy, it's sure wet and cold out here. Dad is struggling in the wind to pull the canvas back over our belongings.

– All this junk! Dad mutters. No wonder the canvas came away.

He takes a box from the top and dumps it on the side of the road. My books spill out and the pages fly away like birds in the wind.

– Dad. No, Dad . . .

I run out into the road in panic because they are my school books and among them is my best book. My best book.

– Matiu! Get off the road! Mum screams.

My best book. In the wind and the rain. My best book.

– *Matiu.*

And there it is. Lying there on the road. I run to get it and car brakes scream in my ears.

But I have it in my arms and hold it safe to me. And I don't care if I get a hiding. I don't care. . . .

Mum hits me very hard.

– What you want to do that for, you stupid kid.

But I don't care. I don't care. . . .

And the driver of the other car is saying angry words to Dad:

– What the bloody hell do you think you're up to, eh? Letting you kid run out like that, what's wrong with you! Look, never mind about bloody arguing. Christ, you shouldn't be on the road at all. Your car's bloody dangerous loaded like that. And why the hell didn't you pull further off the road, eh? Oh, what's the use. You Maoris are all the same. Dumb bloody horis.

He steps back into his car and roars off. Dad comes towards me and his face is full of anger.

Go ahead, Dad. Hit me. I deserve it.

But he doesn't. Instead, he hugs me and asks:

– You all right, son?

– Yes, Dad. I'm sorry, Dad. That man. . . .

– That bastard. Never mind about him.

I clutch my book tightly. I carry it into the car with me. Mum starts to get angry with me again.

– Turi turi, woman, Dad says. It's all over now. Let's forget it.

– It wouldn't have happened if you'd tied down our things properly like Sam told you to do, Mum answers.

Sam is my uncle and we stayed at his place in Hastings last night. Uncle Sam didn't even know we were on our way to Wellington!

– Down to that windy place? he'd said. You fullas better tie yourselves down or you'll be blown away! Don't you know how cold it is down there? Brother, it's liquid sunshine all the year round!

– We don't care, I'd answered him. We're going to make lots of money down there. Not much room left for pa living anymore. That's what you said, ay Dad.

Dad had looked at me strangely.

– No more jobs back home, he told Uncle. Plenty of the seasonal work, yes, but me and Hine had enough of that. We had enough of shearing, the fruit-picking and the going down South to shear some more. No, plenty of work in Wellington. Plenty of factories.

– Who told you that! Uncle snorted.

– Jim, Dad answered.

Uncle Jim is Dad's brother. He lives in Petone and we're going to stay with him until we find our own house.

Uncle Sam had shrugged his shoulders.

– Well, Jim should know, he'd said.

– I want us to have a good life, a new start, Dad tried to explain. A new start for my kids. Me and Hine, we've always had nothing. But my kids? They're going to grow up with everything. I'll fight for it, because they must have it.

But I'd seen Uncle Sam hadn't understood Dad's words. He'd simply shaken his head and wished us luck. And in the morning before we left he'd told Dad to tie the canvas down tight.

– Otherwise that wind will get under it and before you know it you'll be flying into Wellington!

Dad had tried his best with the ropes. He'd said to Mum:

– How about getting rid of some of this junk, ay?

She'd answered him:

– This junk is all we've ever had. I'm not throwing away one piece of it, wind or no wind.

It sure is windy all right, outside the car. The clouds are rushing in the night sky just like the Winged Monkeys. The wind moans and chatters and cackles among our belongings, and I must close my eyes and put my hands to my ears to shut out the sights and sounds of this night.

Then, suddenly, all the noises stop. Even the car has stopped.

– There it is, Dad says.

I open my eyes. Far away are the lights of Wellington, streaming with the rain down our window like glistening towers. And it looks so . . . so . . . beautiful. Just as I'd imagined it to be. Just as I'd pretended it would be. Emerald City.

– Isn't it neat, Mum?

She stares ahead. Her face is still.

– Roha? I ask.

My sister's face is filled with a strange glow.

– Dad?

He looks at me and smiles.

– You and your dreams, son.

He starts the car. We begin to drive down from the hill. I look at Dad and Mum and Roha, puzzled. How come I'm the only one to be happy! Can't they see this is where our live begins and this is where our dreams begin?

And dreams, they come true, don't they? Don't they?

I look out the car. I see a sign: STEEP GRADE. All along the yellow brick road there have been signs like that. STEEP GRADE. CHANGE DOWN. ONE

WAY. LIMITED SPEED ZONE. ROAD NARROWS. STOP. WINDING
ROAD. GO. CONCEALED EXIT. TRAFFIC LIGHTS AHEAD. GREASY
WHEN WET. NO EXIT. NO PASSING. NO STOPPING.
Many signs, all telling us where we have to go and. . . .
I begin to feel scared.
If ever we want to, will we be able to find our way back?
I begin to sing to myself. Not because I'm happy, but because I think I want to
feel sure myself everything will turn out all right.
It will, won't it?

> *Follow the yellow brick road,*
> *Follow, follow, follow, follow,*
> *Follow . . .*

MICHAEL GIFKINS

Head over Heels

I suppose that you could say of me that I was approaching the 'twilight years', the years of old age. There was a considerable period in my life when I 'threw caution to the winds'; this ensured that my later reactions to people and events were informed by what is popularly called 'understanding'. Now, it seems, the boot is on the other foot. Society at large is unwilling to attribute to me any condition of wisdom; that this is a wasteful misconception I am constantly at pains to point out. You see, I do fight back. All the time – even when no obvious opportunity presents. Lacking a ready-made occasion for self-justification I might even manufacture one. Like now. It is far easier than you would think.

Take the other day, for instance. My grandson, young stud that he is (and I *sometimes* admit to a certain jealousy about various of his physical attributes) dropped in to see me with his latest girl. I knew immediately what was on his mind. He was hoping to cajole me into giving a guided tour of the ancestral home – *his* nonchalant display of the one dessicated root of the burgeoning family tree – and once my back was turned sneak in a bit of a tickle on the side: good fun, undoubtedly, but all at my expense. So I did what I usually do under similar conditions of oppression – acted swiftly on my feelings of the moment. Which were probably excessive, seeing as she was a most attractive girl!

In fact, I 'had my act together' from the moment they set foot inside the door. There she stood, spunky as they make them, a bit on the nuggety side perhaps but ready for anything, believe you me. Which she would have got with Jimmy, I don't doubt. Yet I wasn't worried about the competition. You see, I could tell in a flash that she liked me. As a grandfather, I imagine you smile, some relic from a crazy past. No! Her feelings towards me were for a flesh-and-blood contemporary, one-to-one, I think they say.

Did I stop to ask myself, 'Why?' Of course not, would you? I suggested quickly that they might like tea. And by tea I didn't mean just a cup of tea, but the whole experience. She said yes, looking at Jimmy. We talked a bit, while the water boiled, and I was careful to leave lots of space for her attention to wander round the room, picking up on details of how I lived. When I served the tea in fine china my instincts told me that I had her well and truly hooked. It just happened that I'd bought some carrot cake from the local deli and I cut this up so small that I knew that Jim's interest would not be roused. In fact, he was bored witless. We shared it, she and I, and the icing was fragrant as orange blossom, moving her to remark that she hadn't for a long time had a cup of tea that good.

We had this much in common, that we were both romantics. When Jimmy got up to go I could see that she'd like to stay, but didn't press the point. That's one of the things about age, you know when you've won as much ground as you're going to get. He took the whole interlude in very bad grace – all I can say is serve him right! – and I could see that whatever else happened that afternoon he wasn't going to get it all his own way.

But I'm digressing. The point I'm trying to make is that you can't afford to take anything lying down. Which is part of the reason you see me here like this. How did I start on yoga? It was a long time ago, about the period in my life when I realized that since no one was going to give me another body I'd better start taking care of the one I'd got. My wife used to think it was a calculated imposition on her goodwill, my squatting on the living-room carpet and sucking in my stomach till it touched my backbone; that, or standing on my head with my nuts dangling down towards my face. (This latter exercise I was particularly interested in then with regard to its alleged powers of sexual rejuvenation. With all these things it's a bit hard to get to the root of the matter, but I'm inclined to think – and I speak here from carefully observed experience – that the major component of one's sexual energy is a state of mind.)

So anyway, here I am, midsummer and the middle of the week – but that doesn't stop the beach being full of nursing mothers and narcissists. As far as I can see, though, I'm the only crank. Of course there are other ways of telling apart from appearances. Some of those urban peasants down there, solo mums most of them, seem by all accounts to have some pretty strange ideas. On diet, for instance: you are what you eat. All I can say is that they must have discovered some very strange foods. Or astrology. Our destiny lies in the stars. Virgo is as virgo does, I'll go along with that. Talk about placebos for the underprivileged!(Not that their men would fall into that category. I mean, just how privileged can you get, free-loading on a mother-and-child benefit? And always nurturing some precious talent that requires you to spend till mid-afternoon in bed! Who can blame them, they ask, when their old ladies blow up a second time and become so disgusting that they're obliged to move on to someone new?)

Now there's a sight! I do sympathize with her, poor thing, keeping all her clothes on to take a dip. So would I if I'd gone that far to seed. It's a fine line once you've stopped trying. Unattractiveness becomes a major point of self-assertion – you can feel superior to the offence that other people take.

It occurs to me that you might think that I am talking about myself. No, my eccentricity is an entirely different kettle of fish. For one thing – and you must trust me to give me an objective account – I'm not bad-looking. I certainly don't carry any excess weight! And summer brings me up in quite a nice shade of brown that seems to last throughout the year. Wrinkles are another matter. I remember long ago that feeling of panic when they began to march across my face. But now that they're everywhere, top to bottom, front and back, and since I've identified certain literary antecedents for my condition, I can tell myself that I'm getting away with it or even that it's become a definite strength. 'There goes the ancient mariner!' I'll say. 'Carved like driftwood by the elements, but with age belied by a twinkling eye!' (There's also the wiry Yaqui shaman whose body is but the husk of the spirit that has transcended flesh and time. . . . I won't bore you with the rest, but believe me I've got them all off pat.)

I take care that my khaki shorts are always freshly laundered, and I wear them to that fashionable length just above the knee – they're really cut-down trousers, so they roll up to quite good effect. And when I'm standing on my head there's sufficient puckering in the material to confuse anyone who wants to get a look. Down a leg, that is. You'd be surprised how many eyes stray in that direction as people drift past. Curious as to whether there's anything there at all at my age, I don't doubt. Well, for the record, that's one of the few bits that doesn't seem to have changed a lot. All in good working order, thank you very much.

I find it constantly stimulating upside down here on the promenade. Kids of course do it all the time, stand with their heads between their legs, looking at everything the wrong way up. It's a new perspective that makes colours brighter and seems to sharpen forms. I've even been guilty of employing it for unsavoury ends, like in that lonely period of my life I'd much rather forget, when short on women and much else besides I'd masturbate by turning the centrefold pages through 180° to get the novelty of inverted breasts and thighs. One can only marvel at the ingenuity with which we pursue our pleasures.

That part of me that demands recognition is satisfied here less often than you might think. You do get to hear the odd snide comment, but by-and-large the heat seems to take the malice out of people and on a beach the weirdest sights pass without comment. Another point: largely naked as most of us are here we tend to feel vulnerable. Bodies are something that perhaps each of us would rather hide. Ooops! I can't be mistaken, not at this distance! Surely I'm not going to be struck dumb with shyness, like a schoolboy. Ah, that's better.

The old ticker races a bit as I fold my knees down and do rather a neat back roll to end up squatting on my heels. Yes, it is her (I mean, it is *she*: perhaps I really am more nervous than I think). No, I'm composed actually, and should be able to manage to look quizzical. Let's not be *too* self-conscious – curious is about half the way I feel. Talk about people hiding themselves! (Not much left to hide on her! And why haven't I seen her here before? Am I to think that after yesterday she's come looking just for me?)

'Hello,' she says brightly, now that I'm the right way up. (And now that I'm the right way up it seems a very good way to be, especially when she sits down beside me on the wall.) 'Going well?' she smiles, and tells me that Jimmy said she would find me on the beach.

Well, I'm not one for beating about the bush, so I'll tell her how nice I think she looks. Which is both the right and the wrong thing to say, because the fact that she is topless is for her a commonplace, 'no big deal'. Yet part of her must *surely* exist in the knowledge that she looks so stunningly good, so I'll say it in a way that both parts might be happy to hear! And how does she reply? She comes right out with it, says that I don't look too bad myself (which as you know I've been telling myself for years, but it's a bit different when the words are actually spoken and flutter like humming-birds inside your ears) so I have a quick look round me wondering if anyone else on the beach is listening, whether there seems to be anything out of the ordinary in the way that we are seated here. But no, the kids still play in the shallows, the woman to my right rubs sunshade on her arms, and the well-built hair-dresser rolls over to toast his other side. But curiously – and this is a phenomenon that I have often observed at times like this (though again, not for a few years now) – the little waves that are creeping up the sand seem to sparkle with just that much more vigour, and the sky has suddenly become a deeper, wondrous blue. So I grasp the least part of my fantasy, and tell her that I'd hoped that I would see her again. And she replies that there could be no doubt about it, just meeting me that once, she'd flipped for me completely, had fallen headfirst and hopelessly in love!

Well! My initial reaction to this (which fortunately I am able to check) was to giggle; but now I start to feel very, very sober indeed. This is a stage, too, and passes just as quickly as the first. So we are left, the two of us, sitting here talking quite seriously about a number of things, and each finding something familiar (how can I tell if I'm presuming too much?) written in the other's face. Shall I bore you with an analogy? It's like starting a book at the last chapter and being able to accept everything that's gone before as read.

Yes she has got problems with Jimmy, but indicates that when she took him on she knew precisely what she might expect. She thinks she can handle them. Jimmy's father (that's my son) is an entirely different proposition: she can't honestly say that she's got much time for him and it's quite a problem that Jimmy lives at home. (I tell her that I know exactly what she means. It's true that Jeremy is an unfeeling prick and I've long ago stopped blaming myself for *that*.) But she's not here, she says, to complain. She's going to tell me what happened yesterday.

It seems that after she and Jimmy had argued she'd dropped a trip (she says this in such a matter-of-fact way that the words don't raise my hackles in the way that so much cult-talk seems to do) and come down late to this very beach, trying to find me. (I'd popped up to the local to have a cold glass of hock and to meditate on the happenings of the day.) When I wasn't about she'd stripped off, it being dinner time and the beach almost empty, and gone for a swim. It was very warm from the retreating tide's crawl out over the mud in the hottest part of that blazing afternoon. As she lay down in the shallows she knew immediately that she was a fish. With the water only shin deep (it's difficult at low tide to get more water than that without wading halfway to Hawaii) she was obviously a flounder. She bellied further into the warm mud. Opening her eyes beneath the water she saw the fish's world around her. Then she began to move. By wriggling slightly she could lift up a fraction from the bottom and scull through the shallows with amazing ease.

Did she find any difficulty in breathing? She doesn't think so, she says. But it was then that she began to notice the other denizens of her chosen environment, hermit crabs, sea-lice and shrimps – and there, out of the corner of her eye, a plume of mud and the slip stream from some rapidly departing form. Excited now, she followed the trail to where it ended and there was the other fish, wriggling and shuffling nervously into the ooze. Another flounder! Its eyes were the biggest giveaway, and there lightly sketched against the bottom was that familiar shape. Other creatures just like her! Her mind was bursting with the discovery. The shallows were full now of their darting forms, exploding out of their soft beds of mud. They were quick to their new places of rest, oh yes. But never so quick that her eyes could not follow them. Under her benevolent gaze they would sink once again into the welcoming bed of the sea.

As you might imagine, this little tale leaves me almost speechless. It's seductively easy to say something that indicates your right to be impressed, like 'wow!', 'far out!' and 'too much!' which have all enjoyed their vogue. But really, the only genuine form of approval is silence. So this is how we sit for some minutes, in silence. Because of the speed at which our . . . *relationship* (it is difficult to find a better word, so this will have to do) has evolved, there's a tendency in both of us – well in me at any rate, and I shall take the liberty of presuming on her behalf – to revert in this period of silence to an essential shyness. It is my thesis that all worthwhile communication must rely finally on this overwhelming sense of otherness to rest its case. But I'm pleased to say that on this occasion it's a tendency we both anticipate and are able to resist. She is looking across at me and smiling slightly – how they speak volumes, these brief smiles! – and I am doing the same to her. (I can recommend it as a most pleasant way of passing time on a moderately crowded summer beach.) Eyes become my fetish, for her eyes are very frank and not without a hint of mischief. Has she read ahead, and does she know how this last chapter is going to proceed?

Well if she doesn't I certainly do. I can't say that sitting here looking into these large brown eyes I am *entirely* unaware of her breasts, and of the glow from this warm brown skin. But I encourage myself to notice more of these things and soon she catches my eye. 'Well, shall we go then?' she asks. She scrambles to her feet and I must say I like the way her heels dig into the sandy concrete of the wall and the way she moves in close beside me as I uncoil from the position I have elected throughout to take. We climb the long flight of steps to the road and there is, I confess, an impulse to take her hand: what stops me is not my sense of the ridiculous but a knowledge that such a gesture might be unnecessary in the light of the understanding we both have reached.

The house is only a hundred yards up the road so it seems logical that we go there straight away. Conceding the incandescence of this particular event, I'm still a touch relieved when she slips a short grey jersey over her breasts. I do worry a bit about the neighbours, from time to time; after all, in a certain sense they are the closest thing to a family I've got. But I forget all this in the delicious touch as she opens up the gate. 'Your place or mine?' is what she says.

Once inside the house – and it really is most pleasantly cool in here – we go straight to the sofa in the living-room and shuck off the three garments that we share between us. With the coital act complete it really is most relaxing curling around and over each other on the sofa – like an extension of the beach, I suppose – and I can see how much sand and salt there is on each of our bodies and am moved to comment on how sunbleached and tousled is her hair. The room surprises me with its benevolence towards us. I've always felt at home here, but today it seems especially considerate of its occupants, dusting our bodies and the grave but friendly furniture with feathery touches of coloured sunlight as the evening seeps so steadily in through the rather ordinarily-patterned glass. And then it is very pleasant too just to paddle around the house, making a lemon drink in the kitchen, hearing the birds outside, walking naked in the overgrown back garden where the neighbours would find it impossible to see. We're chattering about all sorts of things and I must say it's one of the better afternoons I've ever spent. Yes I *do* feel I've deserved it. I only mention it because it's crept up on me in the way that I've always known these things should.

'What next?' I can hear you ask. I hope for your sake it's not a loaded question. A sceptic's tone indicates a fatal inability to enjoy these simple things. If you are confused I can only suggest that you urgently examine your own priorities. You must above all recognize how essentially irrelevant you have become in this.

It seems like hours since I last had anything to eat and I know that Susan shares my appetites to a T. Clothes will be the only problem, for her, that is. In societies more discerning about what has passed between us there are restaurants where if she went in her bikini they'd be pleased to have her eat.

'Your wife's clothes?' she suggests.

It's a natural enough thought but I find that I can go one better. Somewhere in this old family home are trunks and trunks of my mother's clothes (I'm really quite attached in a heedless sort of way to the past). Undergarments she does not need. There is a long dress, hugging her body in yellow silk but no shoes – or none that fit. And this feather boa. I've got my new cream shirt and freshly-pressed khakis.

We hold each other's hand going home because each of us knows that dinners like the one we've just had should end . . . like this . . . and inside the door I get straight on the phone to Jeremy. He's engaged, of course, for what seems like hours. 'Jeremy?' I say, when I finally get through. 'Come on over will you Jeremy? Now. Yes, that's right. Come straight away.'

I tell him to bring Jimmy too and hang up before his speech. He might think it's a heart attack (though he's got me down for cancer); more likely he'll be terrified that I'm making changes in the will.

Anyway, it doesn't take them long to get here. The car always slips so . . . *sumptuously* right in beside the kerb, and as I open the door to them they must be able to see Susan behind me in the light.

'Come in, come in,' I say, because I'm really very impatient and want to get the whole thing through.

Susan goes straight over to Jimmy and takes him by the arm, but I'm buggered if I'll offer Jeremy, who's gaping like a trout, any liquor of mine to drink.

'You've probably got an inkling of why I've brought you here,' I begin, and I see Susan slip her hand into Jim's and twine round him until he's just the beanpole holding her up.

So I continue. 'But you won't be able to claim that it comes as much of a surprise.' They seem reluctant to listen to what comes next.

'It's to tell you that you're disinherited. Both of you,' I insist.

These things take time to sink in, I know, so I spell it out for them: 'D-I-S-I-N-H-E-R-I-T-E-D. Disinherited. Got it?'

I can see now that Jim is taking it quite hard, but as for my son. . . . I must say that only today do I realize the extent of the dislike for the other that each of us bears.

'Don't you understand me?' I confront him. 'The house will be yours and the flats and the boat and the stocks and shares and every last vestige of my worldly goods.' His face distorts with covetousness and relief.

'But that's not what's at stake!' Honestly, I have to shout to make him hear.

Well, we all flounder about for a while and they seem determined not to leave. It's as though they're waiting for the happy ending that I'm quite disinclined to give. I could say, for example, that Susan will take care of Jimmy, as well she should. Family characteristics are said to skip a generation so he can't possibly turn out all bad. And that if Jeremy's head goes any further up his own arse he might one day meet someone there he recognizes.

But you've heard me say before, priorities are what matters. It really is a most attractive smile. Tomorrow, I don't doubt, I'll only be spending *part* of the day down at the beach.

IAN WEDDE

The Gringos

The Gringos, a former rock and roll band of the nineteen fifties, seldom met these days. When they did it was by accident. Though none of them now played professionally they'd all kept their gear, with the exception of Nigel who'd sold his kit after the band's breakup because he'd felt stupid playing the drums by himself especially when his wife was listening.

But he still had his suit and since his attachment to performing days had increased over the years he'd also guarded those potent accessories: two pairs of blue suede ripple soles, a couple of chunky rings set with huge fake rubies, some velvet Mississippi string ties.

He was pretty sure the other *Gringos* had hung on to their clobber too. In their heyday they'd had a band suit: a midnight blue threequarter length jacket shot with silver lurex, shoulders padded right out, wide scarlet silk lapels plunging to a single button at navel level, a scarlet Edwardian waistcoat with a rich paisley pattern, pegleg pants with a zipper on the inside of each ankle, blue silk shirts with a foam of blue lace on the front and scarlet piping on the cuffs. *The Gringos* had been good enough to afford this number and they'd played anywhere there was a hop between Christchurch and Invercargill, though Dunedin was their base and summer at Caroline Bay in Timaru what really took care of the brass.

There they'd got the cops out more than once as local bodgies and yahoos packed dances to pick fights with kids on holiday at Caroline Bay. Of course *The Gringos* got the blame, or rock and roll did. But they played four summers anyway. In those days there was no bullshit. The lead guitar's pickup went straight into the amp and the metallic music came straight back out again. The two saxaphones blew right in the faces of rock and rolling kids. *The Gringos'* bass went electric long before that was common but he still marched it up and down, solid and even, that splitsecond ahead of the beat, the notes sliding out from under the guitar's syncopation.

From time to time they used a second guitar but they found it complicated the music too much. Then there was Nigel with his basic kit: snare, foot-bass, hihat, one tomtom to the side, and one cymbal, a pair of seldom-used danceband brushes, and a rack of hickory clubs. The rim of the snare was battered, the paint and chrome flaking off down the side. But he wasn't just a walloper. If Pete had the knack of keeping his marching bass just an eyelid-bat ahead of the beat, Nigel had an equally necessary talent for staying that splitsecond behind: this was what gave the music its truculence: 'shootin' the agate'.

After the old rock and rollers stopped being heard – those endlessly interchangeable pros who blasted away behind Chuck Berry and Bo Diddley and even Elvis Presley – Nigel thought the only rock drummer who got close was Charlie Watts of the *Rolling Stones*. But he didn't listen to much 'modern' rock music. After *The Gringos* stopped playing there didn't seem to be much point in listening either. And after about two and a half minutes of any rock track he listened to these days he kept hearing a coda asking to be played, some final chop, a chord that would stamp down like a shoe on a cigarette butt. But the music went on, *nah nah nah*, like jazz. He didn't like jazz, never had. Years back a friend had tried to get him to listen to Charlie Parker.

'That's bullshit mate. The bastard doesn't know shit from clay.'

It was Chuck Berry from the start and it was still Chuck Berry as far as he was concerned when the band broke up. A few years later he'd listened in disbelief as a new English group called *The Beatles* sang 'Roll Over Beethoven'. The music had been ironed out a bit, he could hear how the equipment had changed, but it was the old Chuck Berry number all right.

Only it wasn't the same. Why he felt like this he didn't know. When he thought about it he decided it was because he wasn't playing any more. When he talked to the band they said the same. Also Lorraine didn't like rock and roll any more. She said it was all right when you were a kid, but. . . .

But *he* could remember her dancing back then in 1959.

It had occurred to him that *The Gringos* lasted only a short professional time: '56 to '59. It was a thought whose meaning he couldn't catch. The *real* time was more than four years. Here he was in '73, he had one kid who'd be leaving school soon, and two more as well, he had a house up Brockville and an okay job with Cooke Howlison, it was fifteen years since *The Gringos* had played 'Maybellene', the last song they played as a band, Chuck Berry's first hit, their homage to Chuck. But *then* was still the most important time in his life.

'It was okay when we were kids,' said Lorraine.

And his son, who was fourteen, said he liked the old records but it made him laugh to think of his dad playing in a rock and roll band at Caroline Bay in Timaru.

'I can't imagine it.' Ha ha.

All the same the boy would skite to his friends. Sometimes a bunch of them would turn up, look at Nigel, and listen to some of his collection: 'Maybellene', 'Johnny B. Goode', 'Sweet Little Sixteen', 'Memphis'. Then he'd play them Little Richard, Elvis, and even Muddy Waters. The records were scratchy and worn. Down in the basement rumpus room of his house he longed to put on his gear and show them what it had been like. They stood around, amused, *listening*. He played his collector's item, a recording of Chuck Berry from the film *Jazz on a Summer's Day* at the 1958 Newport Jazz Festival, a performance of 'Sweet Little Sixteen' with Jack Teagarden's trombone blasting in behind. It made him sweat. He wanted to say, 'It took over, see?' They jigged awkwardly, shifting their feet. Then he'd play 'Rock and Roll Music' or 'Roll Over Beethoven', knowing what was going to happen, and sure enough one of the kids would always say, 'But that's a Beatles' song. . . . '

When he went back upstairs with his records carefully under his arm they'd put on *Osibisa* or *The Moody Blues* or *Grand Funk Railroad* or for fucksake *Simon and Garwhatsit*. It was rubbish. He'd hear the *clok* of pool balls on the miniature table and from time to time the fizz of aerosol freshair as they doused their cigarette smoke with Pine Fragrance.

At fifteen he'd been a chippy's apprentice and smoking a packet of cigarettes a day. He couldn't afford it. But like everything else it had to be done with style. You spent hours practising, letting the smoke dribble from your lips and back again up your nostrils. You practised lighting matches inside the open half of a matchbox. Kidstuff. . . .

It was no coincidence that *The Gringos* all had similar jobs. Nigel was a warehouseman. So were two of the others. The other two were clerks. They were all married. They all lived in suburbs near Dunedin. So it was natural that they all got home on a certain day and saw a photograph of Chuck Berry on the front page of the evening paper, and all reached to ring each other up for the first time in months or in some cases years. It took a while before any of them was able to get through the scramble of lines. And then, as if by telepathy, there was nothing to say.

'D'ja. . . . '

'Yeah it's. . . . '

'When I got home. . . . '

No sooner had Nigel hung up, heart thumping, than the phone rang again.

'Hey, d'ja see. . . .'
'Yeah Chuck. . . .'
'Inna paper. . . .'
'Fuck me dead. . . .'
They met in the pub. What had happened? Where had the time gone? They went over a half forgotten litany of names and dates and places. They remembered songs. They swallowed tears.

The day before the concert Nigel gave in to a nagging temptation. In the bedroom he took a large box down from the top of the wardrobe and from it he carefully lifted out The Suit. It was wrapped in tissue and then polythene and had been impregnated with thymol crystals. The Shirt was there too. He hadn't got it all out for so long he'd forgotten the texture and feel of the heavy cloth. It was perfectly preserved. He held the jacket up by the shoulders. He felt furtive and exalted. Quickly he buttoned himself into The Shirt with its chemical smell and its frenzy of lace. The neck button wouldn't do up. No matter, he'd. . . .

Sitting on the edge of the bed he undid the inside zips of the trousers and stepped in pointing his toes like a dancer. In spite of their generous forward pleats he couldn't get the trousers past the tops of his thighs. They'd have to be altered.

Spreading his legs to hold the pants up as far as they'd gone, he grunted into The Jacket. Though cut to drape full and free, tapering not to the waist but to a point below his backside, The Jacket crushed his armpits and wouldn't button. Lorraine could let it out for sure.

Keeping his legs spraddled, his arms held out from his trunk by the crushing jacket, he pushed his feet into the Blue Suedes. They fitted.

He shuffled sideways to the wardrobe mirror. There he saw a fat-faced man of forty with a shiteating smile, whose hair, still black, had receded from his temples along the path the comb still took it, straight back. The fat man's hornrim glasses had slipped a little down his nose. He was standing with his trousers half-up like someone caught having a nasty in a bus shelter. Between the straining buttons of a lacey blue shirt came tufts of black chest hair. The man's arms were held out sideways. The bottoms of his trousers were concertina'd against the insteps of blue shoes whose scarlet laces trailed on the floor.

Skip the waistcoat.
'Jesus Christ. . . .'
But he stood outside the town hall with a dry mouth and a pounding happy heart. The other *Gringos* were there too with their wives. That made ten altogether. They felt like a club. It was a cold spring evening. The rest of the crowd was mostly young. *The Gringos* felt conspicuous but proud. They exchanged derisive glances as the crowd whooped it up. Some of *them* had got dressed nineteen fifties style: there were kids of nineteen and twenty with makeshift ducksarse hairstyles and there was even one beautiful girl wearing pedal pushers, a sweater and a pony tail, and bright red lipstick. Nigel's eyes wandered her way. He wondered if she could rock and roll. It was certainly news to him that Chuck Berry was still appreciated or was being appreciated again. Lots of these kids were only a few years older than his own son! What did they know about the old style?

'The old style . . .': he caught at the phrase as it sidled through his mind. Then they were going in. He was still examining the phrase as they took their seats. The ten of them sat in a row. All around was the racket of a young excited audience. But no dance floor. A *town hall*. Like for concerts, the symphony orchestra.

He was still thinking 'the old style' when the backing group came on: guitar, bass, drums, electric piano. They powered straight into some standards beginning with 'Johnny B. Goode' and going without a pause into Little Richard's 'Awopbopaloobop'. It was deafening. The amps were six feet high. There was wire all over the stage. The bass player kept getting off licks like cracks of thunder which jabbed at Nigel's ears. He could *feel* it in his guts. The guitarist and singer had beanpole legs. He banged his knees together as he sang and played. He appeared to be chewing at the microphone. You couldn't really hear what he said. The audience sat somewhat sullenly.

Then there was a pause. There were groups chanting 'Chuck Chuck Chuck!' It just wasn't like rock and roll. The Kiwi backing group came on again and began tuning up. They looked scared. The phrase 'old style' was still whining away in Nigel's ears which he felt had been damaged by the preceding hour of noise. He watched the drummer up there as he straightened out his kit. He had about twice as much gear as Nigel had ever played with. For a start he had two tomtoms mounted on the foot-bass and another to the side as well. Then he had a total of four cymbals including a sizzle and not counting the hihat. What for? You didn't need it. Nigel admitted the joker was quick and fancy. But he couldn't play rock and roll. He was whipping the music along like a jockey taking his nag away in the home straight but what you wanted to get into rock and roll was slouch, you had to shoot the agate. You had to feel the slug of it like the sexy splitsecond between the thud of a girl's heart and the squirm of the artery in her neck, her breath gasping as she swings back under your arm, catching her flying hand as she goes past again, then rocking back in close. Or it was like not letting a fuck accelerate away with you before the lights changed, yeah. . . .

This thought struck him as original. Leaning sideways to confide it to another *Gringo* he missed Chuck Berry's entry. When he heard the crowd go mad he looked up and saw a lean wolfish Negro wearing a check shirt and narrow peglegs grinning back over his shoulder as he slung his guitar and moved across to the electric piano to tune. This he did with such care and absorption, moving from member to member of the backing group, that the audience thought it was a puton and began to howl.

But *The Gringos* knew better. Nigel was sweating but he sat like a boulder. The wolfish man struck a few elegant licks off his guitar. The sound was simple and familiar. The amps had been turned right down but he waved to turn them down further.

Then he cracked off a couple more licks with a bit more velocity behind them, grinned, rode rubber legs to the front of the stage and all at once was into 'Reelin' and Rockin'' while *The Gringos* sat petrified in their seats three-quarters of the way back from the stage of the town hall with all around them a howling audience of kids not much older than their own.

At one point as Chuck lolloped into 'Too Pooped to Pop' a group in front of *The Gringos* struggled out into the aisle with a banner which read 'We love you Chuck'. They ponced round the front of the stage with it and back down the next aisle. Chuck Berry acknowledged this gesture with an ironical double-take. But the music rode on. He swung his gat arm knocking the steely chords off the instrument as though brushing lint from a coat. He rode one heel across stage, the other leg stretched out in front. He did a pretty good splits and never stopped playing. Lowering the guitar between his legs he shot wads of sound into the audience which was by now dancing wildly in the aisles, not rock and roll, just. . . .

But *The Gringos* sat without moving, as though turned to stone. They didn't miss a thing. They noted the glances Chuck shot at the electric piano player who couldn't rock the instrument. Nigel noted with satisfaction the looks Chuck sent from time to time in the direction of the drummer who was sweating blood. The bass player had been briefed. He marched it up and down.

And Chuck Berry, lean as a knife, lazy as calm water, mean as a wolf, sang and strutted and rubberlegged and licked away at that guitar whose pickup went straight into the amp while the music came straight back out again, no bullshit, metallic, 'in the old style', as though Chuck could never get old, as though rock and roll could never die, and *The Gringos* sat there with their wives while their Suits stayed at home with the real *Gringos* folded up inside somehow with the thymol crystals.

Oh Maybellene
Why can't you be true?

sang Chuck Berry. *The Gringos* had been a good rock and roll band for four years and that had been a lifetime. It was fifteen years since they'd played 'Maybellene' for the last time at Caroline Bay in Timaru in the summer of '59, and that had been even longer.

KERI HULME

Hooks and Feelers

On the morning before it happened, her fingers were covered with grey, soft clay.

'Charleston,' she says. 'It comes from Charleston. It's really a modeller's clay, but it'll make nice cups. I envisage,' gesturing in the air, 'tall fluted goblets. I'll glaze them sea blue and we'll drink wine together, all of us.'

I went out to the shed and knocked on the door. There's no word of welcome, but the kerosene lamp is burning brightly, so I push on in.

She's pumping the treadle potter's wheel with a terrible urgency, but she's not making pots. Just tall, wavery cones. I don't know what they are. I've never seen her make them before. The floor, the shelves, the bench – the place is spikey with them.

'They've rung,' I say.

She doesn't look up.

'They said he'll be home tomorrow.'

The wheel slowed, stopped.

'So?'

'Well, will you get him?'

'No.'

The wheel starts purring. Another cone begins to grow under her fingers.

'What are you making those for?'

She still won't look at me.

'You go,' she says, and the wheel begins to hum.

Well, you can't win.

I go and get him and come home, chattering brightly all the way.

He is silent.

I carry him inside, pointing out that I've repainted everywhere, that we've got a new stove and did you like your present? And he ignores it all.

But he says, very quietly, to his ma, 'Hello.' Very cool.

She looks at him, over him, round him, eyes going up and down but always avoiding the one place where she should be looking. She says, 'Hello,' back.

'Put me down please,' he says to me then.

No 'Thanks for getting me.' Not a word of appreciation for the new clothes. Just that polite, expressionless, 'Put me down please.'

Not another word.

He went into his bedroom and shut the door.

'Well, it's just the shock of being back home, eh?'

I look at her, and she looks at me. I go across and slide my hands around her shoulders, draw her close to me, nuzzle her ear, and for a moment it's peace.

Then she draws away.

'Make a coffee,' she says brusquely. 'I'm tired.'

I don't take offence. After grinding the beans, I ask, 'What are you making the cones for?'

She shrugs.

'It's just an idea.'

The smell from the crushed coffee beans is rich and heavy, almost sickening.

His door opens.

He has his doll in his hand. Or rather, parts of his doll. He's torn the head off, the arms and legs apart.

'I don't want this anymore,' he says into the silence.

He goes to the fire, and flings the parts in. And then he reaches in among the burning coals and plucks out the head, which is melted and smoking. He says, 'On second thoughts, I'll keep this.'

The smoke curls round the steel and lingers, acridly.

Soon after, she went back to the shed.

I went down to the pub.

'Hey!' yells Mata, 'c'mon over here!'

'Look at that,' he says, grinning hugely, waving a crumpled bit of paper. It's a Golden Kiwi ticket. 'Bugger's won me four hundred dollars.' He sways. 'Whatta yer drinking?'

I never have won anything. I reach across, grab his hand, shake it. It's warm and calloused, hard and real.

'Bloody oath, Mat, what good luck!'

He smiles more widely still, his eyes crinkling almost shut. 'Shout you eh?'

'Too right you can. Double whisky.'

And I get that from him and a jug and another couple of doubles and another jug. I am warm and happy until someone turns the radio up.

'Hands across the water, hands across the sea . . .' the voices thunder and beat by my ears, and pianos and violins wail and wind round the words.

The shed's in darkness.

I push the door open, gingerly.

'Are you there?'

I hear her move.

'Yes.'

'How about a little light on the subject?' I'm trying to sound happily drunk, but the words have a nasty callous ring to them.

'The lamp is on the bench beside you.'

I reach for it and encounter a soft, still wet, cone of clay. I snatch my fingers away hurriedly.

'Are you revealing to the world what the cones are for yet?'

I've found the lamp, fumble for my matches. My fingers are clumsy, but at last the wick catches a light, glows and grows.

She sniffs.

'Give me the matches please.'

I throw the box across and she snatches them from the air.

She touches a match to a cigarette, the match shows blue and then flares bright, steady, gold. The cigarette pulses redly. The lamp isn't trimmed very well.

She sighs and the smoke flows thickly out of her mouth and nose.

'I put nearly all of them back in the stodge-box today.'

What? Oh yes, the cones. The stodge-box is her special term for the pile of clay that gets reworked.

'Oh.' I add after a moment, apologetically, 'I sort of squashed one reaching for the lamp.'

'It doesn't matter,' she says, blowing out another stream of smoke.

'I was going to kill that one too.'

I take my battered, old, guitar and begin to play. I play badly. I've never learned to play properly.

He says, out of the dark, 'Why are you sad?'

'What makes you think I am?'

'Because you're playing without the lights on.'

I sigh. 'A man can play in the dark if he wants.'
'Besides I heard you crying.'
My dear cool son.
'. . . so I cry sometimes. . . .'
'Why are you sad?' he asks again.
Everlasting questions ever since he began to talk.
'Shut up.'
'Because of me?' he persists. He pauses, long enough to check whether I'm going to move.
'Or because of her?'
'Because of me, now get out of here,' I answer roughly, and bang the guitar down. It groans. The strings shiver.
He doesn't move.
'You've been to the pub?'
I prop the guitar against the wall and get up.
'You've been to the pub,' he states, and drifts back into his room.

My mother came to visit the next day, all agog to see the wreckage. She has a nice instinct for disasters. She used to be a strong little woman but she's run to frailty and brittle bones now. Alas; all small and powdery, with a thick fine down over her face that manages, somehow, to protrude through her make-up. It'd look so much better if she didn't pile powder and stuff on, but I can't imagine her face without pink gunk clogging the pores. That much has never changed.
    She brought a bag of blackballs for him. When he accepts them, reluctantly, she coos and pats him and strokes his hair. He has always hated that.
    'Oh dear,' she says, 'your poor careless mother,' and 'You poor little man' and (aside to me) 'It's just as well you didn't have a daughter, it'd be so much worse for a girl.' (He heard that, and smiled blandly.)
    She asks him, 'However are you going to manage now? Your guitar and football and all? Hmmm?'
    He says, steadily, 'It's very awkward to wipe my arse now. That's all.'
    For a moment I like him very much.
    My mother flutters and tchs, 'Oh, goodness me, dear, you mustn't say. . . .'
    He's already turned away.

As soon as my mother left, I went out to the shed.
    'You could have come in and said hello,' I say reproachfully.
    'It would have only led to a fight.' She sits hunched up on the floor. Her face is in shadow.
    I look round. The shed's been tidied up. All the stray bits and pieces are hidden away. There's an innovation, however, an ominous one. The crucifix she keeps on the wall opposite her wheel has been covered with black cloth. The only part that shows is a hand, nailed to the wooden cross.
    'Is that a reminder for penitence? Or are you mourning?'
    She doesn't reply.

Early in the morning, while it's still quite dark, I awake to hear him sobbing. I lift the bedclothes gently – she didn't stir, drowned in sleep, her black hair wreathed about her body like seaweed – and creep away to his room.
    The sobbing is part stifled, a rhythmic choking and gasping, rough with misery.
    'Hello?'
    'E pa . . .' he turns over and round from his pillow and reaches out his arms. He doesn't do that. He hasn't done that since he was a baby.

I pick him up, cradling him, cuddling him.

'I can still feel it pa. I can feel it still.' He is desperate in his insistence and wild with crying. But he is also coldly angry at himself.

'I know it's not there anymore,' he struck himself a blow, 'but I can *feel* it still. . . .'

I kiss and soothe and bring a tranquillizer that the people at the hospital gave me. He sobs himself back to sleep, leaning, in the end, away from me. And I go back to bed.

Her ocean, her ocean, te moananui a Kiwa, drowns me. Far away on the beach I can hear him calling, but I must keep on going down into the greeny deeps, down to where her face is, to where the soft anenome tentacles of her fingers beckon and sway and sweep me onward to the weeping heart of the world.

He stays home from school for another week. It's probably just as well, for once, the first time he ventured outside the house, the next door neighbour's kids shouted crudities at him.

I watched him walk over to them, talk, and gesture, the hook flashing bravely in the sun. The next door neighbour's kids fell silent, drew together in a scared huddled group.

'What did you do to stop that?' I ask, after he has stalked proudly back inside.

He shook his head.

'Tell me.'

'I didn't have to do anything.' He smiles.

'Oh?'

'I don't imagine,' he says it so coolly, 'that anyone wants this in their eyes.'

The hair on the back of my neck bristles with shock.

'Don't you dare threaten anybody like that! No matter what they say!' I shout at him in rage, in horror. 'I'll beat you silly if you do that again.'

He shrugs. 'Okay, if you say so pa.'

(Imagine that cruel, steel curve reaching for your eyes. That pincer of unfeeling metal gouging in.) The steel hook glints as he moves away.

How can he be my son and have so little of me in him? Oh, he has my colouring, fair hair and steelgrey eyes, just as he has her colour and bone structure; a brown thickset chunk of a boy.

But his strange cold nature comes from neither of us. Well, it certainly doesn't come from me.

Later on that day – we are reading in front of the fire – a coal falls out. He reaches for it.

'Careful, it's hot,' I warn.

'I don't care how hot it is,' he says, grinning.

The two steel fingers pick up the piece of coal and slowly crush the fire out of it.

It hasn't taken long for him to get very deft with those pincers. He can pick up minute things, like pins, or the smallest of buttons. I suspect he practises doing so, in the secrecy of his bedroom. He can handle almost anything as skilfully as he could before.

At night, after he's had a shower, I ask, 'Let me look?'

'No.'

'Ahh, come on.'

He holds it out, silently.

All his wrist bones are gone. There remains a scarred purplish area with two smooth, rounded knubs on either side. In the centre is a small socket. The hook, which is mounted on a kind of swivel, slots into there. I don't understand how it works, but it looks like a nice practical piece of machinery.

He is looking away.

'You don't like it?'

'It's all right . . . will you string my guitar backwards? I tried, and I can't do it.'

'Of course.'

I fetch his guitar and begin immediately.

'There is something quite new we can do, you know.' The specialist draws a deep breath of smoke and doesn't exhale any of it.

The smell of antiseptic is making me feel sick. This room is painted a dull grey. There are flyspots on the light. I bring my eyes down to him and smile, rigidly.

'Ahh, yes?'

'Immediately after amputation, we can attach an undamaged portion of sinew and nerve to this nyloprene socket.'

He holds out a gadget, spins it round between his lean fingers, and snatches it away again, out of sight.

'It is a permanent implant, with a special prosthesis that fits into it, but the child will retain a good deal of control over his, umm, hand movements.'

He sucks in more smoke and eyes me beadily, eagerly. Then he suddenly lets the whole, stale lungful go, right in my face.

'So you agree to that then?'

'Ahh, yes.'

Later, at night, she says, 'Are you still awake too?'

'Yes.'

'What are you thinking of.'

'Nothing really. I was just listening to you breathe.'

Her hand creeps to my side, feeling along until it finds a warm handful.

'I am thinking of the door,' she says thoughtfully. You know the way a car door crunches shut, with a sort of definite, echoing thunk?

Well, there was that. Her hurried footsteps. A split second of complete silence. And then the screaming started, piercing, agonised, desperate. We spun round. He was nailed, pinioned against the side of the car by his trapped hand.

She stood, going, 'O my god! O my god!' and biting down on her hand. She didn't make another move, frozen where she stood, getting whiter and whiter and whiter.

I had to open the door.

'I know it's silly,' she continues, still holding me warmly, 'but if we hadn't bought that packet of peanuts, we wouldn't have spilled them. I wouldn't have got angry. I wouldn't have stormed out of the car. I wouldn't have slammed the door without looking. Without looking.'

'You bought the nuts, remember?' she adds irrelevantly.

I don't answer.

There are other things in her ocean now. Massive black shadows that loom up near me without revealing what they are. Something glints. The shadows waver and retreat.

They stuck a needle attached to a clear, plastic tube into his arm. The tube filled with blood. Then, the blood cleared away and the dope ran into his vein. His eyelids dragged down. He slept, unwillingly, the tears of horror and anguish still wet on his face.

The ruined hand lay on a white, shiny bench, already apart from him. It was like a lump of raw, swollen meat with small, shattered, bluish bones through it.

'We'll have to amputate that, I'm afraid. It's absolutely unsalvageable.'

'Okay,' I say. 'Whatever you think best.'

They say that hearing is the last of the senses to die, when you are unconscious.

They are wrong, at least for me. Images, or what is worse, not-quite images, flare and burst and fade before I sink into the dreamless sea of sleep.

I went out to the shed.

'Tea is nearly ready,' I call through the open door.

'Good,' she replies. 'Come in and look.'

She has made a hundred, more than a hundred, large, shallow wine cups. 'Kraters,' she says, smiling to me briefly.

I grin back, delighted.

'Well, they should sell well.'

She bends her head, scraping at a patch of dried clay on the bench.

'What were the cones?'

She looks up at me, the smile gone entirely.

'Nothing important,' she says. 'Nothing important.'

When she's washing the dishes, however, the magic happens again. For the first time since the door slammed shut, I look at her, and she looks willingly back and her eyes become deep and endless dark waters, beckoning to my soul. Drown in me . . . find yourself. I reach out flailing, groping for her hard, real body. Ahh, my hands encounter tense muscles, fasten on to them. I stroke and knead, rousing the long-dormant woman in her. Feel in the taut, secret places, rub the tender moist groove, caress her all over with sweet, probing fingers.

'Bait,' says a cold, sneering voice.

She gasps and goes rigid again.

'Get away to bed with you,' she says without turning round.

'I'm going to watch.'

An overwhelming anger floods through me. I whip around and my erstwhile gentle hands harden and clench.

'I'll. . . .'

'No,' she says, 'no,' touching me, warning me.

She goes across and kneels before him.

(I see he's trembling.)

She kisses his face.

She kisses his hand.

She kisses the hook.

'Now go to bed e tama.'

He stands, undecided, swaying in the doorway.

Then, too quickly for it to be stopped, he lashes out with the hook. It strikes her on her left breast.

I storm forward, full of rage, and reach for him.

'No,' she says again, kneeling there, motionless. 'No,' yet again.

'Go to bed, tama,' she says to him.

Her voice is warm and friendly. Her face is serene.

He turns obediently, and walks away into the dark.

At the weekend, I suggested we go for a picnic.

'Another one?' she asks, her black eyebrows raised.

'Well, we could gather pauas, maybe some cress, have a meal on the beach.

It'd be good to get out of the house for a while. This hasn't been too good a week for me, you know.'

They both shrugged.

'Okay,' he says.

'I will get the paua,' she says, and begins stripping off her jeans. 'You get the cress,' she says to him.

'I'll go with you and help,' I add.

He just looks at me. Those steely eyes in that brown face. Then he pouted, picked up the kete, and headed for the stream.

He selects a stalk and pinches it suddenly. The plant tissue thins to nothing. It's like he's executing the cress. He adds it to the pile in the kete. He doesn't look at me, or talk. He is absorbed in killing cress.

There's not much I can do.

So I put on my mask and flippers and wade into the water, slide down under the sea. I spend a long peaceful time there, detaching whelks and watching them wobble down to the bottom. I cruise along the undersea rock shelf, plucking bits of weed and letting them drift away. Eventually, I reach the end of the reef, and I can hear the boom and mutter of the real ocean. It's getting too close; I surface.

One hundred yards away, fighting a current that is moving him remorselessly out, is my son.

When I gained the beach, I was exhausted.

I stand, panting, him in my arms.

His face is grey and waxy and the water runs off us both, dropping constantly on the sand.

'You were too far out. . . .'

He cries.

'Where is she?'

Where is she? Gathering paua somewhere . . . but suddenly I don't know if that is so. I put my mask back on, leave him on the beach, and dive back under the waves, looking.

When I find her, as I find her, she is floating on her back amidst bullkelp. The brown weed curves sinuously over her body, like dark limp hands.

I splash and slobber over, sobbing to her. 'God, your son nearly died trying to find you. Why didn't you tell us?'

She opens her brown eyes lazily.

No, not lazily: with defeat, with weariness.

'What on earth gave you the idea I was going to drown?' She rubs the towel roughly over her skin.

I say, haltingly, 'Uh well, he was sure that. . . .'

(He is curled up near the fire I've lit, peacefully asleep.)

'Sure of what?'

'I don't know. He went looking for you, got scared. We couldn't see you anywhere.'

A sort of shudder, a ripple runs through her.

'The idea was right,' she says, very quietly. She lets the towel fall. She cups her hand under her left breast and points.

'Feel there.'

There is a hard, oval, clump amidst the soft tissue.

'God, did he do. . . .'

'No. It's been growing there for the past month. Probably for longer than that, but I have only felt it recently.' She rubs her armpit, thoughtfully. 'It's there too and under here,' gesturing to her jaw. 'It'll have to come out.' I can't stop it. I groan.

Do you understand that if I hadn't been there, both of them would have drowned?

There was one last thing.
    We were all together in the living room.
    I am in the lefthand chair, she is opposite me.
    He is crooning to himself, sprawled in front of the fire.
    'Loo-lie, loo-lay, loo-lie, loo-lay, the falcon hath borne my make away,' he sings. He pronounces it, 'the fawcon have borne my make away.'
    'What is that?' I ask.
    'A song.'
    He looks across to his ma and they smile slyly, at one another, smiles like invisible hands reaching out, caressing secretly, weaving and touching.

I washed my hands.
    I wept.
    I went out to the shed and banged the door finally shut.
    I wept a little longer.
    And then, because there was nothing else to do, I went down to the pub.
    I had been drinking double whiskies for more than an hour when Mata came across and laid his arm over my shoulder.
    He is shaking.
    'E man,' he whispers. His voice grows a little stronger. 'E man, don't drink by yourself. That's no good eh?' His arm presses down. 'Come across to us?'
    The hubbub of voices hushes.
    I snivel.
    'Mat, when I first knew, her fingers were covered in clay, soft grey clay. And she smiled and said it's Charleston, we'll call him Charleston. It's too soft really, but I'll make a nice cup from it. Cups. Tall fluted goblets she said.'
    His hand pats my shoulder with commiseration, with solicitude.
    His eyes are dark with horror.
    'I'll glaze them sea blue and we'll drink red wine together, all three of us.'
    We never did.

STEVAN ELDRED-GRIGG

When Bawds and Whores Do Churches Build

The *Aphrodite* nosed past yellow heads into the black wharves of the harbour.
Minnie stood at the poop in a limp green scarf.

Heavens, she thought.

Withdrawing to her stateroom to supervise Dawson at the last minute
packing. And eyeing closer her tired hand behind which, out of focus, were
white pilasters and the pink *putti* of the room.

Knock knock.

Mr Macintyre, said Dawson.

Minnie rose.

Mr Macintyre, she said. How odd.

His old eyes watering on her waistband.

Miss Lomax, said Mr Macintyre.

Perhaps you had best be seated.

Minnie sat.

I am the bearer, Miss Lomax, of sad tidings.

Minnie raised her eyes. Screwing them up.

Papa? she said.

Macintyre nodded.

Minnie frowned.

She rode and rode until the groom, a young boy, was lost behind her and
Minnie's plaids were streaming in the nor'wester.

She attained the summit and threw herself onto wiry grass. Behind her a row
of black gums. Before her a heaving welter of grassy hills.

Minnie stared and stared. Through tightened eyes.

Mine, she said. *Mon dieu.*

Sere clouds thrusting into alps, a hundred miles away.

Goodness, said Minnie.

But she could not keep it up.

She poked with a gloved finger at the little stones beneath her. Watched a tiny
spider. Stroked some blades of grass.

How it springs back, she thought.

Mais je m'en fiche.

She stood and gasped. Such tight lacing.

Miss Lomax, said Sir Robert. Under such sad auspices.

Minnie held her eyes low.

My dear, said Lady Cunninghame.

Patting Minnie's hand.

Such a lovely wreath, said Minnie.

Lady Cunninghame nodded and deprecated. Her lower lip trembling.

O my dear, said Lady Cunninghame.

She bent forward and kissed Minnie's cheek.

Back at Mount Lomax a string trio played concerti.

Minnie in black, but also with a touch of lilac.

So sad, said Alice de Renzie over a pastry.

My poor Minnie, she added.

Minnie's eyes wandered out through a bay window on to some walnuts in the park.

This room is so frightful, she said.

Alice started.

Look at it, said Minnie without vehemence.

Alice looked.

I suppose, said Alice.

Why should one be required to be grateful, said Minnie.

Alice pouted.

Minnie digging at a turkey carpet.

Is the empire waist catching on in England? said Alice.

Her eyes darting from Minnie to the window.

Yes, said Minnie.

Glancing at Alice.

O my dear it looks adorable.

Positivement dix-huitième siècle on dit, said Alice.

A magpie gargled.

Would you walk with me for a while, said Minnie.

Alice frowned.

Well, she said.

O please, said Minnie.

Alice smiled.

Well there's nothing more exciting.

Did you notice, said Alice, how they stared?

I didn't, said Minnie.

Perhaps they think us a bit . . . . You know, said Alice.

Minnie frowned.

Old maidish? said Minnie.

The park was dying for winter. Wash of yellow over tall English trees. Leaves in drifts, and being swept into heaps. Gardeners nodding at Minnie and Alice. Swans walking on the lake.

On the croquet lawn they halted.

Papa loved this place, said Minnie.

It is nice, said Alice.

Scrutinising.

So much beauty, she added.

I say!

A flash of sunlight had found a window on the upper storey.

We lose the sun so early in the day at our place, said Alice. Downstairs is positively dank by three in the afternoon. This time of year.

I remember, said Minnie.

I forget, said Alice. You've not been away all that long. Only it seems an age.

Minnie flicked a dead leaf out of her veil.

We have the fires lit every day now, said Alice. The servants grumble, but my dear we'd die of pneumonia.

Jessie Mackay says we have a freedom denied married women, said Minnie.

Alice frowned.

I've never met her. She's rather . . . wild.

Not really, said Minnie.

And they say, said Alice, that she has odd . . . penchants.

Nonsense, said Minnie.

She felt a headache beginning. The light rather harsh.

All I object to in her, said Minnie, and all that advanced circle, is that really they're conservatives.

Alice's eyes were wandering.

They're still committed to the same beliefs. Only want to adjust the elements somewhat differently.

I don't know . . ., said Alice.

(Will cook botch up the veal again tonight?)

I'm supposed to be the richest woman in the province, said Minnie.

Alice's eyes sparkled.

The *Press* said so, said Alice.

And yet, said Minnie.

Stooping low over some cream roses.

That's freedom for you, said Alice eagerly.

Minnie straightened up.

I feel as though I'm sitting on the boiler of a steam engine. Enormous pressure inside. But what on earth shall I make the thing drive?

Alice smiled.

You confuse me, she said.

I wish to build, she said with a rustle of crepe.

His eyes rose from some blotted papers.

You have an appointment madam?

Peering at her through a pince-nez.

Why no, she said.

Tch tch, he said. That boy.

Your antechamber was empty, she said. So I walked in.

His fingers resting on a chubby mother-of-pearl pen.

So I see madam, he said.

And I wish to build, she said.

He let the pen down.

And regarded the small thin woman in black and mauve.

I believe we have the ideal design for you madam, he said.

But, said Minnie.

He reached across to some plans. His tweed scuffing dust.

Now here we are, he said.

Unrolling a blueprint. It crackled as he weighted the corners with ink pots.

A nice four-roomed villa, said the architect. Just the thing for . . . if you'll pardon me madam . . . bereaved ladies.

Sir I am not a widow. And I do not wish . . . .

O quite, he said.

Waving a ringed yellow hand.

We have many maiden lady clients.

I do not want a four-roomed villa, said Minnie. I am Miss Lomax of Mount Lomax.

He raised an eyebrow.

Something larger madam?

Something quite other, said Minnie. I wish to build a cathedral.

My dear, said Lady Cunninghame, It does seem rather . . . odd.

The expense! cried Sir Robert.

Minnie breathed into her tea.

Not that one should not serve God, said Lady Cunninghame.

But are you not wanting in proper humility?

Minnie looked at her.

I don't think so, she said. At least . . . I hope not.

Surveying a blue velvet curtain.

I have other measures, she said.

The bishop don't like it, said Sir Robert.

There are, said Lady Cunninghame, more *useful* ways of serving.

Your father, Miss Lomax, spent a great deal on projects of true public worth, said Sir Robert.

Minnie put down her cup.

You mean the band rotunda? she said.

Just so, said Sir Robert. And the riding track at Hagley Park.

Lady Cunninghame hemmed.

Minnie began to caress a sleeve.

If, said Lady Cunninghame, your preference is for a charity specifically religious in nature, then should you not, my dear, at least consult with synod. The diocesan fund is very low.

I do not wish to be sectarian, said Minnie.

Lady Cunninghame started.

But my dear you do talk of a cathedral . . . .

One hopes, Miss Lomax, you don't mean a chapel, said Sir Robert.

Minnie smiled.

Shall we say a basilica, she said.

Papistry? said Sir Robert.

My dear, said Lady Cunninghame. One does not wish to seem intolerant . . . .

Minnie stood.

I'm sorry to be so silly. I simply mean a great church.

Smoothing down her skirts.

I hardly know yet.

Madness, said the architect. To build on the island.

Nevertheless, said Minnie.

Just shingle, said the architect. Scrape away the grass and the inch or so of soil and all you've got is shingle. And in springtime the river floods.

Can it be done? said Minnie.

If we drove pylons down. But to such great depths. And at such cost Miss Lomax. And so unnecessary.

The money is there, said Minnie.

Such extravagance, said the architect. Seems criminal. When only a mile away on the north bank of the river is an ideal site.

Minnie let a small fart filter between her layers of lace and crepe.

I think a cathedral should occupy a low place, not a hilltop.

We can overcome the problem of shingle under the foundations, said the architect. But the flooding. Miss Lomax, the Waimakariri is notorious for its flooding.

Can you not build against that? said Minnie.

Levees, said the architect. But once again, at great cost.

Minnie made an impatient gesture.

And even then, said the architect. One can guarantee nothing.

Can one ever? said Minnie.

The architect glared.

Do your best, said Minnie.

He bowed his yellow head.

A white sky flat over a still plain. Three courses of limestone rising from jaundiced grass. Wooden scaffolding. The shouts of men. A myriad of small activities from her vantage point on the bridge.

Shall you lay out grounds? said Alice.

No, said Minnie. Nothing. Just the grass, the river.

But just . . . three oaks, said Alice. There.

Inclining her head a little to picture it.

No, said Minnie. Nothing.

They stood in the flat air. The points of their parasols poking into the bridge.

Minnie sighed. It takes so long, she said.

Alice pouted, and glanced at the mountains.

Miss Lomax, said the servant.

The bishop noticed a great deal of white among her black and lilac.

Excuse my – grunt – slowness, said the bishop.

Struggling to his feet.

Not at all, said Minnie.

Well Miss Lomax? said the bishop bowing slightly.

This is my last appeal, said Minnie.

Pray be seated, said the bishop.

Will you not, said Minnie, give me your aid?

The bishop sniffed.

I am sorry Miss Lomax. I have been in contact – informally you understand – with the primate himself. On several occasions. I have discussed this matter with him, in the most general way. I have hinted at your proposals – your wishes.

You have explained your opposition? said Minnie.

The bishop bowed.

I have advised him of my belief in the . . . unwisdom of the scheme. But be assured, Miss Lomax, that in my representations I have been as little guilty of partisanship as my deep lack of friendship with your idea would allow. Indeed I have striven to be generous.

All that in a hint? said Minnie.

The bishop folded his hands.

Your present mood appears to me to give ample substance to the fears which I have entertained regarding your project. It seems to me that from the very beginning, Miss Lomax, you have been moved by vanity, by self-will, by. . . .

Minnie stood.

The bishop began to strain to his feet.

I do not mean to seem abrupt, Miss Lomax. But I represent, in a sense, a paternal wisdom greater than that vouchsafed to you.

Standing with his weight against the desk.

The patriarchate of the church. Puff. My episcopal duty. To admonish you where it seems necessary.

My father is dead, said Minnie.

Take care, said the bishop. Lest your spleen lead your tongue to blaspheme.

Stuff, said Minnie.

The bishop bent forward.

My dear Miss Lomax, will you not be guided by me in this?

Minnie's stomach and colon were broiling with wind.

My lord, said Minnie. The cathedral is an accomplished fact. It is there. Will you help me find a priest for it?

I cannot condone the division of my see, said the bishop.

Then I shall be priest, said Minnie.

The bishop sighed.

You are very rash Miss Lomax.

Minnie's skirts trailing through the door.

A vast belch erupted from her.

How vile, said Minnie.

The servant staring in astonishment.

Minnie smiled.

Spanking along with a jingle of harness a red barouche turned people's eyes. Inside a froth of men and women, and a soft laugh from a blonde wearing gilded spectacles.

The Cunninghame carriage refused to give way to the red barouche.

Furious driving! said Sir Robert.

As he observed his coachman nudge more forthrightly into the road.

Such a crowd, said Lady Cunninghame.

They approached the first bridge, where the trailing painted carriages slowed to an amble. The blonde woman in the red barouche continued her soft laugh, while a redhead next to her fondled a fan of purple feathers.

Two girls in white sat on the grass beneath two willows, raising porcelain to their lips in entire oblivion.

Seems to be quite the thing indeed, said Lady Cunninghame.

And the cathedral came in sight.

O dear, said Lady Cunninghame. It's very . . . large, isn't it?

Sir Robert sniffed.

It's what comes, he said, of leaving your money to women.

One woman dear, said Lady Cunninghame.

Harrumph, said Sir Robert.

Lady Cunninghame shooed a fly away with her furled yellow parasol.

Drive on Powell, said Sir Robert.

A carriage in front of them had stopped.

I cannot understand, said Sir Robert, why one does this sort of thing.

Lady Cunninghame caught herself chewing at a hang nail.

Minnie swept the altar with her hair.

Alice's forehead knitting in the stained light.

Minnie smiled.

There are millions coming, said Alice. Minnie stared.

I don't care. If they want a show.

She looked at a green cushion.

Or perhaps I do. But I don't know.

Every Saturday afternoon, said Alice. More popular even than the polo at Hagley Park.

Minnie laughed.

For a society that prides itself on its power, this one gets remarkably nervous when confronted with a manifestation of it.

Alice's forehead under the stained glass.

Is that not arrogant? she said. Even from you?

Minnie laughed again.

No, she said. Not from me.

Alice frowning.

Minnie laughed and began to process down the nave.

Listen to the hubbub outside, said Alice.

If only I could get a priest, said Minnie.

She broke wind again.

And a good doctor, she laughed.

And, said Alice, when I said, Where shall you live, in the cathedral?, she said, why Alice, in the belfry of course. And laughed.

My dear, said Lady Cunninghame.

Alice twisted her gloves together.

Plus de thé? said Lady Cunninghame.

Non, merci, said Alice.

Their eyes travelled across a white balustrade to rest upon a marble cupid.

Mount Lomax will be sold next month, said Lady Cunninghame. Eighty thousand acres.

Alice frowning at the cupid.

It's so extraordinary, she said. One doesn't know whether or not one has . . . failed.

One's responsibility, began Lady Cunninghame.

But ceased.

I see that waists will be lower this season, said Alice.

I'm glad, said Lady Cunninghame. The empire waist is not entirely compelling on figures beyond – shall we say – a certain limit of radial generosity.

Only hats are getting hideously wide, said Alice. And mutton chop sleeves. It's like going back to the early nineties.

Each raised a napkin to her lip.

Such a sweet day, said Alice.

Yes, said Lady Cunninghame.

A small fountain splashing around the feet of cupid, and from a window on the third floor the sound of a Cunninghame grandchild doing scales on a piano.

Imagine Minnie living in a belfry, said Alice.

Lady Cunninghame stared at her.

My dear, I can't.

And of course, said Alice, there's bound to be a flood some day. And the whole thing will be washed away.

And Minnie killed, said Lady Cunninghame.

They looked at one another in surprise.

Heavens, said Alice.

Glossary of Maori Words and Phrases*

* Place-names are not included

Aanei nga roimata o Rangipapa *These are Rangipapa's tears*
ae *yes*
ariki *high chief*; Te Ariki *the Lord*
aroha *love*

e *O; oh; of*
E hika e! *a term of address*
E! Kua hinga a Tane! *Tane has fallen*
E moe, e te whaea: wahine rangimarie *sleep, Mother (of God): lady of peace*

haere mai *come here, welcome*
haere ra *farewell, goodbye*
haka *chants of defiance accompanied by a stylized dance*
hangi *earth-oven; by common usage, a feast*
Hawaiki *ancestral home of the Maori*
he mea Maori *things Maori*
Hine-nui-te-po *Death Goddess*
hinu *fat*
hoha *nuisance (n); embarrassed, bored (a)*
Hongi Hika *warrior chief of the Ngapuhi, d. 1828*
hori *Maori (derog., from Maori form of George)*
huhu *larvae of beetle found in decaying wood, used for food*

Io *supreme god of Maori pantheon*

ka pai *good*
kahawai *species of fish, used for food*
kai *food, to eat (v)*
kainga *home, village*
kamakama *lively, talkative*
karaka *tree with orange berries*
kauri *massive coniferous forest tree, prized for its timber*
kia ora *greeting*
kina *sea egg*
Te Kooti *nineteenth-century warrior chief of Rongowhakaata who became religious leader*
kotiro *girl*
kowhai *small tree with golden blossom*
kuia *old woman*
kumara *sweet potato*

mana *authority, prestige*
manuka *shrub or small tree*
marae *tribal meeting ground*
matagouri *species of hardy shrub or tree, covered with spikes*
matai *species of forest tree*
Maui *mythological Maori hero, one of whose exploits was to try to kill the Death Goddess by entering her body*

Me he manurere au e *'If I were a bird . . .', opening line of a song*
mere *hand weapon*
mimi *pee*
te moananui a Kiwa *Pacific Ocean*
mokopuna *grandchild*

pa *fortified settlement, by extension, Maori village*
pakeha *New Zealander of European descent*
paua *univalve mollusc, used for food*
pipi *bivalve mollusc, used for food*
pipiwharauroa *shining cuckoo, migratory bird which returns to New Zealand in spring*
piupiu *fringed flax skirt*
pohutukawa *evergreen coastal tree with bright red blossom*
pukeko *swamp-hen*
puku *stomach*
punga *tree-fern*
puriri *tree with red berries*

Te Ra *the sun; by extension, God*
rangatira *chief*
Te Rauparaha *nineteenth-century warrior chief of Ngati Toa*
rata *vine or tree with bright red blossom*
raupo *bulrush*
rewarewa *large forest tree*
rimu *large coniferous forest tree*

ta ra ra, te kita kita *onomatopoeic, song of cicada*
taiaha *long wooden club*
tama *son*
Tane *Maori god of the forest*
tangi *funeral (n), to cry (v)*
taniwha *mythical beast inhabiting waterways and lakes*
tapu *(under) religious restriction, sacred*
taro *root vegetable*
tawa *large forest tree*
te *definite article*
teka *liar*
tenaa koe, e hine *hello, young lady*
tohunga *Maori priest or wizard*
toi-toi *tall tussocky grass with whitish-yellow plumes*
totara *large coniferous forest tree, prized for its timber*
tui *songbird*
turituri *keep quiet!*

waiata *song*
whanau *family*
Te Whiro *death*

Select Bibliography

Only volumes of prose fiction and poetry have been listed. Works written for children are excluded. Most small pamphlets have been ignored. New Zealand is the place of publication unless otherwise indicated.

FLEUR ADCOCK

Poetry

The Eye of the Hurricane, A. H. and A. W. Reed, 1964
Tigers, Oxford University Press, London, 1967
High Tide in the Garden, Oxford University Press, London, 1971
The Scenic Route, Oxford University Press, London, 1974
Below Loughrigg, Bloodaxe Books, Newcastle upon Tyne, 1979
The Inner Harbour, Oxford University Press, 1979

RENATO AMATO

Fiction

The Full Circle of the Travelling Cuckoo, Whitcombe and Tombs, 1967

K. O. ARVIDSON

Poetry

Riding the Pendulum, Oxford University Press, 1973

JAMES K. BAXTER

Poetry

Beyond the Palisade, Caxton Press, 1944
Blow, Wind of Fruitfulness, Caxton Press, 1948
Poems Unpleasant (with Anton Vogt and Louis Johnson), Pegasus Press, 1952
The Fallen House, Caxton Press, 1953
The Iron Breadboard: Studies in New Zealand Writing, Mermaid Press, 1957 (verse parodies)
The Night Shift: Poems on Aspects of Love (with Charles Doyle, Louis Johnson, and Kendrick Smithyman), Capricorn Press, 1957
In Fires of No Return, Oxford University Press, London, 1958
Howrah Bridge and Other Poems, Oxford University Press, London, 1961
Pig Island Letters, Oxford University Press, London, 1966
The Lion Skin, Bibliography Room, University of Otago, 1967
The Rock Woman: Selected Poems, Oxford University Press, London, 1969
Jerusalem Sonnets, Bibliography Room, University of Otago, 1970
Jerusalem Daybook, Price Milburn, 1971 (prose and poems)
Autumn Testament, Price Milburn, 1972
Four God Songs, Futuna Press, 1972
Letter to Peter Olds, Caveman Press, 1972
Ode to Auckland and Other Poems, Caveman Press, 1972
Six Faces of Love, Futuna Press, 1972
Runes, Oxford University Press, London, 1973
Two Obscene Poems, Mary Martin Books, Adelaide, 1973
The Labyrinth: Some Uncollected Poems, 1944–72, Oxford University Press, 1974
The Bone Chanter: Unpublished Poems 1945–1972, ed. J. E. Weir, Oxford University Press, 1976
The Holy Life and Death of Concrete Grady, Oxford University Press, 1976
Collected Poems, ed. J. E. Weir, Oxford University Press, 1979
Selected Poems, ed. J. E. Weir, Oxford University Press, 1982

PETER BLAND

Poetry

Habitual Fevers in *3 Poets* (with John Boyd and Victor O'Leary), Capricorn Press, 1958
Domestic Interiors, Wai-te-ata Press, 1964
My Side of the Story: Poems 1960-1964, Mate Books, 1964
The Man with the Carpet Bag, Caxton Press, 1972
Mr Maui, London Magazine Editions, London, 1976
Primitives, Wai-te-ata Press, 1979
Stone Tents, London Magazine Editions, London, 1981

CHARLES BRASCH

Poetry

The Land and the People and Other Poems, Caxton Press, 1939
The Quest, a verse play, The Compass Players, London, 1946
Disputed Ground: Poems 1939-45, Caxton Press, 1948
The Estate and Other Poems, Caxton Press, 1957
Octonary, Bibliography Room, University of Otago, 1963
Ambulando, Caxton Press, 1964
Not Far Off, Caxton Press, 1969
Home Ground, Caxton Press, 1974

ALISTAIR CAMPBELL

Poetry

Mine Eyes Dazzle: Poems 1947-49, Pegasus Press, 1950; revised editions 1951 and 1956
Sanctuary of Spirits, Wai-te-ata Press, 1963
Wild Honey, Oxford University Press, London, 1964
Blue Rain, Wai-te-ata Press, 1967
Drinking Horn, Bottle Press, 1970
Walk the Black Path, Bottle Press, 1971
Kapiti: Selected Poems 1947-71, Pegasus Press, 1972
Dreams, Yellow Lions, Alister Taylor, 1975
The Dark Lord of Savaiki, Te Kotare Press, 1980
Collected Poems 1947-81, Alister Taylor, 1982

GORDON CHALLIS

Poetry

Building, Caxton Press, 1963

JOHN REECE COLE

Fiction

It Was So Late, and Other Stories, Caxton Press, 1949; ed. Cherry Hankin, AUP/OUP, 1978

JAMES COURAGE

Fiction

One House, Gollancz, London, 1933
The Fifth Child, Constable, London, 1948
Desire Without Content, Constable, London, 1950
Fires in the Distance, Constable, London, 1952
The Young Have Secrets, Jonathan Cape, London, 1954
The Call Home, Jonathan Cape, London, 1956

A Way of Love, Jonathan Cape, London; Putnam, New York, 1959
The Visit to Penmorton, Jonathan Cape, London, 1961
Such Separate Creatures, ed. Charles Brasch, Caxton Press, 1973

JOY COWLEY

Fiction

Nest in a Falling Tree, Doubleday, New York; Secker and Warburg, 1967
Man of Straw, Doubleday, New York, 1970; Secker and Warburg, 1971
Of Men and Angels, Doubleday, New York, 1972; Hodder and Stoughton, London, 1973
The Mandrake Root, Doubleday, New York, 1975; Hodder and Stoughton, London, 1976
The Growing Season, Doubleday, New York, 1978; Hodder and Stoughton, London, 1979

ALLEN CURNOW

Poetry

Valley of Decision, Phoenix Miscellany I, Auckland University College Students'
    Association, 1933
Three Poems, Caxton Club Press, 1935
Enemies: Poems 1934-1936, Caxton Press, 1937
Not in Narrow Seas, Caxton Press, 1939
Island and Time, Caxton Press, 1941
Recent Poems (with A. R. D. Fairburn, Denis Glover, and R. A. K. Mason), Caxton Press,
    1941
Sailing or Drowning, Progressive Publishing Society, 1943
Jack Without Magic, Caxton Press, 1946
At Dead Low Water, and Sonnets, Caxton Press, 1949
The Axe: A Verse Tragedy, Caxton Press, 1949
Poems 1949-57, Mermaid Press, 1957
A Small Room with Large Windows, Oxford University Press, London, 1962
Trees, Effigies, Moving Objects, Catspaw Press, 1972
An Abominable Temper, Catspaw Press, 1973
Collected Poems 1933-1973, A. H. and A. W. Reed, 1974
An Incorrigible Music, AUP/OUP, 1979
You Will Know When You Get There: Poems 1979-81, AUP/OUP, 1982
Selected Poems, Penguin, 1982

RUTH DALLAS

Poetry

Country Road and Other Poems, 1947-52, Caxton Press, 1953
The Turning Wheel, Caxton Press, 1961
Day Book, Caxton Press, 1966
Shadow Show, Caxton Press, 1968
Walking on the Snow, Caxton Press, 1975
Song for a Guitar and Other Songs, ed. Charles Brasch, University of Otago Press, 1976
Steps of the Sun, Caxton Press, 1979

DAN DAVIN

Fiction

Cliffs of Fall, Nicholson and Watson, London, 1945
For the Rest of Our Lives, Nicholson and Watson, London, 1947; Michael Joseph, London;
    Blackwood and Janet Paul, 1965
The Gorse Blooms Pale, Nicholson and Watson, London, 1947
Roads from Home, Michael Joseph, London, 1949; ed. Lawrence Jones, AUP/OUP, 1976
The Sullen Bell, Michael Joseph, London, 1956

No Remittance, Michael Joseph, London, 1959
Not Here, Not Now, Hale, London; Whitcombe and Tombs, 1970
Brides of Price, Hale, London; Whitcombe and Tombs, 1972; Coward, McCann and
    Geoghegan, New York, 1973
Breathing Spaces, Hale, London; Whitcoulls, 1975
Selected Stories, Victoria University Press/Price Milburn, 1981

BASIL DOWLING

Poetry

A Day's Journey, Caxton Press, 1941
Signs and Wonders, Caxton Press, 1944
Canterbury and Other Poems, Caxton Press, 1949
Hatherley: Recollective Lyrics, Bibliography Room, University of Otago, 1968
A Little Gallery of Characters, Nag's Head Press, 1971
Bedlam: A Mid-Century Satire, Nag's Head Press, 1972
The Unreturning Native and Other Poems, Nag's Head Press, 1973
The Stream: A Reverie of Boyhood, Nag's Head Press, 1979

CHARLES DOYLE

Poetry

A Splinter of Glass, Pegasus Press, 1956
The Night Shift: Poems on Aspects of Love (with James K. Baxter, Louis Johnson, and
    Kendrick Smithyman), Capricorn Press, 1957
Distances, Paul's Book Arcade, 1963
Messages for Herod, Collins, 1965
A Sense of Place, Wai-te-ata Press, 1965
Earth Meditations: 2, Charles Alldritt, 1968
Abandoned Sofa, Soft Press, Victoria, B. C., 1970
Earth Meditations: 1-5, Coach House Press, Toronto, 1971
Quorum/Noah (with Robert Sward), Soft Press, Victoria, B. C., 1971
Earthshot, Exeter Books, England, 1972
Preparing for the Ark, Weedflower Press, Toronto, 1973
Planes, Seripress, Toronto, 1975
Stonedancer, Auckland University Press, 1976

YVONNE DU FRESNE

Fiction

Farvel and Other Stories, Victoria University Press/Price Milburn, 1980
The Book of Ester, Longman Paul, 1982

EILEEN DUGGAN

Poetry

Poems, New Zealand Tablet, 1922
Poems, Allen and Unwin, London, 1937
New Zealand Poems, Allen and Unwin, London, 1940
More Poems, Allen and Unwin, London; Macmillan, New York, 1951

MAURICE DUGGAN

Fiction

Immanuel's Land, Pilgrim Press, 1956
Summer in the Gravel Pit, Blackwood and Janet Paul; Gollancz, London, 1965

O'Leary's Orchard and Other Stories, Caxton Press, 1970
Collected Stories, ed. C. K. Stead, AUP/OUP, 1981

LAURIS EDMOND

Poetry

In Middle Air, Pegasus Press, 1975
The Pear Tree, Pegasus Press, 1977
Salt from the North, Oxford University Press, 1980
Seven: Poems, Waysgoose Press, 1980
Wellington Letter: A Sequence of Poems, Mallinson Rendel, 1980

MURRAY EDMOND

Poetry

Entering the Eye, Caveman Press, 1973
Patchwork, Hawk Press, 1978
End Wall, Oxford University Press, 1981

STEVAN ELDRED-GRIGG

Fiction

Of Ivory Accents, Exposition Press, Hicksville, N.Y., 1977

CHRIS ELSE

Fiction

Dreams of Pythagoras, Voice Press, 1981

A. R. D. FAIRBURN

Poetry

He Shall Not Rise, Columbia Press, London, 1930
Dominion, Caxton Press, 1938
Recent Poems (with Allen Curnow, Denis Glover, and R. A. K. Mason), Caxton Press, 1941
Poems 1929-1941, Caxton Press, 1943
The Rakehelly Man, Caxton Press, 1946
Strange Rendezvous: Poems 1929-1941, with additions, Caxton Press, 1952
Three Poems: Dominion, The Voyage, To a Friend in the Wilderness, New Zealand University
    Press, 1952
Poetry Harbinger (with Denis Glover), Pilgrim Press, 1958
The Disadvantages of Being Dead, Mermaid Press, 1958
Collected Poems, Pegasus Press, 1966

RODERICK FINLAYSON

Fiction

Brown Man's Burden, Unicorn Press, 1938
Sweet Beulah Land, Griffin Press, 1942
Tidal Creek, Angus and Robertson, Sydney, 1948
The Schooner Came to Atia, Griffin Press, 1952
Brown Man's Burden and Later Stories, ed. Bill Pearson, AUP/OUP, 1973
Other Lovers, John McIndoe, 1976

JANET FRAME

Poetry

The Pocket Mirror, Braziller, New York; W. H. Allen, London, 1967; Pegasus Press, 1968

Fiction

The Lagoon, Caxton Press, 1951; as *The Lagoon and Other Stories*, Caxton Press, 1961
Owls Do Cry, Pegasus Press, 1957; Braziller, New York, 1960; W. H. Allen, London, 1961;
    Sun Books, Melbourne, 1967
Faces in the Water, Pegasus Press; Braziller, New York, 1961; W. H. Allen, London, 1962;
    Avon Books, New York, 1971
The Edge of the Alphabet, Pegasus Press; Braziller, New York, W. H. Allen, London, 1962
Scented Gardens for the Blind, Pegasus Press; W. H. Allen, London, 1963; Braziller, New
    York, 1964
Snowman Snowman: Fables and Fantasies, Braziller, New York, 1963
The Reservoir: Stories and Sketches, Braziller, New York, 1963
The Adaptable Man, Pegasus Press; Braziller, New York; W. H. Allen, London, 1965
A State of Siege, Braziller, New York, 1966; Pegasus Press; W. H. Allen, London, 1967;
    Angus and Robertson, Sydney, 1982
The Reservoir and Other Stories, Pegasus Press; W. H. Allen, London, 1966
The Rainbirds, W. H. Allen, London, 1968; Pegasus Press, 1969; as *Yellow Flowers in the
    Antipodean Room*, Braziller, New York, 1969
Intensive Care, Braziller, New York; Doubleday, Toronto, 1970; A. H. and A. W. Reed;
    W. H. Allen, London, 1971
Daughter Buffalo, Braziller, New York; Doubleday, Toronto, 1972; A. H. and A. W. Reed;
    W. H. Allen, London, 1973
Living in the Maniototo, Braziller, New York, 1979; Women's Press/Hutchinson, 1981

A. P. GASKELL

Fiction

The Big Game and Other Stories, Caxton Press, 1947
All Part of the Game: the Stories of A. P. Gaskell, AUP/OUP, 1978

MAURICE GEE

Fiction

The Big Season, Hutchinson, London, 1962
A Special Flower, Hutchinson, London, 1965
In My Father's Den, Faber, London, 1972; Oxford University Press, 1977
A Glorious Morning, Comrade, AUP/OUP, 1975
Games of Choice, Faber, London, 1976; Oxford University Press, 1977
Plumb, Faber, London, 1978
Meg, Faber, London; Penguin, 1981

MICHAEL GIFKINS

Fiction

After the Revolution and Other Stories, Longman Paul, 1982

DENIS GLOVER

Poetry

Thistledown, Caxton Club Press, 1935
Six Easy Ways of Dodging Debt Collectors, Caxton Press, 1936
The Arraignment of Paris, Caxton Press, 1937

Thirteen Poems, Caxton Press, 1939
Cold Tongue, Caxton Press, 1940
Recent Poems (with Allen Curnow, A. R. D. Fairburn, and R. A. K. Mason), Caxton Press,
   1941
The Wind and the Sand: Poems 1934-44, Caxton Press, 1945
Summer Flowers, Caxton Press, 1946
Sings Harry and Other Poems, Caxton Press, 1951
Arawata Bill: A Sequence of Poems, Pegasus Press, 1953
Since Then, Mermaid Press, 1957
Poetry Harbinger (with A. R. D. Fairburn), Pilgrim Press, 1958
Enter Without Knocking: Selected Poems, Pegasus Press, 1964; enlarged edition, 1972
Sharp Edge Up: Verses and Satires, Blackwood and Janet Paul, 1968
To a Particular Woman, Nag's Head Press, 1970
Diary to a Woman, Catspaw Press, 1971
Dancing to My Tune, ed. Lauris Edmond, Catspaw Press, 1974 (verse and prose)
Wellington Harbour, Catspaw Press, 1974
Clutha: River Poems, John McIndoe, 1977
Come High Water, Dunmore Press, 1977
Or Hawk or Basilisk, Catspaw Press, 1978
To Friends in Russia, Nag's Head Press, 1979
Towards Banks Peninsula, Pegasus Press, 1979
Selected Poems, ed. Allen Curnow, Penguin, 1981

Fiction

Three Short Stories, Caxton Press, 1936
Till the Star Speak, Caxton Press, 1939
Men of God, Dunmore Press, 1978

PATRICIA GRACE

Fiction

Waiariki, Longman Paul, 1975
Mutuwhenua: The Moon Sleeps, Longman Paul, 1978
The Dream Sleepers and Other Stories, Longman Paul, 1980

RUSSELL HALEY

Poetry

The Walled Garden, The Mandrake Root, 1972
On the Fault Line, Hawk Press, 1977

Fiction

The Sauna Bath Mysteries and Other Stories, The Mandrake Root, 1978

MICHAEL HENDERSON

Fiction

The Log of a Superfluous Son, John McIndoe, 1975

PAUL HENDERSON (RUTH FRANCE)

Poetry

Unwilling Pilgrim, Caxton Press, 1955
The Halting Place, Caxton Press, 1961

Fiction

The Race, Constable, London, 1958
Ice Cold River, Constable, London, 1961

J. R. HERVEY

Poetry

Selected Poems, Caxton Press, 1940
New Poems, Caxton Press, 1942
Man on a Raft: More Poems, Caxton Press, 1949
She Was My Spring, Caxton Press, 1955

NOEL HILLIARD

Fiction

Maori Girl, Heinemann, London, 1960
A Piece of Land: Stories and Sketches, Hale, London; Whitcombe and Tombs, 1963
Power of Joy, Michael Joseph, London, 1965
A Night at Green River, Hale, London; Whitcombe and Tombs, 1969
Maori Woman, Hale, London; Whitcombe and Tombs, 1974
Send Somebody Nice: Stories and Sketches, Hale, London; Whitcoulls, 1976
Selected Stories, John McIndoe, 1977
The Glory and the Dream, Heinemann, 1978

KERI HULME

Poetry
The Silences Between, AUP/OUP, 1982

SAM HUNT

Poetry

Bracken Country, Glenbervie Press, 1971
From Bottle Creek, Alister Taylor, 1972
South into Winter: Poems and Roadsongs, Alister Taylor, 1973
Time to Ride, Alister Taylor, 1975
Drunkard's Garden, Hampson Hunt, 1977
Collected Poems, Penguin, 1980
Running Scared, Whitcoulls, 1982

WITI IHIMAERA

Fiction

Pounamu, Pounamu, Heinemann, 1972
Tangi, Heinemann, 1973
Whanau, Heinemann, 1974
The New Net Goes Fishing, Heinemann, 1977

KEVIN IRELAND

Poetry

Face to Face, Pegasus Press, 1963
Educating the Body, Caxton Press, 1967
A Letter from Amsterdam, Amphedesma Press, London, 1972
Orchids, Hummingbirds, and Other Poems, AUP/OUP, 1974
A Grammar of Dreams, Wai-te-ata Press, 1975
Literary Cartoons, Islands/Hurricane House, 1977
The Dangers of Art: Poems 1975-1980, Cicada Press, 1980

MICHAEL JACKSON

Poetry

Latitudes of Exile, John McIndoe, 1976
Wall, John McIndoe, 1980

M. K. JOSEPH

Poetry

Imaginary Islands, the author, 1950
The Living Countries, Paul's Book Arcade, 1959
Inscription on a Paper Dart: Selected Poems 1945-72, AUP/OUP, 1974

Fiction

I'll Soldier No More, Paul's Book Arcade; Gollancz, London, 1958
A Pound of Saffron, Paul's Book Arcade; Gollancz, London, 1962
A Hole in the Zero, Blackwood and Janet Paul; Gollancz, London, 1967
A Soldier's Tale, Collins, 1976
The Time of Achamoth, Collins, 1977

OWEN LEEMING

Poetry

Venus Is Setting, Caxton Press, 1972

RACHEL McALPINE

Poetry

Lament for Ariadne, Caveman Press, 1975
Stay at the Dinner Party, Caveman Press, 1977
Fancy Dress, Cicada Press, 1979
House Poems, Nutshell Books, 1980

BILL MANHIRE

Poetry

Malady, designed by Ralph Hotere; Amphedesma Press, London, 1970
The Elaboration, Square and Circle, 1972
How to Take Off Your Clothes at the Picnic, Wai-te-ata Press, 1977
Good Looks, AUP/OUP, 1982

OWEN MARSHALL

Fiction

Supper Waltz Wilson, Pegasus Press, 1979
The Master of Big Jingles, John McIndoe, 1982

O. E. MIDDLETON

Poetry

Six Poems, Handcraft Press, 1951

Fiction

Short Stories, Handcraft Press, 1953
The Stone and Other Stories, Pilgrim Press, 1959

A Walk on the Beach, Michael Joseph, London, 1964
The Loners, Square and Circle, 1972
Selected Stories, John McIndoe, 1975
Confessions of an Ocelot and Not for a Seagull, John McIndoe, 1979

PHILIP MINCHER

Poetry
Heroes and Clerks, Handcraft Press, 1959

Fiction
The Ride Home: A Story Sequence, Longman Paul, 1977

BARRY MITCALFE

Poetry
Thirty Poems, Hurricane House, 1960
Harvestman, Coromandel Press, 1979

Fiction
Squid, Glenco, 1951
Moana, Seven Seas, 1975
I Say, Wait for Me, Outrigger, 1976

DAVID MITCHELL

Poetry
The Orange Grove, Poets' Co-operative, 1969
Pipe Dreams in Ponsonby, Stephen Chan, 1972; Caveman, 1975

MICHAEL MORRISSEY

Poetry
Make Love in All the Rooms, Caveman Press, 1978
Closer to the Bone, Sword Press, 1981
Dreams, Sword Press, 1981
She's Not the Child of Sylvia Plath, Sword Press, 1981

Fiction
The Fat Lady and the Astronomer, Sword Press, 1981

PETER OLDS

Poetry
Lady Moss Revived, Caveman Press, 1972
The Habits You Left Behind, Caveman Press, 1972
4 V8 Poems, Caveman Press, 1972
The Snow and the Glass Window, Caveman Press, 1973
Freeway, Caveman Press, 1974
Doctor's Rock, Caveman Press, 1976
Beethoven's Guitar, Caveman Press, 1980

W. H. OLIVER

Poetry

Fire Without Phoenix: Poems 1946-54, Caxton Press, 1957
Out of Season, Oxford University Press, 1980
Poor Richard, Port Nicholson Press, 1982

VINCENT O'SULLIVAN

Poetry

Our Burning Time, Prometheus Books, 1965
Revenants, Prometheus Books, 1969
Bearings, Oxford University Press, 1973
Butcher & Co., Oxford University Press, 1976
From the Indian Funeral, John McIndoe, 1976
Brother Jonathan, Brother Kafka, Oxford University Press, 1980
The Butcher Papers, Oxford University Press, 1982
The Rose Ballroom and Other Poems, John McIndoe, 1982

Fiction

Miracle: A Romance, John McIndoe, 1976
The Boy, the Bridge, the River, John McIndoe, 1978
Dandy Edison for Lunch and Other Stories, John McIndoe, 1981

ALISTAIR PATERSON

Poetry

Caves in the Hills, Pegasus Press, 1965
Birds Flying, Pegasus Press, 1973
Cities and Strangers, Caveman Press, 1976
The Toledo Room: A Poem for Voices, Pilgrims South Press, 1978
Qu'appelle, Pilgrims South Press, 1982

GLORIA RAWLINSON

Poetry

Gloria's Book, Whitcombe and Tombs, 1933
The Perfume Vendor, Hutchinson, London, 1936
Music in the Listening-Place, Cassell, London, 1938
The Islands Where I Was Born, Handcraft Press, 1955
Of Clouds and Pebbles, Paul's Book Arcade, 1963

FRANK SARGESON

Fiction

Conversation with My Uncle and Other Sketches, Unicorn Press, 1936
A Man and His Wife, Caxton Press, 1940; Progressive Publishing Society, 1944
When the Wind Blows, Caxton Press, 1945
That Summer and Other Stories, John Lehmann, London, 1946
I Saw in My Dream, John Lehmann, London, 1949
I for One, Caxton Press, dated 1954 but actually published in 1956
Collected Stories, 1935-1963, Blackwood and Janet Paul, 1964; Longman Paul, 1969;
    reprinted with additional stories as *The Stories of Frank Sargeson*, Longman Paul, 1973;
    Penguin, 1982
Memoirs of a Peon, MacGibbon and Kee, London, 1965; Heinemann, 1974
The Hangover, MacGibbon and Kee, London, 1967
Joy of the Worm, MacGibbon and Kee, London, 1969

Man of England Now, with *I for One* and *A Game of Hide and Seek*, Martin Brian and O'Keefe, London; Caxton Press, 1972
Sunset Village, Martin Brian and O'Keefe, London; A. H. and A. W. Reed, 1976
Tandem (with Edith Campion, *The Chain*), *En Route*, A. H. and A. W. Reed, 1979

MAURICE SHADBOLT

Fiction
The New Zealanders: A Sequence of Stories, Whitcombe and Tombs; Gollancz, London, 1959; Atheneum, New York, 1961
Summer Fires and Winter Country, Whitcombe and Tombs; Eyre and Spottiswoode, 1963; Atheneum, New York, 1966
The Presence of Music: Three Novellas, Cassell, London, 1963
Among the Cinders, Whitcombe and Tombs; Eyre and Spottiswoode; Atheneum, New York, 1965
This Summer's Dolphin, Cassell, London; Atheneum, New York, 1969
An Ear of the Dragon, Cassell, London, 1971
Strangers and Journeys, St. Martin's Press, New York; Hodder and Stoughton, London, 1972; Coronet Books, London, 1975
A Touch of Clay, Hodder and Stoughton, London, 1974
Danger Zone, Hodder and Stoughton, London, 1975
Figures in Light: Selected Stories, Hodder and Stoughton, London, 1979
The Lovelock Version, Hodder and Stoughton, London, 1980

KEITH SINCLAIR

Poetry
Songs for a Summer, Pegasus Press, 1952
Strangers or Beasts, Caxton Press, 1954
A Time to Embrace, Paul's Book Arcade, 1963
The Firewheel Tree, AUP/OUP, 1974

ELIZABETH SMITHER

Poetry
Here Come the Clouds, Alister Taylor, 1975
You're Very Seductive William Carlos Williams, John McIndoe, 1978
The Sarah Train, Hawk Press, 1980
Casanova's Ankle, Oxford University Press, 1981
The Legend of Marcello Mastroianni's Wife, AUP/OUP, 1981

KENDRICK SMITHYMAN

Poetry
Seven Sonnets, Pelorus Press, 1946
The Blind Mountain, Caxton Press, 1950
The Gay Trapeze, Handcraft Press, 1955
Inheritance, Paul's Book Arcade, 1962
Flying to Palmerston, AUP/OUP, 1968
Earthquake Weather, AUP/OUP, 1972
The Seal in the Dolphin Pool, AUP/OUP, 1974
Dwarf with a Billiard Cue, AUP/OUP, 1978

CHARLES SPEAR

Poetry
Twopence Coloured, Caxton Press, 1951

Fiction

Rearguard Actions, Methuen, London, 1936; with L. A. Baigent under pseudonym C. L. Spear-Baigent.

MARY STANLEY

Poetry

Starveling Year, Pegasus Press, 1953

C. K. STEAD

Poetry

Whether the Will is Free: Poems 1954-62, Paul's Book Arcade, 1964
Crossing the Bar, AUP/OUP, 1972
Quesada: Poems 1972-74, The Shed, 1975
Walking Westward, The Shed, 1979
Geographies, AUP/OUP, 1982

Fiction

Smith's Dream, Longman Paul, 1971; revised edition 1973
Five for the Symbol, Longman Paul, 1981

MARGARET SUTHERLAND

Fiction

The Fledgling, Heinemann, London, 1974
The Love Contract, Heinemann, London, 1976
Getting Through and Other Stories, Heinemann, London, 1977; as *Dark Places, Deep Regions, and Other Stories*, Stemmer House, Owings Mills, Maryland, 1980

BRIAN TURNER

Poetry

Ladders of Rain, John McIndoe, 1978
Ancestors, John McIndoe, 1981

HONE TUWHARE

Poetry

No Ordinary Sun, Blackwood and Janet Paul, 1964; enlarged edition John McIndoe, 1977
Come Rain Hail, Bibliography Room, University of Otago, 1970
Sapwood & Milk, Caveman Press, 1972
Something Nothing, Caveman Press, 1974
Making a Fist of It, Jackstraw Press, 1978
Selected Poems, John McIndoe, 1980

RAYMOND WARD

Poetry

Settler and Stranger, Caxton Press, 1965

IAN WEDDE

Poetry

Homage to Matisse, Amphedesma Press, London, 1971
Made Over, Stephen Chan, 1974
Earthly: Sonnets for Carlos, Amphedesma Press, London, 1975
Pathway to the Sea, Hawk Press, 1975
Don't Listen, Hawk Press, 1977
Spells for Coming Out, AUP/OUP, 1977
Castaly: Poems 1973-1977, AUP/OUP, 1980

Fiction

Dick Seddon's Great Dive, Islands/John McIndoe, 1976
The Shirt Factory and Other Stories, Victoria University Press/Price Milburn, 1981

HUBERT WITHEFORD

Poetry

Shadow of the Flame: Poems 1942-47, Pelorus Press, 1950
The Falcon Mark, Pegasus Press, 1951
The Lightning Makes a Difference, Brookside Press, 1962
A Native, Perhaps Beautiful, Caxton Press, 1967
How Do Things Happen? Flowering Hand Press, London, 1972
A Possible Order, Ravine Press, Harrow, Middlesex, 1980

Index

Poetry titles are in *italic*, first lines in roman; prose titles are in **bold**.